165.00

Dictionary of Literary Biography

Documentary Series

1 *Sherwood Anderson, Willa Cather, John Dos Passos, Theodore Dreiser, F. Scott Fitzgerald, Ernest Hemingway, Sinclair Lewis,* edited by Margaret A. Van Antwerp (1982)

2 *James Gould Cozzens, James T. Farrell, William Faulkner, John O'Hara, John Steinbeck, Thomas Wolfe, Richard Wright,* edited by Margaret A. Van Antwerp (1982)

3 *Saul Bellow, Jack Kerouac, Norman Mailer, Vladimir Nabokov, John Updike, Kurt Vonnegut,* edited by Mary Bruccoli (1983)

4 *Tennessee Williams,* edited by Margaret A. Van Antwerp and Sally Johns (1984)

5 *American Transcendentalists,* edited by Joel Myerson (1988)

6 *Hardboiled Mystery Writers: Raymond Chandler, Dashiell Hammett, Ross Macdonald,* edited by Matthew J. Bruccoli and Richard Layman (1989)

7 *Modern American Poets: James Dickey, Robert Frost, Marianne Moore,* edited by Karen L. Rood (1989)

8 *The Black Aesthetic Movement,* edited by Jeffrey Louis Decker (1991)

9 *American Writers of the Vietnam War: W. D. Ehrhart, Larry Heinemann, Tim O'Brien, Walter McDonald, John M. Del Vecchio,* edited by Ronald Baughman (1991)

10 *The Bloomsbury Group,* edited by Edward L. Bishop (1992)

11 *American Proletarian Culture: The Twenties and The Thirties,* edited by Jon Christian Suggs (1993)

12 *Southern Women Writers: Flannery O'Connor, Katherine Anne Porter, Eudora Welty,* edited by Mary Ann Wimsatt and Karen L. Rood (1994)

13 *The House of Scribner, 1846-1904,* edited by John Delaney (1996)

14 *Four Women Writers for Children, 1868-1918,* edited by Caroline C. Hunt (1996)

15 *American Expatriate Writers: Paris in the Twenties,* edited by Matthew J. Bruccoli and Robert W. Trogdon (1997)

16 *The House of Scribner, 1905-1930,* edited by John Delaney (1997)

17 *The House of Scribner, 1931-1984,* edited by John Delaney (1998)

Yearbooks

1980 edited by Karen L. Rood, Jean W. Ross, and Richard Ziegfeld (1981)

1981 edited by Karen L. Rood, Jean W. Ross, and Richard Ziegfeld (1982)

1982 edited by Richard Ziegfeld; associate editors: Jean W. Ross and Lynne C. Zeigler (1983)

1983 edited by Mary Bruccoli and Jean W. Ross; associate editor: Richard Ziegfeld (1984)

1984 edited by Jean W. Ross (1985)

1985 edited by Jean W. Ross (1986)

1986 edited by J. M. Brook (1987)

1987 edited by J. M. Brook (1988)

1988 edited by J. M. Brook (1989)

1989 edited by J. M. Brook (1990)

1990 edited by James W. Hipp (1991)

1991 edited by James W. Hipp (1992)

1992 edited by James W. Hipp (1993)

1993 edited by James W. Hipp, contributing editor George Garrett (1994)

1994 edited by James W. Hipp, contributing editor George Garrett (1995)

1995 edited by James W. Hipp, contributing editor George Garrett (1996)

1996 edited by Samuel W. Bruce and L. Kay Webster, contributing editor George Garrett (1997)

1997 edited by Matthew J. Bruccoli and George Garrett, with the assistance of L. Kay Webster (1998)

Concise Series

Concise Dictionary of American Literary Biography, 6 volumes (1988-1989): *The New Consciousness, 1941-1968; Colonization to the American Renaissance, 1640-1865; Realism, Naturalism, and Local Color, 1865-1917; The Twenties, 1917-1929; The Age of Maturity, 1929-1941; Broadening Views, 1968-1988.*

Concise Dictionary of British Literary Biography, 8 volumes (1991-1992): *Writers of the Middle Ages and Renaissance Before 1660; Writers of the Restoration and Eighteenth Century, 1660-1789; Writers of the Romantic Period, 1789-1832; Victorian Writers, 1832-1890; Late-Victorian and Edwardian Writers, 1890-1914; Modern Writers, 1914-1945; Writers After World War II, 1945-1960; Contemporary Writers, 1960 to Present.*

Dictionary of Literary Biography® • Volume One Hundred Ninety-Nine

Victorian Women Poets

Dictionary of Literary Biography® • Volume One Hundred Ninety-Nine

Victorian Women Poets

Edited by
William B. Thesing
University of South Carolina

A Bruccoli Clark Layman Book
Gale Research
Detroit, Washington, D.C., London

Printed in the United States of America

Library of Congress Cataloging-in-Publication Data

Victorian women poets / edited by William B. Thesing.
    p. cm.–(Dictionary of literary biography; v. 199)
"A Bruccoli Clark Layman book."
Includes bibliographical references and index.
ISBN 0-7876-1854-3 (alk. paper)
1. English poetry–Women authors–Bio-bibliography–Dictionaries. 2. Women and literature–Great Britain–History–19th century–Dictionaries. 3. Women and literature–Great Britain–History–20th century–Dictionaries. 4. English poetry–19th century–Bio-bibliography–Dictionaries. 5. English poetry–20th century–Bio-bibliography–Dictionaries. 6. Women poets, English–19th century–Biography–Dictionaries. 7. Women poets, English–20th century–Biography–Dictionaries. 8. English poetry–Women authors–Dictionaries. 9. English poetry–19th century–Dictionaries. 10. English poetry–20th century–Dictionaries. I. Thesing, William B. II. Series.
PR595.W6V49 1998
821'.8099287–dc21   98-35216
                                                                            CIP

10 9 8 7 6 5 4 3 2 1

For my parents, with love and gratitude,

William V. "Popo" Thesing
(3 August 1911–   )
Father, Golfer, and Survivor

and

Harriet C. "Fifi" Thesing
(26 May 1914–   )
Mother, Teacher, and Muse

Contents

Plan of the Series

. . . Almost the most prodigious asset of a country, and perhaps its most precious possession, is its native literary product — when that product is fine and noble and enduring.

Mark Twain*

The advisory board, the editors, and the publisher of the *Dictionary of Literary Biography* are joined in endorsing Mark Twain's declaration. The literature of a nation provides an inexhaustible resource of permanent worth. We intend to make literature and its creators better understood and more accessible to students and the reading public, while satisfying the standards of teachers and scholars.

To meet these requirements, *literary biography* has been construed in terms of the author's achievement. The most important thing about a writer is his writing. Accordingly, the entries in *DLB* are career biographies, tracing the development of the author's canon and the evolution of his reputation.

The purpose of *DLB* is not only to provide reliable information in a convenient format but also to place the figures in the larger perspective of literary history and to offer appraisals of their accomplishments by qualified scholars.

The publication plan for *DLB* resulted from two years of preparation. The project was proposed to Bruccoli Clark by Frederick C. Ruffner, president of the Gale Research Company, in November 1975. After specimen entries were prepared and typeset, an advisory board was formed to refine the entry format and develop the series rationale. In meetings held during 1976, the publisher, series editors, and advisory board approved the scheme for a comprehensive biographical dictionary of persons who contributed to North American literature. Editorial work on the first volume began in January 1977, and it was published in 1978. In order to make *DLB* more than a reference tool and to compile volumes that individually have claim to status as literary history, it was decided to organize volumes by

From an unpublished section of Mark Twain's autobiography, copyright by the Mark Twain Company

topic, period, or genre. Each of these freestanding volumes provides a biographical-bibliographical guide and overview for a particular area of literature. We are convinced that this organization—as opposed to a single alphabet method—constitutes a valuable innovation in the presentation of reference material. The volume plan necessarily requires many decisions for the placement and treatment of authors who might properly be included in two or three volumes. In some instances a major figure will be included in separate volumes, but with different entries emphasizing the aspect of his career appropriate to each volume. Ernest Hemingway, for example, is represented in *American Writers in Paris, 1920–1939* by an entry focusing on his expatriate apprenticeship; he is also in *American Novelists, 1910–1945* with an entry surveying his entire career, as well as in *American Short-Story Writers, 1910–1945, Second Series* with an entry concentrating on his short stories. Each volume includes a cumulative index of the subject authors and articles. Comprehensive indexes to the entire series are planned.

Since 1981 the series has been further augmented by the *DLB Yearbooks*, which update published entries and add new entries to keep the *DLB* current with contemporary activity. There have also been *DLB Documentary Series* volumes which provide biographical and critical source materials for figures whose work is judged to have particular interest for students. One of these companion volumes is entirely devoted to Tennessee Williams.

We define literature as the *intellectual commerce of a nation*: not merely as belles lettres but as that ample and complex process by which ideas are generated, shaped, and transmitted. *DLB* entries are not limited to "creative writers" but extend to other figures who in their time and in their way influenced the mind of a people. Thus the series encompasses historians, journalists, publishers, book collectors, and screenwriters. By this means readers of *DLB* may be aided to perceive literature not as cult scripture in the keeping of intellectual high priests but firmly positioned at the center of a nation's life.

DLB includes the major writers appropriate to each volume and those standing in the ranks behind them. Scholarly and critical counsel has been sought in deciding which minor figures to include and how full their entries should be. Wherever possible, useful references are made to figures who do not warrant separate entries.

Each *DLB* volume has an expert volume editor responsible for planning the volume, selecting the figures for inclusion, and assigning the entries. Volume editors are also responsible for preparing, where appropriate, appendices surveying the major periodicals and literary and intellectual movements for their volumes, as well as lists of further readings. Work on the series as a whole is coordinated at the Bruccoli Clark Layman editorial center in Columbia, South Carolina, where the editorial staff is responsible for accuracy and utility of the published volumes.

One feature that distinguishes *DLB* is the illustration policy–its concern with the iconography of literature. Just as an author is influenced by his surroundings, so is the reader's understanding of the author enhanced by a knowledge of his environment. Therefore *DLB* volumes include not only drawings, paintings, and photographs of authors, often depicting them at various stages in their careers, but also illustrations of their families and places where they lived. Title pages are regularly reproduced in facsimile along with dust jackets for modern authors. The dust jackets are a special feature of *DLB* because they often document better than anything else the way in which an author's work was perceived in its own time. Specimens of the writers' manuscripts and letters are included when feasible.

Samuel Johnson rightly decreed that "The chief glory of every people arises from its authors." The purpose of the *Dictionary of Literary Biography* is to compile literary history in the surest way available to us–by accurate and comprehensive treatment of the lives and work of those who contributed to it.

The *DLB* Advisory Board

Introduction

Dictionary of Literary Biography 199: Victorian Women Poets, the first of two volumes on British women poets writing between 1832 and 1920, complements the two books in the DLB series previously published on Victorian poets: *DLB 32: Victorian Poets Before 1850* (1984) and *DLB 35: Victorian Poets After 1850* (1985). Only four poets discussed in those volumes—Emily Jane Brontë, Elizabeth Barrett Browning, Dora Greenwell, and Adelaide Anne Procter—appear in *DLB 199*. That thirty-three poets included in this volume were not discussed in the earlier volumes suggests not so much previous neglect as it indicates increased scholarly interest in women writers during the last fifteen years. More and more scholars have come to agree with Angela Leighton's assertion in the introduction to her anthology of *Victorian Women Poets* (1995): "It is the sheer variety of this poetry, in verse form as well as subject matter, which makes it worthy of recovery and reassessment." It is also true   that the lives of these women provide an important perspective on the social history of England in the nineteenth century. The central poet of *DLB 199* is Elizabeth Barrett Browning, around whom the volume is organized. All of the poets included were born before she died in 1861. Seven poets were born before Elizabeth Barrett was born in 1806, while thirty-two of the writers outlived her, six of them living into the twentieth century. However, though the lives of the included poets span 135 years, from Charlotte Elliott's birth in 1789 to Lady Lindsay's death in 1924, these writers published their most important poems during the forty-eight-year period between 1832 and 1880. Browning was the leading woman poet of this period and published significant volumes of poetry during the decades of the 1830s, 1840s, 1850s, and 1860s. The women chosen for this volume were her contemporaries and knew her work. Some were influenced by her tastes, ideas, and outlooks; others reacted against her poetic and political directions. All shared the challenge of writing poetry in an age that was generally cautious or hostile toward literary ambitions for women. The planned follow-up DLB volume on Victorian and Edwardian women poets will feature the second great English woman poet of the nineteenth century, Christina Rossetti, and will focus on poets whose most significant writ-

ing occurred in the years after 1880 through the death of King Edward VII.

Browning once made the plaintive statement that she saw no clear models or mentors who were not drowned in domesticity or sentimentality for her serious work as a poet: "England has had many learned women . . . and yet where are the poetesses? . . . I look everywhere for the grandmothers and see none." At times she could be sharply critical of the works of other female poets. For example, she was uncomfortable with the sentimental popularity and domestic messages of fellow poet Eliza Cook. Although she contemplated at length the circumstances of fulfilling her role as wife, mother, and poet in *Aurora Leigh* (1857), there is little evidence that she participated directly in a network assisting other female poets. Nor do most critics feel that she established a school or movement or left a clear set of poetic descendants. Rossetti, by contrast, has been more completely embraced and celebrated by twentieth-century feminist critics because of her connections with other women writers and the subtexts of revolutionary statements against patriarchy contained in her works.

In the early years of Queen Victoria's reign Browning received the lavish praise of critics and reviewers. In the spring of 1850 there was much speculation as to whom would be named poet laureate after the passing of William Wordsworth. Henry Fothergill Chorley placed a notice in the June 1850 *Athenaeum* proposing Browning as his candidate for the vacant post. He listed three compelling reasons why the appointment of a woman to the position might be suitable: it would be "an honourable testimonial to the individual, a fitting recognition of the remarkable place which the women of England have taken in the literature of the day, and a graceful compliment to the Sovereign herself." He concluded that "there is no living poet of either sex who can prefer a higher claim than Mrs. Elizabeth Barrett Browning." Although the appointment of poet laureate went to Alfred, Lord Tennyson, throughout the 1850s Browning's reputation continued to grow as readers responded to the emotion recorded in her *Sonnets from the Portuguese* (1850) and *Aurora Leigh.* Her role as a humanitarian and social critic was also valued and appreciated by Victorian readers.

Dictionary of Literary Biography 199: Victorian Women Poets takes as its beginning date 1832, the traditional end of the Era of British Romanticism as defined by Parliament's passage of the First Reform Act, which enfranchised the middle classes and increased the number of voters from five hundred thousand to more than one million, though women were not included. When Parliament passed the Second Reform Act in 1867 that expanded the vote to more men but again excluded women, woman suffrage societies began to form at an increasing rate. Parliament did grant women taxpayers the right to vote in municipal elections in 1869, but women did not achieve the right to vote for members of Parliament until the twentieth century, in part because of the opposition of Queen Victoria to the women's movement.

Although the campaign to win the vote was only gaining momentum before 1880, women were winning increased legal rights. Poet Caroline Norton was one of the women vigorously lobbying for the passing in 1839 of the Infant Custody Bill, legislation that granted women the right to apply to the courts for the custody of their children. She also worked to pass the Divorce and Matrimonial Causes Act, which in 1857, transferred decisions from ecclesiastical courts to a divorce court in London, thus making divorce and separation agreements easier to procure. Also, new provisions covering adultery, bigamy, and cruelty were added. The effect was to allow women greater opportunities of protection or release from threatening or difficult marital situations.

When a woman married in Victorian society her identity was largely subsumed under that of her husband. Before Parliament passed the Married Women's Property Acts of 1870 and 1882, a wife had almost no independent legal status. Incrementally, these laws gave all married women the right to own their own property. The 1870 legislation allowed married women the right to possess wages that they earned after marriage and legacies less than £ 200. The 1882 measure permitted a married woman to possess all of the property that she held before and after marriage.

During the decades of reform there were many political and social changes that slowly worked to expand intellectual and economic opportunities for women. Industrialism in the form of new steam engines, railroads, and factories made its black mark on the British rural landscape. By 1850 in Great Britain more inhabitants lived in urban areas than in rural communities, the first time such a pattern was recorded in human history. Women found new employment opportunities in urban and industrial areas. The Society for the Employment of Women, which encouraged women to enter such trades as publishing, was founded in 1860. The temper of the times encouraged new thinking and expanded aspirations.

Progressive ideas for reform were in the air throughout the Victorian period. Prominent liberal intellectuals in England, including John Stuart Mill and his wife, Harriet, took up the demand for the recognition of women's rights in the 1850s. In 1866 reformers Barbara Leigh Smith Bodichon and Emily Davies proposed a plan for the extension of university education to women and succeeded in 1869 in establishing Girton College, Cambridge. Mill, who believed that "the proper sphere of all human beings is the largest and highest which they are able to attain to," indicted sexual inequality and argued for expanded intellectual opportunities for women in his controversial work *The Subjection of Women* (1869). By 1876 a medical education and university classrooms were opened to British women.

Women, though, had to fight against a tide of resistance to gain respect and new opportunities—and this was as true in literature as in any other field. Maria Jane Jewsbury describes "a life so painfully, so laboriously domestic that it was an absolute duty to crush intellectual tastes. . . . I could neither write nor read legitimately till the day was over." A striking example of what was likely the prevailing nineteenth-century attitude regarding the roles of women is expressed in a letter from Robert Southey, the poet laureate of Great Britain, to the young Charlotte Brontë, concerning some poems that Brontë had sent him. He replied in 1837: "Literature cannot be the business of a woman's life, and it ought not to be. The more she is engaged in her proper duties, the less leisure will she have for it, even as an accomplishment and a recreation." He warned her that her poetic efforts would lead her to "day dreams" that were "likely to induce a distempered state of mind" and render her "unfit" for the daily duties that she must perform.

Even those who were open to women writers often had strong prejudices regarding their capabilities. The words of George W. Bethune in the preface to his 1848 anthology *The British Female Poets* are revealing. He finds that nineteenth-century British women poets are "averse to critical restraints" and argues that most "seem to have inverted their pen. As the line came first to the brain, so it was written; as it was written, so it was printed." In Bethune's judgment, the prominent fault of female poetical writers is that they "write from impulse, and as rapidly as they think."

Though women writers faced resistance and bias, they did have opportunities to publish. Many women wrote on a regular basis for periodicals, annuals, or gift books. Some of the leading periodicals that accepted women's poetry included *Household Words, The Spectator, All the Year Round, Punch, Longmans Magazine,* and *The St. James Gazette.* One of the more important outlets for women's writings was the *English Woman's Journal.* Edited by women and focused on women's writing and issues, it flourished from 1858 to 1862 and had a definite feminist agenda. Feature articles held up successful women as role models. As the second half of the nineteenth century progressed women were more often given important editorial responsibilities.

Some of the more well-known annuals or album books of the nineteenth-century include *The Keepsake, Forget Me Not,* the *Amulet,* the *Gem,* the *Literary Souvenir,* and *Friendship's Garland.* Sentimental in tone, they were read by young girls and cultivated women who led a lifestyle of leisure. In the introduction to her *British Women Poets of the 19th Century* (1996) Margaret Randolph Higonnet succinctly summarizes the growing demands and outlets for women's verse: "Over the course of the century, lending libraries, periodicals, and annual gift-books sought female poets in order to reach a growing audience of literate young women. They gathered women's poems in the printed equivalent of a drawing room conversation or girl's keepsake book." By 1857, the year in which *The Keepsake* ceased publication, more cheaply produced magazines had extinguished the popularity of the expensive, decorative annuals.

Anthologies of poetry by women also began to appear in the nineteenth century. The titles include *Specimen of the British Poetesses* (1825), *The British Female Poets, The Female Poets of Great Britain* (1849), and *Women Poets of the Victorian Era* (1891). The seventh volume of Alfred H. Miles's collection *The Poets and the Poetry of the Nineteenth Century* (1905–1907) contains works by women poets as does Edmund Clarence Stedman's *A Victorian Anthology* (1895).

Despite his condescending observations on women writers, anthologist Bethune in compiling *The British Female Poets* clearly sensed that there had been a marked increase in the quantity and quality of verse in the period: "Nothing shows the superiority of women in our days to those of past centuries, more than a comparison of their writings." The limitation of his critical judgment, however, is that he sees this development of energy and productivity in narrow moralistic terms, and this perspective causes him to restrict rather severely the types of themes that he identifies in poetry written by Victorian women. Thus, he observes:

> The manifestation of female talent is a striking characteristic of our age, and a very interesting proof of its moral advancement. . . . It is, therefore, consistent with her character that the genius of woman should yield peculiar delight when its themes are love, childhood, the softer beauties of creation, the joys or sorrows of the heart, domestic life, mercy, religion, and the instincts of justice. Hence her excellence in the poetry of the sensibilities.

Bethune's list of themes accurately describes some of the major themes found in the work of Browning, who explores in her verse the various strains of love and passion–romantic, disappointed, and unrequited–as well as devotion to God and the experiences of soul and spiritualism. However, Bethune neglects to mention the attention given by Browning and other women poets to less stereotypical female subjects.

A recurrent topic treated in both long and short poems throughout the nineteenth century is the fallen woman, a figure that symbolizes the unequal status of the sexes in Victorian society. Browning devoted entire sections of her long epic poem *Aurora Leigh* to the unfortunate plight of the seamstress Marian Erle. Other notable fallen-woman poems are Isa Blagden's "The Story of Two Lives," Mathilde Blind's "The Russian Student's Tale," Caroline Norton's "The Sorrows of Rosalie," Dora Greenwell's "Christina," and Adelaide Anne Procter's "The Requital." In all of these works, the poet empathizes with the woman who is shunned by society.

Although slavery was abolished in British colonies in 1833, the exploitative institution of American slavery was a focus of many poems written by Victorian women poets between 1830 and 1865. Despite her father's ownership of slaves on his plantation in Jamaica, Browning recognized that slavery was an unjust system of human oppression that must end, regardless of the economic consequences for her own family fortunes. Two of her most famous poems on the subject are "The Runaway Slave at Pilgrim's Point" and "A Curse for a Nation." Janet Hamilton referred to "Slavery's Vile Draconian Code" in her poem commemorating the visit of Harriet Beecher Stowe to Glasgow in 1853. Some poets link the oppression of women and children to that of the slaves.

The exploitation of women and children in factories and mines was also a topic of some moving poetry by women. One of the best known is Browning's "The Cry of the Children" (1843), a poem that was inspired by her reading detailed investigative reports on children who were forced to work long hours in factories and coal mines. Ellen Johnston's "The Factory" captures the "low appealing cry" of "A thousand children [who] are asign'd / to sicken and to die!" Caroline Norton's long poem *A Voice from the Factories* (1841) expresses compassion but offers no social or political solutions: "Poor little creatures, overtasked and sad, / *Your* Slavery hath no name, —yet is its Curse as bad!" Other poems attempt to offer consolation for tragic coal mining accidents that sometimes caused hundreds of men and boys to lose their lives. One such treatment occurs in Henrietta Tindal's "On the Hartley Colliery Accident, January, 1862."

In the many poems about social and political injustices the progressive courage of Victorian women can be seen. Such poems highlight the paradoxes contained in traditional or conservative stereotypes of what the Victorian woman should be and do. Leighton in her introduction to her anthology encapsulates these tensions: "Thus, at a time when 'woman' was being hailed as the last bastion of the values of domesticity, chastity, religious faith, sincerity and true feeling, women poets, it would appear, were actually writing about homelessness, sexual desire, unbelief, the self as a masked or mirrored secret, as well as the subversive new sciences."

Some Victorian women poets chose to write about science and humor. In general, women writing about Darwinism and scientific discoveries avoided the gloom and regret expressed by Alfred, Lord Tennyson in his long poem *In Memoriam: Arthur Henry Hallam* (1850). Some of the women who read Herbert Spencer and Charles Darwin found inspiring messages for possible social change and development. The topic of science can be found in poems by Louisa Sarah Bevington, Mathilde Blind, Dora Greenwell, Constance Naden, and May Probyn. To some of these poets, the writings of Darwin and Spencer suggested a new outlook on nature that endorsed progressive social improvement and a more liberal expression of sexual instincts. Inspired by her reading of Darwin's evolutionary theories, Blind composed her epic poem *The Ascent of Man* (1889). Bevington and Naden in their poetry not only questioned religious belief but also ultimately espoused atheism. In her poetry Bevington sees links between inevitable scientific and social change. Naden wrote such poems as "The Pantheist's Song of Immortality," "Scientific Wooing," "Natural Selection," and "Poet and Botanist" in which she looks forward to the liberating forces of change and the cycles of natural process.

Although it was rare for a woman to satirize a political figure, women such as Naden, Probyn, and Menella Bute Smedley used humor, ranging in tone from the light and entertaining to the ironic and sardonic, to satirize social restraints and hypocrisies in Victorian society. Women poets often used the guise of fantasy or the perspective of childhood to register points that were comic or slightly askew. In her poems of fantasy Sara Coleridge sometimes offered wry or ironic critiques of such earnest Victorian institutions as love and marriage. Smedley displays her playfulness in two poems written for children, "The Irish Fairy" and "The Sorrowful Seagull."

Sometimes nineteenth-century women poets addressed each other publicly in their verse. Browning's "L.E.L.'s Last Question" belongs among the memorable elegies of the century. In many poems one woman poet addresses another in a conversation-like style. Some examples of these dialogues include Charlotte Brontë's two poems addressed to her sisters, Isa Blagden's "To George Sand on her Interview with Elizabeth Barrett Browning," and Bessie Rayner Parkes's "For Adelaide"—a poem addressed to Adelaide Anne Procter. While such poems are often tributes, as Dora Greenwell's "To Christina Rossetti," on occasion one writer will criticize another, as Blagden does Sand.

For all their interest in the world outside the domestic circle, Victorian women poets wrote mainly about passion in human relationships and devotion to God. In various forms, from lyrics to dramatic monologues, they treat the range of experiences possible in human love relationships, from satisfaction and unhappiness in marriage to relationships featuring false, disenchanted, late, lost, or parted soul mates. Perhaps the most enduring poetic form used by women poets was the sonnet, best represented by Browning's *Sonnets from the Portuguese*. The rhetoric of the heart is certainly not the exclusive domain of feminine experience, but the poems by women on this topic written throughout Victoria's reign (some of them read and treasured by the queen) were a lasting contribution to literature.

Victorian women poets often wrote to glorify God, and *DLB 199* is notable for featuring women hymn writers. Because they were set to music and popular, the famous works of such writers as Sarah Flower Adams, Frances Ridley Havergal, Charlotte Elliott, and Cecil Frances Alexander in the past have been sometimes overlooked in discussions of the poetry of the era. The year 1997, though, marked a revival of scholarly interest in the Victorian hymn, as three important books on the subject were published: John Richard Watson's *The English*

Hymn: A Critical and Historical Study (1997) is a major study of the history and significance of this type of writing; Peter Newman Brooks in his *Hymns as Homilies* (1997) offers a study of twelve popular hymns; and Ian Bradley's authoritative *Abide with Me: The World of Victorian Hymns* (1997) focuses specifically on the Victorian period.

The importance of hymns in Victorian popular culture was enormous. Bradley argues that "in the last century hymns played much the same role in Victorian culture as television and radio soap operas do today . . . familiar, pervasive and subtly addictive, they both reassured and shocked, comforted and consoled, and occasionally challenged and disturbed . . . and inspired an extraordinary level of loyalty among their fans who bitterly resented change to words or tunes, and felt a sense of bereavement when old favorites were dropped." The range of Victorian hymns mirrored the social class structure of Great Britain—from the High Church hymns to the Nonconformist tunes to the popular Salvation Army choruses. Serious writers and composers devoted their talents to hymnody. Victorians sang their hymns in public churches and evangelical meetings as well as at home with family members around the piano in the parlor. Indeed, Victorian printing technology made possible for the first time the general circulation of hymn books during the nineteenth century. By 1900 the High Church collection, *Hymns Ancient and Modern* (1861), had sold more than 35 million copies. Hymns such as Elliott's "Just As I Am" and Adams's "Nearer, My God, to Thee" remain a central part of the British and Christian heritages.

Although Browning was well regarded in her own time, she and other women poets except Rossetti have been neglected for much of the twentieth century. In the 1920s and 1930s the Modernist reaction against all things associated with the "eminent" Victorians set in with a vengeance. Browning's life story and her poetry were condemned as "sentimental." Even a serious and particularly sympathetic reader such as Virginia Woolf in 1932 had to admit her low level of interest in Browning's work. In an essay that was published in both the *Yale Review* and the *Times Literary Supplement,* Woolf observes that *Aurora Leigh* is not much read or studied anymore. Although she admires the "speed and energy, forthrightness and complete self-confidence" of the speaker's voice, she asserts that it is a voice that also "overwhelms and bewilders." Echoing contemporary criticisms of the poem, Woolf maintains that in displaying such "ardor and abundance" in the long poem Browning "poaches upon a novelist's preserve and gives us not an epic or lyric but the story of many lives."

Until the rise of feminism in the 1970s only polite attention was paid to the works of Browning and lesser Victorian women poets. Four major critical studies appeared in the 1980s: Angela Leighton's *Elizabeth Barrett Browning* (1986), Helen Cooper's *Elizabeth Barrett Browning, Woman and Artist* (1988), Dorothy Mermin's *Elizabeth Barrett Browning: The Origins of a New Poetry* (1989), and Glennis Stephenson's *Elizabeth Barrett Browning and the Poetry of Love* (1989). Mermin argues forcefully that Browning "is for most practical purposes the first woman poet in English literature." Mermin admires her ambition and creativity—"She was always looking for a new subject, a generic innovation, a new way to touch the world"—and believes that Browning's place in the tradition of nineteenth-century poetry by women is central: "her place at the wellhead of a new female tradition remains the single most important fact about her in terms of literary history."

Behind the towering reputation of Browning are the lives and poems of scores of other significant Victorian women poets. Readers are just beginning to appreciate the range, depth, and diversity of texts by Victorian women poets that have been recently made available by publishers in Great Britain and the United States. A few of the more important recent anthologies are: *Victorian Women Poets,* edited by Leighton and Margaret Reynolds; *British Women Poets of the 19th Century,* edited by Higonnet; *Victorian Women Poets 1830–1900: An Anthology* (1994), edited by Jennifer Breen; *Winged Words: Victorian Women's Poetry and Verse* (1994), compiled by Catherine Reilly, with a preface by Germaine Greer; and *Nineteenth-Century Women Poets* (1996), edited by Isobel Armstrong and Joseph Bristow with Cath Sharrock.

Critical books and essay collections are beginning to appear that are helping to define the patterns and approaches needed to understand these writers and their times. Especially useful are books such as Kathleen Hickok's *Representations of Women: Nineteenth-Century British Women's Poetry* (1984), Leighton's *Victorian Women Poets: Writing Against the Heart* (1992) and *Victorian Women Poets: A Critical Reader* (1996), and Tess Cosslett's *Victorian Women Poets* (1996). There is yet much more that needs to be done. For example, there is no complete index or bibliography or series that lists comprehensively the reviews of women's poetry during the Victorian period. Also, many poems published in periodicals remain unexamined and uncollected. Critical, bibliographical and biographical, studies that make connections between Victorian women poets and that examine influence and interaction are sorely needed. Additional research should define more fully the support networks that women writers and editors engaged in during the Victorian period. Also, more study is needed to delineate the relation of female and male poets of the Victorian age.

–William B. Thesing

Acknowledgments

This book was produced by Bruccoli Clark Layman, Inc. Karen L. Rood is senior editor for the *Dictionary of Literary Biography* series. In-house editors are George Anderson, Charles Brower, Jan Peter van Rosevelt, Penelope Hope, and Philip B. Dematteis.

Administrative support was provided by Ann M. Cheschi, Renita Hickman, and Tenesha S. Lee.

Bookkeeper is Neil Senol.

Copyediting supervisor is Phyllis A. Avant. The copyediting staff includes Christine Copeland, Thom Harman, Melissa D. Hinton, Jannette L. Giles, Nicole M. Nichols, and Raegan E. Quinn. Freelance copyeditors are Rebecca Mayo and Jennie Williamson.

Editorial associate is Jeff Miller.

Layout and graphics staff includes Janet E. Hill, Mark J. McEwan, and Alison Smith.

Office manager is Kathy Lawler Merlette.

Photography editors are Margo Dowling and Paul Talbot. Photographic copy work was performed by Joseph M. Bruccoli.

Production manager is Marie L. Parker.

SGML supervisor is Cory McNair. The SGML staff includes Linda Drake, Frank Graham, Jennifer Harwell, and Alex Snead.

Systems manager is Marie L. Parker.

Database manager is Javed Nurani. Kim Kelly performed data entry.

Typesetting supervisor is Kathleen M. Flanagan. The typesetting staff includes Karla Corley Brown, Pamela D. Norton, and Patricia Flanagan Salisbury. Freelance typesetters include Deidre Murphy and Delores Plastow.

Walter W. Ross and Steven Gross did library research. They were assisted by the following librarians at the Thomas Cooper Library of the University of South Carolina: Linda Holderfield and the interlibrary-loan staff; reference-department head Virginia Weathers; reference librarians Marilee Birchfield, Stefanie Buck, Stefanie DuBose, Rebecca Feind, Karen Joseph, Donna Lehman, Charlene Loope, Anthony McKissick, Jean Rhyne, and Kwamine Simpson; circulation-department head Caroline Taylor; and acquisitions-searching supervisor David Haggard.

The editor would like to thank Denis Thomas for his advice on the introduction. My former graduate research assistants–James Richard Simmons Jr., Lee Anna Maynard, Sarah Barnhart, Jordan Harris, Connie Karickoff, Ivan Young, Lucy Morrison, Charles Brower, and Kelly Frank–helped with the preparations. I am also grateful to Patrick Scott and Roger Mortimer for gathering photos and materials from the rare-books collection at Thomas Cooper Library. I thank Ezra Greenspan, the University of South Carolina English Department library representative, for ordering some letters written by Victorian women. Finally, I am grateful to my colleague Paula Feldman and all of the members of the Nineteenth-Century Club of the University of South Carolina for their enthusiasm and interest in British women writers.

Dictionary of Literary Biography® • Volume One Hundred Ninety-Nine

Victorian Women Poets

Dictionary of Literary Biography

Sarah Fuller Flower Adams
(22 February 1805 – 14 August 1848)

Crys Armbrust
University of South Carolina

BOOKS: *Vivia Perpetua, A Dramatic Poem* (London: Charles Fox, 1841);
The Flock at the Fountain (London: Palmer and Clayton, 1845).

OTHER: Fourteen hymns, in *Hymns and Anthems,* compiled by William Johnson Fox (London: Charles Fox, 1841);
"Autumn" and "The Opening of the Royal Exchange," in *Lectures Addressed Chiefly to the Working Classes,* by Fox, 4 volumes (London: Charles Fox, 1849), 4: pp. 145–147.

SELECTED PERIODICAL PUBLICATIONS–UNCOLLECTED:

POETRY

"Winds and Clouds," *Monthly Repository,* 8 (March 1834): 203;
"What Care We for Falling Leaves," *Monthly Repository,* 8 (October 1834): 717;
"Come to Thy Home, Beloved!," *Monthly Repository,* 8 (November 1834): 762;
"A Portrait," *Monthly Repository,* 9 (January 1835): 56;
"Ruth," *Monthly Repository,* 9 (March 1835): 204;
"The Royal Progress," *Illuminated Magazine* (April 1835);
"To an Invalid, with Some Violets," *Monthly Repository,* 9 (April 1835): 258–259;
"Morning, Noon, and Night," *Monthly Repository,* 9 (August 1835): 562;
"The Dead Grasshopper," *Monthly Repository,* 9 (October 1835): 675;
"Lines Suggested by Macready's 'Hamlet,'" *Monthly Repository,* 9 (November 1835): 749–750.

Sarah Fuller Flower Adams; drawing by Margaret Gillies (from Richard Garnett's The Life of W. J. Fox, Public Teacher and Social Reformer 1786–1864, *1910)*

DRAMA

Charade Drama, Monthly Repository, 9 (February 1835): 122–133;
Valentines' Day, Monthly Repository, 10 (February 1836): 94–106.

FICTION

"The Luxembourg," *Monthly Repository,* 8 (January 1834): 54–63;

"The Welsh Wanderer," *Monthly Repository,* 8 (July 1834): 514–520;

"The Three Visits," *Monthly Repository,* 8 (October 1834): 724–733;

"Buy Images," *Monthly Repository,* 8 (November 1834): 756–762;

"A Chapter On Chimnies," *Monthly Repository,* 9 (January 1835): 57–59;

"An Evening with Charles Lamb and Coleridge," *Monthly Repository,* 9 (March 1835): 162–168;

"The Actress," parts 1–3, *Monthly Repository,* 9 (July, August, September 1835): 460–475, 514–530, 571–591;

"An Odd Subject," *Monthly Repository,* 9 (December 1835): 795–802;

"York Minster and the Forest Bugle," *Monthly Repository,* 10 (January 1836): 38–43.

The literary remains of Sarah Fuller Flower Adams are small, comprising only two books, fourteen published hymns, twenty-three uncollected pieces of prose and poetry in periodical publications, and several unlocated manuscript poems on social and political subjects—poems formerly in the possession of Adams's friend and mentor, the noted Unitarian minister and social activist William Johnson Fox. Her modern reputation rests upon a single poetic text, the hymn "Nearer, My God to Thee." Yet while that hymn is familiar to many, its author remains practically unknown.

Although Adams's writings are minor productions within the broader scope of nineteenth-century literary culture, they nonetheless serve as a useful index for the examination of the interplay among varying religious, social, and political ideologies during the highly volatile early days of the British reform movement in the 1830s and 1840s. Thematically, Adams's productions most often detail working-class concerns; rhetorically, they exhibit the argumentative posture and ideological base of Chartism; stylistically, they yield abundant evidence of competing Romantic and Victorian aesthetic sensibilities. The immediate context of her highly personal vision is characteristically religious and most often devotional and meditative—a stance appropriate to her initial readership, which was largely Unitarian. However, her prose and poetry transcend the traditional concerns and boundaries of orthodox religious sectarianism mainly because Adams invariably politicizes her writings with the larger social issues confronting her and her contemporaries.

In her works Adams advocates such issues as political enfranchisement, national education, social acculturation, and gender equity—each of which is informed by a probing awareness of the inadequacies inherent within the social and political systems. These anomalous inclusions in "religious" texts are in part explained by the dissenting nature within Unitarianism itself, wherein great emphasis is placed upon free thought and individual action as opposed to the emphasis upon unquestionable orthodoxy and rigid hierarchy of the established Anglican Church. Adams apparently made few distinctions between her private and her public self, and the matters of intellect, religion, and politics were part and parcel of an integrated whole. The conflation of seemingly incongruent elements in her works, though conspicuous, was decidedly appropriate to her and apparently enthusiastically received by her readers.

Adams was born Sarah Fuller Flower at Great Harlow, Essex, on 22 February 1805. She was the youngest daughter of Benjamin Flower (1755–1829), a political writer, religious dissenter, and printer who had traveled extensively in Holland, Germany, Switzerland, and France. Flower's early political writings focused first on the French constitution and later on England's war with France. The latter works were in fact little more than thinly veiled attacks on the defects within the English constitution. His writings garnered for him in 1793 the editorship of the *Cambridge Intelligencer,* an early radical newspaper espousing highly liberal working-class political and social principles. His hostile criticism in the journal, especially of the Anglican Church, reached such a feverish pitch in 1799 that he was summoned before the House of Lords upon libel charges against Bishop Watson, adjudged guilty, heavily fined, and sentenced to six months' imprisonment in Newgate. Of Adams's mother, Eliza Gould Flower, little is known, but according to Richard Garnett in the *Dictionary of National Biography,* she too had been a martyr for her liberal opinions. Shortly after Flower's release from prison, they married and moved to Great Harlow. Flower set himself up as a printer and continued his political agitation, establishing, for example, *The Political Register,* a monthly magazine that he edited from 1807 to 1811. Flower's wife died in 1810, leaving him to care for Sarah and her elder sister Eliza, who was named after her mother.

In early childhood Sarah developed an intense desire to pursue a serious career upon the stage, and domestic entertainments early on provided her an important artistic outlet in which to nurture and develop both her musical and dramatic skills. According to the biographical sketch by Eliza F. Bridell-Fox, Sarah possessed a rich contralto voice and habitually chose vocal pieces "in which she could unite dramatic action and costume," often to quite good effect. The range of her musical repertoire was varied. Notable among her standards were Franz Schubert's "The Erl King," John Lodge Ellerton's "The Cid," Thomas Campbell's "Lord Ullin's Daughter," the lighter folksongs "My Boy Tammie" and "There's Nae Luck about the House," and her sister Eliza's settings of Sir Walter Scott's "Hallowmas Eve" and "Madge Wildfire's Song." Her impromptu at-home performances usually included dramatic monologues as well, particularly those drawn from William Shakespeare. These amateur parlor performances in the 1820s and early 1830s served as valuable training for Adams's later public stage debut and are useful indicators of her serious musical and dramatic intent.

Sarah's sister Eliza was a talented musician in her own right, publishing several highly popular compositions, including *Fourteen Musical Illustrations of the Waverley Novels* (1831), *Songs of the Seasons* (n.d.), and such political songs as "The Gathering of the Unions," said to have been performed at the Great Birmingham political rally in May 1832. Moreover, she composed many accompaniments for her sister's hymn texts, many of which became musical standards at the Unitarian South Place Chapel, Finsbury, where the sisters led the musical services: one singing and the other playing.

In 1820 Flower and his daughters moved to Dalston, a neighborhood of London, where he established a draper's business and, not surprisingly, resumed his zealous agitating for social and political reform. As he began to assert himself within the community, he and subsequently his daughters made connections with London's literary and intellectual circles, which included many reform sympathizers. Conspicuous among those who would become Adams's lifelong friends were Harriet Martineau, William James Linton, John Stuart Mill, and especially the young Robert Browning. According to Joshua E. Wills, Browning's early religious doubts and avowed atheism inspired Adams to write "Nearer, My God to Thee," composed in 1826 when she was only twenty-one and he only fifteen.

Prior to her association with *The Monthly Repository,* Sarah mainly wrote religious verse of a characteristically evangelical kind. Her hymns, written mostly between 1826 and 1836, total fourteen original works: "Nearer, My God to Thee," "He Sendeth Sun, He Sendeth Shower," "Creator Spirit! Thou the First," "Darkness Shrouded Calvary," "Gentle Fall the Dews of Eve," "Go, and Watch the Autumn Leaves," "O Hallowed Memories of the Past," "O Human Heart! Thou Hast a

Song," "O I Would Sing a Song of Praise," "O Love! Thou Makest All Things Even," "Part in Peace! Is Day before Us?," "Sing to the Lord! For His Mercies Are Sure," "The Mourners Came at Break of Day," and "Living or Dying, Lord, I Would be Thine." She also translated several hymns by Portuguese and Spanish authors.

Upon the death of their father in 1829, Sarah and Eliza came to live with the family of the Reverend George J. Fox, a dissenting minister and close friend whom Flower had designated as his executor and his daughters' guardian. This familial association was to become one of the most influential ones in Adams's life, for it marked the subsequent path of her religious and intellectual life. Indeed, her career became almost exclusively a Fox family production. George's son William Johnson Fox, an eminent Unitarian minister, working-class educator, and art critic, became a close confidant and enthusiastically championed the young author's budding talent, later providing her with important publication and performance opportunities. Charles Fox, William Johnson's brother, became Sarah's principal publisher. In the 1890s Eliza F. Bridell-Fox, William Johnson's daughter, continued to perpetuate Sarah's reputation in privately printed editions of her five-act dramatic poem *Vivia Perpetua* and hymns.

The early 1830s proved auspicious for Sarah. In 1834 she began to publish her work in William Johnson Fox's *The Monthly Repository,* in which she ultimately placed many prose essays and poems and two short one-act dramas. Her works appeared under the pseudonym "S.Y.," claimed by Bridell-Fox to indicate "her pet name Sally to her personal friends." An editorial note in the August 1833 number of *The Monthly Repository,* written by Fox, characterizes the journal as aspiring "to become the People's Magazine, teaching their duties, refining their enjoyments, asserting their rights, and promoting their interest." Fox's declaration aligns the journal's ideology with other Chartist periodical publications of the 1830s such as William James Linton's *The National.* A broad-based emphasis on the educational and cultural agenda of Chartism permeates Sarah's prose contributions to the journal, regardless of whether the discussion at hand be art and literary criticism as in "The Luxembourg" and "An Evening with Charles Lamb and Coleridge" or political enfranchisement and national education as in "The Welsh Wanderer" and "An Odd Subject." Adams's published poetry from this period onward also reveals her politicized vision, and in her poetry one can trace the shift from the Keatsian romanticism of her early devotional lyrics to the Shelleyan socialism of later verses such as her Anti-Corn-League songs.

The year 1834 marked another important event in the life of Sarah Fuller Flower: her marriage on 24 September at St. John's, Hackney, to William Brydges Adams, an engineer and the pseudonymous "Junius Redivivus" of Fox's *Monthly Repository,* whom she had first met through Mrs. John Taylor (later Mrs. John Stuart Mill). Although the couple had no children, their married life was apparently an extraordinarily happy one. William Adams wholly supported the professional endeavors of his wife, including her dramatic aspirations as well as her literary productions.

Sarah Adams's first public dramatic performance occurred in 1837 when she appeared as Shakespeare's Lady Macbeth at the Richmond theater, a performance that met with considerable success. As an anonymous reviewer for the *Court Journal* (most probably Fox) favorably detailed, her "performance was strongly marked by original conception and dramatic power." The success of the play led to further engagements for Adams, notably as Portia in Shakespeare's *Merchant of Venice* and Lady Teazle in Richard Brinsley Sheridan's *School for Scandal*. These successes, coupled with a highly laudatory letter of introduction from Macready, the leading Shakespearean actor of the day, led to an extended engagement at the Bath Theatre, a feeder training program for the London theaters. Unfortunately, just when she was beginning to savor public acclaim for her dramatic talent, her health began to fail. Unable to withstand the rigorous schedule of public performances, Adams again turned her attention to literature.

In this last phase of her literary career Adams produced her largest work, the five-act dramatic poem *Vivia Perpetua,* published in 1841. The poem details the conflict between paganism and Christianity in the personage of the courtesan Vivia, a votary to Jupiter, who experiences martyrdom for her conversion to Christianity. William Johnson Fox, who had earlier published two of Adams's closet dramas in *The Monthly Repository,* described the play in his *Lectures Addressed Chiefly to the Working Classes* (1849):

> At some times, there is the vivacity of stage action, and the force of tragic passion and situation; at others, we only watch the current of thought or emotion; but reality is never lost in either; the whole is pervaded by the grace, beauty, and power of a mind in perfect harmony with its theme; and the result is one of the purest and loveliest specimens ever yet produced of the dramatic poem.

Less glowing approval of the play comes at the century's end from the Celtic scholar Richard Garnett, then director of the British Museum's Reading Room, who in the introduction to an 1892 edition of the play stresses its biographical significance:

> "Vivia Perpetua" is unsatisfactory as a play but has deep human interest as an idealized representation of the author's mind and heart. In the character of Vivia she has shadowed forth her own moral affections and intellectual convictions, and the intensity of her feelings frequently exalts her diction . . . into genuine eloquence. The moral charm, however, takes precedence of the artistic, as is to be expected in the work of a true woman. Lyrical enthusiasm atones in no small measure for the lack of the constructive faculty, and "Vivia Perpetua" fulfils better than many more ambitious works Milton's demand that poetry should be "simple, sensuous, and passionate."

Adams's hymns were first collectively published in Fox's *Hymns and Anthems* (1841), a collection compiled for the use of Fox's congregation at South Place Chapel, Finsbury. Their immediate popularity at South Place Chapel set the tone for their inclusion in many later Victorian hymnals. Fox summarizes her religious poetry in his *Lectures Addressed Chiefly to the Working Classes,* asserting that it finds "its sympathies and congenialities not in the profundity of reflection, nor in the endeavor to give permanence to a shadowy world, but in looking round on the real, and seeing how rich even the surface of the real is in fruits and flowers for human enjoyment." The general tenor of Fox's criticism finds its representative source in her hymn "He Sendeth Sun, He Sendeth Shower," which was sung at the funerals of both Sarah and Eliza. Adams's periodic excess of emotion and sentiment notwithstanding, the contemporary popularity of her hymns allowed her poetic reputation to survive into the twentieth century. In no instance is this more true than in the case of "Nearer, my God, to Thee," upon which her posthumous modern reputation wholly came to rest.

"Nearer, My God, to Thee" shares with Cardinal John Newman's "Lead Kindly Light" the distinction of being the two most well-known hymns written during the nineteenth century. It has been widely reprinted in its original form, in many translations, and in various ideologically-altered versions adapted, as hymnologist John Julian puts it, "to bring the hymn more in harmony with the [sectarian] views of the editors by whom it has been adopted." Its subsequent inclusion in *Hymns Ancient and Modern* (1861) to a tune by John Bacchus Dykes assured its dissemination among more mainstream religious circles, and Sir Arthur Sullivan's much later musical setting of the text further popularized it too. Beyond its appearance in hymnals, the hymn between 1876 and 1911 went through no less than ten frequently reprinted British and American illustrated book editions. Beyond their appeal to a general religious readership, these sumptuously bound, embossed and gilded volumes were standard items in the giftbook and presentation volume trade. Moreover, the hymn's dramatic use aboard the sinking HMS *Titanic* in April 1912–it was the final musical selection played before the ship went down– certainly gave the hymn global notice if not mythic appeal.

Adams's last publication, a catechism for adolescents titled *The Flock at the Fountain,* was published in 1845. A publication notice of the work in the November issue of the *Westminster Review* calls it "a small work for the young, explaining and enforcing the principal points of religion and morals in verse and in prose; and displaying the rare union of a clear head, a fervent heart, and considerable poetical powers. . . . Its object is to convey ideas that will act upon the heart and understanding, and not impress upon the memory a mere religious phraseology barren of useful results." In a sense this work represents Adams's having come full circle in her literary career, ending in a metaphorical way back where she began. The epic dramatic canvas of *Vivia Perpetua* no longer interests her, and her final literary effort focuses what remains of her poetical and intellectual genius in an instructive text of moral power addressed to subsequent generations of young readers–readers who in the best case scenario will continue as she did to strive to make a better, more ethical world, one where neither religious perfidy nor social injustice can exist.

Devastated by the death of her sister Eliza in December 1846, only one month after the publication of *The Flock at the Fountain,* Adams ceased writing literature of any kind. Subsequently, her own health, already tenuously consumptive, began to decline steadily over the next year, and she died 14 August 1848, leaving many to mourn the passing of an extraordinary woman. One of the important litmus tests for literature is its durability, the perennial appeal of a work to following generations of readers. For Sarah Fuller Flower Adams, that test was met by "Nearer, My God, to Thee," a hymn so favored by subsequent generations that it compels the reexamination of the other works of its author.

References:

William Johnson Fox, "On Living Poets; and Their Service to the Cause of Political Freedom and Human Progress; Miss Barrett and Mrs. Adams," in his *Lectures Addressed Chiefly to the Working Classes,* 4 volumes (London: Charles Fox, 1849), 4, pp. 131–161;

Alfred H. Miles, *The Sacred Poets of the Nineteenth Century* (London: George Routledge & Sons, 1906);

Joshua E. Wills, *An Historical and Biographical Sketch of the Hymn "Nearer My God to Thee"* (Philadelphia, 1921).

Cecil Frances Alexander

(1818 – 12 October 1895)

Gloria G. Jones
Winthrop University

BOOKS: *Verses for Holy Seasons, with Questions for Examination,* edited by Walter Farquhar Hook (London: Francis and John Rivington, 1846; Philadelphia: Hooker, 1852);

The Lord of the Forest and His Vassals, An Allegory (London, 1847);

Hymns for Little Children (London: Masters, 1848; Philadelphia: Hooker, 1850);

The Baron's Little Daughter and Other Tales in Prose and Verse (London: Masters, 1848; Philadelphia: Hooker, n.d.);

Moral Songs (London, 1849);

Narrative Hymns for Village Schools (London: Masters, 1853);

Poems on Subjects in the Old Testament, 2 volumes (London: Masters, 1854);

Hymns Descriptive and Devotional, for the Use of Schools (London: Masters, 1858);

The Legend of Golden Prayers and Other Poems (London: Bell and Daldy, 1859);

Easy Questions on the Life of Our Lord (London: Griffeth and Farran, 1891).

Collections: *Poems,* edited, with a preface, by William Alexander (London: Macmillan, 1896; New York: Macmillan, 1896);

Selected Poems of William Alexander and C. F. Alexander, edited by A. P. Graves (London: Society for Promotion of Christian Knowledge, 1930; New York and Toronto: Macmillan, 1930).

OTHER: *The Sunday Book of Poetry,* edited by Alexander (London & Cambridge: Macmillan, 1864; Cambridge, Mass.: Sever and Francis, 1865).

From a young age Cecil Frances Alexander was drawn to writing poetry, frequently preparing a weekly newsletter of comic and serious verse for her family. As an adult she followed the Victorian tradition of writing poems on medieval subjects, but the works that brought her the most recognition were her devotional poems and her hymns, which were inspired by the Oxford Movement. Noted Victorian

Cecil Frances Alexander (photograph by Elliot and Fry)

authority G. B. Tennyson, who defines devotional poetry as verse that is tied to acts of worship, notes that the verse growing out of the Oxford movement, especially its Tractarian phase, is characteristically devotional.

While other Victorian women poets such as Christina Rossetti wrote poetry, religious and otherwise, expressly for publication, no other woman poet was as consistently didactic in her public verse as Alexander. Considered by many as one of the finest English women hymn writers, she desired to make doctrinal subjects such as Baptism, the Ten Commandments, and the Apostles' Creed understandable to children. Almost all of the four hundred poems and hymns written by Alexander were intended for a young audience. Even though instructing children was her goal, her three most famous hymns–"Once in Royal David's City," "There is a Green Hill Far Away," and "All Things Bright and Beautiful"–appear in modern adult hymnals of many denominations. Although some may agree with Geoffrey Faber's observation that the poetry of the Oxford Movement was weak and not particularly memorable, these three hymns certainly exhibit staying power.

Information about the private life of Cecil Frances Alexander is scarce. Since her husband and elder daughter burned most of her papers after her death, one must rely almost entirely on her published writings and remarks that others attribute to her. Even her birthplace is a matter of dispute, with *The Times* (London) obituary and the *Dictionary of National Biography* claiming Wicklow, and Valerie Wallace, her most recent biographer, insisting on No. 25 Eccles Street in Dublin. Alexander's date of birth is similarly vague and can only be said to be some time in 1818. She was born Cecil Frances Humphreys, the third of seven children of Maj. John Humphreys and Elizabeth Reed Humphreys. The major had retired from the Royal Marines in 1806 with some prize money and a pension for an arm lost in a sea battle. He settled in Ireland, where he invested in land, organized the yeomanry on the Irish estate of the first marquis of Abercorn, and held a position at Dublin Castle.

In 1825 the family moved to Ballykeane in County Wicklow, and Major Humphreys became manager of the estates of the earl of Wicklow. Fanny, as Alexander was called by family and friends, showed early signs of literary gifts. She also evidenced extraordinary piety, and both of these tendencies were encouraged by her early friendship–amounting almost to sisterhood–with Lady Harriet Howard, a daughter of the earl of Wicklow, who lived at Shelton Abbey, six miles from Ballykeane. Here the two young ladies visited the sick and needy and performed daily private devotions. They also began teaching Christian doctrine, with heavy emphasis on the memorizing of the catechism, creeds, the Lord's Prayer and the Ten Commandments, preparing the way for their later literary collaboration. Beginning in 1842 they would produce a series of pamphlets expounding the doctrines of the Oxford Movement, with Howard writing the prose and Humphrey contributing verses.

In 1833, however, they were separated by Major Humphreys's moving to County Tyrone in Ulster to take up the management of the estates of the second Marquis of Abercorn, who lived nearby at Baronscourt. In 1835 Fanny presented the Marquis with an unpublished poem in praise of Baronscourt, apparently inspired by Felicia Hemans's "The Stately Homes of England" but focused on a single estate. Another early poem is "The Yellow Damask Chair," a thoroughly uncharacteristic piece of whimsy, consisting of a "complaint" in heroic couplets about decadent changes in fashion. According to the headnote of the poem this criticism was "heard to proceed" from a chair that had been consigned to "a lumber room in a remote part of a nobleman's mansion in the North of Ireland," presumably Baronscourt. The chair links aesthetic fashion with moral depravity and denounces those who simply replace the old with the new, be it fashion or virtue. That somebody as thoroughly conservative as Fanny Humphreys could create a comic conservative curmudgeon suggests that the sentimental, serious, and pious tones of her best-known poems reveal only part of her personality.

In the late 1830s and 1840s Humphreys continued in Tyrone the good works that had occupied her in Ballykeane, with an emphasis on teaching children, particularly deaf children, for whom she established a day school and ultimately in 1850 a small charity boarding school. During this period she came under the influence of the Oxford Movement, particularly John Keble, whose *The Christian Year* (1827), a collection of poems meant to accompany the scripture passages listed in the *Book of Common Prayer* for reading in Anglican churches on the various days of the liturgical calendar, was the best-known volume of Tractarian poetry. While most of the Church of Ireland in the nineteenth century tended toward Low Church or evangelical Anglicanism, Humphreys was a Tractarian throughout her life, and she first appeared in print as a Tractarian.

Alexander's early books appeared under her maiden name. Her first book, *Verses for Holy Seasons, with Questions for Examination* (1846), edited by the Reverend Dr. Walter Farquhar Hook, a well-known Anglican clergyman in Leeds, was described in the dedication as an "attempt to adapt the great principles of [Keble's] immortal work to the exigencies of the schoolroom." This book was followed by her one extended attempt at prose narrative, *The Lord of the Forest and His Vassals, An Allegory* (1847); *The Baron's Little Daughter and Other Tales in Prose and Verse* (1848); *Hymns for Little Children* (1848), which included a brief and rather non-committal prefatory note by John Keble; and *Moral Songs* (1849).

The title poem of *The Baron's Little Daughter and Other Tales in Prose and Verse* deals with a characteristic example of childhood female piety and its beneficial effects on a wayward man in a setting of medieval

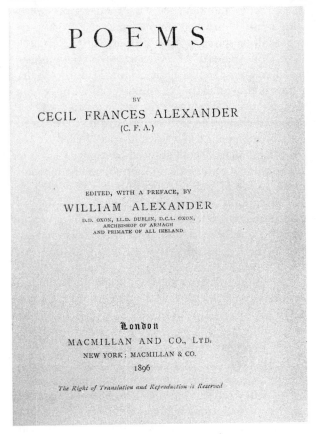

POEMS

BY

CECIL FRANCES ALEXANDER
(C. F. A.)

EDITED, WITH A PREFACE, BY
WILLIAM ALEXANDER
D.D. OXON, LL.D. DUBLIN, D.C.L. OXON,
ARCHBISHOP OF ARMAGH
AND PRIMATE OF ALL IRELAND.

London
MACMILLAN AND CO., LTD.
NEW YORK: MACMILLAN & CO.
1896

The Right of Translation and Reproduction is Reserved

Title page for the first posthumous collection of Alexander's poetry

feudal violence. "The Rising at Aix," in ballad stanzas similarly contrasts a grief-stricken husband's despair at his wife's death from plague with the faith of a child who repeats the refrain "Christ raiseth up the dead." When grave robbers open the wife's tomb, she rises from it and walks home to be reunited with her husband. While Humphreys never definitively suggests whether the Lady Joscelind has been miraculously restored or was mistakenly buried, the character never again smiles after her "resurrection," casting some doubt on the Christian nature of the miracle.

Hymns for Little Children, which sold 546,000 copies by 1878, is by far the most important of these books of the 1840s and contains Alexander's best-remembered hymns. After the introductory morning and evening hymns and a hymn to the Trinity, the forty hymns in the collection are intended to help Sunday school children understand particular passages from the baptismal service, the Apostles' Creed, the Ten Commandments, and the Lord's Prayer. "All Things Bright and Beautiful," for example, illustrates the second statement in the creed, that God is the "maker of Heaven and Earth." "Once in Royal David's City" expounds the proposition that Christ was "conceived by the Holy Ghost, born of

the Virgin Mary." "There is a Green Hill Far Away" expands on the terse description in the *Book of Common Prayer* of the Passion, that Jesus "suffered under Pontius Pilate, was crucified, dead, and buried."

Some of these hymns are reminiscent of William Blake's *Songs of Innocence* (1789) not only in their simple language, meters, and rhymes but also in their celebration of childhood. The "Hymn of the Holy Trinity" begins "We are little Christian children / We can run and talk and play"; similarly "Once in Royal David's City" refers to Christ's "wondrous childhood" and proclaims "He is our childhood's Pattern, / Day by day like us he grew." On the other hand, the poems sometimes carry a stern message. The hymn on the second commandment, forbidding graven images, opens by deploring the idolatry of "strange countries far away / Where God's name is unknown" and warns Christian children that, "They must not think of other things, / Light toys or merry play, / When they are listening to God's Word, / Or kneeling down to pray."

Humphreys's Tractarianism did not lead her to contemplate spinsterhood or nunneries. Beginning in 1846, she established a potentially serious attachment to the Reverend William Archer Butler, a brilliant clergyman who held the chair of moral philosophy at Trinity College, Dublin, but he died in 1848 of "famine fever." Since her best friend Lady Harriet had died in December 1846, these were particularly sad years for the author as well as the ones in which she produced her most enduring verse. In 1849 she met the Reverend William Alexander, a well-connected clergyman six years her junior. He was related to eminent clergymen, landowners, and politicians but at the time was just a country rector who had acquired Tractarian opinions, poetic inclinations, and tradesmen's bills at Oxford while taking six years to graduate. The wedding took place on 15 October 1850; like Elizabeth Barrett, who married Robert Browning, Fanny Humphreys, an established poet, married an obscure younger man who was only aspiring to gain recognition as a poet.

Between 1850 and 1867, while her husband served as rector of three parish churches in County Tyrone and County Donegal, Alexander continued her charitable and educational work in his various parishes. She also published vigorously in the 1850s. *Narrative Hymns for Village Schools* (1853) and *Hymns Descriptive and Devotional, for the Use of Schools* (1858) continued her work as a didactic hymnist for children. The two-volume work *Poems on Subjects in the Old Testament* (1854) included the once well-known poem "The Burial of Moses," which is often claimed, on no stated authority, to have been admired by Alfred, Lord Tennyson and Mark Twain.

The Legend of Golden Prayers and Other Poems (1859) is the most interesting collection that Alexander published in the first decade after her marriage. The title poem deals with a medieval Italian legend, cited in Lord Lindsay's *Christian Art,* about Beata, the new bride of the count of Rome, who is torn between her domestic duties as a wife and "lady of rank" and her personal inclination to say the daily liturgical offices. The lengthy, three-part poem contains an ambitious variety of stanzaic patterns and rhyme schemes. Its medievalism is characteristically Tractarian, and its conflict between the active and contemplative lives presumably reflects some of the dilemmas that Alexander encountered in making the transition from independence to marriage.

Other poems in the volume, which often treat death, have a more somber tone. In 1859 the boarding school for deaf children that Alexander had helped establish nine years earlier burned, killing six of the children. The proceeds from the book were contributed to the rebuilding of the school, and the poem "Voices for the Dumb" dealt specifically with this tragedy. Dividing the poem into three sections, "The Voice of Lamentation," "The Voice of Hope," and "The Voice of the Mother," Alexander expresses the hope that the children's present comfort in heaven outweighs their past sufferings on earth. The collection also includes both graveyard meditations on those who enjoyed normal longevity, such as "Southey's Grave" and "The Grave of Mrs. Hemans (In St. Anne's Church, Dublin)," and many poems about people who died young. "Euthanasia" is a long poem on the death of Lady Harriet Howard; "Lines" memorializes the Reverend William Archer Butler: "The beautiful and gifted dead / The noblest of our kind."

Many of the poems, such as "The Graveyard in the Hills," probe fictional deaths. In the poem "The Solitary" a religiously skeptical humanist communing with nature and a widow weeping by her husband's grave encounter a "Pastor" of the Church of Ireland for some spiritually uplifting consolation in blank verse that is reminiscent of William Wordsworth. In "The Legend of Stumpie's Brae" Alexander tells a didactic story of a murder and haunting in the Ulster version of Robert Burns's Scots dialect. However, the effectiveness of the didacticism and the grisliness are undermined by Alexander's use of dialect and a jaunty rhythm as well as by the comic activities of the "ghaist" who comes "clattering in" at nine o'clock sharp every evening.

Between 1852 and 1860 the Alexanders had two sons and two daughters. Since both boys were sickly, Fanny Alexander and the children spent many winters in the 1860s near Bordeaux at Arcachon and Bagneres de Bigorre, where the English colony was large enough to support an Anglican church. Here the Alexanders expanded their list of aristocratic and distinguished acquaintances, thus improving the career prospects of William Alexander and those of their children. Among their friends were two men who became great favorites of Fanny Alexander: William Edward Hartpole Lecky, the historian of eighteenth-century Britain and Ireland and member of Parliament for Trinity College, Dublin; and Matthew Arnold, who admired William's poetry and in 1867 supported his unsuccessful candidacy to succeed him as professor of poetry at Oxford.

In 1864 Fanny Alexander edited *The Sunday Book of Poetry* (1864) for Alexander Macmillan's Golden Treasury series. Macmillan wanted a collection of poems that could be "safely put into Children's hands on a Sunday." In her preface Alexander expresses the hope in the high tide of Victorian Sabbatarianism that the book "may in some measure make Sunday a *pleasant* day to children." Her reputation as a hymn writer presumably contributed to the commercial success of the venture.

Alexander became mistress of the bishop's palace in the walled city of Derry, Ireland, when the combination of powerful friends and her husband's late-flowering but substantial abilities resulted in his being named bishop of Derry and Raphoe in 1867. That year he preached before Queen Victoria and was invited to stay at Windsor Castle. Two years later the long series of attacks on the Church of Ireland—which had begun with the campaign for Catholic Emancipation in the 1820s and continued with the Tithe Wars in the 1830s—finally resulted in Disestablishment. Though Disestablishment cost William Alexander his seat in the House of Lords, the family still had a carriage, a large house full of servants, a settlement of £56,079 in cash, and an annuity of £2,215.

As a bishop's wife Alexander continued to write poems and often wrote hymns for adults. As early as 1852 she had published the still well-known adult hymn that begins "Jesus calls us; o'er the tumult / Of our life's wild, restless sea." While this hymn is a general call for Christian discipleship, it makes full sense in a liturgical context, intended for St. Andrew's Day, 30 November. The second stanza begins "As of old St. Andrew heard it [Christ's voice] / By the Galilean lake," and the whole hymn illustrates the Gospel for St. Andrews Day, Matthew 4:18–22, which records Christ's calling of St. Peter and St. Andrew. Other once popular adult hymns include "The roseate hues of early dawn," a hymn for morning prayer, and "His are the thousand sparkling rills" (1875), a meditation on the thirst that Christ suffered on the cross. Perhaps the most enduring of Fanny's adult hymns is the one known as "St. Patrick's Breastplate" (1884), an English rendering of the ancient Gaelic hymn to the Trinity attributed to Ireland's patron saint. Alexander did not read Gaelic but worked from several literal and unmusical English translations sent to her by H. H. Dickinson, dean of the Chapel Royal at Dublin Castle.

Some of Alexander's last poems were protests against the Liberal Party's repeated attempts to establish Home Rule in Ireland. "The Loyalists of Ulster" contrasts Fenian "treason" with the "determined, brave, and peaceable" Orangeman of the North, who will stand "for faith, for country, and for home, and for his lady Queen." Much more successful as poetry is "The Siege of Derry," written in 1890. This poem, spoken by a father to his daughter, begins just before an English fleet brings relief to the Protestant population of the city in 1690, ending the long siege by the Roman Catholic army of James II. The poem marked the bicentennial of that battle and indirectly expressed a hope that England would continue to stand by Ulster.

In Alexander's last twenty-eight years her life centered on the rather pallid echo of English splendor provided by St. Columba's Protestant Cathedral in Derry. She attended daily services and continued to involve herself in charitable works, often among the Roman Catholic poor. While her poetry exudes a somewhat pugnacious and intolerant doctrinal confidence, Alexander seems in practice to have gotten along as well with her Roman Catholic neighbors as with skeptics such as Arnold and Lecky. Her last decade was highlighted by two memorable social events. In 1885 she hosted the Prince and Princess of Wales at the bishop's palace for lunch. In 1893, when her younger daughter married George Bowen in South Africa, her husband performed the ceremony, and the bride was given away by no less a dignitary than Cecil Rhodes.

Fanny Alexander died on 12 October 1895 following what was apparently a series of strokes. Her funeral was a large public ceremony with Anglo-Irish grandees, masses of Anglican clergymen, and large crowds of humble folk joining the procession; there were also many memorials testifying to her good works and kindnesses to the poor and distressed of all faiths. By the time of her death her hymn books had gone through many editions to meet the demands of religious primary schools and Sunday schools in Britain and North America: *Moral Songs* was already in its ninth edition by 1867; *Narrative Hymns for Village Schools* was in its sixteenth edition in 1894; topping them all, *Hymns for Little Children* was in

its sixty-second edition in 1884. In 1896 William Alexander edited a collection of his wife's poetry and provided a preface describing her personality and analyzing her work. In 1930 A. P. Graves edited a volume of *Selected Poems of William Alexander and C. F. Alexander.*

A massive change in sensibility would be required for most of Mrs. Alexander's poetry to become popular again. The Irish Protestantism and High Church Anglicanism that she represented are far more embattled today than in her time; her views on childhood, femininity, sentiment, and the didactic role of poetry are, if possible, more embattled still. Her adherence to an idea such as the Elizabethan "Doctrine of Plentitude," where every entity is seen as filling a particular position in the chain of being, is apparent in "All Things Bright and Beautiful." But while the third verse of the hymn, which proclaims, "The rich man in his castle, / The poor man at his gate, / God made them, high or lowly, / And ordered their estate," is omitted from most modern hymnals, the hymn retains an enduring popularity. This popularity was demonstrated in the 1970s when James Herriot used the lines of its first stanza as the titles of his four best-selling volumes reminiscent of his life as a Yorkshire veterinarian. For many years the BBC world service Christmas broadcast of Lessons and Carols from King's College, Cambridge, has begun with "Once in Royal David's City." Furthermore, her being the subject of two sympathetic modern biographies shows that Alexander's character still commands a certain respect and her vanished world a certain historical interest. While her name was once far better known, it is nonetheless a considerable achievement to have written or translated several of the best-known hymns in the English language.

Biographies:
Ernest W. Lovell, *A Green Hill Far Away: The Life of Mrs. C. F. Alexander* (London: Society for the Promotion of Christian Knowledge, 1970);
Valerie Wallace, *Mrs. Alexander: A Life of the Hymn-Writer Cecil Frances Alexander, 1818–1895* (Dublin: Lillliput Press, 1995).

References:
William Alexander, preface to *Poems,* by Alexander (London: Macmillan, 1896; New York: Macmillan, 1896);
Geoffrey Faber, *Oxford Apostles: A Character Study of the Oxford Movement* (London: William Clowes and Sons, 1933);
G. B. Tennyson, *Victorian Devotional Poetry: The Tractarian Mode* (Cambridge, Mass.: Harvard University Press, 1981).

Louisa Sarah Bevington

(14 May 1845 – 28 November 1895)

Eijun Senaha
Hokkaido University

BOOKS: *Key-Notes,* as Arbor Leigh (London: Privately printed, 1876); republished, as by L. S. Bevington (London: Kegan Paul, 1879);

Poems, Lyrics, and Sonnets (London: Stock, 1882);

Common-Sense Country (London: "Liberty" Press, 1890?);

Chiefly a Dialogue: Concerning Some Difficulties of a Dunce (London: "Freedom" Office, 1895).

Liberty Lyrics (London: "Liberty" Press, 1895).

OTHER: "The Moral and Religious Bearings of the Revolution Theory," in *Religious Systems of the World* (London: Swan Sonnenschein, 1892), pp. 768–786.

SELECTED PERIODICAL PUBLICATIONS-UNCOLLECTED:

POETRY

"Sonnet" and "A Double Sonnet," as L. S. B., *Friends' Quarterly Examiner; Religious, Social, and Miscellaneous Review,* 5, nos. 17–20 (1871): 523, 558;

"Teachings of a Day," *Popular Science Monthly,* 12 (January 1878): 327–330;

"Pope and Kaiser," *Commonweal,* 1 (10 June 1893);

"Wishes," *Liberty: A Journal of Anarchist Communism,* 3 (January 1896): 9.

NONFICTION

"The Personal Aspects of Responsibility," *Mind: A Quarterly Review of Psychology and Philosophy,* 4 (April 1879): 244–255;

"Modern Atheism and Mr. Mallock," *Nineteenth Century,* 32 (October 1879): 585–603; 33 (December 1879): 999–1020;

"Determinism and Duty," *Mind: A Quarterly Review of Psychology and Philosophy,* 5 (January 1881): 30–45;

"The Moral Colour of Rationalism," *Fortnightly Review,* 30 (August 1881): 179–194;

"Dynamitism," *Commonweal,* 1 (24 June 1893);

"Why I Am an Expropriationist," *Liberty: A Journal of Anarchist Communism,* 1 (May 1894): 37;

"The Last Gasp of Propertyism," *Liberty: A Journal of Anarchist Communism,* 1 (September 1894): 66–67;

"The Prejudice against Property," *Liberty: A Journal of Anarchist Communism,* 2 (February 1895): 111–112;

"The Whereabouts of Property Ethics," *Liberty: A Journal of Anarchist Communism,* 2 (June 1895): 141–142;

"Anarchism and Violence," *Liberty,* 3 (November 1896): 110–112.

As Louisa Sarah Bevington wrote in "My Little Task" (1882), "What, with this fenced human mind, / What can I do to help my kind? / I such a stammerer, they so blind!" Bevington's concern for the individual human rights of her "kind" against the expanding power of British imperialism changed her life dramatically. Far from a "stammerer," she was a poet, essayist, and activist who represented the political as well as the literary scene of the fin de siècle.

She was born on 14 May 1845 to Quaker parents, Alexander Bevington and Louisa De Horne, at St. John's Hill, Battersea, in the county of Surrey. Her father's occupation was described as "gentleman" on her birth certificate; one of his ancestors had been confined in Nottingham Gaol with George Fox, a founder of the Society of Friends. Louisa Bevington was the eldest of eight children, seven of whom were girls. Her father encouraged her in the observation and love of nature, and at an early age she wrote childish verses about natural objects. Throughout her career as a poet she used verse to express her love of science, poetry, music, and metaphysical thinking. Like George Eliot and Constance Naden, Bevington was influenced by the philosopher and sociologist Herbert Spencer, whose evolutionist view of the universe and society she came to accept. Bevington sustained her belief in Spencer's theories throughout her adulthood; she developed a personal relationship with him as well, and Spencer's

Title page for the second edition of Louisa Sarah Bevington's first collection of poems. It is the first book in which her name appears on the title page.

the use of violence as a final resort against institutionalized injustice, and privately she remained an atheist, refusing any religious ceremony for her funeral. During these years she suffered from mitral disease of the heart, but despite her declining health she remained dedicated to her creative and political activities. Finally, on 28 November 1895, after a six-month bout with dropsy, Bevington died at Willesden, Middlesex. Her death was reported a week later in London by a Helen Glennie, who registered the poet's occupation as "a 'wife' of Ignatz Felix Guggenberger, an artist painter," and her name as Louisa Sarah Guggenberger. Her obituary notice was carried by the 18 December issue of *Torch of Anarchy*.

Bevington's poetic career can be divided into three periods. Up until the 1870s she wrote naturalistic poems with Christian as well as evolutionist tendencies. Her questions were answered by her faith, scientific observation, and a transcendentalist understanding of nature. In the 1880s, as her attention moved toward society, she left Quakerism behind and began writing critical poems and essays while struggling to find a better solution for society's problems. When she came back to England in the 1890s, she identified herself as an anarchist and wrote against the self-evident injustices and evils of late-Victorian England. Her personal evolution from innocent Quaker to agnostic ideologist and political activist is expressed in her representative works of each decade: *Key-Notes* (1876), *Poems, Lyrics, and Sonnets* (1882), and *Liberty Lyrics* (1895).

Bevington started her poetic career in 1871 by privately circulating some of her poems. Her first published verses were "Sonnet" and "A Double Sonnet," which appeared under her initials only in one of the earliest numbers of *Friends' Quarterly Examiner*, a Quaker journal. "Sonnet" is a religious and romantic poem in which Bevington describes her innocent belief in God, on whose divine intentions she "used to wonder when I was a child / And saw a tempest mounting in the sky." She eventually learns that "Lest 'neath a too fair sky man should forget / God sometimes in his life dark clouds doth set." In "A Double Sonnet," likewise, Bevington first admonishes impatience with God's holy will and in the second sonnet stanza asks readers to "do the duty of the hour / Leaving results to time, and God's unfettered power."

Herbert Spencer read her poems and in 1876 asked her for four more to be reprinted in the American journal *Popular Science Monthly*. "Morning," "Afternoon," "Twilight," and "Midnight" appeared in January 1878 as a sequence under the title "Teachings of a Day." Dividing a day into four peri-

sponsorship led to her recognition among both scientific and literary circles.

Shortly after the publication of her second volume of poems in 1882 Bevington traveled to Germany, where in 1883 she married a Munich artist named Ignatz Felix Guggenberger without registering the marriage in England. The marriage lasted nearly eight years; by 1890 she had returned to London and resumed her career under her maiden name, never using her married name in public writings. In the years leading up to her death she became involved with anarchist groups based in London and also associated herself with international revolutionary movements. This political stance coincided with her contributions of poems and articles to anarchist and socialist journals that forcefully put forth a case for anarchism as a viable political philosophy.

By the mid 1890s Bevington was familiar with many London anarchists and was a recognized anarchist poet. She condoned from a political standpoint

ods of progress—from dawn, when "There is effort all the morning / Through the windy sea and sky," until midnight, when "There is action in the stillness, / There is progress in the dark"—the poem asserts an evolutionary view of creation and humanity's part in it:

> So we sing of evolution,
> And step strongly on our ways;
> And we live through nights in patience
> And we learn the worth of days.

The evolutionary lesson Bevington propounds is optimistic: "Nothing hinders, all enables / Nature's vast awakening."

Bevington's first major collection of poems, *Key-Notes,* was published in 1876 under the pseudonym of Arbor Leigh, an obvious allusion to Elizabeth Barrett Browning's *Aurora Leigh.* The collection included the poems Bevington had privately printed and the four poems of "Teachings of a Day." Many of the poems in *Key-Notes* are philosophically based on Charles Darwin's theories of evolution and the transcendentalism of Ralph Waldo Emerson.

The title of this volume was taken from Emerson's conception of a poet's role, used as an epigraph: "Melodious poets shall be hoarse as street ballads when once the penetrating Key-Note of nature and spirit is sounded—earth-beat, sea-beat, heart-beat, which makes the tune to which the sun rolls, and the globule of blood, and the sap of trees." Writing an elegiac dedication to Aimée W., to whom Bevington promises to "send some key-notes of life's journeying moods," she divides the volume of forty-eight poems into twelve months. The collection is that of a nature poet who likens her passions to the changing climates and, by transcending them, finds metaphoric meanings in the universe, but it is also that of an evolutionist who observes cycles and progress. In the opening January section the four poems of "Teachings of a Day" are included, intended to chart the evolution not only of a day but also of a year. In the June section "The Stammerer" and "Summer Song" are included. The former poem, which invokes a young poet's doubts about her abilities, nonetheless demonstrates her mastery of the strict verse form of the French villanelle. In the latter poem, the poet celebrates the coming of summer: "Sing! sing me a song that is fit for to-day," that is "Full of the scent, and the glow, and the passion of June." The conclusion of the poem again suggests an evolutionist conception of nature: "While you sing me a song of the summer that's ancient and new."

Bevington also wrote about woman and her situation. "For Woman's Sake" in the August section introduces a tension between the poet's feminist stance and her religious faith; in the poem she asks her "brother," Jesus Christ, on woman's behalf to "Teach her well" because "Thy code is writ in her belief in thee." "Love and Pride" and "Unfulfilled," in September and October, respectively, both treat the subject of unfulfilled love, for a lover and for God. The last poem of the volume, "Listening," brings up her own religious questioning as well as that of society. The conclusion of her poem affirms a positivist conception of the universe as well as a form of evolutionary meliorism:

> Let them not sob themselves to sleep again
> Till each has felt the universal Heart
> Waking within him, and the great "worth while"
> Of Time and Nature claiming his least deed
> To weave in fabric of a new world-blessedness.

The volume found favor in intellectual and scientific rather than literary circles. According to Alfred H. Miles, "Professor Ray Lankester brought it under the notice of Darwin, who read it after not having opened a volume of verse for fifteen years"; Miles concludes that it "is not surprising that Mrs. Guggenberger should have broken the spell which for fifteen years had confined Darwin to the world of prose, for her part is emphatically that of the poetess of evolutionary science." For Miles, Bevington's first volume of poetry "discerned more accurately than many contemporaries, the immense poetical development which the acceptance of the evolutionary view has made possible for science, and her best poems are attempts, by no means feeble or unskillful, to bring out the poetic significance of scientific principles." Bevington's first collection was republished by Kegan Paul under her own name in 1879.

On the strength of her poems Herbert Spencer asked Bevington to write articles on evolutionary theory as well. Her first two articles appeared in the journals *Mind* ("The Personal Aspects of Responsibility") and *Nineteenth Century* ("Modern Atheism and Mr. Mallock") in 1879; the latter of these refutes from a scientific standpoint the cynical pessimism of W. H. Mallock's "Is Life Worth Living?," in which the cleric attacks the morality of evolutionary theory. The article garnered some literary recognition and many literary friends both in England and America. Other essays followed: "Determinism and Duty" appeared in *Mind* in 1881, again at the suggestion of Spencer, and in August of the same year "The Moral Colour of Rationalism" was published in *Fortnightly Review* as a response to Goldwin Smith's article on the ethics of evolutionary theory titled "Data of Ethics." In the article Bevington argues that Smith's perception of evolutionary theory provides the political ideology that supports colonial exploitation, exemplified by the British suppression of the Morant Bay uprising in Jamaica. "Orthodox Conservatism," she declares, "is inclined to keep its theory of world-wide humanity for its wife and children to listen to, duly couched in Jewish phraseology, on Sunday." As a result, she concludes, "one may long for the time when religion shall no longer have the power to paralyse the morality it professes to patronise." Clearly by this time Bevington's early Quakerism was being displaced by a personal commitment to evolutionism that had political ramifications later in her life.

In 1882 Bevington's second volume of verse, *Poems, Lyrics, and Sonnets,* appeared; it found more success in literary rather than scientific circles. As the personal understanding of nature, religion, and people expressed in *Key-Notes* broadened to include various social problems of late-Victorian England, her provocative expressions became more polished and literary. In the epigraph, along with Wathen Mark Wilks Call and an anonymous German philosopher, Bevington again quotes Emerson: "You must have eyes of science to see in the seed its nodes; you must have the vivacity of the poet to perceive in the thought its futurities." The volume comprises two parts: forty-two poems in "Poems and Lyrics" and twenty-one in "Sonnets." Her dedication to "C.A.V.," written in sonnet form, declares her role as a literary activist:

> Not that the theme is worthy, nor the lay
> Such as your heart would have, one time in three;
> Yet, battling, I would chaunt of victory
> All life's night through: though dubious dream of day
> Scarcely suffices me to shed one ray
>
> O'er the fierce field where you must fighting be;
> Yet you have brought a little sword to me
> Of strange new metal that I would essay.

Thus Bevington indicates her concern about the poet's literary as well as social roles; the collection also includes six other poems on the subject of the poet. Throughout the collection Bevington utilizes companion poems such as "Steel or Gold (A Question)" and "Gold and Steel (The Answer)," "Unperfected" and "Perfected," "Hope deferred" and "Hope Preferred," and "Love's Height" and "Love's Depth" to present her ambivalence and meditative process with respect to various subjects. The tone of the collection is more serious than *Key-Notes,* with poems describing problems of society, home, and individual relationships. Her ideological

shift from a Romantic nature poet to a political anarchist is evident in this volume. As Angela Leighton and Margaret Reynolds assert, "her verse draws on evolutionary theory to decentre, as do Field, Naden and Blind, the egocentric power of human passion ('Egoisme à Deux' and 'Measurements'). Darwinism, with its large-scale, natural, geological imagery, provided a useful model for the idea of inevitable social change."

"Egoisme à Deux" and "One More Bruised Heart" are the most discussed poems in the volume. "Egoisme à Deux" is a love poem that seems to invoke cosmic theory by using such terms as "nebulous," "chaos-elements," and "accidents"; as Kathleen Hickok suggests in a 1995 article in *Victorian Poetry,* the poem is a product of "metrical experimentation" that serves to fuse scientific objectivity with romantic themes: "The first two lines of each stanza present scientific descriptions of creation, geologic time, and evolution of species. The second two lines of each stanza raise the possibility that natural forces at work were commanded by a Will, a Thought, a Longing." However, the poem ends with a question, "Was it divine?," to which Hickok infers an answer: "Not only is the love, 'you' and 'I,' probably accidental; the very presence of life on the planet, of human breath, may be accidental as well. The philosophy of the poem is agnostic at best."

In "One More Bruised Heart," echoing William Blake's condemnation from nearly a century before of socially endemic child abuse, Bevington exposes the ongoing horror of domestic violence:

> One more bruised heart laid bare! One victim more!
> One more wail heard! Oh, is there never end
> Of all these passionate agonies, that rend
> Young hopes to tatters through enslavements sore?

The angry and helpless poet indicates that this abuse takes verbal, physical, and even sexual forms, as in a line that seems to suggest the deflowering of a virgin: "what love of mine can ever mend / Again for you the veil your tyrant tore?" This image also suggests wife abuse, with the tyrannizing husband symbolically tearing a bridal veil. Bevington's choice of the courtly sonnet form, therefore, would seem to be an ironical statement about the volatility of domestic relationships. As Bevington confesses in "The Poet's Tear," there is another level of irony in the fact that human suffering may serve as a source of inspiration for art, but she also expresses the hope that she might influence the reader's sympathy on behalf of the less fortunate: "I cannot cure; I may in part express."

Bevington's accusations of social injustice are vehemently repeated in such poems as "The Unpardonable Sin" and "Hated." In "How Do I Know?" Bevington offers an ironic portrayal of marital discord in which the husband holds all the power over the wife; "Bees in Clover" is addressed to a "wife-shriek" and exhorts the reader to "Help the woman bear her fetter" so that "the woman shall be free." The latter poem displays a newfound interest in allegorical expression that Bevington continues to develop in her next collection. *Poems, Lyrics, and Sonnets* also includes several philosophical poems, such as "The Valley of Remorse," "The Pessimist," and "Three," that deserve attention.

Soon after the publication of *Poems, Lyrics, and Sonnets* Bevington left England and married Ignatz Guggenberger in Germany in 1883. Little is known about her marriage, but the pessimistic attitudes toward marriage and men expressed in her poems and essays may reflect her personal experience. Meanwhile, in the 1880s and 1890s London witnessed the growth of socialist and trade-union movements, and anarchism, with its utopian goals, was also gaining a certain amount of public favor. Women such as Edith Nesbit, Beatrice Webb, and Charlotte Wilson were actively involved in these movements. Bevington returned to London's literary stage in about 1890, when she met Wilson and became a vocal activist, leaning strongly toward an anarchist ideology. She published a series of articles in various anarchist journals and lectured at the Autonomie Club on atheism and Christianity.

In 1893 Bevington published her inflammatory article "Dynamitism," a response to a so-called Christian lady's assertion that anarchism might well be called "dynamitism." This article demonstrates that Bevington had become a strong advocate of anarchist terrorism: "Dynamitism is the bringing 'not of peace but a sword' as a reply to the 'scribes, pharisees, and hypocrites' who prate of 'peace, peace,' when there is no peace." Bevington concludes, "Meanwhile, dynamite is a last and very valuable resource, and as such not to be wasted on side issues." The legitimacy of terrorist violence was not an idle topic for Bevington: in February of that year a suspected anarchist blew himself up while carrying a bomb to the Greenwich Observatory (the incident that inspired Joseph Conrad's 1907 novel *The Secret Agent*). The extent of Bevington's direct involvement in the incident is unclear, but her letters seem to indicate that she was more than a mere bystander. Nevertheless, despite the possibility of criminal indictment, she wrote another agitative article for *Torch* in October, concluding "Demos! Where's our Dynamite?"

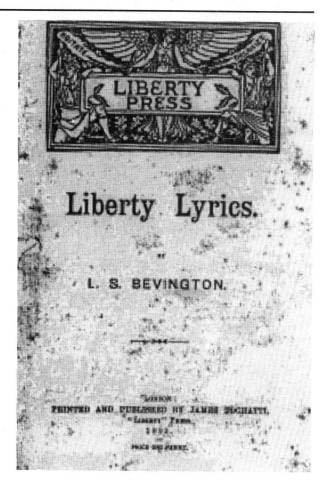

Title page for Bevington's collection of poems that endorse radical anarchism

In 1895, at the age of fifty, Bevington was experiencing failing health but was still active; that year she published two articles on property for James Tochatti's "Liberty" Press and *Chiefly a Dialogue: Concerning Some Difficulties of a Dunce* for Charlotte Wilson's "Freedom" Office. In the same year Bevington published her third and last collection of poems, *Liberty Lyrics,* which comprises fifteen poems, including three reprints from anarchist journals. The collection is probably her most balanced in terms of its aesthetic qualities and its intellectual content, especially her revolutionary perspectives on religion, evolution, and anarchism. In the first poem of the collection, "The End of the World," Bevington proclaims that "the end of the world is here," adopting a cosmic perspective to contrast the political instability of the period with the immutable laws of the universe: "Our round earth planet? Ah, no; / The planet shall roll, and the great sun stand." "Looking Dawnwards" affirms an anarchist ideology, balancing a utopian vision of personal freedom with a sense of responsibility to the less fortunate:

Free to live and have my being–
  Free to choose or deprecate;
Free to keep law or to mend it,
  Free to recognize my mate.
Free, by all consent around me;
  Free by all consent within;
Free from human rule and precept;
  Free from human hurt and sin.
Very gently will I take it,
  Very careful will I be,
Lest the crucified and wistful
  Miss their chance, in vain, through me.

Toward the end of the poem Bevington sees the present as "the very Day of Judgment" and concludes mysteriously that "the Letter's reign is over / And the Spirit waxes fast," which perhaps suggests the end of her literary career and the beginning of her intense involvement with radical anarchist communism. This apocalyptic vision is echoed in another of the collection's poems, "Revolution."

In other poems of the collection Bevington's political fervor seems tinged with the religious faith of her earliest verse. In "Dreamers?" she calls Christ "our comrade of long, long ago," predicting, "That 'Kingdom' *is coming*, on earth as 'within you.'" "In and Out of Church" also seems to unite her earlier religious belief with her mature political vision: "the great Hope warms the fighter, / And the broad New Day grows brighter / And more just." Originally published in the 11 November 1893 issue of *Commonweal*, "In Memoriam" is dedicated to Bevington's deceased comrades and identifies the anarchist's task as "handing the torch as it glows / To all who may ask."

As she had in "Bees in Clover," in several poems in *Liberty Lyrics* Bevington uses that social insect as an appropriate literary image for life in an ideal community. In "The Secret of the Bees" the poet first ponders the difference between the lives of the insect and human: "Economy, Liberty, Order, and Wealth!– / Say, busy bee, how you reached Social Health?" A bee answers that its kind has freedom, no money, and no hypocritical press, "And we got our good habits through sheer Common-Sense." "The Spider and the Bee, A Tale for the Times" is another allegorical poem, of a more meditative tone than the other. A man who believes that the "world must be saved by sympathies" finds a bee trapped in the spider's web. The man says, "I wish you may both–*survive* (?)." The man pities the bee while acknowledging that the spider also needs its prey to survive; baffled by his conflicting sympathies, he sighs and goes home to bed. At that point the poet takes over:

What of the tale? Well, it isn't exact;
Yet it hints at an ugly and pitiful fact.
"Philosophy" severing language from fact–

Sympathy's name is a shibboleth spoken;
Dreams of web-spinners be speedily broken!–
This story one tiny superfluous token.

The poem has a childlike simplicity, but it is obviously intended to be seen also as a political allegory. The bee represents the individual and the spider with its web stands for social institutions. The poem suggests that a natural, perhaps inevitably predatory, relationship exists between the two. Bevington's anarchist ideology allows no room for compromise.

The last poem of the volume, "Dinner," marks the only occasion in Bevington's verse that she attempts to offer an explicit autobiographical statement:

Perhaps mine is a tenth-rate soul, not worth the while to save;
Perhaps a quite incorrigible soul that can't behave;
But it is mine, and I shall have to wear it to my grave.

This poem is not as critical or scornful of society as some of Bevington's other poems were. It is rather a poem that celebrates the individual manner in which she had lived her life. Later that year Bevington succumbed to the heart disease with which she had struggled for years.

Two works by Bevington appeared in the anarchist journal *Liberty* in the year after her death: the poem "Wishes" was published in the January issue and the article "Anarchism and Violence" in November. Though the date of its composition is unknown, the article is in keeping with Bevington's mature views on the legitimacy of terrorist violence: "there are cases where poison becomes medicinal, and there is such a thing as warring against the cause of war." "Wishes," according to the note that accompanied its publication in *Liberty,* was "among the last of the contributions received from our late comrade, L. S. Bevington," most probably written after the poems in *Liberty Lyrics*. It offers Bevington's familiar vision of an anarchist utopia:

Oh, would it could be shared by all,
  That vision of the soul,
Whose will, in tune with social due,
  Needs but its own control:
For then a brave "new earth" would be
Where all should love, and *all were free*.

Yet the poem seems to represent a step back from the more militant attitude Bevington expresses in her prose. She may have been suggesting a middle ground, no doubt realizing that the anarchists' espousal of violence was alienating the general public. Yet it may be more appropriate to conclude that her poetic diction of "Dinner" and "Wishes" reflects that Bevington had adopted a more meditative perspective at the end of her life.

The project of evaluating Louisa Sarah Bevington's literary career is yet to be completed. Alfred H. Miles included her in *The Poets and the Poetry of the Nineteenth Century* (1892), but he introduced her carelessly as "Louisa S. Guggenberger" while admitting she was "better known to the public by her maiden name." He asserted that her "chief defects are over-facility common to so many poetesses, and a deficient perception of the humorous," a judgment that ignores the politically progressive intent of her poetry. Bevington's poetic achievements were subsequently neglected until the 1980s, when entries on the poet began to appear in literary encyclopedias and her poems were reprinted in several anthologies. Yet Miles's brief essay remains the only real source for information of Bevington's life, and there are few critical essays on her individual poems. Bevington's intense political involvement may have overshadowed her poetic contributions, but Angela Leighton and Margaret Reynolds's comparison of Bevington to her contemporary, Christina Rossetti, in their *Victorian Women Poets: An Anthology* (1995) may serve as a starting point for further scholarly

consideration: "Bevington's poetry lacks the darker, imaginative recesses of Rossetti's, and often sounds, in spite of its secularist goals, more religious and high-minded than hers."

References:

Isobel Armstrong, Joseph Bristow, and Cath Sharrock, *Nineteenth-Century Women Poets* (Oxford: Clarendon Press, 1996), pp. 678–682;

Virginia Blain, Isobel Grundy, and Patricia Clements, *The Feminist Companion to Literature in English: Women Writers from the Middle Ages to the Present* (New Haven: Yale University Press, 1990), pp. 91–92;

Kathleen Hickok, "'Intimate Egoism': Reading and Evaluating Noncanonical Poetry by Women," *Victorian Poetry*, 33, no. 1 (1995): 13–30;

Hickok, *Representations of Women: Nineteenth-Century British Women's Poetry* (Westport, Conn.: Greenwood Press, 1983), pp. 67–68, 224;

Irving Louis Horowitz, ed., *The Anarchists* (New York: Dell, 1964);

Alfred H. Miles, ed., *The Poets and the Poetry of the Nineteenth Century*, volume 9 (London: Hutchinson, 1892), pp. 227–244;

Hermia Oliver, *The International Anarchist Movement in Late Victorian London* (London & Canberra: Croom Helm, 1983), pp. 86–87, 107, 123, 152.

Isabella Blagden

(1817? – 20 January 1873)

Kathleen McCormack
Florida International University

BOOKS: *Agnes Tremorne,* 2 volumes (London: Smith, Elder, 1861);

The Cost of a Secret, 3 volumes (London: Chapman & Hall, 1863);

The Woman I Loved and the Woman Who Loved Me (London: Chapman & Hall 1865); republished with "A Tuscan Wedding" (Leipzig: Tauchnitz, 1872; New York: Munro 1886);

Nora and Archibald Lee, 3 volumes (London: Chapman & Hall, 1867);

The Crown of a Life, 3 volumes (London: Hurst & Blackett, 1869);

Poems by Isa Blagden, compiled by Linda White Mazini and Alfred Austin, with a memoir by Austin (Edinburgh: Blackwood, 1873).

SELECTED PERIODICAL PUBLICATIONS— UNCOLLECTED: "Felice de Fauveau," *English Woman's Journal,* 2 (1858): 83–94;

"A Model and a Wife. In Three Chapters," *Fraser's Magazine,* 64 (July 1862): 95–113;

"A Tuscan Village, a Tuscan Sanctuary," *Cornhill Magazine,* 10 (October 1864): 461–476;

"A Holiday in Venice," *Cornhill Magazine,* 12 (October 1865): 441–451;

"Gibson's Studio," *All the Year Round,* 15 (10 March 1866): 205;

"Recollections of Gibson the Sculptor," *Cornhill Magazine,* 17 (May 1868): 540–546.

Isabella Blagden; drawing by Hilda Wilcox Phelps (from Edward C. McAleer, ed., Dearest Isa: Robert Browning's Letters to Isabella Blagden, *1951; courtesy of the Armstrong Browning Library, Baylor University, Waco Texas)*

One of the nineteenth-century Florentine *Inglese*—a label used for all English speakers—Isabella Blagden has gained more fame as a good friend of Robert and Elizabeth Barrett Browning than as a nineteenth-century poet and novelist. This fame results partly from Edward C. McAleer's 1951 collection of the letters Blagden received from the Brownings, the bulk of them written as part of an arranged monthly exchange with Robert Browning during the decade following his wife's death in 1861. The intimacy of McAleer's title, *Dearest Isa: Robert Browning's Letters to Isabella Blagden,* hints at Blagden's reputation of great charm and her importance among the British expatriates in Italy.

The simplicity of Blagden's grave on the Piazzale Donatello in Florence befits the obscurity of her birth. A wreath of sculpted flowers rests on an unadorned crucifix on the top of an otherwise plain slab. Whereas the inscriptions on the tombs of other English women who died single in Florence note their relationships as daughters and sisters (and often allude to the purity of their lives), Blagden's tomb bears only a now-faded inscription of her name and the date of her death.

This dearth of details about Blagden's birth and ancestry almost certainly stems from her illegitimacy. In the nineteenth century a rumor was circulated that her dark coloring was accounted for by an Indian mother and that she owed her lifelong status as an Englishwoman to a British officer as her father. No official register records her birth, and her date of birth can only be estimated as having occurred between 1817 and 1820. Although an occasional letter might make reference to family connections, neither Browning ever mentions a childhood memory, a beloved person, or a specific place that is associated with Blagden's earliest years.

Although she wrote poetry, prose, and novels, Blagden offers few hints of her origins within her works. One melancholy poem, "Orphanhood," describes a lonely childhood. The first line of each stanza repeats the phrase, "The shadow of the forest trees," and the poem's voice reports just one flash of happiness in an isolated, stormy setting. The poem names the most important effect of the overhanging trees in its first stanza, "My childhood withered 'neath their spell," and describes conditions likely for an illegitimate daughter raised in a remote location.

Blagden appeared in Florence and began to establish her place in the expatriate community at the beginning of the 1850s. She spent her first season in the Villa Moutier overlooking the city from the northern slope of the Poggio Imperiale. Later she moved into a villa on the next, more desirable hill of Bellosguardo, where many literary figures clustered. She became a visible figure there, a brightly dressed diminutive figure tending to her orchards and flowers in her garden, attended by well-loved dogs. By 1850 Blagden was comfortably lodged at little cost, and by 1853 she was on first-name terms with Elizabeth Barrett Browning. Despite interludes of living in Rome, she became an intimate member of the Florentine English-speaking community. She not only welcomed guests and gave frequent parties but also cared for strays both canine and human, located lodgings, arranged for servants, and nursed several of her compatriots in their illnesses.

Blagden shared her lodgings, and this circumstance served to widen her social circle. During the early 1850s Blagden lived with the sickly Louisa Alexander until she left for India in 1855. The American sculptor Harriet Hosmer helped gain the villa its reputation as a ménage of independently eccentric women. Frances Power Cobbe remembered enthusiastically her time living with Blagden at Villa Brichieri. She liked the social life, the efficient servants, and the low cost: ten pounds apiece per month enabled the two women to live well and entertain often. In 1857 young Annette Bracken moved into Villa Brichieri and then accompanied Blagden and Robert Lytton on an ill-starred expedition to Bagni di Lucca, where Robert Browning had tempted them with attractive apartments. After they arrived Lytton fell sick, and Blagden had to assume again the nursing duties that she performed for friends all her life.

Life in Florence for Blagden sometimes meant social events at all hours of the day—breakfast, tea, dinner, and evening gatherings—but at times of sickness and death among her many friends it also required her constant attendance and service. In 1861 the last illness of Elizabeth Barrett Browning demanded all of Blagden's emotional fortitude and experience dealing with sickness. Ill at the time herself and much challenged by the instructions of the physician and Robert Browning to maintain silence at the bedside, she remained with her friend for most of her last week. When the end came, the bereaved husband sent for Blagden immediately, and she removed the Brownings' only child, little Pen, from Casa Guidi to care for him at Villa Brichieri. Soon after, she accompanied the grieving Brownings to Paris, where she left them to return to Italy while they proceeded to England.

Despite the death of Browning and the departure of her husband, the English of the Bellosguardo hill continued to make literature a favorite subject of impassioned conversations and in the case of Blagden and several others a serious occupation. Along with novels and articles, Blagden's poems appeared in English periodicals during the 1850s and 1860s. After Blagden's death on 20 January 1873, Linda White Mazini and Alfred Austin collected many of these poems into Poems by Isa Blagden (1873). Mazini and Austin do not order the poems chronologically and only rarely assign them dates. But Blagden's own datings as well as her references to specific public events indicate that she wrote and published poetry for some fifteen years, beginning in her mid thirties. In much of her writing Blagden draws on her residence in Italy to appeal to an English audience. Making the most of her expatriate status, she appeals to armchair travelers with poems, novels, and prose about Italian art, politics, and people.

The Risorgimento, always a popular cause among the English, offered her material for several poems. The speaker in "Rome from the Ripetta" draws inspiration from the arches of the buildings and aquaducts and the dome of St. Peter's and begs Giuseppe Mazzini, "august, yet erring dreamer," to take heart for his efforts from the sight of the dome.

Manuscript for a poem by Blagden (courtesy of the Armstrong Browning Library, Baylor University, Waco, Texas)

A spy, a monk, and a beggar who represent the backwardness and corruption of Italy's government, religion, and economy inspire a similar call in "A Roman Street." The sight of an "undefiled" blossom growing there encourages the speaker of the poem to envision and pray for an Italy united to achieve glorious goals of freedom and independence. The Risorgimento poems culminate with "Rome 1870: Written on the Eve of the Entrance of the Italian Troops into Rome," which happily celebrates the success of Garibaldi's army.

Italy's artistic resources also provided much material for Blagden's poetry. Several of her poems take individual locations or specific artworks in Rome or Florence as occasions for praising Victorian virtues of fellow feeling and dutiful behavior. In "The Church of the Gesù," one of Blagden's most ambitious efforts, the Protestant persona seeks a moment of quiet in the Jesuit church. He pauses at the dazzling altar dedicated to St. Ignatius Loyola, founder of the order, whom he perceives as a knight with a "loyal heart who gave / Its chivalry to Faith." Loyola's lonely death on the threshold of his cherished mission to China elicits the Englishman's fellow feeling: "Though alien my clime, my faith / My human sympathy was strong." Then, finding inadequate consolation in the solitariness of his hero's death, he shifts his attention to a calmer, more reassuring *Madonna with Child* on the ceiling above. In the end the universality of inevitable death implies a universal fellowship that finally consoles the Englishman.

Another art-inspired poem centers on the artist rather than the work. Blagden draws on her visit to John Gibson's workplace in "In a Studio," an overwrought paeon to the sculptor's art, inspired by an encounter that also led her to write a short piece, "Gibson's Studio," in the 10 March 1866 issue of *All the Year Round* and a longer essay, "Recollections of Gibson the Sculptor," in the May 1868 *Cornhill Magazine*. Indeed, beginning with her 1858 article about the sculptor Felice de Fauveau for *English Woman's Journal*, Blagden looked to the studio and the various artists who paint or sculpt there for important settings and characters. All of her five novels—*Agnes Tremorne* (1861), *The Cost of a Secret* (1863), *The Woman I Loved and the Woman Who Loved Me* (1865), *Nora and Archibald Lee* (1867), and *The Crown of a Life* (1869)—but especially the first and last demonstrate Blagden's enthusiasm for the art of Italy and repeat the studio settings and artist characters.

Beyond the artist characters Blagden's picturesque representations of Italians include models, spies, children, and lovers. In the article "A Tuscan Village, a Tuscan Sanctuary" for the October 1864 issue of *Cornhill Magazine* she describes the Tuscan face as "broad and uncontrolled in its expressiveness as an animal's . . . the secret of their picturesqueness." In "A Holiday in Venice" for the October 1865 issue of that same magazine she writes, "In every corner of Italy one finds these exquisite bits of picturesqueness, but Venice is the consecrated home of that seven-robed daughter of light which men call colour." She devotes sections of her essays to descriptions of Italian women, and she characterizes the city of Venice as an attractive widow looking for a new suitor. These methods distance Blagden's persona from her subject, just as the expatriate community in Bellosguardo remained aloof from the rest of Florence.

In *The Stones of Florence* (1959) Mary McCarthy lays the blame for the distance between the Florentines and the Inglese squarely on "the Brownings and their readers" who "expropriated Florence, occupying villas in Fiesole or Bellosguardo, studying Tuscan wildflowers, collecting ghost stories, collecting triptychs and diptychs, burying their dogs in the churchyard of the Protestant Episcopal church, knowing (for the most part) no Florentines but their servants." There is certainly some truth to McCarthy's observation in regard to Blagden. Several of the activities McCarthy catalogues are concerns found in the poems of Blagden, who titled one Italian poem "Wildflowers" and addressed another to a dog. Robert Browning affirms the distance between the Inglese and their hosts in stating his agreement with Blagden: "I agree with you, and always did, as to the uninterestingness of the Italians individually, as thinking, originating souls: I never read a line in a modern Italian book that was of use to me." Blagden too fits McCarthy's pattern in taking a proprietary approach to Florence as "a dear bit of the Old World."

The poems Blagden writes that are set in England contrast with her Italian poems. The English settings are more vaguely described and often include aged ancestral mansions in which occur melodramatic events. In the English poems she sometimes involves orphans in Gothic plots of passion and abandonment. The suffering connected with love is a dominant theme, and she explores other typically Victorian topics: the predicament of the fallen woman, the need for human sympathy, and the demands life makes on responsibility.

During the 1860s, her most productive decade, Blagden visited England every two or three years, often taking up residence near Browning. She once lived in London's Little Venice, but she also spent time outside of the city. In 1862 she passed a good part of the year on the Kentish coast in the

P O E M S

BY THE LATE

ISA BLAGDEN

WITH A MEMOIR

WILLIAM BLACKWOOD AND SONS
EDINBURGH AND LONDON
MDCCCLXXIII

Title page for Blagden's only volume of poetry

North Foreland area overlooking the treacherous Margate Sands. Stone House, a large, pale Georgian building whose curves billow gracefully out over the bluff, offers views as dramatic as those in Bellosguardo but entirely different. The spectacular outlook from the Villa Brichieri extends from the east, where all of the golden city lies mistily below, around to the west, where the Arno River valley sweeps off toward Pisa. In Kent, Blagden looked out from Stone House at tempestuous seas whose waters concealed many shipwrecks. Lighthouses and other singular buildings dotted the North Foreland, notably the Captain Digby public house, whose steps down to the sea made it a frequent refuge for rescued sailors and for smugglers. Broadstairs, the nearby fishing village, has had a pier since the fifteenth century, and its history dwells on storms, smuggling, and shipwrecks.

Blagden stayed at Broadstairs from late winter through the summer of 1862. Despite the beauty of the setting, she was having a difficult period. In February Browning's failure to visit en route from Paris disappointed her. Arriving at Folkestone at four in the morning with his sister and his son, he could not resist the lure of an express train to London and home rather than undertaking a thirty-mile journey up the coast to Broadstairs. During the early months of the year Blagden was fighting an illness that caused her severe pains in the side. Nevertheless, she was working hard, writing *The Cost of a Secret* and "A Model and a Wife."

The English poetry, none of it joyous, reflects this general sense of strenuous effort as well as the more specific struggles of life by the sea in Kent. The view from the North Foreland bluff found its way into her poetry in frequent nautical wreck metaphors. In "The Wrecked Life" the title refers to a victim of a marriage who is set free from her misery and confinement by the too-late death of an unloved, absent husband. In "The Story of Two Lives" the speaker describes his despair: "The mast is down . . . the ship has struck a rock." "The Angels of Life" begins with another nautical description of despair:

Prostrate beside the rock-bound shores of time,
Alone, storm-tossed and harbourless, I wept–
I wept o'er all the buried wrecks sublime
Which in its flood irrevocably slept.

Eventually the sunrise over the sea brings relief, but it also is the harbinger of the arrival of the angel of death.

Blagden's admiration for Charles Dickens, who had stayed in Broadstairs and whose *David Copperfield* (1849–1850) and *Bleak House* (1852–1853) had settings inspired by the village, is evident in her writing, especially *The Crown of a Life* with its circus-performer characters and male bildungsroman narration. On the day of his death in 1870 she wrote an elegy she called "Charles Dickens Is Dead." The poem, set in London where the "Grey Abbey" is to receive the body of England's "second Shakespeare," begins with fertility metaphors applied to Dickens's achievement–"Our noblest fruit was plucked the first"–and then slyly alludes to one of his periodicals, lamenting that "our household words have lost a tone." It concludes that Dickens's major achievement lay in his deftness with the English language, which in "spoken word and written song / Our race's Saxon rule attest."

Such references to Anglo-Saxon heritage are part of the pattern of ethnic generalization that appears in Blagden's Italian characters. Writing of Carlo Goldoni in her essay on Venice, she distances Italy from her English readers on the basis of differing attitudes toward theater: "Anglo-Saxon nations can scarcely know what a power the stage is in the South." In her 1868 essay on Gibson, she compliments the sculptor by praising his "Anglo-Saxon fibre." This recurring praise for the Anglo-Saxon depends partly on an implied contrast with the childish Italians.

Returning to Florence at the end of the summer of 1862, Blagden was well launched on her writing career. She was fretting over placing her novels, complaining about the advertising, calling on Browning and Anthony Trollope for help in negotiating with publishers, and taking much to heart the generally mixed reviews of her first novel and Browning's frank comments on the flaws and virtues of her writing. Although in his letters Browning often praises her articles and parts of her novels, he remains silent about her poetry. Despite the intermittent publication of her poems in periodicals such as *All the Year Round, The Athenaeum,* and *Once a Week,* Browning does not note its appearance as he does her other writing.

In addition to comments on her novels, stories of his struggles raising Pen, and discussions of Euro-

pean politics, Browning in his letters to Blagden mentions hundreds of their friends and acquaintances. The two correspondents could scarcely keep track of each other's addresses, much less keep up with the peregrinations of this huge group. Blagden's published writing alludes mainly to the most famous of them. In "A Holiday in Venice" she quotes Browning's "A Toccata of Galuppi's"; she heads another article with a quatrain from his "Casa Guidi Windows." A full-length poem, "To Georges Sand, on Her Interview with Barrett Browning," grants Barrett Browning a kind of holiness in contrast with the other author's earthy sinfulness. She also admired George Eliot although Gordon Haight implies that when Eliot and George Henry Lewes visited Florence they alone remained immune to the charm so appreciated by the Trollopes, the Storys, Kate Field, Robert Lytton, Julian Fane, Walter Savage Landor, and many others.

Blagden's poetry has much in common with the writing of other midcentury poets, including attitudes, favorite topics, and metaphors. Victorian values of duty and fellow feeling appear didactically in many poems. In "Say Which Were Best," for example, she presents a choice between lethargic self-indulgence and striving hope. A Victorian sense of duty is evident in "My Monogram: Written in Rome, Jan 7th, 1867," which describes her initials, IB, as a "Circle of love and of pleasure, / Barred by a cross of flame." In the fifth and final stanza the speaker interprets the lesson of the figure:

Through yearning, fruition, and loss,
To make duty my goal and my aim,
As the circles are held in the Cross!
My life's motto is writ in my name.

Blagden addresses a popular Victorian interest in "Mesmerism: A Death-Bed Confession" in which the persona tries to prolong the life of his delicate wife by calling in a mesmerist with designs on her love. Challenged not to release her from the life-saving trance, the husband nevertheless awakens her. True to the mesmerist's caution, the lady dies, and the persona shows signs of madness as he transports her bleeding body back to their home where his bloodhounds welcome him:

Through my old hall; its banners stirred
As moved by a strong wind,
Yet as we passed no sound, no step was heard;
The burnished shield which lined
The walls were lit as with a flame

And clashed together as we came!

The fascination with mesmerism, spiritualism, and seances that agitated many Victorians recurs in Blagden's novels as well.

A strain of Pre-Raphaelitism appears mainly in Blagden's Italian poems in which she uses rich diction to describe settings of stained glass and jewel-studded sculpture. In "The Church of the Gesu," for example, the speaker notes the lush details in the interior of the church: "Votive jewels . . . golden bars . . . burnished casements and jasper pillars." In "Alice" the persona clutches her missal as

Rubies red, and glowing
  Pearls and emerald sheaves—
Sapphire rivers flowing,
  Glitter through the leaves.

Blagden's ornate diction is also evident in her choosing as her pseudonym, Ivory Beryl, combining in the name both preciousness and the pale sparkle of the gemstone.

The poetry of Victorian women differs from that of their male contemporaries mainly in its ubiquitous angel metaphors, its many fallen-women narratives, and its references to dogs and other animals. *Poems by Isa Blagden* begins with "The Story of Two Lives," a fallen-woman poem similar to poetic narratives in Mathilde Blind's "The Russian Student's Tale" and the Marian Erle section of *Aurora Leigh*. The poem opens in "an English Park," where a husband is recalling the shock of his wife's sympathetic summary of a newspaper story about the death of an abandoned woman. His guilt prompts him to anguished ravings: "We loved. She was an orphan, poor and young, / My mother's ward. . . . in yon dark ancient hall." After he encounters his former playmate on a London street the man returns with relief to the life expected of him. He marries an earl's daughter, and the sight of his wife sitting among their daughters in his park distracts him momentarily from his anguish. Nevertheless, as he surveys his land, "Yon woods glare vengeful red in day's decline, / For there, a young bright life was poured like wine." The character rejects religious dogma but justifies his actions on the basis of his obligation to act as an example to the "herd."

At this point the narrative becomes the fallen woman's. She describes her efforts to gain admission to a refuge and her temporary friendship with a charitable Evangelical preacher, but she nevertheless, like so many others, ends up under a bridge by the Thames. The poem concludes with her seducer's vision of his victim as an avenging angel; she dies recalling a painting of the Holy Family by

Raphael hanging in the old hall, the site of her seduction.

Again like many women poets of the Victorian period, Blagden also wrote a poem about a dog. Through her kindness to Frolic, Venezia, Keeley, Teddie, and others, Blagden gained local fame for her devotion to animals, and she sometimes complicated her travel by insisting on carrying an occasional canine companion along. "To dear old Bushie, from one who loved her" praises the animal's fidelity and sympathy and calls the pet "noble, yet tender too." Like Elizabeth Barrett Browning's "Flush or Faunus," Mary Howitt's "The Cry of the Animals," and Katherine Harris Bradley and Edith Emma Cooper's "Trinity," this poem dignifies the animal and praises attributes that human friends would do well to imitate.

References to angels appear in more than half of Blagden's poems. "A Love Rhapsody" combines Plato's sundered and reunited loving souls with Christian beliefs: "Those angels on God's missions sent, / Whose grand and sexless beauty awes the soul, / Were severed lovers once." The husband in "Mesmerism" contrasts the demonic mesmerist with his angelic wife, and her unbound hair spreads out "like angel wings." Angels are also characters. In "To Georges Sand" seraphs listen eagerly to Barrett Browning's poetry, and guardian angels smile on her until the poet herself attains sanctity partly by kissing Sand, her stern-voiced, earth-bound predecessor. As a result of this act she replaces Sand in eminence.

At the same time Blagden pursued her writing she persisted in her peripatetic ways. In Florence she moved from villa to villa: Giglioni, Columbaja, Isetta, and Castellani. During the Brownings' time, she occupied their Casa Guidi when heating on the hillside became difficult during the winter months. In 1871 she enjoyed an elaborate jaunt to Austria, returning by way of Trieste and Venice.

Blagden's active social life also continued. Her ability to sustain friendships with both Robert Browning and Austin, whom Browning detested, is a significant measure of her grace and charm. Passionate discussions of Italy, art, spiritualism, and each other went forth in parties until marriages, remarriages, and deaths began dispersing the members of the old group. Blagden undertook her last trip to England in the summer of 1872, specifically because of her ill health, and five months later she died at the age of fifty-five. Her illness and death followed the pattern with which she was quite familiar. She was nursed by Mazini, a member of the English-speaking community, and then joined many of the those she had once similarly comforted in

Florence's Protestant cemetery on the Piazzale Donatello.

In "The Seasons in Italy–Winter" the poet anticipates a winter death and addresses "pale December roses" with a request that when she dies the roses will cover her "lonely tomb and peaceful rest!" Blagden's actual tomb, though, cannot be called either lonely or peaceful, for it is set amid the graves of many of her friends, and the cemetery is now bordered by busy traffic lanes. But despite its unquiet situation, the tomb fulfills the poem by bearing a sculpted bunch of the roses its speaker desires.

Soon after Blagden's death Mazini initiated the publication of her friend's poetry. She gathered the copy for the posthumous edition, financing the project largely by subscription while Austin edited the poetry and wrote its prefatory memoir. Austin praises Blagden's poems, believing them superior to the moderately successful novels despite what he describes as flaws of form and finish. McAleer, on the other hand, has little respect for anything Blagden wrote. Recently published anthologies of Victorian women's poetry include little of Blagden's work. In one the only example of Blagden's poetry appears solely because the poem "Georges Sand" offers a flawless example of the application of the virgin-whore dichotomy and, once again, because of her friendship with Elizabeth Barrett Browning.

The list of honored figures associated with Bellosguardo and named on the memorial plaque affixed to a wall on its piazza starts with Galileo Galilei and ends with Violet Trefussis. It lists Isa Blagden along with Henry James, Nathaniel Hawthorne, Florence Nightingale, and Ouida. However varied the literary achievements of the members of this group, Blagden's name belongs among them, at the geographical center of the community that loved literature, on the piazza at Bellosguardo.

Letters:
Robert Browning, *Dearest Isa: Robert Browning's Letters to Isabella Blagden,* edited, with an introduction, by Edward C. McAleer (Austin: University of Texas Press, 1951).

References:
Angela Leighton and Margaret Reynolds, *Victorian Women Poets: An Anthology* (Cambridge: Blackwell, 1995);
Mary McCarthy, *The Stones of Florence* (New York: Harcourt Brace Jovanovich, 1963).

Papers:
Letters to and from Blagden can often be found in collections that also contain papers associated with the Brownings, primarily at the Armstrong Browning Library, Baylor University, in Waco, Texas, but also in the Boston Public Library, the New York Public Library, and the British Library.

Mathilde Blind
(21 March 1841 – 26 November 1896)

James Diedrick
Albion College

BOOKS: *Poems,* as Claude Lake (London: Bennett, 1867);

Shelley: A Lecture (London: Taylor, 1870);

The Prophecy of Saint Oran and Other Poems (London: Newman, 1881);

George Eliot (London: Allen, 1883; Boston: Roberts, 1883);

Tarantella, A Romance, 2 volumes (London: Unwin, 1885; Boston: Roberts, 1885);

The Heather on Fire: A Tale of the Highland Clearances (London: Scott, 1886);

Madame Roland (London: Allen, 1886; Boston: Roberts, 1886);

The Ascent of Man (London: Chatto & Windus, 1889; revised edition, London: Unwin, 1890);

Dramas in Miniature (London: Chatto & Windus, 1891);

Songs and Sonnets (London: Chatto & Windus, 1893);

Birds of Passage: Songs of the Orient and Occident (London: Chatto & Windus, 1895);

Shakespeare Sonnets (London: Delamore, 1902).

Collections: *A Selection from the Poems of Mathilde Blind,* edited by Arthur Symons (London: Unwin, 1897);

The Poetical Works of Mathilde Blind, edited by Symons, with a memoir by Richard Garnett (London: Unwin, 1900).

OTHER: *A Selection from the Poems of Percy Bysshe Shelley,* edited with a memoir by Blind (Leipzig: Tauchnitz, 1872);

David Friedrich Strauss, *The Old Faith and the New, a Confession,* translated by Blind (London: Asher, 1874);

The Letters of Lord Byron, edited with an introduction by Blind (London: Scott, 1887);

"Shelley's View of Nature Contrasted with Darwin's," *The Shelley Society's Papers,* first series 1 (London: Published for the Shelley Society by Reeves and Turner, 1888);

The Journal of Marie Bashkirtseff, translated with an introduction by Blind (London: Cassell, 1890);

Mathilde Blind

"A Study of Marie Bashkirtseff," in *Jules Bastien-Lepage and His Art: A Memoir,* by André Theuriet (London: Unwin, 1892).

SELECTED PERIODICAL PUBLICATIONS–UNCOLLECTED: "Shelley," review of *The Poetical Works of Percy Bysshe Shelley, Westminster Review,* 38 (July 1870): 75–97;

"Lilja," review of "The Lily," by Eystein Asgrimsson, edited by Eirikr Magnusson, *The Dark Blue,* 1 (June 1871): 524–528;

"Nocturne," *The Dark Blue,* 3 (March 1872): 25–26;

"Maxims and Reflections, from the German of Goethe," translated by Blind, *Fraser's Magazine,* 93 (March 1876): 338–348;

"Mary Wollstonecraft," *New Quarterly Magazine,* 10 (July 1878): 390–412;

"The Tale of Tristram and Iseult," *National Review,* 2 (February 1884): 826–837;

"Marie Bashkirtseff, The Russian Painter," *Woman's World,* 1 (January 1885): 351–356, 454–457;

"Personal Recollections of Mazzini," *Fortnightly Review,* 55 (May 1891): 702–712;

"The Moat," *Eclectic Magazine,* 2 (July 1899): 146.

Mathilde Blind's career as an English poet and woman of letters is best understood in the context of the European revolutions of 1848, which brought her and her family to England in 1852 as permanent political exiles when she was nine years old. Her own fervently idealistic, politically engaged poetry, which germinated in the rich soil of her stepfather's radical engagements, was nurtured by the expatriate community that formed around his and his wife's home in west London. Blind's ardent feminism, nationalism, and religious skepticism developed distinctively English coloration, but they were rooted in the cosmopolitan experiences that initially nourished them.

Blind was born Mathilde Cohen in Manheim, Germany. She was the second of two children born to an elderly retired banker, who died in Blind's infancy. In 1847 her mother, Friederike Ettlinger, became involved with the movement for a united and democratic Germany and in 1849 married Karl Blind, a radical political writer and activist. He had been expelled from Heidelberg University in 1846 for writing an article denouncing the punishment of a freethinking soldier, and he and Ettlinger were both condemned to prison in Durkheim in 1847 for circulating a pamphlet that the government deemed treasonable. Blind became one of the leaders of the Baden insurrections during the revolutions of 1848; the suppression of this movement led to his exile from Germany. By 1849 Blind and his new family had also been exiled from France, and in 1851 they were expelled from Belgium under pressure from the reactionary government of Napoleon III. Granted asylum in England, they settled in St. John's Wood, just west of Regent's Park. For the next thirty years their household became both a haven for Europe's radical exiles and an influential intellectual salon.

Much of the evidence concerning Mathilde Blind's formative years comes from an unpublished and fragmentary autobiography composed late in her life and now preserved in the British Library. The fifty-five-page fragment reveals little about her family experiences, but it reveals much about her intellectual development and her determination to refashion herself as an Englishwoman. It began in 1855, when Blind (fictionalized in the narrative as "Alma") was fourteen and was sent to the Ladies' Institute, St. John's Wood. There she formed emotionally intense relationships with five other young girls, and together the six of them wrote novels and verses, edited their own journal, and acted out scenes from the novels of Charles Dickens. Blind's favorite poets at that time were all male–George Gordon, Lord Byron; Alfred, Lord Tennyson; and "the divine Shelley"–and she described her fifteen-year-old self as "an incurable dreamer of dreams."

Within a year she was abruptly awakened from her reveries. One member of her intimate circle was Rosa Carey (given a pseudonym in the narrative), who went on to become a best-selling writer of wholesome stories with conventional morals directed at young girls. She and Blind fell out over religious differences that the autobiography casts as the central drama of Blind's young life. Although at sixteen she claimed "the Christ ideal seized hold of my imagination," and soon Blind was reading Thomas Carlyle's *Sartor Resartus,* William Paley's *Evidences of Christianity,* and Max Muller's *Comparative Mythology* and feeling "a keen relish in exercising my brain on the arguments that proved Christianity a myth." She and a fellow student "again and again came back to the strange discrepancies between the account of Creation in Genesis and the history of our globe as revealed to us by the rocks and stones." Like Thomas Carlyle's alter ego in *Sartor Resartus,* Blind believed that "to live truly and to any purpose on this earth one must have faith," but she also believed that "the living faith that inspired the lips of martyrs to sing amid flames" no longer answered to contemporary realities and thus "turns into a rigid formalism which mummifies the mind."

As a result of her questioning spirit Alma is accused of being "a spiritual leper" by the school's minister and expelled. At this point a physical gap opens up in the narrative–symbolizing the trauma of this decisive turning point in her life–and when the narrative resumes six months later she is in Zurich, at the end of 1858, living in the home of her maternal uncle. He arranges for her to take courses in Middle German, Gothic, and Latin at the University of Zurich. She studies under a husband and wife who are both accomplished scholars and is soon introduced to a wider circle of Swiss intellectuals and radicals. "It was a big leap from the schoolroom of the Plymouth sister schoolmistress to the group of brilliant Revolutionists with whom after a week or two I was on the most intimate terms," she writes.

Blind's stepfather, Karl Blind, a German activist who was exiled from his homeland in 1849

"So many witty, original, fascinating, dare-devil spirits as formed Madame Helder's circle it is rare to meet together."

Blind's reimmersion in the European radical community of her mother and stepfather freed her from the constraints she experienced at the Ladies' Institute and allowed her to reinvent herself in the manner of the English Romantic poets she most admired at this time. In addition the remarkable independence that would characterize her entire adult life began to emerge. Ellipses in the autobiography indicate the omission or excision of details concerning her private life (she begins an Alpine walking tour on a beautiful summer day that causes her to forget "all my imaginary love troubles"); in their place is a narrative of a solitary poetic wanderer through the Alps, "those Mothers of Europe," where "for once I felt truly free! My body pliant to my soul moved rhythmically to the sound of the rushing stream. . . . I felt then to the utmost the poetry of the road. The charm which gypsies, vagabonds and outcasts of all times must feel in that kind of existence." Like William Wordsworth before her, she experiences the kind of spiritual epiphany via nature that her religious schooling at St. John's Wood never enabled:

The Alps, aglow like mountains of roses round a heavenly Jerusalem, receding range beyond range into ever

airier infinitudes of light, a vision like the last part of Beethoven's Ninth Symphony turned into visible form and beckoning something usually ignored or apparently non-existent in some depth of being below our habitual consciousness—something latent within leaping up, irresistibly yearning to that glorified region as if they too belonged to each other from everlasting to everlasting—what a sensation, momentary and yet to be kept through life as one of its few treasures.

Nature also becomes the anchor of Blind's emerging feminism. When she meets a young woman and her mother in a mountain lodge, they question her prudence in traveling unaccompanied. She answers that fear "makes us slaves." When asked if women are not "predestined to be dependent," that "nature and society play into each other's hands," Blind answers that nature is egalitarian. "I don't know about nature, I cried eagerly. There seems very little difference in the habits of male and female eagles, seagulls and swallows." The autobiographical fragment ends when Blind meets one of her former schoolmates who is vacationing in the Alps with her father. They spend an evening by the fire in an inn talking of school friends, and the next day Blind boards a train back to Zurich—all the while yearning to head for the Caucasus, "having heard from a traveler I met at Grindelwald that its mountain scenery far surpassed anything in the Alps."

Blind was back in London in 1859, where she continued her rigorous program of self-education. She was encouraged and assisted in this endeavor by her mother—and the British Library, where she received a reader's card in May. Blind's association with the library enriched her intellectual development for the rest of her life; but in the meantime she was receiving a liberal education in radical politics from many of the leading revolutionary figures in nineteenth-century Europe, who were regular visitors to her family's home: Louis Blanc, who led the socialists in overthrowing King Louis Philippe and establishing the Second Republic in France; Karl Marx, who also took up permanent exile in London following the revolutions of 1848; and the Italian revolutionary Giuseppe Mazzini, who had a lasting influence on Blind's thought and poetic values. These continental influences on her thinking are evident in her first known poem, a German ode recited at Bradford on the occasion of the Friedrich von Schiller centenary in 1859.

Blind's second work, never printed and now lost, was her first work in English: a tragedy about the French revolutionary Robespierre. Among other things it reveals the influence on her thinking of Louis Blanc, who went on record praising the play. A much greater influence at the time was Mazzini, who she commemorated in an 1891 essay in *The Fortnightly Review*. Blind recollects that she met Mazzini when she was in constant "ferment and unrest," and he showed her a way out of despair. "The materialist school of thought, which recognized force and matter as the only factors in the world, the notion that we are ephemeral creatures here today and gone tomorrow, that the life in us is as the flame of a candle which burns down to the socket and goes out, left a void which it required Mazzini's essentially spiritual doctrine to bridge over." Mazzini's doctrine was a doctrine of social salvation, social brotherhood; he vehemently rejected Blind's early idol Carlyle because he was "a worshipper of force." "If, instead of loving and admiring nations and humanity, you only love, admire, and reverence individuals, you must end by being an advocate of despots," Mazzini told her, anticipating a judgment that history itself has made against Carlyle's later pronouncements. Blind parted company with Mazzini, however, when it came to his essentialist views of women. Calling skepticism and analysis "the bane of our age," Mazzini tells Blind that "women, even women, who should be all compact of faith and devotion, are beginning to question and to analyze!"

Blind's questioning and analysis continued throughout the 1860s, a decade marked by personal tragedy, artistic growth, and the establishment of friendships that shaped the remainder of her life and career. In early 1866 she received an ominous letter from her brother Ferdinand, who was in Germany participating in the left-wing opposition to Otto von Bismarck. Bismarck, architect and first chancellor of the German Empire, had been named minister-president of Prussia in 1861 and had ruthlessly suppressed dissent and unconstitutionally expanded the army in order to wage war against Austria and other German states. Ferdinand's letter reveals the depth of his opposition to Bismarck: "As I wandered through the blooming fields of Germany, that were so soon to be crushed under the iron heel of war and saw the number of youths pass by that were to lose their lives for the selfish aims of the few, the thought came quite spontaneously to punish the cause of so much evil, even if it were at the cost of my life." Acting on his convictions, Ferdinand undertook a failed assassination attempt, and in 1866 he hanged himself while in prison.

One year later, still dressed in mourning clothes, Blind published her first book of poetry under the pseudonym Claude Lake. The poems were written in the years leading up to the death of her brother and are dedicated to "Joseph Mazzini, the Prophet, Martyr, and Hero." They reflect the seminal influence of the British Romantic poets on her own poetic sensibility—especially the pantheism and apocalyptic yearning of Percy Shelley and the early Wordsworth and Samuel Taylor Coleridge. Many of the poems also embody the same revolutionary ardor that motivated her brother. Echoes of Shelley's "Mont Blanc" can be heard in "The Torrent," the first and best poem in the volume, a hymn to Mazzini's revolutionary heroism that also expresses Blind's ambivalent desire to break free of the chains of her gender and speak in the voice of a male heroic poet:

> But I, behold, like to the tiny thing,
> The forest bird; I feel a magic spell,
> That draws me strongly on uncertain wing
> Away from all the violet woodland smell,
> To hear the words that from thy spirit well:
> Enchained, entranced, oh! Let me list, while flame
> And dazzling light in billows round me swell;
> Then flying back to shades from whence I came
> I will heroic deeds, prophetic words, proclaim.

The language of Coleridge and Wordsworth is woven throughout the rest of the volume, apparent in many of the poem's titles: "Am I, indeed, th' Aeolian harp," "I move amid a golden cloud," "My heart is hushed and holy."

Ironically, this first volume of poetry, which self-consciously embraces a male poetic tradition, appeared just when Blind was becoming preoccupied with the oppressive gender system and the status of women. According to her longtime friend and literary advisor Richard Garnett, "from the age of about five-and-twenty onwards the question of raising the status of women occupied a large share in Mathilde's thoughts." She told Garnett that women should be allowed to pursue all vocations (excepting military careers), and when he countered that this would throw a large number of men out of work she responded sharply that these men could emigrate. Like Mary Wollstonecraft, about whom she published an important essay in 1878, Blind located the source of gender inequity in education. "Among the numerous companions of her girlhood," Garnett writes, "she was the only one who could be considered well educated, and she had educated herself. It was not from want of talent, or of desire to excel; within the range of her own acquaintances she had seen numbers of lives intellectually wrecked by parents' obstinate adherence to conventional schemes of education and of life."

It is no surprise that the women Blind came most to admire during this decade—George Sand, George Eliot, and Elizabeth Barrett Browning—all defied Victorian conventions. Blind was reading women writers in earnest in the 1860s, including

Illustration for Blind's Dramas in Miniature *(1891), in which she attempted to "give poetic expression to some of the tragic phases of human life and passion"*

Eliot, Christina Rossetti, and especially Browning, whose *Aurora Leigh* (1857) impressed her more than any other contemporary poem. Recollecting their conversation on the subject, Garnett writes that in *Aurora Leigh* Blind said she "found the confirmation of her own thoughts on 'soulless, unspiritual education, where everything is nipped in the bud and crushed to nothingness,' and 'the first revelation of the world through poetry.'" During the latter half of the 1860s Blind developed a feminist voice that achieved its fullest expression in the poetry, essays, and biographies she would write in subsequent decades.

The most important influence on Blind's emerging poetic voice at this time, however, was her friendship with the Pre-Raphaelite painter Ford Madox Brown and the community of artists and intellectuals that regularly gathered at Brown's Fitzroy Square home. She began associating with this group in the early 1860s, forming lifelong friendships with Brown, his wife, and several of their close friends.

Brown's grandson, the future novelist Ford Madox Hueffer, describing this informal salon in his wry 1898 memoir *Ford Madox Brown: A Record of his Life and Work,* recalled that Blind was one of the promising younger members of the group that gathered at Fitzroy Square: "In the younger generation Miss Blind, Miss Spartali, now Mrs. Stillman, and Lucy, Catherine, and Oliver Madox Brown promised much." The men who gathered around Blind at this time were clearly dazzled—and daunted—by what Hueffer called her "extreme beauty and fire." William Michael Rossetti described her in a letter to the visiting American poet Walt Whitman as "a woman of singular ability and independence of mind." Rossetti's daughter later described her as "self-assertive, high-minded, and altogether formidable."

Blind formed three other important friendships with members of Brown's informal salon, all of them grounded in a common devotion to the memory and poetry of Shelley. William Rossetti, brother of the painter and poet Dante Gabriel Rossetti, was a writer and editor who was preparing an edition of Shelley's poems when he met Blind in 1869. In *Some Reminiscences* (1906), Rossetti records meeting her at the Browns'. "She was of Jewish race," Rossetti writes, "with fine, animated, speaking countenance, and an ample stock of interesting and pointed conversation." He adds that "later on I was continually in her company, in the society of my wife or of the Browns, up to the close of 1892."

Blind also met Richard Garnett, another Shelley scholar, at the Browns'. Garnett worked in the British Library and was appointed assistant keeper of printed books and superintendent of the Reading Room in 1875. He quickly became a trusted friend and advisor to Blind; as early as February 1870 he begins a letter to her "My dear Mathilde (if I may call you so)." Their twenty-five-year correspondence, most of it preserved in the British Library, records a remarkable literary friendship and constitutes an important chapter in the cultural history of late-nineteenth-century London. Their first letters, written in the spring of 1869, concern everything from Algernon Swinburne's essay on Shelley in *The Fortnightly Review* to Eliot's new poem in *Blackwood's Magazine* to the paucity of good criticism on William Shakespeare. From the beginning of their correspondence Blind often enclosed fragments and drafts of her poems in her letters, to which Garnett consistently responded with enthusiasm, praise, and frequently pointed criticism. His advice concerning technical matters was unfailingly helpful; he helped her avoid many mistakes of diction, phrasing, and metrics that troubled her as a poet employing English as a second language. As for his more general influence on her literary career, and his later judgments of her oeuvre, the modern reader is entitled to some skepticism. Garnett is the author of the *Dictionary of National Biography* entry on Christina Rossetti, about whom he concluded that except for "Goblin Market" "she is, like most poetesses, purely subjective, and in no respect creative."

The most famous member of this quartet of Shelleyites was the poet Swinburne. Some contemporaries believed that Blind was "infatuated" by Swinburne; others claimed Swinburne's friends thought a marriage to Blind would "save" him from a life of dissolution. The few letters that survive between the two are silent on these questions but reveal that each admired the other's poetry and maintained an intense interest in revolutionary politics. Blind wrote to him on 7 September 1870, for instance, after the surrender of Napoleon III to the king of Prussia, exclaiming "what astounding times these are! One has scarcely time to recover from one surprise than even more marvelous a one follows close on its footsteps, but certainly the last few days have teemed with fate."

Blind's commitment to Shelley quickly assumed a public character. On 9 January 1870 she delivered a lecture on the poet to the Church of Progress in St. George's Hall (published in pamphlet form the same year by the Shelley Society). Later that month, Garnett wrote Blind that Lady Shelley (the wife of Mary and Percy Shelley's son) heard the lecture and then reported her words to him: "I was much pleased . . . and think Miss Blind's outline of Shelley's life . . . describes what Shelley really was a thousand times better than Rossetti's memoir." She refers to W. R. Rossetti's *The Poetical Works of Percy Bysshe Shelley, With Notes and a Memoir,* which Blind reviewed anonymously in the July 1870 issue of the *Westminster Review* (she acknowledged authorship in an 1872 letter to *The Athenaeum*). While Blind praises Rossetti as the first to combine the disparate threads of biographical detail "into a symmetrical whole," she also carefully details his editorial errors and his reductive emphasis on technical matters in the poetry, revealing her own superiority to Rossetti as a scholar and critic of Shelley (further demonstrated in her 1872 publication *A Selection from the Poems of Percy Bysshe Shelley,* which contains her own memoir of the poet).

Blind insists, as did Shelley, that poetry is inherently political. Pointing to *Prometheus Unbound,* Blind notes that Shelley, when he "launched that *enfant terrible* of a poem into the world, fully believed in his power of making a breach in the solid rampart of custom, so as to take by storm and overnight, as it were, that great stronghold in which theology, mon-

archy, and matrimony have hitherto braved even the sap of Time and Change." Calling him "the poetic forerunner of John Stuart Mill," Blind argues that Shelley was the first poet to embody "the most momentous of all our modern ideas—that of the emancipation of women from . . . subjection to men." Objecting to Rossetti's slighting of "The Revolt of Islam," she notes that Shelley's poem "holds that woman, just as man, is or should be a being whose sympathies are too vast—whose thoughts too multiform to converge to the one focus of personal love, and that in the self-same way it is at once her right and her duty to take an active share in the general concerns of humanity . . . and to influence them, not only indirectly through others, but directly by her own thoughts and actions." She concludes her essay by proposing a rough division of all poets into "witnesses and interpreters." In describing Shelley as an interpreter she is also proclaiming her own aesthetic ideal: "The internal workings of the human mind, the mighty questions of religion, of the development of humanity, of the hidden laws of nature, sway their thoughts and throb audibly through their solemn rhythms."

During most of her lifetime the politically engaged nature of Blind's poetry was downplayed or obscured, not just because of her gender but by her close association with the Pre-Raphaelite circle and the aesthetic movement it helped inspire. In 1871 she moved out of her parents' house and established her own residence. About this same time she became, in Ford Madox Hueffer's words, "one of the most intimate friends of the Madox Brown family" and spent a considerable part of each year living in their household. Her first published poem, "Nocturne," appeared in the March 1872 issue of *The Dark Blue,* a short-lived but influential journal whose contributors included Brown, Swinburne, William Morris, W. M. and D. G. Rossetti, and Edward Dowden. These contributors, like Blind, were in conscious revolt against bourgeois conventions and proprieties and looked to predecessors like Shelley, Alfred, Lord Tennyson, and Robert Browning for inspiration. *The Dark Blue* propagated the ideas and ideals of aestheticism, serving as a bridge between the Pre-Raphaelite and art for art's sake movements. Blind's poem, never collected in any of her subsequent volumes, is a haunting, lyrical fantasy reminiscent of Robert Browning's "Porphyria's Lover" that provocatively blends eroticism, madness, and death.

Despite her continuing association with the "aesthetes" Blind's subsequent poetry diverged from theirs in important ways. Like Eliot, about whom she wrote an important biography (published in 1883, it

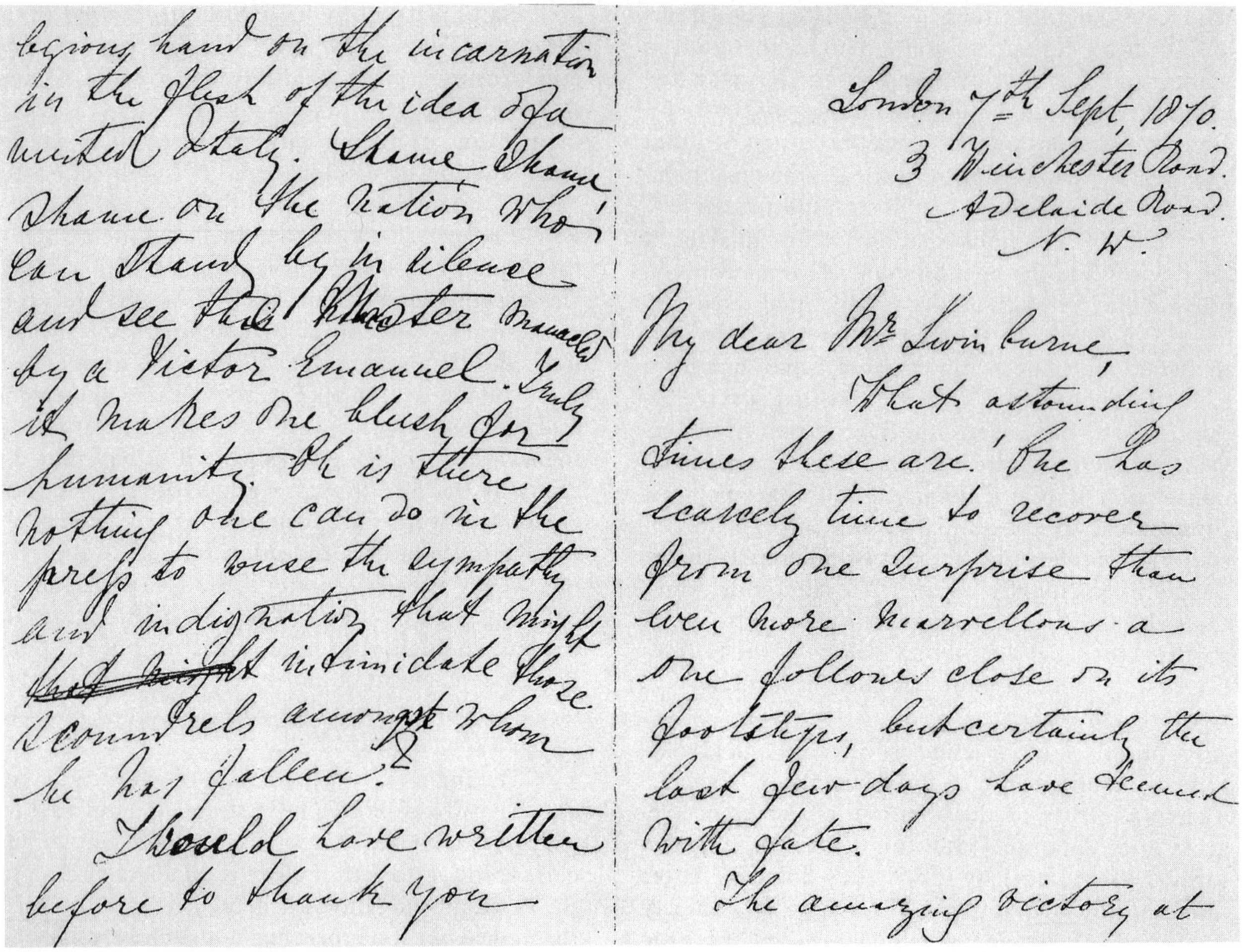

[Handwritten letter reproduced — left page]

> legions hand on the incarnation
> in the flesh of the idea of a
> united Italy. Shame Shame
> Shame on the nation who
> can stand by in silence
> and see this blunder made
> by a Victor Emanuel. Truly
> it makes one blush for
> humanity. Oh is there
> nothing one can do in the
> press to rouse the sympathy
> and indignation that might
> intimidate those
> scoundrels amongst whom
> he has fallen.
> I should have written
> before to thank you

[Handwritten letter reproduced — right page]

> London 7th Sept, 1870.
> 3 Winchester Road.
> Adelaide Road.
> N. W.
>
> My dear Mr Swinburne,
>   What astounding
> times these are. One has
> scarcely time to recover
> from one surprise than
> even more marvellous a
> one follows close on its
> footsteps, but certainly the
> last few days have teemed
> with fate.
>   The amazing victory at

Letter from Blind to her friend Algernon Charles Swinburne celebrating the surrender of Napoleon III to the King of Prussia

was the first biography of Eliot written by a woman), Blind believed that "art for art's sake" threatened to render literature merely decorative. This attitude is apparent in her introduction to *The Letters of Lord Byron,* which she edited in 1887: "words always stood as signs for things to Byron, his object being to get hold of the one that most adequately expressed the image in his mind: a manner of writing which differs entirely from the aesthetic method, where the luxuriant beauty of expression becomes of such supreme importance that it weakens, undermines, and finally destroys the sap and marrow of thought, as the enlacing ivy the tree that is its stay." Blind's own thought was increasingly engaged with religious and social issues in the 1870s, and this had profound consequences for her poetry. In 1874 she translated David Friedrich Strauss's *The Old Faith and the New, A Confession* into English, a project that identified her as a religious skeptic and freethinker (Eliot had translated Strauss's *The Life of Jesus, Critically Examined* in 1846). In 1878 she published a long essay on Mary Wollstonecraft in the *New Quarterly Magazine*—one of only two extended discussions of the pioneering feminist to appear in English periodicals since Wollstonecraft's death (the other was by Eliot).

While writing her translation of *The Old Faith and the New,* Blind made the first of several trips to Scotland. Visiting the island of Iona, she discovered the legend of Saint Oran, which became the subject of her first major poem, "The Prophecy of Saint Oran." The legend concerns the experiences of a group of Irish monks who spread Christianity throughout Scotland and northern England in the sixth century, led by St. Columba. According to the legend, Oran consented to being buried alive in order to appease certain demons of the earth who were preventing Columba from building a chapel. But when Columba ordered the body to be dug up after three days, Oran arose from the dead to proclaim that there is no God, final judgment, or future state. Columba silenced Oran by ordering his body to be buried once again, a command that subsequently became the Gaelic proverb used as the epigraph to

Blind's poem: "Earth, earth on the mouth of Oran, that he may blab no more."

Blind's revisions of the legend are significant. In her account, a four-part narrative comprising 148 stanzas, Oran falls in love with the daughter of a native chieftain, whose paganism eloquently resists his attempts to convert her (she calls Christianity a "joy-killing creed"). In addition he is condemned to burial by St. Columba rather than offering himself as a sacrifice. Finally, it is his beloved Mona who releases him from the grave, not some supernatural agency. The entire poem may be read as Blind's poetic representation of what Oran might have said if allowed to continue speaking after rising from the earth, filtered through her own feminist, freethinking perspective. The final words St. Oran speaks in the poem express the "religion of humanity" Blind absorbed from Strauss and the feminism celebrated in her essay on Wollstonecraft:

Cast down the crucifix, take up the plough!
Nor waste your breath which is the life in prayer!
Dare to be men, and break your impious vow,
Nor fly from woman as the devil's snare!
For if within, around, beneath, above
There is a living God, that God is Love.

The radical implications of the poem were not lost on contemporary readers. Indeed, the publisher, Newman and Company, withdrew *The Prophecy of Saint Oran and Other Poems* from circulation in September 1881, as revealed in a 24 September letter from W. M. Rossetti to Ford Madox Brown: "I was sorry to see . . . the bother about Mathilde's book. It looks to me very much as if the Publisher had got frightened by somebody about the atheistic character of the book, and had determined to sell it no more. Not long ago he was similarly frightened—but here chiefly or wholly on the ground of morals—about a volume of poems by George Moore which he had published, and he withdrew it from circulation. Mathilde at our house was very weak, and in that sense ill. . . ."

Always acutely sensitive to criticism, Blind was pained by her publisher's suppression of her first (and one of her best) volumes of poetry. But she would have been heartened by the reviews in the leading literary journals, including *The Athenaeum* and *The Academy,* which praised her dramatic economy and the maturity of her poetic voice. London's daily press was equally enthusiastic. The 26 September *Times* (London) called it "a remarkable contribution to English literature." *The Daily Telegraph* for 1 September singled out another poem in the volume for special praise in a comparison that doubtless pleased the author: "'The Street Children's Dance,'

. . . wherein the spectacle of poor children dancing round a barrel organ is pathetically moralized, is as tender and full of loving pity as Browning's 'Cry of the Children.'"

The controversy over "The Prophecy of Saint Oran" did not dissuade Blind from her continuing quest to marry poetic and political representation. Her next major poem, *The Heather on Fire: A Tale of the Highland Clearances* (1886), was published in the midst of the Highland land war of the 1880s. Known as the Crofters' War (crofters were the Scottish peasant farmers and fisherman who had earned a subsistence living from the land for generations), it was fought with such bitter ferocity that the British government sent gunboats to the west coast of Scotland and stationed policemen and troops on the Hebrides Islands. This conflict was rooted in the Highland Clearances that began in the eighteenth century and accelerated in the 1830s, the decade that is the setting of Blind's poem.

One of the most infamous mass evictions of a class of people in British history, the clearances were part of the transformation of the west of Britain from a paternalistic society based on ties of kinship to a capitalist one based on commercial and exploitative landlordism. Crofters were brutally evicted from their homes and property, first to make way for sheep grazing then for hunting grounds for wealthy British and American sportsmen. In the preface to her poem Blind assures the reader that the atrocities rendered in her narrative are historical, not imaginative, and that "the uprooting and transplantation of whole communities of Crofters from the straths and glens which they had tilled for so many generations must be regarded in the light of a national crime."

The Heather on Fire gives this crime a local habitation and a name. Its 181 octave stanzas, all composed of heroic couplets, tell the story of a family destroyed by actions of English landlords, one of whose agents boasts: "of all these dirty huts the glen we'll sweep, / And clear it for the fatted lowland sheep." At the beginning of the poem the patriarch of this peasant family, Rory MacKinnon, is already crippled from injuries he suffered as a soldier fighting for the English king in the Peninsular War; his son Michael delays marriage to his beloved Mary for nine years to provide for his parents. Their eventual union has produced four children, with another on the way, when the long-threatened evictions begin—at a time when Michael is away at one of his annual migrations to the herring fishery. The agents set the heather on fire, wreck the cottages, and smoke the villagers out of their hovels. Rory's bedridden wife dies in the flames; Mary is turned out

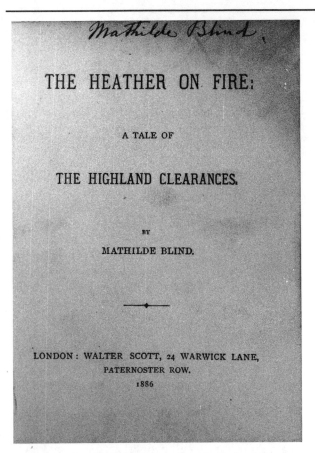

Title page for Blind's long poem about the Crofters' War in Scotland in the 1880s

cal energy or attraction with little of the real marrow of human life, the flesh and blood of man and woman. . . . we have them here."

Written at a time Blind had come to identify her own poetic project with that of Barrett Browning, *The Heather on Fire* represents her decisive break with the art for art's sake wing of the aesthetic movement. It embraces the vision of the poet's role as expressed in book 5 of *Aurora Leigh,* in which Browning criticizes the contemporary poet who seeks to escape the present and "trundles back his soul five hundred years, / Past moat and drawbridge, into a castle-court." Asserting that the poet's sole work is to represent "this live, throbbing age, / That brawls, cheats, maddens, calculates, aspires," Browning's concluding counsel aptly describes *The Heather on Fire:* ". . . Never flinch, / But still, unscrupulously epic, catch / Upon the burning lava of a song / The full-veined, heaving, double-breasted Age." *The Manchester Examiner and Times* explicitly connected the two poets and poems in its 1 September review of *The Heather on Fire:* "Miss Blind does not possess her theme; she is possessed by it, as was Mrs. Browning when she wrote *Aurora Leigh.*"

Blind hoped that *The Heather on Fire* would enter the contemporary debate on Britain's Scotland policy, and it clearly did so. On 30 July 1886 *The Morning Post* reported: "a subject which has painfully preoccupied public opinion is in the poem *The Heather on Fire,* treated with characteristic power by Miss Mathilde Blind." Prime Minister William Gladstone, while never politically radical like Blind, was also seeking to aid the crofters. In February 1883 his government set up a commission under Lord Napier to inquire into their living conditions, and in 1855 a bill was introduced in Parliament to grant them security of tenure and fair rents. Gladstone's government fell before the bill passed, but his third government, prompted by the newly elected Crofter's Party in the House of Commons, pushed the legislation through in 1886, the year *The Heather on Fire* was published. Letters exchanged between Blind and Gladstone in the 1880s record the fact that he read and praised *The Heather on Fire;* her last letter to him, in 1891, praises the liberal statesman for his "intellectual and political achievements."

In the same year that she published *The Heather on Fire,* Blind gave a lecture to the Shelley Society that anticipated the title poem of her next book on an epic theme, *The Ascent of Man* (1889). "Shelley's View of Nature Contrasted with Darwin's" asserts a central role for poetry in reconciling the Rousseauian vision of a "good, sinless, and be-

with her youngest child, who dies of exposure. Michael returns and flees with the remainder of his family to a ruined stronghold, where his wife gives birth to their fifth child, who dies. The agents burst in, gather them together with the other villagers, and prepare to put them on a ship to be taken to a distant colony (Canada was the usual destination). The family's eldest daughter dies of grief and exhaustion at the churchyard where they gather to bury their dead, and Michael, along with his remaining boy and twin girl, is hurried onto the ship. Rory escapes his captors and remains ashore to witness the final catastrophe: soon after starting out the ship is driven back to the rocky coast in a storm, and everyone aboard perishes.

Although *The Heather on Fire* clearly employs extremes of incident and sensation, the result is never mere sensationalism. In fact, the reviewer for *The Athenaeum* congratulated Blind "upon her boldness in choosing a subject of our own time, fertile in what is pathetic and awe-inspiring, and free from any taint of the vulgar or conventional. Poetry of late years has tended too much towards motives of a merely abstruse and fanciful, sometimes a plainly artificial, character; and we have had much of lyri-

neficent" nature with the evolutionist's view of nature as a site of "lust, hunger, rapine, and cruelty." For Blind "the true conflict consists in man's struggle with the irresponsible forces of Nature, and the victory in his conquest over them, both as regards the subjection of his own lower animal instincts and in his continually growing power through knowledge of turning these elemental forces, that filled his savage progenitors with fear and terror, into the nimblest of servants." "The Ascent of Man," dedicated to Barrett Browning, is her own poetic attempt to represent this struggle. Like *The Heather on Fire,* it is concerned with violence, but this time the violence of both creation and civilization are represented and the relationship between the two explored. "The Ascent of Man" struggles to discover what can be redeemed from blind violence; as in Tennyson's "In Memoriam," the quality of its doubt is more compelling than the quality of its faith.

What affirmation does emerge in "The Ascent of Man" emerges out of love, but a love that is most profoundly grounded in the physical experiences of mothers. As Isobel Armstrong noted in *Victorian Poetry: Poetry, Poetics and Politics* (1993), "Mathilde Blind may have been the first nineteenth-century woman poet to describe the birth of a child, where for a moment violence is productive." Part two of "The Ascent of Man" ends with the sonnet "Motherhood," which begins with a memorable octave:

> FROM out the font of being, undefiled,
> A life hath been upheaved with struggle and pain;
> Safe in her arms a mother holds again
> That dearest miracle—a new-born child.
> To moans of anguish terrible and wild—
> As shrieks the night-wind through an ill-shut pane—
> Pure heaven succeeds; and after fiery strain
> Victorious woman smiles serenely mild.

The phrase "font of being" refers to the mother's womb, but as Kathleen Hickok has noted in *Representations of Women: Nineteenth-Century British Women's Poetry* (1984), the modifier "undefiled" could refer either to the mother or the child. "If the former," Hickok writes, "then this mother is the Virgin Mary herself; if the latter, then the poem stands in defiance of the doctrine of original sin." Given the secular perspective of Blind's other poetry, it makes sense to read the sonnet, as Hickok does, as "an attempt to translate the myth of the Madonna into the experience of the ordinary woman," one that asserts that every mother's womb, and every new life, is "undefiled."

The experiences of women and mothers is also central to Blind's next volume of poetry, *Dramas in Miniature* (1891). As she wrote in a letter to William

Gladstone accompanying a gift copy of the book, "this volume mainly aims at giving poetic expression to some of the tragic phases of human life and passion." *Dramas in Miniature* is almost evenly divided between narrative poems on tragic themes and shorter lyrics, some steeped in loss but others ecstatic and affirmative. An impressive range is evident in the slim volume, from the novelistic realism of "The Russian Student's Tale" to the seductive gothicism of "The Song of Willi." Many of the poems were written at considerable emotional cost, as Blind acknowledged in a January 1891 letter to Richard Garnett: "I think the volume of poems is nearly complete now, for I shall have no peace till they are done. I was writing at one, 'A Mother's Dream,' till five o'clock in the morning last week. I didn't mean to but could not help myself; the emotional intensity was such that it went over me like waves and each time I lay down I had to start up and go on again. I paid for it with two days of sickness and suffering, however if the poems should be really fine I must not grudge it; as nothing worth doing was ever done without pain."

Out of this pain emerged some of Blind's most intensely personal lyrics, at least one of which, "Only a Smile," may allude to her relationship with Ford Madox Brown:

> I feed my love on smiles, and yet
> Sometimes I ask, with tears of woe,
> How had it been if we had met,
> If you had met me long ago,
> Before the fast, defacing years
> Had made all ill that once was well?
> Ah then your smiling breeds such tears
> As Tantalus may weep in hell.

Dramas in Miniature was published the same year Brown died. Brown's wife, Emma, who had been sick for several years, had died the previous year. Brown drew a frontispiece for *Dramas in Miniature* depicting the deathbed scene in Blind's poem "The Message," and both works obliquely allude to Emma's death. Although Blind was informally "adopted" by the Browns in the early 1870s after their son died and both their daughters married, her relationship to the painter eluded conventional categories. The two shared many intellectual interests, and Brown was an ardent supporter of Blind's poetry, which she often read aloud to him in draft form. He completed a portrait of the poet in three chalks in 1876, and she was with him (along with his daughter Catherine) the day he died. In fact, Ford Madox Hueffer reports that "his last quite coherent words must, I think, have been uttered whilst advising some alterations to a work of Miss Blind's." W. M.

Rossetti's daughter (and Brown's granddaughter) wrote in her memoir that Brown was "the most devoted and distinguished" of all Blind's friends. "Miss Blind was his junior by some 10 or 12 years [they were in fact twenty years apart in age], and his feelings for her toward the close of his life were perhaps more romantic than those of mere friendship."

Whatever the precise nature of Blind's relationship to Brown, it did not quell her independent spirit. During the last decade of her life she traveled widely, increasingly so after becoming sole heir to the fortune of her stepbrother Max Cohen in 1892. Freed from economic worries, she was allowed to once again embrace the cosmopolitan culture that originally nurtured her talent. Plagued throughout her adult life by chronic bronchitis, she often sought warmer climates—southern France, where she met Oscar Wilde, who commissioned the article for *The Woman's World* that led to the translation of *The Journal of Marie Bashkirtseff* (1890); Italy; and Egypt. The latter two countries inspired her last volume of poetry, *Birds of Passage: Songs of the Orient and Occident* (1895). The section titled "Songs of the Orient" includes the important poem "The Tomb of the Kings," resembling in spirit Shelley's "Ozymandias" but set inside a pharoah's tomb and comprising forty-six stanzas of eight-foot rhyming couplets. "Songs of the Occident" contains some of Blind's best sonnets and short lyrics, including "On a Torso of Cupid," "The Agnostic," "Rest," and seven "Shakespeare Sonnets" inspired by an extended stay in and around Stratford in 1894.

During the last few years of her life Blind spent considerable time in the company of her close friend Mona Caird, the novelist and feminist whose 1888 *Westminster Review* essay "Marriage" set off a storm of controversy and elicited twenty-seven thousand letters to *The Daily Telegraph*. In her essay Caird argues that as an institution marriage is a "vexatious failure." She also states that chastity "has virtually no connection with the woman's own nature." Two years later, in *Dramas in Miniature,* Blind published "The Message," a poem about the death of a prostitute whose speaker declares "she was not worse than all those men / Who looked so shocked in public, when / They made and shared her sin." It is poetically fitting that Blind spent some of her last years in the company of this kindred radical spirit; together they formed an important part of a larger Victorian literary sisterhood. Some of the time the two writers spent together is preserved in a Commonplace Book that Blind kept from 1892 to 1895, now at the Bodleian Library, Oxford. It records many of the walks she and Caird took in the countryside around Wendover, east of Oxford, and their discussions of everything from the condition of the rural peasantry ("Mona said and I agree with her that it would well repay the state to organize free lectures on physiology and hygiene in every town and village in the country") to their mutual love of nature to their current writing projects.

Mathilde Blind died in an invalid's home in south London on 26 November 1896. In her will she bequeathed the greater part of her considerable estate to Newnham College, Cambridge, to encourage and support higher education for women. The London *Times* inadvertently emphasized her boldly independent and unconventional career in its 2 December 1896 notice of her cremation and memorial service by printing it directly after the funeral notice for Coventry Patmore. Patmore achieved best-seller status with "The Angel in the House," an immensely popular poem about courtship, marriage, and the separation of spheres, which Virginia Woolf would later criticize for its oppressive effect on women's lives. Patmore was given a high-church funeral, and at the end of the service the religious poet Alice Meynell "lowered into the grave a wreath of laurels inscribed 'From the women of England.'" Blind's funeral discourse was pronounced over her remains in a Unitarian Chapel by her longtime friend Moncure Conway, who had been compelled to leave his Unitarian ministry at Harvard in the 1850s for his sermons against slavery. In addition to Conway, Richard Garnett, Ford Madox Hueffer, Theodore Watts-Dunton, and Mona Caird were members of what Garnett later described as a "large audience of men and women, many of much distinction, who had esteemed and loved and admired her in life."

In his obituary essay on Blind for *The Athenaeum,* Theodore Watts-Dunton remembered her as "one of the noblest of women . . . combining the artlessness of the very child with the strong intellect of the strongest man." He also wrote that "the chains with which women are loaded by convention irritated her, and no wonder. A period when the old idea of woman's submissiveness to man is fled, but only to leave a great woman more isolated than she was before, is hardly the period in which a woman like Mathilde Blind—a woman of genius—daring of thought, and independent of attitude—can find herself at ease." Four years later Richard Garnett created a fitting memorial to Blind in the biographically rich and honorific memoir of the poet he wrote for Arthur Symons's edition of *The Poetical Works of Mathilde Blind* (1900). The poems Garnett celebrates in his introduction seem likely to experience new life in the wake of renewed interest in Blind's remarkable career.

References:

Isobel Armstrong, *Victorian Poetry: Poetry, Poetics, and Politics* (New York: Routledge, 1993);

Ian Bradley, "The Highland Land War of the 1880s," *History Today,* 37 (December 1987): 23–28;

Moncure Daniel Conway, *Autobiography: Memories and Experiences of Moncure Daniel Conway* (Boston: Houghton Mifflin, 1904);

Richard Garnett, "Memoir," in *The Poetical Works of Mathilde Blind,* edited by Arthur Symons (London: Unwin, 1900), pp. 2–43;

Margaret Morganroth Gullette, "Afterword," in *The Daughters of Danaus,* by Mona Caird (New York: Feminist Press, 1989), pp. 493–534;

Kathleen Hickok, *Representations of Women: Nineteenth-Century British Women's Poetry* (Westport, Conn.: Greenwood, 1984);

Ford Madox Hueffer, *Ancient Lights and Certain New Reflections: Being the Memories of a Young Man* (London: Chapman & Hall, 1911);

Hueffer, *Ford Madox Brown: A Record of His Life and Work* (London: Longmans, Green, 1896);

Alexander Mackenzie, *The History of the Highland Clearances* (Aberdeen: Mackenzie, 1883);

Helen Angeli Rossetti, *Dante Gabriel Rossetti: His Friends and Enemies* (London: Hamish Hamilton, 1949);

William Michael Rossetti, *The Diary of W. M. Rossetti, 1870–1873,* edited by Odette Bornand (Oxford: Clarendon Press, 1977);

Rossetti, *Selected Letters of William Michael Rossetti,* edited by Roger W. Peattie (University Park: Pennsylvania State University Press, 1990);

Rossetti, *Some Reminiscences of William Michael Rossetti,* 2 volumes (London: Brown, Langham, 1906);

Algernon Swinburne, *Letters of A. C. Swinburne,* volume 1, edited by Cecil Y. Lang (New Haven: Yale University Press, 1960);

Donald Thomas, *Swinburne: The Poet in His World* (New York: Oxford University Press, 1979);

Theodore Watts-Dunton, obituary, *The Athenaeum,* 5 December (1896): 796–797.

Papers:

The major collection of Blind's manuscripts and letters is in the British Library, including fragments of an unpublished and incomplete autobiography (add ms. 61930, fol. 1r–55r). The Commonplace Book that Blind used from 1892 to 1895 is held by the Bodleian Library, Oxford (ms. Wapole e.1).

Anne Brontë

(17 January 1820 – 28 May 1849)

James R. Simmons Jr.
Louisiana Tech University

See also the Anne Brontë entry in *DLB 21: Victorian Novelists Before 1885.*

BOOKS: *Poems by Currer, Ellis, and Acton Bell,* by Brontë, Charlotte Brontë, and Emily Brontë (London: Alyott & Jones, 1846; Philadelphia: Lea & Blanchard, 1848);

Agnes Grey, as Acton Bell (London: Newby, 1847; Philadelphia: Peterson, 1850);

The Tenant of Wildfell Hall, as Acton Bell (3 volumes, London: Newby, 1848; 1 volume, New York: Harper, 1848).

Collections: *The Life and Works of Charlotte Brontë and Her Sisters,* Haworth Edition, 7 volumes, edited by Mrs. Humphry Ward and C. K. Shorter (London: Smith, Elder, 1899–1900);

The Shakespeare Head Brontë, 19 volumes, edited by T. J. Wise and J. A. Symington (Oxford: Blackwell, 1931–1938);

The Poems of Anne Brontë: A New Text and Commentary, edited by Edward Chitham (London: Macmillan, 1979).

Anne Brontë, painting by Charlotte Brontë (Brontë Society)

While Anne Brontë remains the least known of the Brontë sisters, often referred to as the "other one" even by scholars, it should be remembered that upon her death at age twenty-nine in 1849 she was actually more accomplished than either Charlotte or Emily. Brontë not only had published a volume of poetry with her sisters, *Poems by Currer, Ellis, and Acton Bell* (1846) but also had seen some of her poetry published independently. In addition she had two novels published, *Agnes Grey* (1847) and *The Tenant of Wildfell Hall* (1848). Considering that neither Emily nor Charlotte were as productive by their twenty-ninth year, it seems likely that the youngest of the Brontë sisters might have been a major literary figure had she lived into her thirties, as did her sister Charlotte. Anne Brontë's tentative fame today is to some degree due to her famous surname, and even with a critical reappraisal of her work during the last twenty years she is still recog-

nized primarily as a novelist. Yet just as her talents as a novelist are being reexamined, so too are her skills as a poet. With the emergence of the critical recognition of many noncanonical Victorian women poets and owing to the work of scholars and critics such as Edward Chitham, Tom Winnifrith, and Derek Stanford—who considers her one of the best Victorian women poets—Brontë's poetry is at last receiving the long-overdue recognition it deserves.

Born in Yorkshire, England, on 17 January 1820, Anne Brontë was the youngest daughter of the Reverend Patrick and Maria Branwell Brontë. She spent most of her early life in the village of Haworth at her home at the parsonage, and although her mother died in 1821, her Aunt Branwell joined the family and served as the household supervisor until her death in 1842. Perhaps to lessen the strain on Aunt Branwell and to help educate his daughters, Patrick Brontë decided to send his daughters away to get an education. Brontë was fortunate that as the youngest daughter she was unable to join her elder sisters, Maria, Elizabeth, Charlotte, and Emily at the Clergy Daughter's School at Cowan Bridge because it was there that an epidemic occurred in 1825 that took the lives of Maria and Elizabeth and forced Emily and Charlotte to return to Haworth. Brontë did, however, receive some formal education between 1835 and 1837 at Margaret Wooler's boarding school at Roe Head and later when Wooler's school relocated to Dewsbury Moor near Leeds.

The Brontës were never wealthy, and Brontë was forced to find employment in 1839. She first worked as a governess in the home of Joshua Ingham of Blake Hall, and in 1840 she became governess to the three daughters of the Reverend and Mrs. Edmund Robinson of Thorp Green Hall, near York. Her brother Branwell was hired as a tutor for the Robinson's son Edmund in 1843, and it was probably because of an affair Branwell may have been having with Mrs. Robinson that Brontë left this position by June 1845. While it is clear that her days as a governess influenced her later literary output, it is not clear to what extent her brother's indiscretions may have influenced her writing. Brontë did write, however, that while at Thorp Green Hall she "had some unpleasant and undreamt-of experience of human nature." Thus, after resigning in June 1845 she returned to Haworth, where she would remain with her father, Charlotte, Emily, and Branwell until she died a few years later.

Brontë's early years—both before and after her tenure as a governess—were extremely productive in a literary sense although her early poetry demonstrates a tendency toward extremes. One such example is the poem "A Voice from the Dungeon," written in October 1837 when Brontë was at Dewsbury Moor.

I'm buried now; I'm done with life;
I've done with hate, revenge, and strife;
I've done with joy, and hope and love
And all the bustling world above.

Long have I dwelt forgotten here
In pining woe and dull despair;
This place of solitude and gloom
Must be my dungeon and my tomb.

This poem has a rather gruesome tone, as the narrator claims to "dream of fiends instead of men." The narrator, in a trancelike state, is awakened by "one long piercing shriek. / Alas! Alas! That cursed scream," which portends that she must "die alone." Indeed, the eerie nature of the verse is more emblematic of Emily's work than Brontë's, and for some time this was considered to be Emily's poem despite the fact that Brontë signed the manuscript. It is perhaps an indication of the extent to which Brontë's reputation as a poet has been reclaimed that she is now justly given credit for this poem that, like much of Emily's work, is preoccupied with death. Although the Brontës often wrote poetry about death, Brontë did so much less than Emily, with the exception of later poems written in reference to specific individuals.

Although "A Voice from the Dungeon" is rather atypical of Brontë's early poetry in some ways, other poems written during this period have more consistent thematic connections. Throughout her childhood, at least up until the time she left Haworth for Blake Hall, Brontë and Emily collaborated on a series of imaginative adventures about the fictitious land known as Gondal. While none of their Gondal prose is known to be extant, much of the poetry from that period is still available. One of Brontë's earliest poems known to exist, dated 1 July 1837, is a Gondal poem titled "Alexander and Xenobia":

Fair was the evening and brightly the sun
Was shining on desert and grove,
Sweet were the breezes and balmy the flowers
And cloudless the heavens above.

It was Arabia's distant land
And peaceful was the hour;
Two youthful figures lay reclined
Deep in a shady bower.

One was a boy of just fourteen
Bold, beautiful, and bright;
Soft raven curls hung clustering round
A brow of marble white.

These first stanzas of the poem, which depict the reunion of two young lovers after a period of separation, demonstrate Brontë's teenage infatuation for romantic poetry. The tone of the poem is cheerful and optimistic although that outlook became less common in Brontë's poetry after she reached maturity and was beset by a variety of woes.

This youthful enthusiasm for romance was apparently tested in 1839 when Brontë developed an infatuation for her father's curate, the Reverend William Weightman. While the exact nature of their relationship has long been a point of debate, it seems beyond conjecture that Weightman was never a serious suitor for Brontë but that he was in fact more of a flirt; as Charlotte wrote, "he would

Haworth Parsonage, Brontë's home for all but the two years she attended boarding school

fain persuade every woman under thirty whom he sees that he is desperately in love with her." While Charlotte had apparently censured Weightman for his flirtatiousness, she also seemed to recognize that Weightman had at least a passing interest in her sister. In 1842 Charlotte wrote to her friend Ellen Nussey that Weightman "sits opposite to Anne at church sighing softly and looking out of the corners of his eyes to win her attention–and Anne is so quiet, her look is so downcast–they are a picture." Despite the fact that their relationship was never consummated in any sense, many critics have noted that Weightman's death in September 1842 may have left Brontë regretting that she had allowed her best and perhaps only opportunity for romance to slip away. This sense of loss has been discerned in her poetry although critics such as Edward Chitham warn against interpreting her verse on that basis because of the "uncertainty of the external evidence concerning her relations" with Weightman. Though some of her verse seems clearly to be written about Weightman, other references cannot be taken literally due to the arbitrary nature of their fledgling "romance."

"Self-Congratulation," which was written in 1840 when Weightman had been at Haworth for several months, is apparently the first of Brontë's poems about her feelings for the young curate. It tells of a young maiden with a secret passion for a young man. Despite this early indication that Brontë may have harbored feelings for Weightman, critics usually agree that the majority of poems she wrote about him were composed after his death from cholera in September 1842. One of these, "To

_____," written in the December following Weightman's death, is of special interest:

> I will not mourn thee, lovely one,
>   Though thou art torn away,
> 'Tis said that if the morning sun
>   Arise with dazzling ray
>
> And shed a light with burning beam
>   Athwart the glittering main,
> 'Ere noon shall fade that laughing gleam
>   Engulfed in clouds and rain.
>
> And if thy life as transient proved,
>   It hath been full as bright,
> For thou wert hopeful and beloved;
>   Thy spirit knew no blight.

Few critics doubt that this poem is about the young curate who may have captured Brontë's romantic interest.

Yet it is another poem, "Severed and Gone" (written in 1847), that is perhaps the best known of those ostensibly about Weightman. Brontë seems to be mourning the loss of Weightman:

> Severed and gone, so many years!
> And thou art still so dear to me,
> That throbbing heart and burning tears
> Can witness how I clung to thee.
>
> I know that in the narrow tomb
> The form I loved was buried deep,
> And left in silence, and in gloom,
> To slumber out a dreamless sleep.

In this poem Brontë also makes reference to the departed loved one as "mouldering dust, alone– / Can this be all that's left of thee?," which echoes "To ____ ." Although the debate about Weightman's influence on Brontë's poetry has raged for years, no scholar has offered a more plausible inspiration for these poems than the deceased curate.

Not all of Brontë's poetry is about love or death. Religion is a common topic in her verse, just as it has similar prominence in her sisters' works. Perhaps more so than either Charlotte or Emily, however, Anne's piousness has often led critics to be dismissive about her work. Some critics have assumed from the prevalence of religious themes in her poetry that she was a bored country girl with little else to write about although this assessment belies the careful consideration with which Brontë pursued theological questions. "A Word to the 'Elect'" (written in May 1843), for example, expresses her firm opposition to Calvinist doctrines regarding predestination. Brontë's personal theology rejected the belief that punishment could be eternal:

And when you, looking on your fellow men
Behold them doomed to endless misery,
How can you talk of joy and rapture then?
May God withhold such cruel joy from me!

That none *deserve* eternal bliss I know;
Unmerited the grace in mercy given:
But none shall sink to everlasting woe
That have not well deserved the wrath of heaven.

Indeed, Brontë's opinions on religion and her relationship with God is so prevalent in her poetry that it could be considered the most intrinsic element of her verse. Often she addresses the part that her faith in God plays in overcoming the many tragedies in her life, as in "If this be all" (written in May 1845):

O God! if this indeed be all
　　That life can show to me:
If on my aching brow may fall
　　No freshing dew from Thee:
. . . .
If life must be so full of care,
　　Then call me soon to Thee;
Or give me strength enough to bear
　　My load of misery.

During the next two years Brontë experienced the high and low points of her life, and she doubtless needed all the strength she could draw from her faith. It was in May 1846 that the book of poetry by the Brontë sisters appeared under their pseudonyms as *Poems by Currer, Ellis, and Acton Bell*. While the sisters considered publication of the book an accomplishment in itself, the collection, which was mod-

*Pencil sketch of Brontë by her sister Charlotte (*The Bookman *[New York] 3, no. 4 [1896])*

estly priced and the beneficiary of several good reviews, had by June 1847 sold only two copies.

Yet even as sales of the collection failed to live up to expectations, the sisters had turned to other literary endeavors. They each wrote a short novel and then searched for a publisher who would release Brontë's *Agnes Grey*, Emily's *Wuthering Heights*, and Charlotte's *The Professor* as a three-volume set. After a series of rejections the quasi-reputable firm of Thomas Cautley Newby of London agreed to publish *Agnes Grey* and Emily's *Wuthering Heights* together if the sisters agreed to contribute fifty pounds to offset expenses. Despite the harsh conditions of the offer and Newby's refusal of Charlotte's novel, Brontë and Emily agreed to the terms, and *Agnes Grey* and *Wuthering Heights* were published in December 1847. While *Agnes Grey* was and still is overshadowed by its companion novel, it was nevertheless at the time warmly received.

The reviews of Brontë's second novel, *The Tenant of Wildfell Hall*, however, were in some cases far from kind. Unlike Charlotte, who essentially gave up writing poetry after the publication of *Jane Eyre* in 1847, Brontë did not let her interest in novel writing end her career as a poet. It was about this time, in fact, that Brontë accomplished what her more famous sisters did not: she had one of her poems published independently in a magazine.

Like much about the Brontë sisters' lives, even the facts regarding the publication of this poem are

Portrait of Brontë by her sister Charlotte (Brontë Society)

shrouded in mystery. As Elizabeth Gaskell reports in *The Life of Charlotte Brontë* (1857) Charlotte's friend Ellen Nussey, when on a visit to Haworth,

> saw Anne with a number of *Chamber's Journal,* and a gentle smile of pleasure stealing over her placid face as she read.
>
> "What is the matter?" asked the friend. "Why do you smile?"
>
> "Only because I see they have inserted one of my poems," was the quiet reply;

and not a word more was said on the subject.

In *The Poems of Anne Brontë: A New Text and Commentary* (1979), Edward Chitham notes that this is a somewhat enigmatic report in that Nussey was not at Haworth when Brontë's poem was first published and the wrong magazine is mentioned in the anecdote. What is a fact is that Brontë's poem "The Three Guides" was published in the August 1848 issue of *Fraser's Magazine,* and while it could be that Nussey was mistaken about the magazine, it seems doubtful that Brontë would have first been aware of this magazine in January, some five months after its publication, which was the actual time of Nussey's

visit. Even though an alternative solution has been explored—that Brontë may have had a heretofore unknown published in *Chamber's* in January—no evidence has been found to substantiate this. Thus it seems likely that the questions surrounding this episode, like much else about the Brontës, will remain a mystery.

"The Three Guides," one of Brontë's longest and most didactic poems, displays a more mature point of view, combining those elements of religiosity and underlying morbidity found in much of her early work.

> Spirit of earth! thy hand is chill.
>   I've felt its icy clasp;
> And shuddering I remember still
>   That stony-hearted grasp.
> Thine eye bids love and joy depart,
>   O turn its gaze from me!
> It presses down with sinking heart;–
>   I will not walk with thee!
> . . . .
> Dull is thine ear; unheard by thee
>   The still small voice of Heaven
> Thine eyes are dim and cannot see
>   The helps that God has given.
> There is a bridge, o'er every flood,
>   Which thou canst not perceive,
> A path, through every tangled wood;
>   But thou wilt not believe.

Critics have debated the identities of the three guides of the poem's title. It has been suggested that the guides are the three Brontë sisters, yet a close reading of the poem suggests that the solution may not be so obvious. Whatever Brontë's specific symbolic intent, the poem was clearly written as a message of Christian faith.

Written after "The Three Guides," between November 1847 and April 1848, "Self-Communion" is the longest poem Brontë wrote as an adult, and it is also one of her best works. This poem, which most critics agree explores her relationship with her sister Emily, transcends much of her earlier poetry. For pure lyric beauty it ranks among the best poetry composed by the Brontë sisters.

> The mist is resting on the hill;
> The smoke is hanging in the air;
> The very clouds are standing still;
> A breathless calm broods everywhere.
> Thou pilgrim through this vale of tears
> Thou, too, a little moment cease
> Thy anxious toil and fluttering fears,
> And rest thee, for a while, in peace.

As in most of Brontë's poetry, the presence of God is emphasized. However, this poem is written

Brontë's grave in the seaside resort of Scarborough, the site of her death in May 1849

with such grace that there is no evidence of didacticism or moralizing. Were this poem representative of the majority of her work, Brontë might rank as one of the greatest of Victorian women poets. Unfortunately, just as she seemed to be reaching maturity as a poet, as well as a measure of success as a novelist, her life shortly thereafter came to an end.

On 24 September 1848, a little more than a month after the publication of "The Three Guides," Brontë's brother Branwell died. Although his profligate living had caused his health to deteriorate rapidly over the years, his death was still a staggering blow to his sisters. By 9 October Emily's health seemed in question as well; refusing medical attention until her last day alive, she died of tuberculosis on 19 December 1848. Brontë had been closer to Emily than any of her other siblings, and her loss so soon after the death of her brother nearly prostrated her with grief.

Thus by 1849 Charlotte and Anne Brontë, both in their twenties, found themselves the lone survivors of six children. It is not surprising, perhaps, that Brontë's health, which had been delicate even before Emily's death, began to fail rapidly. In January 1849 she wrote "A dreadful darkness closes in," a poem that seems not only to address Emily's recent death but anticipates her own as well.

A dreadful darkness closes in
    On my bewildered mind
O let me suffer and not sin,
    Be tortured yet resigned.

Through all this world of whelming mist
    Still let me look to Thee,
And give me courage to resist
    The Tempter till he flee.
. . . .
Should Death be standing at the gate
    Thus should I keep my vow;
But, Lord, whate'er my future fate
    So let me serve Thee now.

The poem seems to represent Brontë's acceptance of her impending demise although she clearly does not relish the prospect of leaving this world. In many ways her lot has been a hard one–"Weak and weary though I lie / Crushed with sorrow, worn with pain"–yet she does not question God, maintaining her faith until the last.

"A dreadful darkness closes in" was Brontë's last poem, about which Charlotte wrote in 1850 that "These lines written, the desk was closed, the pen laid aside–for ever." While this was not entirely true–Brontë wrote at least one letter, to Ellen Nussey on 5 April 1849–it was indeed Brontë's last contribution to literature. In May 1849 Charlotte and Ellen Nussey took Brontë to the seashore at Scarborough, hoping that the salt air might improve her rapidly worsening condition. Just three days after her arrival, however, on 28 May, Brontë succumbed to consumption. She was buried at Scarborough.

Brontë's reputation as a novelist and poet was for many years dominated by Charlotte's influence. Charlotte disliked *The Tenant of Wildfell Hall* to such an extent that she perhaps tried to compensate for what she saw as its sordid subject matter (it is about an abused woman who deserts her alcoholic and adulterous libertine husband) by stressing her sister's piety and quiet nature. Charlotte's most famous description of Brontë appears in the preface to the 1850 edition of *Wuthering Heights and Agnes Grey*:

> Anne's character was milder and more subdued.... She wanted the power, the fire, the originality of her sister, but was well-endowed with quiet virtues of her own. Long suffering, self-denying, reflective, and intelligent, a constitutional reserve and taciturnity placed and kept her in the shade, and covered her mind, and especially her feelings, with a sort of nun-like veil, which was rarely lifted.

This largely well-intentioned character painting represents the reputation Charlotte sought to create for her sister, as did her championing of Brontë's religious poems and her more reverent novel, *Agnes Grey*. The assessment of her character was echoed by publisher George Smith, who recalled Brontë as "a gentle, quiet, rather subdued person, by no means pretty, yet of a pleasing appearance. Her manner was curiously expressive of a wish for protection and encouragement, a kind of constant appeal which invited sympathy." These efforts to protect Brontë's reputation succeeded perhaps too well: literary historians have tended to assume that Brontë lacked the fire and passion of her sisters, that her success was almost entirely due to their fame. Few critics have believed in her abilities as fervently as did George Moore, who claimed on the basis of novels alone that had Brontë "lived ten years longer she would have taken a place beside Jane Austen, perhaps even a higher place." Yet her novels and poetry are receiving new attention as scholars consider the previously overlooked works of a diverse group of women writers of the era. Without question, at the time of her death at age twenty-nine Brontë had published more than either of her sisters at a comparable age, and had she lived she might have rivaled them in reputation today as well. Perhaps Derek Stanford's assessment of Brontë's poetry is the most fitting: "Anne's voice, in

poetry, is still a small voice. Compared with it, many other voices of 'louder lay,' however much lacking in purity or integrity, have often seemed more important. . . ." Yet Brontë's small voice possesses much emotional power; Stanford asserts that if "we respond sympathetically to aspirations after the 'good life,' if the existence of sin appears real, and the idea of deity desirable but distant, if hope seems difficult and human love unsmooth, we shall not read Anne Brontë's poems unrewarded."

Biographies:
W. T. Hale, *Anne Brontë, Her Life and Writings* (Bloomington: Indiana University Press, 1929);
Winifred Gerin, *Anne Brontë* (London: Nelson, 1959);
Ada Harrison and Derek Stanford, *Anne Brontë: Her Life and Her Work* (London: Methuen, 1959).

References:
Miriam Allott, ed., *The Brontës: A Critical Heritage* (London: Routledge & Kegan Paul, 1974);
Phyllis Bentley, *The Brontës* (London: Home & Van Thal, 1947);
Charlotte Brontë, "Biographical Notice of Ellis and Acton Bell," introduction to *Wuthering Heights and Agnes Grey* (London: Smith, Elder, 1850), pp. 1–12;
Timothy J. Holland, "The Image of Anne Brontë," *Brontë Newsletter*, 9 (1990): 1–3;
Bettina L. Knapp, *The Brontës: Branwell, Anne, Emily, and Charlotte* (New York: Continuum, 1991);
Elizabeth Langland, *Anne Brontë: The Other One* (New York: Macmillan, 1989);
George Moore, *Conversations in Ebury Street* (London: Heinemann, 1924), pp. 235–248;
F. B. Pinion, *A Brontë Companion* (London: Macmillan, 1975);
P. J. M. Scott, *Anne Brontë: A New Critical Assessment* (London: Vision, 1983);
W. S. Stevenson, *Emily and Anne Brontë* (London: Routledge & Kegan Paul, 1968);
Tom Winnifrith, *The Brontës and Their Background* (London: Macmillan, 1973).

Papers:
Locations with significant holdings include the Brontë Parsonage Museum, Haworth, which holds three of Anne's four extant letters and manuscripts of some of her poems; the Ashley Library, British Museum, which holds the fourth extant letter and other manuscripts; the Berg Collection, New York Public Library; the Bonnell Collection, J. Pierpoint Morgan Library, New York; and the Humanities Research Center, University of Texas.

Charlotte Brontë
(21 April 1816 – 31 March 1855)

Carol A. Bock
University of Minnesota, Duluth

See also the Brontë entry in *DLB 21: Victorian Novelists Before 1885* and *DLB 159: Short-Fiction Writers, 1800–1880.*

BOOKS: *Poems by Currer, Ellis and Acton Bell,* by Charlotte, Emily, and Anne Brontë (London: Aylott & Jones, 1846; Philadelphia: Lea & Blanchard, 1848);

Jane Eyre. An Autobiography, as Currer Bell (3 volumes, London: Smith, Elder, 1847; 1 volume, New York: Harper, 1847);

Shirley: A Tale, as Currer Bell (3 volumes, London: Smith, Elder, 1849; 1 volume, New York: Harper, 1850);

Villette, as Currer Bell (3 volumes, London: Smith, Elder, 1853; 1 volume, New York: Harper, 1853);

The Professor: A Tale, as Currer Bell (2 volumes, London: Smith, Elder, 1857; 1 volume, New York: Harper, 1857);

The Twelve Adventurers and Other Stories, edited by C. K. Shorter and C. W. Hatfield (London: Hodder & Stoughton, 1925);

Legends of Angria: Compiled from the Early Writings of Charlotte Brontë, edited by Fannie E. Ratchford and William Clyde De Vane (New Haven: Yale University Press, 1933);

Five Novelettes, edited by Winifred Gérin (London: Folio Press, 1971);

The Secret & Lily Hart: Two Tales by Charlotte Brontë, edited by William Holtz (Columbia: University of Missouri Press, 1979);

The Poems of Charlotte Brontë: A New Annotated and Enlarged Edition of the Shakespeare Head Brontë, edited by Tom Winnifrith (Oxford & New York: Blackwell, 1984);

The Poems of Charlotte Brontë: A New Text and Commentary, edited by Victor A. Neufeldt (New York: Garland, 1985);

An Edition of the Early Writings of Charlotte Brontë, edited by Christine Alexander, 2 volumes to date (Oxford: Blackwell, 1987–);

Charlotte Brontë

The Belgian Essays, by Brontë and Emily Brontë, edited and translated by Sue Lonoff (New Haven: Yale University Press, 1996).

Collections: *The Life and Works of Charlotte Brontë and her Sisters,* Haworth Edition, 7 volumes, edited by Mrs. Humphry Ward and C. K. Shorter (London: Smith, Elder, 1899–1900);

The Shakespeare Head Brontë, 19 volumes, edited by T. J. Wise and J. A. Symington (Oxford: Blackwell, 1931–1938).

OTHER: "Biographical Notice of Ellis and Acton Bell," in *Wuthering Heights, Agnes Grey,* together with a selection of poems by Ellis and Acton Bell, as Currer Bell (London: Smith, Elder, 1850).

Although Charlotte Brontë is one of the most famous Victorian women writers, only two of her poems are widely read today, and these are not her best or most interesting poems. Like her contemporary Elizabeth Barrett Browning, she experimented with the poetic forms that became the characteristic modes of the Victorian period—the long narrative poem and the dramatic monologue—but unlike Browning, Brontë gave up writing poetry at the beginning of her professional career, when she became identified in the public mind as the author of the popular novel *Jane Eyre* (1847). Included in this novel are the two songs by which most people know her poetry today. Brontë's decision to abandon poetry for novel writing exemplifies the dramatic shift in literary tastes and the marketability of literary genres—from poetry to prose fiction—that occurred in the 1830s and 1840s. Her experience as a poet thus reflects the dominant trends in early Victorian literary culture and demonstrates her centrality to the history of nineteenth-century literature.

Charlotte Brontë was born on 21 April 1816 in the village of Thornton, West Riding, Yorkshire. Her father, Patrick Brontë, was the son of a respectable Irish farmer in County Down, Ireland. As the eldest son in a large family, Patrick normally would have found his life's work in managing the farm he was to inherit; instead, he first became a school teacher and a tutor and, having attracted the attention of a local patron, acquired training in the classics and was admitted to St. John's College at Cambridge in 1802. He graduated in 1806 and was ordained as a priest in the Church of England in 1807. In addition to writing the sermons he regularly delivered, Patrick Brontë was also a minor poet, publishing his first book of verse, *Cottage Poems,* in 1811. His rise from modest beginnings can be attributed largely to his considerable talent, hard work, and steady ambition—qualities his daughter Charlotte clearly inherited.

Charlotte's mother, Maria Branwell Brontë, died when her daughter was only five years old. Born to a prosperous tea merchant and grocer, Maria Branwell was raised in Penzance, Cornwall, married Patrick Brontë in 1812, bore six children in seven years—Maria (1813), Elizabeth (1815), Charlotte (1816), Patrick Branwell (1817), Emily (1818), and Anne (1820)—and died of cancer at the age of thirty-eight. Though the loss of their mother certainly made a difference in the lives of all the Brontë children, the younger ones—Charlotte, Branwell, Emily, and Anne—seem not to have been seriously affected by her death. A remarkably observant child with a good memory, Charlotte nevertheless remembered little of her mother; when, as an adult,

she read letters that her mother had written to her father during their courtship, she wrote to a friend on 16 February 1850, "I wish She had lived and that I had known her."

During Maria Brontë's illness her sister, Elizabeth Branwell, came from Penzance to care for the family temporarily and, because Patrick Brontë's attempts to remarry after his wife's death were unsuccessful, she stayed until she died in 1842. "Aunt Branwell" has often been characterized as a gloomy and rigid Methodist who cast a pall of moral reproval over the lives of the little Brontës, but Charlotte's close friend Ellen Nussey remembered her in an 1871 memoir as "lively and intelligent" and capable of arguing "without fear" in conversations with her brother-in-law. She seems to have had more influence over Anne, who was still an infant when her aunt arrived in Haworth, than over the older children, who had considerable freedom in choosing their activities. Often left to their own devices, they played on the wide expanse of moors that surrounded their parsonage home; they also read voraciously and engaged in the imaginative play that was to develop quickly into literary inventiveness.

Charlotte's eldest sister, Maria, appears to have been especially influential in the creative development of her siblings. Unusually bright and mature for a nine-year-old, Maria became somewhat of a companion to her father after her mother's death, reading to him and her siblings from the pages of *Blackwood's Magazine.* She also directed little dramas through which the children early developed skill at speaking in the voices of imagined characters. Under the tutelage of her father and at the encouragement of Maria, Charlotte, like her younger brother and sisters, was attracted to the literary life at an early age.

In 1824, when she was eight years old, Charlotte and Emily joined their older sisters at the newly opened Clergy Daughters' School at Cowan Bridge in the parish of Tunstall. Although later made infamous by Charlotte's scathing depiction of "Lowood School" in *Jane Eyre,* Cowan Bridge had, in fact, much to recommend it to Patrick Brontë's notice. Having five daughters and one son to educate on a small income, he clearly qualified as a "necessitous clergy" and, moreover, he would have found the mission of the school compatible with his expectations for his daughters. According to a December 1823 advertisement in the *Leeds Intelligencer,* the aim of the school was to provide a "plain and useful Education" that would allow young women "to maintain themselves in the different Stations of Life to which Providence may call them" and to offer "a more liberal Education for any who may be

Brontë, second from left, with her siblings Anne, Branwell, and Emily; drawing by Branwell

sent to be educated as Teachers and Governesses." Patrick Brontë's decision to send his four eldest daughters to Cowan Bridge thus reflects his concern for their material as well as intellectual and spiritual welfare, a concern that he passed on to Charlotte, who of the three Brontë sisters that survived to adulthood came to feel most anxious about her need to establish herself in a fulfilling and yet economically viable career.

Charlotte Brontë's earliest experience with school life could not have made teaching seem an attractive career. As Juliet Barker notes in *The Brontës* (1994), the record of her abilities in the school register hardly suggests that her potential was noticed: "Reads tolerably–Writes indifferently–Ciphers [arithmetic] a little and works [sews] neatly. Knows nothing of Grammar, Geography, History or Accomplishments [such as music, drawing, French]." Since the assessment of every other student is essentially the same, the register tells little about Charlotte but certainly reveals that Cowan Bridge was unlikely to recognize individual talent, much less foster it. The evaluation concludes with a telling comment: "Altogether clever for her age but knows nothing systematically."

Charlotte found the rigors of boarding school life harsh in the extreme. Food was badly prepared under unsanitary conditions and, as a consequence,

outbreaks of "low fever," or typhus, forced the withdrawal of many students, some of whom died. Maria developed consumption while at Cowan Bridge and was harshly treated during her incapacitating illness, an incident Charlotte drew upon in portraying Helen Burns's martyrdom at the hands of Miss Scatcherd in *Jane Eyre*. Patrick Brontë was not informed of his eldest daughter's condition until February 1825, two months after Maria began to show symptoms; when he saw her, he immediately withdrew her from the school and she died at home in early May. Elizabeth, in the meantime, had also fallen ill. When the entire school was temporarily removed on doctor's orders to a healthier site by the sea, Elizabeth was escorted back to Haworth where she died two weeks after Charlotte and Emily were brought home by their father on June 1.

The loss of Elizabeth and Maria profoundly affected Charlotte's life and probably helped shape her personality as well. Suddenly becoming the eldest child in a motherless family forced her into a position of leadership and instilled in her a sometimes almost overwhelming sense of responsibility, one that conflicted with a streak of rebelliousness and personal ambition. From this point on, Charlotte took the lead in the children's activities, a position of sibling dominance that she maintained throughout their lives and literary careers.

Following the tragic experience at Cowan Bridge, Patrick Brontë tutored his four remaining children at home and provided them with music and art instruction from competent teachers. The children were responsive scholars who also read avidly on their own and continued their imaginative play under Charlotte's direction. They were allowed to choose freely from their father's library, which included requisite family reading such as John Bunyan's *Pilgrim's Progress* (1678-1684), Hannah More's *Moral Sketches* (1784), John Milton's *Paradise Lost* (1667), Sir Walter Scott's *The Lay of the Last Minstrel* (1805), James Thomson's *The Seasons* (1726-1730), and, of course, the Bible. The family regularly received *Blackwood's Magazine,* which heavily influenced Charlotte and Branwell's early writing, and, beginning in 1832, *Fraser's Magazine For Town and Country,* both lively and influential conservative periodicals with a heavy emphasis on literature. The Brontës also apparently had access to the library at Ponden House, a private residence nearby, and belonged to the Keighley Mechanics' Institute library as well as one or more of the local circulating libraries that carried popular contemporary novels and poetry.

The seminal event of the Brontës' literary apprenticeship occurred on 5 June 1826, when Mr. Brontë returned from a trip to Leeds with a present for Branwell—a box of toy soldiers—to which all four children immediately laid claim. Each child selected a soldier as his or her own and, naming them for their respective childhood heroes (Charlotte's was the Duke of Wellington), they began to construct plays and narratives around and through the voices of these characters. The earliest of such works were written in an almost microscopic hand in minuscule manuscripts so they would be compatible in size with their supposed authors—the toy soldiers.

Charlotte Brontë's juvenile tales revolve around the imagined adventures of the Duke of Wellington's two sons, Charles and Arthur Wellesley, and the social elite of "Glass Town," later transformed into the kingdom of "Angria." Arthur, soon elevated to the "Duke of Zamorna," is a recognizably Byronic hero who engages in romantic intrigues as well as in political treachery; his younger brother Charles is a less powerful, often humorous figure, who spies and reports on the scandalous doings of his Angrian compatriots—particularly his brother and his many paramours. Both Wellesleys are authors, and it is significant that Brontë's attractive but morally reprehensible Duke of Zamorna develops into the poet of the family while Charles emerges as a storyteller and her favorite narrator.

These early tales not only reveal the themes that preoccupied Brontë as a young writer and which reemerge in her adult writing—themes of romantic passion and sexual politics, desire, betrayal, loyalty, and revenge—but also reflect her early awareness of an issue central to early Victorian literary culture: the concern that poetry writing was a self-indulgent and even morally questionable activity. Romantically alluring but destructively egotistical, Brontë's "self-concentered" poet-duke is one of the means by which she represents her own early ambivalence about being a poet. This ambivalence—also experienced by male Victorian poets such as Alfred Tennyson, Robert Browning, and Matthew Arnold—was surely later intensified by social proscriptions against feminine subjectivity.

While the juvenile writings of the Brontës have been justly compared to fantasies, they were not merely uninformed imaginings. For example, early stories such as "A Romantic Tale," dated 15 April 1829, reflect the young writers' familiarity with articles on British colonizing in Africa published by *Blackwood's Magazine* in 1826 as well as more expected sources such as the Bible (especially the Book of Revelations), standard educational texts such as J. Goldsmith's *Grammar of General Geography* (1825), the works of Bunyan, the *Arabian Nights Entertainments,* and *Tales of the Genii* (1820) by Sir Charles Morell (pseudonym of James Ridley).

Characters in the children's stories debate contemporary issues such as the Catholic Emancipation Act of 1829, indulge in political gossip about prominent figures such as the Duke of Wellington, and conduct military campaigns informed by the children's knowledge of actual military engagements such as the Peninsular War, 1808-1814. The fictitious setting for the tales, supposedly on the coast of West Africa, owes much to the popular oriental cityscape paintings of John Martin, and the Angrians are based on contemporary engravings that Charlotte patiently copied from such books as *Finden's Illustrations of the Life and Works of Lord Byron* (1833-1834) and popular annuals such as *The Literary Souvenir.*

By 1829 Branwell was "editing" *Branwell's Blackwood's Magazine*—the title changed, ironically, to *Blackwood's Young Men's Magazine* when Charlotte assumed editorship seven months later—and the two collaborators were producing tiny, hand-sewn volumes that imitate in striking detail *Blackwood's Edinburgh Magazine,* the original upon which they were based. Like their prototype, Charlotte and Branwell's magazines are gatherings of writings in various genres—plays, stories, poems, imagined conversations, letters, sketches, anecdotes, essays—and include the advertising, editorial notes, and informa-

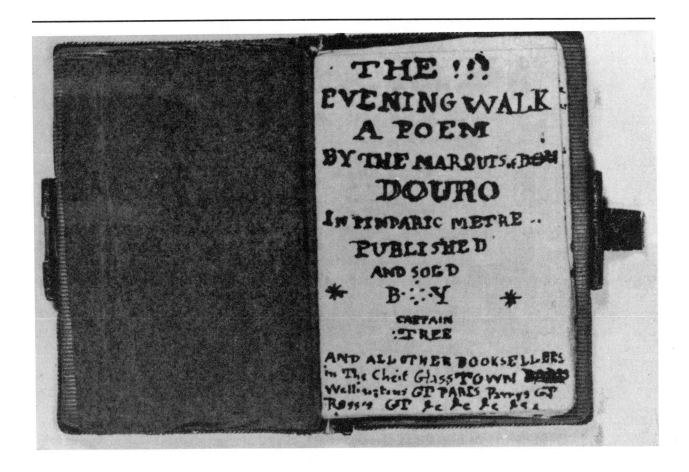

Title page for a miniature book by Brontë (Brontë Society); other miniature books created by the Brontë children (Brontë Parsonage Museum). The coin is about the size of a half-dollar (Brontë Parsonage Museum).

tion about publication and marketing that are typically found in such periodicals. Reproducing the material form of *Blackwood's Magazine*, Charlotte and Branwell also engaged in literary gossip and controversies like those they learned about through their reading, filling the pages of their narratives with literary reviews and vituperative personal exchanges between Glass Town literati.

It was during this early period of playful yet intense immersion in make-believe literary life that Charlotte Brontë first experimented with poetry. Producing sixty-five poems and a satirical play about poetry writing in 1829–1830, the fourteen-year-old self-consciously attempted to define herself as a poet. Though most of these early poems have a Glass Town context, being embedded within her narratives and spoken or sung by fictitious characters, some are only loosely connected to the stories. Many are interesting in that they reveal Brontë's exposure to current literary debates such as those concerning "neglected genius," the role of tradition and imitation versus originality and inspiration, and the public reception of poetry in a changing literary economy. The various poetic forms that Brontë experimented with during this time reflect her self-designed apprenticeship through imitation of earlier poets. For example, her many descriptions of natural landscapes are indebted to the eighteenth-century topographical poem that had been developed by "nature poets" such as James Thomson and William Wordsworth. Also, the influence of the popular Thomas Moore can be seen in Brontë's many poems written as songs.

Brontë deliberately imitates Thomas Gray's "Progress of Poetry" (1754) in "The Violet," dated 14 November 1830, in which she traces the history of Western literature beginning with Homer and then beseeches admission to that "bright band" of poets who have preceded her:

> Hail army of immortals hail!
> Oh Might I neath your banners march!
> Though faint my lustre faint & pale
> Scarce seen amid the glorious arch
>
> Yet joy deep joy would fill my heart
> Nature unveil thy awful face
> To me a poets pow'r impart
> Thoug[h] humble be my destined place

Such an early poem of course reflects Brontë's poetic immaturity as well as her enthusiasm for her chosen métier. In other pieces Brontë shows the ability to view her own literary pretensions with humorous detachment. She concludes one lushly descriptive poem with the self-deflating observation that "such a charming dogge[re]l / as this was never wrote / not even by the mighty / & high Sir Walter Scott."

Although the early poems contain visionary, lyre-playing bards and other romantic poet-figures, Brontë in her stories and plays repeatedly satirizes the romantic conception of the poet as a self-inspired original genius. She deploys parodic characters, such as Henry Rhymer in "The Poetaster," a story dated 6–12 July 1830, to debunk her own romantic posturing and that of her siblings. "The Poetaster" also humorously depicts the changing literary culture of England in the 1830s, a time when technological advances in printing allowed for the entry of many new writers into the literary marketplace. The "noble profession [of authorship] is dishonoured," wails a Glass Town publisher who soon expects to see "every child that walks along the streets, bearing its manuscripts in its hand, going to the printers for publication." Making fun of her own and her siblings' precocious literary aspirations, Brontë shows a good-humored awareness of both the opportunities and the complexities involved in pursuing a literary career in her day.

This spate of poetic production was interrupted in January 1831, when Brontë left Haworth for a second time, traveling twenty miles to become a student at Roe Head School in Mirfield, near Dewsbury. Owned and run by Margaret Wooler, whom her father called a "clever, decent, and motherly woman," Roe Head was a small school that usually enrolled only about seven boarding students at a time, all girls around the same age, and therefore was able to attend closely to the needs and abilities of individuals. Although Brontë was initially homesick and isolated from the other students because of her differences from them—her outdated dress, slightly eccentric behavior occasioned by poor eyesight and timidity, and her ignorance of grammar and geography as well as her precocious knowledge of literature and the visual arts—in time she won the respect and affection of her peers and came to feel quite at home in her new school environment.

At Roe Head, Brontë made two contrasting yet equally enduring friendships. One friend was Ellen Nussey, an entirely conventional and affectionately loyal girl with whom Brontë corresponded throughout her life. After the writer's death, Nussey jealously guarded her friend's reputation, in part by heavily editing her letters. Brontë's other friend, Mary Taylor, was as radical as Nussey was conservative. Boisterous, intelligently opinionated, and more intellectual than Nussey, Taylor apparently appealed to the bright, rebellious, and ambitious side of Brontë. Late in her life Taylor published *The*

First Duty of Women (1870), in which she argued that the first priority for women should be to prepare to support themselves financially. She had acted upon this conviction in 1845 by immigrating to New Zealand, where she ran a successful business as a shopkeeper until she returned to England in 1860 to live out her life in comfortable economic independence. It is unfortunate that only one of the many letters that Brontë wrote to Taylor survives.

Although she was considerably behind most of the other girls when she entered the school, Brontë quickly moved to the top of the class and stayed there until she left eighteen months later, carrying away several prizes and medals awarded for outstanding academic achievement. Often continuing her studies while the other girls were relaxing at the end of the day, Brontë apparently recognized that her education was a necessary investment in the future: she was not attending Miss Wooler's establishment merely to gain polish but rather to train herself for a career as a governess. Due to her dedication to her studies she wrote only three poems during her time at the school.

After her departure from Roe Head in May 1832, the rather uneventful round of life at Haworth, where she was in charge of her younger sisters' educations, eventually led Brontë back to the exciting world of Angria and the occupation of writing. From 1833 to 1834 she produced approximately 2,200 lines of poetry, most of it tightly embedded within the context of the passionate tales that she and Branwell were spinning around the political and romantic experiences of their beloved Angrians. Many of these poems are songs whose meaning and effect depend on a knowledge not only of the subject matter alluded to but also of the singer's character and the situation in which the lyric is sung. Other poems are lengthy narratives that develop the Angrian saga, deepening and sometimes complicating the plots developed in the accompanying prose narratives. These poems are formally more competent than the ones she produced prior to her stay at Roe Head, but they also show less willingness to experiment with poetic form and more absorption in the characters and content of the tales. The literary self-reflectiveness of her earlier writing gave way to an almost total absorption in the Angrian world of fantasy, with its emphasis on military conflict (largely Branwell's contribution) and romantic betrayal (Charlotte's main interest).

The few exceptions to Brontë's Angrian writings include a group of poems written in normal-sized script on lined paper, apparently from the same notebook, and preceded by instructions from her father: "All that is written in this book, must be

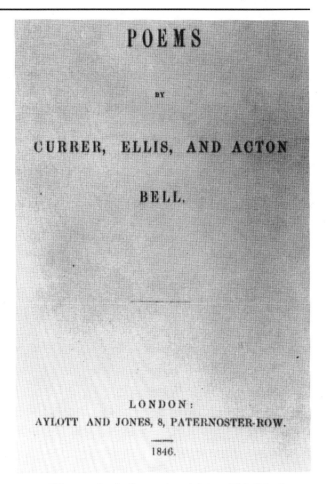

POEMS

BY

CURRER, ELLIS, AND ACTON

BELL.

LONDON:
AYLOTT AND JONES, 8, PATERNOSTER-ROW.
———
1846.

Title page for the Brontë sisters' first published book

in a good, plain *and legible hand.* PB." Several of these non-Angrian poems—"Richard Coeur de Lion & Blondel," "Death of Darius Codomanus," and "Saul"—may suggest that Brontë recognized the need to develop a public poetic mode to complement the private writing she and her siblings indulged in their literary fantasies. Thus, evidence of conflict in Brontë's poetry emerges in a way that connects literary differences—in poetic modes, voices, subject matters, even penmanship—with a perceived division between the private life of communication with a coterie audience, her siblings, and a public life of responsibility to authority figures, such as her father and teachers (the poems on historical and Biblical figures are similar to school exercises she later wrote in Brussels). This division eventually led Brontë to abandon poetry for prose fiction, but not until she had gained significant poetic skill and struggled through much anxiety related to this perceived conflict between the lure of the private imagination and the call of public duty.

The decision that Brontë should return to Roe Head as a teacher in July 1835 certainly contributed to this anxiety since there was little opportunity to "play out" the Angrian tales at Miss Wooler's school. As her journal testifies, Brontë grew increasingly resentful of what she saw as her "wretched bondage" to the teaching profession, with its long hours, lack of privacy, and tedious duties. She was able to write only in snatches and during vacations, so it is not surprising that her rate of production at this period fell well below that of her partner, Branwell, who installed himself in a Halifax studio with the intent of earning his living as a portrait painter and who found considerable time for both writing and socializing.

Brontë's poems after her return to Roe Head reflect her longing for home and for Angria as well as her anxious need to reconcile her desire to write with the necessity of continuing to teach to earn a living. The most famous of these poems, sometimes anthologized as "Retrospection," begins poignantly:

> We wove a web in childhood
>   A web of sunny air
> We dug a spring in infancy
> Of water pure and fair
> We sowed in youth a mustard seed
> We cut an almond rod
> We are now grown up to riper age
> Are they withered in the sod. . . .

The poem continues for 177 more lines, developing into vividly realized scenes featuring the Duke of Zamorna. The poem then breaks into a retrospective prose narrative that is rudely interrupted by "a voice that dissipated all the charm" as a student "thrust her little rough black head into [her teacher's] face" to demand, "Miss Brontë what are you thinking about?"—a striking example of the incompatibility of Brontë's inner, imaginative life with her actual experience while at Roe Head.

Gradually, Brontë was able to resume a pace of writing comparable to that of her earlier productive times, but even when she was writing prolifically there is evidence of distraction and dissatisfaction. The stories of 1836, for example, show that she was often unable to settle on a subject or identify new topics to write about, and many poems from this period end abruptly or trail off rather than draw to a close. Poems such as "But Once Again . . . ," dated 19 January 1836, explicitly articulate Brontë's concern about the conflict between the demands of her teaching career and her desire for romantic, social, and intellectual stimulation, which she associated with the imaginary world of Angria and, especially, with her poet-duke, who emerges as an enthralling poetic muse in the poem:

> I mean Zamorna!
> . . . he has been a mental King
>   That ruled my thoughts right regally
> And he has given me a steady spring
>   To what I had of poetry.
>
> . . . I've heard his accents sweet & stern
>   Speak words of kindled wrath to me
> When dead as dust in funeral urn
>   Sank every note of melody
> And I was forced to wake again
>   The silent song the slumbering strain.
>
> . . . to his altar I am bound
>   For him the consecrated ground
>   My pilgrim steps have trod
>
> . . . grovelling in the dust I fall
>   Where Adrian's shrine lamps dazzling glow. . . .

In December of 1836 Brontë decided to try her hand at professional writing, with the hope of earning her living as a publishing poet. To this end she sought the advice of no less a figure than Robert Southey, then poet laureate of England, to whom she sent a selection of her poems. The discouraging response in his letter of 12 March 1837 has become infamous:

> Literature cannot be the business of a woman's life: & it ought not to be. The more she is engaged in her proper duties, the less leisure she will have for it, even as an accomplishment & a recreation. To those duties you have not yet been called, & when you are you will be less eager for celebrity.

Brontë's reply to Southey and the fact that she preserved his letter in a wrapper inscribed "Southey's Advice | To be kept forever" seem to suggest that she submitted to his masculine authority, but her prodigious literary output during this period, particularly of poetry, tells a different story. Between January 1837 and July 1838 Brontë wrote more than sixty poems and verse fragments, including drafts of what were eventually to be some of her best poetical works. However, they remained fragmentary and defective; it was not until 1845 that she was able to revise them into poems she was willing to publish.

Brontë left Roe Head for good in December 1838 and spent the next four years attempting to reconcile her need to earn a living with her desire to remain at Haworth and write. She accepted two positions as a governess, working for the Sidgwick family in nearby Lothersdale from May to July in 1839 and for the Whites at Upperwood House in Rawdon from March to December 1841. Both experiences ended badly, largely because she could not accommodate herself to her situation. On 3 March 1841 she confided to Nussey:

> ... no one but myself can tell how hard a governess's work is to me—for no one but myself is aware how utterly averse my whole mind and nature are to the employment. Do not think that I fail to blame myself for this, or that I leave any means unemployed to conquer this feeling. Some of my greatest difficulties lie in things that would appear to you comparatively trivial.... I am a fool. Heaven knows I cannot help it!

In the summer of 1841 Brontë began negotiations for a loan from Aunt Branwell to establish a school that she and her sisters might operate. In December she declined Miss Wooler's generous proposal that she replace her as director of Roe Head, turning down a fine opportunity to take charge of an established school with a good reputation. This remarkably bad business decision is explained by her having become committed in the meantime to a new and more exciting plan suggested to her by Mary Taylor: that she and Emily attend school on the Continent in order to improve their command of French and Italian, and acquire "a dash of German" so to attract students to the school they would open upon their return. Inspired by Taylor's descriptions of Europe and emboldened by the Taylors' presence in Brussels, where she intended to study, on 29 September 1841 Brontë wrote a letter to Aunt Branwell in a manner characteristic of her self-confident mood:

> I feel an absolute conviction that, if this advantage were allowed us, it would be the making of us for life. Papa will perhaps think it a wild and ambitious scheme; but who ever rose in the world without ambition? When he left Ireland to go to Cambridge University, he was as ambitious as I am now. I want us *all* to go on. I know we have talents, and I want them to be turned to account.

Charlotte and Emily Brontë left England in February 1842 to enroll as the oldest students in a school run by Madame Claire Zoë Heger and her husband, Constantin. English and Protestant in a school of Roman Catholic Belgians, the Brontës were isolated from their younger peers by differences in language, culture, age, and faith, not to mention Emily's austere reserve and Charlotte's social timidity. Although both young women made considerable academic progress in Brussels and were praised for their success, neither ever felt entirely comfortable there, and when they went back to Haworth for Aunt Branwell's funeral in November 1842, Emily chose not to return to Brussels.

Drawing of Brontë by her brother, Branwell (Brontë Society)

For Charlotte Brontë, though, there was an attraction at the Pensionnnat Heger beyond the opportunity for academic achievement; or rather, such achievement was inextricably involved for her with the attractive presence of Constantin Heger. He was an excellent teacher of literature, who, unlike Southey, encouraged Brontë's literary talent, giving her close, individual attention and challenging her to clarify her thinking about writing as well as to refine her writing skills. In the essays she wrote under Heger's direction, Brontë returned to the literary issues raised in her earliest poems with a new sense of urgency. To her Romantic insistence on the spontaneity of poetic "genius, [which] produces without work," Heger wrote extensive marginal notes, arguing for the neoclassical values of control, learning, and imitation. He did not simply dismiss Romantic ideas about genius and poetic creativity as Brontë had often done when she was younger; rather, he took such arguments seriously and patiently explained the need for mechanical expertise and careful craftsmanship in her writing.

Although she apparently composed little new poetry in Brussels, Brontë did continue to transcribe revised versions of earlier poems into a copybook she had brought with her from Haworth, an indication that she may have been contemplating publishing them in the future. Encouraged in her literary efforts as she had never been before, Brontë's regard for Heger quickly developed into a grateful infatuation with the man whom she addressed in a 24 July 1844 letter as "my literature master . . . the only master that I have ever had." Understandably, Madame Heger soon tried to put some distance between her husband and his interesting English pupil. Hurt and angry, Brontë withdrew from the Belgian school in January 1844 and returned to England nursing her wounded pride and unrequited affections.

The letters she wrote to Heger from Haworth in 1844 painfully display her feelings for "Monsieur," while at the same time they reveal Brontë's increasing anxiety about establishing herself in a fulfilling line of work. Always troubled by extreme nearsightedness, she experienced a temporary further weakening of her sight at this time, writing Heger, a bit histrionically, that since too much writing would result in blindness "*a literary career is closed to me*—only that of teaching is open to me." In November the Brontë sisters abandoned their plan for opening a school in Haworth since not one prospective applicant had responded to their advertisements. The eldest Brontë's prospects—romantic, professional, and literary—seemed dim indeed, and she sank into a state of hopeless lethargy.

Brontë suddenly recovered from this period of enervating depression in the fall of 1845, when she stumbled upon a notebook of Emily's poems. As she remarked in her "Biographical Notice" to the 1850 edition of *Wuthering Heights,* she recognized that these were "not common effusions, nor at all like the poetry women generally write." She eagerly pressed her sister to publish her poems with a selection of her own verse, to which were added poems contributed by Anne. The sisters agreed to publish the poems pseudonymously (perhaps at Emily and Anne's insistence), and Charlotte Brontë energetically set about the task of finding a publisher for *Poems by Currer, Ellis, and Acton Bell* (1846), which the small London firm of Aylott & Jones agreed to print at the authors' expense, a common practice for unknown writers.

Charlotte Brontë cheerfully took sole responsibility for corresponding with their publisher and for seeing the *Poems* through the press; as she later recorded in the "Biographical Notice," "the mere effort to succeed had given a wonderful zest to existence; it must be pursued." Her enthusiasm for the business end of authorship, as well for its creative aspect, demonstrates her determination to succeed as a professional author in the literary economy of early Victorian England—a quality that she shared with successful contemporaries such as her future biographer, Elizabeth Cleghorn Gaskell. It is a quality that also explains why she wrote almost no poetry after 1845 and why she was already attempting to secure a contract for her first novel, *The Professor* (1857), before the *Poems* had even appeared in print.

Unlike her sisters' contributions, nearly all of Charlotte Brontë's poems in the 1846 volume are reworkings of much earlier compositions, mostly from the prolific period of 1837–1838, which she revised expressly for publication in this volume. In preparing her poems Brontë not only deleted all references to their original narrative contexts, as her sisters did for their "Gondal poems"; she additionally changed them to suit her new readership, invoking popular motifs (such as the sailor's return in "The Wife's Will") and expressing sentiments that were culturally resonate in 1846. For example, "Pilate's Wife's Dream"—originally a monologue spoken by the Duchess of Zamorna in a quite different fictitious situation—concludes with lines that anticipate the final affirmation of faith expressed in Tennyson's *In Memoriam* (1850):

> I feel a firmer trust—a higher hope
> Rise in my soul—it dawns with dawning day;
> . . . .
> Ere night descends, I shall more surely know
> What guide to follow, in what path to go;
> I wait in hope—I wait in solemn fear,
> The oracle of God—the sole—true God—to hear.

The poems that Brontë chose to present to the public in 1846 were not composed spontaneously and "without work" but deliberately altered to suit their new environment and purpose—a sure sign that Brontë had begun to modify her Romantic notions about literary genius and accommodate herself to the demands of professional authorship.

Because Charlotte Brontë's poems are longer than those of her sisters, she contributed only nineteen to their twenty-one each, so that each writer is given approximately the same amount of space in the book. Each poem is clearly attributed to either "Currer," "Ellis," or "Acton," and the contributions by the three are presented alternately, so that no one poet dominates any portion of the volume. The effect invites comparison between the three writers and makes Emily's superiority as a poet noticeable.

The arrangement of the poems also obscures a coherence between Charlotte Brontë's poems, many of which are connected through continuing narrative lines and/or through consistencies in character. For example, four of her poems—"The Wife's Will," "The Wood," "Regret," and "Apostasy"—together constitute a single story of an English wife who chooses to accompany her husband into political exile in France, where she affirms at the end of her life a loyalty to her native faith, the religion of romantic love:

'Tis my religion thus to love,
  My creed thus fixed to be;
Not Death shall shake, nor Priestcraft break
  My rock-like constancy!

Presented through extended monologues, this story effectively develops the character of the speaker through four dramatically realized situations in which she addresses an implied audience—William in the first three poems, a French-Catholic priest in the last. These poems thus resemble both the long narrative poem that was to become popular in Victorian England—Elizabeth Barrett Browning's *Aurora Leigh* (1857), for example—but also the dramatic monologue, perhaps the most distinctively Victorian poetic form, one refined by poets like Tennyson and the Brownings. Other Brontë monologues include "Frances," "The Missionary," "Pilate's Wife's Dream," and "The Teacher's Monologue."

Some of Brontë's poems are clearly lyrical—the companion pieces "Evening Solace" and "Winter Stores," for example—but most of the poems have a narrative component. Such narrative poems as "Gilbert" and "Mementoes," include Gothic elements like those that made *Jane Eyre* so popular; other poems, such as "The Letter," use precise imagery and details of setting to project a character's state of mind into his or her external environment, much as she did later in her novels and as Tennyson did in poems such as "Mariana." Others are linked together through narrative compatibility: for instance, "Preference" seems to be an indignant woman's response to the aggressive declaration of love asserted by the male speaker of her preceding poem, "Passion"; and "Gilbert" seems to be exactly the kind of

Brontë's husband, Arthur Bell Nicholls

arrogant lover who seduced and betrayed "Frances," whose troubled monologue precedes the story in which he is brought to retributive justice (though his victim is identified as "Elinor").

The sense of coherence in Charlotte Brontë's published poems derives in part, of course, from their common origin in the juvenile writings, which initiated the themes that appear so often in her novels; but their unity is also due to formal similarities based on a new purpose in her writing: to develop characters that are psychologically interesting through monologues and narratives that reveal personality within the context of dramatic situation. This purpose links the poems that Brontë published in 1846 to the dominant poetic modes of the Victorian period—the long narrative poem and the dramatic monologue—as well as to the literary form by which she ultimately became identified as an author in the public sphere: the novel.

Though Brontë made every effort to publicize *Poems*, paying for advertising and requesting that Aylott & Jones send review copies to fourteen periodicals, the volume sold poorly—only two copies in the first year—and received only three reviews, which were, however, rather favorable. Originally priced at 4 shillings, the volume was republished by the publishers of *Jane Eyre* in 1848, and received more insightful critical attention after the publication of Gaskell's *The Life of Charlotte Brontë* in 1857. Though most critics have acknowledged the superiority of Emily Brontë's poems, a few reviews published in 1848 to 1849, when *Jane Eyre* was selling very well, favored Charlotte Brontë's; for example, the anonymous reviewer for the 10 November 1849 *Britannia* praised her "mastery in the art of word painting" and her "faculty of exhibiting in words the shadowy images of mental agony." E. S. Dallas, in a July 1857 review in *Blackwood's Magazine,* remarked that her poetry is distinguished from that of her sisters' by her "faculty of forgetting herself, and talking of things and persons exterior to herself"–a quality shared by novelists and poets who write in the narrative and dramatic monologue forms. Brontë, however, adamantly agreed with those who thought her sister's poetry superior, and in a 26 September 1850 letter to Gaskell she dismissed her own contributions to the 1846 volume as "juvenile productions; the restless effervescence of a mind that would not be still."

In 1847, before she had secured her public reputation as a novelist, Brontë sent presentation copies of *Poems* to several important literary figures–a common strategy for unknown authors who wished to attract the attention of influential critics. She also persistently tried to publish her first novel, *The Professor,* which was rejected nine times before she received an encouraging reply from the firm of Smith, Elder, who declined to publish the book but asked to review any other novel she might be working on. Heartened by this request, Brontë finished *Jane Eyre* rapidly–in about two weeks– and had the satisfaction of seeing the novel in print shortly thereafter. The book was immediately popular and "Currer Bell" quickly became known by the reading public as "the author of *Jane Eyre.*"

After the success of her novel, Brontë wrote no poetry except for three unfinished poems on the occasions of her sisters' deaths. Though greatly saddened by the tragically early deaths of Branwell (24 September 1848), Emily (19 December 1848), and Anne (28 May 1849), she continued to publish novels–*Shirley* in 1849, *Villette* in 1853– and enjoyed stimulating literary correspondences with several people, including George Henry Lewes and William Smith Williams, the perceptive and kindly reader for her publishing firm, Smith, Elder. Letting her identity become known, she achieved the literary celebrity that Southey had warned her to eschew and became acquainted with several important authors, including William Makepeace Thackeray, Harriett Martineau, and Gaskell. At the age

of thirty-eight, Brontë married her father's curate, Arthur Bell Nichols and died, possibly of either hyperemesis gravidarum (severe vomiting caused by pregnancy) or a serious infection of the digestive tract, on 31 March 1855. She is buried, along with the rest of her remarkable family (except for Anne, who died in the seaside town of Scarborough), in the Church of St. Michael and All Angels, immediately across from her parsonage home.

Charlotte Brontë was not a successful poet in her own day, and today she is still rightfully known for her novels rather than for her poems. The inevitable comparisons between Emily's terse romantic lyrics and her sister's more discursive poetic style have produced a lower estimate of her poems than they probably deserve. "Pilate's Wife's Dream," for example, is arguably a much better poetic monologue than Elizabeth Barrett Browning's well-known "The Runaway Slave at Pilgrim's Point." Brontë is an important figure in the history of nineteenth-century poetry because her career illustrates the shift in literary tastes from poetry to prose fiction and because she employed, sometimes quite skillfully, the poetic modes that became characteristic of the Victorian period.

If one agrees with Virginia Woolf's claim in "'Jane Eyre' and 'Wuthering Heights'" that Charlotte Brontë's novels are read "for her poetry," one might argue that Brontë never did entirely abandon her career as a poet. Adapting her creative impulses to the demands of the market, Brontë incorporated poetic features into the more viable form of the novel, and so became a successful literary professional in Victorian England and a "major author" in the accepted canon of British literature.

Letters:

The Letters of Charlotte Brontë, with a selection of letters by family and friends, edited by Margaret Smith, 1 volume to date (Oxford: Clarendon Press, 1995–).

Bibliographies:

Thomas J. Wise, *A Bibliography of the Writings in Prose and Verse of the Members of the Brontë Family* (London: Clay, 1917);

Jami Parkison, "Charlotte Brontë: A Bibliography of 19th Century Criticism," *Bulletin of Bibliography,* 35 (1978): 73–83;

G. Anthony Yablon and John R. Turner, *A Brontë Bibliography* (London: Hodgkins, 1978; Westport, Conn.: Meckler, 1978);

Anne Passel, *Charlotte and Emily Brontë: An Annotated Bibliography* (New York: Garland, 1979);

Christine Alexander, *A Bibliography of the Manuscripts of Charlotte Brontë* (Westport, Conn.: Meckler, for The Brontë Society, 1982);

Rebecca W. Crump, *Charlotte and Emily Brontë: A Reference Guide,* (Boston: G. K. Hall, 1982–1986).

Biographies:

Elizabeth Cleghorn Gaskell, *The Life of Charlotte Brontë,* third edition, revised, 2 volumes (London: Smith, Elder, 1857);

Clement Shorter, *The Brontës: Life and Letters,* 2 volumes (London: Hodder and Stoughton, 1908);

Thomas James Wise and John Alexander Symington, eds., *The Brontës: Their Lives, Friendships, and Correspondence,* The Shakespeare Head Brontë, 4 volumes (Oxford: Blackwell, 1932);

Winifred Gérin, *Charlotte Brontë: The Evolution of Genius* (Oxford: Clarendon Press, 1967);

Margot Peters, *Unquiet Soul: A Biography of Charlotte Brontë* (New York: Doubleday, 1975);

Rebecca Fraser, *Charlotte Brontë* (London: Methuen, 1988);

Lyndall Gordon, *Charlotte Brontë: A Passionate Life* (London: Chatto & Windus, 1994; New York: Norton, 1995);

Juliet Barker, *The Brontës* (New York: St. Martin's Press, 1994).

References:

Christine Alexander, *The Early Writings of Charlotte Brontë* (Oxford: Blackwell, 1983);

Miriam Allott, *The Brontës: The Critical Heritage* (London: Routledge & Kegan Paul, 1974);

Carol Bock, "Gender and Poetic Tradition: The Shaping of Charlotte Brontë's Literary Career," *Tulsa Studies in Women's Literature,* 7 (1988): 49–67;

Sue Lonoff, "Charlotte Brontë's Belgian Essays: The Discourse of Empowerment," *Victorian Studies,* 32 (1989): 387–409;

Virginia Woolf, "'Jane Eyre' and 'Wuthering Heights,'" in her *The Common Reader,* first series (London: Hogarth Press, 1925), pp. 196–204.

Papers:

Significant manuscript collections including Charlotte Brontë's poems are held at the Pierpont Morgan Library, New York; the Brontë Parsonage Museum, Haworth; the British Library; the Brotherton Library, University of Leeds; the Houghton Library of Harvard University and Harvard College Library; the New York Public Library; Princeton University Library; University Libraries of the State University of New York at Buffalo; the Humanities Research Center at the University of Texas, Austin; and the Henry E. Huntington Library, in San Marino, California. Christine Alexander's *A Bibliography of the Manuscripts of Charlotte Brontë* provides precise information on the locations of the individual manuscripts.

Emily Brontë

(30 July 1818 – 19 December 1848)

Siobhan Craft Brownson
Winthrop University

See also the Brontë entries in *DLB 21: Victorian Novelists Before 1885* and *DLB 32: Victorian Poets Before 1850.*

BOOKS: *Poems by Currer, Ellis, and Acton Bell,* by Brontë, Charlotte Brontë, and Anne Brontë (London: Aylott & Jones, 1846; Philadelphia: Lea & Blanchard, 1848);

Wuthering Heights: A Novel, as Ellis Bell (2 volumes, London: Newby, 1847; republished as 1 volume, Boston: Coolidge & Wiley, 1848);

The Complete Poems of Emily Jane Brontë, edited by C. W. Hatfield (New York: Columbia University Press, 1941; London: Oxford University Press, 1941);

Five Essays Written in French by Emily Jane Brontë, translated by Lorine White Nagel, edited by Fannie E. Ratchford (Austin: University of Texas Press, 1948).

Collection: *The Poems of Emily Brontë,* edited by Derek Roper and Edward Chitham (Oxford: Clarendon Press, 1995).

The only poems by Emily Brontë that were published in her lifetime were included in a slim volume by Brontë and her sisters Charlotte and Anne titled *Poems by Currer, Ellis, and Acton Bell* (1846), which sold a mere two copies and received only three unsigned reviews in the months following its publication. The three notices were positive, however, especially with respect to the contributions of Ellis Bell–Emily Brontë. The writer of the review in the 4 July 1846 *Athenaeum,* for example, noted her "fine quaint spirit" and asserted that she had "things to speak that men will be glad to hear,–and an evident power of wing that may reach heights not here attempted." It seemed in 1848, the year of Emily's death, as if this potential were never to be realized. However, Brontë's twenty-one contributions to *Poems* represented only a fraction of the nearly two hundred poems collected by C. W. Hatfield in his noteworthy edition, *The Complete Poems of Emily Jane*

Emily Brontë

Brontë (1941). Several factors combined to delay the publication of a complete, accurately edited collection of Brontë's poems: her sister Charlotte, who in her heavy-handed revision of seventeen unpublished poems by Brontë to accompany the 1850 edition of *Wuthering Heights,* first published in 1847, went so far as to add lines and whole stanzas; the wide dispersal of Brontë's manuscripts after their sale in 1895 by Charlotte's widower, Arthur Bell Nicholls; and finally the difficulty in reading the manuscripts, some of which Brontë wrote in a tiny, crabbed script on irregular bits of paper. Ranging from 1836 to 1846–fortunately, Brontë dated all but about a dozen of her poems–these verses reveal that she had indeed reached the heights attempted in the poems in the 1846 volume.

Unfortunately the student of Brontë's biography cannot rely on the signposts she left on her manuscripts and must try to reconstruct her life from a scarcity of material. The plays and stories she wrote with her sister Anne about the imaginary land of Gondal have not survived. Her other prose consists of seven essays in French, a few notes, and four birthday letters she exchanged with Anne. Much of what we know about Brontë is seen at a remove, through Charlotte's writings about her or Elizabeth Gaskell's biography of Charlotte. Myths about the family abound, but Brontë seems to be the most mysterious figure of all of them. She is alternately the isolated artist striding the Yorkshire moors, the painfully shy girl-woman unable to leave the confines of her home, the heterodox creator capable of conceiving the amoral Heathcliff, the brusque intellect unwilling to deal with normal society, and the ethereal soul too fragile to confront the temporal world. There is probably an element of truth as well as hyperbole in each of these views. Again, the fault lies in part with Charlotte, who in her effort to assuage the critical charge of "coarseness" aimed at the author of *Wuthering Heights* wrote a "Biographical Notice of Ellis and Acton Bell" to accompany the 1850 edition of that novel and Anne's *Agnes Grey*. Of Brontë she wrote, "Under an unsophisticated culture, inartificial tastes, and an unpretending outside, lay a secret power and fire that might have informed the brain and kindled the veins of a hero; but she had no worldly wisdom; her powers were unadapted to the practical business of life. An interpreter ought always to have stood between her and the world." The real identity of the poet who created the fierce queens of Gondal and the visionaries of the subjective poetry lies somewhere between the shadowy myths about Brontë and the documented facts.

Emily Brontë was born on 30 July 1818 in the parsonage at Thornton in Yorkshire to the Reverend Patrick Brontë and Maria Branwell Brontë, the fifth of their sixth children after Maria, Elizabeth, Charlotte, and Branwell and the only daughter to be given a middle name. Both parents displayed literary ambitions; Patrick Brontë's *The Cottage in the Wood,* an Evangelical tale supporting Sunday schools and castigating the evils of drinking, was published in 1815, and during the same year Maria Branwell wrote an apparently unpublished piece titled "The Advan-

tages of Poverty, in Religious Concerns," a typically Methodist yet sincere and pious essay exhorting the faithful to care for the poor. In the year of Emily's birth Patrick's novella *The Maid of Killarney* was also published. Though Brontë continued throughout her life to observe her father's writing of sermons, articles, fiction, and poetry, she lost the example of her bright and vivacious mother shortly after the family's move to Haworth in 1820. Weakened by the birth of six children in as many years (Anne was born 17 January 1820), Maria Branwell was unable to fight off illness and died of cancer on 15 September 1821. Her sister, Elizabeth Branwell, moved into the parsonage that same month to help Patrick care for his young family.

That Yorkshire played an important role in Brontë's life and art is indisputable. Except for several brief absences, she chose to spend her remaining years at the parsonage. However, many of the myths surrounding her life arise from the time immediately after her mother's death, including the isolation of Haworth, the harsh eccentricities of her father, the dour Methodism of Aunt Branwell, and the abnormal upbringing of the Brontë children. Elizabeth Gaskell's *The Life of Charlotte Brontë* (1857), while admirable in many ways, was responsible for some of these errors. Recent biographies, especially Juliet Barker's *The Brontës* (1995), have sought to correct these misconceptions. Barker points out that Haworth was a "busy, industrial township," that Patrick was an involved and caring father, that Aunt Branwell's upbringing as a Wesleyan Methodist brought her closer to the gentler Church of England than to severe Calvinist beliefs, and that the six Brontë children enjoyed a "perfectly normal childhood" filled with games, lessons, religious education, and walks on the moors. Close in age and temperament, they provided each other with plenty of diversions. The Brontës' nursemaid, Sarah Garrs, reported that the children's games "were founded upon what Maria read to them from the newspapers, and the tales brought forth from the father's mines of tradition, history, and romance." Emily's participation in the playacting and daily walks would later significantly influence both her poetry and her fiction.

In 1824 several important changes occurred in the Brontë household. First, Sarah Garrs and her sister Nancy left the family, and Tabitha Aykroyd was engaged. Tabby remained with the Brontës until her death in 1855 and was accorded a place in the Haworth parsonage that far exceeded that of a mere servant. One of the few recorded incidents from Brontë's childhood also occurred during this year and illustrates the normalcy of the Brontë children's upbringing as well as the interest of their father in their development. Patrick Brontë, in helping Gaskell collect appropriate information for her biography of Charlotte, wrote her in a 30 July 1855 letter that he had used a mask to elicit honest responses from his children to his individual queries, "thinking that they knew more than I had yet discovered." He gave each one the mask and "told them all to stand and speak boldly." He asked Brontë, then aged about six, what he should do with her brother, Branwell, "who was sometimes a naughty boy." She answered, "Reason with him, and when he won't listen to reason, whip him." This answer seems to have arisen more from Emily's experience as a member of a large, active, and noisy set of siblings than from a quiet, doleful, and studious group.

More importantly, 1824 was the year that Patrick sent all of his daughters except Anne to Cowan Bridge School, a "School for Clergymen's Daughters." Patrick, though in possession of a perpetual curacy at Haworth, owned no land or inheritance and therefore had few options for providing for the future of his children. As in most Victorian families the bulk of the family income would be spent on the son's education. Yet Patrick knew he needed to enable his daughters to seek livings, most probably as teachers or governesses, and hence they needed to be educated. Miss Evans, the superintendent of the new school, called Brontë a "darling child" and "little petted Em," and the admissions register referred to her as "quite the pet nursling of the school." Tragically for the Brontë sisters, during the time they attended Cowan Bridge School it closely resembled the fictional Lowood School presented by Charlotte in *Jane Eyre* (1847). The staff at Cowan Bridge School was careless with respect to food preparation, and during the winter the rooms were often cold. The Brontë sisters had always been susceptible to coughs and colds, and the difficult physical conditions at Cowan Bridge most likely hastened Maria's and Elizabeth's contraction of consumption. They were sent home to die in 1825; after Patrick saw how ill Elizabeth was, he went to Cowan Bridge to collect Charlotte and Brontë himself. According to most biographers the deaths of their elder sisters most profoundly affected Charlotte, who had more complete memories of their deceased mother and now had also lost the sisters who had filled the maternal role. As Barker notes, all of Charlotte's heroines were orphans, and nearly all of the children in *Wuthering Heights* also become motherless. In her poetry many of Brontë's Gondal characters are also motherless, orphaned, or the children of parents who abandon them.

Between 1826 and 1829 Emily began music lessons, completed samplers, and made drawings and sketches of the natural subjects such as birds to which she was drawn for the remainder of her life. Her close observations of birds, animals, plants, and the changing skies over Haworth form a significant part of her poetry. During this time Branwell acquired several sets of toy figures such as soldiers, Turkish musicians, and Indians. These toys were the impetus for the founding of the imaginary lands of Angria and Gondal. The children began to write plays about the figures, with Emily and Charlotte composing "bed plays" that they kept secret from the adults as well as from Branwell and Anne. In "Tales of the Islanders" (1829) Charlotte gave a history of the early plays, underscoring Emily's early affiliation with the works of Sir Walter Scott, for she chose the Isle of Arran for her island and Scott for her "cheif [*sic*] man." This affinity grew with Aunt Branwell's 1828 New Year's gift to "her dear little nephew and nieces," a copy of Scott's *The Tales of a Grandfather* (1827–1829). In addition to Scott's works the Brontë children drew material for their plays from the family library of Aesop's *Fables, The Arabian Nights' Entertainment,* and wood-engraver Thomas Bewick's *History of British Birds.* Their most important influence during these early years was most likely *Blackwood's Magazine,* whose satires, political commentaries, and extensive book reviews provided them with a wealth of detail that seeded their imaginations throughout their early years of creativity.

In 1831, after Charlotte left for Roe Head School, Emily and Anne began to concentrate their energies exclusively on the Gondal saga, distinct from the Angrian fantasies of their brother and sister, a special form of imaginative play in which the two younger sisters alone engaged for the remainder of their lives. Emily's first mention of Gondal occurs in her diary paper for 24 November 1834, a series of notes written by Emily and Anne about every four years and the earliest piece of Brontë's writing to have survived. The first paragraph of the entry reads, "Taby said just now Come Anne pilloputate (i.e. pill a potato) Aunt has come into the kitchen just now and said where are you feet Anne Anne answered On the floor Aunt papa opened the parlour door and gave Branwell a letter saying here Branwell read this and show it to your Aunt and Charlotte—The Gondals are discovering the interior of Gaaldine Sally Mosley is washing in the back kitchen." In addition to noting the astonishing absence of punctuation conventions in the sixteen-year-old Emily's diary entry, critics uniformly point

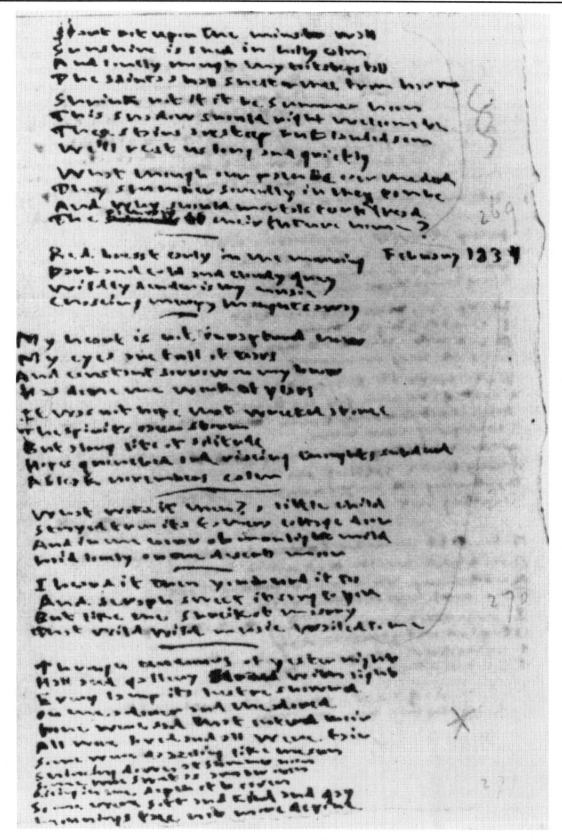

Manuscript for three of Brontë's poems, including "Start not upon the minster wall," one of her earliest extant works (John Howell Books, 1982 Anniversary Catalogue)

to her seamless fit of the imaginary Gondal into the fabric of everyday events in the Brontë kitchen.

Scholars such as W. D. Paden in *An Investigation of Gondal* (1958) have deftly recovered much of the history of Gondal despite Charlotte's destruction of the plays and prose after her sisters' deaths, from the birthday notes, the undated lists of character names Anne wrote, the list of place names she wrote into a copy of J. Goldsmith's *A Grammar of General Geography* (1819), and Emily's and Anne's Gondal poems. Most recognize, however, their own creative responsibility in such a reconstruction, for while Brontë wrote almost seventy poems that are undoubtedly part of the Gondal story, the majority of her poems cannot always be attributed to Gondal, and many are clearly more personal lyrics. Scholars therefore find Fannie Ratchford's *Gondal's Queen: A Novel in Verse* (1955), an attempt to fit the whole of Brontë's poetic output into the Gondal fantasy, an interesting but far-fetched effort. What can be determined is that Gondal, according to Anne, was "a large island in the North Pacific" and that Gaaldine was "a large island newly discovered in the South Pacific." The rigorous scenery of these islands derives much from Scott's fiction and is filled with mountains, heather, and snow. The Gondal stories concern impetuous royalty, political intrigue, love thwarted and abandoned, wars, murders, and assassinations. In a noteworthy article in 1939 Helen Brown was one of the first critics to point out the influence of George Gordon, Lord Byron, on Brontë's Gondal characters and their isolation, passions, dark crimes, and darker thoughts. The main character in Brontë's Gondal poems, the speaker of at least fourteen and the subject of many others, is the passionate, dark-haired queen Augusta G. Almeda, or A.G.A., perhaps based on Mary, Queen of Scots and the young Queen Victoria, in whose accession to the throne Brontë took a good deal of interest. A secondary character is Julius Brenzaida, king of Almedore in Gaaldine.

Critical reception of the Gondal poems has been uneven. Some critics reject them for their melodrama, formulaic qualities, and simplistic meters and rhymes. Recently, however, feminist critics have taken special note of the prominent role played by the queen, A.G.A. Christine Gallant, for example, calls attention to the fact that Gondal is "a mythic world emphatically excluding the real world" known to Victorian women, controlled by a "dominating presence of female figures." Teddi Lynn Chichester believes that Brontë was continually working through her own loss of significant female figures, that "through Augusta, Brontë could explore, in private, her need to create a powerful,

even indestructible" woman, and that A.G.A. "ultimately reinforced the disturbing connection between mortality and the feminine" that is such a potent undercurrent in Western literature. Richard Benvenuto points out that without the years Brontë spent "developing her Gondal imagination, the mature imagination she did attain would have been a considerably different mode of vision." While a knowledge of the facts of Gondal can deepen the reader's understanding of Brontë's creative life, we can still appreciate the poems for their merits apart from their place in the Gondal saga. In writing the Gondal poems Brontë took on different voices and personae, and the themes of imprisonment and death that inform her better-known poetry were first explored therein. The dark and overpowering emotions first manifested in these poems certainly fed her invention of Catherine and Heathcliff in *Wuthering Heights*.

The luxury Brontë enjoyed of freely flowing from domestic responsibilities at the parsonage to the world of Gondal and the mental and emotional sustenance she found therein was cut short in July 1835, when she accompanied Charlotte, now a teacher, to Roe Head. For Brontë—removed from her routine for the first time since she was six years old, extremely reticent and impatient with the other pupils in the school—the experiment was unhappy and unsuccessful. Moreover, because her daily schedule was now rigidly proscribed, she had no time to engage in the intellectually sustaining creation of the Gondal stories, and she was no longer living with Anne, her partner in the fantasy. Charlotte later recalled her firm belief that Brontë "would die if she did not go home, and with this conviction obtained her recall." Charlotte understood only too well the void caused by the absence of "sources purely imaginary": she too grieved for her inability to interact with her visions of Angria. The combination of homesickness and creative deprivation forced Brontë home in October 1835, but her dependence on Yorkshire to free her poetic originality should not be overstated. She forced herself to leave home again two more times, to teach at Law Hill and to study in Brussels, and these journeys broadened rather than stultified her inventive abilities.

Brontë spent the three years following her return from Roe Head at home, and since Anne had replaced her at the school, she became responsible for many of the domestic duties at the parsonage, especially after Tabby broke her leg. Brontë found time, however, to continue the Gondal saga and, more importantly, to practice her poetic craft. Though traumatic, her brief time at Roe Head and subsequent return to Haworth evidently intensified

Painting of Brontë (center) and her sisters Anne and Charlotte by their brother, Branwell, circa 1835 (National Portrait Gallery, London)

a new resolve to concentrate on her poetry. Her first extant poems are from 1836 and display some of the treatments of nature and death she was to concentrate on for the remainder of her life. For example, in "Will the day be bright or cloudy?" and "High waving heather 'neath stormy blasts ending," a poem Stevie Davies calls a "precocious bravura piece," Brontë adapts her close observation of natural phenomena to poems that examine and accept the two-faceted essence of the day's evolution and the changing weather. In "Start not upon the minster wall" she explores the comforting rather than threatening affinity of the living and the dead.

Brontë's diary paper of 26 June 1837 records Anne's writing of a poem, her own work on a volume of Augusta Almeda's life, Queen Victoria's accession to the throne, and her corresponding interest in the coronation of the emperors and empresses of Gondal and Gaaldine. She wonders where she and her siblings will be in four years and expresses three times the hope that whether they are in "this drawing room comfortable" or "gone somewhere together comfortable" that all will be for the best. The note is observant and cheerful and perhaps reflects the satisfaction Brontë took in her extensive composition of poetry during the year. Poems such as "The night of storms has passed," "A.G.A. to A.E.," "Now trust a heart that trusts in you," and "Song by Julius Angora" reveal a poetic exploration of Gondal corresponding to her Gondal prose. Her other poems from this period are somewhat problematic for critics in that, as Derek Roper says, they "plainly deal with fictional situations" yet do not belong to the Gondal cycle. Throughout her poetic career Brontë assumed personae who did not necessarily speak for her, and while it is difficult to assign certain poems to her own voice, it is important to be wary of attaching too much significance to the thoughts and feelings expressed in this fictional poetry. However, a poem from 1837 underscores in what seems to be Brontë's voice her need to express herself in poetry. The speaker asks heaven why it has denied the "glorious gift to many given / To speak their thoughts in poetry" and wonders why she cannot transmute her visions, available to her since "careless childhood's sunny time," into poetry. An aspect of this need can also be found in "I'll come when thou art saddest," a poem written in 1837, in which the speaker is the imagination, what Barker calls "the great comforter," upon which all of the Brontës relied for sustenance and consolation.

Brontë continued her poetic productivity throughout 1838, from which twenty-one dated poems have survived. Also surviving from this time are fragments of her translation of Virgil's *Aeneid* and notes on Greek tragedies, evidence that tends to contradict the fallacy that Brontë's was an uneducated mind from which sprang an amazing quantity of poetry and the remarkable *Wuthering Heights*. Sometime in the autumn of 1838 she made the surprising decision to accept a teaching position at Law Hill, a girls' school outside Halifax, a fact recorded in a letter from Charlotte to Ellen Nussey that, though dated October 1836, Edward Chitham revealed was postdated October 1838. Benvenuto speculates that Brontë went to Law Hill because she felt guilty enjoying the pleasures of home while her sisters were laboring at Roe Head. Though Charlotte wrote to Ellen Nussey that Brontë's duties at Law Hill constituted "slavery," Barker points out that Brontë had time to write what she calls "three outstanding poems." One of these was "A little while, a little while," a poem in which Brontë synchronizes the "dungeon bars" of her duties at school and her disparate choices of imagining during her "hour of rest" either the comforts of Hawthorn, the "spot 'mid barren hills," or Gondal with its "distant, dreamy dim blue chain / Of mountains circling every side." Charlotte was correct in surmising that Brontë would "never stand" the "hard labour" at Law Hill—she left the school in March or April 1839, worn out by homesickness and the lack of time she could devote to poetry and Gondal. Her return home again freed her from the "dungeon bars"; though she apparently wrote no poetry during the first three months of 1839, she left twenty-nine dated poems from the remainder of the year. She re-

visits some of her favorite natural subjects in poems such as "Mild the mist upon the hill" and "The starry night shall tidings bring," though often nature is unable to give solace to grief-stricken speakers. Brontë takes a more philosophical approach in "I am the only being whose doom," in which the speaker despairs to find "the same corruption" in "my own mind" as she has seen in all of "mankind," and "There was a time when my cheek burned," in which the speaker finds that her ardent devotion to truth, right, and liberty are misplaced, for the "same old world will go rolling on" unaffected by her passion or her indifference.

In her 30 July 1841 birthday note Brontë, though pleased that she and her family are all "stout and hearty," expressed her wish that four years hence she and her sisters will no longer be "dragging on" but will have carried out their "scheme" for setting up a school of their own. Though ultimately the plan was never realized, Emily and Charlotte attempted to improve their teaching prospects by studying French with Constantin Heger at the Pensionnat Heger, a boarding school for girls in Brussels, arriving in February 1842. After he recognized the sisters' intellectual strengths and their aptitude for French, Heger personally tutored them, having them read and analyze works in French and then compose their own essays based on these models. Though Brontë was unable to complete any poems while she was in Brussels, her composition of a prose allegory, "Le Palais de la Mort," influenced the second of the two poems she began, "Self-Interrogation." Both essay and poem personify Death, and in the poem Death logically convinces the human speaker in the dialogue that his life has been empty and that he has nothing left to live for. As Janet Gezari points out, "despite the ray of hope in the last two lines, this poem is among Brontë's glummest," its bitterness surely reflective of Aunt Branwell's November 1842 death, which caused Brontë and Charlotte to depart the Pensionnat for Haworth. Though Charlotte returned to Brussels in January 1843, Brontë remained in Yorkshire for the remainder of her life.

In February 1844 Brontë began to copy her poems into two notebooks, one titled "Gondal Poems," the other left untitled. Though early critics such as Winifred Gérin distinguished Gondal poems from "personal" poems on the basis of Brontë's division, later critics such as Roper and Barker caution against rigidity in approaching the poetry in this way. The act of copying itself suggests that Brontë took her poetry seriously and wanted to have a more permanent structure for it than scraps of paper allowed, even if at this point she did not even contemplate publication. In the autumn of 1845, however, a momentous discovery occurred. Charlotte recalled, "I accidentally lighted on a MS. volume of verse in my sister Emily's handwriting." Despite Brontë's anger and sense of betrayal at her sister's "unlicensed" intrusion, its "taking hours to reconcile her to the discovery" Charlotte had made and "days to persuade her that such poems merited publication," Brontë eventually was won over to the idea of sending her work out to publishers along with some by Charlotte and Anne. The sisters spent the remainder of the year selecting and revising their poetry, Brontë choosing poems largely written in 1844 and 1845 and being careful to delete any references to the private Gondal. They took the pseudonyms Currer, Ellis, and Acton Bell and agreed to publish *Poems* at their own expense with the publishing company of Aylott and Jones in 1846.

Many critics agree that Brontë's poetry from *Poems* is her strongest. Lawrence J. Starzyk, for example, calls attention to the "beautiful lyrics" of "A Day Dream," where the "sustained dialogue of the mind with itself is masterfully executed as the despondent narrator converses with the joyous spirit of nature." Davies refers to "To Imagination" as "that classic, rational and balanced defence of imagination as an alternative faculty to reason." Barker believes that "The Prisoner," originally a Gondal poem, is "rightly one of Emily's most famous, as it includes the powerful and intensely emotional description of the captive's vision." Perhaps because Derek Stanford thinks that Brontë wrote only six major poems, his reading of "Death" and the "vertiginous and vertical excitement that seems to give this poem wings" is particularly striking. In one of the few stylistic analyses of Brontë's poetry C. Day Lewis finds that the effect of the rhythm in "Remembrance" is "extremely powerful, extremely appropriate" and that "it is the *slowest* rhythm I know in English poetry, and the most sombre." Roper concludes simply that "the selection that Emily made for 1846 includes some of her best poems."

Other than a long narrative Gondal poem from late 1846 and a shorter incomplete revision of the same from May 1848, Emily's last poem, much anthologized and perhaps the most commented upon, was "No Coward Soul Is Mine," written in January 1846. Tom Winnifrith calls it a "fitting culmination of Emily's poetic work," admiring the fineness of its "pantheistic vision"; Starzyk finds that the contradiction in the poem "represents a profound insight into the nature of the universe and man's attempt at finding permanence therein." This creation of a Methodist minister's daughter is indeed astonishing for its blunt rejection of orthodox religion—

> Vain are the thousand creeds
> That move men's heart, unutterably vain
> Worthless as withered weeds
> Or idlest froth amid the boundless main

—coupled with its embrace of a truer and more sustaining omnipresence of God:

> With wide-embracing love
> Thy spirit animates eternal years
> Pervades and broods above,
> Changes, sustains, dissolves, creates and rears.

Brontë reveals her ability to actually know the supreme being who is the Alpha and Omega of whom she learned in the Bible when she was but a small child:

> Though Earth and moon were gone
> And suns and universes ceased to be
> And thou were left alone
> Every existence would exist in thee.

Barker points out that "No Coward Soul Is Mine" is the "only statement of its kind in all of Brontë's extant writings," and so readers should not be quick to assume that the speaker is Brontë herself. However, the immediacy of the poem and the authenticity of the voice suggest that Brontë was not taking on a persona but indeed sharing her deeply felt relationship with God. We will unfortunately never know if she intended to continue to write poetry in this vein. Whether she was too dismayed by the lack of response to *Poems* or too distracted by the composition of *Wuthering Heights,* Brontë devoted little of her remaining two years to writing poetry.

In a 6 April 1846 letter Charlotte wrote to Aylott and Jones that "C., E., and A. Bell are now preparing for the press a work of fiction, consisting of three distinct and unconnected tales": Charlotte's *The Professor* (1857), Emily's *Wuthering Heights,* and Anne's *Agnes Grey.* Thomas Newby eventually consented to publish the latter two novels, which came out in December 1847. The first reviewers were mystified and puzzled by the strangeness and savagery of *Wuthering Heights,* although nearly all recognized the seductive power of the novel and the original vision of its author. Twentieth-century critics have recognized the ways in which the Gondal poetry, with its isolated and terrifying scenery, its passionate and grief-stricken characters, provided Emily with a wide stage on which to rehearse the similar scenery of Wuthering Heights and the characters of Cathy and Heathcliff in the novel. How-

Manuscript page for one of Brontë's poems concerning the mythical kingdom of Gondal (courtesy of the Trustees of the British Library)

ever, the critic who perhaps most perceptively synthesized the poetic and fictional halves of Emily's creative aptitude wrote at the end of the nineteenth century. A fellow poet, Algernon Swinburne, referred to *Wuthering Heights* in a 16 June 1883 article as "essentially and definitely a poem in the fullest and most positive sense of the term."

Little is known of the last two years of Emily's life, although her family endured some severe trials. Patrick was nearly blinded by cataracts, and Branwell, who had never realized his artistic potential, had returned home dependent on alcohol and disgraced because of an affair with his employer's wife. Branwell became ill with what probably was consumption in early September 1848 and died later that month. Emily Brontë fell ill with consumption in October 1848 and refused all medical help, claiming that even homeopathy "was only another form of quackery." She steadily grew weaker and died on 19 December 1848. She was thirty years old.

The student of Emily Brontë's poetry must sort through various contradictions in order to approach her work with even a little confidence. She wrote most of her poetry during what is technically the Victorian period, but her exploration of the self, the imagination, and the visionary associate her more closely with Romantic poets such as Samuel Taylor Coleridge and William Wordsworth than with Alfred, Lord Tennyson, and Robert Browning. She was a woman poet who did not bemoan the lack of "literary grandmothers," as Elizabeth Barrett Browning did, and seemed to have little familiarity with female predecessors such as Felicia Hemans and Letitia Elizabeth Landon. She was a serious poet who, like her peers Emily Dickinson, John Clare, and, later, Gerard Manley Hopkins, wrote dozens of poems with no intention of publishing or even showing them to her family. She is far better known for her one mind-searing novel than for her poetry, but since early in the twentieth century few years have passed without some article, book, or new edition devoted to her verse. Her life remains an enigma; her poetry refuses easy classification. Yet Brontë's fierce willingness to confront in her poetry the most profound intellectual, theological, and emotional challenges to the human spirit assures her a continuing place in the minds of readers who seek guidance through those obstacles in poetry.

Letters:

The Brontë Letters, edited by Muriel Spark (London: Peter Nevill, 1954).

Bibliographies:

Anne Passel, *Charlotte and Emily Brontë: An Annotated Bibliography* (New York & London: Garland, 1979);

Rebecca W. Crump, *Charlotte and Emily Brontë, 1846–1915: A Reference Guide* (Boston: G. K. Hall, 1982);

Janet M. Barclay, *Emily Brontë Criticism, 1900–1982: An Annotated Checklist* (Westport, Conn.: Meckler, 1984);

Crump, *Charlotte and Emily Brontë, 1955–1983: A Reference Guide* (Boston: Hall, 1986).

Biographies:

A. M. F. Robinson, *Emily Brontë* (London: W. H. Allen, 1883);

Winifred Gérin, *Emily Brontë: A Biography* (Oxford: Clarendon Press, 1971);

Edward Chitham, *A Life of Emily Brontë* (Oxford & New York: Blackwell, 1987);

Katherine Frank, *A Chainless Soul: A Life of Emily Brontë* (Boston: Houghton Mifflin, 1990);

Juliet Barker, *The Brontës* (New York: St. Martin's Press, 1995).

References:

Miriam Allott, ed., *The Brontës: The Critical Heritage* (London & Boston: Routledge, 1974);

Richard Benvenuto, *Emily Brontë* (Boston: Twayne, 1982);

Charlotte Brontë, "Biographical Notice of Ellis and Acton Bell," in her edition of *Wuthering Heights and Agnes Grey* (London: Smith, Elder, 1850);

Helen Brown, "The Influence of Byron on Emily Brontë," *Modern Language Review,* 34 (July 1939): 374–381;

Kathryn Burlinson, "'What language can utter the feeling': Identity in the Poetry of Emily Brontë," in *Subjectivity and Literature from the Romantics to the Present Day,* edited by Philip Shaw and Peter Stockwell (London & New York: Pinter, 1991), pp. 41–48;

Teddi Lynn Chichester, "Evading 'Earth's Dungeon Tomb': Emily Brontë, A.G.A., and the Fatally Feminine," *Victorian Poetry,* 29, no. 1 (Spring 1991): 1–15;

Edward Chitham and Tom Winnifrith, *Brontë Facts and Brontë Problems* (London: Macmillan, 1983);

Stevie Davies, *Emily Brontë: The Artist as a Free Woman* (Manchester: Carcanet, 1983);

Denis Donoghue, "The Other Emily," in *The Brontës: A Collection of Critical Essays,* edited by

Ian Gregor (Englewood Cliffs, N.J.: Prentice-Hall, 1970), pp. 157–172;

Emma Francis, "Is Emily Brontë a Woman? Feminity (*sic*), Feminism and the Paranoid Critical Subject," in *Subjectivity and Literature from the Romantics to the Present Day,* edited by Shaw and Stockwell (London & New York: Pinter, 1991), pp. 28–40;

Christine Gallant, "The Archetypal Feminine in Emily Brontë's Poetry," *Women's Studies, 7* (Spring 1980): 79–94;

Elizabeth Gaskell, *The Life of Charlotte Brontë,* edited by Angus Easson (New York: Oxford University Press, 1996);

Janet Gezari, notes to *Complete Poems,* by Emily Brontë, edited by Gezari (London & New York: Penguin, 1992), pp. 222–285;

Jill Dix Ghnassia, *Metaphysical Rebellion in the Works of Emily Brontë: A Reinterpretation* (New York: St. Martin's Press, 1994);

Robin Grove, "'It Would Not Do': Emily Brontë as Poet," in *The Art of Emily Brontë,* edited by Anne Smith (London: Vision, 1976), pp. 33–67;

Margaret Homans, "Emily Brontë," in her *Women Writers and Poetic Identity: Dorothy Wordsworth, Emily Brontë, and Emily Dickinson* (Princeton, N.J.: Princeton University Press, 1980), pp. 104–161;

Bettina L. Knapp, "The Poems: 'No Coward Soul is Mine,'" in her *The Brontës: Branwell, Anne, Emily, Charlotte* (New York: Continuum, 1991), pp. 102–107;

C. Day Lewis, "Emily Brontë and Freedom," in his *Notable Images of Virtue: Emily Brontë, George Meredith, W. B. Yeats* (Toronto: Ryerson, 1954), pp. 1–25;

Barbara and Gareth Lloyd Evans, *The Scribner Companion to the Brontës* (New York: Scribners, 1984);

Dorothy Mermin, "The Damsel, the Knight, and the Victorian Woman Poet," *Critical Inquiry,* 13 (Autumn 1986): 64–80;

Rosalind Miles, "A Baby God: The Creative Dynamism of Emily Brontë's Poetry," in *The Art of Emily Brontë,* edited by Anne Smith (London: Vision, 1976), pp. 68–93;

W. D. Paden, *An Investigation of Gondal* (New York: Bookman, 1958);

"Poetry of the Million," *Athenaeum* (4 July 1846): 682;

Fannie Ratchford, *Gondal's Queen: A Novel in Verse by Emily Jane Brontë* (Austin: University of Texas Press, 1955);

Derek Roper with Edward Chitham, introduction to *The Poems of Emily Brontë,* edited by Roper and Chitham (Oxford: Clarendon Press, 1995);

Muriel Spark and Derek Stanford, *Emily Brontë: Her Life and Work* (London: Owen, 1953);

Lawrence J. Starzyk, "Emily Brontë: Poetry in a Mingled Tone," *Criticism: A Quarterly for Literature and the Arts,* 14 (Spring 1972): 119–136;

Starzyk, "The Faith of Emily Brontë's Immortality Creed," *Victorian Poetry,* 13 (1972): 295–305;

A. C. Swinburne, "Review of Mary Robinson's Emily Brontë," *Athenaeum* (16 June 1883): 762–763;

Irene Tayler, "Emily Brontë's Poetry," in her *Holy Ghosts: The Male Muses of Emily and Charlotte Brontë* (New York: Columbia University Press, 1990), pp. 18–71;

Tom Winnifrith and Edward Chitham, "Poems," in their *Charlotte and Emily Brontë: Literary Lives* (New York: St. Martin's Press, 1989), pp. 96–108;

Winnifrith, "Poetry," in his *The Brontës* (London: Macmillan, 1977), pp. 32–45.

Papers:

Many of Brontë's surviving manuscripts are held by the Brontë Parsonage Museum Library, the British Library, the Pierpont Morgan Library, the New York Public Library, the Princeton University Libraries, and the University of Texas at Austin Library.

Frances Browne
(16 January 1816 – 25 August 1879)

Marya DeVoto
University of North Carolina at Chapel Hill

BOOKS: *The Star of Attéghéi; The Vision of Schwartz; and Other Poems* (London: Moxon, 1844);

Lyrics and Miscellaneous Poems (Edinburgh: Sutherland & Knox, 1848; London: Simpkin, Marshall, 1848);

The Ericksons. The Clever Boy; or, Consider Another (Two Stories for My Young Friends) (Edinburgh: Paton & Ritchie, 1852);

Pictures and Songs of Home (London: Nelson, [1856]);

Granny's Wonderful Chair, and Its Tales of Fairy Times (London: Griffith, Farran, Okeden & Welsh, 1856);

Our Uncle the Traveller's Stories (London: Kent, 1859);

My Share of the World: An Autobiography, 3 volumes (London: Hurst & Blackett, 1861);

The Orphans of Elfholm, Magnet Stories, No. 30 (London: Groombridge, [1862]); republished in *The Magnet Stories for Summer Days and Winter Nights* (New York: J. Miller, 1864);

The Castleford Case, 3 volumes (London: Hurst & Blackett, 1862);

The Poor Cousin (London, [1863]);

The Young Foresters, Magnet Stories, No. 45 (London: Groombridge, [1864]);

The Hidden Sin. A Novel, 3 volumes (London: Bentley, 1866; New York: Harper, 1866);

The Exile's Trust, a Tale of the French Revolution, and Other Stories (London: Leisure Hour, [1869]);

The Nearest Neighbour and Other Stories (London: Religious Tract Society, [1875]);

The Dangerous Guest: A Story of 1745 (London: Religious Tract Society, [1886]);

The Foundling of the Fens: A Story of a Flood (London: Religious Tract Society, [1886]);

The First of the African Diamonds (London: Religious Tract Society, [1887]);

Robin the Runner (London: Religious Tract Society, n.d.).

Frances Browne, although she was known in her time as the Blind Poetess of Ulster, is more famous in the twentieth century as a children's writer. Browne, an industrious poet and journalist whose nineteenth-century poetic reputation was largely bound up with the romance of her struggle with blindness, produced two moderately admired volumes of poems in the 1840s and a third volume of children's verse in 1856. She might be unknown today if several stories from her volume of fairy tales for children, *Granny's Wonderful Chair, and Its Tales of Fairy Times* (1856), had not made an impression on the much more famous children's writer Frances Hodgson Burnett. Burnett, who in the 1870s unwittingly retold several of Browne's stories from hazy childhood memory, was charged with plagiarism and afterwards republished Browne's tales with an explanatory preface. Since 1880 Browne's versions of these stories have been frequently reprinted, often in anthologies of children's tales.

Interest in Browne's poetic work, however, has been evidenced only by the reprinting of a few short excerpts. Scraps from Browne's first two volumes of poems have been reprinted in collections devoted to recovering women's poetry and in anthologies of Irish nationalist verse, where her short lyric "The Songs of Our Land" often appears, sometimes without attribution. Like her contemporary Elizabeth Barrett Browning, Browne was admired in her time for the pathos of her short sentimental lyrics, but many of her poems vividly illustrate political events, religious themes, and, most notably, an adventurous range of geographic territory. Perhaps the most striking thing about her poetic output is its consistent preoccupation with exotic locations. While Browne is a minor poetic talent who was clearly much influenced by the second generation of Romantic poets, both male and female, her longer poems in particular combine these elements in original and ambitious ways.

Frances Browne was born in the small Irish mountain village of Stranorlar, in County Donegal, on 16 January 1816. Browne's father was the village postmaster, but accounts of her great-grandfather's squandered estates gave the family a claim to reduced gentility. Frances, the seventh of twelve children born into her family, lost her sight at the age of

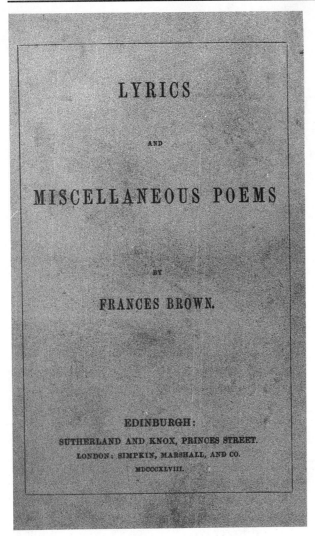

Title page for Frances Browne's collection that includes her popular Irish anthem "The Songs of Our Land"

choice of dry, educational books, she entertained them by telling long stories or repeating the plots of novels. To fix her newfound knowledge in her memory, Browne lay awake at night and reviewed each day's learning.

Books were scarce in Browne's village, so she relied heavily on borrowing. Books she recalled from her childhood include *Robinson Crusoe, The Negro Servant,* and accounts of Mungo Park's African explorations, all works with the element of exoticism so prominent in Browne's poems. Later she managed to acquire the complete works of Sir Walter Scott, whose interest in bards and minstrels is also echoed in her poetry. Her historical interests were first piqued at age twelve by hearing a selection from Edward Baines's *History of the Wars of the French Revolution* (1817), which she credits with introducing her to the "wonderful Romance of History"; although she had access to English histories, the twenty-one-volume *Ancient Universal History,* which comprised a range of material on both the Classical and the ancient world, made a greater and more lasting impression.

Alongside her historical studies Browne developed a strong interest in geography, pursued as were her other studies through interrogating friends and acquaintances as well as by memorizing her sisters' and brothers' schoolroom lessons. Later she asked a friend to place her fingers on a map, so that she could trace distances, boundaries between countries, and topographical features. In childhood Browne once spent a sleepless night puzzling over Christopher Columbus's attempted feat of traveling to Asia by sailing west before she was enlightened on the subject of the earth's roundness.

Browne's first poetic effort, an attempt to render the *Lord's Prayer* in verse, was undertaken around age seven, when "a few psalms of the Scotch version, Watts's *Divine Songs,* and some old country songs (which were certainly not divine) formed the whole of my poetical knowledge." Most of her early verse is imitative of the first poems she memorized: the Psalms, Thomas Grey's *Elegy Written in a Country Churchyard* (1751), or the favorite of her later childhood, Robert Burns. Although it is not recorded whether she learned to write, her later regular employment of secretaries and amanuenses suggests that she probably dictated her poems.

At around age fifteen Browne encountered two models that temporarily interrupted her poetic outflow but strongly influenced her later style: Homer's *The Iliad* and George Gordon, Lord Byron's *Childe Harold's Pilgrimage* (1812–1818). If *The Iliad* convinced Browne, as she tells it, to burn her poems and *Childe Harold* led her to refrain from writ-

eighteen months during an outbreak of smallpox. While her blindness prevented her receiving any formal education, her brothers and sisters attended the village school. According to Browne much of her early education derived from listening to her siblings read their lessons aloud and memorizing their lessons, which often consisted of dictionary excerpts and grammar practice.

Browne's account of her early life, printed in the preface to *The Star of Attéghéi; The Vision of Schwartz; and Other Poems* (1844), emphasizes her early and systematic efforts to pursue an informal education. A sermon heard at age seven at her parents' Presbyterian church, which contained some unfamiliar words, inspired an aggressive policy of grilling friends and acquaintances for definitions. Although unable to read herself, Browne bribed her siblings to read to her by offering to do their household chores. When her readers rebelled at Browne's

ing any more, both had a pervasive effect on the themes and imagery of her poetry when she began to write again at the age of twenty-three. Describing her return to poetry in Romantic terms as a "strange desire" and an "irresistible inclination," Browne composed her first published poems, including the long-lived patriotic lyric "The Songs of Our Land," in 1840, submitting them to the newly formed and short-lived *Irish Penny Journal*.

Encouraged by Gunn and Cameron, the publishers of the *Irish Penny Journal,* Browne approached the London *Athenaeum*—which she had heard of but never read—in 1841, proposing that they publish her poems with a copy of the journal as payment. The editor, C. W. Dilke, responded with enthusiasm. Appearing at first as F.B., later as F. Browne, and by 1843 under her full name, Browne contributed more than thirty poems to the journal between 1841 and 1844. Her poems in *The Athenaeum* were published alongside those of household names such as Elizabeth Barrett Browning, Lydia Sigourney, and Walter Savage Landor. These were probably Browne's most prolific years as a poet, during which she produced many of the lyrics that would appear in her two volumes of poetry for adults, *The Star of Attéghéi; The Vision of Schwartz; and Other Poems* and the 1848 *Lyrics and Miscellaneous Poems.*

Browne's poems also began to appear in *The Keepsake,* edited by the Countess of Blessington, and in *Hood's Magazine.* During the interval between the appearance of her first poems and the publication of *The Star of Attéghéi,* Browne, still living at home, apparently began to receive pay for her efforts. With her earnings she arranged to have a sister educated as her amanuensis and began contributing to her family's support.

Critical response to Browne's first volume (and indeed to all of her work) almost invariably dwells on her biography. While reviewers urged readers to admire the contents of *The Star of Attéghéi* on their own merits, they were unable to resist marveling at Browne's output given her poverty and, most particularly, her blindness. The volume's lengthy, heavily biographical "Editor's Preface," typically, recounts in detail the story of her self-education:

> The flower that has struggled into beauty under unfavourable conditions of air and light, testifies to more than common vigour in the soil whence it sprang:—and they whose sense has, first, been secured by the absolute claims of a work of art, are, for the most part, willing to add something to their admiration, on the score of any particular difficulties under which it may have been achieved.

Whatever they might think of her poems, readers seemed to find Browne's story unfailingly inspiring.

Critics were generally favorable in their estimation of *The Star of Attéghéi,* although their enthusiasm was reserved almost entirely for the "other poems": her short lyrics, or "sweet little pieces," as the reviewer for *The Dublin Review* characterized them in December 1844. While these verses range widely in geography and subject matter, as suggested by titles such as "The French Army at Carnak," "The Australian Emigrant," "The Removal of the Cherokees," "The Bells of Limerick," and "The Promised Land," they share such thematic preoccupations as exile, the fragility of civilizations, the preservation of memory, the enduring role of poets, disillusionment in the glamor of war, and, inevitably, the romance of foreign travel.

Most of them are elegiac in tone; like much of Felicia Hemans's work they often use an historical or political context, as indicated by the titles above, to reflect on one of her favorite themes. Often a theme is reworked in various settings and situations: for instance, several poems explore the thematic possibilities of a portrait or memento. In "The Maid of the Rhone" a young woman falls in love with a crusader's portrait and never marries, while in "The Picture of the Dead" a Native American chief thanks the artist who has preserved his dead child through the marvel of portraiture. In "The Parting Gifts" a young man cherishes locks of hair from his sister and his lover until his death, but the memory of his loved ones is insufficient beside the inducements of fame and valor; he never returns home. Similarly, almost every poem in the volume addresses the theme of exile, which is developed at length in the long title poem.

Victorian readers seem to have overlooked the political dimension to Browne's choice of subjects in favor of a purely aesthetic response. Unlike recent feminist scholars, who have tended to focus on Browne's evident interest in social issues such as poverty and emigration, her contemporary critics generally responded to what was conventionally pleasing in her imagery, her diction and her depiction of what they saw as universal sentiments. A 26 October 1844 review in *The Athenaeum* remarks on her "fine poetical sense, a great sensibility to melody, and at times a rich-toned utterance"; *The Dublin Review,* too, praises her musicality and "pure" diction as well as "the warm and patriotic feelings of her generous Irish heart."

This same perceived sweetness, however, cloyed on some reviewers. *Chambers's Journal,* summing up Browne's poetic career in a 4 May 1861 review of her first novel, is atypical in remarking on

Sir Robert Peel, Browne's benefactor, to whom her Lyrics and
Miscellaneous Poems *(1848) is dedicated; engraving by
J. Cochran of a painting by Sir Thomas Lawrence*

Browne's more active poetic virtues, declaring that her poems display "her energy of mind, her resolution of character, her scorn of mean and soulless men, her love of the brave, the wise and the good." Most felt the poet's virtues to be sweeter and slighter. Although admiring of her lyric gifts, the reviewer for *The Athenaeum* hastened to add that one could "not claim for Miss Browne much originality, either of thought or forms"; *The Dublin Review* complained of the "settled melancholy" that gives a "tone of monotony" to the volume. Sir Charles Duffy opined in a personal letter of 6 January 1845 that the shorter poems "are moulded upon Mrs. Hemans, and have generally the melody but never the occasional strength and picturesque beauty of that writer."

If Browne's short lyrics tended to charm but ultimately bore reviewers, the two lengthy narrative poems mentioned in the title troubled them. "It is our duty now to look to her longer poems," declared the critic at *The Dublin Review*, "and we could really wish that this task were not imposed on us." Ambitious works of epic scope, adorned with an array of historical footnotes and a Romantic atmosphere reminiscent of adventures by Byron and Scott, these lengthy nar-

ratives must have seemed incongruous coming from the pen of the bravely struggling blind poetess critics liked to admire. They are also politically explicit in a way that the volume's short poems are not.

Nevertheless, these more ambitious poems rework many of the same themes that critics found more palatable in the short lyrics. "The Star of Attéghéi," inspired according to Browne by a newspaper account of the Circassian resistance to Russian domination, chronicles the exploits of a nameless hero of Circassian, or Attéghéi, descent, who earns the moniker "Star of Attéghéi" as a freedom fighter for the Circassian resistance. On the eve of battle it is revealed that the Star of Attéghéi is really no hero but a heroine: fleeing an arranged marriage to a Muscovite nobleman, the young Dizila left her long braid on her mother's grave and determined to die in the service of Circassian independence. Fulfilling a gypsy's prediction that he will kill the thing he loves, the spurned Muscovite kills the heroine in the ensuing skirmish as she throws herself in front of the sword meant for her Polish lover and battle companion.

In "The Star of Attéghéi" Browne offers a specific critique of Russia's expansionist political policy as well as making clear her distaste for imperial domination in general. Analogizing her own role as a poet of tiny, embattled Ireland to a warrior minstrel's dual role in commemorating and defending Circassia, Browne declares that while poets (and women) of small nations may not be able to defend themselves against larger political events, their influence as keepers of conscience and memory outlasts imperial power.

The volume's other lengthy narrative poem, "The Vision of Schwartz," is founded on the legend of a twelfth-century monk, Berthold Schwartz, who discovers gunpowder by accident while searching for the Philosopher's Stone. Like "The Star of Attéghéi," "The Vision of Schwartz" takes a spirited stand against imperial subjugation and domination. A supernatural figure appears to Schwartz to show him the horrors his invention will wreak on future civilizations: the sacking of Byzantium by the Turks, the destruction of the Inca Empire by the Spaniards, and finally a gory British sea battle. As in "The Star of Attéghéi," an outspoken narrator interprets the action, denouncing violent conflicts in general and particularly handing down stirring jeremiads against the African slave trade and the Catholic Church's role in Latin American conquest.

Reviewers of the volume were nearly unanimous in disparaging these long narrative poems, which they saw as overly ambitious and inappropriately derivative of Browne's male poetic predecessors. *The Dublin Review,* for example, chided Browne for including in "The Star of Attéghéi" plot elements from *The Iliad* and Byron's *Lara* (1814). Warning against the dangers of unconscious plagiarism, the reviewer expresses the critical consensus that Browne has overreached herself in choosing her subject: "It is no slur on Miss Browne's genius that she did not succeed where there were two such illustrious competitors; but it is a slur against her judgment that she entered the field with them at all." An *Irish Monthly* retrospective piece in 1890 suggests that "The Star of Attéghéi" and "The Vision of Schwartz," seen in this case as derivative of Sir Walter Scott's poetic narratives, were included only because an unfortunate convention of the time required the inclusion of longer works in a volume of poetry. Even Browne's admiring editor feels called upon to remark in the volume's preface that had she consulted her friends about the composition of "The Star of Attéghéi" "they might have warned her off this particular ground."

Ultimately, while the reception of *The Star of Attéghéi* was generally warm, it was also inseparable from the public reception of Frances Browne as a blind poet. Reviewers, uncomfortable in offering critical estimates of a blind woman's poetry, expounded enthusiastically and at length on the moral and scientific lessons to be drawn from Browne's miraculous employment of metaphors drawn from sight. One review even reprinted a poem with every reference to vision italicized, while a fellow poet, Alicia Jane Sparrow, wondered in verse "Oh, what can bring these glorious things before thy darken'd eye?" (*The Athenaeum,* 1 February 1845). The glowing estimation of *The Dublin Review* that "It is perfectly wonderful when we consider that it is the production of a self-taught blind girl of twenty-eight" demonstrates how crucially Browne's biographical situation defined her poetic reputation as a novelty rather than a writer whose ideas should be evaluated seriously.

The Star of Atteghei seems to have marked the high point of Browne's career as a poet; her later works were little reviewed, and her publications in *The Athenaeum* (which began printing fewer poems of any kind around the same time) dwindled over the next few years, although she continued to contribute a poem occasionally through 1853. If her first collection failed to establish her as a poetic celebrity, however, it did win her some permanent financial security. In 1844 she received, through the influence of her admirer Sir Robert Peel, an annual pension of twenty pounds from the Royal Bounty Fund.

In 1847, at the height of the Irish famine, Browne and her sister moved to Edinburgh. In 1848 she published *Lyrics and Miscellaneous Poems,* which she dedicated to her benefactor, Sir Robert Peel. Unlike *The Star of Attéghéi,* which Browne had confidently filled with new and unfamiliar material, this new collection was retrospective, consisting almost entirely of previously published poems, most of them from the early years of her *Athenaeum* career, although she also chose to reprint "The Songs of Our Land." Her brief preface dryly explains the motive for reprinting: "scattered poems become, in process of time, liable to the risk of controverted authorship; and proprietors in general wish to retain their rights, though they should extend over nothing more valuable than rocks or sand."

Whether or not she took her earlier reviewers' advice to heart, Browne's second book contains no poem longer than the five-page "The Returning Janissary," which recounts the return of a single Greek among the thousands sold into Turkish military service as children. As in *The Star of Attéghéi,* the poems, although thematically similar, range across considerable geographical territory. Continuing her earlier volume's preoccupations with childhood memories, passing civilizations, and political exile, Browne includes poems sympathetic to the Jews, to

Frontispiece and title page for Browne's collection of moral poems for young children

the last defenders of Poland, and to Templars unjustly burned at the stake by the Pope in 1314. Characteristically, Browne's wide-ranging sense of time and place continues to link Irish political concerns with a broader sense of political wrongs, as when she notes in a footnote to "On the Death of Thomas Campbell" that "at the interment of Campbell, when the coffin was lowered into the grave, a Polish exile threw upon it some earth he had brought as a relic from the tomb of Kosciusko."

The Athenaeum critic's response to Browne's second volume, reviewed in the 8 January 1848 issue, adds little to the received critical opinion of her "touching story and gift of song." Sounding the familiar biographical note, the reviewer observes that the new collection will provide "additional evidences that the Muse which found out this young girl in her loneliness has not ceased to be her companion" but warns, with some justification, that the poems show "a sameness of tone and similarity of measure—which create a feeling of monotony." Certainly Browne's second volume lacks any poem with

the sustained excitement of her more ambitious and longer works.

In Edinburgh Browne joined a literary circle that included John Wilson, the essayist known in the pages of *Blackwood's* as "Christopher North," and acquired the editorial patronage of *Chambers' Edinburgh Journal.* She became involved with a wide range of literary and journalistic activities, producing not only poems but news articles, reviews, stories, essays, and eventually children's stories for periodicals such as *Chambers', Tait's Edinburgh Magazine,* and *Ainsworth's Magazine.* Among her diverse output at this time was a series of *Legends of Ulster* begun in *Fraser's Magazine* in 1848 and continuing through 1851.

Browne's first book for children, *The Ericksons. The Clever Boy; or, Consider Another (Two Stories for My Young Friends),* was published in Edinburgh in 1852. In that year she and her sister moved to London; soon afterwards, her sister married. Thereafter Browne, who in 1852 received a gift of one hundred pounds from the marquess of Lansdowne, engaged a secretary to assist her in her literary labors. While her subsequent writing seems to have included a book of verse for children, most of her efforts from this point on went into prose, including novels and books of stories for adults and children.

Pictures and Songs of Home, a slim volume of poems for young children, appeared under Browne's name in 1856; according to the date on its title page, her most enduring and celebrated literary work, *Granny's Wonderful Chair, and Its Tales of Fairy Times,* was published that same year, although it actually first appeared in 1857. *Pictures and Songs of Home* lacks any of the sense of imaginative exploration that characterizes *Granny's Wonderful Chair* and the rest of Browne's published verse. The familiar theme of travel serves a sober, didactic purpose here; a foundering toy ship is made to support the gloomy moral that "Many a brave hope that went out in full sail / Has gone down like my boat on the lake," while a baby is reassured in its first steps only to be warned: "But in thy after goings, child!– / For oh this world is wide and wild, / And much more false than fair!" Although there are several poets of the period who share Browne's name, this atypically gloomy didacticism is probably not grounds for concluding that *Pictures and Songs of Home* is not Browne's work; perhaps it was written to the specifications of the publisher. If she did write the volume, which was subsequently printed in elaborately illustrated editions, she never wrote anything like it again, nor did she publish again with Thomas Nelson and Sons.

Quite different in style and subject matter is *Granny's Wonderful Chair,* the volume of stories so fondly misremembered and rewritten by Frances Hodgson Burnett. *Granny's Wonderful Chair* is a set of framed fairy tales, some of which are still reprinted individually in collections of fairy tales or Christmas stories. When Dame Frostyface, the grandmother of the title, goes on a journey, she leaves a storytelling chair to comfort her granddaughter, Snowflower. Since the chair also travels, Snowflower rides in it to court, where its stories win the hearts of a corrupt aristocracy headed by King Winwealth.

The stories illustrate the kind of simple lessons common to fairy tales, but the imaginative embroidery and social criticism recall the excitement of Browne's early verse. The elaborate descriptions of the mer-king's dominions, for example, show Browne's gift for fantastical Gothic scenery, while the denouement of the frame story, in which the wicked Queen and Princess Greedalind spy what they believe is gold at the bottom of a pit and decide

to live there indefinitely until they can recover it, is reminiscent of her stirring declaration in "The God of the World" that the world has "come to the age of gold, / But not the golden age."

From the mid nineteenth century on, as Nina Auerbach and U. C. Knoepflmacher have argued in *Forbidden Journeys: Fairy Tales and Fantasies by Victorian Women Writers* (1992), the writing and rewriting of fairy tales provides an acceptable location for women's imaginative and critical dissent. *Granny's Wonderful Chair* caused Katharine Pyle, editor of a 1916 edition, to wonder:

> Whence came her vision of the old woman who weaved her own hair into grey cloth at a crazy loom; of the fortified city in the plain, with cornfields and villages; of floors of ebony and ceilings of silver; of swallows that built in the eaves while the daisies grew thick at the door?

Browne's fairy-tale depiction of the old woman, self-evidently a figure of the writer weaving her own life and experiences into memory, has clear connections to the more explicit analogies made between the memory-preserving roles of poets and women in "The Star of Attéghéi." The more enthusiastic reception granted to *Granny's Wonderful Chair,* however, suggests that such sentiments were more acceptably shrouded in the guise of purely imaginative children's literature.

While *Granny's Wonderful Chair* quickly went out of print, the publicity generated by Burnett's accidental plagiarism, which took place in the pages of *St. Nicholas* in the 1870s, revived public interest in Browne's original stories and cemented *Granny's Wonderful Chair* as the cornerstone of Browne's literary reputation. The book was reprinted in 1880 and almost every year thereafter throughout the decade; it has continued to reappear in print, both as a complete volume and in excerpts, well into the 1990s.

Browne's career as a novelist for adults began in 1861 with the publication of *My Share of the World.* Subtitled "An Autobiography," and occasionally misidentified as such, *My Share of the World* is the story of one Frederick Favoursham, a young man, as *Chambers' Edinburgh Journal* summarized on 4 May 1861, who is "by turns artist, tutor, phrenologist, writer for the daily press, private secretary, holder of a government office, and finally of a large estate and many thousands." As this diverse description suggests, Browne drew inspiration from Charles Dickens; young Lucien LaTouche, the protagonist of a later novel, *The Hidden Sin* (1866), vacillates like David Copperfield between an ill-educated, girlish fiancée and the prim, angelic daughter of his mentor before he rescues the latter from the clutches of a smarmy bank clerk who has corrupted her father. Both *My Share of the World* and *The Hidden Sin* have Gothic elements and strong, charismatic female characters that recall the Romantic enthusiasms of Browne's poetry. Particularly memorable in *The Hidden Sin* is Madame Palivez, the last heir of a great banking dynasty, a successful businesswoman, and a raving beauty of indeterminate but great age with a passion for flowing purple gowns and midnight horseback rides.

Browne continued to write articles, novels, and children's books throughout her life with only moderate success. Few of her books went into a second edition, and it was only after her death that *Granny's Wonderful Chair* achieved its popularity. She received further financial assistance from 1863 on in the form of a civil list pension of one hundred pounds per year. She died suddenly of heart disease at Rosedale Terrace, Notting Hill, London, on 25 August 1879.

While it can scarcely be argued that Frances Browne was a major influence in the history of nineteenth-century poetry, much of her poetry is still vivid and engaging. Her longer poems, in particular, should be of interest not only because they provide a biographical context for her influential fairy tales but because their ambitious reworking of Romantic themes and imagery are part of the historical record of how women poets of the early-Victorian period dealt with their poetic legacy. Readers of her own day were inclined to receive Browne as a minor sentimental lyricist; however, recent critical work has done much to question the critical assumptions that make such a judgment seem a dismissal. But Browne's poetry further records that she aspired to be something more than her contemporary readers perceived: a socially aware artist whose interests and sympathies were not local but global.

Reference:

"Editor's Preface," in *The Star of Attéghéi; The Vision of Schwartz; and Other Poems* (London: Moxon, 1844).

Papers:

A manuscript of an unpublished prose work, "The Highland Bookseller," and letters to the publishers William Blackwood and Sons dating between 1860 and 1864 are held at the National Library of Scotland; the British Library holds three letters from Browne dating between 1860 and 1863 and concerning her application for a grant from the Royal Literary Fund.

Elizabeth Barrett Browning

(6 March 1806 – 29 June 1861)

Beverly Taylor

University of North Carolina at Chapel Hill

See also the Browning entry in *DLB 32: Victorian Poets Before 1850.*

BOOKS: *The Battle of Marathon: A Poem* (London: W. Lindsell, 1820);

An Essay on Mind, with Other Poems, anonymous (London: Duncan, 1826);

Prometheus Bound, Translated from the Greek of Aeschylus; and Miscellaneous Poems, anonymous (London: A. J. Valpy, 1833; Boston: J. H. Francis / New York: C. S. Francis, 1851);

The Seraphim and Other Poems (London: Saunders & Otley, 1838);

Poems, 2 volumes (London: Moxon, 1844); republished as *A Drama of Exile: And Other Poems,* 2 volumes (New York: Langley, 1845);

Poems: New Edition, 2 volumes (London: Chapman & Hall, 1850); republished as *The Poems of Elizabeth Barrett Browning* (New York: C. S. Francis / Boston: J. H. Francis, 1850);

Casa Guidi Windows: A Poem (London: Chapman & Hall, 1851);

Poems: Third Edition, 2 volumes (London: Chapman & Hall, 1853);

Two Poems, by Browning and Robert Browning (London: Chapman & Hall, 1854);

Poems: Fourth Edition, 3 volumes (London: Chapman & Hall, 1856);

Aurora Leigh (London: Chapman & Hall, 1857; New York & Boston: C. S. Francis, 1857; revised, London: Chapman & Hall, 1859);

Poems before Congress (London: Chapman & Hall, 1860); republished as *Napoleon III in Italy, and Other Poems* (New York: C. S. Francis, 1860);

Last Poems (London: Chapman & Hall, 1862; New York: Miller, 1862);

The Greek Christian Poets and the English Poets (London: Chapman & Hall, 1863); republished as *Essays on the Greek Christian Poets and the English Poets* (New York: Miller, 1863);

Elizabeth Barrett Browning; pastel drawing by Eliza Fox Bridell (the Armstrong Browning Library, Baylor University)

Psyche Apocalypté: A Lyrical Drama, by Browning and Richard Hengist Horne (London & Aylesbury, U.K.: Privately printed, 1876);

New Poems by Robert and Elizabeth Barrett Browning, edited by Frederic G. Kenyon (London: Smith, Elder, 1914; New York: Macmillan, 1915);

The Poet's Enchiridion, edited by H. Buxton Forman (Boston: Bibliophile Society, 1914);

Elizabeth Barrett Browning: Hitherto Unpublished Poems and Stories, with an Inedited Autobiography, edited by Forman, 2 volumes (Boston: Bibliophile Society, 1914);

Diary by E. B. B.: The Unpublished Diary of Elizabeth Barrett Browning, 1831–1832, edited by Philip

Kelley and Ronald Hudson (Athens: Ohio University Press, 1969).

Editions and Collections: *The Poetical Works of Elizabeth Barrett Browning,* 6 volumes (London: Smith, Elder, 1889–1890);

The Poetical Works of Elizabeth Barrett Browning, edited by Frederic G. Kenyon (London: Smith, Elder, 1897);

The Complete Poetical Works of Elizabeth Barrett Browning, Cambridge Edition, edited by Harriet Waters Preston (Boston & New York: Houghton, Mifflin, 1900);

The Complete Works of Elizabeth Barrett Browning, edited by Charlotte Porter and Helen A. Clarke, 6 volumes (New York: Crowell, 1900);

Casa Guidi Windows, edited by Julia Markus (New York: Browning Institute, 1977);

Aurora Leigh, edited by Margaret Reynolds (Athens: Ohio University Press, 1992).

OTHER: "Queen Annelida and False Arcite" and "The Complaint of Annelida to False Arcite," in *The Poems of Geoffrey Chaucer, Modernized* (London: Whittaker, 1841), pp. 237–257;

Richard Hengist Horne, ed., *A New Spirit of the Age,* includes anonymous contributions by Browning, 2 volumes (London: Smith, Elder, 1844);

"The Daughters of Pandarus," two versions, from *The Odyssey,* by Homer, translated by Browning, in *Memoirs and Essays Illustrative of Art, Literature, and Social Morals,* edited by Anna Jameson (London: Bentley, 1846), pp. 137–138.

Rated by her contemporaries among the leading poets—male or female—writing in English, Elizabeth Barrett Browning remained prominent in Great Britain, the United States, and parts of Europe from the 1840s throughout most of the nineteenth century. Scorning the label "poetess" automatically assigned in her era to women writers, she self-consciously joined the poetic tradition tracing back to classical antiquity, penning works in such varied forms as the Homeric epic, Popean didactic verse, Greek tragedy, a hybrid combining verse drama with Miltonic epic, a Petrarchan sonnet sequence, and a novel in verse in addition to many ballads and lyrics. Her themes range from the intensely personal to affairs of state, from loss and love to social oppression and Italian independence. She had achieved sufficient distinction by 1850 that critics proposed her to succeed William Wordsworth as poet laureate, and throughout her lifetime her reputation dwarfed that of her husband, poet Robert Browning. Writers such as Dante Gabriel Rossetti, Algernon Swinburne, and John Ruskin

heralded the importance of her work, and younger poets such as Emily Dickinson and Christina Rossetti attested to her significant influence on their own development. Along with the reputations of most Victorians her critical fortunes declined precipitously as modernist tastes devalued much nineteenth-century literature as too voluble and too earnest, and by the 1950s she was represented in anthologies or literary studies almost entirely by *Sonnets from the Portuguese* (published in *Poems: New Edition,* 1850), revered as a paean of devotion to her husband yet frequently derided for its supposed sentimentality. Her most ambitious work, *Aurora Leigh* (1857), went through more than twenty editions by 1900 but none between 1905 and 1978. Although in anthologies and literary histories after 1900 the tendency of scholars to mention her as an appendix to discussions of Robert Browning and refer to her patronizingly as "Mrs. Browning" or "Elizabeth" has long obscured her significant literary achievement, since the 1970s Elizabeth Barrett Browning has increasingly been recognized as a powerful, independent voice of social criticism and an innovative poet whose experimentation with rhyme and rhythms (frequently lamented by reviewers in her day) anticipated movements in modern versification.

Elizabeth Barrett Moulton-Barrett (nicknamed "Ba") was born 6 March 1806 at Coxhoe Hall, five miles south of Durham, to Edward Barrett Moulton-Barrett, a native of St. James, Jamaica, and Mary Graham-Clarke of Newcastle-upon-Tyne. The oldest of eleven surviving children, she had eight brothers and two sisters. From 1809 until she was past twenty years of age she lived in the idyllic setting of Hope End, an estate of more than four hundred acres in the Malvern Hills, Herefordshire. Her wealthy father converted the stately Georgian home into stables and built a new mansion of opulent Turkish design, including minarets, which his wife described as something from *Arabian Nights Entertainments.* The interior's brass balustrades, mahogany doors inlaid with mother-of-pearl, and finely carved fireplaces were eventually complemented by lavish landscaping: ponds, grottos, kiosks, an icehouse, a hothouse, and a subterranean passage from house to gardens.

Amid such luxury and the region's bucolic beauty, Barrett enjoyed a physically robust, active girlhood. She was intellectually precocious, particularly attracted to the study of classical Greek that she began, along with Latin, under the guidance of her brother Edward's tutor. Although she later described this endeavor to her neighbor, the blind classicist Hugh Stuart Boyd, as being more "guessing

Hope End, Barrett's childhood home, noted for its distinctive, Turkish-style architecture

and stammering and tottering through parts of Homer and extracts from Xenophon than reading," she persisted on her own in studying Greek poets, dramatists, and philosophers—including Pindar, Aeschylus, Sophocles, Euripides, Aristophanes, Plato, Aristotle, and Isocrates. Through corresponding and reading with Boyd she also embraced the Greek Christian Fathers. Almost entirely self-educated, she studied Hebrew, German, French, and Italian as well as the major English and Continental writers, including contemporaries, and she enthusiastically read the works of Voltaire, Thomas Paine, Jean-Jacques Rousseau, and Mary Wollstonecraft.

Barrett was similarly precocious in poetic activity. She stated in an early autobiographical essay that she "first mounted Pegasus" at four and at six (in actuality, probably nine) exhibited "feats of horsemanship" by penning lines on virtue. To reward her efforts her father presented her a ten-shilling note enclosed in a letter addressed to the Poet Laureate of Hope End, a title that stimulated her to compose a series of poems commemorating family birthdays. More ambitiously, she wrote a 1,462-line narrative in heroic couplets on the Battle of Marathon that her father paid to have privately published in fifty bound copies when she was fourteen. Conspicuously imitative of Alexander Pope's rendition of Homer, this youthful work contains

spirited battle descriptions and announces themes prominent in her mature works. In celebrating the earliest important symbolic victory of the Athenians over Persian invaders led by Darius the Great, the poem anticipates a theme of resistance to domination that animated her later works dealing with both gender and politics. Her first poem to be published rather than privately printed, "Stanzas, Excited by Some Reflections on the Present State of Greece," pursued related themes and appeared anonymously in *The New Monthly Magazine* when she was fifteen; "Thoughts Awakened by Contemplating a Piece of the Palm Which Grows on the Summit of the Acropolis at Athens" was also published that year in the same journal.

In the same year Barrett fell ill along with her sisters (ages twelve and seven), all suffering headaches, pains in their sides, twitching muscles, and general malaise. Henrietta and Arabella recovered quickly, but Elizabeth did not, and during an extended convalescence from this undiagnosed malady she and her family began to view her as an invalid. (Despite frequent assertions beginning in early biographical accounts, no evidence exists to link her invalidism to any mishap in saddling or riding a horse.) Sent to recover at the Gloucester spa, she was treated—in the absence of symptoms supporting another diagnosis—for a spinal problem. Recent diagnoses based on the extant evidence have generated hypotheses including tuberculosis of the spine, but most have centered on severe bronchial difficulties, which would plague her for the rest of her life. At this stage her principal complaints were spasms involving swooning, a racing heart, and pain in her right side. During this illness Barrett began to take laudanum (opium powder dissolved in alcohol) to help her sleep, but apparently in such weak doses that she evinced no symptoms of addiction. Whatever their physical causes, her debility may have been accentuated by a sense of diminishment when Edward went to boarding school at Charterhouse and his classics tutor was dismissed, interrupting her own studies. For Barrett these events vividly delineated her culture's strict separation of male and female spheres of experience and opportunity. Having spent nearly a year confined to bed or a suspended spine crib, she returned home weak and under physician's orders not to engage in excessive reading, writing, or intellectual labor.

Barrett nevertheless pursued her omnivorous taste for reading, especially of poetry, and her study of Greek. She sent verses to poet Thomas Campbell, who offered a critique, and published several more poems in periodicals. In 1826 at age twenty she published *An Essay on Mind, with Other Poems,* anonymously and at the expense of her grandmother's companion Mary Trepsack. The title poem, 1,262 lines of didactic heroic couplets again heavily influenced by Pope, attempts to survey the history of poetry, philosophy, and science from ancient Greece to the present day; along the way it celebrates John Locke and George Gordon, Lord Byron, for liberating the mind from repressive systems. Though she later described the poem in a letter to the poet and critic Richard Hengist Horne as "pertness and pedantry," it demonstrates her philosophical erudition and contains felicitous imagery and flashes of the wit and irony found in her mature poetry. Several of the shorter poems in the volume praise rebels against tyranny: "Stanzas on the Death of Lord Byron" and "Stanzas Occasioned by a Passage in Mr. Emerson's Journal . . ." celebrate Byron's support of Greek independence, a cause also extolled in "Riga's Last Song," and "On a Picture of Riego's Widow, Placed in the Exhibition" focuses on the stoic widow of a patriot executed in the Spanish Revolution of 1820. The concluding work in the volume, "A Vision of Fame," invests the writer's life with ominous foreboding by personifying Fame as a beautiful woman who withers to a skeleton before the aspiring poet's eyes. Notice of the volume established what would become a theme in contemporary criticism—Barrett's unusual, even "unwomanly," erudition: *The Literary Gazette* (15 July 1826) judged

that the title poem "displays a much more extraordinary degree of philosophical, we might say metaphysical acumen, than could be expected either from the youth or sex of the writer" and deemed it eloquent but "too learned"; *The Eclectic Review* (July 1826) similarly noted the author's extensive reading but found the theme of "An Essay on Mind" "barren and dazzling" while regarding the shorter poems more "genial."

Before publishing her next volume of poetry Barrett suffered two grievous losses: the death of her beloved mother and the forced sale of her cherished home. In 1828 her mother, Mary, having gone to Cheltenham to recover from an extended illness not considered serious, died unexpectedly. Her mother's death represented a devastating loss to Barrett. Unlike her siblings, she was incapable of experiencing any catharsis by exhibiting her grief. She developed a disposition inclined to fear the worst, and from this time morbidly dreaded separation from any family member. Her mother had represented for Barrett a model of femininity both inspiring and disturbing. For eighteen years Barrett's mother endured continual childbearing, and at her death she left offspring ranging in age from Octavius, four years old, to Elizabeth, twenty-two. The eldest daughter warmly recalled both her mother's encouragement of her poetry and a sweet disposition that she later described to Browning as somewhat soured by her father's "thunder." Since Barrett's delicate health and studious, literary bent made it unthinkable that she would assume her mother's duties in managing the household, the role was soon filled by her maternal aunt Arabella and eventually by her sisters.

Loss of the family home in 1832 further disrupted the family's security. Sugar plantations in Jamaica provided Mr. Barrett's wealth, and his income had been compromised by protracted litigation contesting the will by which his maternal grandfather bequeathed him the bulk of the Jamaican property. The court decision went against him in 1824. His income was further eroded by falling sugar prices and lower production, economic instabilities created by slave insurrections and expectations of emancipation, which finally occurred in 1833. Although Barrett and her father recognized that the end of slavery in the colonies would severely threaten the plantations from which their wealth derived, Barrett fervently supported emancipation; she wrote in 1833 to a former neighbor, a Mrs. Martin, that emancipation "has ruined" the British colonialists: "That is settled. The consternation here is very great. Nevertheless I am glad, and always shall be, that the negroes are—virtually—free!"

Sonnets from the Portuguese

VII

The face of all the world is changed, I think,
Since first I heard the footsteps of thy soul
Move still, oh, still, beside me, as they stole
Betwixt me and the dreadful outer brink
Of obvious death, where I who thought to sink
Was caught up into love, and taught the whole
Of life in a new rhythm. The cup of dole
God gave for baptism, I am fain to drink,
And praise its sweetness, Sweet, with thee anear.
The names of country, heaven, are changed away
For where thou art or shalt be, there or here;
And this .. this lute and song .. loved yesterday,
(The singing angels know) are only dear,
Because thy name moves right in what they say.

Manuscript page for one of Elizabeth Barrett's love poems to her future husband (the Armstrong Browning Library, Baylor University)

83

Following the humiliating auction of Hope End, the family continued to be comfortably wealthy, though lacking the extreme luxury of Barrett's youth. After the sale Barrett's father settled his family in the coastal town of Sidmouth until finally moving them in 1835 to London, which remained Barrett's permanent residence until her marriage.

While at Sidmouth, Barrett in 1833 anonymously published *Prometheus Bound, Translated from the Greek of Aeschylus; and Miscellaneous Poems.* To Boyd, Barrett eventually described the translation of Aeschylus's drama, completed in only twelve days, as a "frigid, rigid exercise," and she exorcized embarrassment over its inferiority by writing a second, much improved translation in 1845 (published 1850). Though a curt, negative notice in *The Athenaeum* (8 June 1833) cited the earlier version as a "warning" that Aeschylus should be avoided by those undertaking poetic translation, the subject of the Greek drama–Prometheus's disobedient theft of fire from the gods–must have exerted strong appeal to a woman aspiring to the lofty ranks of the poets. The "miscellaneous" poems published with the translation include several that emphasize male artists' unnatural silencing of women: "The Picture Gallery at Penshurst" suggests that images of Dorothy Sidney created by poets and painters silenced her own voice, and "The Death-Bed of Teresa del Riego" returns to the valiant widow celebrated in Barrett's 1826 volume to suggest the eloquence of her stoic suffering. Other poems in the collection attest to Barrett's kinship to the Promethean quality of the major Romantic poets. "The Tempest" and "A Sea-Side Meditation," for example, evoke the sublime through imagery of thunder, lightning, and raging winds and seas and describe the interchanges between nature and the human mind, which perceives in nature's threatening grandeur glimpses of immortality. A review in *The Gentleman's Magazine* (June 1833) warned that the young lady author risked being labeled a bluestocking, but the critics commended the study of Greek to more women, judged the translation faithful to the sense of the original, and praised the shorter poems. Both the spirit of resistance expressed in the poems of 1833 and the tensions inherent in her ambitions to write serious verse surface in an unpublished poem from this period, "A True Dream (Dreamed at Sidmouth, 1833)." In it the speaker's creative activities, described as "the magic art," conjure mysterious, menacing figures that threaten their creator. Her brother protectively but ineffectually attempts to slay them. Fleeing, she locks her chamber door only to discover that she has locked herself outside her domestic haven along with her uncontainable, immortal creations.

Once settled in London with her family, Barrett began her literary career in earnest by submitting anonymous verse to the periodical press, especially to *The New Monthly Magazine* and *The Athenaeum.* (She had published a couple of poems in the *Times* (London) in 1831 and 1832.) She also published works in annual gift books, lavishly produced volumes that featured the engravings more prominently than the accompanying poems and stories. Barrett acknowledged that she held the annuals in generally low esteem, but she recognized that being invited to contribute provided her an opportunity to publish along with famous writers. She was still largely unknown, for her two collections and periodical contributions had all appeared either anonymously or bearing only her initials. Her debut in the annuals came about through a personal friendship with the popular prose writer Mary Russell Mitford, introduced to Barrett by John Kenyon. A distant kinsman (his great-grandmother was the sister of Barrett's great-grandfather), Kenyon had been admitted to the Barretts' new home at 50 Wimpole Street on the strength of this connection, which exempted him from Mr. Barrett's eccentric, exaggerated reluctance to admit outsiders into his family circle.

In the years following her prolonged illness in adolescence Barrett was continually plagued by weakness and a severe susceptibility to colds and coughs, and her frequent indispositions and fear of venturing into inclement weather combined with her shyness and devotion to literary occupations to make her quite reclusive. She visited art exhibitions but otherwise avoided the city's bustle. Through Kenyon, however, she was introduced to literary London. A wealthy patron of the arts and a minor poet, he enjoyed wide acquaintance with literary and artistic circles. Although she mostly chose to experience Kenyon's wide contacts with the famous vicariously, through his reports of social engagements and discussions of books and magazines during his visits to her sickroom, in 1836 she accepted his invitations to dine with the renowned poets Wordsworth and Walter Savage Landor and, on an outing to the zoo, to meet Mitford, famous for her fiction and sketches, especially her memorialization of quiet rural life called *Our Village.* Mitford, a gregarious, warmhearted woman nineteen years older than Barrett, quickly became a dear friend. From this meeting they began exchanging thoughtful gifts and lively letters full of literary gossip and personal confidences. (Over two decades Barrett wrote Mitford about five hundred letters.) One result of the friendship was Barrett's contributions to the 1838, 1839, and 1840 issues of the annual *Findens' Tableaux,* edited by Mitford. Barrett's ballads "A Romance of the Ganges" and "The Romaunt of the Page" were often praised by reviewers as the best poems of their collections.

Barrett's name came before the public for the first time in 1838, when her father, proud of her new work, assented to her publishing *The Seraphim and Other Poems* with "Elizabeth B. Barrett" on the title page. The title poem of the volume represents the reactions of two angels to the Crucifixion. Barrett's preface rightly terms it "a dramatic lyric" though it is configured as a drama: its external action is reported in the comments of the angels Ador and Zerah, whose developing appreciation of the ennobling results of Christ's suffering furnishes the poem's true "action." Conceived as a companion of sorts to *Prometheus Bound,* as the preface declares, the poem celebrates not heroic rebellion but the divine submission of Christ. Through Christ's humility and suffering the angels learn to value earthly pain above celestial tranquillity. Most of the collection's shorter poems, some of which previously appeared in the *New Monthly Magazine, The Athenaeum,* and *Findens' Tableaux,* continue related themes. Unlike the Promethean defiance central to the previous collection, the pervasive emphases of these poems are sympathy and stoic endurance. They focus on loss of innocence, experience of suffering, and the compensations afforded by heaven. In "The Deserted Garden," for example, the speaker recalls her childhood delight in a secret bower of roses but declares she would not renounce her sorrowful adult awareness of mortality and "Heavenly promise" in order to reclaim that state of untutored innocence. Similarly, in "Isobel's Child" a grieving mother learns to resign her dying infant to heaven rather than to try to hold him in this "dull / Low earth, by only weepers trod." Barrett's preface remarks on the generally religious character of the collection, observing that "the gravitation of poetry is upwards. The poetic wing, if it move, ascends" and that poets must feel glad and happy if "in turning towards the beautiful, they may behold the true face of God." Among reviewers the volume won praise for its piety and "deep poetical feeling"; many found "The Seraphim" disappointing in execution, preferring the shorter poems as closer to perfection. John Wilson, writing in *Blackwood's Edinburgh Magazine* (August 1838), mused that the simpler poems "will live in the memory of many a gentle girl–and mothers will ask their daughters to recite them."

While concentrating on these "womanly" aspects commentators failed to remark the challenges

Casa Guidi, in Florence, Italy, where Browning wrote her long poem Casa Guidi Windows *(1851)*

posed by other poems in the collection to conventions of feminine resignation. Without overtly unsettling the volume's religious tone, many poems affirm the value of women's perspective and self-assertion. The long ballad "The Poet's Vow," for example, portrays a poet who rejects human beings as despoilers of Earth and withdraws from society to commune with Nature. When he takes this vow, he reassigns his betrothed, Rosalind, to his best friend. She, however, refuses to be merely an object exchanged between men. Before she dies years later, Rosalind directs that her bier be borne to the misanthropic poet's home, where through the means of a scroll written earlier she upbraids him for rejecting humankind–and the individual woman–and for abstracting Nature. Barrett's ballad "The Romance of the Ganges," to cite another instance, complicates a sentimental tale in which a jilted Hindu woman, Luti, commits suicide. Before she drowns herself the heroine protests her wrongs. By requiring her friend Nuleeni, who is to marry Luti's former lover, to remind her husband that he wronged Luti and eventually to repeat the tale to her future son, Luti implies that sisterly bonds supersede those of romantic love and that women can use their maternal influence to shape less misogynistic attitudes in future generations. Barrett's resistance to conventional assumptions about the sort of poetry women should write undergirds her elegiac tribute "Felicia Hemans," dedicated to Letitia Landon and inspired, as her subtitle indicates, by Landon's "monody" on the death of Hemans. While complimenting these two "poetesses" by alluding to their verse, Barrett undercuts what she viewed as their sentimentality by directing the mourner to "Lay only dust's stern verity upon the dust undreaming" and by commanding her to "Be happy" for Hemans's art rather than to dwell on her personal sufferings. Elsewhere in the volume Barrett distinguishes her practices from those of the poetesses, foreshadowing the political and social protest that her later, more outspoken verse would claim as appropriate for women poets as well as men. "The Soul's Travelling," for example, which concludes by affirming the necessity of turning to God, at the outset characterizes the fallen world by describing city scenes that manifest the gulf between rich and poor: "The trail on the street of the poor man's broom, / That the lady who walks to her palace-home, / On her silken skirt may catch no dust."

Although reviewers ignored such elements in the 1838 collection and sometimes also complained that the poems were affected and marred by "outlandish compound words" or unnaturally accented syllables, the volume earned the notice of at least eight significant periodicals, most of which quoted the poetry extensively and judged it highly promising. Anxieties about her transgressions of gender expectations punctuated even admiring reviews, however. H. F. Chorley in *The Athenaeum* (7 July 1838) discerned "evidence of female genius and accomplishment" but viewed the poetry deficient in the feminine charm of simplicity. *The Quarterly Review* (September 1840), evaluating nine women poets, judged Barrett superior in "her extraordinary acquaintance with ancient classic literature" and "the boldness of her poetic attempts," but concluded that she failed to achieve "success . . . in proportion to her daring."

Just when she was poised to enjoy growing literary recognition, Barrett in 1838 experienced a serious illness that necessitated her departure from London. She suffered severe bronchial or pulmonary distress (possibly tuberculosis although never diagnosed as such), which between 1838 and 1841 left her bedridden, struggling to breathe, spitting blood, and afflicted by chronically weak lungs, phlegm, racking cough, hemorrhaging, and loss of appetite. Dr. Chambers, the physician-in-ordinary to the young Queen Victoria, sent Barrett to the warmer climate of Torquay on England's south coast, where she was initially accompanied by her sister Henrietta and two brothers, including her favorite, Edward. Her heart irregularities were treated with digitalis and her insomnia—unsurprising in a patient confined to bed—with regular doses of morphine. Her physician in Torquay also forbade her to write poetry or undertake serious reading—instructions she ignored.

During her second winter in the coastal town, in February 1840, grief over the death of her brother Sam in Jamaica compromised her health, but a second bereavement precipitated a complete emotional and physical breakdown. In July, Edward was lost at sea on a calm day during a sailing party. His body was not recovered for several days. Barrett was shattered by the blow, which she always regarded as the greatest sorrow of her life. Not only was "Bro" her dearest companion, but she held herself directly responsible for his death, for she had kept him in Torquay against their father's express desires. Barrett's father had expected Edward, who was past thirty, to settle the patient at the coast and return to London, presumably to make a start in some sort of work. Barrett, however, had pleaded that she could not part with him, and he was allowed to stay. His death was so painful that she was for many years completely unable to speak of it. Though she wrote guardedly about the tragedy in her courtship correspondence with Browning, even five years after their marriage she had never spoken openly about it.

After three miserable years in Torquay, Barrett was finally able to return to London in September 1841, apparently convinced that the future stretching before her held only an invalid's confinement. She lived in near isolation for the next five years, not leaving her room for months at a time and receiving few visitors outside her family. Besides Kenyon and Mitford, visitors later included the clergyman George B. Hunter, whom she had known in Sidmouth, and her Wimpole Street neighbor, the art critic Anna Jameson. Constantly attended by her sister Arabella and a spaniel named Flush, sent to her in Torquay by Mitford as a consolation after Bro's death, Barrett lived surrounded by her books, busts of Geoffrey Chaucer and Homer, and framed engravings of contemporary writers—Wordsworth, Browning, Alfred, Lord Tennyson, Thomas Carlyle, and Harriet Martineau. Gradually, partly through work, she regained vitality, as her correspondence indicates. In 1842 she began an epistolary friendship with Benjamin Robert Haydon, the painter of large canvasses on historical subjects, which continued until 1845, about a year before he committed suicide; Haydon requested that Barrett edit his voluminous diary for publication, but she declined. She also developed a correspondence and several literary projects with the poet and critic Richard Hengist Horne. They collaborated on *Psyche Apocalyptè,* (1876), a drama never completed; on his 1841 modernized edition of Chaucer, for which Barrett wrote "Queen Annelida and False Arcite" and "The Complaint of Annelida to False Arcite"; and on his 1844 collection of essays on contemporary writers, *A New Spirit of the Age.* For this project Barrett provided most of the sections on Wordsworth, Landor, Carlyle, Tennyson, and Richard Monckton Milnes, and many of the epigraphs. In 1843 Harriet Martineau, a famous author of fiction as well as travel writings, reviews, and essays on politics, economics, and theology, joined Barrett's list of correspondents as well. Barrett continued her wide reading and study, reflected in two substantial critical essays written for *The Athenaeum* in 1842. "Some Account of the Greek Christian Poets" surveys the writers in an energetic, entertaining manner and includes about eight hundred lines of her translations. "The Book of the Poets," which originated as a book review, surveys English poetry from Chaucer to the present, viewing eighteenth-century poetry as a nadir, Romantic verse as a return to greatness, and Tennyson and Browning as the most gifted among her contemporaries. In addition to these prose works, by 1843 Barrett was writing some of her best poetry to date and was regaining strength and beginning forays into the world beyond her room.

Publication of her 1844 two-volume collection *Poems* established Barrett as one of the major poets of the day. The collection begins with two prose reconsiderations of her relationship to male literary tradition, the first a personal dedication to her father that acknowledges her ambition for other readers' praise, the second a preface that examines her relationship to John Milton by justifying the subject of the collection's long opening poem, "A Drama of Exile." Resuming the story told in *Paradise Lost,* this verse drama dares to take Milton's epic in new directions, in a form that the preface declares approaches "the model of the Greek tragedy." While asserting her reluctance to till soil so nobly cultivated by Milton, Barrett boldly revises his perspective by exploring the loss of Eden from Eve's point of view: "My subject was the new and strange experience of the fallen humanity, as it went forth . . . into the wilderness; with a peculiar reference to Eve's alloted [*sic*] grief, which, considering that self-sacrifice belonged to her womanhood, and the consciousness of originating the fall to her offence,—ap-

peared to me imperfectly apprehended hitherto, and more expressible by a woman than a man." Though focusing on so-called womanly subjects such as grief and self-sacrifice and venturing self-consciously into traditionally male preserves in subject and genre, Barrett's treatment is not timid but aggressive. As her preface declares, she "took pleasure in driving in, like a pile, stroke upon stroke, the Idea of EXILE"—a subject that she as a woman writer knew firsthand—"I also an exile!" The preface also vigorously defends her ostensible presumption in treating sacred subjects and introducing figures such as Christ into her poems, a practice criticized by some earlier reviewers. As though to stress her distance from typical assessments of "poetesses," she concludes the preface, "I never mistook pleasure for the final cause of poetry; nor leisure, for the hour of the poet." Barrett's concentration on Eve's viewpoint clearly disturbed some reviewers, as illustrated by the comment in *Blackwood's* (November 1844) that Eve's grief is a subject too trivial "to sustain the weight of a dramatic poem." Yet other reviewers recognized in the work "mental energy and daring imagination" (*The League,* 7 December 1844), "enough of fine thought and imagination to furnish a hundred inferior but still beautiful conceptions" (*Athenaeum,* 30 November 1850), and "power such as we do not remember in any lady's poetry" (*The Critic,* 1 November 1844).

Though critics did not generally comment directly on the neatly wrought sonnets of the 1844 collection—bearing titles such as "Irreparableness," "Tears," "Grief," "Comfort," "Work," and "Discontent"—their subject matter probably contributed to the consensus that Barrett's poetry was "eminently religious" and "calculated to be a blessing and a benefit to mankind" (*Blackwood's,* November 1844) and could be termed "poetry of endurance" (*The Atlas,* 31 August 1844). The sonnets also included two titled "To George Sand" that interrogate gender stereotypes, a tendency that would become alarming to critics of Browning's late volumes. Addressed to the French novelist whom Barrett, as she confessed to Mitford, found thrilling but sometimes indecent, these sonnets publicly acknowledged regard for a figure still deemed scandalous for gender anomalies—anomalies converted to strengths in the first sonnet's opening line: "Thou large-brained woman and large-hearted man." In celebrating Sand's defiance of the period's gender stereotypes the two sonnets provide a precedent for the many reviewers who commended Barrett herself for joining "womanly" heart and delicacy to "manly" intellect and nerve.

Browning with her husband, poet Robert Browning, 1853; painting by Anna de L'Epinois (University of Texas at Austin)

The ballads in the 1844 volumes, which aroused both critical and popular admiration, subtly anticipate the more outspoken critiques of gender stereotypes and conventions to be found in Barrett's later works. "The Romaunt of the Page," for example, narrates the story of a medieval damsel who disguises herself as a page in order to accompany her new husband on a crusade to the Holy Land. On the eve of returning to England she tests his attitudes before revealing her ruse, only to discover that he would never value a wife who had thus "unwomaned" herself. At this point the female page chooses to die at the hands of pursuing pagans rather than submit to her husband's commitment to conventional gender roles. "The Duchess May" depicts a similarly willful wife. Having married for love against the designs of her guardian, May and her husband are besieged in his castle by the disappointed suitor. Seeing no escape, May's husband plans to leap from his castle tower, consigning his wife to the arms of his enemy. She rejects his solu-

tion, instead joining him in the fatal jump, astride his powerful steed. The irony and complexity of these situations permitted readers to see both women as fulfilling conventionally feminine roles—serving their husbands, sacrificing themselves for love—yet simultaneously asserting themselves against their husbands' wishes and choosing death rather than the destinies defined by their culture. Barrett partially disguised her critique of her own society's strict gender codes by locating these tales in a medieval setting, as in "The Romance of the Swan's Nest," which questions the standard myths of courtly love by contrasting a young girl's dream of courtship with unromantic reality. "Lady Geraldine's Courtship" more directly challenges readers' assumptions by depicting a wealthy woman in the Victorian present who chooses to marry a poet beneath her social class. While these and other ballads frequently excited praise for their sentimental features, their disruptive implications went unremarked.

The collection's social protest poems posed their challenges to Victorian readers more directly. Barrett attacked child labor in "The Cry of the Children," which reflects her reading of "Report on the Employment of Children and Young Persons in Mines and Manufactories," compiled by her correspondent R. H. Horne for Parliament, and she protested economic oppression in "The Cry of the Human," which alludes to the poor starving while protective tariffs levied by the Corn Laws artificially elevated the price of bread. The 1844 volumes were widely discussed—some thirty-five reviews appeared in that year and the first months of the next, many others subsequently—and widely praised. Critics regarded the collection as truly "poetical" and even when they criticized Barrett's work as affected or her rhythms awkward judged the poetry inspiriting (though melancholy), original, powerful, and ennobling. Perhaps the view of Chorley in *The Athenaeum* (24 August 1844) most accorded with Barrett's intentions, for he distinguished her seriousness of purpose from that of most women writers.

Of the 1844 poems "Lady Geraldine's Courtship" holds special importance in Barrett's life, for it opened the doors of 50 Wimpole Street to her future husband. In one passage citing verse read by the poet narrator to the lady who comes to love him, Barrett named Browning, deftly alluding to his concurrent series of pamphlets titled *Bells and Pomegranates:* "Or from Browning some 'Pomegranate,' which, if cut deep down the middle, / Shows a heart within blood-tinctured, of a veined humanity." The passage sets Browning apart from the other contemporary poets mentioned (Wordsworth, Tennyson, and William Howitt), awarding him the longest reference and a finely turned metaphor. The compliment was not lost on Browning. After reading a copy of *Poems* presented by their mutual friend Kenyon to Browning's sister Sarianna, he soon posted a letter to the reclusive poet, the first of 574 (all but one are extant) that they exchanged over the next twenty months. Postmarked 10 January 1845, it began abruptly: "I love your verses with all my heart, dear Miss Barrett," amplifying further on, "I do, as I say, love these Books with all my heart—and I love you too." Browning recalled an occasion when Kenyon had wanted to introduce the two poets, but she had declined to receive them because she was unwell.

Browning was at this time frustrated in his efforts to build a literary reputation; initially encouraged by the actor and theatrical manager William Charles Macready, since 1836 he had unsuccessfully endeavored to establish himself as a verse playwright. Most disastrously, the reviews of his ambitious, long narrative poem *Sordello* (1840) derided his work as obscure, a label that stuck to him for decades. Although he was regarded in literary circles as a highly promising poet, his pamphlet series *Bells and Pomegranates,* initiated in 1841 with *Pippa Passes* (much admired by Barrett), did little to rehabilitate his reputation with the critics and public. Barrett highly esteemed his work, however, and her correspondence with Mitford reveals her keen curiosity about the man as well.

Living with his doting parents and younger sister in the suburb of Camberwell, Browning at thirty-three was six years younger than Barrett. Their lives differed markedly, for he traveled and mixed freely in literary society. Because of her health and cloistered situation Barrett at the outset of their correspondence entertained no notion that a romantic relationship was possible for her. Recognizing her skittishness, Browning mostly concentrated early letters on their mutual interest in poetry. He observed contrasts between their writing, praising her personal passion, so unlike his studied dramatic approach: "You speak out, you,—I only make men & women speak—give you truth broken into prismatic hues, and fear the pure white light, even if it is in me" (13 January 1845). She in turn commended his capacity to be both subjective and objective (15 January 1845). Pressed by him, she offered suggestions for revising his poems in progress; he generally made changes where she suggested, but not always as she suggested. In May 1845 Barrett yielded to his importuning for personal acquaintance and received him in her room at Wimpole Street, where he quickly became a frequent visitor—he recorded ninety-one visits in all. By September 1845 she had tentatively agreed to marry him.

As their love developed so did Barrett's anxiety that her father might suspect the state of her affections. Although he himself had married at twenty, apparently enjoyed a happy relationship with his wife, and sired twelve children, Edward Barrett harshly and rather unaccountably opposed the desires of any of his adult children to marry. (Julia Markus has argued that he feared a generation of grandchildren might have revealed miscegenation in his family history.) Whatever his motives, he never forgave Barrett's elopement, never read any of the conciliatory letters she wrote over succeeding years, and similarly cast off two other children who dared to marry in his lifetime. At age forty Barrett was alone among her siblings in being financially independent, thanks to bequests from her grandmother and her uncle, yet she shrank from alienating her father. She not only remembered his affection and encouragement in her girlhood but also gratefully appreciated his tender solicitude after Edward's death, when she felt she deserved his blame. After she returned to London, Papa had nightly prayed alone with her in her room, and she felt strongly devoted to him despite his despotic temperament. Eventually, however, her attachment to Browning won out, and her letters grew increasingly critical of her father. When he opposed her plans to seek a more temperate winter climate in Italy, he finally seemed to prove himself indifferent to her welfare, to reveal that he did not love her as she understood the term. Filial duty was thus removed as the final obstacle to her marriage.

Her health, which intimates and strangers alike assumed would preclude her marrying, had improved greatly, especially with Browning encouraging her to take exercise outdoors. Without question, her bronchial/pulmonary condition continued to be serious. However, the regimen she had followed after she returned from Torquay in late 1841 had doubtless contributed to her continuing weakness, for she rarely left her room or even rose from a semireclining position. Lack of exercise left her weak and depressed her appetite, but morphine enabled sleep and calmed her inevitable frustrations. (Though she would continue using morphine regularly throughout her life, she did not exhibit typical signs of addiction such as continuous headache, memory lapses, or hallucinations.) The invalid's life in real ways had facilitated her poetry, excusing her from domestic and social duties and reserving her time for study and writing. But invalidism also proved a prison that increasingly limited her experience of a world she wanted to write about: contemporary life and its social problems. To Browning, contrasting her limited sphere to his immersion in society, she complained that she was like a blind poet.

Barrett and Browning quietly married on 12 September 1846, attended only by her faithful maid Elizabeth Wilson and his cousin James Silverthorne. Keeping all her siblings ignorant to shield them from her father's anger, Elizabeth Barrett Browning left Wimpole Street a week later, bound for Italy with her new husband, Wilson, and Flush. For posterity their courtship produced a series of engrossing letters, entertaining, humorous, and tender. In his 1903 study of Robert Browning, G. K. Chesterton commented that the letters would always be private, no matter how many times published, for their author might as well have been writing in "the dialect of the Cherokees." Though the syntax of both poets is sometimes tortuous, their letters are not merely decipherable but fascinating; in rich metaphors and dramatic details they not only tell an exciting romantic story but also afford unique insight into the aesthetic principles and themes of two remarkable poets. Besides the letters the courtship also inspired Browning's series of forty-four Petrarchan sonnets, recognized as one of the finest sonnet sequences in English. Written during their 1845–1846 correspondence, Sonnets from the Portuguese remained Browning's secret until 1849, when she presented them to her husband. Despite his conviction that a writer's private life should remain sealed from the public, he felt the quality of these works demanded their publication. They appeared in Browning's 1850 edition of Poems, their personal history thinly concealed by omitting sonnet 42, which refers to one of her earlier poems, and by using a title that seems to imply the poems are translations. In actuality the title confirms the intimacy of the subject matter, for it alludes to Robert's great affection for her 1844 poem "Catarina to Camoens," which expresses a dying woman's love for the sixteenth-century poet exiled from the Portuguese court because his poverty and low rank made him an unacceptable suitor.

The sequence is markedly innovative. Browning breaks with the conventions of the Renaissance sonnet sequence—so closely associated with Dante Alighieri, Petrarch, and William Shakespeare—by making the speaker and lover a woman. While the speaker seems to adopt the usual posture of the Petrarchan lover, claiming a position of inferiority from which she worships a superior beloved, by doing so she also claims the power of speech. These poems are highly unusual in English literature up to this time in directly expressing female desire; the female lover is a speaking subject rather than a silent muse, and despite the frequent references to angels and spirits, the love she evokes is conspicuously physical and sensuous. She further transforms the sonnet convention of portraying the beloved woman muse as beautiful and the male lover as wounded or made ill by love. Instead Browning depicts the woman as initially faded and ill almost to the point of death but restored to life and vigor by love. The poems further challenge Petrarchan conventions by making marriage not the impediment to love but its fulfillment. While readers have been perennially engrossed by the biographical components of the series, the sonnets' intricate artistry—which prompted critics to rank them with those of Shakespeare—is too often overlooked. The poems work their gender transformations and variations on the traditional tropes of courtly love in artfully crafted verse that purposefully varies the traditional structural and rhythmic patterns of Petrarchan sonnets, alludes resourcefully to classical literature, and develops richly resonant metaphors and ingenious conceits. Whereas Victorian critics and readers prized these sonnets as sincere expressions of conjugal devotion, recent generations of readers have found them rather embarrassingly sentimental for precisely the same reason, without recognizing either their technical accomplishment or their daring in revising the sonnet tradition to articulate from a woman's viewpoint an ideal of amatory and poetic equality.

Along with the *Sonnets from the Portuguese*, Browning's *Poems: New Edition* of 1850 included most of the titles previously published in the 1838 and 1844 collections—many of them heavily revised—plus her new and improved translation of *Prometheus Bound*, some miscellaneous translations, and thirty-six poems that had appeared in periodicals but not in book form. Her subject matter was increasingly bold. "The Runaway Slave at Pilgrim's Point," a dramatic monologue composed during her honeymoon, powerfully indicts institutionalized slavery. A slave woman who has witnessed the killing of her slave lover murders the infant conceived during her rape by white men. The poem conveys the rage and the poignancy of her agony. Unable to tolerate "the master's look" in her child's too-white face, she can love it only after death restores it to consoling blackness. Symbolically captured at the location where the Pilgrims claimed their own freedom in the New World, the runaway curses the slave catchers and the white women who scorn their black sisters, questions God's neglect of his black children, and declares, "white men / Are, after all, not gods indeed." As she wrote to her old friend Boyd, Browning thought the poem might be "too ferocious" even for the Boston Anti-Slavery League, which first published it in their 1848 *Liberty Bell*. The poem's startling demand that readers sympathize with a woman guilty of infanticide implies that her autonomy as an individual takes precedence over even the maternal role so widely celebrated by Victorian culture as woman's transcendent destiny.

More subtle in its effects but perhaps equally intense about imbalances of power in gendered relations, the sonnet "Hiram Powers' 'Greek Slave'" interrogates the relationship between the beauty and the suffering of the woman depicted in a sculpture, a Greek Christian enslaved by non-Christian Turks. Having seen the chained nude figure, which eventually caused popular sensations at the Great Exhibition in London (1851) and the first World's Fair in New York (1853), in Powers's Florence studio, Browning poetically transformed its silent feminine suffering into eloquent "thunders of white silence"

Browning with her son, Pen, in Rome in 1860

that can "shame" the masculine strength that perpetrates such crimes. Adopting a different tone, "Hector in the Garden" seems to evoke nostalgia for an idyllic girlhood; yet in it, too, Browning subverts cultural assumptions about gender hierarchies. It whimsically recalls the speaker's play at age nine, when, stirred by epic accounts of the Trojan War, she planted a flower bed in the form of an effigy of the Trojan hero. The deceptively light, lilting verse implies a telling contrast between the militarism of the masculine ideal and the nurturance of the girl, who restrains and reshapes the "hero" by snipping and pruning. In other tonal registers "A Year's Spinning" and "Confessions" sympathetically evoke the experience of ostensibly fallen women. These poems that strike modern readers as stirringly feminist were balanced in the collection by others more conventionally "feminine" in spirit—poems commemorating friends and relatives, evoking a child's intuitive belief in God, stressing the pathos of a child's death, and, most prominently, displaying conjugal devotion in *Sonnets from the Portuguese*. Consequently the 1850 collection further enhanced Browning's reputation, though it received less critical attention than her earlier volumes, perhaps because it included so much previously published material.

Reviewers generally failed to note her technical improvements and criticized her again for obscurity, diffuseness, grotesque imagery, and stylistic carelessness resulting in faulty rhymes and rhythms. Again they praised her scholarship—sometimes condescendingly—and admired her pathos, purity, and "womanly" spirit, though some suggested she chose subjects beyond the reach of women. Nonetheless, in *The Athenaeum* (30 November 1850) Chorley, who had recommended in April 1850 that she be appointed poet laureate, judged her "probably, of her sex, the first imaginative writer England has produced in any age:—she is, beyond comparison, the first poetess of her own." The reviewer in *Fraser's Magazine* (February 1851) echoed this view, calling her "the best poetess . . . whom England has yet produced" because she combined a "delicate, pure, and intense . . . spirit of womanly love" with a "masculine and far-reaching intellect."

Browning's next volume ventured more directly into what her culture deemed a province of "masculine intellect" but in a manner also foregrounding "womanly love." *Casa Guidi Windows*, published in 1851, records her reactions to the stirring events in Florence as the Italian Risorgimento challenged Austrian rule. After spending the first winter of their marriage in Pisa, the Brownings had in April 1847 settled in Florence, eventually renting the second floor of a fifteenth-century palazzo, the Casa Guidi, which was their home base for the rest of their married life though they made extended visits to England, Paris, and Rome as well as shorter sojourns in Vallambroso, Lucca, Siena, Milan, and Venice. They traveled to see books through the press, to visit family, and to protect Browning's health in milder winter and summer climates. But Florence remained their center and was the birthplace in March 1849 of their only child, Robert Weidemann Barrett Browning (nicknamed "Pen"). Browning also endured four miscarriages, one in their first year of marriage and the last in 1850 at age forty-four, when she almost died after hemorrhaging more than six pints of blood. While living in Florence and wintering in Rome the Brownings made wide acquaintance among the Anglo-American community, numbering among their English friends Landor, Tennyson's brother Frederick, and Isa Blagden and among the Americans sculptors Hiram Powers, Harriet Hosmer, and William Wetmore

Story; the writer Margaret Fuller Ossoli; and the consul Mr. Kinney. Their visitors included Jameson, Kenyon, Thomas and Jane Carlyle, William Makepeace Thackeray, Owen Meredith, and Harriet Beecher Stowe as well as the actress Fanny Kemble and painters Frederick Leighton and Val Prinsep. In their first five years in Italy, when Browning enjoyed surprisingly robust health, she explored her surroundings, delighting in Italy's cultural treasures and countryside. Although the Brownings sometimes experienced anxieties when the quarterly payments on her investments were delayed or proved smaller than expected, they lived comfortably, often overpaying because they failed to bargain, happy to have their meals sent in by the local trattoria and other needs attended by her maid and a manservant. In Florence, Browning thoroughly fell in love with Italy and embraced the cause of unification and independence, the subject of her next volume.

The windows of Casa Guidi afforded Browning a dramatic view of events associated with Florentine resistance to Austrian occupation. Begun in late 1847, the long, iambic pentameter rhyming poem *Casa Guidi Windows* records her eyewitness account of a joyous assembly that occurred on the Brownings' first wedding anniversary, when a crowd gathered at the Pitti Palace to celebrate what was construed as a harbinger of Tuscan independence—Grand Duke Leopold II had granted Florence liberty to maintain a civic guard. Browning expressed her passionate support of the independence movement in the germ of the poem, titled "A Meditation in Tuscany," and sent it to *Blackwood's Magazine*. The editor refused the poem on the grounds that its subject matter was too local to interest English readers. This rejection intensified Browning's critical view of English provincialism and lethargy regarding humanitarian causes. Though specific to Italian current events, *Casa Guidi Windows* also expressed her continuing preoccupations, for it manifested her increasing conviction that poetry should be actively involved in life and her confidence that a woman poet should speak out on political and social issues. The poem as published in 1851 has two parts, each responding to a political demonstration she witnessed. Whereas the first section catches the euphoria of the 1847 celebrations, part 2 registers the poet's crushing disappointment, shared by silently protesting throngs, when in 1849 the Tuscan grand duke, having previously aroused hopes for independence, returned to Florence at the head of Austrian troops, signaling the failure of the liberal movement. Although the topical references of the poem may daunt modern readers unfamiliar with

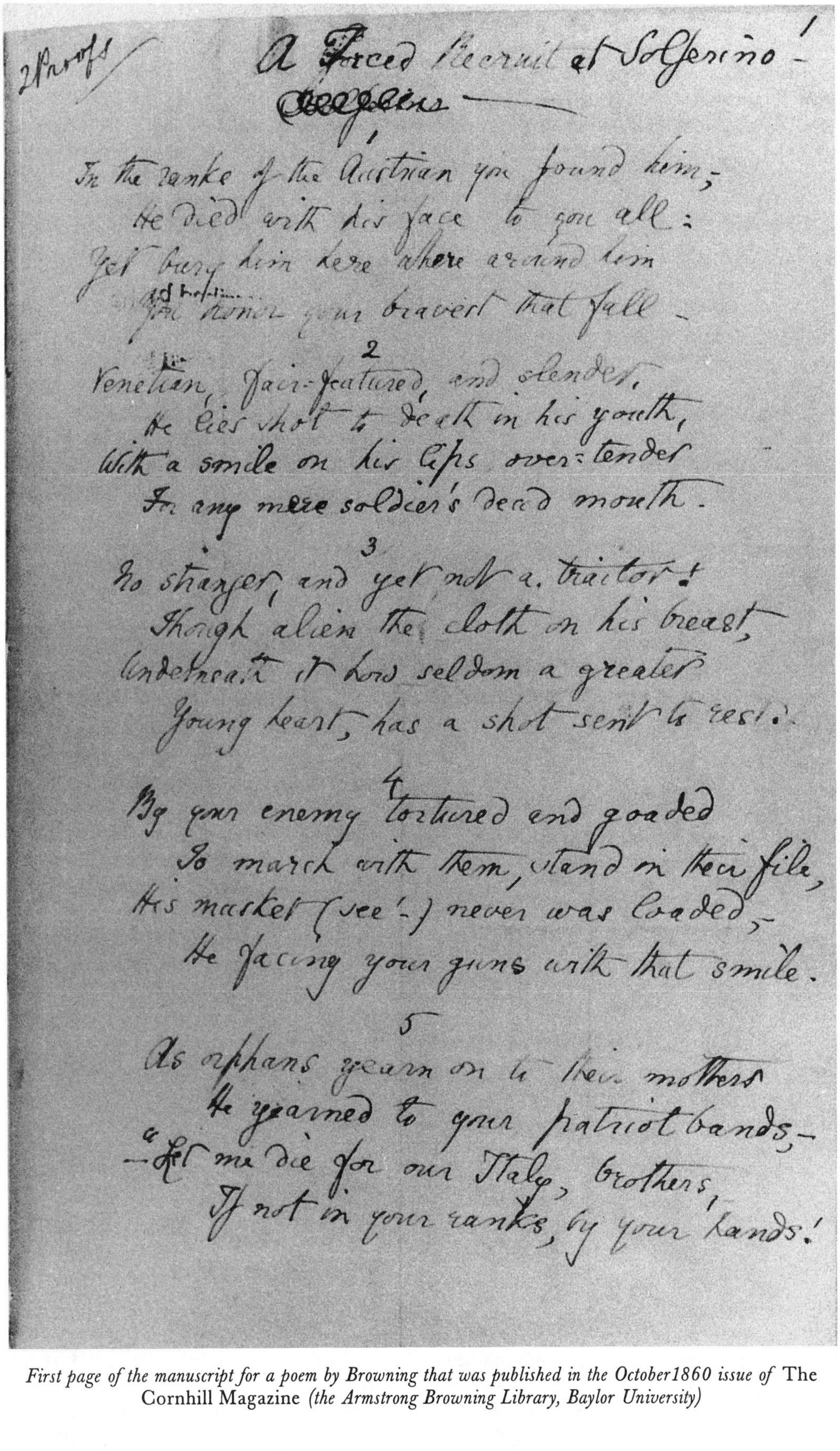

2 Proofs

A Forced Recruit at Solferino ~

1

In the ranks of the Austrian you found him,
 He died with his face to you all:
Yet bury him here where around him
 You honor your bravest that fall.

2

Venetian, fair-featured, and slender,
 He lies shot to death in his youth,
With a smile on his lips over-tender
 For any mere soldier's dead mouth.

3

No stranger, and yet not a traitor,
 Though alien the cloth on his breast,
Underneath it how seldom a greater
 Young heart, has a shot sent to rest.

4

By your enemy tortured and goaded
 To march with them, stand in their file,
His musket (see) never was loaded,—
 He facing your guns with that smile.

5

As orphans yearn on to their mothers
 He yearned to your patriot bands,—
"Let me die for our Italy, brothers,
 If not in your ranks, by your hands!"

First page of the manuscript for a poem by Browning that was published in the October 1860 issue of The
Cornhill Magazine *(the Armstrong Browning Library, Baylor University)*

the events to which it refers, *Casa Guidi Windows* remains powerful in its assumption that the female poet can use feminine subjectivity and emotion to claim authority on political issues. She speaks in part 2, for example, not in spite of her experience as a mother but because of it. Self-consciously critiquing men's mismanagement of government, she also discusses her relationship as a woman to a male poetic tradition. Her commitment to the Risorgimento has conspicuously personal dimensions, for Italy's warmth and light nurtured her own rebirth in health, marriage, and motherhood. Moreover, the political passions expressed in the poem connect directly with her early enthusiasm for Greek resistance to the Persians and Byron's support of Greek independence and with her horror of slavery. Throughout the poem Browning refers to the artistic and cultural history of Italy to represent the humane spirit now crushed by the Austrian yoke.

Casa Guidi Windows inspired mixed reviews, but critics frequently characterized Browning as combining "masculine" and "feminine" qualities, which must have gratified the poet who in earlier sonnets praised Sand on precisely those grounds. *The Athenaeum* (7 June 1851) commended a new direction in Browning's work, away from the earlier poetry's "record of personal feelings" "tinged" with "sentimental melancholy" to a more "courageous and wise" attention to the interests of mankind. *The Prospective Review* (1851) recognized "something at once manly and womanly in the character of her mind—energy large, and feeling deep." Though *The Eclectic Review* (1851) deplored her plea for England to promote Italy's unification as "wrong, illogical, and halting in her otherwise manly and prominent progression," it judged the poem "one of the noblest productions of female genius," combining a "deep and most womanly" pathos with "scathing vigour" and "the perfection of satiric art." *The Spectator* (28 June 1851) discerned "womanly faith and trust . . . enlightened by a manly power of analyzing events and facing disagreeable truths" and recommended the poem as a corrective to those who think women and politics "should be wide as the poles asunder": it demonstrates "the feminine warmth of heart that may coexist with a vivid sympathy with the public affairs of nations, and of the deeper human interest those affairs themselves assume when thus viewed in relation to family life and from the centre of the natural affections."

The Brownings journeyed to London in the spring of 1851 and the summer of 1852. Her father's refusal to reconcile with her, even to read her letters or meet her child, and the difficulties he posed to her visits with her siblings pained her deeply. The intervening winter in Paris (when she met Sand) marked a notable decline in her health, and in January 1855 her bronchial illness and racking cough recurred. The Brownings repeated their visits to London in the summer of 1855 to correct proof for his masterpiece collection, *Men and Women,* which received disappointingly scant and obtuse reviews, and again in summer 1856 (after a winter in Paris), this time to proof her masterpiece, *Aurora Leigh,* which was printed at the end of 1856 but bore 1857 on its title page.

This blank-verse poem—longer than *Paradise Lost* at nearly eleven thousand lines—constitutes a new genre, for it is simultaneously an epic and a novel. Published two years before Tennyson's first installment of *Idylls of the King, Aurora Leigh* bluntly argues that the stuff of ambitious poetry should not be the remote chivalry of a distant past, neither King Arthur nor Charlemagne, but the pulsing life of the present day as experienced by ordinary people. In a sense her version of modern epic develops from Wordsworth's own revision of the genre for his time, *The Prelude* (1850), but whereas he took the autobiography of the poet as his subject, Browning contrived a spirited fiction that is simultaneously a love story, a *Kunstlerroman* (autobiography of an artist), and a social protest poem. The poem intertwines the stories of three major characters: the heroine, Aurora Leigh; her cousin Romney Leigh, who loves her; and a working-class woman named Marian Erle, whom Romney tries to rescue. Orphaned at puberty by the death of her English father, her Italian mother having died earlier, Aurora is sent from Italy to England to be raised by her strict, conventional aunt. Aurora satirizes the narrow "feminine" education mandated by her aunt, surreptitiously educates herself among her father's books, and dreams of becoming a great poet, a goal Romney declares impossible for a woman.

Rejecting Romney's proposal of marriage and liberated by her aunt's death, Aurora supports herself through journalism and wins popularity as a poet. Romney, meanwhile, proposes to Marian, a seamstress, hoping to save her from poverty and make her a partner in his philanthropic endeavors, the role he had envisioned for Aurora. Lady Waldemar, a wealthy aristocrat who wants Romney for herself, involves Aurora in Marian's life and eventually—perhaps unknowingly—facilitates Marian's abduction to a French brothel, which leaves Romney waiting at the altar. Aurora, sick of her poetry's superficiality (and suppressing her unacknowledged love for Romney), abandons London. She coincidentally discovers Marian—now a mother—in Paris. Marian's story of being drugged, raped, and reviled

as a fallen woman teaches Aurora to shed her pi-
ously conventional assumptions about sexual purity, and she establishes a home in Italy with Marian
and her infant son. When Romney seeks them out,
he feels morally obligated to marry Marian, but she
refuses. He too has been stripped of naive assumptions, having failed in his philanthropic efforts to
aid the poor. Blinded in a fire that destroyed the ancestral home he tried to turn into a utopian community, he has gained insight into both the limits of his
socialist vision and the value of Aurora's poetry.
The poem concludes with the engagement of
Aurora and Romney and the prophecy that through
her poetry she may effect social reforms that he has
failed to accomplish.

Browning had projected such a work ever
since 1844. Reiterating a conception described to
both Kenyon and Mitford at that time, she in an
early letter to Robert declared her intention to write
"a sort of novel-poem—a poem as completely modern as 'Geraldine's Courtship,' running into the
midst of our conventions, & rushing into drawing-
rooms & the like . . . & so, meeting face to face &
without mask the Humanity of the age, & speaking
the truth as I conceive of it, out plainly." In book 5
of the nine-book poem she writes a manifesto for
such contemporaneity, insisting that the business of
poets in the modern world is to confront its problems—"this live, throbbing age, / That brawls,
cheats, maddens, calculates, aspires." *Aurora Leigh*
admirably achieves this relevance, for it deals with
an array of Victorian social problems such as the exploitation of seamstresses, the limited employment
opportunities for women, the sexual double standard, sexual hypocrisy including sanctimonious
views of the Fallen Woman, rape, prostitution,
drunkenness, domestic violence, schisms between
economic and social classes, and various schemes
for reform. While maintaining the equality of the
woman poet and her capacity to write seriously
philosophical and socially redemptive works, the
poem scathingly criticizes women's conventionally
meager education and limited property rights and a
wide array of affectations and human foibles.

Browning braced herself for harsh reviews because of the work's bold sexual content and unflinching candor. Most of the critics formulated
their objections in terms of decorum. While admiring "glorious chords and melodies," the reviewer
for *The Athenaeum* (22 November 1856) complained
that "Milton's organ is put by Mrs. Browning to
play polkas in May-Fair drawing-rooms" and protested that she mixed the "precious" with the
"mean." *The Dublin University Magazine* (1857) judged
that Browning had transgressed gender limits in

both her manner and her subject matter: she "as-
sumes as it were the gait and the garb of man, but
the stride and the strut betray her. She is occasionally coarse in expression and unfeminine in
thought; . . . the authoress has written a book which
is almost a closed volume for her own sex." Even so,
the reviewer commended her for protesting the "social wrongs of woman" and judged *Aurora Leigh* her
"greatest poem," a judgment expanded by *The Daily
News* (26 November 1856), which labeled it "the
greatest poem ever written by a woman." Despite
critics' carping about sordid subject matter, coarse
language, an overly independent heroine, and offensive feminism, the poem within a fortnight went into
a second edition and earned intense praise from
Landor, Leigh Hunt, Meredith, Ruskin, Dante Gabriel Rossetti, Swinburne, and George Eliot, who
said she read it at least three times and declared
Browning "the first woman who has produced a
work which exhibits all the peculiar powers without
the negations of her sex." Browning enjoyed thinking she had stirred up a scandal. She wrote Jameson
that she had "expected to be put in the stocks and
pelted with the eggs of the last twenty years' 'singing birds' as a disorderly woman and freethinking
poet!" She was surprised to hear of "quite decent
women taking the part of the book in a sort of effervescence," requiring her to "modify my opinions
somewhat upon conventionality, to see the progress
made in freedom of thought." Defending herself
against charges of coarse attention to such "unfeminine" topics as rape and prostitution, she wrote her
Hope End neighbor Mrs. Martin, "If a woman ignores these wrongs, then may women as a sex continue to suffer them; there is no help for any of
us—let us be dumb and die."

Having reached the height of her fame, Browning was frequently ill during her remaining four and
one-half years. She was less able to accompany her
husband, but she encouraged him to pursue an active social life that sometimes took him to several
engagements in the same evening. Over the years
they had disagreed on a number of issues: She preferred unusual and colorful costumes for Pen and
wide indulgence in his deportment and education
whereas his father inclined toward a more disci-
plined and "masculine" upbringing. She was deeply
enthralled by spiritualism, a rage among many intelligent and educated people of the day, whereas he
was thoroughly skeptical. She became emotionally
agitated about Italian politics whereas he shared her
general views but with less obvious passion. Yet
only three months before she died Browning described their closeness to her sister-in-law by asserting that she was "inside of him": "For the peculiarity

of our relation is, that even when he's displeased with me, he thinks aloud with me and can't stop himself."

Her passionate engagement in Italian politics furnished the subject matter of her 1860 collection, the last to be published in her lifetime. The title, *Poems before Congress,* suggests her desire to influence current events through her poetry. In 1859 open conflict between the Italians and Austrians had resumed, with Napoleon III of France intervening against the Austrians. After winning battles promoting the Italian cause, however, he had struck a truce with the Austrians in the treaty of Villafranca, which left Venice in Austrian hands and essentially squandered what had seemed to be progress toward Italian independence. Browning's title refers to a scheduled meeting of the major powers involved in the conflicts, a congress she hoped would negotiate terms favorable to Italian liberty—instead the conference was indefinitely postponed. Of the volume's eight poems seven deal with current events in Italy. The other one, "A Curse for a Nation," condemns American slavery but connects with the Italian subject matter by attacking political inaction that allows crimes against individual liberty, by focusing on a nation's moral identity, and by asserting woman's responsibility to speak on political issues.

Although addressed to the United States, this poem aroused considerable hostility in England, where reviewers interpreted her native land as the real object of its criticism, a view implied in the volume's preface, which insists that "non-intervention does not mean, passing by on the other side when your neighbour falls among thieves." "Napoleon III in Italy," while praising the French ruler's intervention against Austria, both exhorts Italians to live up to their nation's past and obliquely criticizes England for putting financial gain ahead of moral right in military decisions. The poems collectively sneer at the failure of leaders to sustain momentum in the liberal cause. "A Tale of Villafranca," for example, sarcastically refers to widespread timidity that vacated the promise of "the great Deed" achieved by Napoleon III against the Austrians, and "Christmas Gifts" shames the Pope for ignoring the wrongs suffered by his native land. Other poems adumbrate women's roles in the conflicts. "The Dance" memorializes a dance spontaneously initiated by Florentine ladies with French soldiers in elegant tribute to their aid, and "A Court Lady" poignantly evokes the visit to a military hospital of an aristocratic woman in formal dress. Published soon after the famous endeavors of Florence Nightingale in the Crimea, both poems strikingly emphasize women's symbolic power rather than their nursing capacities,

recalling Browning's protest in a letter to Jameson that by worshiping women's nursing talents but objecting to their thinking or creating, men perpetuated the ideology of separate spheres and denigrated women's intellectual abilities: "I do not consider the best use to which we can put a gifted and accomplished woman is to make her a hospital nurse. If it is, why then woe to us all who are artists! The woman's question is at an end."

Instead of praising Browning's combination of womanly feeling and manly thought, as notices of earlier works had done, reviews of this late volume complained that she had transgressed into masculine subjects. The *Blackwood's* reviewer declared in 1860 that "it is a good and wholesome rule that women should not interfere in politics . . . the case is worse when women of real talent take part in political affray" and counseled that "To bless and not to curse is woman's function." If women do not limit their concerns to their household duties, they should enter the public arena in more-feminine roles—becoming nurses, like Florence Nightingale. More brutally, *The Edinburgh Review* (1861), assessing all Browning's work through *Poems before Congress,* savaged her poetical ambition, "grotesque ideas," "intolerable conceits," and "coarsely masculine" tone, concluding that "considering the great capabilities she possessed, her career may be accepted as some proof of the impossibility that women can ever attain to the first rank in any imaginative composition."

Browning's anxiety over events in Italy contributed to her physical decline, and she collapsed in the summer of 1859, later acknowledging that she had nearly died. The Brownings left for restorative climates, summering in Siena and wintering in Rome. But a series of severe emotional blows had also eroded her health. The death of Kenyon in late 1856 left the Brownings financially comfortable, with bequests to the two of them totaling £ 11,000, but his death cost them their dearest mutual friend. Browning's father's death in April 1857 renewed her grief over a breach now eternally past healing. Their old friend Jameson, who assisted them on their honeymoon flight to Italy, died in 1860, and in the same year Browning's sister Henrietta, who had also been cast off by their father when she married, died a painful death from cancer. First elated in the spring of 1861 by thinking Italian independence was imminent, Browning was then devastated in June by the death of Camillo di Cavour, whom she viewed as the principal force for unifying Italy. In a low state of mind and having endured severe bronchial attacks every winter for the previous six years, Browning fell ill with a sore throat and cold on 20

Browning's tomb in the Protestant cemetery in Florence, designed by Sir Frederic Leighton

June 1861. She suffered from difficult breathing and pulmonary phlegm; she nevertheless insisted that this episode was not serious. But a rupture of abscesses in her lungs proved fatal; she died on 29 June, cradled in her husband's arms. Robert Browning and Pen left Florence within a month, and though Browning returned annually to northern Italy for each of his last twelve years until his death in 1889, he never returned to Florence, where a tomb designed by Sir Frederic Leighton and a tablet on the Casa Guidi erected by the city commemorated his wife. The obituary notices generally designated Browning the greatest woman poet in English, and some maintained she was the greatest in world history.

In early 1862 Robert Browning published a final collection of his wife's verse as *Last Poems,* compiled from a list she had drawn up herself. Some of the twenty-eight poems, including translations from Greek and Latin, were written prior to her marriage, some on recent political and personal events. Among the political poems "Mother and Poet" deepened the pathos of her Risorgimento poetry by voicing the misery of a woman who wrote verse urging

patriotic self-sacrifice and then suffered the deaths of her two sons in battle. The collection included the only poem the Brownings had ever published jointly, a social protest called "A Song for the Ragged Schools of London," which had been printed in an 1854 pamphlet to benefit one of her sister Arabella's charities. Some of the pieces in *Last Poems* address the power imbalance in relationships between men and women. "Void in Law" and "Bianca among the Nightingales," for example, articulate the woe of women abandoned by false husbands and lovers. In "Lord Walter's Wife" a woman wittily inverts the normal power structure; she ironically exposes the hypocrisy and sexual double standard implicit in the flirtatious advances of her husband's friend. When Thackeray refused to publish "Lord Walter's Wife" in his family periodical *The Cornhill Magazine,* Browning's reply indicated how purposefully she penned such challenges to conventional attitudes:

I don't like coarse subjects, or the coarse treatment of any subject. But I am deeply convinced that the corruption of our society requires not shut doors and windows, but light and air: and that it is exactly because pure and prosperous women choose to ignore vice, that miserable women suffer wrong by it everywhere. Has paterfamilias, with his Oriental traditions and veiled female faces, very successfully dealt with a certain class of evil? What if materfamilias, with her quick sure instincts and honest innocent eyes, do more towards their expulsion by simply looking at them and calling them by their names?

A similar purpose undergirds "A Musical Instrument," which on one level alludes to the myth of Pan and Syrinx to convey the truism that an artist must suffer but also describes the male artist's transformation of the female into art as a brutal ravishment. Reviews of this final volume sounded familiar inconsistencies: they commended Browning for her purity and womanly nature while charging that her verse was coarse, irreverent, and infected by excessive and, some charged, anti-English political fervor.

These contradictions forecast the trajectory of her reputation between her death and the 1990s. The critical view that Browning had been a major poet and unquestionably the greatest of women poets persisted nearly to the end of the nineteenth century, when attention increasingly shifted to her life, fueled by publication of collections of her letters and by the appearance of biographies, which Robert Browning had discouraged in his lifetime. Though *Sonnets from the Portuguese* remained continuously in print, frequently in beautifully produced gift volumes, her great work *Aurora Leigh* sank into obscurity despite Virginia Woolf's praise. Interest in her life led inevitably to devaluation of her work, for as she became romanticized as a doting wife—pure, womanly—her outspoken critique of her culture, her bravely visionary social critique, and even her technical daring faded from the picture, leaving in its place a sentimental parody of both the work and the woman. Reconsideration of her poetry by feminist critics since the 1970s, however, increasingly values its modernity, especially in its depiction of sexual politics but more broadly in its exposition of economic and political issues. In this regard Browning believed herself to be breaking new ground for the woman poet. Though she early expressed enthusiasm for the work of Letitia Landon and Felicia Hemans, for example, she also felt them to be too narrow in their subject matter and too ladylike in their execution. Instead she admired the intensity and reforming zeal of prose writers such as Mary Wollstonecraft, Madame de Staël, and Sand. She specifically lamented the dearth of women in her poetic ancestry. Writing to Chorley, she remarked, "I look everywhere for grandmothers and see none."

Women poets who followed Elizabeth Barrett Browning suffered no comparable lack.

Letters:

Letters of Elizabeth Barrett Browning, edited by Frederic G. Kenyon, 2 volumes (London & New York: Macmillan, 1898);

Elizabeth Barrett Browning: Letters to Her Sister, 1846–1859, edited by Leonard Huxley (London: John Murray, 1929);

Twenty-two Unpublished Letters of Elizabeth Barrett Browning and Robert Browning Addressed to Henrietta and Arabella Moulton-Barrett (New York: United Feature Syndicate, 1935);

Letters from Elizabeth Barrett to B. R. Haydon, edited by Martha Hale Shackford (New York: Oxford University Press, 1939);

Elizabeth Barrett to Mr. Boyd: Unpublished Letters of Elizabeth Barrett Browning to Hugh Stuart Boyd, edited by Barbara P. McCarthy (London: John Murray, 1955; New Haven: Yale University Press, 1955);

Letters of the Brownings to George Barrett, edited by Paul Landis and Ronald E. Freeman (Urbana: University of Illinois Press, 1958);

Letters of Robert Browning and Elizabeth Barrett Barrett, 1845–1846, 2 volumes, edited by Elvan Kintner (Cambridge, Mass.: Belknap Press/Harvard University Press, 1969);

Invisible Friends: The Correspondence of Elizabeth Barrett Barrett and Benjamin Robert Haydon, 1842–1845, edited by Willard Bissell Pope (Cambridge, Mass.: Harvard University Press, 1972);

Elizabeth Barrett Browning's Letters to Mrs. David Ogilvy 1849–1861, edited by Peter N. Heydon and Philip Kelley (New York: Quadrangle/New York Times and the Browning Institute, 1973);

The Letters of Elizabeth Barrett Browning to Mary Russell Mitford, 1836–1854, edited by Meredith B. Raymond and Mary Rose Sullivan (Waco, Tex.: Armstrong Browning Library of Baylor University, 1983);

The Brownings' Correspondence, 13 volumes to date, edited by Philip Kelley, Ronald Hudson, and Scott Lewis, (Winfield, Kans.: Wedgestone Press, 1984–).

Bibliographies:

H. Buxton Forman, *Elizabeth Barrett Browning and Her Scarcer Books* (London: Privately printed, 1896);

Thomas J. Wise, *A Bibliography of Writings in Prose and Verse of Elizabeth Barrett Browning* (London: Privately printed, 1918);

Wise, *A Browning Library: A Catalogue of Printed Books, Manuscripts, and Autograph Letters by Robert Browning and Elizabeth Barrett Browning, Collected by T. J. Wise* (London: Privately printed, 1929);

Warner Barnes, *A Bibliography of Elizabeth Barrett Browning* (Austin: University of Texas/Baylor University, 1967);

William S. Peterson, *Robert and Elizabeth Barrett Browning: An Annotated Bibliography, 1951–1970* (New York: Browning Institute, 1974);

Philip Kelley and Ronald Hudson, eds., *The Brownings' Correspondence: A Checklist* (New York & Arkansas City, Kans.: Browning Institute /Wedgestone Press, 1978);

Kelley and Betty Coley, *The Browning Collections: A Reconstruction* (Waco, Tex.: Armstrong Browning Library of Baylor University, 1984):

Sandra Donaldson, *Elizabeth Barrett Browning: An Annotated Bibliography of Commentary and Criticism, 1826–1990* (New York: G. K. Hall, 1993).

Biographies:

Jeannette Marks, *The Family of the Barrett: A Colonial Romance* (New York: Macmillan, 1938);

Dorothy Hewlett, *Elizabeth Barrett Browning: A Life* (New York: Knopf, 1952; London: Cassell, 1953);

Gardiner B. Taplin, *The Life of Elizabeth Barrett Browning* (New Haven: Yale University Press; London: John Murray, 1957);

Mary Jane Lupton, *Elizabeth Barrett Browning* (Old Westbury, N.Y.: Feminist Press, 1972);

Edward C. McAleer, *The Brownings of Casa Guidi* (New York: Browning Institute, 1979);

Rosalie Mander, *Mrs. Browning: The Story of Elizabeth Barrett* (London: Weidenfeld & Nicholson, 1980);

Daniel Karlin, *The Courtship of Elizabeth Barrett and Robert Browning* (Oxford: Oxford University Press, 1985);

Margaret Forster, *Elizabeth Barrett Browning: A Biography* (Garden City, N.Y.: Doubleday, 1988);

Julia Markus, *Dared and Done: The Marriage of Elizabeth Barrett and Robert Browning* (New York: Knopf, 1995).

References:

Helen Cooper, *Elizabeth Barrett Browning, Woman and Artist* (Chapel Hill & London: University of North Carolina Press, 1988);

Deirdre David, *Intellectual Women and Victorian Patriarchy: Harriet Martineau, Elizabeth Barrett Browning, George Eliot* (Ithaca, N.Y.: Cornell University Press, 1987);

Alethea Hayter, *Mrs. Browning: A Poet's Work and Its Setting* (London: Faber & Faber, 1962);

Gladys W. Hudson, *An Elizabeth Barrett Browning Concordance,* 4 volumes (Detroit: Gale Research, 1973);

Angela Leighton, *Elizabeth Barrett Browning,* Key Women Writers series (Bloomington: Indiana University Press, 1986);

Leighton, *Victorian Woman Poets: Writing against the Heart* (Charlottesville: University Press of Virginia, 1992);

Tricia Lootens, *Lost Saints: Silence, Gender, and Victorian Literary Canonization* (Charlottesville: University Press of Virginia, 1996);

Dorothy Mermin, *Elizabeth Barrett Browning: The Origins of a New Poetry* (Chicago: University of Chicago Press, 1989);

Glennis Stephenson, *Elizabeth Barrett Browning and the Poetry of Love* (Ann Arbor: UMI Research Press, 1989);

Marjorie Stone, *Elizabeth Barrett Browning* (New York: St. Martin's Press, 1995).

Papers:

The Wellesley College Library, Berg Collection at the New York Public Library, Henry E. Huntington Library, British Library, Folger Library, Harvard College Library, Yale University Library, Pierpont Morgan Library, Library of the University of Texas, Armstrong Browning Library at Baylor University, and Boston Public Library hold important collections of Browning manuscripts, letters, and books.

Elizabeth Cecilia Clephane

(10 June 1830 – 19 February 1869)

Tony Perrello
University of South Carolina

BOOKS: *The Ninety and Nine* (Boston: Lothrop, 1877).

SELECTED PERIODICAL PUBLICATIONS—
UNCOLLECTED: "Beneath the Cross of Jesus," *Family Treasury of Sunday Reading* (1872): 398;
"Dim Eyes Forever Closed," *Family Treasury of Sunday Reading* (1872): 398–399;
"In the Vale," *Family Treasury of Sunday Reading* (1872): 552;
"Into His Summer Garden," *Family Treasury of Sunday Reading* (1873): 245;
"From My Dwelling 'Midst the Dead," *Family Treasury of Sunday Reading* (1873): 365–366;
"The Day Is Drawing Nearly Done," *Family Treasury of Sunday Reading* (1873): 389;
"The Victory," *Family Treasury of Sunday Reading* (1874): 595.

Elizabeth Cecilia Clephane left a mere eight hymns to posterity; but these are among the finest examples of evangelical hymnody, one of the dominant types of devotional writing of her time. During the explosion of hymn writing in the nineteenth century, such religious verse—many of which were written by women—was published in newspapers and religious magazines and eventually made its way into one or more of the hundreds of nineteenth-century hymnbooks. Clephane's hymns are vital cultural material because they were part of the communal religious lives of thousands of people, both British and American. Hymns provided literary experiences for many Victorians, whether or not they read what is conventionally treated as canonical poetry.

Clephane probably lived to see only one of her hymns in print. However, that hymn caught the attention of the American evangelist Ira D. Sankey, who, along with Dwight Moody, captivated thousands of working-class and lower-middle-class members of nonconformist churches with his rollicking and rousing musical performances. Evangelical services such as those presided over by Moody and Sankey drew enormous crowds. In *A History of the*

Evangelical Party in the Church of England (1933), George R. Balleine estimates that half a million people heard the gospel preached during the Moody-Sankey campaigns of 1873–1875. These men campaigned most actively in the years following the death of Clephane, but her verses energized and helped popularize their gatherings. Thanks largely to the efforts of Sankey, Clephane's hymns were printed within a few years of her death.

The *Edinburgh & Leith Post Office Directory* for 1830–1831 shows that Clephane's father, Andrew Clephane, and his family lived at 5 West Circus Place, a short street leading off Royal Circus in Edinburgh's New Town. It was here, in the city of Edinburgh, that Elizabeth Cecilia Douglas Clephane was born, of noble Scottish lineage on both sides, on 10 June 1830. She was eight years old when her father, Andrew Clephane, an advocate and sheriff of Fifeshire, died. Clephane's mother, Anna Maria Douglas Clephane, was obliged to move the family, first to another residence in Edinburgh in 1841 and then to the small coal-mining town of Ormiston. In 1844, when Clephane was thirteen years old, her mother died as well. Thereafter the movements of the Clephane family become difficult to trace. With both parents dead the eldest child, George, abandoned his siblings and traveled to Canada. Elizabeth's elder sisters, Anna Maria and Anna Jane, were seventeen. There were also two younger brothers, Andrew and William, and a seven-year-old sister, Margaret, to care for. Elizabeth and her sisters moved to a small town in the Scottish Borders named Melrose, about thirty miles south of Edinburgh, the site of the famous ruin of a twelfth-century Cistercian abbey. They settled at Bridgend House, close to Abbotsford, and over the years they gained local fame for their generosity and selfless devotion to their community.

St. Aidan's, a small Scottish Free Church, became the spiritual home of the Clephane sisters. The resident minister, the Reverend William Cousin, called them "succourers of many" and went on to cite their charitable natures: "Just by way of

The Eildon Hills near Abbotsford, Scotland, which inspired Elizabeth Cecilia Clephane to write "The Ninety and Nine"

encouragement to others in the matter of good works I may mention that at the end of the financial year it was the custom of the sisters to send for the treasurer, and if he had to report a deficit he always came away with a cheque for the amount. They gave up their horses and carriage that they might have the more to devote to charity." Working in the obscurity of the sparsely populated Borders, Elizabeth C. Clephane was a symbol of holy works and single-minded devotion to God.

The hymn upon which Clephane's fame rests is "The Ninety and Nine." Various stories circulate about the composition of the hymn. According to one version, the death of Clephane's eldest brother, George, was the occasion for the piece. The tale of his dissolute end and its subsequent effect on Clephane is told by D. P. Thomson:

> He was known as a "Remittance man." That means one who is supported from home, and draws a monthly allowance. He was possibly a failure in the Old Country, and had been given a chance in the New. Unfortunately he fell in with companions who helped him to spend his allowances in an unwise way, and one morning he was picked up at the roadside. He was carried to the house of Dr. Mutch. There he died. . . .

Elizabeth learned of her brother's death shortly before her twenty-first birthday in 1851. In her room at Bridgend she gazed out at the surrounding Eildon Hills, where flocks of sheep often grazed, and, meditating upon her wayward brother, scribbled the first stanza of her great poem:

> There were ninety and nine that safely lay
>   In the shelter of the fold;
> And one was out on the hills, away
>   Far off from the gates of gold—
> Away on the mountains wild and bare,
> Away from the tender Shepherd's care.

Whether or not there is any truth to this apocryphal story, the agricultural imagery—gleaned from the Gospels (Matthew 18 and Luke 15)—is significant, given the historical milieu.

Against the socioeconomic upheaval of the Industrial Revolution, with its social dislocations and rapidly growing cities, the Anglican Church upheld the ideal of a rural society. In fact, William Booth, founder of the Salvation Army, called for the urban poor to move back to the country as a relief from the ills of poverty in the late nineteenth century. Long

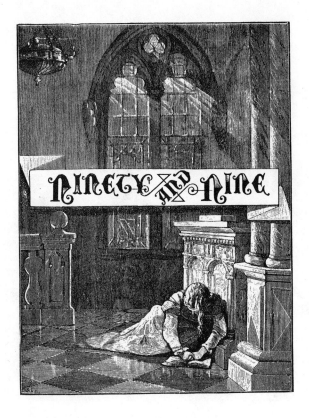

Frontispiece for the 1877 edition of Clephane's best-known hymn

gave her passing only a brief notice (23 February 1869). By all accounts, however, Clephane was in frail health for most of her brief life.

Over the next several years "The Ninety and Nine" was published in a variety of periodicals. In 1874 it appeared in *The Family Treasury of Sunday Reading,* a Presbyterian serial that published eight of Clephane's hymns under the heading "Breathings on the Border" between 1872 and 1874. "The Ninety and Nine" was the final poem by Clephane to appear. It was next printed in a London religious journal titled *The Christian Age,* where it came to the attention of Sankey as he rode a train from Glasgow to Edinburgh. Sankey was charmed by the piece and pasted it in his musical scrapbook. In his memoirs Sankey recalled the first public performance of the hymn, which occurred at a religious service at the Free Assembly Hall in Edinburgh before the verses were even set to music:

> At this moment I seemed to hear a voice saying: "Sing the hymn you found on the train!" But I thought this impossible, as no music had ever been written for that hymn. Again the impression came strongly upon me that I must sing the beautiful and appropriate words I had found the day before, and placing the little newspaper slip on the organ in front of me, I lifted my heart in prayer, asking God to help me so to sing that people might hear and understand. Laying my hands upon the organ I struck the key of A flat, and began to sing. Note by note the tune was given, which has not been changed from that day to this. As the singing ceased a great sigh seemed to go up from the meeting, and I knew that the song had reached the hearts of my Scotch audience.

Moody was moved to tears on this occasion, as was Sankey. Sankey later "discovered" that the tune to which he sung his hymn on that day was derived from a slave song, "A Wonderful Stream Is the River of Time."

"The Ninety and Nine" became the signature hymn of the Moody and Sankey revivals. "When you hear 'The Ninety and the Nine' sung," said one of Moody's Edinburgh helpers, "you know of a truth that down in this corner, up in that gallery, behind the pillar which hides the singer's face from the listener, the hand of Jesus has been finding this and that and yonder lost one, to place them in His fold." Indeed, "The Ninety and Nine" seems to have a history that speaks of an unusual power to transform the wayward listener. In his autobiography Sankey details seven instances of conversion connected with "The Ninety and Nine," in settings as far-flung as Massachusetts and South Africa. The style of "The Ninety and Nine" best characterizes the spirited evangelical missionary music that was popular

after the urbanization and industrialization of England, recurring images—such as the metaphorical sowing and reaping of the missionary and the paired images of Christ as shepherd and mortal sinners as sheep—demonstrate that Victorian hymn writers still thought of their national identity as rural and agricultural. Such images are present throughout Clephane's small canon.

"The Ninety and Nine" made its first appearance in print in 1868 in *The Children's Hour* (which raises questions about the alleged 1851 composition date). According to Reverend James Dodds, Clephane, a lover of children and reputedly a Sunday School teacher, had been a regular contributor to this obscure children's paper. Clephane's cousin, a woman named Hornsburgh, was editor. When she solicited a contribution to the paper from Clephane, her cousin expressed a desire to compose upon the parable of the lost sheep and soon submitted "The Ninety and Nine." Within a year after the hymn was published, on 19 February 1869, Clephane had died. The cause of death is obscure; the *Scotsman* newspaper

after mid century, which Sankey is credited with introducing to Great Britain.

After Sankey had introduced "The Ninety and Nine" to the public he published it, along with "The Cross of Jesus" (as he had retitled another Clephane composition, "Beneath the Cross of Jesus") in a relatively slender volume of sheet music titled *Gospel Hymns and Sacred Songs* in 1875. D. Lothrop and Company published a special edition of "The Ninety and Nine" in 1877, replete with designs, engravings, and a preface by Clephane's sister Anna Maria. Sankey republished "The Cross of Jesus" and "The Ninety and Nine" in his collection *Sacred Songs and Solos* (1880) and in *Gospel Hymns Nos. 1 to 6 Complete* (1895), which he compiled with P. P. Bliss. In 1884 Booth included "The Ninety and Nine" in his collection, *Salvation Army Music*. With their appearance in the *Church Hymnary* of 1928, the lasting influence of "The Ninety and Nine" and "Beneath the Cross of Jesus" seemed assured.

"Beneath the Cross of Jesus," the first of "Breathings on the Border" series, appeared in an 1872 issue of *The Family Treasury of Sunday Reading*. A quick-moving, five-stanza piece, it begins:

> Beneath the Cross of Jesus
>   I fain would take my stand—
> The shadow of a mighty rock
>   Within a weary land—
> A home within the wilderness,
>   A rest upon the way,
> From the burning of the noontide heat,
>   And the burden of the day.

A. E. Bailey notes that in most hymnals "Beneath the Cross of Jesus" is cut from its original five stanzas to three in order to soften the effect of the stern Calvinistic theology it embraces. In his memoirs Sankey calls it "The Cross of Jesus" and mistakenly refers to it as one of only two hymns that Clephane ever wrote, although these may indeed be the only of Clephane's verses ever to be set to music. Sankey fondly recalls the occasion of the hymn's first performance, comparing its effect on audiences to that of "The Ninety and Nine."

"Beneath the Cross of Jesus" celebrates the most important of Christian symbols, considering the cross in light of a series of metaphysical conceits. The crossbeams, for example, are envisioned as the intersection of heavenly love and justice; at the conclusion of the second stanza they form "A ladder up to heaven," evoking Jacob's dream from the Book of Genesis. Finally, they become "Two arms outstretched to save," emphasizing both God's embrace as a haven from worldly woe ("O safe and happy shelter! / O refuge tried and sweet!") and the intimacy of

American evangelist Ira D. Sankey, whose revival meetings helped popularize Clephane's hymns

Christ's love, which perhaps suggests an erotic component ("O trysting place where Heaven's love / and Heaven's justice meet!").

Clephane's verses embody the major tenets of Presbyterian evangelism in its emphasis on the depravity of the individual and the necessity of divine grace, symbolized by the cross:

> I take, O Cross, thy shadow
>   For my abiding place;
> I ask no other sunshine
>   Than the sunshine of his face;
> Content to let the world go by,
>   To know no gain nor loss,—
> My sinful self my only shame,
>   My glory, all, *the Cross!*

Clephane's verse celebrates salvation in Christ, but there is certainly a morbid element to her hymns as well. The dominant images in her verse are of life adumbrated by shadow, darkness, and mists. The only joy is in death and the return to the enfolding arms of God. Such a view, based on the evangelical gnostic rejection of the world, was a popular vision for the Victorian Christian, as Ed-

Score for Clephane's hymn. Sankey later "discovered" that his musical setting was derived from an American slave song.

ward Palmer Thompson notes in *The Making of the English Working Class* (1963):

> Those who could read were deluged, throughout the early nineteenth century, with the tracts which celebrated "Holy Dying." No Methodist or evangelical magazine, for the mature or for children, was complete without its death-bed scene in which (as Leigh Hunt has also noted) death was often anticipated in the language of the bride or bride-groom impatient for the wedding night. Death was the goal which might be desired without guilt, the reward of peace after a lifetime of suffering and labour.

"The Victory," the seventh hymn in the "Breathings on the Border" series, published in *The Family Treasury of Sunday Reading* in 1874, begins:

> Life-light waneth to an end;
>   Pitiful look, dying eyes,
>   Asking of Death's mysteries,
> Passing round from friend to friend—
> Death! Thou hast the victory!
>
> Slowly round the dying bed
>   Daylight faded into gloom;
>   Noiseless weeping filled the room,
> Trembling lips say, "He is dead"—
> Death! Thou hast the victory.

There is a sonnetlike turn in stanza 5, however, when Death's conquering power is called into question by Jesus' abandoned tomb.

> From the answering grave they rise,
>   My beloved dead again;
>   But I knew them weary then
> Now, no weeping dims their eyes:
>   Death, thou hast no victory!

No doubt the reference to "my beloved dead" was inspired by Clephane's early loss of her parents and her prodigal brother, George.

In the sixth installment of "Breathings on the Border," "The Day Is Drawing Nearly Done" (1873), most of Clephane's favorite elements recur: children as sheep returning to the fold, the strangely commercial image of heaven's "golden gate," the movement from life's dim shadows toward the awaiting light of death, the enfolding arms of the Savior as a refuge. The entire hymn is presided over by Jesus, figured as an elder brother, a common metaphor in hymns of the time that must have been especially poignant for Clephane:

> The day is drawing nearly done—
>   Come home, children, come home!
> The night lamps shine out one by one—

> Come home, children, come home!
> The Elder Brother stands at the threshold of the door;
>   He holdeth out his loving hands—come in for evermore.
> Come home, children, come home,
>   For the darkness draweth quickly on, and the day is nearly done.

"The Day Is Drawing Nearly Done" also reminds readers of Clephane's status as a spiritual guide to those less fortunate in Melrose and a keeper and educator of small children. In one of the clearest portraits of Clephane available, her sister Anna Maria writes: "Gathering little forlorn children, both on week days and on Sundays, she taught them for this life and the life to come. Among the sick and sorrowful, she won the name of 'My Sunbeam.'"

The Reverend William Arnot eulogized Clephane in a short introductory note preceding the first two hymns to appear under the heading "Breathings on the Border" late in 1872:

> These lines express the experiences, the hopes, and the longings of a young Christian lately released. Written on the very edge of this life, with the better land fully in the view of faith, they seem to us footsteps printed on the sands of Time, where these sands touch the ocean of eternity. These footprints of one whom the Good Shepherd led throughout the wilderness into rest may, with God's blessing, contribute to comfort and direct succeeding pilgrims.

Arnot's eulogy makes use of images that match those in Clephane's verse, suggesting that he must have known Clephane and her poems well. These images in turn seem to reflect the way in which she lived her life—as an unassuming, hardworking pilgrim and evangelist.

Clephane is commemorated by a memorial brass plaque that hangs in St. Aidan's Church, which touts her as "Authoress of the Favorite Hymn *The Ninety and the Nine.*" Clephane, both in her verses and in her secluded, almost ascetic existence, offered an alternative vision of life in a Victorian culture that was becoming increasingly worldly and urbanized, filled with what William Wordsworth called "The still, sad music of humanity."

References:
Ira D. Sankey, *My Life and the Story of the Gospel Hymns* (Philadelphia: Sunday School Times, 1907), pp. 296–298, 304–313;
D. P. Thomson, "The Sweet Singer of Melrose: The Story of Elizabeth Clephane and Her Famous Hymn," *Women of the Scottish Church—II* (Galashiels: Walker, 1946).

Caroline Clive
(V)
(24 June 1801 – 13 July 1873)

Linda A. Julian
Furman University

BOOKS: *IX Poems by V,* as V (London: Saunders & Otley, 1840; revised and enlarged, London: Saunders & Otley, 1841);

I Watched the Heavens: A Poem, as V (London: Saunders & Otley, 1842);

Saint Oldooman: A Myth of the Nineteenth Century, Contained in a Letter from the Bishop of Verculanem to the Lord Drayton, anonymous (London: Simpkin, Marshall, 1845);

The Queen's Ball: A Poem, as V (London: Saunders & Otley, 1847);

The Valley of the Rea, as V (London: N.p., 1851);

The Morlas: A Poem, as V (London: Hope, 1853);

Paul Ferroll: A Tale, as "the author of *IX Poems by V*" (London: Saunders & Otley, 1855; enlarged edition, London: Saunders & Otley, 1856; New York: Redfield, 1856; Leipzig: Tauchnitz, 1856);

Poems, by the Author of "Paul Ferroll," Including a New Edition of IX Poems by V, with Former and Recent Additions (London: Saunders & Otley, 1856); enlarged as *Poems by V., Author of "Paul Ferroll," Including the "IX Poems"* (London: Longmans, Green, 1872);

Year After Year: A Tale, as "the author of *Paul Ferroll*" (London: Saunders & Otley, 1858; Leipzig: Tauchnitz, 1858);

Why Paul Ferroll Killed His Wife, as "the author of *Paul Ferroll*" (London: Saunders & Otley, 1860; Leipzig: Tauchnitz, 1861; New York: Carleton, 1862);

John Greswold, 2 volumes, as "the author of *Paul Ferroll*" (London: Hurst & Blackett, 1864);

Editions: *Poems by V. Including the IX Poems,* edited, with an introduction, by Alice Greathed (London: Longmans, Green, 1890);

IX Poems by V, edited, with an introduction, by Eric Partridge (London: Scholartis Press, 1928);

Paul Ferroll, introduction by Partridge (London: Scholartis Press, 1929);

Caroline Clive in 1846; portrait by her husband's cousin, Theophilus Clive (frontispiece for The Diary and Family Papers of Mrs. Archer Clive [1801–1873], *1949, Mary Clive, ed.)*

Paul Ferroll, introduction by Charlotte Mitchell (Oxford & New York: Oxford University Press, 1997).

PERIODICAL PUBLICATION: "The Great Drought," *Blackwood's Edinburgh Magazine,* 56 (December 1844): 433–453.

OTHER: *Guy of Warwick: A Knight of Britain Who in His Day Did Many Deeds of Prowess and Conquest in Germany, Italy, and Denmark, and Also Against the Infidels, the Enemies of Christianity, As May Be Seen More at Large in This Present Book Newly Printed at Paris in the Year 1525,* translated by Caroline Clive, edited by William B. Todd (Austin: University of Texas Press, 1968).

Death overshadows all other themes in the single volume of collected poems by Caroline Clive, and, ironically, Clive's own death on 13 July 1873 was gruesome and tragic. Clive, who had been an invalid for several years, was writing in her boudoir when a spark set fire to her dress, books, and papers. She died the following morning, survived by her husband, the Reverend Archer Clive, and two children. The accident was shocking enough to merit news reports in both *The Times* (London) and *The New York Times*.

At the time of her death Clive's poetic achievements, favorably received though somewhat obscure, had been eclipsed by several novels. Writing as *V*, she steadily published her poems from 1840 to 1872, the year before her death. Her collected poems appeared in 1890. Although Clive's heavily moralistic and somewhat predictable style and tone make her poems unpalatable to most readers today, the poems are nevertheless intriguing because they reveal a sensitive appreciation of nature, an imaginative view of death, and a genuine emotional power. Most rely on a heavy-handed use of apostrophe, allegory, and personification; and they do not offer much variety in verse form. Most often they are in rhymed couplets or lines with alternating end rhyme and are usually iambic tetrameter or iambic pentameter. The later poems have fewer strained and unidiomatic lines than do the early works. Despite their technical lapses, however, the number of reprints and editions suggests that during Clive's lifetime her poems were in steady demand, and the reviews of her poetry, though not frequent, are generally positive.

Born in London on 24 June 1801, Caroline Wigley was the daughter of Edmund Meysey-Wigley and Anna Maria Meysey, the last of the Meysey family and the owner of Shakenhurst, the family estate in Worcestershire, where Caroline spent her youth. She had two brothers and two sisters. Her father, who practiced law, was recorder for Leicester and a member of Parliament, losing his seat a year after Clive's birth. Her childhood was profoundly unhappy, largely because of her lameness caused by infantile paralysis. According to Mary Clive, editor of the family diary, she may also have been unhappy because she was "an ugly little thing" whose "bright eyes were squinny, her mouth enormous, her jowl heavy." Caroline's greatest pleasures were riding horseback and listening to and reading stories, especially sensational and macabre works. As a young adult she divided her time between Shakenhurst and Malvern Hall, near Birmingham, in Solihull parish. Malvern Hall had been inherited from a cousin by Caroline's brother Edmund, who as a condition of his inheritance had to adopt the name Greswolde, a name significant as that of the protagonist of her novel *John Greswold* (1864). Caroline, who loved Malvern Hall and the surrounding countryside, was forced from it, however, by the untimely deaths of her two brothers. Perhaps these sudden deaths increased her already-keen interest in death, which was to become the major subject of her poems.

By her early twenties Wigley was debating the merits of poetry as a vocation. Seeking advice, she wrote to Isaac D'Israeli, the author of *Calamities of Authors* (1812–1813) and *Quarrels of Authors* (1814), signing her letter "George Ferrol," a name similar to that of the protagonist of *Paul Ferroll: A Tale* (1855), her best-known novel. D'Israeli suggested that she seemed to be compromising too much of her "personal happiness" in her concern to be a poet and that she be wary of sacrificing happiness and wisdom in an effort to be known as a poet. She seems not to have been discouraged by D'Israeli's advice. She sent some poems to the philosopher Dugald Stewart, signing the cover letter "P. Ferrol." In the family diary Mary Clive says that Stewart's wife, not he, answered the letter, praising the poems but advising her not to rely on poetry as a livelihood. Nevertheless, Wigley continued to write poems, and in the early 1830s when she became acquainted with her future husband, the Reverend Archer Clive, rector of Solihull parish, she sought his criticism of her work.

In 1840 two major events occurred: in the spring Wigley published her first book of poetry, *IX Poems. By V,* and in November, at age thirty-nine, she married the Reverend Clive. The *V* stands for Vigolina, perhaps the Latin form of her maiden name, Wigley, and was Archer Clive's nickname for her. Some readers believed that the *V* stood for Victoria though others believed the poems had been written by a man. Among those who identified a male tone was Henry Nelson Coleridge, who wrote an anonymous review of the volume for the *Quarterly Review* of September 1840. Caroline Clive's volume was the eighth of nine books by women being reviewed by Henry Nelson Coleridge in the lengthy essay, which included his assessment of poems by Caroline Norton, Elizabeth Barrett, and his wife, Sara Coleridge. Henry Nelson Coleridge wrote of Clive's poems that "these few pages are distinguished by a sad Lucretian tone, which very seldom comes from a woman's lyre. But V. is a woman, and no ordinary woman, certainly." Coleridge praised the poems effusively, saying that some stanzas "are, in our judgment, worthy of any one of our greatest poets in his happiest moments," and he predicted

POEMS

BY

THE AUTHOR OF "PAUL FERROLL."

INCLUDING A NEW EDITION OF

IX POEMS BY V,

WITH FORMER AND RECENT ADDITIONS.

" Of IX Poems by V, we emphatically say, in old Greek, Βαιὰ
μὲν ἀλλὰ ΡΟΔΑ. It is an Ennead to which every Muse may have
contributed her Ninth. The stanzas printed by us in Italics are,
in our judgment, worthy of any one of our greatest poets in his
happiest moments."—*Quarterly Review*, September, 1840.

LONDON:
SAUNDERS AND OTLEY, CONDUIT STREET.
1856.

Title page for Clive's 1856 collection that includes "Venice, 1853," one of her highly praised poems (courtesy of Special Collections, Thomas Cooper Library, University of South Carolina)

that this volume would not be the last from this poet. Coleridge found the nine poems of "equal merit," but he singled out four: he quoted most of "The Grave" and labeled "Youth Took One Summer Day His Lyre" and "Former Home" as "the sweet poems." He ended his comments on Clive by quoting all forty lines of "Written in Health," which, he wrote, "we admire more for their terseness and force than for the spirit which animates them."

All nine poems concern death, approaching the subject in both predictable and imaginative ways. Two are complementary: "Written in Illness" (twenty-eight lines) and "Written in Health " (forty lines) are both first-person examinations of death. "Written in Illness," composed in 1829 and one of the few poems dated, comprises seven four-line stanzas. The alternating rhymes and line lengths slow the pace of this poem in which the

speaker seems to be approaching death in an increasingly languid state of mind. "Written in Illness" is reminiscent of William Wordsworth's poetry in its suggestion that the soul learns from nature, but in contrast to Wordsworth's vision in "Ode: Intimations of Immortality from Recollections of Early Childhood" (1807), where birth begins the human separation from glory, Clive's poem presents illness as beginning the process through which "the shapes of joys and ills" gradually recede and "All indistinct they grow." This poem is the third in the volume to use the worn metaphor of life as a ship: "My bark floats on the sea of death, / Of deepening waves the sport." "Written in Health" is an apostrophe to Fate in which the speaker ironically asks for a quick death. The speed with which the speaker wants to die is reflected in the speed with which the reader is moved through the rhymed couplets in iambic tetrameter. The speaker wishes to die quickly so that he or she can die in the full flower of "my love, my hope, my strength" and not dwindle into a shell containing only "the baser part of man." The speaker begs to end life "Like comets when their race is run, / That end by rushing on the sun," and the structure and pace of the poem give the sense of hurtling toward death.

In "The Grave," one of the poems praised by H. N. Coleridge, the speaker is in a tomb, lights a lamp, and walks through the realms of the dead. In its emphasis on dying generations, "wither'd Empires," and war and other calamities, the poem reminds one of Thomas Gray's *Elegy Written in a Country Churchyard* (1750) though the poem lacks the complexity of Gray's poem. The speaker realizes that all tongues and symbols are useless before the power of death. Although Clive never names Christ in this poem—or in any poem in the volume—she alludes to Christ as the only one ever to escape the tomb. The poem ultimately suggests that those who grieve for their dead shall soon be soothed by Death themselves. Like most of the verse in the volume, this poem has lines that are marred by odd syntax or strained rhymes. A good example is provided by the lines of the verse "for my strained eye sought / For other limit to its width in vain," where "in vain" is misplaced, probably so that Clive could rhyme with "domain," two lines above.

The last line in the first stanza of "At Llyncmstraethy" is also difficult because of ambiguity: "And fain would seek beyond a calmer land" is problematic because of the placement of "beyond." Does the speaker want to seek beyond a calmer land or seek a calmer land beyond? The weakest of the nine, this poem also uses the image of the ship upon the sea of life in its reflection that the speaker is weary of life's battles and would like to have eternal rest. Similarly, in "Starlight," the twenty-line opening poem in the volume, the speaker thinks of death but is somewhat comforted by the realization that he or she senses around the home fire the presence of dead friends now at peace. As does "At Llyncmstraethy," this poem reveals a speaker's struggle to find the path of eternal rest. The speaker's one comfort is the realization that he or she is "not without a guide."

Also elegiac are the remaining three poems, "Former Home," "Heart's Ease," and "Frontispiece of an Album. Filled with Works of Art of Three Sisters for Their Mother." "Former Home" is seventeen four-line stanzas of iambic tetrameter with alternating lines rhyming. The male speaker is visiting a childhood scene, comparing the changes in the natural scene since his early life there and the changes in himself since childhood. He recalls how as a boy he had hoped to have a life of "Glory, Faith, and Truth" but now realizes that his youthful idealism has given way in the face of "sin and time." The poem ends with a desperate apostrophe: "Ah, paint old feelings, rock sublime, / Speak life's fresh accents, mountain flood!"

"Heart's Ease" is an apostrophe to the flower of that name, a plea that it renew the speaker and that it "change the past" and bring again youth and hope. As the speaker holds the leaves of the flower to her breast, she sees them wither and realizes that she will not have ease from her suffering. This poem, six stanzas of iambic pentameter lines, alternately rhyming, is the best in the volume, in spite of its plentiful abstractions and few concrete images. The sincere questioning and longing of the speaker give it a kind of emotional power lacking in the other poems, and it avoids the wrenched syntax and presumably unintended ambiguities found elsewhere.

"Frontispiece of an Album," the poem that ends the volume, is the strongest piece, though it is omitted from many subsequent editions. This single-stanza, twelve-line poem arranged in three quatrains begins:

> As on a lake the water-flow'rs arise,
> Nurs'd by its bosom to the forms they wear,
> And floating o'er it, paint it with their dyes,
> And shed a tribute of their perfume there;
> So, mother, by thy cares all gently brought
> From the dark nothingness of infancy....

The poem's emotional restraint gives it power and interest, and it avoids the poor versification and rhymes found in most of the poems in Clive's first volume.

In 1841 Clive published a revised and enarged edition of *IX Poems. By V,* which included nine additional poems. Most of these are about death though several also explore kinds of love. "The Mosel," fourteen four-line stanzas, is about the power of romantic love to alter memory. The speaker describes a day's outing on the Mosel River alone with the boatman and "mine own dear friend," sharing the joyous sensations of being in nature and of feeling part of the natural order. At the end the speaker addresses the river, saying that if the future brings happiness, looking back on this day will give great pleasure, but if the future brings sorrow, remembering this day will evoke sadness. Presumably the speaker is defining that happy future in terms of the likelihood that he or she will still be in the company of the friend. Although one could consider this poem a statement about friendship, the poem's tone seems more romantic. It likely reflects Clive's own feelings about her experience in the spring of 1840, when she and her future husband, traveling together through the Rhine valley, spent the day in a boat on the Mosel River.

Two of the additions, both titled "Bessy," also concern love, perhaps romantic love. Both poems imagine scenes with the title character, who is dead. The relationship between Bessy and the speaker is not clear; however, the speaker clearly longs for her companion's company. In the first poem, hearing a song often sung by Bessy brings on a flood of scenes in the speaker's mind of Bessy at the hearth, singing and laughing. The second poem describes Bessy as having a "radiant bloom" and "laughing wile." The speaker reasons that grief for Bessy should have diminished with time but that it often appears in tears and "thoughts unworded."

Similar to the "Bessy" poems in its theme about the pain of separation by death is "We Two Have Sate and Sung Together." The speaker feels a sense of deep loss when remembering the past, but this poem focuses less on the loss than on the possibility of the two friends being reunited in death. The strong part of the poem is in the fifth and sixth stanzas, where the speaker imagines the now-dead friend viewing the speaker's death. Similar in their themes but less effective are "Death, Death! Oh! Amiable, Lovely Death!" and "Maesyneudd. On the Shore of a Small Lake Above the House." The latter poem both looks forward to death as a glorious end for those who have suffered earthly affliction and celebrates the virtues of a quiet life removed from striving for the trappings of fortune.

The first poem among the new works is "Youth and Age (Part II)," which seems to be a companion to "Youth Took One Summer Day His

Clive, circa 1860

Lyre," published in the 1840 *IX Poems by V*. The 1840 poem focuses on Youth's recognition that both Youth and Age are part of life. Unlike the earlier poem, in which Youth celebrates the virtue of Age in withstanding life's grief, here Age's sadness at the death of Youth is lessened by his realization that he can bear this death with patience and a "quiet mood," knowing that soon he will come "near the shore / Where friends who meet shall part no more." Among the few concrete and original images in the poem is a striking extended simile:

> As streams engulph'd in yawning caves,
> Will foam and strive before they cease:
> Not like the lapse of quiet waves,
> Uniting with the Seas in peace.
> His lip, erewhile so fresh and red,
> Was ghastly white as is the dead.

However, the power of the few original and vital images is diluted in the poem by many abstractions and threadbare images.

The two most imaginative additions are "Invitation After Pulling Down and Rebuilding a House" and "The Lady." "Invitation," comprising two four-line stanzas, is the only poem in the volume that has even a suggestion of humor. It addresses the ghosts dispossessed of their dwelling place after the speaker's house has been demolished, inviting them to "flit, old Ghosts, and live with me" and watch for the "companion Ghosts" sure to inhabit the new house eventually. "The Lady" is a ten-stanza ballad that, as a note explains, was set to music as "The Old English Lady" by the Chevalier Neukomm. The poem simply describes an old lady who lives in wealth and cares for her tenants and neighbors so generously that when she dies they mourn her greatly. The poem ends by stating that the tombstone will never be moved and "That childless Lady was the last / Of her old name and race," suggesting that neither wealth nor good deeds can save one from the grave.

Clive's next work, *I Watched the Heavens: A Poem* (1842), is a fifty-eight-page canto, presumably part of an unfinished, larger work. The male speaker, looking at the night sky, sees a star and imagines that it is "some new world, all fresh and bright / With its ten thousand hopes, and not one fear." When the speaker is inexplicably transported there, he finds a world that appears to be like Earth but is, in fact, a place without death. A manlike spirit urges the speaker to return to the Earth, "man's happiest dream to know– / Dream thou shalt die." As he surveys this new world, the speaker finds that even there, the beings have divided themselves into torturers and the tortured. They have built great monuments to pride and torn them down again in boredom, and some have attempted to introduce time into this timeless world.

The most alarming discovery, however, is that the inhabitants have built tombs even though they can never die: "Whatever told of death they copied there." They also lie in the tombs, longing for death. The speaker meets a distraught spirit who mourns for all eternity the lover from whom he has been separated by death. A female specter tells about the loss of her firstborn child in infancy and her unbounded grief. She says she has learned that "Grief to human soul is like the breeze / What wafts the bark, that lengthen'd calms would sink, / In triumph home across the conquered seas!" The canto ends with her statement that death is a minor part of a life whose "future home is all the breadth of space."

Clive's choice of a mother as the final speaker is interesting in light of the fact that her own children were born in 1842 and 1843. During this early part of her marriage she was writing steadily and leading an active social life which allowed her to meet such writers as Walter Savage Landor, Harriet Martineau, Mary Russell Mitford, and Elizabeth Barrett Browning. The Clives, well-read and sophisticated conversationalists, enjoyed playing cards, reading aloud to one another, attending art exhibitions, and traveling, both in England and on the Continent. During this period she wrote two unusual works, one a lengthy and gruesome story, "The Great Drought," which appeared in *Blackwood's* in December 1844, and *Saint Oldooman: A Myth of the Nineteenth Century, Contained in a Letter from the Bishop of Verculanem to the Lord Drayton* (1845), a satirical attack on the Oxford Movement.

The Queen's Ball: A Poem, a brief and intriguing volume, appeared in 1847. A prefatory note suggests that a comment in a friend's letter gave Clive the idea for the poem: "I hear that one hundred and fifty people were invited to the ball, last Friday, who are dead." The poem describes a ball attended by spirits of the dead whose names, presumably, had been inadvertently left on the invitation list. The deity who allows the spirits to attend the ball is Pluto, a surprising choice for a poet whose poems generally refer to Christianity, though not blatantly.

The poem describes the spirit of a dead girl who has left her lover alive. Now she sees him enjoying the "fair and gay," heedless of the past. Next, the spirit of "the guest of guests," one always in demand on social occasions, is gratified to hear that he is remembered still in the conversation of friends. Another ghost, that of an old woman, sees her jewels worn by a young replacement, and the spirit of a mother, dead only six months, looks into the face of her beautiful daughter to find no real sorrow. Still another ghost hears his heir reveling in his newfound wealth. The last ghost is that of a man who sees a woman; when alive the two had been "actors in a fearful scene" though the poem does not explain their past. However, as the living woman shines amid the glamor of the ball, she suddenly thinks of the dead man: "Herself, and him, and all that lay / Behind in that eventful day, / And what was done and suffer'd then." The most disappointing part of the poem is the abrupt and silly couplet with which it ends: "More Ghosts! I know their stories well, / But stories more, I will not tell."

The Valley of the Rea (1851) and *The Morlas: A Poem* (1853), Clive's next two books, approach the subject of death in strikingly different ways. *The Valley of the Rea* is a fourteen-page narrative poem prefaced by an apostrophe to the Rea, a "little stream which rises in the Brown Clee-hills and falls into the Teme," according to the headnote. Vaguely medieval in setting and tone, the poem centers on the tragically thwarted love of Mabel and Reuben. Through a series of misinterpreted communications, Reuben allows Mabel to think that her indifference to him has driven him off to war, and to almost certain death. He means to let her know the next day that his threats to go to war were just a ruse to test her, but when he arrives at Mabel's house the next day, he learns that in despair she has drowned herself, clutching a ribbon he had given her. Some of the poem's power and interest comes from its understatement and restraint by the unnamed third-person narrator.

The Morlas, on the other hand, a fifty-nine page, first-person narration, is largely descriptive and philosophical. Although Clive's headnote says she worked on the poem "all the best years of my life," it is not as interesting as either *The Valley of the Rea* or Clive's earlier poems. The narrator discovers a remote and beautiful glade where he hopes to "soothe my labour-harassed mind." He is struck by the idea that this natural scene is never changing, in contrast to the flux of human generations, ever dy-

Clive's husband, the Reverend Archer Clive, in 1862

ing and being born. As he finds himself in a melancholic mood, he hears the voice of a spirit who tells him that these melancholic thoughts have been common to many others sitting in the same spot. The Spirit of the Valley says it will tell the man about some of the other people, now phantoms, who were "actors of a common scene," which he further explains: "A thousand tales their doom has told, / But one conclusion ended all. / Death waited still by ev'ry path." The spirit says that often the suffering mortals who have sought comfort in his haunts have prayed to him, but "A holier shrine receiv'd their pray'r" and bore "the tribute up to Heaven." Hearing the spirit say that human life is short and that people must decide to enjoy or endure it, the speaker "stood amaz'd with happiness, / A stranger to his own new-bliss."

Clive's next work, and the one for which she was best known in her lifetime, is the novel *Paul Ferroll*, which appeared to wide acclaim in England in 1855. *Paul Ferroll* was so widely read that the title pages of Clive's subsequently published verse often identified her as the author of *Paul Ferroll*. In an 1897 essay discussing Clive's novels, Adeline Ser-

geant says that *Paul Ferroll* is the "precursor of the purely sensational novel, or of what may be called the novel of mystery." She argues that it differs from Charlotte Brontë's *Jane Eyre* (1847) because Brontë was interested in character whereas Clive pays no attention to motive. In 1860 Clive's *Why Paul Ferroll Killed His Wife* appeared; a much weaker work than *Paul Ferroll*, it describes the events leading up to the action in the earlier novel. Of her other two novels, *Year After Year: A Tale* (1858) and *John Greswold*, the first is more highly regarded. An attack on the insurance business, *Year After Year* perhaps reflects Clive's frustration over a long-running suit to force payment of her brother's life insurance. *John Greswold* is, according to Sergeant, "the autobiography of a young man who has very little story to tell and does not know how to tell it."

In 1856 Saunders and Otley published *Poems, by the Author of "Paul Ferroll," Including a New Edition of IX Poems by V, with Former and Recent Additions*. It incorporates *The Queen's Ball, I Watched the Heavens, The River Rea,* and *The Valley of the Morlas,* each of which had been previously published in single volumes. The volume also reprints eight of the original *IX Poems,* omitting only "Frontispiece of an Album," and it includes only four poems from the 1841 edition: "The Mosel," "Death, Death! Oh! Amiable, Lovely Death!," "We Two Have Sate and Sung Together," and "The Lady." The eight new poems are "Written for a Friend Who Wished to Have in Verse the Persian Sentence," "A Last Day," "I'm Young, and It Is Early," "Age," "Adon," "The Half-Way House," "A Fragment," and "Venice, 1853."

Of the new poems in the volume, "A Last Day" poignantly reveals the emotions of a speaker watching the last fire in her fireplace before leaving her house for a new dwelling. This poem perhaps grew out of Clive's experiences when in 1845 her husband inherited the Clive family estate, Whitfield, left the clergy, and moved the family from Solihull parish. "I'm Young, and It Is Early," spoken by one who is going blind, is unusual because it is iambic hexameter, not Clive's usual shorter lines. "The Half-Way House," like "Adon" and "Age," is about crossing the threshold of death. The implicit contrast between age and youth is central to several poems in the first two volumes of Clive's poems.

The longest of the new poems is "Venice, 1853," an eighteen-page description (in rhymed couplets) of the city by a speaker who is viewing it from a gondola. The speaker is particularly moved by St. Mark's and the Rizzi Palace, where the poor now inhabit the former halls of splendor. The poem celebrates the history and beauty of Venice, described as "Transparent, clear-cut, delicate, / Like cameo, on an opal set." "Venice" was one of Clive's poems according to the 1917 edition of the *Cambridge History of English Literature,* which states that "few [of Clive's poems] will be found unsatisfactory, unless the reader's nature, or his mood, be out of key with them."

Writing in the *Edinburgh Review* (October 1856), an unnamed reviewer of this 1856 volume compares Clive's poems to those of Matthew Arnold, but without giving much evidence for the claim: "Not unlike the poems of Matthew Arnold, for quality and style, are the poems by 'V.'" The reviewer finds that the description in Clive's poems "displays that coexistence of the synthetic and analytic modes of looking at things, the general want of which is the great defect of most modern poetry, even of a high class." Singling out "The Valley of the Morlas" as the best poem in the volume, the reviewer says that its effect is difficult to describe because it results from "the sustained loftiness and individuality of moral tone, which more or less distinguish all the verses of 'V' from the ordinary poetry of the day."

Little is known about Clive's literary efforts during the 1860s. Following the marriage of their daughter, Alice, in 1862, Clive and her husband traveled frequently. On a trip to Rome in 1865 she suffered a paralytic stroke and was taken to Cannes to recuperate. In Cannes their son, Meysey, met Lady Katharine Fielding, the woman he later married. Dates on some poems make it clear that Clive continued to write during this period, publishing *Poems by V., Author of "Paul Ferroll," Including the "IX Poems"* in 1872, the year before her death.

This volume contains twelve new poems, many written during the 1860s and one written in 1842. The early poem, "The Mother," is spoken by a woman who fears that her child will be stillborn and is comforted only by realizing that if it were, it would nevertheless rise on the last day. This poem likely reveals Clive's own apprehension about childbirth, fears compounded by the fact that both of her children were born when she was in her early forties. Her diary during this period records some surprisingly explicit thoughts about her pregnancies.

Three others of the new poems are especially interesting: "The Crab Tree" and "An August Evening, 1865" because of their delicate lyricism and "Beaten to Death" for its grotesque power. It imagines what a mother must be feeling after hearing that her child, whom she thinks is being safely cared for at boarding school, has been beaten so savagely by a teacher that the child suffers horribly for two hours after the beating and then dies. This poem was based on a news story Clive had read in *The Times* (London).

The 1890 *Poems by V. Including the IX Poems,* edited by Clive's daughter, Alice Greathed, went largely unnoticed by critics as did the one twentieth-century attempt to kindle interest in her work—Eric Partridge's 1928 edition of *IX Poems by V.* E. G. Twitchell, who reviewed Partridge's edition in *The London Mercury* (November 1928), ridiculed Clive for "doing her best all the time to fall into male attitudes." Further, he found Clive's poems "unusually crude in feeling and often melodramatic," praising them only to the extent that "she treated her unalterably grim subjects with earnestness if not with sincerity." He speculated about whether or not the young Thomas Hardy might have known Clive's work.

This scathing review shows the degree to which poetic taste had changed by 1928. What had been acceptable and even praiseworthy verse to many Victorian readers was less acceptable as Edwardian tastes became modern. Partridge's fourteen-page introduction to the 1928 volume is the most comprehensive treatment of Clive's literary career. He says that Clive's work is somewhat similar to that of Elizabeth Barrett Browning and even more like that of the French poet Louise Ackermann. Few would argue with Partridge's assessment that, although Clive is "not indeed of the first rank," she had more skill than some poets who are better known. Clive's religious sensibility, her narrow range of subject matter, and her limited ability with versification make it unlikely that her poems will undergo a revival of interest.

Bibliographies:
"Bibliographical," *Academy,* 61 (July–December 1901): 6;
"Bibliographical," *Academy,* 62 (January–June 1902): 78.

Biography:
Mary Clive, ed., *Caroline Clive, from the Diary and Family Papers of Mrs. Archer Clive, 1801–1873* (London: Bodley Head, 1949).

References:
"Mrs. Archer Clive," *Athenaeum* (19 July 1873): 84;
"New Poets," *Edinburgh Review,* 104 (October 1856): 173–186;
Adeline Sergeant, "Mrs. Crowe. Mrs. Archer Clive. Mrs. Henry Wood," in *Women Novelists of Queen Victoria's Reign: A Book of Appreciations* (London: Hurst & Blackett, 1897).

Sara Coleridge

(22 December 1802 – 3 May 1852)

Daniel Robinson
Widener University

BOOKS: *Pretty Lessons in Verse for Good Children; with Some Lessons in Latin, in Easy Rhyme,* anonymous (London: J. W. Parker, 1834);

Phantasmion, anonymous (London: William Pickering, 1837); republished as *Phantasmion: Prince of Palmland,* edited by Grenville Mellen, 2 volumes (New York: Samuel Coleman, 1839); republished as *Phantasmion, A Fairy Tale,* with an introduction by John Duke Coleridge, first Baron Coleridge (London: Henry S. King, 1874; Boston: Roberts, 1874).

OTHER: Martin Dobrizhöffer, *An Account of the Abipones, an Equestrian People of Paraguay,* translated by Sara Coleridge (London: John Murray, 1822);

[Jacques de Mailles?], *The Right Joyous and Pleasant History of the Feats, Gests, and Prowesses of the Chevalier Bayard, the Good Knight without Fear and without Reproach, By The Loyal Servant,* 2 volumes, translated by Sara Coleridge (London: John Murray, 1825); republished in 1 volume (London: G. Newnes / New York: Scribners, 1906);

Samuel Taylor Coleridge, *The Literary Remains of Samuel Taylor Coleridge,* edited by Henry Nelson Coleridge and Sara Coleridge, 4 volumes (London: William Pickering, 1836–1839; New York: Harper, 1853);

Samuel Taylor Coleridge, *Aids to Reflection in the Formation of a Manly Character,* edited by Henry Nelson Coleridge, introduction by Sara Coleridge, 2 volumes (London: William Pickering, 1843);

Samuel Taylor Coleridge, *Biographia Literaria,* edited, with an introduction, by Sara Coleridge, 2 volumes (London: William Pickering, 1847);

Samuel Taylor Coleridge, *Notes and Lectures upon Shakespeare and Some of the Old Poets and Dramatists With Other Literary Remains,* edited by Sara Coleridge, 2 volumes (London: William Pickering, 1849; New York: Harper, 1853);

Samuel Taylor Coleridge, *Essays on His Own Times; Forming a Second Series of The Friend,* edited by Sara Coleridge, 3 volumes (London: William Pickering, 1850);

Samuel Taylor Coleridge, *The Poems of Samuel Taylor Coleridge,* edited by Derwent Coleridge and Sara Coleridge (London: Edward Moxon, 1852).

Sara Coleridge's considerable efforts to rehabilitate and preserve for the Victorian period the literary reputation of her father, Samuel Taylor Coleridge, have tended to overshadow her achievements as a poet in her own right. With her husband, Henry Nelson Coleridge (also her cousin), she prepared editions of all of her father's important works, often prefixing introductory essays that demonstrate her critical acumen and devotion to her father's literary legacy. Like her brother Hartley, who enjoyed moderate success as a sonneteer, Sara Coleridge lived in her father's shadow but without the intense disappointment and resentment that haunted the self-destructive, alcoholic Hartley. As her biographer Bradford Keyes Mudge notes, she was an accomplished essayist as well as a competent editor. Her poetic instincts, moreover, were keen, and she recognized the passionate and even erotic nature of her father's poetry. While not prolific in comparison with many of her contemporaries, Sara Coleridge demonstrated something of the poetic genius that ran in her blood, particularly evident in her wildly fantastic fairy tale, *Phantasmion* (1837), a novel that includes much of her best poetry. She also published a successful volume of poetry for children, *Pretty Lessons in Verse for Good Children; with Some Lessons in Latin, in Easy Rhyme* (1834), which ran through five editions. Although Virginia Woolf, commenting on her in 1940, was disappointed by her unfulfilled potential, calling her an "unfinished masterpiece," Sara Coleridge's achievements, like those of Dorothy Wordsworth, sister to William, though meager in comparison to their more famous relatives, stand on their own merits and suggest that

*Sara Coleridge, circa 1827; an engraving based on a painting by
Charlotte Jones (from the frontispiece for Edith Coleridge's*
Memoir and Letters of Sara Coleridge, *1873)*

the mind behind them fulfilled its own intellectual enterprise.

Born on 22 December 1802 at Greta Hall, Keswick, Sara Coleridge was the fourth child born to Samuel Taylor Coleridge and his wife, Sara Fricker Coleridge. Their youngest child and only daughter, she grew up without knowing her father, who, though he was absent for her birth and for most of her life, considered her an intelligent child and, later, a capable woman. The estrangement of her parents from one another impressed her deeply but did not deter her subsequent loyalty to her father. As precocious as her brother Hartley, she did grow up, however, under the influence of her father's most famous literary friends. In addition to the encouragement of her mother, her uncle, poet Robert Southey, whom she affectionately called "fat Sall," contributed greatly to her education by giving her access to his fine library. Though he later considered her something of a bluestocking, William Wordsworth, who had collaborated with her father

on *Lyrical Ballads* (1798) but later grew distant from his friend, did not allow his own differences with Samuel Taylor Coleridge to interfere with his esteem for the young Sara and his encouragement of her educational pursuits, which, despite her persistent poor health, included learning Latin, Italian, French, and Spanish (later Greek and German) as well as music. Years later, Sara Coleridge, poignantly and somewhat ironically, would dedicate her edition of her father's *Biographia Literaria* (1847) to Wordsworth, referring to herself as his "Child in heart and faithful Friend." Although Samuel Taylor Coleridge seldom came home, Sara met, at Greta Hall, such literary notables as Sir Walter Scott, Thomas De Quincey, and Charles Lamb, who were impressed by her beauty and intelligence.

Because of her father's chronic indigence, Sara Coleridge began her first literary effort in an attempt to raise money to send her brother Derwent to Cambridge. Though her brother eventually found a patron in J. H. Frere, Coleridge assiduously

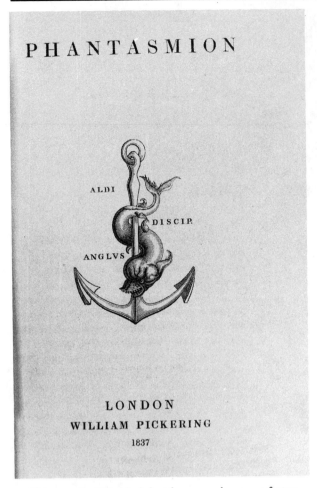

PHANTASMION

ALDI

DISCIP.

ANGLVS

LONDON
WILLIAM PICKERING
1837

Title page for Coleridge's best-known work, a prose fantasy

completed her translation of Martin Dobrizhöffer's *Historia de Abiponibus* (1784), finding a publisher in John Murray. Upon the anonymous publication of *An Account of the Abipones, an Equestrian People of Paraguay* in early 1822, Sara Coleridge was a professional author at age nineteen; although it did attract her father's notice and impressed Southey and Lamb, the book was only a modest success. Moreover, while Hartley tended to discourage his sister's literary ambitions, Derwent formed with his sister an intellectual affinity that would last most of their lives as a result of this particular endeavor. During this year, much to the distress of the entire Coleridge family, Hartley ignominiously left Oxford under a dark cloud, charged with habitual drunkenness, and Derwent performed poorly on his examinations at Cambridge. Sara, however, spent a quiet three weeks in Highgate, London, with her father. While in London she made the acquaintance of her accomplished first cousin Henry Nelson Coleridge. A graduate of King's College, Cambridge, and a future barrister, her cousin Henry impressed her so much that they secretly became engaged. Shortly after returning home, in poor health and feeling the strain of her separation from her beloved and guilt over their stealth, Sara began a lifelong addiction to opium—an illness she shared with her father and that was not unlike her brother Hartley's alcoholism. Her impaired health, however, did not deter Sara from completing a more ambitious literary project, a translation from the medieval French of the elaborately detailed memoirs of the Chevalier Bayard, a sixteenth-century knight. Murray published the book in 1825, but Southey, concerned for her health, discouraged her from publishing another book for the time being.

Despite confessing to her brother Derwent some anxiety over her imminent nuptials, Sara married Henry Nelson Coleridge on 3 September 1829, after a six-year engagement. Wordsworth's eldest son, John, officiated. The couple moved to Hampstead, not far from her father's home. The next year would find Coleridge pregnant and yearning for her mother, who dutifully took up residence to assist with the baby. Her son, Herbert, was born in October 1830, followed within two years by a daughter, Edith, who was born in July 1832. In 1834 Sara and Henry suffered through the deaths of infant twins; Sara, again suffering from depression and severe anxiety, found relief in writing and opium.

The same year, J. W. Parker published Coleridge's only volume of poetry, *Pretty Lessons in Verse, for Good Children,* which she had composed for Herbert and Edith. The book was influenced by the children's poetry of Ann and Jane Taylor, whose famous poem "The Star" ("Twinkle, twinkle, little star") had appeared in their hugely successful *Original Poems for Infant Minds* (1804). Coleridge admired their poetry but found the moral lessons bleak and disturbing, resolving that her volume should have only happy, positive messages. The book went through five editions in five years—no small success. Most of the poems are simplistic lessons in Latin vocabulary, English history, world geography, the months of the years, and the days of the week. "Good Things from Distant Places," for example, teaches children that: "Tea is brought from China / Rice from Carolina, / India and Italy— / Countries far beyond the sea." Coleridge addresses several poems to her son, under such titles as "To Herbert, When Objected to a Walk," "Herbert and His New Crib, A Present from a Lady," and "Herbert's Beverage." Coleridge herself was ambivalent about the book despite its success; her brother Derwent openly disdained the verse as doggerel.

As do the Taylors' poems or, for that matter, the poems in William Blake's *Songs of Innocence and*

Experience (1794), Coleridge's poems for children sometimes demonstrate an adult complexity. "Poppies," for instance, frankly contrasts young Herbert's delight in the beautiful flowers—"they to him are nothing more / Than other brilliant weeds"—with his mother's much less innocent reverie:

> O how should'st thou with beaming brow
> With eye and cheek so bright,
> Know aught of that gay blossom's power,
> Or sorrows of the night?
>
> When poor Mama long restless lies,
> She drinks the poppy's juice;
> That liquor soon can close her eyes,
> And slumber soft produce:
>
> O then my sweet, my happy boy
> Will thank the Poppy-flower,
> Which brings the sleep to dear Mama,
> At midnight's darksome hour.

Coleridge's candid depiction of her opium addiction offended her family, given her father's struggle with the drug, and she later regretted publishing the poem. Recalling her father's poem "The Pains of Sleep" (1816), "Poppies" provides a remarkable insight into Coleridge's "sorrows of the night" as mother, as opium addict, and as poet and into the ways in which addiction may be shared by father and daughter and powerfully expressed through poetry.

One poem in the volume, "The Nightingale," specifically takes up Coleridge's father's poem of the same title from the 1798 *Lyrical Ballads.* It reiterates the ways in which melancholy poets of the past have misinterpreted the song of the nightingale through their own melancholy emotional perception. Samuel Taylor Coleridge asserts in his poem that nothing in nature is melancholy, that only "some night-wandering Man" tortured by his own grief hears the bird's song as sad; Sara Coleridge borrows her father's line to address her own children and similarly correct this view: "No, 'tis the merry Nightingale . . . ." This poem has an additional layer of biographical complexity in the implicit recognition on Sara Coleridge's part that, like her, her father wrote the poem to impart such wisdom to his son Hartley, who appears at the end of "The Nightingale" of 1798 accompanied by his father's prayer that he be brought up as "Nature's playmate." Painfully aware of her father's absence, Coleridge concedes in her poem that the nightingale sings mournfully, like other birds, only when cruel little boys rob her nest: she asks, "What mother would not weep and cry / To lose

her precious darling?" Unlike her father's poem, Coleridge's poem recognizes, through allusion, that, for whatever reason, parents do become estranged from their children; from a new perspective she sees how painful it is for the parent as well as for the child.

Coleridge was deeply grieved but not surprised by her father's death in 1834, shortly after the publication of *Pretty Lessons in Verse.* The event determined the course the rest of her life would take. With her husband's aid and support, she committed herself to defending his reputation, which had been steadily deteriorating for years and now suffered, in addition to a general consensus that his work was incoherent at best, new attacks on his moral character, including the public's morbid fascination with his opium addiction and accusations of plagiarism by Thomas De Quincey. In an unpublished poem titled "To My Father on His Lines Called 'Work without Hope,'" written sometime between 1825 and 1845, Coleridge identifies with the personal note of despair and failure in her father's sonnet "Work Without Hope" (1825). Ironically invoking the Petrarchan language of poetic aspiration, her poem looks forward to her father's canonization as a great poet and to her own role in protecting his fame while admitting the defeat of her own poetic aspirations in the painful recognition of his disappointments. As her father's literary executor Coleridge turned her attention away from her own compositions to the editing, annotating, and introducing of his literary remains. She and her husband, while doing much to rehabilitate Samuel Taylor Coleridge's public image and to explain and interpret his work, did his literary fame the greatest service by keeping his work in print for most of the nineteenth century. By the twentieth century, due in large part to his daughter's efforts, Samuel Taylor Coleridge was firmly installed in the literary canon.

While Henry prepared his edition of her father's *Table Talk* (1835), Coleridge busied herself with transcribing her father's marginalia and notes and with raising their two children. Despite her persistent ill health, she wrote *Phantasmion* primarily for Herbert and Edith's enjoyment but revised it considerably for publication in 1837. Ostensibly a fairy tale, *Phantasmion* concerns the adventures of the title character, a young prince, who is given the wings of a fairy and who pursues the beautiful Iarine. Unlike most fairy tales however, the book also develops mature themes of parental death, sexual seduction, violence, murder, and metaphysical evil. Coleridge wrote to her hus-

Drawings by George Richmond of Coleridge's son, Herbert, in 1848, and her daughter, Edith, in 1850 (Harry Ransom Humanities Research Center, The University of Texas at Austin)

band in a letter of 29 September 1837 that she hoped the book would help children develop their imaginative capacities while treating "human hopes, and fears, and passions, and interests, and of those changeful events and varying circumstances to which human life is liable." Interpolated lyrical poetry throughout the story develops the characters and their motivations, juxtaposing serious and whimsical tones and demonstrating the palpable influence of her father's poetry in the use of synaesthesia to evoke a world of passions, dreams, and the imagination. Like much of her father's poetry, Coleridge's *Phantasmion* resists the determinacy of allegorical interpretation, urging a more subjective, imaginative reading.

In June of 1837 *Phantasmion* was published anonymously by William Pickering, the publisher who brought out Coleridge's editions of her father's work. Unsure of the book's merits, Coleridge nonetheless recognized a critical tendency to dismiss works of the genre: she wrote in a letter on 29 July 1837 that she understood that "to print a Fairy Tale is the very way to be *not read,* but shoved aside with contempt." Like many of her contemporaries, such as her father, Scott, and Lamb, she believed that fairy tales in general were beneficial to the development of the intellect and

imagination. Reviews were mixed. In the September 1840 issue of the *Quarterly Review* one reviewer recognized the generic hybridity of *Phantasmion* and its originality, pointing out that the book "is not a poem, but it is poetry from beginning to end, and has many poems within it." The reviewer goes on to remark defensively that *Phantasmion* "is one of a race that has particularly suffered under the assaults of political economy and useful knowledge;—a Fairy Tale, the last, we suppose, that will ever be written in England, and unique in its kind." Hartley Coleridge praised the book, claiming that it established his sister's precedence over all other women writers of the day, with the exception of poet and playwright Joanna Baillie. Although it was not widely influential, the book was published in the United States in 1839 and republished in both London and Boston with an introduction by John Duke Coleridge, first Baron Coleridge, in 1874.

Henry Nelson Coleridge died on 25 January 1843 after a prolonged illness of the spine that intensely distressed his wife. Coleridge subsequently renewed her commitment to republishing her father's work by studying the German philosopher Friedrich von Schelling in order to counter the persistent accusations of her father's plagiarism. For her 1847 edition of the *Biographia Literaria* Coleridge wrote a 180-page introductory essay defending the integrity and philosophical acuity of her father's vision. Though a poet herself, she devoted the last years of her life to a new edition of her father's poetry, upon which she collaborated with Derwent until her death from breast cancer on 3 May 1852. Arguably Coleridge's most significant contribution to Victorian poetry was her last project, *The Poems of Samuel Taylor Coleridge* (1852), because it offered the public a new perspective on one of the most important poets of the early nineteenth century. For this she deserves recognition and the gratitude of later readers and scholars. Although it may seem that she subjugated her own literary ambitions to the preservation of her father's fame, Coleridge nonetheless pursued her endeavors with a tenacity and resolve that her father lacked. Scholars have consistently found the individual figures of the Coleridge family fascinating for the insight their lives and careers offer. More recently, feminist archival recoveries of women writers of the Romantic and Victorian periods have paid particular attention to Sara Coleridge not merely to lament her untapped potential but to study her remarkable achievements as a poet, editor, and professional author as well as the extent to which she participated, along with scores of other women, in a feminine Romanticism decidedly different from that more famously associated with her father and his male contemporaries.

Letters:

Leslie Nathan Broughton, ed., *Sara Coleridge and Henry Reed: Reed's Memoir of Sara Coleridge, Her Letters to Reed, Including Her Comment on His Memoir of Gray, Her Marginalia in Henry Crabb Robinson's Copy of Wordsworth's Memoirs* (Ithaca, N. Y: Cornell University Press /

London: H. Milford/Oxford University Press, 1937).

Biographies:

Edith Coleridge, *Memoir and Letters of Sara Coleridge,* 2 volumes (London: Henry S. King, 1873; New York: Harper, 1874);

Eleanor Towle, *A Poet's Children: Hartley and Sara Coleridge* (London: Methuen, 1912);

Earl Leslie Griggs, *Coleridge Fille: A Biography of Sara Coleridge* (London: Oxford University Press, 1940; Folcroft, Pa.: Folcroft Library Editions, 1973);

Bradford Keyes Mudge, *Sara Coleridge, A Victorian Daughter: Her Life and Essays* (New Haven: Yale University Press, 1989).

References:

Nathan Cervo, "Sara Coleridge: The Gigadibs Complex," *Victorian Newsletter,* 78 (Fall 1990): 3–9;

Katherine T. Meiners, "Reading Pain and the Feminine Body in Romantic Writing: The Examples of Dorothy Wordsworth and Sara Coleridge," *Centennial Review,* 37 (Fall 1993): 487–512;

Bradford Keyes Mudge, "Sara Coleridge: A Portrait from the Papers," *Library Chronicle of the University of Texas,* 23 (1983): 15–35;

Virginia Woolf, "Sara Coleridge," in her *Death of the Moth and Other Essays* (New York: Harcourt Brace, 1970), pp. 111–118.

Papers:

The Harry Ransom Humanities Research Center at The University of Texas at Austin holds many unpublished materials relating to Sara Coleridge, including manuscripts, journals, and correspondence.

Eliza Cook
(24 December 1818 – 23 September 1889)

Suzanne Ozment
The Citadel

BOOKS: *Lays of a Wild Harp* (London: Bennett, 1835);

Melaia and Other Poems (London: Wood, 1838; New York: Langley, 1842);

Poems, Second Series (London: Simpkin, Marshall, 1845);

The Poetical Works of Mary Howitt, Eliza Cook, and L. E. L. (Boston: Phillips & Sampson, 1849);

Jottings from My Journal (London: Routledge, Warne & Routledge, 1860);

New Echoes and Other Poems (London: Routledge, Warne & Routledge, 1864);

Diamond Dust (London: Pitman, 1865);

The Poetical Works of Eliza Cook (London: Warne, 1869; New York: Scribner, Welford & Armstrong, 1869; revised edition, New York: Crowell, 1882).

Collection: *The Eliza Cook Songster, Containing a Collection of Her Most Admired Ballads, and Many of the Most Popular Songs of the Day* (London: Ryle, n.d.).

OTHER: *Eliza Cook's Journal,* edited by Cook, 1849–1854.

When Eliza Cook died on 23 September 1889, *The Times* (London) noted that many readers would be surprised to learn "that she was alive but yesterday." Thirty years before, the obituary in *The Times* continues, her name had been "a household word." However, ill health had caused her to put down her pen and lead a more retired life; thus she had faded from public view. From the 1830s to the 1850s Cook's verses attracted favorable reviews and a wide readership in Great Britain and the United States and were well represented in the popular annuals of the day such as *Forget Me Not, The Keepsake of Friendship, The Young Ladies' Offering; or Gems of Prose and Poetry,* and *The Illustrated Ladies' Keepsake.*

Cook came from humble and inauspicious beginnings. She was born on 24 December 1818, the youngest of eleven children, to Joseph Cook, a London brazier and tinsmith. When she was nine years old her father retired and moved his family to a farm in Sussex. Almost entirely self-educated, Cook received support and encouragement from her mother. She began writing poetry as a girl and by the time she was fifteen had composed several of her most popular verses, including "Star of Glengary," a love lyric written in Scots dialect, and the sentimental "Lines to My Pony."

Cook published her first collection of verses, *Lays of a Wild Harp,* in 1835, when she was seventeen. Her poems, submitted anonymously, began to appear in such periodicals as *The Metropolitan Maga-*

zine, *The New Monthly Magazine,* and *The Weekly Dispatch.* The death of her mother when Eliza was about fifteen inspired the composition of several poems, including her most popular lyric, "The Old Armchair," which appeared in *The Weekly Dispatch* in 1837. In this poem the speaker takes a nostalgic tone as she laments her loss. She recalls the days when her mother graced "the hallowed seat" that now stands empty and recollects the "gentle words that mother would give; / To fit me to die, and teach me to live." The chair becomes a shrine consecrated to the memory of the idealized mother and worshiped by the bereft child: "But I love it, I love it; and cannot tear / My soul from a mother's old Arm-chair." When her second volume of poems, *Melaia and Other Poems* (1838), appeared in a second edition in 1840, the editors included a frontispiece showing Cook bending over "The Old Arm-Chair."

Over the course of her career Cook published nearly five hundred poems. *Poems, Second Series* appeared in 1845, and Cook's last collection of new verses, *New Echoes and Other Poems,* was issued in 1864. Most of her works celebrate home and hearth, natural beauty, friendship, and love. Some of them were set to music and became well-known songs, which were collected in *The Eliza Cook Songster.* The attraction of Cook's poetry to a popular audience is clear to see. Her poems consistently endorse middle-class virtues and values in traditional post-Romantic terms, seldom moving beyond sentimental commonplaces.

Predictable sentiments surface in narrative verses such as "Melaia," a poem set in ancient Greece. One evening an elderly stranger appears in the doorway of the studio of Melonian, a renowned sculptor, to commission a statue of his dog. At first offended by the idea of modeling such a lowly, ignoble subject, the sculptor is nonetheless intrigued by the request and asks to hear the old man's story. The stranger maintains he was once a king who rescued a wounded hound from the battlefield. His other strong attachment, he confesses, was to his "queenly bride," whom he describes as "My worshipped star, my joy, my pride." The attachment was not equally returned, however. By chance the king learns that his wife has dishonored him and allied herself with those who have plotted his murder. To escape certain death he leaves "Crown, sceptre, throne" to become "a friendless fugitive." His sole companion is his "gallant dog." Relentlessly pursued across the desert, Melaia is forced to advance on foot when his horse dies. Delirious, overcome by exhaustion and thirst, he collapses just after he sees his dog race away. The next thing he knows, the dog has returned with "A small and lifeless beast of

prey." The "raw repast" restores Melaia, who from that time on wanders the land, accompanied by Murkim, his "one friend," until at last the dog dies "Of sheer old age." The poem closes with a description of future visitors to Melonian's studio who pass by grand masterpieces to pause before the marble form of "a bold and couchant hound," inscribed "Melaia's Friend."

One of her short lyrics, "The Happy Mind," illustrates Cook's didactic tendencies through the voice of a speaker who scolds the malcontent and praises the obstinately cheerful:

> Out upon the calf, I say,
> Who turns his grumbling head away,
> And quarrels with his feed of hay
>   Because it is not clover.
> Give to me the happy mind,
> That will ever seek and find
> Something fair and something kind,
>   All the wide world over.

Similarly, in "Time" the moralizing speaker warns the young:

> Time is indeed a precious boon,
>   But with the boon a task is given;
> The heart must learn its duty well,
>   To man on earth and God in heaven.
> Take heed, then, play not with thine hours,
>   Beware, unthinking youth, beware!
> The one who acts the part he ought,
>   Will have but little time to spare.

Often the titles, borrowed from familiar platitudes, proclaim the poems' moral messages, as is the case with "Let Not the Seed of Anger Live," "Let Not the Sun Go Down upon Your Wrath," "Where There's a Will There's a Way," "Live and Let Live," and "Be Kind When You Can."

Cook's poetry was repeatedly praised for its simple, unadorned style. As Sarah Hale, author of the 1855 volume *Woman's Record; or, Sketches of All Distinguished Women from the Creation to A. D. 1854,* put it, "there is hardly a trace of labor or study in her poetry." Hale went on to quote an unidentified critic as saying of Cook

> There is a heartiness and truthful sympathy with human kind, a love of freedom and of nature in this lady's productions, which, more even than their grace and melody, charms her readers. She writes like a whole-souled woman, earnestly and unaffectedly, evidently giving her actual thoughts, but never transcending the limits of taste or delicacy. The favour with which her numerous pieces have been received, and the ease with which she writes, encourage us to hope for much future delight and instruction from her generous pen.

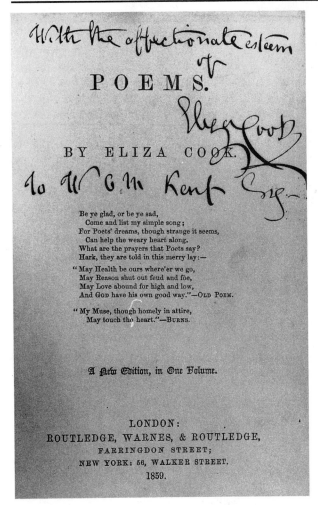

POEMS.

BY ELIZA COOK.

Be ye glad, or be ye sad,
   Come and list my simple song;
For Poets' dreams, though strange it seems,
   Can help the weary heart along.
What are the prayers that Poets say?—
Hark, they are told in this merry lay:—

" May Health be ours where'er we go,
   May Reason shut out feud and foe,
   May Love abound for high and low,
And GOD have his own good way."—OLD POEM.

" My Muse, though homely in attire,
   May touch the heart."—BURNS.

A New Edition, in One Volume.

LONDON:
ROUTLEDGE, WARNES, & ROUTLEDGE,
FARRINGDON STREET;
NEW YORK: 56, WALKER STREET.
1859.

Title page, inscribed by the author, for the first edition of Cook's collected verse (Collection of William B. Thesing)

illustrate further, in the Cook canon there are more than a dozen poems about Christmas, eighteen about time, eighteen more that take up patriotic themes, two dozen that contemplate death, two dozen about sailors and the sea, more than forty that consider love and friendship, and scores of others celebrating natural beauty or promoting traditional values and wholesome character traits.

Part of Cook's appeal seems to have been that she kept the image of herself as a "natural poet" constantly before her audience. Acknowledging herself untutored, she stated in the preface to *Poems, Second Series:*

I can only write from my heart, and that heart has been left from infancy to the mercy of its own intense impulses. My rhyming tendency developed itself at a very early age, but the tones of judicious praise, or improving censure, never met my ear. The advantage of an enlightened, nay even a common education was denied me, lest Knowledge should only serve to foster Poetry, and make "a sentimental fool" of me. I was left like a wild colt on the fresh and boundless common of Nature to pick up a mouthful of Truth where I could. The woods and forests became my tutors: the rippling stream and bulrush sighing in the wind whispered to me in sweet and gentle breathings: the silver stars in the measureless night-sky, and the bright flowers in my morning path awoke my wonder, and opened the portals that led to the high and mysterious temple of Thought. God and Creation were before my eyes in all their glory, and as an untaught child I worshipped the Being who had endowed me with power to contemplate his works, and "rejoice therein."

Four years later Cook prefaced the inaugural issue of *Eliza Cook's Journal* with "A Word to My Readers," in which she again described her initiation into a literary career, presenting herself as a simple, passionate child of nature:

My earliest rhymes, written from intuitive impulse, before hackneyed experience or politic judgment could dictate their tendency, were accepted and responded to by those whose good work is a "tower of strength." The first active breath of nature that swept over my heart strings, awoke wild but earnest melodies, which I dotted down in simple notes; and when I found that others thought the tune worth learning—when I heard my strains hummed about the sacred altars of domestic firesides, and saw old men, bright women, and young children scanning my ballad strains, then was I made to think that my burning desire to pour out my soul's measure of music was given for a purpose. My young bosom throbbed with rapture, for my feelings had met with responsive echoes from honest and genuine Humanity, and the glory of heaven seemed partially revealed, when I discovered that I held power over the affections of earth.

At the same time the critic notes the lack of polish in Cook's work: "It may be hoped, also, that she will take more pains in the finishing of her verses, than she has hitherto done, and avoid a repetition of ideas, a fault to which she is somewhat prone."

Without question, Cook was prone to dwell on favorite subjects and themes. For example, the titles of some of her many poems devoted to the seasons of the year indicate the narrowness of her range: "Winter Is Coming," "Winter Is Here," "Summer Is Nigh," "Summer's Farewell." A series of devotional lyrics borrow their titles and messages from the Lord's Prayer: "Hallowed Be Thy Name," "Thy Kingdom Come," and "Thy Will Be Done." The formulaic approach is also evident in verses such as "The Old Farm-Gate," "The Old Water-Mill," "The Old Mill-Stream," and "Old Story Books," in which predictable objects and sites become the subjects of clichéd nostalgic reflection. To

In "The Poet's Heart," one of several lyrics about poets and the writing of poetry, Cook gives thanks for her literary gift:

> I would not lose the poet power
> That feels the thorn and sees the flower
> With sharper thrust, and gladder mirth,
> Than more undreaming ones of earth.
> No, not for worlds would I resign
> This fond, weak, poet-heart of mine.

Cook targeted middle- and working-class readers and proudly defended her role as a poet of the people. In the preface to *Poems, Second Series* she quotes a reviewer of her earlier works who condemned her as "a poet of and for the lower classes." "Did he dream of the compliment he paid me?" asks Cook. "Surely it is no mean end to lay fast hold on sentiments unwarped by classic learning, and excite sympathy with feelings that live in simple bosoms, deep, strong, and unbiassed [sic]." Referring to other literary masters from humble origins—Robert Burns, William Shakespeare, John Milton, Geoffrey Chaucer—Cook finds herself in good company. In an effort to ensure circulation of her poems among lower-income readers Cook published an economical reprint of her works, asserting that she would be as pleased "in meeting the plain book on the deal table of the mechanic as in finding myself richly bedight in the boudoirs of the wealthy." Much critical praise was focused on her uplifting influence on a popular audience. At the turn of the century John H. Ingram contended that "She carried pathos and true sentiment into hearts and homes where little but vulgarity and commonplaceness dwelt."

While critics such as Ingram praised her for penning verses "filled with sympathy for the downtrodden and helpless, the earth-weary and oppressed," her sympathy is expressed in orthodox terms. Though she may condemn materialism and satirize social pretension, and though she may endorse the spread of knowledge and promote philanthropy, her verses are not calculated to be deeply unsettling. Cook's poems about work are illustrative. Even those sympathetic to the plight of the working poor and critical of the privileged classes nonetheless call for devotion to duty, self-denial, and humility on the part of the laborer until reforms are effected.

In "The Poor Man to His Son" a father, insisting that all work is honorable, urges his son to strive diligently and accept his place in life:

> Work, work, my boy, be not afraid,
>   Look Labor boldly in the face;

> Take up the hammer or the spade,
>   And blush not for your humble place.

Echoing the principles of Thomas Carlyle, the father tells the son to be satisfied if he can but earn remuneration sufficient to keep on working:

> God grant thee but a due reward,
>   A guerdon portion fair and just;
> And then ne'er think thy station hard,
>   But work, my boy, work, hope, and trust!

Cook's representations of those who earn their living from the land are conventionally idealized. While she acknowledges the hard work and the meager return field hands receive, Cook romanticizes agricultural labor in poems such as "Harvest Song" and "The Ploughshare of Old England." Despite their hard life, farmers are sustained by the wholesomeness and beauty of their natural surroundings. The "merry" laborers rejoice in "Song of the Haymakers":

> We dwell in the meadows, we toil on the sward,
>   Far away from the city's dull gloom;
> And more jolly are we, though in rags we may be,
>   Than the pale faces over the loom.

We hear from the pale face bent over the loom in "Song of the City Artisan." In this poem the weaver affirms at the outset his willingness to work and his acceptance of his lowly position:

> Labor is good, my strong right hand
>   Is ever ready to endure;
> Though meanly born, I bless my land,
>   Content to be among its poor.

His only request is that he be allowed to earn his bread under the "open sky":

> Give me a spade to delve the soil
>   From early dawn to closing night;
> The plough, the flail, or any toil
>   That will not shut me from the light.

Even in poems that graphically depict the abuse of workers, Cook moderates her message. For example, "Our Father," like Elizabeth Barrett Browning's "The Cry of the Children," was written in response to a government report by R. H. Horne on the employment of children in mines and factories. The children Horne interviewed claimed to say their prayers each night, but when he examined them further he discovered that the only two words they knew were "Our Father." Like Browning, Cook describes the shameful bondage of ignorant young laborers:

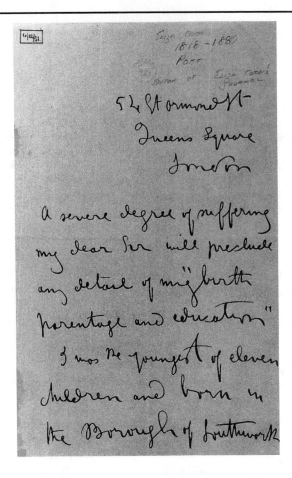

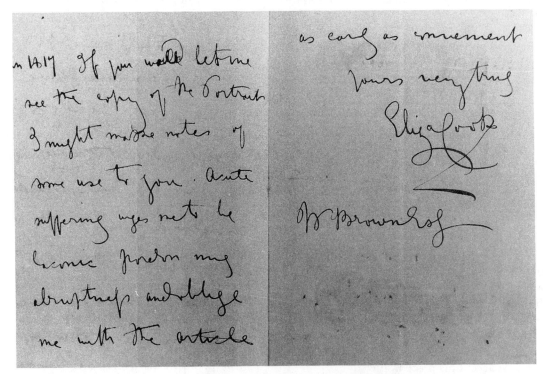

December 1851 letter from Cook responding to a request for biographical information (courtesy of Special Collections, Thomas Cooper Library, University of South Carolina)

Pale, struggling blossoms of mankind,
　　Born only to endure,
White helpless slaves whom Christians bind,
　　Sad children of the poor!

She tempers her criticism with a lesson on piety rather than making a demand that the sufferings of working children be alleviated, however in the final stanza of the poem, the speaker appeals to those "who have fairer lots; / Who live with plenty, love, and mirth" to learn from those less fortunate the value of prayer.

In two other poems the misery of the workers is similarly undermined. "A Song for the Workers" censures the greedy, heartless "despots" who enslave the workers, making them "unceasing drudges." The subtitle indicates that the poem was "Written for the Early Closing Movement," a campaign aimed at reducing working hours. Yet, as she details the grim effects of ceaseless toil and proclaims, "Right is up and asking / Louder for a juster lot," the speaker appeals to the masters to reform the system, not to the workers to revolt. In fact in the final stanza she urges them, "Work on bravely, God's own daughters! / Work on staunchly, God's own sons!" In "Stanzas to My Starving Kin in the North," written by Cook in 1863 in support of the "Fund for the Relief of the Distressed Operatives in the Cotton Districts," the speaker praises the workers for "showing *souls* like the *hero*, not *fangs* like the brute" in their steady endurance of hardship. Because they have patiently borne their sufferings, she assures them that "God and the People" will send them the assistance they deserve.

Despite the preponderance of sentimental, domestic, and patriotic verses, Cook broached unorthodox subjects and themes as well. "The Sacrilegious Gamesters," for instance, is based on the true story of some riotous young men who held a midnight gambling party with the corpse of a friend at the communion table in a village church. To her contemporaries Cook seemed quite outspoken. In "Three Hundred Pounds a Year" she mockingly satirizes materialism and social ambition. The speaker, Charles Adolphus, professes love to Florence Isabel, swearing, "Thou art the dearest of the dear; / My fate! my soul! my life!" Nevertheless, he poses the question, "But on 'three hundred pounds a year' / How can you be my 'wife?'" He points out: "Love, now, is an expensive thing." Calculating the wages for a housemaid, cook, page, and footman and the costs of a brougham, an opera box, fine clothes, and jewels, he concludes he "really can't afford it."

At mid century Cook received glowing praise from Frederic Rowton, who maintained that she had "the boldest spirit of any Poetess in our language." Comparing her to male poets, Rowton claimed, "She has a man's sense of freedom; a man's self-reliance; a man's sceptical spirit; a man's wide, grasping, general, original vision; and to these qualities she adds the quick instinctive perceptions, the pure love of Beauty, and the ardent, sensitive affectionateness which so eminently distinguish woman." He defended her against criticisms that her boldness was unfeminine. Rowton saw her

as one of the best and most powerful of all our female poets, and one who is greatly raising and purifying our estimate of woman's mind. She has by her example disproved the long prevalent dogma, that the female soul cannot rise above the trifling, minute, and evanescent affairs of life; and has clearly shown that when the mind of woman is emancipated from its petty restraints, and lifted above life's conventionalisms, it is at least as strong in essence, and as striking in its developments, as the mind of the male.

Rowton offered as an example of her "sense of freedom" a poem titled "The Gipsy's Tent," which closes with the following stanza:

Pant ye for beauty? Oh, where would ye seek
Such bloom as is found on the tawny one's cheek?
Our limbs that go bounding in freedom and health,
Are worth *all* your pale faces and coffers of wealth;
There are none to control us; we rest or we roam;
Our will is our law, and the world is our home;
Even Jove would repine at *his* lot if he spent
A night of wild glee in the gipsy's tent.

Rowton's positive opinion was not universally shared, however. Among others, Browning, whose poems appeared in annuals and keepsakes alongside Cook's, found nothing in her work to admire. In a 13 December 1839 letter to her American friend Mary Russell Mitford, Browning cited recent favorable notices of Mitford's *Findens' Tableaux: A Series of Thirteen Scenes of National Character, Beauty, and Costume* (1837) "by all the critics . . . except Mr. [William] Jerdan of the *Literary Gazette* who is so out of breath with lauding Miss Eliza Cook's poems that he cant do it for anything else." Later in the same letter Browning expressed her inability to share Jerdan's enthusiasm. Her perusal of a volume of Cook's poems prompted her to say mockingly, "The sight of the book & its whole tone amused me very much." She ridiculed Cook's "modest" introduction and the frontispiece showing "a full length of the lady in mourning à la mode & hair à la Brute & a determination of countenance 'to be poetical' whatever nature might say to it." Even the facsimile signature beneath Cook's portrait provoked Browning's scorn: it has been "obligingly appended to show how great geniuses dot their i[']s like vulgar clay." Of the poems themselves Browning maintained, "I c^d read nothing in it worth reading again."

Browning was not the only one to comment on Cook's decidedly masculine appearance. Her short hair and tailored clothes attracted considerable attention, as did her personal relationships. Cook never married. While there is no concrete evidence of love affairs, rumors circulated from time to time that Cook was romantically involved with various editors and literary men who helped to advance her career. Moreover, she openly acknowledged a "romantic friendship" with Charlotte Cushman, an American actress to whom she dedicated two poems. In "To Charlotte Cushman, Seeing Her Play 'Bianca' in Milman's Tragedy of 'Fazio'" Cook described the profound effect of Cushman's performance on her:

> I had seen many "fret and strut their hour";
>   But my brain never had become such slave
> To Fiction, as it did beneath thy power;
>   Nor owned such homage as to thee it gave.

At the height of her popularity Cook founded, edited, and wrote the majority of a successful periodical called *Eliza Cook's Journal,* a publication aimed at working-class readers that was issued weekly from May 1849 to October 1854. Selling for pennies, the magazine enjoyed slightly higher circulation than Charles Dickens's *Household Words* though only half that of the *London Journal,* according to Sally Mitchell. Characterized by clear, straightforward prose, Cook's magazine focused on issues affecting women and children, with articles supporting expanded educational and employment opportunities for women and a more enlightened and tolerant view of spinsterhood. The journal also included didactic articles, stories, book reviews, and biographical sketches. Moreover, many of Cook's poems appeared for the first time or were reprinted.

Poor health caused her to stop publication after only five years, though a substantial portion of the magazine was republished in 1860 as *Jottings from My Journal.* Five years later Cook published *Diamond Dust,* a collection of aphorisms drawn from her journal column of the same title.

In 1863 Cook was awarded a Civil List pension of £100 annually. In later life she resided with relatives and published little, but she continued to receive royalties from her books until her death. Assessing her position early in the twentieth century, John H. Ingram pointed out that her accomplishments must be gauged in light of her intentions. "She did not attempt to please poets or philosophers—her audience was the people. . . ." For several decades the people responded enthusiastically. Yet, despite the efforts of those such as Ingram to keep her poems in print, when Eliza Cook died at Wimbledon at age seventy-one her name as a poet largely died with her.

References:

Sarah Josepha Hale, *Woman's Record; or, Sketches of All Distinguished Women from the Creation to A. D. 1854* (New York: Harper, 1855), pp. 629–630;

John H. Ingram, "Eliza Cook," in *The Poets and the Poetry of the Century,* volume 7, edited by Alfred Henry Miles (London: Hutchinson, n.d.): 269–272;

Sally Mitchell, *The Fallen Angel: Chastity, Class and Women's Reading 1835–1880* (Bowling Green, Ohio: Bowling Green University Popular Press, 1981);

Frederic Rowton, *The Female Poets of Great Britain, Chronologically Arranged: with Copious Selections and Critical Remarks* (Philadelphia: Baird, 1854), pp. 480–482.

Papers:
The Mortlake Collection at the Pennsylvania State University Library holds a small sampling of Cook materials, including seven signed poems, sixteen letters, original watercolors from the 1840 edition of *Melaia and Other Poems,* and several engravings.

Helen Lady Dufferin, Countess of Gifford
(1807 – 13 June 1867)

Denise K. Comer
University of South Carolina

BOOKS: *The Dandies Rout,* by Dufferin and Caroline
Norton (London: Marshall, 1819);

*Selections. A Set of Ten Songs and Two Duets. The words
and music by two sisters,* by Dufferin and Norton
(London: Power, 1829);

The Charming Woman, anonymous (London, 1835);

Ten Songs (London, 1861);

*Lispings from Low Latitudes, or Extracts from the Journal
of the Hon. Impulsia Gushington,* as Impulsia
Gushington (London: Murray, 1863);

*Songs, Poems and Verses, edited with a memoir and some
Account of the Sheridan family, by her son, The Marquess of Dufferin and Ava* (London: Murray,
1894);

*A Selection of the Songs of Lady Dufferin (Countess of Gif-
ford),* edited by Frederick Dufferin (London:
Murray, 1895).

PLAY PRODUCTION: *Finesse, or A Busy Day in
Messina,* London, Haymarket Theatre, 1863.

PERIODICAL PUBLICATION: "A Few Thoughts
on Keys," *Cornhill Magazine,* 12 (November
1865): 623–628.

Helen Lady Dufferin, Countess of Gifford

Helen Lady Dufferin emerged from the rich literary heritage of the Anglo-Irish Sheridan family. Associated most commonly today with the tradition of Irish ballads, Dufferin was known and adored within Victorian literary circles, and such ballads as "The Charming Woman," "The Irish Emigrant," and "Terence's Farewell" achieved widespread popularity throughout the nineteenth century. Dufferin's poetry, often set to music by herself or others, reflects important concerns traceable throughout the early and middle periods of Victorian literature: a biting criticism of social class, a spotlight on Irish poverty and emigration, and a despair over loss and separation. While Dufferin infused her early and later writing with an arch wit (particularly in her social satires), the songs and poems written during the middle of her life are marked by sentimentality and often a profound sadness.

Despite her nineteenth-century popularity, Dufferin's work is now largely obscured, in part by the current critical focus on her sister, Caroline Norton. Contributing as well to Dufferin's current obscurity is the fact that much of her work initially appeared anonymously as single-sheet publications and was then incorporated into musical scores and songbooks for publication in England and America. Thus, the few existing records of Dufferin's work often exhibit discrepancies as to titles and dates of publication. The most valuable source of information on Dufferin is her son, Frederick Temple Hamilton Blackwood, who nearly thirty years after her death compiled Dufferin's published and unpublished works into *Songs, Poems, and Verses* (1894) and

127

provided a biographical sketch of his mother. While Frederick Dufferin's tribute is useful, he frequently sets Dufferin against the background of the Sheridan family, his father, himself, and the literary and political community within which he and his mother circulated. Thus the most extensive repertory of information on Dufferin defines her in relation to those around her and casts her as the epitome and perfection of, progressively, daughterhood, wifehood, motherhood, and Victorian "Ladyhood."

Born in 1807 on Charlotte Street, Fitzroy Square, in London, to Caroline Henrietta (born Callander) and Thomas Sheridan, Helen Serina Sheridan was the second eldest of seven children. Dufferin's father co-owned the Drury Lane Theatre with his father, playwright Richard Brinsley Sheridan, until it burned down on 24 February 1809, taking with it what little was left of the family fortune. Thomas Sheridan, suffering from poor health in the years after the financial downfall, accepted an appointment as colonial paymaster in the Cape of Good Hope in 1813. He was accompanied by Dufferin and her mother, while Dufferin's two brothers, Brinsley and Thomas, and two sisters, Caroline and Georgina, stayed with relatives in Scotland. Soon after moving to Africa, Thomas and Caroline Sheridan had two more children, Frank and Charles. Thomas Sheridan's health continued to deteriorate, however, and he died of consumption on 12 September 1817, when Dufferin was ten years old.

Caroline Sheridan, now a penniless widow with seven children, returned to England with her three children, where they were reunited with the four other siblings. Frederick, the Duke of York, provided the family with private apartments at Hampton Court, and to further support the family Dufferin's mother wrote novels, of which *Carwell* (1830) was the best known. Though beset by financial difficulties, Dufferin's childhood was spent among the privileged classes, and her education was extensive. Under her mother's tutelage Dufferin mastered French before she was sixteen and also became proficient in German and Latin. Though never formally trained, Dufferin became skilled at sketching, drawing, and watercolor painting, and, encouraged by her mother and her uncle, Charles Sheridan, Dufferin began writing poems and composing music at an early age. She and her siblings performed theatrical skits, and in collaboration with her sister Caroline she would often write poems, sketches, and songs—a practice the sisters would continue throughout their lives. One of these early collaborative efforts between Dufferin and Caroline resulted in their first publication, *The Dandies Rout* (1819), a collection of rhymes and sketches that satirized a popular series of books known as the "Dandy Books."

Despite the rich literary environment at Hampton Court, the family's finances continued to suffer, and it became increasingly important for the Sheridan daughters to marry. In 1824, at the age of seventeen, Dufferin met Price Blackwood, heir to the marquess of Dufferin, who was at that time a navy captain. Blackwood immediately proposed, and, despite disapproval from the Blackwood family over Dufferin's lack of dowry, they married on 4 July 1825 when Dufferin was eighteen years old. Dufferin and Price Blackwood left immediately after the wedding for Florence, Italy, in order to avoid further strife with his family. They remained in Italy for two years while Dufferin continued writing, mostly in the form of illustrated journals and letters. Soon after arriving in Florence she became pregnant; the pregnancy was a difficult one, during which Dufferin required careful nursing, and as a result she was plagued with health difficulties for the rest of her life. Dufferin's son, in fact, doubts whether "there was a day of her life which she passed quite free from pain."

Dufferin gave birth to a son, Frederick Temple, on 21 June 1826. An anecdote that Frederick Dufferin relates in *Songs, Poems, and Verses* about his birth illustrates the manner in which he portrays Dufferin as the epitome of the self-sacrificing Victorian mother. During the birth Dufferin's health was so precarious that at one point doctors were considering whether to preserve mother or child. Purportedly Dufferin, upon hearing the discussion, cried out, "Never mind me! Save my baby!" Both mother and child survived, however, and soon after the birth Dufferin moved with her husband and son to Tuscany and then on to the Apennines.

Unlike her sister Caroline's abusive marriage, Dufferin's marriage seems to have been quite happy, though marked by a long period of absence and ultimately cut short by her husband's early death. Apparently, Dufferin was did not consider herself in love with Price Blackwood initially but had agreed to marry him because of pressure from her mother and friends. When Caroline was considering marriage to George Chapple Norton in 1827 Dufferin wrote her a letter from Italy in which she professed a newly developed love for her husband and exhorted Caroline to follow her example.

A year after Frederick's birth, Dufferin and her husband were encouraged by signs of reconciliation with the Blackwood family, and they returned to England in 1827, where they purchased a small cottage at Thames-Ditton, near Dufferin's mother. For three years they remained at Thames-Ditton

Illustration for Lady Dufferin's Lispings from Low Latitudes *(1863), a parody of the travel memoirs popular at the time*

and often visited London, where Caroline Norton introduced Dufferin to the literary society she entertained. Here, at the Norton's home, Story's Gate, Dufferin socialized with authors such as Theodore Hook, Fanny Kemble, and Sydney Smith.

Dufferin and her two sisters, Georgina Lady Seymour, Duchess of Somerset, and the Honorable Caroline Norton, were collectively dubbed the "Three Graces" throughout London society. With characteristic wit Dufferin said years later to Benjamin Disraeli: "Georgey's the beauty, Carry's the wit, and I ought to be the good one, but I am not." Peppered throughout various "reminiscences" from the period, such as those of Mary Somerville and Lord Beaconsfield, are laudatory accounts of the "Three Graces" and their "gracious" mother, Caroline Sheridan. Lord Beaconsfield, who called Duf-

ferin his "chief admiration" of the "Three Graces," recalls "how delightful were the dinners in old days at Mrs. Norton's, the wit and humour that flowed more copiously than did the claret." Referred to by her friends as "Nelly" and characterized by her son as having an "innocent gaiety" and a "sunny temperament," Dufferin charmed everyone who met her and became quite popular and admired.

Continuing their tradition of collaborating, Dufferin and Caroline together published anonymously a selection of vocal music titled *Selections. A Set of Ten Songs and Two Duets. The words and music by two sisters* (1829). Unfortunately, no record remains of how Dufferin and her sister divided the work.

Writing and composing by herself as well, Dufferin, between 1827 and 1830, wrote "The Fine Young English Gentleman," a witty satire on social class inspired by her brother Charles and his fellow clerks at the Admiralty. It was first presented to the public in 1850, when it was printed with another poem as a one-page publication. The poem enters the debate of the day over what constituted a "gentleman." Running contrary to stipulations set forth by John Ruskin and Cardinal John Newman that a true "gentleman" must be of a pure and moralistic character, Dufferin's "gentleman" possesses selfish, extravagant and haughty traits reminiscent of Pip of Charles Dickens's *Great Expectations* (1860–1861).

Set to music by Dufferin, "The Fine Young English Gentleman" narrates a "day in the life" of a "young pate," living beyond his means, keeping up "appearances at a very dashing rate," and "lounging" around on a "borrowed horse." After dining at the Clarendon Hotel and being surprised that "common folks should ask such a fine young man to pay," he spends an hour "admiring Duvernay, / Like a fine young English gentleman, one of the present time!" The gentleman drinks late into the night, impetuously challenging "three men friends" to a duel (which is somehow later abandoned). He wakes up late for work the next day, and then reminisces with "his brother clerks" about these drunken adventures. Dufferin's witty censure of Victorian youth of a certain class became quite popular; it was republished in various collections and also sung during the comedy *Catching an Heiress,* first performed at the Adelphi Theatre.

As Dufferin continued to write and to enjoy a happy, though financially meager, existence, her husband was suddenly commissioned to the frigate *Imogene* in 1831, headed for destinations including Africa, India, and Australia. In an excerpt from his journal published in *Songs, Poems, and Verses,* the newly appointed Commander Blackwood writes, "In the morning I was most unexpectedly ordered to accompany the squadron to the Downs, and had to take leave of my dear wife and lovely boy almost on the instant." Though this separation caused a "poignancy of grief," as Blackwood reported, the family needed the money. Dufferin's husband was absent for nearly four years.

While her husband was at sea Dufferin and he engaged in avid correspondence, in which she often included songs and poems dedicated to Blackwood. These poems, unpublished during Dufferin's life, are included in *Songs, Poems, and Verses.* "Song," for instance, written and set music on 30 April 1833, exhorts her husband to "Let each friendly look thou greetest / Seem a message, Love, from *me!*" During Blackwood's absence Dufferin lived alternately at Hampton Court Palace and in Ireland at Clandeboye, the estate to which Blackwood was heir. She continued to socialize with her sister Caroline in the London literary circles, where she met Benjamin Disraeli in 1832, marking the beginning of a long-lasting friendship. In 1834 Dufferin traveled with her sisters and their husbands, as well as her eldest brother, Brinsley Sheridan, on an extended family trip to Belgium, Germany, Amsterdam, and France, and then returned to London by Christmas. It was on this trip that the family witnessed the abuse Caroline suffered at the hands of George Norton.

In 1835, after an absence of nearly four years, Price Blackwood returned to England, and the family took residence in Bookham Lodge cottage in the parish of Stoke, still regularly visiting London. That same year Dufferin published anonymously a small collection of poetry, *The Charming Woman,* which met with enormous success. The title ballad became one of her most famous, a favorite in "the streets and theatres as well as in the drawing-rooms of London."

A complement to Dufferin's witty treatment of the new class of young English gentlemen, "The Charming Woman" satirically censures their female counterparts. Just as the "Fine Young English Gentleman," with his flippancy, extravagance, and shallowness, acts altogether against the ideas of how a "true" Victorian gentleman should behave, the "Charming Woman" acts in direct antithesis to Victorian ideals of feminine modesty, domesticity, and innocence. This so-called New Woman of the 1830s has been characterized by Katherine Hickok as "immodest, flirtatious, strong-willed, politically inclined, imprudent with money, or even a bit 'Blue.'" "The Charming Woman," in fact, became a proverbial expression for a unladylike lady, and Elizabeth Barrett Browning borrowed the phrase in *Aurora Leigh* as a scornful description of Lady Waldemar, "The charming woman there."

Dufferin's charming woman, Miss Myrtle, though penniless, somehow owns dresses that "would make Maradan stare," wears her hemlines a little too high, keeps herself "a little too thin," and stays out a little too late. Rather than learning "how to hem and to sew," Miss Myrtle's mother (a charming woman, as well), taught her how to speak Latin and Greek and "how to solve problems in Euclid / before she could speak."

The speaker of the poem, a gossiping female voice, criticizes Miss Myrtle for discussing matters outside the traditional "private sphere": "She can chatter of Poor-laws and Tithes, / And the value of labour and land,– / 'Tis a pity when charming women / Talk of things which they don't understand!" For the speaker, what is perhaps most alarming of all is that "these charming women / Are inclined to have wills of their own!" The poem closes with a warning to Miss Myrtle's fiancé, whom she is scheduled to marry the following day, and any other young men who might be swept away by the charms of such a woman: "O young men, if you'd take my advice, / You would find it an excellent plan,– / Don't marry a charming woman, / If you are a sensible man!"

The witty social criticism of "The Charming Woman" and "The Fine Young English Gentleman" is also found in other, unpublished poems by Dufferin. "The Mother's Lament," for instance, also written during the 1830s, depicts a mother's utter despondence over the fact that her five "gawky girls" have all inherited from their father the dreaded "Spriggins nose." "Mrs. Harris's Soliloquy While Threading Her Needle" laments how "things are sadly altered" with all the "fine new-fangled ways" of sewing that have replaced a simple needle and thread.

Whereas the speaker in "The Charming Woman" looks critically on women who "chatter of Poor-laws and Tithes," Dufferin herself felt no compunctions about discussing political issues of the day. Throughout her life she closely advised Frederick on his own political aspirations, which (after her death) landed him such positions as governor-general of Canada (1872–1878), ambassador to Russia and Constantinople (1879–1883), and viceroy of India (1884–1888).

Dufferin's interest in politics is also reflected in other poems collected in *Songs, Poems, and Verses.* "Meditations on the Poor Law," for instance, written when her older brother, Brinsley Sheridan, was standing for Parliament, presents a scoffing voice: "Why should I support my neighbour / On my goods–against my will? / Can't he live by honest labour? / Can't he beg–or can't he steal?" The speaker, in favor of maintaining the status quo of "We–the Feasts, and they–the Fasts!," vows henceforth to participate in politics and to "rally" around "everything."

Though Dufferin continued to write about the political and social issues of Victorian England, Dufferin's next publication shifts in focus to Ireland. One explanation for this critical shift is that in 1839 with the death of his father, Price Blackwood became Lord Dufferin, owner of the sprawling Clandeboye estate in Northern Ireland. Before they were able to move to Clandeboye, though, Helen's health faltered and doctors urged her to spend time in Italy instead.

While Dufferin was in Italy, two of her poems were published as single sheets in 1840 in London: "The Irish Emigrant" and "Terence's Farewell."

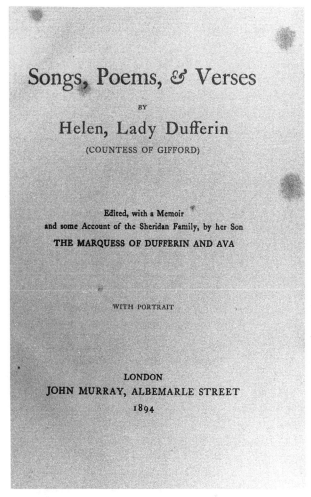

Songs, Poems, & Verses

BY

Helen, Lady Dufferin

(COUNTESS OF GIFFORD)

Edited, with a Memoir
and some Account of the Sheridan Family, by her Son
THE MARQUESS OF DUFFERIN AND AVA

WITH PORTRAIT

LONDON
JOHN MURRAY, ALBEMARLE STREET
1894

Title page for a posthumous collection of Lady Dufferin's verse compiled by her son, the Marquess of Dufferin and Ava

"The Irish Emigrant," also titled "The Ballad of the Irish Emigrant," "The Lay of the Irish Emigrant," and "The Lament of the Irish Emigrant," would become one of Dufferin's most famous ballads. The two ballads reflect not only Dufferin's shift in focus to Ireland but a concomitant shift in tone from satiric wit to sentimentality and sadness. "The Lament of the Irish Emigrant" and "Terence's Farewell to Kathleen" are two of the many ballads, songs, and poems about Ireland written during the 1840s, when the country was stricken by poverty. This genre of verse, as Brian Folliard describes it, depicts "patriotism for a down-trodden land . . . ; the tragic sorrow of poverty and famine; the bitter anger of eviction; the sentimental emotion of the emigrant."

"The Lament of the Irish Emigrant" was subsequently set to music in America by William Dempster, "attained world-wide fame," and remains popular in the musical community today. It portrays a speaker sitting alone on a hillside "stile," where he used to sit with his beloved wife, Mary, before her death. He misses the "soft clasp" of her hand, her "breath warm" on his cheek, and the voice that she "never more may speak." Having decided to leave Ireland because of his poverty and loneliness—"I'm very lonely now, Mary, / for the poor make no new friends"—the speaker closes with optimistic hope: "But I'll not forget you, darling, / In the land I'm going to. / They say there's bread and work for all, / And the sun shines always there."

Such portrayals of Irish emigration and exile, told from the point of view of parting lovers, became a hallmark of Dufferin's poetry and music. In "Terence's Farewell to Kathleen," for example, Kathleen departs for England, leaving Terence "All alone by myself in this place!" Speaking in the Irish vernacular, Terence reminds Kathleen, "Och! Them English, decaivers by nature! / Tho' may be you'd think them sincere, / They'll say you're a sweet charmin' creature, / But don't you belave them, my dear!" In "The Emigrant Ship," printed in *Songs, Poems, and Verses,* the speaker conveys the same misguided optimism expressed in "The Lament of the Irish Emigrant": "A little toil,—a little care,—and in a world of bliss / We shall forget the poverty that parted us in this. / How small a thing 'twill seem to us upon that blessed shore, / Where the 'hundred thousand welcomes' shall be ours evermore!" Another of Dufferin's musical explorations of the same subject, a complete score titled "O, Bay of Dublin" first printed in the 1840s, has since been republished in collections of Irish ballads.

The sense of exile and separation emanating from Dufferin's poetry about Ireland no doubt reflects the tragedy in Dufferin's own life—her husband's early and sudden death. In the summer of 1841, while Dufferin remained in Italy, Price Blackwood traveled to England to visit their son at Eton and also to run (unsuccessfully) for election to Parliament at Chatham. After the elections he intended to visit Clandeboye to manage some personal affairs and boarded a ship headed for Belfast, Ireland. But before the ship left the dock he lapsed into a fever, and, after taking a fatal dose of morphine prescribed by an inattentive chemist, died on board the ship on 20 July.

Dufferin's depiction of lost love and loneliness expressed previously in her poetry about Ireland now found its way into more personal poetry of mourning, with titles such as "And Have I Lost Thee?" and "They Bid Me Forget Thee." In "I Am Weary" the speaker sadly observes that "the green earth in its beauty, hath a mournful look to me, / And a dream of sadness dwells within the voice of stream and tree. / The kindly looks are vanished

that made home Paradise, / The glorious sunshine is not worth the light of loving eyes!"

Now a widow at age thirty-five, Dufferin settled at Clandeboye in 1842; during a winter visit to her sister Georgina in Italy, she met George Hay, Lord Gifford, a melancholy Cambridge undergraduate who at eighteen years of age was barely older than Dufferin's son. Dufferin offered Gifford companionship and solace, and subsequently the young man fell passionately in love with her. Dufferin refused Gifford's proposal of marriage, assuming the young man's love would subside as he grew older. Gifford, however, proposed to Dufferin several more times over the next twenty years.

Dufferin instead turned to two other relationships: that with her son and that with God. Upon his father's death Frederick had left Eton for six months to console Dufferin, and the relationship between mother and son became one of remarkable intimacy. Frederick Dufferin's nephew and biographer, Harold Nicolson, writes in *Helen's Tower* (1937) that "She shared his every interest and his every pleasure; she shared his friendships and his adventures; they enhanced each other's merriment and inspired each other's wit."

A group of Dufferin's poems written for her son's birthdays, which he included in *Songs, Poems, and Verses,* documents both the "passionate partnership" between mother and son and Dufferin's new emphasis on faith. All titled with some variation of "To my son . . ." and accompanied by various gifts such as a chain made from her hair, these poems depict Dufferin looking expectantly toward heaven, hoping for a reunion with her "beloved" (son, not husband) after they both die. In "To My Dear Son on his 21st Birthday" (21 June 1847), for example, Dufferin asserts that "human love / Is all too poor in passionate words." As an alternative to inadequate words she presents her son with a silver lamp, which will continue to "bless" him with "light" after she has gone to "God's own glorious light." The following year's birthday poem, "To My Son," conveys an intense sadness: Dufferin seeks escape from "human ill," from "cares that kill, from joys that pall." Looking to Heaven, she consoles herself by asserting that "when all things else are dust / Our love shall make a part of Heaven."

As her son became the focal point of Dufferin's life, she advised him on his political aspirations and on his own writing, although apparently her advice on the latter subject was more often critical than approving. Returning from Italy in 1843, Dufferin settled in London, living alternately there and at Clandeboye. Dufferin continued to travel, visiting France, Germany, and Scotland, and continued en-

Helen's Tower, a "monument of devotion" to Lady Dufferin erected by her son on the family estate in Clandeboye, Northern Irleand

gaging in literary and political circles, becoming acquainted with (among others) Charles Dickens, Thomas Babington Macaulay, Edward Bulwer-Lytton, and William, king of the German state of Württemberg. In 1849 Dufferin moved with her mother to 29 Grosvenor Place, a home Frederick Dufferin had bought after attaining his majority and becoming a lord in waiting to the queen. In June 1851, after a brief period of sickness, Caroline Sheridan died, and Dufferin, feeling that the "air of Grosvenor Place did not agree with her," moved to Hampstead and then to Highgate, where she lived at Dufferin Lodge.

Though Dufferin had continued writing throughout these years, she did not publish anything for nearly fifteen years after her husband's death. In 1846 Frederick Dufferin traveled throughout Ireland to document the disastrous effects of the failed Irish potato crops and then published his *Narrative of a Journey from Oxford to Skibbereen during the year of the Irish Famine* in 1847. Influenced by her son's narrative, Dufferin continued to write poetry about Irish poverty, separation, and exile.

Published in 1857 as the title poem of another single-sheet publication, "Katey's Letter," set to mu-

sic by Dufferin, is written from an Irish "girl" to her departed "love," who is now working near Boston. "Altho' he cannot read," Katey writes anyway, because "the manin' was so plain / I loved him faithfully." Sadly, no response comes, but Katey attributes it to the fact that her "love can neither read nor write," and she knows "he loves me faithfully / . . . That he is true to me." Illustrating the limitations of language and the power of a communication beyond words, the nameless love in Boston, in the companion poem, "Sweet Kilkenny Town," receives Katey's letter and, though unable to read the words, observes: "Oh! The folks that read and write (though they're so mighty clever), / See nothin' but the words, and they're soon read through; / But Katey's unread letter would be spakin' to me ever / Of the dear love that she bears me. . . ."

Though she continued to write poetry and music, *Katey's Letter,* which enjoyed widespread popularity, marked the end of Dufferin's professional poetic career. Henceforth she focused her literary ambitions on drama and prose, returning to the wit and satire that marked her earlier writing. From 1858 to 1860 Dufferin and her son sailed the Mediterranean on a yacht, visiting Egypt, Greece, Constantinople,

Beirut, and Jerusalem; in 1861, after a brief interval at home, she again set off for Syria with her friend Cyril Graham. These trips—and the journal and sketches she composed during them—would later serve as the basis for *Lispings from Low Latitudes* (1863). In between these two trips, from 1860 to 1861, Dufferin wrote a play, *Finesse, or A Busy Day in Messina.*

Alternately titled *Spy and Counter Spy,* Dufferin wrote the three-act comedy, set in 1811, specifically for the Wigan acting company, of which Alfred Wigan was known for playing the part of a Frenchman speaking broken English and John Baldwin Buckstone was known as a leading farcical actor. Performed at the Haymarket Theatre in 1863, where it enjoyed moderate success, *Finesse* depicts two spies from Napoleon's army intending to overthrow the English army, which was at that time holding Messina and other Sicilian ports for King Ferdinand IV. As a concurrent theme Dufferin includes in the play a mad scientist, the Baron, in search of everlasting life. After a variety of misunderstandings and questioned identities, the plans of both the French spies and the Baron are overthrown by English soldiers.

In the years after her husband's death, as Dufferin had devoted herself primarily to her son, her writing, her family, and her religion, George Gifford had continued his courtship of her. Following his initial proposal in Rome in 1842, he proposed a second time in 1856, and Dufferin again refused him. Two events in 1862 finally prompted Dufferin to accept Gifford's third proposal. First, over the twenty-year courtship, Dufferin had told Gifford that she would not marry him until her son married, and in October Frederick Dufferin married Hariot Rowan Hamilton. Second, Gifford was injured while renovating his home, Castle Gifford. Though doctors at first thought the injuries were minor, Gifford's condition soon deteriorated, and he retired to Highgate, where Dufferin nursed him. Gifford again proposed and after asking doctors for assurance that his injuries were indeed fatal, Dufferin agreed to marry him. They married over Gifford's sickbed in October 1862, and only two months after the marriage, on 22 December 1862, Gifford died.

To ease Gifford's pain during his final days Dufferin wrote and illustrated the brilliantly witty *Lispings from Low Latitudes, or Extracts from the Journal of the Hon. Impulsia Gushington.* Compiled from her various travels, *Lispings* parodies Frederick's travel narrative *Letters from High Latitudes* (1857), which recounts his journey across the Baltic Sea and Sweden. Published under the pseudonym Impulsia Gushington in March 1863, four months after Gifford's

death, the inscription to *Lispings* reads, "Although the contents of the Volume are of a light and humorous character, they served an earnest purpose, in lightening the tedium and depression of long sickness in the person of a beloved friend."

Recalling Dufferin's early social satires, *Lispings* is a journal consisting of twenty-three "Plates" and diary entries recounting Impulsia Gushington's journeys through Egypt and "edited" by a nameless "Editor" to eliminate sections of extreme effusiveness and "gushiness." Gushington, a naive, wealthy, unmarried woman, has a "sudden inspiration" to travel and, within a month, finds herself at the port of Alexandria, Egypt, abandoned by her "faithful" domestics. Gushington narrates her misadventures through Egypt: a negligent guide, Dimitri, allows her dog to die; a family of misfits, the MacFishys, take advantage of her; and an alarming camel ride, during which camel herders steal her belongings, lands Gushington destitute, friendless, and "clotheless" (the windy ride has caused her dress to fall off). She at last finds solace in the affections of a rather suspect gentleman, Monsieur de Rataplan, whom she agrees to marry. Through it all, though continually taken advantage of, Gushington maintains a naive innocence and trust, along with a misinformed reliance on false gestures of civility and propriety.

Following Gifford's death, Dufferin moved from Highgate to Clandeboye, where her health began to decline. The last work published during her lifetime was a short essay titled "A Few Thoughts on Keys," published anonymously in *The Cornhill Magazine* in 1865. This essay, characteristic of her quick wit and satirical bent, discusses the paramount importance of keys in the English household, particularly for women. Dufferin wittily traces the various uses for keys as well as the history of keys (both literally and as used figuratively in speech). "What household," Dufferin asks, does not have "legendary reminiscences of keys strangely lost . . . that have gone and hung themselves . . . on wrong rings and wandered madly into wrong pockets?"

In 1866, while at Clandeboye, Dufferin was diagnosed with breast cancer. After an operation she enjoyed peace for a short time, only to relapse seven months later. She died on 13 June 1867 at Highgate, where she is buried next to her second husband, George Gifford.

Distraught by his mother's death, Frederick Dufferin resolved to pay tribute to Dufferin. Even as early as 1848, with this aim in mind, he had commissioned leading domestic designer William Burn to erect "Helen's Tower" at Clandeboye. Helen's Tower, Frederick's "monument of devotion," is composed of three stacked rooms with a "roof-bastion" at the top. On the second floor is a sitting room lined by "golden tablets," on which are etched various poems dedicated to Dufferin, which Frederick had solicited from famous writers. With the tower's completion on 8 October 1861 a commemorative publication titled *Helen's Tower* (1861) was privately printed. The first edition contains Dufferin's "To My Son on His 21st Birthday" and Alfred Lord Tennyson's "Helen's Tower." Subsequent editions of *Helen's Tower,* as Frederick continued to solicit dedication poems from various writers, include "Helen's Tower," by Robert Browning, and "The Song of Women," by Rudyard Kipling. As further tribute to Dufferin, Frederick compiled *Songs, Poems and Verses,* which includes a biographical sketch, a selection of her published and unpublished poetry, her essay on "Keys," and her play, *Finesse.* As a companion volume, Frederick also published *A Selection of the Songs of Lady Dufferin* (Countess of Gifford) (1895), which contains a selection of the many musical scores either contributed to or written by Dufferin. Despite Frederick's efforts at disseminating Dufferin's work among the public, her expressive and lively poetry and songs have since fallen into obscurity. With the exception of "The Lament of the Irish Emigrant," Dufferin's writing, though popular during the nineteenth century, is largely unknown in the twentieth. Foretelling the later obscurity of her work is "The Dead Language," the last poem Dufferin wrote. Included in *Songs, Poems, and Verses,* "The Dead Language" focuses on forgotten words over the passage of time. Just as the languages of "ancient empires" were once vital and alive, Dufferin writes, the language "that love taught us" contained words that were once "Living their life—dreaming their dream" but are now "Ne'er to be uttered nor heard again." And, sadly, in the case of Dufferin and many forgotten nineteenth-century female poets, this may be the fate of their words as well.

References:

Alice Acland, *Caroline Norton* (London: Constable, 1948);

Percy Fitzgerald, *The Sheridans,* volume 2 (London: Grolier Society, 1900), pp. 357–380;

Brian Folliard, *Irish Poems of Love and Sentiment* (Girard, Kans.: Haldeman-Julius, 1927), pp. 6–7, 54–55, 61–64;

Katherine Hickok, *Representations of Women: Nineteenth Century British Women's Poetry* (Westport, Conn.: Greenwood, 1984), pp. 68, 188, 226;

Sir Alfred Lyall, *The Life of the Marquis of Dufferin and Ava,* 2 volumes (London: Murray, 1905);

Alfred H. Miles, *The Poets and the Poetry of the Nineteenth Century,* volume 8 (London: Routledge, 1892), pp. 235–236;

Harold Nicolson, *Helen's Tower* (London: Constable, 1937);

Edmund Clarence Stedman, *Victorian Poets* (Cambridge: Osgood, 1887), p. 260.

Charlotte Elliott
(18 March 1789 – 22 September 1871)

James I. St. John
Forest Lake Presbyterian Church, Columbia, S.C.

BOOKS: *Hours of Sorrow Cheered and Comforted; or Thoughts in Verse,* (London: Seeley, 1836; Philadelphia: Lindsay & Blakiston, 1856);
Morning and Evening Hymns for a Week (London, 1836; Philadelphia: Protestant Episcopal Book Society, 1860);
Thoughts in Verse on Sacred Subjects (London: Hunt, 1869); enlarged as *Thoughts in Verse, on Sacred Subjects; with Some Miscellaneous Poems Written in Early Years and Now Published* (London: Hunt, 1871);
Selections from the Poems of Charlotte Elliott (London: Religious Tract Society, 1873);
Leaves from the Unpublished Journals, Letters, and Poems of Charlotte Elliott (London: Religious Tract Society, 1874).

OTHER: *The Invalid's Hymn Book,* edited by Elliott (Dublin: Robertson, 1834).

Charlotte Elliott is not counted among the powerhouses of Victorian poets. She did not create poems that were quoted in literary salons across the channel, nor was she typically given to presenting lectures and readings. Her name was not on the lips of the literati of London or Oxford, and she is not even listed in either the first or second series of Catherine Jane Hamilton's *Women's Writers: Their Works and Ways* (1892, 1893). Yet Elliott was noted in her day for her faithfulness to God, her verses that described her understanding of ideal faith, and the intensity of her vision. The challenges she faced seem pointedly rendered in her hymn "Just As I Am, Without One Plea" her best-known work and the single piece that has preserved her name for generations. Without "Just As I Am" it is likely that Elliott's name would not have made it into any anthologies at all.

Elliott was born on 18 March 1789 in Clapham, North Yorkshire. A daughter of Charles Elliott, she was on her mother's side the granddaughter of the Reverend H. Venn of Huddersfield. Her

Charlotte Elliott

mother's brother was John Venn, a leader within the evangelical movement in the Church of England during the early decades of the nineteenth century. After a severe illness left her a permanent invalid in 1821, she came under the spiritual influence of Dr. Cesar Malan of Geneva, whom she first met at her father's residence in Clapham on 9 May 1822. According to Elliott's sister, Eleanor (Ellen) Babington, Malan led her "to the true remedy for her anxiety—namely, simple faith in God's own Word." For forty years Malan exerted what Babington terms a "strong" influence upon Elliott's will, which lessened as her religious principles deepened.

Babington reports that prior to Elliott's introduction to the views of Malan she had read widely, especially English poets, finding them "an unceasing delight." Her advisor, however, had grave reservations about her continuing to do so: "Dr. Malan perceived the spiritual danger of such pursuits, so eagerly followed, to one of her temperament." At his urging she set aside the authors she had once found so attractive and confined herself to listening to the Holy Spirit. As Babington remarks, from "this time her poetical talents became consecrated to religion; and though she had in earlier years composed humorous poems, which were much admired by competent judges, she willingly renounced the *éclat* which this style of writing secured, and . . . devoted all the efforts of her pen henceforward to one object—the glory of God, and the benefit of others."

Elliott's invalidism in part led her family south in 1823 to Brighton, where her brother, Henry Venn Elliott, was the minister in charge of St. Mary's. He had conceived a plan to create a residence at Brighton to provide care for the needy daughters of poor clergy. To promote the creation of this home and to raise necessary funds for it he urged all the members of his family to become involved in a bazaar. It was for this project that the ill Elliott, frequently at home alone and consumed by feelings of uselessness, came upon the inspiration to write the text of "Just As I Am" as her contribution to the fundraiser. The poem was included in *The Invalid's Hymn Book* (1834), which Elliott edited.

Elliott lived out the rest of her life in Brighton and its environs. She took advantage of the healing powers of the springs, finding there at least a slight measure of peaceful hope in life. Although she did do some traveling in France in her later years, Babington records that Elliott mostly "became too weak to leave her room." She died peacefully in her sleep on 22 September 1871.

Elliott's poems were collected in volumes that she and other family members had published. Her hymns, numbering about 150, clearly reveal the religious influence of Malan as a glance at the titles of her primary works makes plain: *The Invalid's Hymn Book, Hours of Sorrow Cheered and Comforted; or, Thoughts in Verse* (1836), *Morning and Evening Hymns for a Week* (1836), and *Thoughts in Verse on Sacred Subjects* (1869). Her poems also appeared in *The Christian Remembrancer Song Pocket Book* (1834) and *Psalms and Hymns for Public, Private, and Social Worship; Selected by*

the *Rev. H. V. Elliott, &c* (1835–1848). Two posthumous collections round out Elliott's literary career: *Selections from the Poems of Charlotte Elliott* (1873), which includes the memoir by Babington that was published separately in 1874, and *Leaves from the Unpublished Journals, Letters, and Poems of Charlotte Elliott* (1870).

These volumes contain verse of uneven quality, ranging from the dignified "Just As I Am" to selections as maudlin as "Hymn for a Dying Bed," which appeared in *Selected Poems*:

> While ceaseless love and ceaseless care
>   By all are fondly shown,
> A voice within me cries, "Beware!
>   For thou must die alone"
> . . . .
> But oh! I view not now with dread
>   That shadowy vale unknown;
> I see a light within it shed:
>   I shall not die alone!
>
> One will be with me there, whose voice
>   I long have loved and known:
> To die is now my wish, my choice,
>   I shall not die *alone*!

While commentators such as Tom Ingram and Douglas Newton in *Hymns as Poetry* (1956) maintain that a "hymn is at the same time a poem" and argue that "for incalculable numbers of people, [hymns] are an intensely formative influence on their taste in poetry," modern readers may consider much of Elliott's writings as verse rather than as poetry.

Elliott's better hymns, as Alfred Miles contends in "Sacred, Moral, and Religious Verse," are those that "are cast in the same form, in four-line stanzas with a short line for the fourth. It seems as though she needed the restraint of form to check the diffuseness of facility. Her hymns are characterized by simplicity, directness, and sincerity; they breathe a sweet and elevated poetry." One can sense the difficulty Elliott has in sustaining imagery in longer stanzas such as those in "The Better Country," another poem included in *Selections*:

> Oh yes! there is a land of light!
>   One where the Sun no more goes down;
> Wherein there shall be no more night,
>   Where darkening skies no more shall frown,
> And when this earth so dark appears,
>   Onward I look, and dry my tears.

The stanza seems static as the poet uses conventional images for the darkness that will never trouble the "land of light."

The surest hallmarks of Elliott's writings derive from her sense of loneliness, depression, and

SELECTIONS

FROM THE

Poems of Charlotte Elliott,

AUTHOR OF "JUST AS I AM."

WITH A MEMOIR BY HER SISTER,

E. B.

LONDON:
THE RELIGIOUS TRACT SOCIETY;
56, PATERNOSTER ROW, 65, ST. PAUL'S CHURCHYARD,
AND 164, PICCADILLY.
MANCHESTER: CORPORATION ST. BRIGHTON: WESTERN ROAD.

Title page for the first posthumous collection of Elliott's work,
published in 1873

sometimes even despair; on occasion, though, these emotions are coupled with an openness and a directness that does not always dissolve into outright sentimentality. In *Hymns and Human Life* (1952) Erik Routley argues that the last verse of "Just As I Am" is a "magnificent example" of Elliott at her best:

> Just as I am—of that free love,
> The breadth, length, depth, and height to prove,
> Here, for a season, then above—
> O Lamb of God, I come!

Routley also observes that "Miss Elliott's preference for meters which use a short final line . . . gives an impression of softness and resignation to her hymns which, if it is not to be overdone, requires careful musical treatment." Elliott's poems that have well stood the test of the decades are those such as "Just As I Am" that have been set effectively to pleasing hymn tunes and are thereby enhanced—sometimes greatly so—by the music.

While Elliott's place in the pantheon of Victorian poets is not as elevated as that of many of her contemporaries, she belongs among the ranks of those women and men who were creating thousands of hymns, in her case espousing doctrines that were not those of the elite but most assuredly were those of that great body of ordinary citizens with evangelical and revivalist sentiments. This trend was later to culminate near the close of the nineteenth century in the emotional, dramatic, rhythmic gospel music tradition that achieved an enduring popularity. In a real sense, Elliott—poet, versifier, hymnist—was a product of her age, shaped by Malan's evangelical teachings but mostly molded by the limitations she faced as an invalid. It is little wonder that the moving verses that were most popular in her own day constitute her chief legacy:

> Just as I am—poor, wretched, blind;
> Sight, riches, healing of the mind,

Yea, all I need, in Thee I find—
      O Lamb of God, I come!

A 28 July 1849 letter to Elliott from Edward Quillinan, the son-in-law of William Wordsworth, testifies to the power that many of Elliott's best poems—"Just As I Am" in this instance—had upon her contemporaries. "Dear Miss Elliott," Quillinan writes,

> The day I received your very kind and welcome note, with the music of the hymn, I was moving from home, and I did not return till last night. I need not say how much I am obliged to you. That hymn was originally sent to us, for my dying wife, by a relation of ours, a clergyman's wife in Kent; and it is rather remarkable that *her* daughter, who is on a visit to us, was the first person (as yet the only one) from whom I heard the music, which is exactly what it should be. This young lady was in the room when I received it, and she immediately, at my request, sang it without difficulty to her own accompaniment. I should be ashamed of having deprived you of your only copy; but you tell me that you have access to another. I cannot desire a more touching and appropriate melody for the words, but, if you will not think me obtrusive or unreasonable, I *should* like to have the other air, when your niece may have the leisure to copy it; for everything connected with those words cannot but be of deepest interest to me, and to Mr. and Mrs. Wordsworth.

> When I first got the letter enclosing them, from Kent, I said to the beloved sufferer who knew she was soon to leave us, "Here is a hymn from your friend Charlotte ——— of Barham. Shall I read it to you?" She answered hesitatingly, "Yes, I *must* hear it since it comes from *her*. She is so good, it ought to be worth hearing." I read it; and had no sooner finished than she said very earnestly, "That is the very thing for me." At least ten times that day she asked me to repeat it to her; she desired me to write it in "Horne's Manuel for the Afflicted," a little book which she kept by her pillow, and which is now one of my melancholy treasures; and, every morning, from that day till her decease nearly two months later, the first thing she asked me for was her hymn. "Now *my* hymn," she would say—and she would often repeat it after me, line for line, many times in the day and night. You may judge from this whether the volume you propose to send us will be acceptable to her father and mother and husband.

> Mrs. Wordsworth has told me that your hymn forms part of her daily solitary prayers. I do not think that Mr. Wordsworth could bear to have it repeated aloud in his presence, but he is not the less sensible of the solace it gave his one and matchless daughter.

Elliott's reputation rests more on a single six-stanza hymn than on her collected works, yet the power of that one poem and perhaps a few others has made her reputation secure. It was so during her own lifetime. It is so today.

Just as I am—without one plea
But that thy blood was shed for me,
And that Thou bid'st me come to Thee—
      O Lamb of God, I come!

Biographies:
Eleanor Babington, *Memoir of Charlotte Elliott* (London, 1874);
Erik Routley, *Hymns and Human Life* (London: John Murray, 1952), pp. 207–209;
Tom Ingram and Douglas Newton, *Hymns as Poetry* (London: Constable, 1956).

Dora Greenwell
(6 December 1821 – 29 March 1882)

Janet Gray
Princeton University

See also the Greenwell entry in *DLB 35: Victorian Poets After 1850.*

BOOKS: *Poems* (London: Pickering, 1848);
Stories That Might Be True (London: Pickering, 1850; London & New York: Strahan, 1866);
Poems (Edinburgh: Strahan, 1861; London: Hamilton, Adams, 1861);
The Patience of Hope (Edinburgh, 1855; Boston: Ticknor & Fields, 1862);
Two Friends (Boston: Ticknor & Fields, 1863; Edinburgh: Strahan, 1867);
A Present Heaven (Edinburgh, 1860; Boston: Ticknor & Fields, 1864);
Essays (London & New York: Strahan, 1866);
Lacordaire (Edinburgh: Edmonston & Douglas, 1867; London: Isbister, 1874);
Poems (London: Strahan, 1867);
Carmina Crucis (London: Bell & Daldy, 1869; Boston: Roberts, 1869);
On the Education of the Imbecile (London: Strahan, 1871);
Colloquia Crucis (London: Strahan, 1871);
John Woolman (London: Kitto, 1871);
Songs of Salvation (London: Strahan, 1873);
The Soul's Legend (London: Strahan, 1873);
Liber Humanitatis: A Series of Essays on Various Aspects of Spiritual and Social Life (London: Daldy, Isbister, 1875);
Camera Obscura (London: Daldy, Isbister, 1876);
A Basket of Summer Fruit. Dedicated to the American Evangelists who Lately Visited England (London, 1877);
Poems (London: Scott, 1889; New York: Whittaker, 1889);
Poems (London: Eyre Methuen, 1904);
Everlasting Love, and Other Songs of Salvation (London: Allenson, 1906);
Selected Poems (London: Allenson, 1906);
Selections from the Prose of Dora Greenwell (London: Epworth, 1950).

Dora Greenwell; painting by Hastings (Henry Betti, Dora Greenwell, *1950)*

Dora Greenwell was among the most highly praised of the women poets whose careers flourished just after Elizabeth Barrett Browning's death. She is often grouped with Jean Ingelow and Christina Rossetti, and like them she worked in the traditions of religious and love lyrics, exploring and redefining their limits. New anthologies of nineteenth-century women's poetry published in the 1990s have formed a canon of Greenwell's work that shows her stylistic range, from the sentimental to the political to the metaphysical. She made her literary reputation, however, with prose writings that articulate an eclectic Protestantism, anticipating Christian existentialism in their concern with modern struggles for faith. These writings reveal a vigorous, cultivated mind attuned to intellectual and social change. They also help to illuminate inconsistencies in Greenwell's poetic craft. Late in her career, in *Li-*

ber Humanitatis: A Series of Essays on Various Aspects of Spiritual and Social Life (1875), she wrote that poetry and Christianity share a sympathy for humanity, but they depart in their dealings with nature and natural passions. The poet intensifies wildness, loves luxury, and drives anguish deeper, demanding objects shaped to his desires. Christ purges nature, and the Christian tries to heal anguish and accept austerity. Both extremes of this conflict appear in Greenwell's poems.

Greenwell was the middle child and only daughter of William Thomas Greenwell, a country squire and magistrate, and Dorothy Smales Greenwell, the aristocratic daughter of a Durham lawyer. She was born on 6 December 1821 and raised at Greenwell Ford, a modern mansion built on property near Lanchester, Durham, that the family had held since the sixteenth century. Her four brothers were sent away to school, but, typical for girls of her class, Dora stayed home, where she was bred to the "Lady Bountiful" tradition of charitable condescension to the lower classes. As a young adult she plunged into an ambitious program of self-education with help from a neighbor who lent her books. Besides becoming adept in French, Italian, German, and Latin, she explored every field of knowledge—from medieval lore to social economy to physiology—about which she could find anything to read.

The only known representation of Greenwell is a conventional portrait of a young gentlewoman newly eligible for marriage. She never married. In her essay "Our Single Woman" (1866), Greenwell hints that she did not remain single by choice, but she satirizes the Victorian stereotype of the "dove-like" old maid nursing a broken heart. She urges the creation of institutions through which single women can do work expressive of their inner growth. She illustrated by her own example a modernized version of the noncloistered religious life that had for centuries offered women creative and often influential alternatives to marriage. A chronic illness (nowhere specified) that struck in her early twenties frequently disabled her later in life, but writing served her as an intellectual and social outlet.

No event had a greater impact on Greenwell's life than her father's loss of the family property due to a failed investment in 1847. While traumatically separating her from the places and expectations of her childhood, the loss of Greenwell Ford also partially freed her from a class whose way of life was becoming obsolete. The songs she chose for a musical commonplace book that she assembled during her twenties show that, with her loss of status, her religious longings deepened and her political sympathies shifted away from her Tory origins toward

struggles for liberation. Her writings reflect a sense of cataclysmic original loss and show much internal struggle as she worked to adapt her gentlewoman's breeding to a helping role in the modern world.

Living amid competing Christian denominations, Greenwell did not strictly adhere to Anglicanism. The range of her religious views shows in the biographies she wrote of a French Dominican, *Lacordaire* (1867), and an American Quaker, *John Woolman* (1871), figures who shared the traits of devoutness, severe self-discipline, and commitment to human liberties. Her enthusiasm for the popular American revivalists who visited Britain in the 1870s even shocked admirers of her eclecticism, who felt these preachers were beneath her in class and intellect. While avoiding dogma, Greenwell believed the cross on which Christ died to be the "one great fact," the signifier of God's susceptibility to the same embodiment and loss as humans. Greenwell's religious writings were part of the Victorian transformation of Christianity into a social gospel, the investment of Christ with feminine attributes, and the affirmation of affective and sensuous experiences repressed by modern economic ideology. Yet she viewed science and social progress as potential supports for religious life, since science showed that pain and death had always ruled nature and belief in human betterment directed attention toward lives in which misery still reigned.

Greenwell published her first book, *Poems* (1848), soon after the sale of Greenwell Ford. She and her parents had moved in with her oldest brother William, who was substituting for the rector at Ovingham in Northumberland. She assisted William in his pastoral work with the poor and in the summertime wandered the romantic grounds of nearby Castle Prudhoe. Several times during her career Greenwell used her own books to make contact with literary figures, sending an autographed copy with a letter. The earliest such correspondence that survives, addressed to Henry Wadsworth Longfellow, begins with a letter accompanying her first book and extends from 1848 to 1852. None of Greenwell's early verse attracted sustained critical attention, but it was well enough received to encourage her to publish a second book, *Stories That Might Be True* (1850). Among narrative poems about frustrated love, erotic inability, and unmarked passing, "Madana" stands out as an early illustration of Greenwell's affinity for sensual mysticism. In short couplets the poem describes the effects of the flower-tipped arrows of Madana or Kama, "the Hindu Cupid." Five arrows give a fleeting, harmless pleasure that leaves only sensory memories of summer; but Madana's greater power is concentrated in an arrow with a

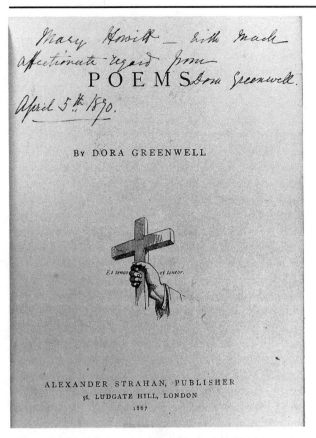

Title page, inscribed by the author, for Greenwell's volume that includes memorial sonnets to Elizabeth Barrett Browning (courtesy of Special Collections, Thomas Cooper Library, University of South Carolina)

honeycomb head that wounds incurably with its addictive sweetness.

When William Greenwell gave up his position in 1850, Dora and her parents had to leave Ovingham rectory and depend on the hospitality of friends for several months before they could settle with Alan, Greenwell's second youngest brother, who was newly appointed the rector at Golbourne, Lancashire. Again Greenwell involved herself in ministry to the poor. She also began seriously writing prose and shared her work with a younger friend, Josephine Grey (later Butler), who became well known for her campaign against the sexual exploitation of lower-class women during the 1860s. "Christina," a 380-line, blank-verse dramatic monologue that Greenwell wrote in 1851, is prescient of Grey's future career and must owe much to the friendship between Greenwell and Grey, who introduced her to evangelicalism. The speaker, a dying woman being cared for at an inn, asks a priest to return her crucifix to her childhood friend Christina. She tells of her own sexual corruption and emotional hardening, her separation from Christina, and her secret

watching of Christina's life. Greenwell revises the popular genre of the seduction narrative to relieve the fallen woman of the conventional consequences of her sexual exploitation. Rather than dying young, the fallen woman lives on for some time before the death scene. It is not the speaker but Christina who bears a child that dies: misery also strikes the pure.

The speaker tells of secretly leaving flowers on the grave of her friend's child until one day Christina finds her there. In the dialogue that follows, the speaker takes the jaded voice of secular modernity and Christina answers with loving fervor, praying over her friend, who experiences spiritual conversion in Christina's embrace—one of many instances of Greenwell's bringing erotic intensity to a relationship between women:

> And o'er the chaos of the void within
> A breath moved lightly, and my soul stretched out
> Its feelers darkly, as a broken vine
> Puts forth its bruisèd tendrils to the sun:
> A mighty yearning took me, and a sigh
> Burst from my bosom, cleaving for my soul
> A way to follow it, and in that hour
> Methought I could have died, and known no pain. . . .

Greenwell's father died in 1854. Her brother Alan, in ill health, resigned his position the same year. Greenwell and her mother settled comfortably with a few servants in a house in the bailey (the outer fortification) of Durham. Founded in medieval times, Durham was still economically dominated by the church in the early nineteenth century, although it was undergoing modernization as it became a hub of the coal industry. Greenwell became involved in visiting inmates at the prison and the poorhouse, experiences she wrote about in essays published in *The North British Review*. Her irascible and overprotective mother, keeper of the household finances, often refused to give Greenwell money for fear that she would give it away.

During the eighteen years the two women lived together in Durham, Greenwell wrote the works that established her reputation. She also initiated several correspondences that proved of lifelong value. In 1857 she wrote to poet and artist William Bell Scott, a friend of her brother Alan, praising Scott's biography of his brother. Scott invited her to his home in nearby Northumberland, where she met writers and artists visiting from London. In 1859 Greenwell began corresponding with Thomas Constable, the Edinburgh printer of her books. She built close friendships with Constable, his wife Lucy, and their children, who became a surrogate family for her and welcomed her for extended visits. In 1860

Greenwell sent *The Patience of Hope* to the American poet John Greenleaf Whittier with a letter applauding his antislavery activism. Whittier, a consistent promoter of women writers, secured an American publisher for Greenwell's prose works and wrote an introduction to the 1862 American edition of *The Patience of Hope*. Greenwell's third prose book, *Two Friends* (1863), a philosophical dialogue dedicated to Thomas Constable, elicited a letter of praise and critique from William Angus Knight, then a young Scottish divine and later a professor. They corresponded for many years about theology and writing. In 1862 she made contact with Rossetti, whom she had not yet met despite their having Scott as a common acquaintance.

Greenwell's first two theological books reflect Josephine Grey Butler's influence, with letters from Butler incorporated in the text. *A Present Heaven* (1855) argues for a spirituality immanent in life, not to be deferred until death. In *The Patience of Hope* (1860) Greenwell claims that the central crisis of modern faith is a contradiction between the natural will to greatness and the Christian commitment to the defeated, weak, and marginalized. Both prose books were enthusiastically received. Visiting Edinburgh soon after the publication of *The Patience of Hope,* Greenwell wrote excitedly to her mother about discovering its popularity among young intellectuals, one of whom told her that "none of his friends would believe it was written by a woman."

Greenwell's publishers followed up the success of her prose by publishing dozens of her poems, old and new, in a new periodical, *Good Words,* founded in 1860. Among the new poems, "When the Night and Morning Meet" simply illustrates Greenwell's theological quarrel with the Romantic view of nature. The poet tells of her vigil at the deathbed of a man who spent his life in the "dark and narrow street" of a city, far from the natural sights and sounds that Romanticism associated with spirituality. Yet the man dies in spiritual triumph, having won the soul's "Rich heritage."

Greenwell's new poems and selected older ones were collected in *Poems* (1861), whose author was identified simply as "The author of 'The Patience of Hope.'" The three-hundred-page collection includes ballads on medieval subjects with heroines and allegorical female figures; poems of pain, suffering, and physical disability; and nostalgia translated to the hope of heaven. Writing to Scott in 1857, Greenwell had expressed her dissatisfaction with her "homegrown" poems and her ambition to improve her art by exercising the "temperance and restraint" modeled by Johann Wolfgang von Goethe and preached by John Ruskin. A few of her shorter poems, organized into separate sections headed "Valentines and Songs" and "Sonnets," demonstrate her application of this discipline. In three stanzas the valentine "The Broken Chain" describes the sense of loss that comes of breaking bonds, whether imposed or deeply internal. The first stanza speaks of slavery, the second of "sister" flowers linked "With a Name and with an Hour, / Running down its Rosary," and the third of a chain "Firm as gold and fine as hair": "Would not something sharp remain / In the breaking of the chain?"

With a section of the 1861 volume later expanded and given the title "Liber Veritatis" (book of truth), Greenwell began to organize poems in a thematic sequence. In "Old Letters" the poet tells of finding a box of love letters in an ancient hall. A series of poems traces them from their first meeting— "We date / Our marriage from our meeting day"— until their separation. Their love is a godsend, although not sanctioned by convention:

> here a steadfast law
> Doth hold or rend asunder hearts that draw
> Together, restless till they meet, then soon
> Divided, and for ever; it would seem
> That God hath made these loving hearts and bold
> . . . not to fold
> Their warmth within each other, but to stream
> Afar and wide. . . .

Greenwell's writings on social issues for *The North British Review* were collected in *Essays* (1866), followed by a new edition of her poems. *Poems* (1867) is dedicated to the memory of Elizabeth Barrett Browning, who died in 1861. Added to the contents of *Poems* are new political poems on the Italian unification movement, American slavery, and the poverty British weavers suffered when the Civil War made American cotton unavailable.

A sonnet to Browning from the earlier volume is now titled "To Elizabeth Barrett Browning in 1851" and paired with a second sonnet, "To Elizabeth Barrett Browning in 1861." Together the sonnets illustrate the overwhelming power of Browning as a model to women poets who followed her and Greenwell's almost hopeless desire to be her literary heir. The earlier poem resembles one of Greenwell's fan letters, heightened to eroticism by its borrowing from the love sonnet tradition. Greenwell compares herself as a reader of Browning's poems to the Queen of Sheba swooning over Solomon's wealth, a bee in a rose, and a nightingale that risks its life competing with Orpheus, poet of the gods. The second sonnet has almost no figurative embellishment; Greenwell simply states, "I only loved thee—love thee!" She describes a single meeting with Browning when they exchanged kisses and Greenwell received Browning's blessing.

Greenwell had concentrated on writing short lyrics in the years since her earlier collection was published. The "Valentines and Songs" section is much expanded, including several imitations of medieval love lyrics. She had written to Knight that studying Provençal literature brought "a fresh breath . . . full of charm and allurement" to her own poetry.

Among the new poems, "Home" and "A Scherzo" (A Shy Person's Wishes) contrast both in craft and in their stances toward convention. "Home" was a favorite of Greenwell's contemporaries, but twentieth-century critic Angela Leighton finds it "sludgy," and for Kathleen Hickok it epitomizes Victorian domestic ideology:

> Two birds within one nest;
> Two hearts within one breast;
> Two spirits in one fair
> Firm league of love and prayer,
> Together bound for aye, together blest.

"A Scherzo (A Shy Person's Wishes)" strains against the enclosure extolled in "Home," and late twentieth-century critics such as Isobel Armstrong consider it one of Greenwell's finest poems. "Scherzo" means joke, and, in a rollicking meter, the shy person of the subtitle tells of wishing to be in a long list of places—"Anywhere, anywhere, out of this room!" This final line echoes a line from Thomas Hood's popular poem about a fallen woman's suicide, "The Bridge of Sighs": "Anywhere, anywhere / Out of the world!" Greenwell's revision expresses restlessness about being contained in domesticity and constrained by social forces. The alternate places she lists show a longing to join natural things in their seclusion, growth, and freedom:

> With the wasp at the innermost heart of a peach,
> On a sunny wall out of tip-toe reach,
> With the trout in the darkest summer pool,
> With the fern-seed clinging behind its cool
> Smooth frond, in the chink of an aged tree,
> In the woodbine's horn with the drunken bee. . . .

In *The Patience of Hope* Greenwell wrote that the soul, like natural things, "must pass through strange metamorphoses, through sundry successive kinds of death." But the list of natural transformations in "A Scherzo" leads back to the social world in the figure of a weaver, a worker whose livelihood was under threat in Greenwell's day and whose making of textiles parallels the poet's making of texts:

> To be couched with the beast in its torrid lair,
> Or drifting on ice with the polar bear,
> With the weaver at work at his quiet loom;
> Anywhere, anywhere, out of this room!

In 1869 Greenwell published a book of poems she had been planning since 1863. She described this book to Rossetti as an "inward" history with a connecting thread. *Carmina Crucis,* which included nothing previously published, became her most highly regarded book of poetry.

In "Desdichado" and "The Sunflower" Greenwell brought to maturity a stanza that she apparently invented, a quatrain composed of one trimeter line, two pentameter lines, and another trimeter line, usually rhymed ABAB. The stanza reads as an incomplete synthesis of the ballad meter of folk verse and the longer, literary poetic line. It has an unsettling, evocative effect; something seems to have been left out.

"Desdichado" and "The Sunflower" also capture contrasting spiritual states. The title "Desdichado" refers to the motto of a knight in Sir Walter Scott's novel *Ivanhoe* (1819) and means disinherited or fatal destiny. It is also the title of a sonnet by the French symbolist poet Gérard de Nerval. Greenwell's poem responds to the epigraph, quoted from Jean Paul, for *Les Chimères* (1854), the book in which the sonnet appears: "God is dead, the sky is empty. Children, you have no fathers." Greenwell advises not to weep for people who have lost loved ones or are suffering from guilt:

> But weep for him whose eye
> Sees in the midnight skies a starry dome
> Thick sown with worlds that whirl and hurry by,
>   And gives the heart no home;
>
> Who hears amid the dense
> Loud trampling crash and outcry of this wild
> Thick jungle world of drear magnificence,
>   No voice which says, *my child.* . . .

In "The Sunflower" the sky contains the object of the flower's obsessive adoration:

> I lift my golden orb
> To his, unsmitten when the roses die,
> And in my broad and burning disk absorb
>   The splendours of his eye.
>
> His eye is like a clear
> Keen flame that searches through me; I must droop
> Upon my stalk, I cannot reach his sphere;
>   To mine he cannot stoop.

This poem was the first of Greenwell's to attract attention from twentieth-century feminist critics. Cora

Kaplan found the sunflower's self-abnegation—so characteristic of Greenwell—sexual and submissive with "troubling masochistic nuances." Yet the poem ends on a note of pride and triumph:

> All ray'd and crown'd, I miss
> No queenly state until the summer wane,
> The hours flit by; none knoweth of my bliss,
> And none has guess'd my pain;
>
> I follow one above,
> I track the shadow of his steps, I grow
> Most like to him I love
> Of all that shines below.

The sunflower is a traditional symbol of Christ, and in the Victorian "language of flowers" the sunflower represents haughtiness or aristocratic bearing. The combined symbolism makes the sunflower someone like Greenwell herself, a gentlewoman striving to imitate Christ.

Greenwell's most effective writing on social issues resulted from her being asked by the director of the new Royal Albert Asylum for Imbeciles to compile statistics and literature on mental disability for a fund-raising pamphlet. *On the Education of the Imbecile* (1871) was welcomed by clergy and physicians as the latest thinking in the field. Countering the trend of Darwinian eugenics, Greenwell urged loving and hopeful treatment of the mentally disabled.

Greenwell's mother died in the fall of 1871, and in 1872 she traveled south, living for several years in Torquay, Clifton, and different parts of London. Settled in a house near Westminster Abbey in 1874, Greenwell became a part of London literary life and attracted a growing circle of intellectual companions.

After visiting Greenwell in the summer of 1875 Christina Rossetti noted their shared aging and copied out her "Autumn Violets," a sonnet about the passing of youth, for Greenwell. Greenwell's response, the celebratory poem "To Christina Rossetti," contradicts the modesty of Rossetti's sonnet by asserting that Rossetti's own poetry invites a sensual communion:

> The grapes in their amber glow
> And the strength of the blood-red wine
> All mingle and change and flow
> In this golden cup of thine,
> With the scent of the curling vine,
> With the balm of the rose's breath. . . .

Despite their similarities, Greenwell disagreed so strongly with Rossetti about some poetic matters that Rossetti's opposition could strengthen Greenwell's opinion. She wrote to William Michael Rossetti that his sister did not agree with her about the "pagan element" in art—"which makes me feel sure I am right."

In *Liber Humanitatis,* her second collection of essays, Greenwell tackled large philosophical and scientific questions such as the relationship between spirituality and physiological pathology. She chose the name *Camera Obscura* (1876) for her last book of poems to signify the human intellect's condition of bondage and limitation. The title refers to a Bible verse from First Corinthians that Greenwell often quoted: "For now we see through a glass, darkly; but then face to face: now I know in part; but then shall I know even as I am known."

In two poems about mothers and daughters Greenwell seems to seek reconciliation between nature and the soul. In "Demeter and Cora" Demeter, the goddess of corn, speaks with her daughter, who has been abducted into the underworld by "the King of Hell." Invisible to one another, the two women talk about their lives and passions in separate worlds, having difficulty hearing one another through the earth:

> "But, mother, tell me of the wet
> Cool primrose! of the lilac bough
> And its warm gust of rapture, met
> In summer days!—art listening yet?"
> "Art near me, O my Cora, now?"

In "The Homeward Lane" Greenwell makes a rural homecoming an allegory of reunion in death. The speaker approaches "The father's house" as two rustic gatekeepers wait for her. But the speaker turns away from the gate, having recognized an old woman picking a wild rose on the heath:

> in her deep-set eye
> Dwelt untold ecstasy,
> And in her eye was bliss,
> And rapture in her kiss,
> And heaven in her embrace.

During her last years Greenwell lent her voice to the campaigns for animal rights and woman suffrage. An uncollected poem, "Fidelity Rewarded," was written for the antivivisection campaign but also chillingly resonates to women's oppression. The dog who speaks shows devotion to its master in a power relationship that recalls the sunflower's devotion to the sun, but instead of ending with a secret triumph like the sunflower's, the later poem ends in torture and death, making

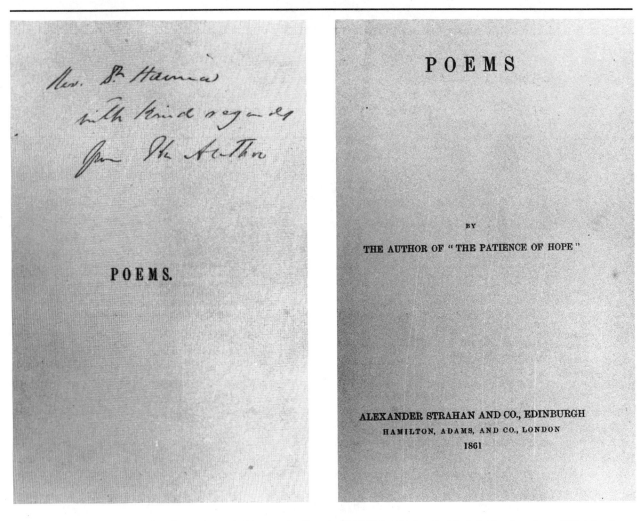

Half-title page, inscribed by the author, and title page for Greenwell's 1861 collection that includes her long poem "Christina"

it an agonized outcry against abuse. As a brute the dog has no choice but to love its master, but when it grows old, the master crucifies it for the sake of science:

Some secret hint to track
 Of life's poor trembling flame,
He nailed me to a rack,
 He pierced and tore my frame.

Greenwell's earliest poems and a continuing thread of later poems reflect their origins in private life. They are responses to readings, messages to friends whose names are disguised, keepsake verses to be copied into albums, and lyrics to be sung to the accompaniment of a parlor piano. During her thirties and forties her engagement with Christian thought and service, enhanced by a keen awareness of embodiment and physical pain, enriched her writing while placing disruptive pressures on her poetics. In her essay "Popular Religious Literature" (1866) Greenwell quoted Frie-

drich Schiller's claim that an artist aiming to create "a work of high imagination" must not pursue any "direct object." She added that a writer wishing to reach a wide audience with a religious message must reject this advice and address the audience's needs and desires. For a reviewer in *The Athenaeum* (1867), Greenwell succeeded in making the writing of poetry a kind of social service:

Miss Greenwell is specially endowed as a writer of sacred poetry: and it is the rarest realm of all, with the fewest competitors for its crown. She seems to us to be peculiarly fitted with natural gifts for entering into the chambers of the human heart, and to be spiritually endowed to walk there, with a brightening influence, cheering, soothing, exalting, with words of comfort and looks of love, as a kind of Florence Nightingale walking the hospital of ailing souls.

A Present Heaven and *The Patience of Hope* established Greenwell's reputation as a theological writer and created a receptive audience for her poetry. Her subsequent efforts to raise the level of her poetic craft resulted in compact lyrics that were praised for their artistic maturity but drew criticism for being obscure and spiritually narrow. Before repeating the format of *Carmina Crucis* with *Camera Obscura,* which drew similar criticism and praise, Greenwell turned away from the elite poetic tradition to compose *Songs of Salvation* (1873), consisting of hymns and ballads for uneducated readers. The beginning line of the most enduring of these hymns, "I am not skilled to understand," reflects the audience Greenwell imagined while expressing her own habits of self-deprecation and her belief that intellect is inadequate in spiritual matters.

As a social presence Greenwell eluded easy description. Ingelow speculated that she was "a new kind of person." William Michael Rossetti described her as elegant, serious, and pleasing—suitable attributes for a gentlewoman. Yet she was capable of scandalizing a genteel gathering: when in her forties, for example, she was asked if she would try to parlay her literary success into marriage, and she responded that the husband of a woman present was the only man in Durham worth pursuing. The Constables' son Thomas remembered her as a great talker and delightful playmate who was "always true and fearless." An American friend who called Greenwell "a gypsy among theologians," found her manner charismatic and socially levelling. William Dorling, a young scholar when she lived in London and her first biographer after her death, recorded the candor and intellectual intensity she brought to gatherings at her home.

An anecdote originating in *The Athenaeum* (7 August 1897) about Greenwell's having challenged Christina Rossetti and Jean Ingelow to a sewing contest has been repeated many times in biographies of Rossetti. The article is inaccurate, based on misconstrual of correspondence among the three poets in 1863. Told accurately, the anecdote typifies Greenwell's efforts to build literary friendships, her ambivalence about aesthetics, and her struggle between haughtiness and humility. Greenwell had sent the other two women copies of her own poems just as a rivalry began to brew between them. Ingelow's first book of poems (1863) quickly outstripped the sales of Rossetti's book published the year before. Responding belatedly to Greenwell's letter, Rossetti plied her with questions about Ingelow. Ingelow responded to Greenwell's gesture of literary sisterhood by embroidering her an elaborate workbag and promising to challenge Rossetti to give evidence of her needlework skills. Greenwell wrote with amuse-

ment to Lucy Constable about Ingelow's "old-fashioned, Clarissa Harlowe" gift. She deprecated the "humble" kettle-holder she was making in return; yet she placed high value on useful mementos. In her essay "Hardened in Good" (1866) she wrote of giving women convicts practical objects she had sewn as reminders of her care for them—gifts that she thought were a more effective form of outreach than were religious tracts.

Greenwell died on 29 March 1882, having suffered a near-fatal accident the year before. She never achieved the popularity of Ingelow or the critical acclaim of Rossetti, but her reputation survived her; volumes of her poems were published in 1889 and in 1906. The introduction to a selection of her poems in *The Poets and the Poetry of the Century* (1892) sums her up as "a poet of rare sweetness, penetration, and individuality" while noting that her "desire to interpret exceptional phases of spiritual existence" worked against her popularity. In the early 1900s she still had devoted admirers in both Britain and the United States, among them the scholar Paul Elmer More, who recommended her work to T. S. Eliot in 1933. Her admirers disagreed about whether her prose or poetry most deserved to endure. Frequent criticisms from her contemporaries were that her writing seemed unfinished, that she exaggerated conflict and failed to achieve a transcendent principle. Her most compact verse invited comparison to the poetry of the seventeenth-century metaphysical poet George Herbert, but her vacillating poetics caused some admirers to consider her just below first-rate, a lesser poet than Rossetti because of her unevenness.

In the late twentieth century "Christina" has been of interest to critics such as Hickok and Leighton because the Victorian preoccupation with sexual fallenness helps to illuminate beliefs about gender, sexuality, and women's roles. Kaplan places Greenwell among long-neglected women poets whose works help to reveal the historical "structuring of femininity through language" and suggests comparison of Greenwell's "The Sunflower" with Emily Dickinson's "My Life had stood—a loaded Gun," both fantasies of power. In her explorations of the sublimity of small things and the modern landscapes of religious doubt, Greenwell's territory often resembles Dickinson's. Armstrong calls attention to images of overflow and projection in Greenwell's poetry and to her account in "Our Single Women" of the conflicts that the Romantic poetics of emotional expression produced for women writers. In social life, Greenwell wrote, women are required to withhold and suppress feeling, but in their writing they reveal secret selves with fine minds, strong passions, and exacting consciences made morbid by social constriction. The assertion in this essay that "To be Man's help-meet is Woman's true vocation" has led some historians of gender to call Greenwell's views conservative, but, as Armstrong points out, the essay also subverts conventionality. Greenwell envisioned women arming themselves to slay the "bugbear" of "the safe and mediocre."

Biographies:

William Dorling, *Memoirs of Dora Greenwell* (London: Clarke, 1885);

Constance Maynard, *Dora Greenwell* (London: Allenson, 1926);

Henry Bett, *Dora Greenwell* (London: Epworth, 1950).

References:

Isobel Armstrong, *Victorian Poetry: Poetry, Poetics and Politics* (New York & London: Routledge, 1996);

Janet Gray, "Dora Greenwell's Commonplace Book," *Princeton University Library Chronicle,* 57, no. 1 (1995): 47–74;

Gray, "The Sewing Contest: Christina Rossetti and the Other Women," *a/b: Auto/Biography Studies,* 8 (Fall 1993): 233–257;

Kathleen Hickok, *Representations of Women: Nineteenth-Century British Women's Poetry* (Westport, Conn. & London: Greenwood, 1984), pp. 30–31, 65–66, 99, 108, 119, 122;

Cora Kaplan, "Introduction," in *Salt and Bitter and Good: Three Centuries of English and American Women Poets* (New York: Paddington, 1975), pp. 13–25;

Kaplan, *Sea Changes: Essays on Culture and Feminism* (New York: Verso, 1987), pp. 86–87;

Angela Leighton, "'Because men made the laws': The Fallen Woman and the Woman Poet," in *New Feminist Discourses: Critical Essays on Theories and Texts,* edited by Armstrong (London & New York: Routledge, 1992), pp. 342–360;

Leighton, *Victorian Women Poets: Writing against the Heart* (Charlottesville: University Press of Virginia, 1992), pp. 123–125;

M., "A Poetic Trio," *The Athenaeum,* 3641 (7 August 1897): 193–194.

Janet Hamilton

(14 October 1795 – 30 October 1873)

Florence S. Boos
University of Iowa

BOOKS: *Poems and Essays of a Miscellaneous Character on Subjects of General Interest* (Glasgow: Thomas Murray / Edinburgh: Paton & Ritchie / London: Arthur Hall, 1863);

Poems of Purpose and Sketches in Prose of Scottish Peasant Life and Character in Auld Langsyne, Sketches of Local Scenes and Characters, with a Glossary, by Janet Hamilton, Authoress of "Poems and Essays" (Glasgow: Thomas Murray / Edinburgh: William Ritchie / London: James Nibet, 1865);

Poems and Ballads (Glasgow: James Maclehose, 1868);

Poems, Essays and Sketches. A Selection from the First Two Volumes, "Poems and Essays," and "Poems and Sketches," with Several New Pieces (Glasgow: James Maclehose, 1870); enlarged as *Poems, Essays, and Sketches: Comprising the Principal Pieces from Her Complete Works*, edited by James Hamilton (Glasgow: James Maclehose, 1880); republished as *Poems, Sketches, and Essays* (Glasgow: James Maclehose, 1885).

Janet Hamilton may have been the most widely read and appreciated working-class poet of Victorian Scotland. Her vigorous, satiric, and recollective poems in English and her native Doric (Lowland Scots) exemplified the values of a region and vanished time and provided rare insight into the developed views of an imaginative elderly woman who never attended school, remained poor all her life, raised a large family, and overcame illiteracy and blindness to record verses she composed in her head. An upright woman of mildly reformist inclinations, angered by the devastating consequences of urban industrial blight, Hamilton eventually became an articulate spokeswoman for the working class and a remarkable example of an elderly oral poet whose verses found wide circulation in print.

She was born on 14 October 1795 at Shotts, in Lanark (formerly a county in central Scotland), the child of James Thomson, a shoemaker, and Mary Brownlee Thomson. Through her mother Janet

Thomson was descended from John Whitelaw of Stand, Monkland, a devout Covenanter who was executed for his beliefs at the Old Tolbooth, Edinburgh, in 1683, four years after he took part in the battle of Bothwell Bridge. Hamilton memorialized her great-great-grandfather's death in prose and verse and celebrated in other reminiscences the words and deeds of other strong-minded Presbyterian ancestors, among them her grandparents.

When Janet was about seven, her parents' bad health led them to move to Langloan in the parish of Old Monkland, then a small village and later a subdivision of Coatbridge, and she lived there until her death. Her parents worked for two years as field laborers on the nearby Drumpellier estate, and Janet sat at home to complete her day's labor of spinning "two hanks of sale yarn." When she was nine, she began to work as a tambourer, or weaver and embroidress, and she followed this occupation until she became blind at about sixty. Her mother "left the out-door labour," and it seems likely that mother and daughter worked side by side, perhaps discussing points of faith and the biblical lore dear to Mary Thomson. Hamilton believed throughout her life that women should contribute to their family's income as well as instruct their children at home, a pattern made easier by the home-based craftwork she and her mother both plied.

As a child Janet Thomson received no formal schooling, but taught by her mother, she read before she was five and quickly applied herself to ballads, songs, and stories, as well as to the constantly available religious texts. Hamilton's accounts of her ancestors' strict Sabbatarian practices blended respect with memories of the restiveness she recalled feeling when she could not hear tales or explore the outdoors. At eight she saw a copy of John Milton's *Paradise Lost* (1674) and a book of Allan Ramsay's poetry on a loom in a weaver's cottage, borrowed the books, and read them with delight. In the village library she found and read a number of histories and collections of essays (including Plutarch's *Lives* and volumes of *The Spectator* and *The Rambler*) and the poems of Robert Fergusson and Robert Burns, but few novels were available to her since many Presbyterians disapproved of them. Hamilton adhered to the religion of her upbringing in most other ways, but her taste in literature was eclectic, and she avidly read Shakespeare and other literary works disapproved of by her pious friends. She later told Alexander Wallace that she "could scarcely remember the time when her love of books was not her ruling passion," and she continued to read till two or so each morning of her sighted life.

When James Thomson returned to his former occupation of shoemaking in Langloan, he employed as an assistant John Hamilton, whom Janet married in February 1809, when she was thirteen and he twenty-five. She remembered their wedding with fondness: one cold February day the couple walked the twelve miles from Langloan to Glasgow, where they were married by Dr. Lockhart of College Church, a preacher they had never met. They returned after dark and began housekeeping with their "plenishing"(household goods) and one Spanish dollar. Biographical accounts mention that the couple had ten children, whose names were recorded in the Old Monkland Parish registers and in the Hamilton family bible. A daughter and two sons seem to have died in infancy, but the other seven children survived into adulthood and at least five of them outlived their mother. Those whose births

were recorded were Archibald, born June 1810; Mary, born May 1812; James, born July 1814; William, born August 1816; John, born August 1816 (a twin of William, he may have died young since the name was used again); John, born August 1818; Charles, born May 1820; Marion ("Mirren"), born June 1824; and Janet, born July 1825 (who lived only five weeks). Hamilton therefore bore her first child at fourteen and her last before she was thirty. In her "Reminiscences of the Radical Time" she remembers "crying amongst my five young children" in April of 1820, when she feared the Radical militia would attack her husband and other men of the village who refused to join them.

The marriage was evidently a good one and John Hamilton consistently supported his wife's marked desires to read and write. Alexander Wallace, a minister who visited the couple, recorded in a brief sketch prefaced to *Poems and Ballads* (1868) that

It was very amusing to hear her "ain gudeman," John, telling with great glee, how that after she had "used up" the village library, he went to another at some distance, and brought one armful of books after another, and continued his journeys till this other librarian was also compelled to acknowledge that he had never known a case of such *fell* reading before.

At her own expense Hamilton started a small circulating library for the benefit of her neighbors, but this venture failed when users did not return the books, and she lost her entire supply. According to her later memories, Hamilton also turned her attention to her children's education with zeal. She taught sons and daughters alike to perform household tasks, and each child began to read at five, with the Shorter Catechism and the Gospel of John as texts.

Though she could read, Hamilton could not write. Between the ages of seventeen and nineteen she composed in her head about twenty poems, all religious, and her husband transcribed them for her, but after the birth of her third child she left off composition for about thirty years. When she was about fifty she taught herself to write in a rough script (of her own invention) and began to write essays for an annual supplement to Cassell's periodical, *The Working Man's Friend*. She wrote these early essays and her earliest published poems in standard English but gradually began to insert more details of Scottish setting and speech into her later volumes, and her style became more personal and direct as her confidence grew. Hamilton's fervent support for European independence movements suggests that her social and political views may also have broadened somewhat as she made a wider range of choices and interacted more directly with the outside world. At one point a grandson in the colonies sent her a small gold bar to have made into a ring, but she sold it instead and gave the entire proceeds to the Garibaldi Fund for Italian independence. Even after she became blind, she was eager to have the newspaper read to her.

James Hamilton recorded the environment in which she managed to write: "My mother's pieces were mostly all composed amid the bustle and noise incident to the affairs of a family being conducted in a small house, or while she was engaged in conversation with her family and friends." Unfortunately, Hamilton was partially blind by sixty and fully blind by seventy-one. In many of her later poems she laments her inability to see beloved natural objects. Her lifelong habit of memorizing long passages of poetry, including her own verses, helped her write through her blindness, and her son James transcribed her poems—composed, in her husband's words, "when the burning thochts within winna let her rest." Her firm-mindedness and independence are mentioned in James's preface to the 1880 edition of her poems:

Having been my mother's amanuensis, I may say that when I wrote a piece from her dictation, and afterwards read it over to her, she rarely made a correction on it. When her books were being printed, although unable from want of sight to read a line, she never would allow any one but herself to make any correction on the proofs. I read them; she sat and listened, and an alteration of a word or a syllable from her own she would detect at once. She said if her writings possessed any merit, it would be her own; and if there were blemishes in them, they, too, would be her own.

Hamilton's first book, *Poems and Essays of a Miscellaneous Character on Subjects of General Interest,* appeared by subscription in 1863, when the author was sixty-eight. Her later *Poems and Ballads* (1868) was "lovingly and respectfully inscribed by the Authoress to her Brothers, the Men of the Working Class," but the earlier *Poems and Essays* bore a conventional dedication to a member of the upper classes: "To Colonel D. C. R. C. Buchanan, Drumpellier, This Volume is by permission respectfully dedicated." Buchanan was a neighboring landowner and heir of the estate on which Hamilton's parents had worked, and she praised him as "the liberal supporter of every benevolent and educational institution in the large and populous district in which he resides." The 1863 volume also includes a preface and gentle appeal for critical forbearance, which Hamilton signed in her characteristic script:

I hope the critics will lay the rod lightly across the shoulders of an old woman of threescore-and-ten, whose only school-room was a shoemaker's hearth, and her only teacher a hard-working mother, who, while she plied the spinning-wheel, taught me at her knee to read the Bible—the only education she or I, her daughter, ever received.

This first volume earned highly praiseful reviews in many newspapers in London and Scotland, and its immediate successors appeared with introductions by Alexander Wallace, D.D., and George Gilfillian, a well-known critic and patron of Scottish poetry.

Hamilton's work found an unusual range of reviewers in both Scotland and England. As one might expect, reviewers for religious and temperance papers such as *The League Journal, The Christian News,* the *United Presbyterian Magazine,* and the *Evangelical Repository* liked her work, but so did writers for major Scottish newspapers and several London papers, including the *Pall Mall Gazette,* the *Athenaeum,* the *St. James Gazette,* and *Punch.* Reactions tended to follow regional lines—the Scottish newspapers praised her Doric verses and the English ones her clear standard-English style—but most singled out "Effie: A Ballad," the tale of a young motherless woman betrayed by her lover in favor of a wealthier woman, for special praise. A typical Scottish reaction comes from the Glasgow *Herald* (28 November 1868):

The name of Janet Hamilton is one of the most remarkable in the history of Scottish poesy. That a woman in humble life, who did not enjoy the advantages of the usual elementary branches of a school education, should, at the age of 73, and while now blind, be capable of writing or composing verse at all, is singular enough; but that these verses should possess the *verve,* pathos, and genuine truthfulness of a Tannahill, and even, in all but his best pieces, of a Burns, can only be accounted for by the inheritance of genius. The ballad, "Effie," for tenderness, simplicity, and beauty, deserves to be placed alongside of the immortal "Auld Robin Gray" of Lady Ann Lindsay.

In several early poems Hamilton expressed ambivalent support for Britain's military campaign in the Crimea, but none of her political poems thereafter favored any colonial venture or conflict. In other poems she voiced contempt for the "sport" of hunting, attacked wars of oppression, and denounced American "Slavery's vile Draconian code / Of lawless laws, that flout the laws of God" ("Lines Addressed to Mrs. H. B. Stowe"). Hamilton was or became an ardent supporter of assorted liberal-populist revolutionary movements in Europe—praising independence movements in Spain, Hungary,

Poland, Greece, and Italy and expressing particular anger and distress at internecine slaughter in Poland. Some of this political verse affirmed more general democratic and egalitarian political ideals, and she often associated those ideals with "Auld Mither Scotland."

Hamilton's political opinions evolved as she wrote. Initially, for example, she remembered the activists of the 1819–1820 Radical uprising as violent malcontents dissatisfied with a (relatively) "good" lot. Even then, however, she asked rhetorically whether "if our misguided brethren of the times we refer to had enjoyed the same privileges [of electoral representation], they would ever have, even in their trying circumstances, supplied us with materials for writing Radical Reminiscences." Later contacts with a variety of workingmen's organizations acquainted her with a wider range of reformist and educational causes, and she supported them all.

Hamilton expressed her cultural nationalist views rather conventionally in her first volume. Several dramatic narratives record the persecutions of her dissenting ancestors and their fellows, and other poems celebrate Scotland's natural beauty and historic independence. In later poems she began to personify her beloved Scotland in clear self-image, as a loving if contentious old mother and indefatigable source of critical advice. In "Auld Mither Scotland," for example, the speaker frames a sharp critique of unequal British exploitation: "It's England's meteor flag that burns / Abune oor battle plains; / Oor victories, baith by sea an' lan', / It's England aye that gains." She also feared both illiteracy and the disappearance of Doric, and correctly observed that "mang baith auld an' young, / There's mony noo that canna read / Their printit mither tongue." Indeed, the "mither tongue" was more than a metaphor and mark of cultural identity to her—it became the emblematic source of most of her matriarchal memories and literary models. Her nationalism was Scottish-cultural rather than British-imperialist, and her early poems display an unabashed enjoyment of Scots usages, usually in informal contexts. Writing a "bit scrift" verse to "frien' Tammie" in "Verses Inscribed to Mr. Thomas Duncan, Glasgow," she reports that she had bidden her Muse "lea her trantels ahint her," but the Muse had resisted Doric: "An' wow she was cadgie an' gidgin' ful' fain, / An' tae skirl the Doric her pip didna hain." The problem of appropriate usage, however, was firmly resolved by the time she published "A Plea for the Doric" in 1865, in which the speaker apologizes for her "Parnassian" efforts, in standard English, "to busk oot my sang wi' the prood Southron tongue." She also expresses skepticism and regret at the long line of

distinguished Scottish journalists and intellectuals who had left Edinburgh (known affectionately as "Auld Reekie," or "Old Smokey") for London and notes with sarcasm that:

> I'm wae for Auld Reekie; her big men o' print
> To Lunnon ha'e gane, to be nearer the mint;
> But the coinage o' brain looks no a'e haet better,
> Though Doric is banish'd frae sang, tale, and letter.

Hamilton's vigorous defense of Scots vernacular is noteworthy, especially when one considers the social constraints to which elderly women without formal education were subject and the "genteel" emulative pressures to which many male working-class poets succumbed. Her egalitarian pride in her "national" history and language freed her to develop her natural gift for satiric mimicry and vernacular metaphor and fostered her growing respect for others' aspirations to national identity and independence.

During Hamilton's lifetime, local discoveries of extensive coal and iron lodes, explosive growth of rail and canal networks, new iron-smelting techniques, and explicit exemption from the modest constraints of the Public Health Acts (until 1885) inflicted on her natal Coatbridge and its environs some of the most intensely rapacious industrialization ever seen in the British Isles. Coatbridge quadrupled in size between 1821 and 1851 and suffered terribly from the ravages of such unregulated industrial development. Many of Hamilton's poems describe the effects of the new forms of work on Langloan and its surrounding villages—filth, noise, crowding, colliery explosions, and loss of livelihood and craft identity for the region's weavers. Some of Hamilton's most mordant lines appear in background descriptions of these conditions, often embedded in poems on other topics. Here, for instance, the environs of a pub is described in "Our Local Scenery":

> There's chappin' an' clippin' an' sawin' o' airn;
> Burnin' and soterin', reengin' and chokin'.
> Gizzen'd and dry ilka thrapple and mouth,
> Like cracks in the yird in a het simmer drought. . . .

By 1865 she had even begun to question some of the concrete uses to which human knowledge and science were put, as in "Rhymes for the Times. IV.–1865." For although

> . . . knowledge increases, abune an' below;
> The yird's like a riddle, pits, tunnels, an' bores,
> Whaur bodies, like mowdies, by hunners an' scores
> Are houkin', an' holin', an' blastin' the rocks;
> An' dronin's an' burnin's, explosions an' shocks, . . .

Oh, mony's the slain in the battle o' life!
It's Mammon we worship, wi' graspin' an' greed,
Wi' sailin' an' railin' at telegraph speed,
Get gowd oot the ironstane, an' siller frae coal,
An' thoosan's on thoosan's draw oot o' ae hole.

These changes also give a characteristic Hamiltonian inflection to the retrospective poem of memory, in which a speaker walks to a place she has known and contrasts its past and present fortunes. In "A Wheen Aul' Memories," for example, the speaker, cane in hand, visits nearby Gartsherrie, once a rural village in her girlhood:

Noo the bodies are gane an' their dwallin's awa',
And the place whaur they stood I scarce ken noo ava,
For there's roarin' o' steam, an' there's reengin o' wheels,
Men workin', an' sweatin', an' swearin' like deils.

And the flame-tappit furnaces staun' in a raw,
A' bleezin', an' blawin', an' smeekin' awa,
Their eerie licht brichtenin' the laigh hingin' cluds,
Gleamin' far ower the loch an' the mirk lanely wuds.

Hamilton evolved from a mild supporter of working-class causes into a wryly embittered observer of the squalor and depredation of industrial development. She became a marked skeptic about all forms of "progress" and "development" that blighted the lives of working people and destroyed the quiet community and environs of her youth.

Nineteenth-century temperance movements now attract little interest and literary expressions of support for them even less, but many Scottish temperance-movement activists were women, and the Scottish temperance movement fostered a wide range of working-class social organizations, such as the Band of Hope (a children's league), insurance agencies, and Friendly Societies. Hamilton's anger about the consequences of working-class alcoholism brought out some of her sharpest abilities, and the immediacy and passionate specificity of her descriptions suggest that she may have written from personal experience.

About half of the early essays Hamilton began to publish in the 1850s explore the consequences of alcoholism, and her essays on the subject call for personal abstention rather than governmental intervention. Their poetic counterparts dramatize the grim effects of addiction on Scottish working-class family life and provide detailed portrayals of the abuse of wives by alcoholic husbands and of parents by their sons. Some of the best of these poems might be described as satiric Doric rants in a Scottish tradition of stylized oral declamation. The effects of these tours de force are cumulative, and some of them—parts of "Oor Location" and "Our Local

Scenery," for example—shade over into the broader forms of social commentary mentioned above. The opening passage of "Oor Location," for example, segues into a description of the combative atmosphere of yet another Coatbridge pub:

Boatmen, banksmen, rough and rattlin',
'Bout the wecht wi' colliers battlin',
Sweatin', swearin', fechtin', drinkin',
Change-house bells an' gill-stoups clinkin',
Police—ready men and willin'–
Aye at han' when stoups are fillin',
Clerks, an' counter-loupers plenty,
Wi' trim moustache and whiskers dainty–
Chaps that winna staun at trifles,
Min' ye they can han'le rifles.

Like many others, Hamilton felt special contempt for petty profiteers and manipulators of human weakness—the proprietor of "The Three Golden Balls," for example, whose pawnshop shelves are "laden / With spoils of man, wife, child, and maiden, . . . / Vampire like, the blood he drains / From the drunkard's burning veins."

One of Hamilton's "walking poems," "Sketches of Village Character," provides a natural frame for such a blend of informal description, nostalgia, and reflection. The speaker guides her reader through an area once inhabited by prosperous weavers and narrates the fates of seven carefully individuated local pub owners. In one case the owner and his wife had "focht like twa cocks, an' aft she was seen / Gaun stoiten aboot wi' a pair o' black een." The weavers of her youth, of course, were gone ("The men o' the furnace, the forge, an' the mine, / Tak' the place o' the weavers in days o' langsyne"), but the publican's successors would flourish forever: "There's nae change in ae thing, that's drinkin', I trow; / We drink, but oor drouth is ne'er slocken'd, I think." Even better times might not help: "The higher the wages the deeper we drink."

Other poems describe or allude to the suffering of women married to alcoholics and wife beaters. In "The Feast of the Mutches," for example, the speaker recognizes one of her acquaintances among the attenders at a banquet the city has held for some of its old women and observes that "there's a puir heid that's been cutit and clour'd, / But Heaven an' hersel' kens what she endured / Lang years frae a drucken il-deedie gudeman: / He's yirded, an' sae are the sorrows o' Nan."

Hamilton seems to have written most directly about the sorrows and ravages caused by alcoholic children—in the essay "Intemperance *Versus* the Moral Law," for example, she reports:

We have known, ay, and seen—alas! that we should say so; it was not a solitary instance—a grey-haired mother, on her own hearth, shrinking from the presence of her own son, who, with murderous threats, uplifted hand, and eyes flaming with patricidal fires, was demanding from her the means to procure further indulgence in his depraved and brutal tastes. We have seen a father, day after day, forgetting to eat his bread, and nightly steeping his couch with tears, for the dishonour and apparent perdition of his son. . . .

The oldest of Hamilton's sons would have been about forty when this was written, and the most likely source of such details was personal experience. In a poem, "Midnight Vigil," the speaker mourns the "burning wound" of "my sons" who are lost in "depths defiling / Of intemperance. . . ." Another temperance essay, "Counteracting Influences," concludes with an untitled poem that mentions that "a monster so hideous, so hateful, and dire, / It seems as it moved in a circle of fire" has dragged two of a mother's children "to his den, / And turned them to brutes in the likeness of men." That same essay, however, also decries "that monstrous libel on womanhood" that is the "female drunkard" and the fear-inducing "reeling footsteps of him who is misnamed husband and father." One must be careful not to conflate set pieces of propaganda with autobiography but Hamilton's focus on the harm inflicted by adult alcoholics on their parents is unusual.

The mother of seven surviving children, Hamilton also saw mothers and "grannies" everywhere—from "Mother Earth" to "Auld Mither Scotland" to her own mother and those among her friends who grieved at the death of a child—and she constantly viewed events through the eyes of women, often old women. "The Way o' the Warl'" must surely have been one of the few critiques of public opinion that firmly urges its readers to "Lippen [trust] aye maist tae Heaven, tae yersel', an' yer mither," in that order. She also populated many poems with young girls—herself in memory, neighborhood girls, her daughter—and her empathy for her fellow women often extended across class boundaries. In "Craignethan Castle," for example, Hamilton evinces more sympathy for Mary, Queen of Scots than one might expect from someone of her Presbyterian origins, and she decries the pathetic murder of a young heiress in "The Deserted Mansion." Hamilton did not romanticize such class distinctions, but she clearly believed that certain emotions and moral imperatives were independent of the "accidents of birth and fortune."

Many of Hamilton's Scots ballads and cautionary tales also express a particular concern for women deceived or abandoned by men. Seduction and desertion are romantic staples, of course, but Hamilton gave special attention to the harm caused to women and their families. Her wary expectation of male sexual dishonesty gave poems such as "Effie—A Ballad," "Mysie, An Aul' Warl' But Ower True Story," and "The Ballad o' Mary Muiren" at times a mildly feminist tone.

Hamilton also preached quite ardently the need for women to educate their children, a view that gradually led her to embrace wider appeals for women's self-culture and equal status in working-class education reform movements. She became, in fact, an unshakably committed believer in women's education but assumed this need not take place in schools—none of which, after all, she had ever attended. Her poems and essays often praise women who had learned to read and taught their children, enjoin others to follow their example, and return again and again to the cardinal social virtues of such activities. Two of her ten essays on social topics advocate working people's self-education, and three focus specifically on women's self-education and their education of children.

In her advocacy of women's education Hamilton also took note of contemporary debates about women's roles. Quite skeptical of proposals by middle-class women reformers at first, she later came to accept ideas she thought could be adapted to the actual circumstances of working-class life. In the early "On Self-Education," for example, Hamilton still insists that education of the young was more important than public speaking and argues rather dubiously that a woman with a public mission could "always find a vent for her opinions and feelings on such subjects through the press." She had come to accept the work of such politically active women in "Rhymes for the Times, II," however, and asks only that those who would "tak up puir women's quarrels" should also "touch her heart an' teach her saul." When "neebour Johnie," finally, "a douce aul' farrant eldrin 'chiel," sneers at speakers at Glasgow College who advocate women's access to higher education, Hamilton's speaker rebukes him in pointed terms: "Noo, John, quo I, haud aff oor taes, / A woman best kens woman's ways. . . ."

In the same year Hamilton's "Address to Working-Women" (1863) also includes an almost anguished plea for a higher education standard for poor women: "We must confess that we have fallen immeasurably short of the standard attained by the females of the upper and middle classes, who by a zealous improvement of their mental resources—by reading, thinking, and composing—have strengthened and embellished their minds, while they have adorned and enriched the literature of their coun-

Manuscript for an untitled poem by Hamilton, written in the script she invented for herself (from Poems, Essays, and Sketches: Comprising the Principal Pieces from Her Complete Works, *1880)*

try." That some women remained illiterate was especially bitter to her ("Alas for the woman who is thus engaged in the battle of life!"), but she pointedly called working men to task for "that spirit of predominance and exclusiveness which, with a few exceptions, has met [women] at every turn."

Workingmen who truly wished "a good time coming" would also have to include "the females of your class, and more particularly the young, the future mothers of future men, in every movement for furthering the intellectual advance of your order." Hamilton was partly dependent on her working-class "brothers" for the publication and circulation of her works, and some of her views were controversial in a decade marked by the establishment and consolidation of male-only "working-men's" schools and colleges. In this context her criticisms reflected her courage.

Several of Hamilton's poems also celebrate women's economic contributions. In "A Lay of the Tambour Frame," for example, the lifelong tambourer denounces the men who exploits her and her sisters:

> Selfish, unfeeling men!
> Have ye not had your will?
> High pay, short hours; yet your cry, like the leech,
> Is, Give us, give us still.
> She who tambours—tambours

For fifteen hours a day—
Would have shoes on her feet, and dress for church,
Had she a third of your pay.

Hamilton came late to feminism, but she always identified broadly with other members of her sex and devoted herself throughout her work to the experiences and well-being of women. Her particular preoccupation with women's roles as educators and workers was integral to her life experience and eventually led her to criticize the blatant bias against women in working-class movements of her time.

Many of Hamilton's most attractive verses are "ballads of memorie," in which she blends commentary on the present with remembrances of things past. Several of these poems reflect her strong belief in the value of oral history, transmitted within a family from one generation to another, and most record social interactions with an aged and beloved storyteller who points a moral of constancy, integrity, and loyalty in the face of duress. The storyteller is usually a grandmother, whose conversations with a bright little girl, recalled by the girl grown old, reach out to readers in their turn.

Most "grannie poems" pay tribute to Hamilton's paternal grandmother, from whom she learned both songs and the wisdom to value them. These verses therefore bridge fifty years and more and offer a cumulative poetic account of an old woman's sense of personal and communal identity. Many record stories of Covenanters and others who showed great faith or resilience under the tests of poverty, isolation, and famine and experienced striking visions and other quasi-psychic events. Hamilton clearly designed such tales as moral *exempla* but sometimes evoked allegedly divine foreknowledge and prophetic attributes as a means to her end.

In "Grannie's Tale. A Ballad of Memorie," for example, a father who had complained about the birth of a fifth child in a time of famine later struggles to cope with the deaths of the other four and his wife. In "Grannie's Crack Aboot the Famine in Auld Scotlan' in 1739–40" a grandfather feels a flash of anger when his "witless bairns" waste food, but his more tactful wife pauses to tell them about a winter starvation in 1739, when people foraged for nettles and watched their children die. She remarks sadly that "some, perhaps, like silver seven times purified, / Cam' oot the furnace pure at last" but hopes the children will be spared so harsh an alembic.

Hamilton's deepest expression of a bond with her grandmother appears in "Grannie Visited at Blackhill, Shotts, July, 1805." Little Janet is bored

when her grandfather discusses cattle and sheep prices but feels a lovely sense of epiphanic intimacy when grandmother sits spinning, "[a]ye croonin' o'er some godly saum," and her wrinkled face "brichen't wi' a holy calm." Grannie pauses in one of her pious stories to bless the child: "God bless thee, bairn—my Jamie's bairn," / She said, an' straikit doun my hair; / "O may the martyrs' God be thine, / And make thee His peculiar care." The child then lays her head in Grannie's lap, and looks up to see her "dicht / A tear that tremilt on her cheek." The speaker has seen "a length o' days sinsyne" but "ne'er forgat / That simmer gloamin' at Blackhill," when the old woman tries to impart her best values to the child and confers a protective blessing. "Pictures of Memory," by contrast, is Hamilton's only poem of a remembered moment with her venerated but apparently rather austere mother. Unlike the "grandmother poems," it also offers a vignette of a child's assertion of the importance of imagination to her identity. The girl in "Pictures" had eagerly brought her mother a volume of fairy tales and ballads, only to hear the maternal reproof that "such reading may amuse, / But will not make you good and wise." In a noncombative but instantaneous response the little girl "warbled clear an old Scotch ditty," and her mother is moved in spite of herself: "her eyes / Were brimming o'er with love and pity." At last, "She smiled, and softly laid her hand / Upon the fair child's shining hair, / Who, like a dancing sunbeam, pass'd / Away into the summer air." The tie between mother and child is unbroken, but the child remains free to follow "the burning thochts within [that] winna let her rest."

A concomitant belief in the dignity and moral importance of the tale-teller's role informed Hamilton's conception of her own literary purpose. The only surviving depiction of Hamilton shows her in a mutch, and her "Feast of the 'Mutches'" wryly proclaims a sense of community with her fellow old women. Glossed as "verses commemorative of the annual supper given to the poor old women, in the City Hall, Glasgow, on January 3, 1868," when nearly two thousand were present, "all wearing white mutches," Hamilton's poem marvels over the visual effect of two hundred white heads, reflects on the lives of three individual grannies, and closes with a clear self-referential image and benison:

God bless ye, aul' grannies! I wish ye a' weel,
Ye're wearin' awa' to the Lan' o' the Leal;
May ye in the Lan' o' the Leal an' the true
Meet the aul' blin' grannie that sings to ye noo! . . .
We bless ye, kind gentles, an' leddies sae fair,
That oot o' yer plenty hae something to spare

For white heided grannies. O may it be given
To gentles an' grannies to meet yet in Heaven!

In 1868 Queen Victoria granted the seventy-three-year-old poet a Civil List pension. It was no longer possible for Hamilton to use the money for reading or travel, but she was deeply gratified by good reviews, public interest, and the concern of her friends. Hamilton added her final preface to the second edition of *Poems and Ballads* in May 1873, five months before her death, and used the occasion to comment briefly on her blindness and bedridden state, bid her readers farewell, and offer "sincere thanks to my friends, the press and the public, for the genial reception my literary efforts received from them."

After a three-year illness that prevented her from leaving her bed for more than an hour a day, Hamilton died 30 October 1873 at age seventy-eight, and her much older husband followed shortly thereafter. Their daughter Mirren cared for both of them in their final illnesses, and their son James wrote of his mother in her last years:

During all her long years of severe pain and blindness, I never heard her utter a word of complaint or murmuring for herself. . . . Her feelings of sympathy and concern were all for others. I have often heard her express a regret that the want of the means many times prevented her from assisting others to the extent she desired.

Regional newspapers reported her death, and more than four hundred mourners came from Glasgow and nearby towns to the funeral in Langloan. Many may have become acquainted with her through workingmen's organizations and temperance societies in the Glasgow and Coatbridge region, but others must have known her only through her work, which clearly reached a wide range of working- and middle-class readers.

Literary criticism of working-class poetry has tended to focus on issues of middle-class patronage, censorship, and cooptation. Most of the records that might clarify how Hamilton's publications reached a wide audience have disappeared, but she probably benefited from the efforts of regional societies whose members subscribed to her works. Her essays and poems clearly had broad social and political resonance, in any case, and her reception in the 1860s and 1870s also benefited from an interest in "people's literature" fostered by reformist anthologists and newspaper editors.

Eulogistic poems published after her death and poetic echoes of some of her more striking verses in late-century volumes by Scottish working-class women poets suggest that Hamilton's poetic

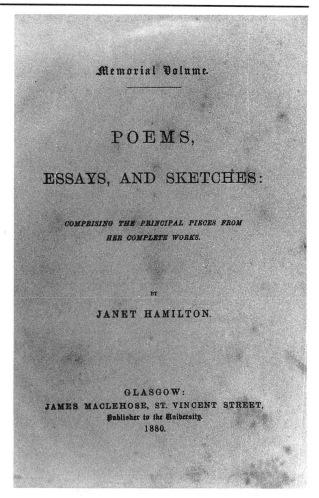

Title page for the collection of Hamilton's works edited by her son James Hamilton (courtesy of Special Collections, Thomas Cooper Library, University of South Carolina)

legacy did influence younger working-class poets, but it is difficult to say how much. No extended later studies of her work have appeared, in part perhaps because her work does not lend itself to certain forms of textual analysis and in part because Scots language and regional verse fell into critical disfavor. Commentators typically dismiss her as "traditional," and Brian Maidment even called her poetry and essays "a compendium of ferociously conservative attitudes" in his *Poorhouse Fugitives: Self-Taught Poets and Poetry in Victorian Britain* (1987). One must temper such judgments with appreciation of her political evolution and the importance of temperance and self-education for nineteenth-century working-class women.

Indeed, Hamilton's works resist neat ideological labels. Unlike many of the authors included in Maidment's study, who struggled to master middle-class tradition, she wrote unapologetically for members of her own class, but her strong-minded advocacy of vernacular usage and oral tradition paradoxically convey a consistent faith in the universality of her work. Her poems also suggest something of the great range of emotional and linguistic experience possible for a nineteenth-century working-class woman, and some of her satiric verse is genuinely brilliant. Her abilities to articulate the values of a regional culture now nearly lost to memory merit serious attention from students of nineteenth-century poetry and Scottish popular culture, for their humor, public spiritedness, and linguistic and social realism convey some of the ideals of Victorian Scottish working-class life.

Hamilton deeply loved literature and education, denounced the illiteracy, wife battering and child abuse she saw, and came to demand a wider range of political opportunities for working-class women. This ideological descendant of non-complying Covenanters also identified the values of her rural past with movements toward European democracy and self-determination, and she responded with growing skepticism to war, empire, and the actions of British imperialism.

Her works are also formally diverse. She was deeply introspective and "sentimental," but her bilingual poems display a wide curiosity and fascination with education and processes of change and deploy an extensive array of dramatic situations and poetic forms. Her Scots satiric poems are virtuoso tours de force, and her "ballads of memorie" are models of the use of poetic narrative for "people's history." Her political poems also have more than antiquarian interest for at least two reasons: her "defenses" of the Doric bluntly denounce the cultural destruction wrought by linguistic conformity, and her mordant descriptions of everyday Glaswegian life brilliantly document the side effects of urbanization and industrial blight.

In short, Hamilton's poems provide some of the clearest views possible of the opinions and sensibility of a nineteenth-century Scottish woman who never attended school and observed her environs evolve in fifty years' time from rural village to industrial working-class tenements. As the author of these works, Hamilton broke several stereotypes and undercut many generalizations. It can no longer be said that no unschooled woman left a significant literary legacy, that all women "dialect" poets shied away from social criticism, or that nineteenth-century women's poetic language lacked iconoclasm or sardonic wit. Hamilton was not only a poet who overcame obstacles but also a Scottish working-class writer who succeeded in conveying a complex maternal sensibility in two languages, and her poems and essays manifest a deep understanding of women's experiences at many levels.

Biography:
John Young, *Pictures in Prose and Verse; or, Personal Recollections of the Late Janet Hamilton, Langloan* (Glasgow: George Gallie, 1877).

References:
Florence Boos, "Cauld Engle-Cheek: Working-Class Women Poets of Victorian Scotland," *Victorian Poetry,* 33 (1995): 51–71;

Boos, "'Oor Location': Victorian Women Poets and the Transition from Rural to Urban Scottish Culture," in *Victorian Urban Landscapes,* edited by Debra Mancoff and Dale Trela (New York: Garland, 1996), pp. 133–156;

D. H. Edwards, *One Hundred Modern Scottish Poets* (Brechin: Edwards, 1880), pp. 248–259;

Janet Hamilton (Coatbridge: Monklands Library Services Department, 1971);

Brian Maidment, *Poorhouse Fugitives: Self-Taught Poets and Poetry in Victorian Britain* (Manchester: Carcanet, 1987);

Julia Swindells, *Victorian Writing and Working Women* (Minneapolis: University of Minnesota Press, 1985);

J. Veitch, "Janet Hamilton, Poetess of Langloan," in *Good Words for 1884,* edited by Donald Macleod (London: Ibister, 1884), pp. 118–124;

Martha Vicinus, *The Industrial Muse: A Study of Nineteenth Century British Working Class Literature* (London: Croom Helm, 1974);

David Vincent, *Bread, Knowledge and Freedom: A Study of Nineteenth-Century Working Class Autobiography* (London: Methuen, 1981);

Joseph Wright, *Laird Nicol's Kitchen and Other Sketches of Scottish Life and Manners* (Paisley: Gardner, 1906).

Frances Ridley Havergal

(14 December 1836 – 3 June 1879)

John Ferns
McMaster University

BOOKS: *The Ministry of Song* (London: Christian Book Society, 1871; New York: De Witt C. Lent, 1872);

Bruey: A Little Worker for Christ (London, 1873; New York: Randolph, 1880?);

The Four Happy Days (London, 1874);

Under the Surface (London: Nisbet, 1874);

Little Pillows; or, Good-night Thoughts for the Little Ones (London, 1875; New York, 1876);

Morning Bells; or, Waking Thoughts for the Little Ones (London, 1875; New York: Dutton, 1879);

My King; or, Daily Thoughts for the King's Children (New York: Randolph, 1876; London, 1877);

Our Work and Our Blessings (New York: Randolph, 1876);

Royal Bounty; or, Evening Thoughts for the King's Guests (London, 1877; New York: Randolph, 1878);

Royal Commandments; or, Morning Thoughts for the King's Servants (London, 1877; New York: Randolph, 1878);

Loyal Responses; or, Daily Messages (London, 1878; New York: Randolph, 1879);

Royal Invitation; or, Daily Thoughts on Coming to Christ (London, 1878; New York: Randolph, 1878);

Echoes from the Word for the Christian Year (London, 1879; New York: Randolph, 1880);

Morning Stars; or, Names of Christ for His Little Ones (London: Nisbit, 1879; New York: Randolph, 1879);

Red Letter Days: A Memorial and Birthday Book (New York: Randolph, 1879);

Kept for the Master's Use (London: Nisbet, 1879; New York: Randolph, 1879).

Editions and Collections: *Under His Shadow: The Last Poems* (London: Nisbet, 1879; New York: Randolph, 1879);

Life Mosaic: The Ministry of Song and Under the Surface (London: Nisbet, 1879; New York: Randolph, 1879);

Life Chords (London: Nisbet, 1880; New York, 1886);

Frances Ridley Havergal (photograph by Elliott & Fry)

Threefold Praise and Other Pieces (London: Nisbet, 1880);

Swiss Letters and Alpine Poems, edited by J. Miriam Crane (London: Nisbet, 1881; New York: Randolph, 1881);

Crimson and Gold Threads from the Life and Works of Frances Ridley Havergal (New York: Dutton, 1882);

Bells Across the Snow (New York: Dutton, 1882);

The Poetical Works of F. R. Havergal, edited by M. V. G. Havergal (London: Nisbet, 1884; New York: Dutton, 1885);

Blossoms from a Believer's Garden (Philadelphia & New York: American Sunday-School Union, 1888);

Coming to Christ (Philadelphia: Henry Altemus, 1897);

159

The Poems and Hymns of Christ's Sweet Singer: Frances Ridley Havergal, edited by Tacey Bly (New Canaan, Conn.: Keats, 1977);

Kept for The Master's Use, introduction by William J. Petersen (Grand Rapids, Mich.: Kregel Publications, 1989).

OTHER: *Songs of Grace and Glory,* edited by Havergal and Charles B. Snepp (London: Nisbet, 1880).

Poet Frances Ridley Havergal is principally remembered as an evangelical, low-church hymn writer. A dozen of her hymns appear in the Anglican *Book of Common Praise,* making her the most fully represented woman hymn writer in that collection. During her lifetime her work was as well known in America as it was in Britain. Shortly after her death Jane McCready of *Faith and Works Magazine* wrote to Havergal's sister and biographer, Maria Vernon Graham Havergal, from Philadelphia in July 1879: "Her little books, 'My King's Royal Commandments and Royal Bounty,' with 'Daily Thoughts on Coming to Christ,' are the constant companions of a very large number of Christians here, whilst 'Little Pillows' and 'Morning Bells' are dear to many a child's heart." Hymnologist Charles B. Snepp wrote to Maria Havergal, "After many years' experience in the study of hymnology, I do not hesitate to affirm that the hymnal compositions of Frances Ridley Havergal must ever rank among the finest in the English language, and portray the fullest and ripest fruits of the Christian character." While she was only a minor Victorian woman poet, Havergal was among the finest hymn writers of the nineteenth century.

Havergal was born on 14 December 1836 to William Henry Havergal, the rector of Astley, Worcestershire, and his wife, Jane. She was the youngest of their four daughters and two sons. Baptized on 25 January 1837, Havergal had two important godmothers: Lucy Emra, author of *Lawrence the Martyr* and *Heavenly Themes and Other Poems,* and Elizabeth Cawood, whose lively intelligence influenced her.

Havergal's godfather was the vicar of Hambleden, the Reverend W. H. Ridley, a descendent of the martyr Nicholas Ridley. In her autobiography, which was written in 1859 and included in Maria Havergal's *Memorials of Frances Ridley Havergal* (1880), the poet contemplates her second name:

> But what the R- doth represent
> I value and revere,
> A diamond clasp it seems to be,

> On golden chains, enlinking me
> In loyal love to England's hope,
> The Church I hold so dear.

Known in her family as "Fanny" and to her musician father as "Little Quicksilver," Havergal preferred her baptismal name "Frances," which she used as her signature beginning with the publication of her first book, *The Ministry of Song* (1871).

Her eldest sister, Jane Miriam Havergal Crane, who taught her reading, spelling, and rhyming, remembered her sister as of fair complexion and light, curling hair, who could speak with "perfect distinctness" by the age of two. By the age of four she could read the Bible and write in a round hand. In a poem addressed to Frances in 1863 and included in *Memorials,* her sister describes their family home at Astley:

> Behold thy birthplace, Frances! The old house
> Entwined with ivy, roses and the vine;
> Beneath the shadow of the ancient shrine
> Where ministered our father twenty years.
> He built the northern aisle, and gave the clock,
> A musical memento of his love
> For time and tune and punctuality!
> Fair is the garden ground, and there the flowers
> Were trained with care and skill by *one* who now
> Rests from her labours in the heavenly land.
> Here life and death together meet; the tombs
> Stand close beside the mossy bank, where once
> Sisters and brothers met in frolic play.
> Around, the wooded hills in beauty rise!
> Earth has not many scenes more fair than this,
> And none more dear to those who called it Home!

In 1842 Havergal's invalid father, who composed hundreds of chants and sacred songs and whose psalter she was later to edit, resigned the living of Astley. The family lived for three years at Henwick House in the parish of Hallow until the Reverend Havergal was appointed rector of St. Nicholas, Worcester, in 1845. In her autobiography, which she calls "a little account of my own *inner* life," Frances recounts the beginning of her "religious ideas": "from six to eight I recall a different state of things. The beginning of it was a sermon preached one Sunday morning at Hallow Church, by Mr. (now Archdeacon) Phillpotts . . . what a fearful thing it is to fall into the hands of the living God. No one ever knew it, but this sermon haunted me, and day and night it crossed me." She remembers yearning to become a Christian:

> I do not think that I was eight when I hit upon Cowper's lines, ending "My Father made them all!" That was what I wanted to be able to say; and after once seeing the words, I never saw a lovely scene again without

being *teased* by them. One spring (I think 1845) I kept thinking of them, and a dozen times a day said to myself, "Oh if God would but make me a Christian before the summer comes!" because I longed so to enjoy His works as I felt they could be enjoyed. And I could not bear to think of *another* summer coming and going, and finding and leaving me still "not a Christian."

The central event in Havergal's young life was the death of her mother on 5 July 1848, when Havergal was eleven. As she records in her autobiography, "A mother's death must be childhood's greatest grief . . . I did not, *would* not, see God's hand in it, and the stroke left me worse than it found me." She never forgot her mother's warning, "Fanny dear, pray to God to prepare you for all that He is preparing for you." Not long before her own death she said that "The words mamma taught me in 1848 have been a *life prayer with me.*" Following his wife's death, the Reverend Havergal took his family to North Wales for a holiday.

In her autobiography Havergal notes that on "August 15, 1850, to my great delight I went to school. And that single half-year with dear Mrs. Teed, formerly of Great Campden House, at Belmont now, was perhaps the most important to me of any in my life." She dates her Christian conversion from this period, "The climax came about the first or second week in December. I shall never, never forget the evening of Sunday, December 8th." The next July her father married Caroline Ann Cooke of Gloucester. In August 1851 Havergal attended school at Powick Court in Worcester, but severe erysipelas of the face and head caused her to leave school in December.

In November 1852 Havergal accompanied her parents to Germany where her father was seeking a cure for his failing eyesight. She attended Louisenschule in Dusseldorf until September 1853 and achieved considerable academic success there. "The year 1853 was unique in some things. I was at school at Dusseldorf part of it; and stood alone (as far as I know) among the 110 girls." Her report read "Frances Havergal, Numero Eins." The Havergals returned to England in December 1853.

On 17 July 1854 Havergal was confirmed by Dr. Henry Pepys, bishop of Worcester. In her manuscript book she wrote a poem titled "Thine For Ever":

Oh! "Thine for ever," what a blessed thing
    To be for ever His who died for me!
My saviour, all my life Thy praise I'll sing,
    Nor cease my song throughout eternity.

Having become proficient in French and German, Havergal studied Greek with her father so that she could study the New Testament in that language.

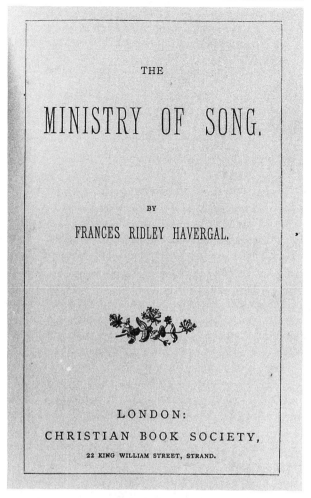

THE

MINISTRY OF SONG.

BY

FRANCES RIDLEY HAVERGAL.

LONDON:
CHRISTIAN BOOK SOCIETY,
22 KING WILLIAM STREET, STRAND.

Title page for Havergal's first book (courtesy of Special Collections, Thomas Cooper Library, University of South Carolina)

She began to submit poems for publication under the pseudonyms "Sabina" and "Zoide." Any payment she received she sent to the Church Missionary Society and other charities.

In May 1856 she visited Celbridge Lodge in Ireland. Her support of the Irish Society, a body dedicated to the spread of scriptural education in Ireland dates from this visit. From 1856 to her death in 1879 she contributed £900 to the society. Also, during the summer of 1856 she began to study Hebrew. Her hymn writing and her relationship with her father are well illustrated in a story from 1858 about her writing of the well-known hymn "I gave My Life for Thee." This hymn, supposedly her first, was written in Germany and first appeared in *Good Words.* Maria Havergal records that her youngest sister

had come in weary, and sat down opposite a picture with this motto. At once the lines flashed upon her, and she wrote them in pencil on a scrap of paper. Reading them over, they did not satisfy her. She tossed them into the fire, but they fell out untouched! Showing them some months after to her father, he encouraged her to preserve them, and wrote the tune "Baca" specially for them.

She would later write of the experience, "I gave 'My Life for thee' to papa's tune 'Baca'. . . . What a privilege it is even to have contributed a bit of music for His direct praise."

In 1860 her father resigned from St. Nicholas, where Havergal had worked since 1846 as a Sunday school teacher. As is noted in *Memorials* Havergal's teaching had become a calling: "Her Sunday School work was a loved employment. In the neatly kept register titled 'My Sunday Scholars, from 1846 to 1860,' each child's birthday, entrance date, occurrences in their home, general impressions of their character, and subsequent events in their life, are all carefully noted." Havergal herself writes that "Among all my St. Nicholas memories, none will be fonder or deeper than my class. . . . It has been to my soul a means of grace . . . seldom have Bible truths seemed to reach and touch me more than when seeking to arrange and simplify them for my children. Therefore, I thank God that these children have been entrusted to me! . . . I trust it has been *true* bread which I have cast upon these waters; my Saviour knows, and He only, my earnest longings that these little ones should be His own." In March 1860 Havergal wrote in her register, "May all whose names are written here / In the Lamb's Book of life appear."

Following her father's resignation the family moved to Shareshill. In February 1861 Havergal began instructing her two youngest nieces (Jane Miriam Havergal Crane's children) at Oakhampton. Maria Havergal notes of her sister that "Her one great object was the education of her nieces for eternity, not for time only; and not merely religious knowledge, but the realities of faith and holy living, were dwelt upon." Her hymn and musical writing were flourishing; however, she found her work a mixed blessing: "A power utterly new and unexpected was given me [singing and composition of music], and rejoicing in this I forgot the Giver, and found such delight in this that other things paled before it."

Havergal felt herself chastened when she fell ill. In the first part of 1865 she was "very poorly" and had to "give up everything, Sunday school and Saturday evening class, visiting, music, etc." During the winter of 1865–1866 she revisited Germany with her parents. In Bonn she met the musician Ferdinand Hiller, who recommended that she devote her life to music. Like her father, Havergal was a talented musician. Maria Havergal records that "such was the strength of her musical memory, that she would play through Handel, much of Beethoven and Mendelssohn, without any notes . . . her touch was instinct with soul, as also was her singing . . . it was in Handel's music that she . . . particularly delighted." On 23 September 1867 Havergal was led by Miss Clara Gedge to join the Young Women's Christian Association. The family moved into Pyrmont Villa, Leamington, on 27 December 1867.

Havergal increasingly felt her talent to be a gift from God. Of her poetry and hymn writing, she observes in 1866, "I have a curious vivid sense, not merely of my verse faculty in general being given me, but also of every separate poem or hymn, nay every line, being given. It is peculiarly pleasant thus to take it as a direct gift, not a matter of effort, but purely involuntarily." The next year she again describes her poetic process as a divine gift:

> I have not had a single poem come to me for some time, till last night, when one shot into my mind. All my best have come in that way, Minerva fashion, full grown. It is so curious, one minute I have not an idea of writing anything, the next I *have* a poem; it is *mine,* I see it all, except laying out rhymes and metre, which is then easy work! I rarely write anything which has not come thus.

On a later occasion she writes,

> Writing is *praying* with me, for I never seem to write even a verse by myself, and feel like a little child writing; you know a child would look up at every sentence and say "What shall I say next?" That is just what I do; I ask that at every line He would give me, not merely thoughts and power, but also every *word,* even the very *rhymes.* Very often I have a most distinct and happy consciousness of direct answers.

She came to a greater appreciation of the blessing of her vocation as a hymn writer: "I never before realized the high privilege of writing for 'the great congregation.'"

Havergal deeply felt the death on 14 April 1868 of her niece Evelyn Emily Crane (presumably one of the nieces she had taught), whom she had led to Christ three years earlier. In May 1869 the Reverend Crane took his wife, their eldest daughter, Miriam, and Havergal to Switzerland by the Rhine route, through Heidelburg, Freiburg, Basle, and Schaffhausen. Havergal composed such poems as "He hath spoken in the darkness," which appeared in *Under the Surface* (1874). In fall 1868 she visited Scotland and particularly enjoyed the Highland scenery.

When thy days on earth are past,
Christ will call thee home at last,
His redeeming love to praise,
Who hath strengthened all thy days.

Frances R. Havergal

Frontispiece and illustration of Ashley Church and Rectory from Memorials of Frances Ridley
Havergal *(1880), prepared by Havergal's sister, Maria*

Havergal's father died two days after Easter 1870. In her poem "Yet Speaketh" she writes of the example he provided her:

Deep teachings from the Word he held so dear,
    Things new and old in that great treasure found,
A valiant cry, a witness strong and clear,
    A trumpet with no dull uncertain sound;
These shall not die, but live; his rich bequest
To that beloved Church whose servant is at rest.

The Reverend Havergal was buried in Astley churchyard. Soon after she began to prepare *Havergals' Psalmody* for publication.

In June 1871 Havergal made what she regarded as her most enjoyable Swiss visit with her friend Elizabeth Clay. She visited the country in summer 1873, 1874, and again with her sister Maria in 1876. Her collaboration with the illustrator Baroness Helga von Cramm dates from the 1876 visit. Her enjoyment of nature often is couched in religious imagery as when she observes that "In the south west the grand mountains stood, white and perfectly clear, as if they might be waiting for the resurrection."

Havergal's perception of herself as a tool of God is clear in her comments on her most famous hymn, "Take My Life." The writing of the piece stems from an experience of "vivid joy" that occurred on 2 December 1873; yet she evidently did not have a high regard for the hymn. About October 1876 she described "The Thoughts of God," which appeared in *The Sunday Magazine,* as "the very best poem I ever wrote," but she noted "I have not heard one word about it doing anybody any real good. It's generally something that I don't think worth copying out or getting printed (like 'I did this for thee', and 'Take My Life'), that God sees fit to use."

Weakened by an illness in 1874, Havergal described herself in 1877 as having "little physical strength." However, pain and suffering she regarded as a blessing. To Havergal they showed "the real *nothingness* of earthly aims and comforts, and the fleetingness and unsatisfactoriness of everything except Christ." Her writing, as always, she saw as dedicated to, dependent on, and entirely inspired by her master, Jesus: "I not only feel that I can't, but *really can't,* write a single verse unless I go to Him for it and get it from Him."

Maria Havergal records that her sister passed the year 1877 "uneventfully at her home, or in visits to her brother or sisters, to Ashley Moor, and to London." She became a member of the Christian Progress Scripture Reading Union and, to relieve its editor Mr. Boys, edited its magazine *Christian Progress* for three months. On 26 May 1878 her much loved stepmother died. In October the family home in Leamington was broken up, and Havergal and her sister Maria moved to the Mumbles in South Wales. On their last Sunday at Trinity Church, Leamington, Havergal's Advent hymn "Thou art coming, O my Saviour" was sung as the concluding hymn.

Havergal's tastes remained simple despite her growing fame. Her room in her new home at Newton, Caswell Bay, near Swansea contained her American typewriter, harp-piano, and favorite books such as *The Life and Works of Rev. W. Pennefather* and Agnes Giberne's *The Upward Gaze.* Prominently displayed was her motto, "For Jesus' sake only." The popularity of her writings (runs of some books topping fifty thousand copies) had reached such a point that, as she noted, "Every post brings more letters from strangers alone than I and my sister can answer. It is nine months since I have had a chance of doing a stroke of new work!"

Havergal was ill at Christmas 1878, and her sister records her New Year's greeting for 1 January 1879: "'He crowneth the year with His goodness', and He crowneth me 'with loving-kindness and tender mercies.' You, dear Marie, are one of my mercies; and I do hope He will let me do something for you up in heaven!" In early March, Havergal completed her last book, *Kept for the Master's Use* (1879). In April she took a YWCA meeting in Swansea. Maria Havergal records that, "At the close of her address she took round to each a copy of 'Take my life, and let it be / Consecrated, Lord, to Thee' with a blank space, where each might sign her name who could do so, in true and loyal allegiance." During the first three weeks of May she received 118 total abstinence pledges from boys and girls who formed the Newton Temperance Regiment.

In June 1879 Havergal was to visit Ireland to work for the Irish Society, but she fell seriously ill on 21 May. On 29 May the diagnosis of peritonitis led Havergal to comment, "It's home the faster! God's will is *delicious;* He makes no mistakes." On 3 June, following "a terrible rush of convulsive sickness," she spoke her last words, "There, now it is all over! Blessed rest!"

Havergal's work was well regarded throughout her life. The poet Charles Tennyson Turner, brother of the laureate, was impressed with her work as early as 1870: "Since I looked critically at 'The Ministry of Song', I have been surprised and delighted with the great beauty and power of a good proportion of the poems, and the sweetness of the residue . . . 'How should they know Me' and 'Making Poetry' are before all others . . . Miss Havergal,

Sappho, and Mrs. Browning constitute my present female trio."

Hymns such as "Take My Life," "Who Is On The Lord's Side?," and her Advent hymn "Thou Art Coming O My Saviour" continue to be widely sung in churches. With its martial apocalyptic imagery "Who Is On The Lord's Side?" (1877) is a typical mid-nineteenth-century hymn in the "Onward Christian Soldiers" (1864) tradition. Both of these hymns appear in the "Pilgrimage and Conflict" section of *The Book of Common Praise*. Martial imagery, as in this first verse, also dominates verses two and four of the hymn:

> Who is on the Lord's side?
> 		Who will serve the King?
> Who will be his helpers
> 		Other lives to bring?
> Who will leave the world's side?
> 		Who will face the foe?
> Who is on the Lord's side?
> 		Who for him will go?
> 				By thy call of mercy,
> 				By thy grace divine,
> 		We are on the Lord's side
> 				Saviour, we are thine!

Repetitive and accumulative questioning in the first eight lines leads to a declaration of faith in the final two lines of the verse, a declaration achieved through the "mercy" and "grace divine" of lines nine and ten. Indeed, "grace divine" forms a thread that runs through the whole hymn since it is named in the tenth line of each stanza.

The third stanza contains apocalyptic jewel imagery of the kind that appears in The Book of Revelation. It is Jesus' "life-blood" that transforms the material into the spiritual and eternal:

> Jesus, thou hast bought us,
> 		Not with gold or gem,
> But with thine own life-blood,
> 		For thy diadem.
> With thy blessing filling
> 		Each who comes to thee
> Thou hast made us willing,
> 		Thou hast made us free.

While "Who Is On The Lord's Side?" can be seen as a characteristic Havergal hymn in its evangelical fervor, "Take My Life" is surely her finest achievement. It expresses her completely, eminently fulfilling her personal motto, "For Jesus' sake only," and is appropriately placed in the "Discipleship" section of *The Book of Common Praise*. The hymn progres-

sively reveals that the author gives everything to Christ. It is written with the "true voice of feeling," in perfect sincerity, for Havergal is known to have sold her jewelry to donate to the Church Missionary Society and distributed the earnings from her writing to charity. As with "Who Is On The Lord's Side?," but even more successfully, accumulation and repetition are used for intensified poetic effect:

> Take my life, and let it be
> Consecrated, Lord, to thee;
> Take my moments and my days,
> Let them flow in ceaseless praise.
>
> Take my hands, and let them move
> At the impulse of thy love;
> Take my feet, and let them be
> Swift and beautiful for thee.
>
> Take my voice, and let me sing
> Always, only, for my King;
> Take my lips, and let them be
> Filled with messages from thee.
>
> Take my silver and my gold,
> Not a mite would I withold;
> Take my intellect, and use
> Every power as thou shalt choose.
>
> Take my will, and make it thine;
> It shall be no longer mine;
> Take my heart, it is thine own,
> It shall be thy royal throne.
>
> Take my love; my Lord, I pour
> At thy feet its treasure store:
> Take myself, and I will be,
> Ever, only, all, for thee.

In its purity of feeling and simplicity of language "Take My Life" not only is the finest example of Havergal's hymn writing but also takes a natural place in the hymn tradition that runs back through John Keble, John Newton, the Wesleys, Isaac Watts, and George Herbert.

Letters:
Letters by the Late Frances Ridley Havergal, edited by Maria Vernon Havergal (New York: Randolph, 1885; London: Nisbet, 1886).

References:
Esther E. Enock, *Frances Ridley Havergal* (London: Pickering & Inglis, n.d.);
Maria Vernon Graham Havergal, *Memorials of Frances Ridley Havergal* (New York: Randolph, 1880).

Emily Hickey

(12 April 1845 – 9 September 1924)

Richard Tobias
University of Pittsburgh

BOOKS: *A Sculptor, and Other Poems* (London: Kegan
Paul, Trench, 1881);
Verse-Tales, Lyrics, and Translations (London: Mat-
thews, 1889);
Michael Villiers, Idealist, and Other Poems (London:
Smith, Elder, 1891);
Poems (London: Matthews, 1896);
*Ancilla Domini: Thoughts in Verse on the Life of the Blessed
Virgin Mary* (London: Printed for the author,
1898);
Our Lady of May, and Other Poems (London: Catholic
Truth Society, 1902);
Lois (London: Washbourne, 1908);
Thoughts for Creedless Women (London: Catholic
Truth Society, 1906);
The Catholic Church and Labour (London: Catholic
Truth Society, 1908);
*Our Catholic Heritage in English Literature of Pre-
Conquest Days* (London: Sands / St. Louis:
Herder, 1910);
Later Poems (London: Richards, 1913);
Devotional Poems (London: Stock, 1922);
Jesukin, and Other Christmastide Poems (London:
Burns, Oates, 1924).

OTHER: Robert Browning, *Browning's Strafford: Ed-
ited and Annotated,* edited by Hickey (London:
Bell, 1884);
Alfred Henry Miles, ed., *The Poets and the Poetry of the
Century,* volume 8, contributions by Hickey
(London: Hutchins, 1891);
Roden Noel, *Livingstone in Africa,* preface by Hickey
(London: Ward & Downey, 1895);
Noel, *The Poetry of the Hon. Roden Noel,* edited by
Hickey and John Addington Symonds (Lon-
don: Privately printed, 1901);
*Havelok the Dane: An Old English Romance, Rendered into
Later English,* translated by Hickey (London:
Catholic Truth Society, 1902);
St. Patrick's Breastplate: A Metrical Translation, Irish
text with verse translation by Hickey, James
Clarence Mangan, and Cecil Frances Alexan-

Emily Hickey

der, prose translation by J. Whitley Stokes
(London: Catholic Truth Society, 1902);
"Roden Noel, Poet," *Nineteenth Century and After,* 91
(April 1922): 624–633.

In volume eight of *The Poets and Poetry of the
Century* (1891) the editor, Alfred Henry Miles, included the work of one unknown poet and one
known poet. The unknown poet was Gerard Manley Hopkins, who had died in 1889 and whose poetry appeared in print for the first time in this collection; the known poet was Emily Hickey, who had
published three books of verse. Inclusion in the anthology was the high point of Hickey's career; Hop-

166

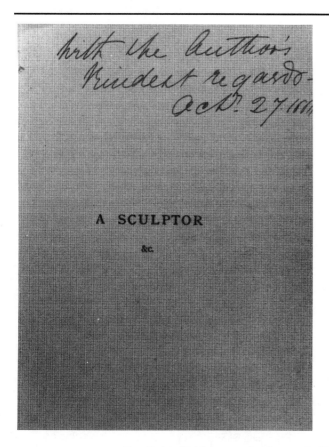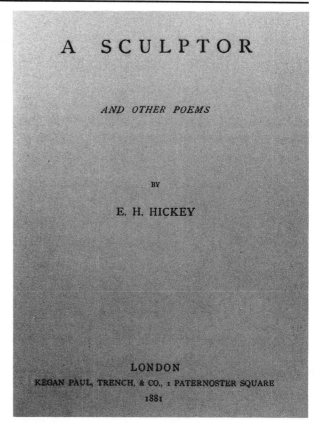

Inscribed half-title page and title page for Hickey's first book (Emory University Library)

kins's reputation did not grow until after 1918, when his friend Robert Bridges published *The Poems of Gerard Manley Hopkins*. Hopkins now occupies an exalted position in Victorian and modern poetry, but Hickey has largely been forgotten. Nevertheless, the two poets shared more than the initial letter of their surnames. Hickey was born in Ireland and lived her adult life in England; Hopkins was born in England and spent his last years in Dublin. Both were converts to Roman Catholicism. Robert Browning, Algernon Swinburne, Dante Gabriel Rossetti, and William Morris influenced both poets. Both Hickey and Hopkins used the difficult Italian sonnet form. Hopkins, a Jesuit priest, subordinated his individuality to his order; Hickey often wrote in a ballad style that suppressed individual insight in favor of general and abstract pictures. On the other hand, Hopkins graduated from Oxford while Hickey had no university degree. Hopkins wrote in complex language about his religious life while Hickey, during the last twenty-three years of her life, wrote highly pious poems in a standard dialect. Hopkins's sonnets are abrasive, angular, and somewhat rebarbative in style; Hickey's are smooth and easy. Hickey's late poems were published in Catholic periodi-

cals in London, Dublin, and New York; Hopkins never saw any of his poems in print.

Emily Henrietta Hickey was born in Macmine Castle, the ancestral estate of her mother, near Enniscorthy, County Wexford, on 12 April 1845. She grew up at the Church of Ireland rectory of her father, the Reverend J. S. Hickey, at Goresbridge, County Carlow. Her grandfather the Reverend William Hickey wrote on political and agricultural issues under the pseudonym Martin Doyle. Her mother, whose maiden name was Stewart, claimed descent from the royal house of Stuart. Hickey was educated in Irish boarding schools.

In 1866, after *The Cornhill Magazine* accepted her poem "Told in the Firelight," Hickey moved to London; thenceforth she only returned to Ireland for family visits. Hickey supported herself by working as a governess, a lady's companion, and a secretary and by writing for magazines, including *Macmillan's* and *The Academy*, until 1878, when she became a lecturer on English literature at the North London Collegiate School for Girls. Essays in the school magazine by Hickey's former students describe her as committed, intelligent, and knowledgeable.

Hickey met Browning and other literary luminaries through her position as secretary of the

Browning Society, which she cofounded with Dr. Frederick Furnivall in 1881. Her 1884 edition of Browning's historical play, *Strafford* (1837), includes questions that would be useful in classrooms.

At the start of her career Hickey thought of herself as a member of the English-language community rather than as an Irishwoman. As a girl she had adored the poetry of Sir Walter Scott; although her father discouraged her from reading the works of William Shakespeare, which he considered to be marred by "Elizabethan coarseness," she recited verse by Shakespeare and Browning. She also read Elizabeth Barrett Browning's *Aurora Leigh* (1857) and borrowed a copy of Alfred, Lord Tennyson's *Maud* (1855), which she learned by heart. She read Anglo-Saxon, and as an associate of Furnivall, founder of the Early English Text Society, the New Shakspere Society, the Ballad Society, and other groups dedicated to discovering and publishing early documents of English verse, she knew the canonic works of English literature.

Later in life Hickey became interested in Ireland and its literature and translated an ancient Irish hymn, *St. Patrick's Breastplate* (1902). She also knew William Butler Yeats's work, and she used Irish legends as a basis for her own poetry. Hickey also admired the minor Victorian poet Roden Noel; she edited or coedited volumes of his poems in 1895 and 1901 and wrote an appreciative introduction for the 1885 edition praising his efforts to connect his art with political issues of the day.

Hickey never married, and many of her poems, both lyric and narrative, concern impossible unions or social pressures blocking lovers from fulfillment. Her biographer, Enid Dinnis, who only knew Hickey during the last two years of the poet's life, speculated that the poems reflected an unhappy love affair.

Robert Browning praised the title piece of Hickey's first book, *A Sculptor, and Other Poems* (1881). The poem is narrated by a woman who has married her foster brother; she had promised their dying mother that she would care for the boy, and three days after the mother's death the two walked "in a dull rain driving slow and small . . . to the church and there were wed." The marriage has not been consummated; the sculptor has no feelings for his wife, who sells her embroidery to buy art supplies for him. The husband, however, cannot sculpt because he cannot love.

The wife is clearly unsatisfied. When she asks her husband to satisfy her desires, he ignores her. In her own room,

> panting as if in struggle fierce,
> She tore off that sombre dress of hers,
> And once, after years, was fain to free
> The storm of her passionate agony.

The wife has worn the dull, gray clothes since her marriage. Standing naked before the mirror, she compares herself to the marble on which her husband lavishes his attention:

> She lookt and started amaz'd because
> She saw how exceeding fair she was,
> And cried with a cry of great despair,
> "Alas! In vain am I made so fair,
>
> For his life is utterly perishing
> At the feet of that dreadful, shapeless thing
> Which never can rise, in face or limb,
> To smile back the strength of his love on him.
>
> O love, my love, who never wilt know
> That I, thy wife, have lov'd thee so,
> I would lie death-doom'd at thy sacred feet
> To hear thee say but, *I love thee, Sweet*,
>
> Wilt thou not open thine eyes to see
> How good perfection can never be
> If Nature and Art, which are its source,
> Be torn from each other in grim divorce?"

When the sculptor invites friends to see his work, they stare uncomprehending at a shapeless lump. The narrator explains:

> There was That within him which was divine;
> But his soul was its prison, not its shrine;
> And the fetter'd Thought could never, free,
> Go forth in its strength and symmetry,
>
> Though its prison-walls at its yearning cry
> Trembled and shook exceedingly.—
> Alas for the man whom God bids live,
> And keep what he fain would die to give.

Since the sculptor has never entered into his sexuality, he can never become an adult. The sculptor is the "eternal boy" of many late-nineteenth-century narratives, from Robert Louis Stevenson's boys in his novels *Treasure Island* (1883) and *St. Ives* (1897) to the hero of James M. Barrie's 1904 play *Peter Pan*. In the sculptor's dreamy extended childhood, imagination is never risked in experience. Art results only from the fulfillment of human nature, and in this poem human nature is adult sexuality.

An imagined audience asks the narrator the meaning of the story. She replies that she cannot

take upon me the mystery
Of things, as if I were God's spy.

Think ye God answers *no* or *yes*
To men as they idly guess and guess,
"If he had lov'd or if—"? that *if*
Is God's undecipher'd hieroglyph.

In "A Sculptor" the woman succeeds as an artist with her embroidery because she has embraced the sexual side of her nature, but Hickey also writes about women who deny this aspect of themselves. In "A Rose," a lyric in *A Sculptor, and Other Poems,* the speaker's lover brings her a rose and asks her to rest from her abstract intellectual toil. The woman is "Unquiet-soul'd," a "seeder for the cause / Of many a thing," who has forgotten that "love, not Knowledge, maketh wise." She accepts the rose,

But woe is me!
I could not let this light and beauty be!
    I pull'd the petals of my rose apart,
With fingers most unkindly tore aside
    The crimson veil that veil'd its golden heart.
I saw the gold, but ah! the flower died.
And, all unwomanly, in pride,
    "Away with ignorance!" I cried,
"My flow'rs shall all be knowledge-bringers!
To what vaileth joy unless one knows
Its why and wherefore?"

She has not only killed the rose with her intellectual questioning but has also silenced her lover: "never now a word of love he speaks." He, too, turns to the realm of thought and talks "of systems and of rules and laws, / And of effect and cause." The speaker yearns "to be a woman once again" and advises herself to "lay down your pen":

For you will never write those deep-ton'd songs
Of Love and Truth, to live on human tongues,
That human hearts may beat more quick and pure.

Intelligence destroys the creative spirit. William Wordsworth made a similar point in "The Tables Turned" (1798):

Our meddling intellect
Misshapes the beauteous forms of things:—
We murder to dissect.

Wordsworth is not condemning science or learning but asking for proportion and balance; Hickey is restating Wordsworth's insight from a feminine perspective: her intellectual woman realizes that her "garden is dead-leav'd." The poem also recalls a line from Wordsworth's "Tintern Abbey" (1798), in which the narrator tells how he has heard and been

changed by "The still, sad music of humanity." Speaking to the rose her lover has given her, Hickey's narrator admits that in destroying it she has

on thy quivering heart unpitying trod,
And evermore that still, sad voice repeat
That whoso wrongeth Nature wrongeth God.

Hickey's poem is an expression of the alienated modern spirit that yearns for closer unions between nature and art, body and soul, earth and heaven.

In "Callimachus: A Sketch" Hickey imagines the renowned Greek sculptor as a painter who has portrayed a young woman slain by the god Thamyris on a sacrificial altar. Callimachus destroys his painting because his audience sees only the beauty of the work and not the truth of the event:

Yea, Beauty, to my deeming, is in sooth
Bastard that springs not from the womb of Truth.

According to Robert Graves's *The Greek Myths* (1955), Thamyris was "the first man who ever wooed one of his own sex." Graves describes this passion for men, introduced by Thamyris, as the Greek mythologizing of "the victory of patriarchy over matriarchy." Thus, the truth that the painter has seen may be that of the destruction of female power and the assertion of male dominance.

In 1884 Hickey resigned as secretary of the Browning Society and traveled on the Continent to restore her broken health. After her return to England, inspired in part by John Henry Newman, she moved from her father's Calvinistic theology to Anglo-Catholicism.

Most of the poems in Hickey's second book, *Verse-Tales, Lyrics, and Translations* (1889), are lyrics that seem appropriate for magazine publication. One celebrates Father Damien, who established a leper colony in Hawaii; another marks the three-hundredth anniversary of the defeat of the Spanish Armada; several are about unfortunate children of suffering mothers. An untitled sonnet retells the biblical story of the foolish virgins who had no oil for their lamps; the final six lines shift the story:

Then turned one virgin of the virgins wise
    To one among the foolish, with a low
Sweet cry, and looked her, lovelike, in the eyes,
    Saying, "My oil is thine, for weal, for woe,
    We two are one, and where thou goest I go,
One lot being ours for aye, where'er it lies."

Hickey wrote several poems about close emotional ties between women. In a later poem in the collection, "From 'M' to 'N,'" the four stanzas begin, respectively, "How sweet are you?," "How true?," "How near?," and "How far?" The third stanza says that the loved one is

> As to the earth her atmosphere;
> As warp to woof when web is wove;
> As strength to hope; as light to love;
> As my own blood, my flesh, my breath;
> As near as life, as near as death.

The final stanza, however, says that the union can never be realized because the lovers are "as far as bliss / Of comradeship from Judas kiss; / As day from Night" and ends by saying that the loved one is farther "than heaven from hell." The lines are rigorously asexual; the poem could be read as another expression of Hickey's demand (*M* standing for Emily) that nature and art be united, for the *N* may stand for Nature. On the other hand, *N* may represent Annie Eleanor Ridley, her colleague at the North London Collegiate School for Girls, to whom her *Poems* (1896) was dedicated. Early reviewers of the volume related Hickey's work to that of the Jacobean metaphysical poet George Herbert, who sought mystical unions.

The final section of *Verse-Tales* is titled "Translations from the First English." "The Battle of Maldon" has a Victorian feel about it: heroism is praised with no blood shed; brave soldiers will not negotiate peace. The epic fragment "Judith" deals with a woman's resistance to rape. "The Dream of the Holy Rood" is a dramatic monologue.

The poems in this collection would have appealed to an audience that wanted comfort, order, and meaning. True to Alexander Pope's dictum that the poet should write "What has often been thought, but ne'er so well expres'd," Hickey gives new expression to familiar thoughts. In "Folk-Song, From the Old French" a woman is yearning for a lover who is gone:

> What shall one do if Love depart?
>   I sleep not night nor day;
> All night I think of my true-love,
>   Him who is far away.

> I got me from my restless bed.
>   And donned my gown of grey,
> And went out through the postern gate
>   To the garden at break of day.

The lover returns, to the sound of the nightingale's song:

> In a brave boat up the Seine river,
>   Wrought of the pleasant pine;
> The sails are all of satin sheen,
>   The ropes of silken twine:

> The mainmast is of ivory,
>   The rudder of gold so fine.

Hickey's words and manner repeat those of the folk songs that her century discovered and imitated. Her magazine readers would be delighted at such a pleasant picture of true love.

In the introduction to *The Poets and the Poetry of the Century* Miles printed seventy-five lines from the title work of Hickey's *Michael Villiers, Idealist, and Other Poems* (1891) and praised this long narrative poem about the English domination and exploitation of Ireland. Michael Villiers is the son of an English absentee landlord and an Irish peasant woman whom the Englishman met on a visit to his Irish property. Both father and mother die while Villiers is still young, and a bachelor English uncle provides a home and education for the boy. Villiers grows up to become a parlor socialist; his practical-minded friend, Arthur Grey, is unable to sway him from his idealism. Villiers decides to be celibate and to devote himself entirely to the cause of the Irish, but later he meets a "true woman," Lucy Vere, who supports him in his crusade. Slavery, Villiers says, hurts both slave and master:

> You have not man and man, but slaves and slaves,
> The enslaver being doubly the enslaved.

Colonialism, in other words, is damaging both to England and to Ireland. Villiers denies that nature justifies domination: "Are we Nature, then, / Or Men?" Like Barrett Browning's *Aurora Leigh,* "Michael Villiers, Idealist" is a novel in verse with lyric interludes. Hickey's characters are types—the unthinking English bachelor uncle, the eager reformer, the pure woman. After she became Roman Catholic in 1901, Hickey tried to suppress the poem because one line in it expresses doubt as to the divinity of Christ. The problem, however, is larger than the single line: Villiers believes that human efforts can solve human problems; such secularism was anathema to Hickey's later religious convictions.

Miles selected "Beloved, It is Morn," which originally was published in *A Sculptor,* as the first poem to reprint in *The Poets and Poetry of the Century.* Composers created musical settings for the poem three times, and phonograph recordings of some of them still existed in the 1920s. It is a direct, uncomplicated lyric with four-line stanzas speaking of morning, daytime, and evening and a three-line refrain. The poem begins:

> Beloved, it is morn!
>   A redder berry on the thorn,
>   A deeper yellow on the corn,

For this good day new-born,
    Pray, Sweet, for me
    That I may be
Faithful to God and thee.

Hickey's fourth collection, *Poems,* opens with three narratives. "The Ballad of Lady Ellen" is based on a story in Yeats's collection *Fairy and Folk Tales of the Irish Peasantary* (1888). Hickey points out that the story is, in fact, of French origin. Yeats used the tale in his play *The Countess Kathleen* (1892); Katharine Tynan also used it in her poem "The Ballad of the Countess Kathleen" (1891). By selling her soul Ellen brings life back to a blighted land and is saved from hell by the Virgin Mary. "The Passion of King Conor" is about the king's conversion. "The Wolf Story" is set in Russia: two men steal the carcass of an animal slain by a wolf, but the wolf cries so piteously that the men return it. The wolf's own pack then kills him for the carcass.

The collection includes many sonnets in the arduous Italian form, which limits the writer to five rhyming words. Hickey is skillful with the form and sometimes deliberately breaks its rules: in "To R. N.," which is probably dedicated to Noel, who died in 1894, an extra syllable in the final line seems to be a sudden breakthrough of grief. Another poem, "Ad Poetem," may also be to Noel, or it may be to Hickey's ideal poet. Of this poet she says, "No pestilential sloughs of decadence, / Have ever clogged your spirit, fouled you." The last line advises the poet to sing about "the strain" of "Heavens' blue road, the earth's brown nest." Again, body and soul must be conjoined in an expression of perfect life. The sonnets visibly show this unity.

Hickey retired from teaching in 1894. After being received into the Roman Catholic faith at the Dominican Priory on Haverstock Hill on 22 July 1901 she served as an editor and secretary for the Catholic Truth Society. The movement from concern for social ills to concern for the state of the soul is apparent in her poetry. Dinnis is eager to praise Hickey's late poems, but even she has to admit that "Certitude . . . does not produce the highly flavoured fruits of speculation." Hickey's early books had been widely reviewed, but after 1901 the secular press ignored her. Her late poetry is correct in language and doctrine, but occasionally words

come to life, as in "The Annunciation" from *Ancilla Domini:*

Hear ye the message, God's earth and the heavens of His
    might,
Borne by the Angel who stands in the infinite light?
  Here on the brows of her, here on the breast of her,
    Strike her, God's glory, and smite.

How can such terrible worship and honour be laid,
Burden of ave and anguish, of sorrow and shade,
  Weighty on brows of her, heavy on heart of her,
    Poor little Nazarene maid.

In 1912 the Vatican awarded Hickey the decoration Cross Pro Ecclesia et Pontifice. She continued to write until her last year. Her penultimate book, *Devotional Poems* (1922), comprises pieces that had previously been printed in *The Irish Monthly* in Dublin, *The Catholic World* in New York City, and *Ave Maria* at the University of Notre Dame. In her last year she wrote a collection of Christmas verse that was published posthumously in 1924. Near the end of her life she was awarded a civil-list pension. She continued writing until her eyesight failed; she underwent an operation for cataracts but died shortly afterward, on 9 September 1924, of heart failure.

Biography:
Enid Dinnis, *Emily Hickey: Poet, Essayist–Pilgrim. A Memoir* (London: Harding & More, 1927).

References:
Alice Furlong, "Emily Hickey," *Irish Monthly,* 53 (January 1925): 16–20;
Eleanor M. Hill, "In Memoriam: Emily Hickey," *North London Collegiate School Magazine,* 49 (October 1924): 107–108;
William S. Peterson, *Interrogating the Oracle: A History of the London Browning Society* (Athens: Ohio University Press, 1969).

Papers:
Emily Hickey's biographer, Enid Dinnis, writes of "Bound volumes, magazine articles, newspaper cuttings, MSS . . . preserved with an orderly care" and "letters and sundry records." Dinnis quotes from such materials, but there is no record of them in archives in Great Britain or the United States. The University of Reading has letters from Hickey to her publishers Elkin Mathews and Macmillan. University College, Dublin, also has letters.

Mary Howitt

(12 March 1799 – 30 January 1888)

Becky W. Lewis
University of South Carolina

See also the William and Mary Howitt entry in *DLB 110: British Romantic Prose Writers, 1782–1832, Second Series.*

BOOKS: *The Forest Minstrel and Other Poems,* by Howitt and William Howitt (London: Baldwin, Cradock & Joy, 1823);

The Desolation of Eyam: The Emigrant, a Tale of the American Woods: and Other Poems, by Howitt and William Howitt (London: Wightman & Cramp, 1827);

The Seven Temptations (London: Bentley, 1834);

Sketches of Natural History (London: Darton, 1834; Philadelphia: Conrad & Parsons, 1834);

Tales in Verse (London: Darton, 1836; Boston: Weeks, Jordan, 1839);

Tales in Prose: For the Young (London: Darton & Son, 1836; Boston: Weeks, Jordan, 1839);

Wood Leighton; or, A Year in the Country, 3 volumes (London: Bentley, 1836; Philadelphia: Carey, Lea & Blanchard, 1837);

Birds and Flowers, and Other Country Things (London: Darton & Clark, 1838; Boston: Weeks, Jordan, 1839);

Hymns and Fireside Verses (London: Darton & Clark, 1839);

Hope on, Hope Ever, or, The Boyhood of Felix Law (London: Tegg, 1840; Boston: Munroe, 1840);

Strive and Thrive: A Tale (London: Tegg, 1840; Boston: Munroe, 1840);

Sowing and Reaping; or, What Will Come of It? (London: Tegg, 1841);

Who Shall be Greatest? A Tale (London, 1841; Boston: Munroe, 1841);

Which is the Wiser; or, People Abroad. A Tale for Youth (London: Tegg, 1842; New York: D. Appleton, 1842);

Little Coin, Much Care; or, How Poor Men Live. A Tale (London: Tegg, 1842; New York: D. Appleton, 1842);

Work and Wages; or, Life in Service (London: Tegg, 1842; New York: D. Appleton / Philadelphia: G. S. Appleton, 1843);

No Sense like Common Sense; or, Some Passages in the Life of Charles Middleton, Esq. (New York: D. Appleton, 1843);

Love and Money: An Every Day Tale (London: Tegg, 1843; New York: D. Appleton, 1844);

Alice Franklin: A Tale; Another Part of "Sowing and Reaping" (London: Tegg, 1843; New York: D. Appleton / Philadelphia: G. S. Appleton, 1843);

The Author's Daughter (New York: Harper, 1845);

172

Fireside Verses (London: Darton & Clark, 1845);

My Own Story; or, The Autobiography of a Child (London: Tegg, 1845);

The Two Apprentices, a Tale for Youth (New York, 1845; London: Tegg, n.d.);

Ballads and Other Poems (London: Longman, Brown, Green & Longmans, 1847; New York: Wiley & Putnam, 1847);

Bright Days; or, Herbert and Meggy (Boston: Lothrop, 1847);

The Children's Year (London: Longman, Brown, Green & Longmans, 1847; Philadelphia: Lea & Blanchard, 1848); republished as *The Story of a Happy Home, or, The Children's Year and How They Spent It* (London: Nelson, 1875);

The Heir of Wast-Wayland: A Tale (London: Simms & M'Intyre, 1847; New York: D. Appleton, 1851);

The Childhood of Mary Leeson (London: Darton, 1848; Boston: Crosby, Nichols, 1854);

Our Cousins in Ohio (London: Darton, 1849; New York: Collins, 1849);

How the Mice Got out of Trouble, and Other Tales. From the "Dial of Love" (London: Darton, 1850);

Popular Moral Tales for the Young (New York: D. Appleton / Philadelphia: G. S. Appleton, 1850);

The Steadfast Gabriel, a Tale of Wichnor Wood (Edinburgh: Chambers, 1850); republished as *Gabriel: A Story of Wichnor Wood* (New York: Collins, 1850);

The Literature and Romance of Northern Europe: Constituting a Complete History of the Literature of Sweden, Denmark, Norway and Iceland, by Howitt and William Howitt, 2 volumes (London: Colburn, 1852);

Pictures and Verses. For Young People (New York: Colby, 1853);

Stories of English and Foreign Life, by Howitt and William Howitt (London: Bohn, 1853);

The Turtle Dove and Other Stories (New York: C. S. Francis / Boston: J. H. Francis, 1853);

The Picture Book for the Young (London: Low & Son, 1855; Philadelphia: Lippincott, 1856);

Mary Howitt's Illustrated Library for the Young, 2 series (London: Kent, 1856);

Stories from the History of the Reformation. For the Entertainment and Instruction of the Young (New York: Francis, 1857);

Marien's Pilgrimage: A Fire-Side Story, and Other Poems (London: Darton, 1859);

A Popular History of the United States of America, from the Discovery of the American Continent to the Present Time, 2 volumes (London: Longman, Brown, Green, Longmans & Roberts, 1859; New York: Harper, 1860);

The Blackbird, the Parrot, the Cat, and Other Stories. A Picture Book for the Young (London: Dean, 1861);

Lillieslea; or, Lost and Found: A Story for the Young (London & New York: Routledge, 1861);

Little Arthur's Letters to his Sister Mary. A Pleasing Picture Book for Young Folks (London, 1861);

A Treasury of New Favorite Tales, for Young People (London: Hogg & Sons, 1861);

Ruined Abbeys and Castles of Great Britain, by Howitt and William Howitt (London: Bennett, 1862);

The Poet's Children (London: Bennett, 1863);

The Story of Little Cristal (London: Bennett, 1863);

The Cost of Caergwyn, 3 volumes (London: Hurst & Blackett, 1864);

Stories of Stapleford, 2 parts (London: A. W. Bennett, 1864);

The Angel Unawares, and Other Stories (New York: Miller, 1865);

Our Four-Footed Friends (London: Partridge, 1867);

John Oriel's Start in Life (London, 1868);

Picture from Nature (London & New York: Routledge, 1869);

Vignettes of American History (London: Partridge, 1869);

A Pleasant Life (Edinburgh & London: Gall & Inglis, 1871; New York: Nelson, 187?);

Birds and their Nests (New York: Routledge, 1871; London: Partridge, 1872);

Natural History Stories for My Juvenile Friends (London: Partridge, 1875);

Tales for All Seasons (London & Guildford: F. Warne, 1881);

Tales of English Life, including Middleton and the Middletons (London: F. Warne, 1881);

Mary Howitt; An Autobiography, 2 volumes, edited by Margaret Howitt (London: Isbister, 1889).

Edition: *The Poetical Works of Howitt, Milman, and Keats* (Philadelphia: Cowperthwait, 1840).

OTHER: *Fisher's Drawing Room Scrap-Book,* edited by Howitt (London: Fisher, Son & Jackson, 1840–1842);

Anders Fryxell, *The History of Sweden,* 2 volumes, translated by Anne von Schaultz, edited by Howitt (London: Bentley, 1844);

Joseph Ennemoser, *The History of Magic,* 2 volumes, translated by William Howitt, with an appendix by Howitt (London: Bohn, 1847);

Howitt's Journal of Literature and Popular Progress, 3 volumes, edited by Howitt and William Howitt (London: Willoughby, January 1847–June 1848);

Biographical Sketches of the Queens of Great Britain from the Norman Conquest to the Reign of Victoria; or, Royal Book of Beauty, edited by Howitt (London: Colburn, 1851); republished as *The Queens of England, from the Norman Conquest to the Regin of Victoria,* revised by Geneva Armstrong (Chicago: Wasson, 1901);

The Dial of Love: A Gift Book for the Young (London: Darton, 1852);

The Dial of Love: A Christmas Book for the Young, compiled by Howitt (London: Darton, 1853; Philadelphia: Lindsay & Blackston, 1854);

Pictorial Calendar of the Seasons Exhibiting the Pleasures, Pursuits, and Characteristics of Country Life for Every Month in the Year, edited by Howitt (London: Bohn, 1854);

Elihu Burritt, *Thoughts and Things at Home and Abroad,* includes a memoir by Howitt (Boston: Phillips, Sampson, 1854; London: Cassell, Petter & Gilpin, 1868);

Margaret Howitt, *Twelve Months with Fredrika Bremer in Sweden,* 2 volumes, preface by Howitt (London: Jackson, Walford & Hodder, 1866).

TRANSLATIONS: Fredrika Bremer, *The Neighbours: A Story of Every-Day Life* (2 volumes, London: Longman, Brown, Green & Longmans, 1842; 1 volume, New York: Harper, 1843);

Bremer, *The Home; or, Family Cares and Family Joys* (2 volumes, London: Longman, Brown, Green & Longmans, 1843; 1 volume, New York: Harper, 1843);

Bremer, *The President's Daughters; including Nina* (3 volumes, London: Longman, Brown, Green & Longmans, 1843; 1 volume, New York: Harper, 1844);

Emilie Smith Flygare-Carlen, *The Rose of Tistelon: A Tale of the Swedish Coast,* 2 volumes (London: Longman, Brown, Green & Longmans, 1844);

Bremer, *New Sketches of Every-Day Life: A Diary. Together with Strife and Peace* (2 volumes, London: Longman, Brown, Green & Longmans, 1844; 1 volume, New York: Harper, 1844);

Bremer, *Domestic Life; or, The H——Family* (London: T. Allman, 1844);

Christoph von Schmid, *The Picture of the Virgin* (London: Orr, 1844);

Wilhelm Hey, *The Child's Picture and Versebook: Commonly Called Otto Speckter's Fable Book* (London: Longman, Brown, Green & Longmans, 1844; New York: D. Appleton / Philadelphia: G. S. Appleton, 1850);

C. Stoeber, *The Curate's Favourite Pupil* (London: Orr, 1844);

Hans Christian Andersen, *Only a Fiddler! and O. T.; or, Life in Denmark,* 3 volumes (London: R. Bentley, 1845);

Andersen, *The Improvisatore* (2 volumes, London: Bentley, 1845; 1 volume, New York: Harper, 1845);

Andersen, *Wonderful Stories for Children* (London: Chapman & Hall, 1846; New York: Wiley & Putnam, 1846);

Henriette Wach von Paalzow, *The Citizen of Prague,* 3 volumes (London: Colburn, 1846);

Adalbert Stifter, *Pictures of Life* (London: Simms & M'Intyre, 1847);

Alphonse de Lamartine, *Genevieve: A Tale* (London: Simms & M'Intyre, 1847);

Andersen, *The True Story of My Life: A Sketch* (London: Longman, Brown, Green & Longmans, 1847; Boston: James Munroe, 1847);

Bremer, *Brothers and Sisters: A Tale of Domestic Life* (London: Henry Colburn, 1848; New York: Harper, 1848);

Sofia Margareta Zelow Knorring, *The Peasant and His Landlord* (New York: Harper, 1848);

Bremer, *The Midnight Sun: A Pilgrimage* (London: Colburn, 1849);

Bremer, *An Easter Offering* (London: Colburn, 1850);

Bremer, *The Homes of the New World; Impressions of America* (3 volumes, London: A. Hall, Virtue, 1853; 2 volumes, New York: Harper, 1853);

Bremer, *Hertha* (London: Arthur Hall, Virtue, 1856; New York: Putnam, 1856);

Bjornstjerne M. Bjornson, *Trust and Trial: A Story from the Danish* (London: Hurst & Blackett, 1858);

Bremer, *Two Years in Switzerland and Italy,* 2 volumes (London: Hurst & Blackett, 1861);

Bremer, *Travels in the Holy Land,* 2 volumes (London: Hurst & Blackett, 1862);

Bremer, *Greece and the Greeks. The Narrative of a Winter Residence and Summer Travel in Greece and Its Islands,* 2 volumes (London: Hurst & Blackett, 1863);

Friedrich Wilhelm Hackländer, *Behind the Counter* (Leipzig: Bernhard Tauchnitz / London: Sampson Low / Paris: Reinwald, 1867).

Mary Howitt's long life bridged the Romantic and Victorian eras. Born and raised in a strict Quaker family, she maintained throughout her life a strong humanitarianism and an interest in diverse religious expressions such as Evangelical Christianity, Anglicanism, Spirtualism, and Catholicism. In her writing she combined the Romantic belief that imagination can improve the world and the Victorian interest in new ideas. With a love of the beauty of nature, poetry, and words, she moved easily in the worlds of art, literature, and politics.

Mary Botham Howitt, the daughter of Samuel and Ann Wood Botham, both Staffordshire Quakers, details in *My Own Story; or, The Autobiography of a Child* (1845) a Quaker childhood of "stillness and isolation" that was also rich in imagination. While her parents held to strict Quakerism, her independence of mind was encouraged by other members of her household, including her older sister and constant companion, Anna; her paternal grandfather who "read . . . and wrote a great deal," collected herbs, and, although irascible, gave books, raisins, and almonds to his granddaughters; and a "singularly gifted" nursemaid with "a turn for all that was picturesque and traditional, considerable superstition, and a remarkable faculty for relating anything clearly and effectively." Howitt recalls that when she began reading books, having been taught by her mother, she "began to compose little poems, and relate, rather than write, tales in prose." This early start in writing explains the practiced ease of the compositions of the mature poet.

The Botham daughters received a short formal education in Quaker schools in Croyden and Sheffield. These schools provided the young girls with their first glimpses of a larger world, making them aware of their isolated and restricted home life. They became especially conscious of their drab dress compared with the dress of girls from wealthier, more liberal Quaker homes. The girls did well in school, and the future poet developed her literary talents. Upon returning home they continued their education on their own, borrowing secular books and periodicals from friendly neighbors. According to Howitt's niece and biographer, Amice Lee, in 1816 the seventeen-year-old Mary Botham "uttered a prayer that she might some day be a famous writer."

In 1824 she married William Howitt, a liberal Quaker, and soon after setting up their home in Nottingham the couple began a productive collaboration. They produced between them seven children (only four survived childhood) and more than 170 books. Their first collaborative publication, *The Forest Minstrel and Other Poems* (1823), contained simple poems about rural life. In regard to their second poetry collection, *The Desolation of Eyam: The Emigrant, a Tale of the American Woods: and Other Poems* (1827), the reviewer for the July 1827 *Eclectic Review* singled out some poems as "anti-quakerish," "licentious," and "atheistical." The volume nevertheless sold well and went into a second edition.

One of the first books that Howitt wrote on her own was *Sketches of Natural History* (1834), a col-

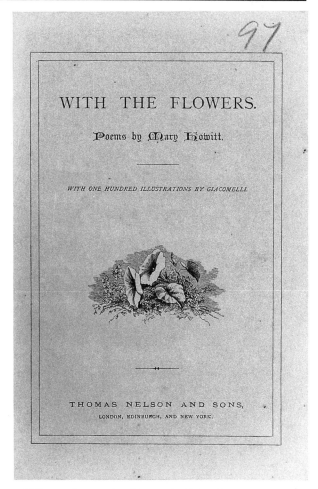

Title page for an 1870 illustrated edition of poems by Howitt (courtesy of Special Collections, Thomas Cooper Library, University of South Carolina)

lection of poems inspired by Thomas Bewick's woodcuts of birds and animals, which she dedicated to her two young children "for their amusement." In *My Own Story* Howitt remembers that the books given to her by her grandfather often "seemed written on purpose to deter children from reading." In her own poetry, however, Howitt delights young readers with humor, energy, and fancy as she provides close observations of nature. She employs simple lyrical verse forms and writes about exotic as well as everyday animals and plants—"The Coot," "The Camel," "The Locust," "The Broom-Flower," and "The Bird of Paradise." She writes that "The Monkey" is "nature's punchinello," who is "full of fun as Puck could be; / Harlequin might learn of thee!" She wonders how the monkey entertained "Little Abel and his brother," frolicked around Noah's ark, and "made both mirth and mischief" throughout biblical history.

Howitt anthropomorphizes plants, giving them human feelings and gender markings. "The

Nettle-King" is "both great and strong," and enjoys the power of his "poison-flowers." He determines to be "king of the plants below." His physical strength allows him to trample on neighboring, weaker plant and animal life. He brags about his power, hoping that he will soon become "as great as a forest-tree! / The great wide world is the place for me." However, he gets his comeuppance when a woodsman, "a simple clown," cuts him down. This theme of the oppressor presages her later work in which she draws attention to the problems of the poor. One of her best-known poems, "The Spider and the Fly: An Apologue. A New Version of an Old Story" appears in this collection and illustrates her striking ability to tell a story and construct dialogue.

A more ambitious effort influenced by Joanna Baillie's *Plays on the Passions* (1798–1812), *The Seven Temptations* (1834) relates in blank verse seven dramatic stories about various character types–the young scholar, the spendthrift turned miser, the rejected lover–who are subjected to temptations. The reviews were mainly positive. The reviewer of the 22 February 1834 issue of *The Athenaeum* applauded the work as "bold," uniting "a purity of feeling . . . closely resembling the life-like pathos of Defoe, with such an occasional sublimity of imagination as is shared by few–very few women."

During the 1830s Howitt and her husband were active members of a literary group who edited and wrote for the popular giftbooks and annuals such as *Winter's Wreath, Literary Souvenir, New Year's Gift, Amulet,* and *Findens Tableaux.* It was through this lucrative market that Howitt met Anna Maria Fielding (Mrs. S. C. Hall), Felicia Hemans, Letitia Elizabeth Landon, Elizabeth Barrett Browning, Eliza Cook, Maria Jane Jewsbury, Mary Mitford, and Caroline Bowles Southey. In 1836 the Howitts moved to Esher, a village close to London and to the publishing world, in order to devote themselves to writing and to live solely on their literary earnings. In *Victorian Samplers: William and Mary Howitt* (1952) Carl Ray Woodring describes Mary Howitt during this period as "turning out poems like thumbtacks for the gilt and satin annuals."

One poem first published in the annuals, "The Voyage with the Nautilus," provides an illustration of Howitt's romantic imagination. This ballad, reminiscent of Samuel Taylor Coleridge's *The Rime of the Ancient Mariner* (1798), describes a sea voyage the narrator takes with an old mariner in a "little boat" made of "a great pearl shell" with "masts of wild sea rush." After a visit to a "charmed isle" the narrator of the poem asks to go home where his mother awaits his return. However, the old mariner takes him away toward the "ocean's verge." The mariner

suggests that the narrator "might desire, / To have some wondrous things to tell, / Beside your mother's fire." He explains,

> What's sailing on a summer sea?
> > As well sail on a pool!
> Oh, but I know a thousand things
> > That are wild and beautiful!

However, the narrator seizes the helm just in time before sailing into the "gulf of eternity" and demands that the mariner steer them back to land. Howitt's treatment of a crazed mariner does not have the darkness of Coleridge's poem but shows a delicate fancy, more comforting and appropriate to a child's imagination.

Howitt continues this rich vein of simple poetry with *Birds and Flowers, and Other Country Things* (1838). The reviewer for the May 1838 issue of *Gentleman's Magazine* commends the "good sense, correct taste, and elegant fancy" of "this our most favourite poetess of the age." An 1871 edition of this volume published by Thomas Nelson includes eighty-seven woodcuts by H. Giacomellii. This graceful edition introduces Howitt as "a deservedly popular English authoress who has made many admirable additions to the literature of Great Britain." Howitt shows a loving regard for nature in these poems, as when she vividly describes in "The Falcon" a hawking day in medieval England:

> The kennelled hounds' long bark is heard;
> The falconer talking to his bird;
> The neighing steed; the angry word
> > Of grooms impatient there.
> But soon the bustle is dismissed;–
> The falconer sets on every wrist,
> A hooded Hawk, that's stroked and kissed
> > By knight and lady fair.

She notes in the poem that the falcon is no longer needed for the hunting skills as the Englishmen of her own time "loathe the sword and love the pen." The falcon is now in control of his own fate but is also remembered and honored for the part he played in England's past in "the minstrel's line." In this poem Howitt reveals her strong objection to war and belief in the power of words to improve the world.

Howitt dedicated her next poetry collection, *Hymns and Fireside Verses* (1839) to Caroline Bowles, "an honoured fellow-laborer" in making "the spirit of Christianity an endeared and familiar fire-side guest." This volume includes a long twelve-part ballad titled *Marien's Pilgrimage* about a girl, a forerunner of Pippa in Robert Browning's *Pippa Passes* (1841), who goes through the "wide world" delivering "service on the earth." Representing the spirit of

Howitt with her husband, William (City of Nottingham Art Museum)

evangelical Christianity, Marien is more angel than human:

> And ever, as she went along,
> Sweet flowers sprang 'neath her feet;
> All Flowers that were most beautiful
> Of virtues strong and sweet.

The volume also contains Easter and Christmas hymns. In her poem "A Christmas Carol" Howitt in the first of fifteen verses echoes W. Sandys's popular "God Rest Ye Merry Gentlemen," written during the same period.

One lucrative source of income for Howitt was writing children's tales that were published by Thomas Tegg. In 1845 Tegg brought out Howitt's *My Own Story,* which was written for a young audience. It eloquently evokes the magical experiences that make up a childhood. One particularly insightful story concerns her imagining in the fields next to her house a "great black elephant" that, of course, her family insists does not exist. Howitt captures the essence of a child's imagination and claims that the memory of this incident gave her "great charity with the exaggerations and even the apparent falsehood of children." In *My Own Story* Howitt relates much memorable and lyrical description, such as this evocation of a change of season:

> The autumn went on—we ate apples and cracked nuts together, and as the days grew colder came out in warm spencers and woolen handkerchiefs, and now and then received an admonition, not always very welcome, not to keep standing so much: that it was getting damp and chilly in the evenings, and we must not go out after tea.

In 1847 William and Mary Howitt began one of the most exciting collaborations of their lifetime when they published the first number of *Howitt's Journal of Literature and Popular Progress* in January 1847. With this "cheap and literary periodical for the people" they promised moral instruction, inspiration, and entertainment. The Howitts listed themselves as coeditors and "Fellow-workers in the Regenerating Path of Life." They hoped to inspire and elevate the impoverished workers of the 1840s by providing, in a weekly periodical, literature and art for them to enjoy. They took pains to make each fourteen-page issue especially beautiful—it had a green-and-silver cover featuring illustrations, including works by artists such as William Blake, Margaret Gilles, and J. C. Horsley. The periodical included works by writers such as Hans Christian Anderson, Lydia Maria Child, Thomas Cooper, Leigh Hunt, Margaret Fuller, Mary Russell Mitford, Camilla Toulman, and Cotton Matter Mills (Elizabeth Gaskell).

Howitt's Journal also contains powerful poetry written by Mary Howitt on the theme of social reform. The first issue of the third volume includes "Eighteen-Hundred-Forty-Seven," a poem in which she grapples with the severe conditions of the hungry 1840s. She rails against the year 1846 which "has used us ill, / Has stripped us to the very bone." She asserts that "he has been a cruel guest, / His gifts have been war, crime and debt. . . . And, as a parting boon, the Cholera-pest!" The illustration to go along with this poem shows a party scene with elegantly clad men and women dancing under graceful chandeliers surrounded by several illustrations depicting grim scenes of poverty—a starving family in a barren room, a casket, an empty plate and cup; a man begging on the street; a man imprisoned in a tiny dark cell; and a homeless, barefoot woman in a flimsy dress.

In "The Benighted Angel," a poem reminiscent of William Blake's work, Howitt attacks the hypocrisy and injustice of social institutions that do nothing to ease conditions for the poor. She tells the story of an angel lost in London who seeks refuge for the night. The Angel walks

> Through lordly streets, by mansions splendid
>
> The powdered lacqueys, smooth and tall,
>   Looked forth into the streets gas-lighted,
> But none took pity on the small
>   Fair stranger homeless and benighted.

Even the church doors are "strongly barred, / Alike by Churchman and Dissenter." Finally the angel turns a corner and finds a welcoming, well-lighted house where

> A miserable crowd rushed in—
>   The night it was so cold and dreary—
> Those doors alone; these halls of gin
>   Were open to the worn and weary!

The angel recognizes the inability of London social organizations to help the poor:

> And "Oh thou London town!" she cried,
>   "Spite of thy churches and thy preachers,
> Thy Christian virtues vaunted wide;
>   Thy books, thy schools, thy many teachers;
>
> Thus dost thou charter death and sin;
>   Thus of God's law art thou a scorner,
> And plan test Hell—by licensed Gin,
>   To snare the poor at every corner."

Despite the Howitts's sympathy for the problems of the powerless, their high ideals did not sell well and the journal failed by the end of the year. As their friend Ebenezer Elliott, the working man's poet of Sheffield, had suggested in a letter, "men engaged in a death struggle for bread will pay for amusement when they will not for instruction. . . . If you were able and willing to fill the Journal with *fun* it would pay." The failure of *Howitt's Journal* left the couple bankrupt and in debt. One bit of good fortune occurred when in February 1850 Mary Howitt received a letter from Charles Dickens eliciting her to write for the "new cheap weekly journal," *Household Words,* that he was about to start. Howitt contributed to Dickens's journal for many years.

Howitt continued her political reform efforts during the 1850s, becoming actively involved in abolition and women's rights. She and Anna Jameson gathered signatures, including those from Elizabeth Barrett Browning and Elizabeth Gaskell, in petitioning Parliament to pass the first Married Women's Property Act. She also supported the London art world and became friends with the Pre-Raphaelites. To the end of her days Howitt continued to embrace new, often radical, ideas and to live her life boldly. She and her husband became deeply involved with the Spiritualism movement in the 1850s and 1860s. In the 1870s the Howitts left England to settle in Italy, spending their summers in the Tyrol and winters in Rome. Both are buried in the Protestant Cemetery in Rome.

Howitt's poetic career reached its peak in the 1840s, and her poems were widely read in both Britain and America. In *Lady Geraldine's Courtship* (1844) Elizabeth Barrett Browning honored Howitt by naming her as one of the modern poets that

Bertrand, the peasant poet, read to Lady Geraldine,

Wordsworth's solemn-thoughted idyl,
Howitt's ballad-verse, or Tennyson's enchanted reverie,–
Or from Browning some "Pomegranate,"

In 1841, when a Philadelphia publishing company decided to introduce a new edition of Keats by giving "preference to those which would be most acceptable to the public–most popular," they chose to list Howitt's name first in the volume *The Poetical Works of Howitt, Milman, and Keats*. Such recognition suggests her importance as a British poet in mid-nineteenth-century America. A portrait graces the frontispiece, and a memoir describes her poems as

always graceful and beautiful, and often vigorous ... they afford evidence of a kindly and generous nature, as well as of a fertile imagination, and a safely-cultivated mind. She is entitled to a high place among the Poets of Great Britain.

Although Howitt is no longer seen as a major poet, *My Own Story* and her nature poems deserve attention. Her unpublished letters are also valuable as they contain lively anecdotes of both British and American nineteenth-century literary and art world luminaries.

Bibliography:
Carl Ray Woodring, "William and Mary Howitt: Bibliographical Notes," *Harvard Library Bulletin*, 5 (Spring 1951): 251–255.

Biographies:
Carl Ray Woodring, *Victorian Samplers: William and Mary Howitt* (Lawrence: University of Kansas Press, 1952);
Amice Lee, *Laurels and Rosemary: The Life of William and Mary Howitt* (London, New York & Toronto: Oxford University Press, 1955).

Reference:
George Paston, "William and Mary Howitt," in his *Little Memoirs of the Nineteenth Century* (Freeport, New York: Books for Libraries Press, 1902), pp. 325–376.

Papers:
The Howitt papers are scattered among private collections and public libraries including those of the University of Nottingham, Harvard University, Dove Cottage, the Mitchell Library (Sydney), the National Library of Scotland, the Nottingham Public Libraries, the John Rylands Library, and the Library of the Society of Friends (London). In her biography Amice Lee (Mary Howitt's grandniece) has drawn on the family collection of Mary Howitt's letters to her sister Anna Harrison.

Maria Jane Jewsbury

(25 October 1800 – 4 October 1833)

Harriet Devine Jump
Edge Hill University College

BOOKS: *Phantasmagoria; or, Sketches of Life and Literature,* 2 volumes (London: Robinson, 1825; Edinburgh: Constable, 1825);

Letters to the Young (London: Hatchard, 1828); revised and enlarged as *Letters Addressed to Her Young Friends: To Which Is Added, Legh Richmond's Advice to His Daughters* (Boston: Perkins & Marvin, 1829);

Lays for Leisure Hours (London: Hatchard, 1829);

The Three Histories: The History of an Enthusiast. The History of a Nonchalant. The History of a Realist (London: Westley & Davis, 1830).

SELECTED PERIODICAL PUBLICATIONS–UNCOLLECTED:

POETRY

"Oceanides, No. I: The Outward-Bound Ship," *Athenaeum* (29 December 1832): 843;

"Oceanides, No. II: My Sea Hermitage," *Athenaeum* (12 January 1833): 25;

"Oceanides, No. III: The Burden of the Sea," *Athenaeum* (13 April 1833): 233;

"Oceanides, No. IV: The Sunken Rock," *Athenaeum* (20 April 1833): 249;

"Oceanides, No. V: Address to the Deep," *Athenaeum* (27 April 1833): 265;

"Oceanides, No. VI: The Voyager's Regret," *Athenaeum* (4 May 1833): 297;

"Oceanides, No. VII: The Spirit of the Cape," *Athenaeum* (11 May 1833): 279;

"Oceanides, No. VIII: A New Year's Day Song," *Athenaeum* (21 September 1833): 635;

"Oceanides, No. IX: The Eden of the Sea," *Athenaeum* (12 October 1833): 682;

"Oceanides, No. X: Sunset and Night," *Athenaeum* (26 October 1833): 721;

"Oceanides, No. XI: To an Infant Afar," *Athenaeum* (30 November 1833): 816;

"Oceanides, No. XII: The Haven Gained," *Athenaeum* (28 December 1833): 896–897.

FICTION

"The Rivals," *Literary Souvenir* (1826): 99;

Maria Jane Jewsbury; portrait by George Freeman (Tamworth Library)

"The Lost Life," *Amulet* (1830): 187;

"The Bergsman and his Guest," *Winter's Wreath* (1830): 128;

"Love Breezes," *Literary Souvenir* (1831): 253;

"The History of a Trifler," *Amulet* (1831): 149;

"The Revenu," *Winter's Wreath* (1831): 116;

"The Lost Bride," *Athenaeum* (5 March 1831): 154.

NONFICTION

"Literary Sketches No. I: Felicia Hemans," *Athenaeum* (12 February 1831): 104–105;

Review of *The Nature and Dignity of Christ,* by Joanna Baillie, *Athenaeum* (28 May 1831): 337;

"Poetry by the People: Review of *Corn Law Rhymes* and *The Mechanic's Saturday Night*," *Athenaeum* (11 June 1831): 369–371;

Review of *Selections from the Poems of William Wordsworth, Chiefly for the Use of Schools and Young Persons, Athenaeum* (25 June 1831): 404–405;

"Shelley's 'Wandering Jew,'" *Athenaeum* (16 July 1831): 456–457;

"Literary Women No. II: Jane Austen," *Athenaeum* (27 August 1831): 553–554;

Review of *Memoirs of Celebrated Female Sovereigns,* by Anna Jameson, *Athenaeum* (12 November 1831): 730–731.

Maria Jane Jewsbury, or M. J. J., as she often signed her literary texts, was an important and respected writer in the 1820s and 1830s. The author of four full-length books as well as more than seventy contributions to literary annuals and at least fifty-one review articles in the well-established weekly journal *The Athenaeum,* she was regarded by both her readers and her friends as greatly gifted. Her early death at age thirty-three was seen as a tragic curtailment of what promised to be an increasingly successful literary career.

The scope of Jewsbury's works is impressive. She began publishing poetry in newspapers and journals while she was still in her teens; at age twenty-four she brought out a two-volume work that included not only poems but also serious essays and satirical sketches; three years later she published a book of religious advice for young people; and her final full-length work was fiction. Her *Athenaeum* contributions, written in the last years of her life and published anonymously, show her considerable intellect at its best, covering a wide range of subject matter from poetry through history, politics, and religion to women's lives and social expectations.

Jewsbury's achievements seem all the more impressive when her background and upbringing are taken into account. The eldest of six children, she was born at Measham, a small and unremarkable colliery town in the English Midland county of Derbyshire, on 25 October 1800. The Jewsburys had lived in Measham for many generations as prosperous coal-mine owners, but Thomas Jewsbury, Maria Jane's father, had branched out into the relatively new business of cotton manufacture, which he had learned initially from Robert Peel Sr., father of the future British prime minister. In 1799 Thomas married Maria Smith of Coleshill in Warwickshire, who was reputedly a clever and accomplished woman, possessed of considerable artistic taste and skill. Presumably she was responsible for encouraging the talents of her eldest child, in the intervals between giving birth to five more children: Thomas and Henry Richard were born in 1802 and 1803, and then, after a nine-year gap, Geraldine Ensor (herself a successful writer later in life) was born in 1812, Arthur in 1815, and Francis (Frank) in 1819.

In a letter written in adult life to a friend and fellow poet Felicia Hemans, Jewsbury recalled, "I was nine years old when the ambition of writing a book, being praised publicly, and associating with authors seized me with a vague longing." The opportunities for achieving these ambitions, especially the last, must have seemed remote when the family was living in such a relative cultural desert as Measham. Jewsbury was sent to boarding school in Shenstone, Staffordshire, but a severe illness when she was fourteen put an end to her formal education. Left largely to her own devices, she began sitting up half the night writing poems, beginning a play, and planning tales and novels. At the age of seventeen she published a poem in a local newspaper, the *Coventry Herald.* Thirty lines long, titled "Curiosity and Scandal," the piece is a lively and witty satire on contemporary modes and manners that gives a good indication of one of the future directions of her talents.

In 1818 Thomas Jewsbury's cotton business declined. In search of improved prospects, the family left Measham and moved north to the thriving industrial city of Manchester. Certainly the move was advantageous for Maria Jane: she could feed her appetite for books by joining libraries, and she had greater opportunities for publishing and socializing. She succeeded in placing poems in the newspapers and journals and in associating, in a limited way, with authors as she had always wished to do. However, shortly after the family arrived in Manchester, her mother gave birth to her youngest brother, Frank, and died a few weeks later. Maria Jane, not yet nineteen, summoned all her resources and stepped into her mother's shoes, running the household and taking responsibility for her five younger siblings.

A less determined young woman would probably have abandoned all thoughts of a literary career at this point. Jewsbury, however, forged on, despite what she later described as "a life so painfully, so laboriously domestic that it was an absolute duty to crush intellectual tastes. . . . I could neither write nor read legitimately till the day was over." She had poems published in the *Manchester Gazette* and made contact with Alaric Watts, editor of the *Manchester Courier* and later of the popular annual *The Literary Souvenir.* Recognizing her talents, he introduced her to a firm of London publishers who agreed to bring

Birthplace of Jewsbury at Measham, Derbyshire; sketch by T. W. Mercer

out a two-volume collection of her poetry, prose sketches, and short fiction. In the summer of 1825 the work appeared anonymously under the title *Phantasmagoria; or, Sketches of Life and Literature.*

There are twenty-six poems in the first volume of *Phantasmagoria* and nineteen in the second. A proportion of them are the kind of sentimental lyrics that were popular with readers of the annuals, as their titles demonstrate: "A Lover's Farewell," "Lines to a Beautiful Rose," "Lines Sent with an Hour-Glass," "Lines Suggested by Seeing Two Lovely Infants at Play," for example. Another popular subgenre that is well represented in the collection is the "historical sketch." These sketches, which include "The Flight of Xerxes," "Regulus before the Roman Senate," "Columbus in Chains," and "Montezuma," are more successful and interesting than the poems. The best examples of this kind, "Joan of Arc" and "The Women of Suli," both in volume one, and "Song of the Hindoo Women, While Accompanying a Widow to the Funeral Pyre of Her Husband" in volume two, share a common theme: female heroism in the face of imminent death. Joan of Arc is celebrated for her service to her king "with the ability of a General and the self-devotedness of a

Woman" but most of all for the fact that after her country turned on her she died "as she lived, severe, serene." The women of Suli, whose town is sacked by an invading army, clasp hands and perform a thrilling circle dance on the edge of a cliff before flinging themselves over the precipice in a heroic mass suicide, while the Hindoo women sing their powerful and evocative song to a young widow who is about to die courageously on her husband's funeral pyre. "To Death: Written in Severe Sickness" foregrounds Jewsbury's recurring obsession with dying, which has, she writes, cast its shadow over her since her earliest years. Although the poem ends with the speaker's reconciliation with her coming death, which follows some kind of spiritual revelation, the writing is at its most powerful in its earlier passages of darkness, horror, and fear.

The opening poem in *Phantasmagoria* is a dedication of the work "To William Wordsworth, Esquire," in which Jewsbury addresses Wordsworth as her "spirit's father" and offers him "the homage of the heart!" As soon as the first volume was published, in the spring of 1825, she sent a copy to the poet, accompanied by a letter explaining her deep indebtedness to him for "whatever merits these efforts may be found to possess." Wordsworth wrote back two days later (4 May 1825) with grateful thanks for "the honour you have done me." Although he went on to say that "on the whole I prefer your Prose to your Verse," he praised one poem, "To Love," as excellent, remarked on the strength of the lines in "To Death," and made many encouraging comments on the contents of the volume as a whole. He also sent a copy to Robert Southey, the poet laureate, to review. Unfortunately he had failed to notice that one of Jewsbury's wittiest prose satires, "First Efforts in Criticism," included an extended parody of Southey's own rambling and discursive review style. Southey evidently did notice, however, and replied that "the best service [he] could render to the misguided young person was to leave her wholly unnoticed."

Within a few days of receiving Wordsworth's letter, Jewsbury traveled to the Lake District and met the poet and his family in person. The whole family took an instant liking to her and she to them, and she developed a close friendship with Wordsworth's daughter Dora, four years her junior, that lasted until Jewsbury's death.

The success of *Phantasmagoria,* her friendship with the Wordsworths, and a correspondence that she began with the successful woman poet Hemans carried Jewsbury happily through the end of 1825 and the early months of 1826. Living at home in Manchester, where she was visited by the Wordsworths, she continued busily writing for the annuals and periodicals. Then, in early May 1826, she was struck down by a mysterious illness that chiefly affected her stomach and seemed at first to be life-threatening; it took her two years to recover fully. In the autumn of that year she was taken to Leamington in Warwickshire to be put under the care of Dr. Jephson. Because of her extreme weakness and debility she published little for more than a year, although she did manage to write copious letters to Dora and to her sister, Geraldine, age fourteen, who had been packed off to boarding school. One letter to Dora, written in October 1826, shows that Jewsbury underwent some kind of intense religious experience at this time, probably under the influence of her friend and "Mentor" Miss Kelsall, during which she became convinced that "[s]elf-aggrandisment–emolument–gaining friends . . . were wrong at the time . . . because *Self*–was their grand centre" and that even though she would probably return to writing after her recovery, she would do so with a "new *motive*–& that motive will be a hearty, honest, constant desire to glorify & serve *God*."

By the autumn of 1827 Jewsbury was well on the road to recovery. Completing her convalescence

in a girls' boarding school run by family friends just outside Manchester, she was encouraged to compose another book. *Letters to the Young,* published in May 1828. A pious advice manual of a highly evangelical nature, this work reiterates many of the sentiments expressed in her letter to Dora from Leamington. Although it does not recommend itself to twentieth-century readers, *Letters to the Young* was extremely popular in its day and was apparently still "cherished by the class of readers for whom it was written" in the late 1870s.

Throughout her illness and convalescence Jewsbury had been corresponding with Hemans. In June 1828 Hemans invited Jewsbury to pay an extended visit to Wales where Hemans was spending the summer with her own large family of five sons. Jewsbury, still delicate, accepted and traveled to Wales with Geraldine and their two younger brothers. The country air and idyllic rural existence quickly restored her to health, and the summer was one of the happiest she had ever spent. Reading, listening to music, walking, and above all talking together, the two women writers developed an intense intimacy that was not only pleasurable but also resulted in renewed literary activity for Jewsbury. She returned to spend the autumn and winter in Manchester, where she continued to produce poetry and stories for the annuals. The most substantial outcome, however, was a volume of poems titled *Lays for Leisure Hours,* dedicated to Hemans, which appeared in early 1829.

Although Jewsbury wrote apologetically to Dora Wordsworth, apropos of this publication, "I only write verse to improve my prose," there is a significant improvement in the quality of the writing in this volume as compared to that in *Phantasmagoria.* The friendship with Hemans certainly contributed to Jewsbury's returning confidence in her own abilities as a poet, but it also enabled her to share her anxieties (derived partly, as she admitted, from conversations with Wordsworth) about "the pains and penalties of female authorship." The conflict for a woman artist between fame and peace of mind, to which Hemans's own poetry frequently recurs (in her "Woman and Fame" and "Properzia Rossi," for example), is expressed in several of the poems in *Lays for Leisure Hours.*

In "To my own Heart," a long, serious poem of self-examination, Jewsbury castigates herself for excessive ambition: "Wild love of freedom, longings for the lyre" and "aimless energies that bade the mind / Launch like a ship and leave the world behind." Despite its apparent message that such aspirations are self-torture leading only to unhappiness and its recommendation of a "calmer mood" of self-

Jewsbury's friend, the poet Felicia Hemans

"the genius with which she was gifted combined to inspire a passion for the ethereal, the tender, the imaginative, the heroic—in one word, the beautiful." It is in the "History of an Enthusiast," however, that Jewsbury most clearly enacts her continuing ambivalence about the possibilites open to a gifted woman.

Julia, the heroine of the tale, is a talented and ambitious artist who, like Jewsbury herself, longs for "a more brilliant sphere . . . intercourse with the gay and gifted." In her early twenties she publishes a book that brings her the fame she has craved, and ignoring warnings such as "Genius [is] the smallpox of the soul," she moves to a glittering life in London. Despite her material and intellectual success, however, she lacks a moral and spiritual center, and six years later a former admirer finds her to be "withered at the root . . . with energies that only kindled their own funeral pyre." His reasons for no longer wishing to marry her are, he tells her, that "I should not like a lioness for a wife . . . high intellect in women . . . interferes with [man's] implanted and imbibed ideas of domestic life and womanly duty." Despite voicing Jewsbury's own misgivings about the price of literary fame, the story ends on what some recent critics have read as a note of defiance, as Julia departs to live alone in Europe—a solitary life, certainly, but one in which she can be herself without compromise.

Despite the awful warnings in *Three Histories* about the dangers of residence in London, Jewsbury herself was increasingly drawn to life in the capital. In 1830 she began a lively correspondence with the hugely popular poet Letitia Elizabeth Landon, whom Jewsbury met in the summer when she stayed in London. Spirited, amusing, and independent, Landon appreciated Jewsbury's wit and intelligence, referring to her in a letter as "an illuminated temple with all the lamps hung outside." In reply to Dora Wordsworth's expressed anxieties about the demoralizing effects of life in the city Jewsbury explained that her working life there would be much easier, since she could make more money without having to work so hard. In August of that year she began contributing articles to the weekly journal *Athenaeum*.

Jewsbury's contributions to *The Athenaeum,* which continued to appear regularly for the next eighteen months, were published anonymously. This anonymity made it possible for her silently to assume a male persona and thus to write with an authority that would otherwise have been denied her. In the issue of 28 May 1831, for instance, she wrote sympathetically about "our elder literary women" (the feminist Mary Wollstonecraft, the

lessness and spiritual hope, the language and imagery suggest that Jewsbury is unable to relinquish completely her "glittering dreams" and youthful aspirations. This ambivalence is even more apparent in "The Glory of the Heights," a fine poem that owes its form and some of its diction to Wordsworth's ode on "Intimations of Immortality from Recollections of Early Childhood" (1807). Jewsbury's theme is the "mockery" of dreaming that genius can be "wed / To quiet happiness," and the poem ends by urging the creative artist to aspire to heaven where all such contradictions will be erased. In the long central section of the poem, however, the mountain heights that represent aspiration and genius are depicted as powerful and sublime, glittering like jewels in the sunset and glorious in the storm, while the vale, image of peace and domestic happiness, seems weak and passive by comparison.

Jewsbury's anxieties about literary ambition (together with a further tribute to Hemans) reappeared in her last full-length work, a collection of three tales published under the title *The Three Histories: The History of an Enthusiast. The History of a Nonchalant. The History of a Realist* (1830). As Hemans's sister Harriett Hughes confirmed, the portrait of Egeria, the female protagonist of the "History of a Nonchalant," was drawn from Hemans:

Gothic novelist Ann Radcliffe, and the playwright Joanna Baillie, for example), whose rational "masculine" intellects she contrasted favorably with the "feminine" elegance of her own female contemporaries. Her views on poetry were decidedly expressed: she wrote on 30 April 1831, "Imaginative Literature, even when second-rate, has a use. . . . It helps to stave off barbarism," and argued that "a metaphor may be untrue as a moral statement, but it ought to be correct as an imaginative statement" (19 March 1831). She wrote one of her most interesting essays (16 July 1831) in praise of Percy Bysshe Shelley, who was still at that time regarded as an eccentric whom it was "suspicious to quote and dangerous to admire." Jewsbury contrasts his reputation with that of George Gordon, Lord Byron, still at the height of his popularity, and argues that Shelley, despite his apparent atheism, was more sincere and his poetry more elevated than that of his more admired contemporary. Moreover, says Jewsbury, his poetry "exhibits the contradiction of inculcating Christian ethics whilst spurning Christian doctrines," since the "spiritual nonentity"–called by Shelley Universal Love, Harmony, Wisdom–only requires to be renamed as God for the poetry to read "religiously, in the true meaning of the term." In its recognition of Shelley's importance, this essay is many years ahead of its time and demonstrates the strength and perceptiveness of Jewsbury's critical abilities.

Living part of the time in London–independent, successful and apparently fulfilled–Jewsbury in early 1831 made a decision that surprised her friends and caused consternation to her family. Writing to Dora Wordsworth on 12 March from Tamworth in Staffordshire, where she had gone, apparently for a period of quiet reflection, she announced that she had decided to marry the Reverend William Kew Fletcher. How long she had known him is not entirely clear, although he appears obliquely in letters written to Geraldine in August of the previous year. She is not in love with him, she writes, but in "a very morally prudential state of mind," a phrase that suggests that she was becoming aware of the passing of time and the financial disadvantages of remaining single. Although Fletcher "wants a good deal of polishing and softening and mellowing," she believes he is someone she can ultimately love and lean on.

Despite Jewsbury's resolve, the wedding did not take place for nearly eighteen months. Part of the delay was owing to Fletcher's lack of a private income; he needed to find a posting, preferably abroad. By the autumn of 1831 Jewsbury was pleased to report that he was negotiating with the East India Company for a chaplaincy in India. The "certain and handsome income" that went with the job would mean that the pressure of having to support herself by writing would be removed. A more serious obstacle, however, was that Jewsbury's father was deeply unhappy about the projected marriage: he had wanted a better match for his daughter, and his opposition continued for more than a year, to the point where he refused to allow Fletcher into his house. Jewsbury reported herself to be "worn to the bone" by April 1832, and her depression cast its shadow over her literary production. Although she was still contributing both to the annuals and to *The Athenaeum,* she was determined not to write another book for several years, as she wrote to Hemans: she was disgusted with most of what she had written, and dissatisfied with anything new she attempted to write.

By July 1832 Thomas Jewsbury had relented enough for Jewsbury to agree that the marriage should go ahead. The ceremony, which took place in Wales on 1 August, was conducted by Hemans's brother-in-law, whose wife, Harriett Hughes, reported to Dora Wordsworth that Jewsbury had "uttered the terrible 'obey,' with edifying distinctness." Geraldine was a bridesmaid and Jewsbury's father had made the journey to Wales to be in attendance. The couple spent a month traveling before arriving in London in early September to make arrangements for their long voyage, and on 22 September they sailed for India. Wordsworth had sent a fine edition of his works for Jewsbury to take to India, and she set off cheerfully with "the *most* comfortable of accommodations–best cabin–maid–and *such* a paragon of a kind, generous, noble-hearted husband!"

Her earlier depression about her writing seems to have dissipated by this time, and on the long journey to India she not only kept a detailed journal, part of which was published in *The Athenaeum* of 1 December 1832, but also wrote a series of twelve poems for that review under the general title "Oceanides." These poems, which have been called her "finest achievement," chart her changing moods on the progress of the voyage. "Oceanides, No. I: The Outward-Bound Ship," for example, follows the journey as far as the first stopping place, Madeira, and shows her fighting her homesickness with self-reminders of the duty that awaits her in India, while "Oceanides, No. II: My Sea Hermitage" pays tribute to the power of the sea, whose omnipotence is seen as second only to that of God. The same theme is developed in "Oceanides, No. III: The Burden of the Sea," but this time the ocean itself is the speaker of the poem. Despite its claim that "'Tis God himself that speaks by me," the exultation of

Jewsbury's sister, Geraldine, also a writer, in 1855

the sea in its own might and its ability to overthrow the pride and ambition of the inhabitants of the "puny world" seems dangerously close to paganism, and in "Oceanides, No. IV: The Sunken Rock," Jewsbury takes this tendency to its logical conclusion by dropping the Christian motif altogether. In this fourth poem the waves lure the ship onward by means of a falsely benign appearance until it wrecks on an unseen rock. The waves then exult in their power, while the drowned passengers are mourned over by the Oceanides, spirits of the deep. The seventh poem in the sequence charts the frightening rounding of the Cape; the ninth celebrates an Edenic interlude in Ceylon (where the Fletchers's host was Benjamin Bailey, a friend of John Keats, whom Jewsbury was delighted to discover was "such a Wordsworthian as I have rarely met"), and the twelfth, "The Haven Gained," commemorates the arrival of the ship in Bombay on 3 March 1833, nearly six months after leaving England.

Jewsbury's initial impressions of India were far from favorable: she described Bombay in her journal as "*alias* biscuit-oven, *alias* brick-kiln, *alias* burning Babel, *alias* Pandemonium, *alias* everything hot, horrid, glaring, barren, dissonant and detestable." It took her several months, during which the couple moved first to Karnai, on the Malabar Coast,

and then to Sholapore, to get over her culture shock and to become reconciled to India and to traveling, an equanimity that is the subject of last poem she wrote, "Ay, up with the tent-pegs," a cheerful celebration of the nomadic life. In early June she recorded in her journal that she had suffered an attack of "demi-semi cholera" and in Sholapore Fletcher became severely ill. After three extremely difficult months he recovered enough to allow the couple to return to the relatively healthier climate of Karnai; but Jewsbury became ill on the journey and died of cholera in Poona on 4 October 1833, just three weeks away from her thirty-third birthday.

When news of Jewsbury's death finally reached England, family and friends were deeply shocked. Wordsworth published a poem, "Liberty," written for her a few years earlier, and in an attached note celebrating her life and achievements, he paid particular tribute to "one quality, viz. quickness in the motions of her mind [in which] she had, within the range of the authors' acquaintance, no equal," while Landon wrote of Jewsbury's unequaled "powers of conversation." Many of her contemporaries' tributes made much of the loss to posterity, suggesting that she had never fulfilled her potential in her literary productions. Hemans, for example, wrote: "How much deeper power seemed to lie, coiled up as it were, in the recesses of her mind than was ever manifested to the world in her writings! Strange and sad does it seem that only the broken music of such a spirit should have been given to the earth; the full and finished harmony never drawn forth." Elizabeth Barrett Browning, writing on 21 June 1845 to her friend Mary Russell Mitford some twelve years after Jewsbury's death, saw her life as "an aspiration . . . no more!" and regretted that despite her exceptional "comprehensiveness of mind and higher logical faculty than are commonly found among women" she had in fact "done little, if anything."

More recent commentators have suggested that such double-edged tributes are unfair to Jewsbury, who in fact achieved a substantial amount in her relatively short years of writing life. It is certainly true, of course, that her contemporaries would have been unaware of the extent of her contributions to the annuals and would not have been able to identify her important and influential *Athenaeum* reviews and essays even if they had known of their existence. In addition, much of the work she had produced, and which she had taken with her to India with the intention of bringing out some kind of collected edition, was lost after her death when her widower refused to answer family letters or to return her collected writings. However, the clear sense of gathering strength and skill that (despite her own self-doubts) is evident in her later poetry, suggests that had she survived she would have become an increasingly important poet.

Biographies:

Jane Williams, *The Literary Women of England* (London: Saunders & Otley, 1861);

F. Espinasse, *Lancashire Worthies: Second Series* (London: Simpkin, Marshall, 1877);

Eric Gillett, ed., *Maria Jane Jewsbury: Occasional Papers, with a Memoir* (London: Oxford University Press, 1932);

Monica Fryckstedt, "The Hidden Rill: The Life and Career of Maria Jane Jewsbury," *Bulletin of the John Rylands Library of Manchester*, 66, no. 2 (Spring 1984), pp. 177–203; 67, no. 1 (Autumn 1984), pp. 450–473.

References:

Isobel Armstrong, Joseph Bristow, and Cath Sharrock, eds., *Nineteenth-Century Women Poets: An Oxford Anthology* (Oxford: Clarendon Press, 1996);

Elizabeth Barrett Browning, *The Letters of Elizabeth Barrett Browning to Mary Russell Mitford: 1836–1854,* edited by Meredith B. Raymond and Mary Rose Sullivan, 3 volumes (Winfield, Kans.: Wedgestone Press, 1983);

Andrew Boyle, *An Index to the Annuals (1820–1850)* (Worcester: Boyle, 1967);

H. F. Chorley, *Memorials of Mrs. Hemans* (London: Saunders & Otley, 1836);

Norma Clarke, *Ambitious Heights: Writing, Friendship, Love—the Jewsbury Sisters, Felicia Hemans, and Jane Welsh Carlyle* (London: Routledge, 1990);

J. E. Courtney, *The Adventurous Thirties: A Chapter in the Women's Movement* (London: Oxford University Press, 1933);

Suzanne Howe, *Geraldine Jewsbury: Her Life and Errors* (London: Allen & Unwin, 1935);

Harriett Hughes, *The Works of Mrs. Hemans, with a Memoir of Her Life,* 7 volumes (Edinburgh: Blackwood; London: Cadell, 1839);

Howard Vincent, ed., *The Letters of Dora Wordsworth* (Chicago: Packard & Son, 1944);

William and Dorothy Wordsworth, *Letters: The Middle Years, Part One, 1821–1829,* edited by Alan G. Hill (Oxford: Clarendon Press, 1978).

Papers:

Jewsbury's manuscripts are located in the Wordsworth Library, Dove Cottage, Grasmere; her letters are housed in the John Rylands Library of the University of Manchester.

Ellen Johnston
(1835 – 1873)

James R. Simmons Jr.
Louisiana Tech University

BOOK: *Autobiography, Poems and Songs of Ellen Johnston, The "Factory Girl"* (Glasgow: William Love, 1867); revised edition (Glasgow: William Love, 1869).

Though not well known during her lifetime, Ellen Johnston has nevertheless found a following as scholars have become increasingly interested in both noncanonical women writers and working-class poets of the nineteenth century. While female poets such as Felicia Hemans and Letitia Landon have garnered increased attention, as have poets who wrote about the working classes, such as Thomas Hood and Thomas Cooper, Johnston is a poet who transcends both categories, as a noncanonical female poet who was both working class and who wrote many poems about working-class life. As an authentic "factory girl," Johnston had a genuine working-class perspective that few other poets in nineteenth-century Britain possessed.

The details of Johnston's early life are sketchy, and even in her *Autobiography* the information is vague and ill defined. Born at Muir Wynd, Hamilton, Scotland, on an indeterminate date in 1835, Ellen Johnston was the only child of James Johnston, a stonemason originally from Lochee, Dundee, and Mary Johnston, nee Bisland, of Glasgow. Though her father had no formal education, he was a poet, and Johnston notes in her autobiography that the duke of Hamilton, her father's employer at the time of her birth, referred to him as "Lord Byron." Her father's literary leanings might have influenced Johnston's own literariness, although only indirectly.

According to Johnston, when she was seven months old, her father and mother decided to immigrate to America, but as they were about to depart from the docks at Broomielaw her mother claimed that she feared that Ellen would die on the voyage and decided to remain in Scotland while her husband went to America. Subsequently, her mother returned to her home in Bridgeton, where

she worked as a dressmaker and milliner to support her young daughter. Eight years later, after having heard that her husband had died in America, Johnston's mother remarried, this time to a power-loom tender whom Johnston does not name. The family then removed to Anderston, and within two years Johnston's happy childhood came to an end.

An autodidact, Johnston claimed that she was able to read both the English and Scottish dialects from an early age and that her favorites included the novels of Sir Walter Scott. Unhappily for Johnston, her stepfather resented her erudition, feeling that her time would be better spent gainfully employed, and like many other working-class children she was soon put to work, first as a power-loom weaver in a factory at age eleven. Johnston soon became unhappy, but not, it seems, merely because she was forced to work at so early an age. Although Johnston is never explicit about the cause of her unhappiness, in her autobiography she seems to imply that her stepfather had sexually abused her. Eventually she ran away from home but was discovered by her uncle and returned to her mother. Though her mother beat her brutally, she refused to tell her why she had run away and preferred to keep "the secret in my own bosom." Nevertheless, the tranquility that her home had provided prior to her mother's remarriage was never again present, and she ran away repeatedly throughout her teenage years.

When she was living at home and employed, Johnston found herself admired by many of her fellow factory workers because of her erudition, but consequently she was also despised by many of her female coworkers who were jealous of her. Johnston claimed that they slandered her, and thus her life at work was as unhappy as was her personal life. She did fall in love with a man whom she does not name, and he was apparently the father of her daughter, Mary Achenvole Johnston, who was born out of wedlock in 1852, when Ellen was seventeen. This man abandoned them. Although she soon found another lover, he did not offer to marry her. By 1852 Johnston was a single mother living with her mother and her despised stepfather.

Amidst so much grief and misery in only seventeen years, Johnston was finally to know some happiness. She started to write poetry, and a poem on the Crimean War, "Lord Raglan's Address to the Allied Armies," was published in the Glasgow *Examiner,* earning a prize of £10. Although she later claimed that the poem gave her some renown, her health declined and she found that she was no longer able to do factory work. Unfortunately, neither her stepfather nor her mother were now able to work, and thus Johnston was the sole wage earner in her family. She was advised by a physician that she would die within three months unless she got out of the factory, but emboldened by the success of her poem, for the first time since her early childhood she discovered that "I did not then want to die, although I had wished to do so a thousand times before." Johnston decided that her best option was to try to earn a living as a poet, or at least enough of a living to provide for her family while she regained her health.

Her next attempt to earn money as a poet was to send a poem titled "An Address to Napier's Dockyard, Lancefield, Finnieston," to the owner of the dockyard, Robert Napier. Napier was so impressed by this poem that he sent Johnston £10. Though this money was sufficient to sustain her family for five months, at the end of that time she was forced, once again, to work in the factory.

Johnston went to work at Galbraith's Mill in Glasgow until 1857, and then for a "change of air" she went to work in Belfast, leaving her family—including her daughter—behind. It was during this period that Johnston would begin the lyric productivity that would characterize the remainder of her life, and she claimed that "I became so notorious for my poetic exploits that little boys and girls used to run after me to get a sight of 'the little Scotch girl' their fathers and mothers spoke so much about." One of the poems from this period, "A Mother's Love," was written for her daughter, and in it Johnston poignantly describes the pain caused by her separation from the one person whom she loved most in the world:

I love thee, I love thee, and life will depart
Ere thy mother forgets thee, sweet child of her heart;
Yea, death's shadows only memory can dim,
For thou'rt dearer than life to me, Mary Achin.

This poem is one of Johnston's earliest to address substantially one of the two main themes found in

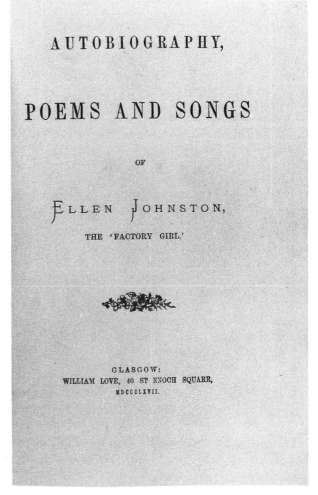

AUTOBIOGRAPHY,

POEMS AND SONGS

OF

ELLEN JOHNSTON,

THE 'FACTORY GIRL.'

GLASGOW:
WILLIAM LOVE, 40 ST ENOCH SQUARE,
MDCCCLXVII.

Title page for Ellen Johnston's only book (courtesy of Special Collections, Thomas Cooper Library, University of South Carolina)

her poetry: her family and her life as a factory girl. As Johnston began to write poems such as this, about matters more personal to her, her poetry was elevated from the earlier work that she had done merely to gain financial reward. Unfortunately fate was to deal Johnston several more blows in rapid succession, each of which would exacerbate her feelings of sorrow and misery.

Johnston left Belfast for Manchester and then returned to her mother and her child. The first event that was to shake Johnston's life was the news that, after being supposed dead for twenty years, her father was in fact alive in America and had written Johnston's mother inquiring after her and Ellen's health. Even more shocking was the news that after being told that his wife had remarried, Johnston's father had committed suicide. At about this same time Johnston apparently chose to tell her mother what she referred to as the "mystery of my life"–her stepfather's abuse of her–and shortly thereafter, in 1861, her mother died.

The first of these events Johnston described in the poem "The Factory Girl's Reply to Edith," a poem which also refers to her stepfather's abuse:

> A Father's love I never knew,
>   He left me when an infant child,
> And sailed Columbia's shore to view,
>   And chase ambition's fancy wild.
> . . . .
>
> Another dozen years had fled;
>   One day a startling letter came–
> O God! my father was not dead,
>   But living in the state of Maine.
>
> Edith, I scarce dare tell the more,
>   Save where the Niagara's wave
> Swells proudly o'er its pebble shore,
>   And points a suicide's sad grave.
>
> Conscience wrung with wild remorse
>   To hear his child, far-famed in song,
> Wept neath a cruel stepfather's curse,
>   That he himself had caused the wrong.

Johnston's poem points not only to the emotional damage she suffered, but it also refers to what she considered her growing fame, although it would be safe to say that her notoriety was strictly localized, in that most of the poetry she was writing during this period was only sporadically published in local newspapers and was aimed at factory operatives and female workers in general. Despite the emotional intensity of the poems detailing her personal trials and tribulations, most scholars consider the poetry relating to her life in the factories as the most worthy of careful consideration. Not only did these poems account for her regional fame, but they are among the most interesting examples of working-class poetry written during the nineteenth century.

"The Last Sark" is often considered one of her most powerful poems. Written in 1859, this poem's bitterness and sense of oppression related to the working-class perspective and the despondency that many working-class families must have felt when they were unable to find work.

> Gude guide me, are you hame again, an ha'e ye got nae wark,
> We've naething noo tae put awa' unless yer auld blue sark;
> My head is rinnin' roon about far lichter than a flee–
> What care some gentry if they're well through a' the puir wad dee!
> Our merchants an' mill masters they wad never want a meal,
> Though a' the banks in Scotland wad for a twelvemonth fail;
> For some o' them have fair more goud than any one can see–

What care some gentry if they're weel through a pure wad dee!

In this poem–which typifies Johnston's use of the Scots dialect–Johnston speaks with the voice of the mother of a starving child and the wife of a husband who is unable to find work. As Johnston points out, the factory owners and the upper classes cannot comprehend the trials that the working classes must go through to survive, nor do they care to. Although it is easy to read some of the poem's lines as overly melodramatic, such as in the sixth stanza when the mother says she is about to drop the baby because "you ken I binna tasted meat for days far mair than three," Johnston's popularity would indicate that her contemporaries found the poem realistic and believable.

Another poem that Johnston wrote recounting the plight of the working classes is "The Working Man." In this poem Johnston describes working men, who can truly be seen as "sons of nature's art," as the backbone of Scotland:

> Let him that ne'er kent labour's yoke but come to Glasgow toon,
> And let him take a cannie walk her bonnie buildings roon,
> And let him wi' his lady hands, his cheeks sae pale and wan,
> Stand face to face, without a blush, before the Working Man.
>
> But the man who wins fair fortune wi' labour's anxious pain,
> He is the man who's justly earned her favour and her fame;
> And may he keep flourishing wherever he may gang,
> And ne'er forget the days now gane when but a working man.

Johnston contrasts the hardiness of the working man to the near effeminacy of the aristocrats (with their "lady hands") whose livelihood depends on the toils of the working classes. It was from poems such as this one that Johnston derived her reputation as a powerful voice of the working classes.

After her mother's death Johnston moved again, this time to Dundee, where she once again went to work in a factory. According to Johnston, she was a superior worker at the Verdant factory, so skilled that "the cloth I wove was selected by my master as a sample for others to imitate." Despite Johnston's high opinion of herself, she was discharged from her position there in December 1863, though she protested that it was without justification. In an act of almost unprecedented boldness, Johnston sued her employer and was awarded a week's wages. Johnston claimed, however, that rather than being celebrated by the factory workers, she was subsequently treated as a pariah and that although "I was envied by my sister sex in the Verdant Works for my talent," after the lawsuit "they hated me with a perfect hatred. . . . I was persecuted beyond description–lies of the most vile and disgusting manner were told upon me, till even my poor ignorant deluded sister sex went so far as to assault me on the streets, spit in my face, and even several times dragged the skirts from my dress." Johnston claimed that anonymous letters were sent to other factories warning them not to employ her, and thus she went for months without work.

Johnston seems not to have realized that her self-promotion probably contributed to her unpopularity with her coworkers. While it is not impossible that her former employers may have slandered her, certainly there was an element of jealousy and outright dislike in the actions of the other factory workers. Johnston's memoirs are so heavily laced with self-congratulatory accounts of her fame as a poet and proclaim so often her superiority to her coworkers that it is easy to imagine that this tendency carried over into her interactions with others. Certainly in a poem such as "The Maid of Dundee to Her Slumbering Muse" she relishes her queenly role, claiming that the public has "crowned thee queen, and all the honors won thee, / And made thee dear old Scotland's favorite boast," and that "they shall welcome forth in a queen-like manner / Thy Factory Girl–the maid of sweet Dundee." Although in this instance her boastfulness is revoltingly blatant, Johnston seemed unaware of this character trait of hers and attributed her misfortunes entirely to jealousy and vindictiveness.

It was after her release from the Verdant Works that Johnston achieved her greatest renown as a poet. She went to work in the Chaplesdale Factory, and while there she started to contribute to the "Poet's Corner" in the Dundee *Penny Post*. Because of the paper's editorial policy, readers were often encouraged to write in and respond to poems that appeared in the paper, and thus Johnston was able to see how her work was received by the community. She began to publicize poetry that she claimed was written by her readers in admiration of her work. One example of this type of poetry is "Lines to Ellen, the Factory Girl," written in 1866.

> Hast thou no mother, Ellen dear, to know thy griefs and
>   fears,
> No sister who hath shared thy joys through all thy childish
>   years,
> No brother's merry coaxing ways to welcome thee at home,

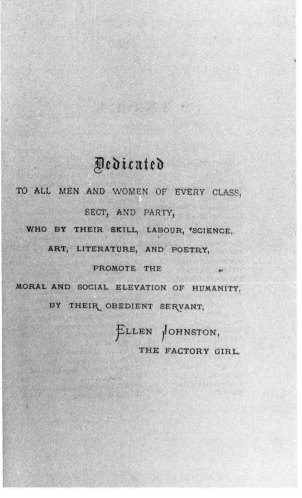

Dedication for Johnston's Autobiography, Poems and Songs *(courtesy of Special Collections, Thomas Cooper Library, University of South Carolina)*

> No father dear, in his arm-chair–are all those loved ones
>   gone?
>
> I know your heart is sensitive, and that you can ill brook
> The sneer from those you work beside, the cold contemptu-
>   ous look;
> Tho' I have met with some of those, the number is but few–
> The most of those I work beside are friends sincere and
>   true.

By this time Johnston was not only writing in her poetry about her family life and her life as a factory worker but was exhibiting a sense of persecution as well. It is clear from her poetry written during the 1860s that her social ostracism was beginning to tell on her, and her poetry is rife with images of the forlorn factory girl, a pariah to all who know her, with neither friend nor family member to whom she could turn for comfort. Undoubtedly, however, her unflattering portraits of her coworkers, painted as tormentors and harridans, did nothing to endear her to the other factory operatives. Coupled with her evident sense of superiority, it may be said that Johnston quite likely exacerbated her own misery by inviting the persecution of others.

In 1867, with the assistance of Alex Campbell, editor of the *Penny Post,* Johnston published her collection of poetry and her autobiography, aptly titled *Autobiography, Poems and Songs of Ellen Johnston, The "Factory Girl."* Published by subscription, this volume has an autobiographical section of twelve pages, followed by some 130 poems, including all of those that had previously appeared in the Glasgow *Examiner,* the Glasgow *Weekly News,* and the Dundee *Penny Post.* The autobiographical section, which relates almost all that is known about Johnston today, details her life up until 1867, including her attempted suicides, her stepfather's abuse, her father's suicide, her persecution by her peers, and even the birth of her daughter out of wedlock. If Johnston's detractors had missed the unsubtle hints that she had given in her previously published poetry regarding her coworkers, certainly her autobiography provided more ammunition for them.

She notes in her autobiography that the "poetic gift bestowed on me by nature's God has brought on me the envy of the ignorant, for the enlightened classes of both sexes of factory workers love and admire me for my humble poetic effusions . . . I merely mention this to clear away any doubt that may arise in the mind of any readers." She goes on to relate that her poetry has the ability to "cast a mystic spell over many of its readers whose numerous letters reached me from various districts, highly applauding my contributions. . . ."

The poems collected in her *Autobiography* include her early works such as "Lord Raglan's Address to the Allied Armies" and "An Address to Napier's Dockyard," as well as later works encompassing all of the issues previously addressed in her poetry. Some of these poems describe Johnston's feelings of persecution and especially her apparent belief that although her poetry was as lyrically beautiful as any being written at the time, it was not afforded the respect it warranted–simply because she was a working-class woman. The poem "An Address to Nature on its Cruelty" typifies the verse she wrote that presents her as a poet undervalued merely because of her humble origins.

> O Nature, thou to me was cruel,
> That made me up so small a jewel;
> I am so small I cannot shine

> Amidst the great that read my rhyme.
> When men of genius pass me by,
> I am so small they can't descry
> One little mark or single trace
> Of Burns' science in my face.
> Those publications that I sold,
> Some typed in blue and some on gold,
> Learned critics who have seen them
> Say origin dwells within them;
> But when myself perchance they see.
> They laugh and say, "O, is it she?
> Well, I think the little boaster
> Is nothing but a fair imposter;"
> . . . .
> At first they do my name exalt,
> And with my works find little fault;
> But when upon myself they gaze,
> They say some other claims the praise.

In this poem Johnston blames her lack of national renown on her working-class status, on her poverty, and even on her personal appearance. Yet it is interesting to note that she acknowledges that she was known as a "boaster," although apparently this did little to curtail her claims that she was an individual who was in many ways better than those with whom she lived and worked. Most clearly manifested in poems such as this, however, is that she was willing to blame anything and everything but her own shortcomings as a poet for her lack of national renown. It seems Johnston was no longer finding the local recognition that she had received fulfilling and that she longed for acceptance on a larger national scale.

However, this was a type of recognition that she would never achieve, although her collection was well enough received that it went into a second edition in 1869. Curiously, in the second edition the autobiographical section was drastically edited, and although the poetic contributions were essentially the same the autobiographical details of her life surrounding her daughter's birth were excised. Even more puzzling is that after the 1869 edition Johnston seems to have disappeared from the literary scene altogether, and the only further information available about her is that she died in the Glasgow Barony Poorhouse in 1873, when she was just thirty-eight years old.

No doubt without her greatest promoter and evaluator of her talents–herself–Johnston's fleeting fame dissipated, and as a result she was little known after her death. Only since the early 1990s, with the recovery of the works of a number of female Victorian poets, has Johnston's poetry been reevaluated, resulting in a critical reappraisal of her work. Examinations of her poetry in anthologies and articles by Angela Leighton and Margaret

Reynolds, Isobel Armstrong, and Florence Boos, among others, have afforded Johnston's work a newfound recognition and appreciation. Perhaps Boos describes the scope of Johnston's work most succinctly, when she writes: "Political anger and personal disappointment—at the emotional damage she had suffered, at fellow poets' facile promises—alternated in Johnston's work with a sense of fellowship, shared struggle, and gratitude for readers' goodwill in her poetry. The 'Factory Girl' fought inequities and injustices in her verse, but she also laid claim to the value of the expressive working woman's inner life. . . ." Ironically, it was not until the end of the twentieth century that Johnston's poetry finally achieved some small degree of the widespread recognition that she so desperately sought—and was denied—in her own lifetime.

References:

Florence S. Boos, "Cauld Engle-Cheek: Working-Class Women Poets in Victorian Scotland," *Victorian Poetry,* 33, no. 1 (Spring 1995): 53–73;

"Ellen Johnston," in *Victorian Women Poets,* edited by Angela Leighton and Margaret Reynolds (Oxford: Blackwell, 1995), pp. 406–414;

"Ellen Johnston," in *Nineteenth-Century Women Poets: An Oxford Anthology,* edited by Isobel Armstrong, Joseph Bristow, and Cath Sharrock (Oxford: Clarendon Press, 1996), pp. 574–575;

Julia Swindells, *Victorian Writing and Working Women: The Other Side of Silence* (Minneapolis: University of Minnesota Press, 1985).

Harriet Hamilton King

(10 February 1840 – 7 May 1920)

Linda A. Julian
Furman University

BOOKS: *Aspromonte, and Other Poems* (London: Macmillan, 1869);

The Disciples (London, 1873; New York: Randolph, 1888);

A Book of Dreams (London: Kegan Paul, Trench, 1883);

Ugo Bassi's Sermon in the Hospital (New York: Pott, 1885); republished as *The Sermon in the Hospital. From "The Disciples"* (London: Kegan Paul, Trench, 1888); republished as *Sermon in the Hospital, Ugo Bassi* (New York: Pott, 1924);

Ballads of the North and Other Poems (London, 1887);

Cardinal Manning: A Character Sketch; or, Foreshadowings (London: Whittingham, 1895);

The Prophecy of Westminster, and Other Poems. In Honour of Henry Edward, Cardinal Manning (London: Whittingham, 1895);

The Hours of the Passion and Other Poems (London: Richards, 1902; New York: Dutton, 1902);

Letters and Recollections of Mazzini (London & New York: Longmans, Green, 1912);

The Religion of Mazzini (London: Burns & Oates, 1913).

Harriet Eleanor Baillie Hamilton King, who wrote seven volumes of poetry with an enviable range of subjects and genres, was best known during her life as the author of a body of poems advocating and celebrating the Italian republican movement and its leaders. Her detailed knowledge of Italian history and politics and her friendship with Guiseppe Mazzini (1805–1872) gave rise to poems and prose notable for their intensity and passion. Her many lyrics, ballads, narrative poems, and devotional poems also reveal a striking imagination and a delicate sensibility as well as skill at versification. The variety and artistry of her work make all the more perplexing the relative lack of information about her life and achievements.

The daughter of Admiral W. A. Baillie Hamilton and Lady Harriet Hamilton, King was born in Edinburgh on 10 February 1840 and spent most of her childhood and adolescence in London and Blackheath. Most of the sketchy information about her life comes from her own comments in *Letters and Recollections of Mazzini,* published in 1912, when she was elderly. In that memoir she says that from the age of six she wrote poetry and that poetry and history were her favorite reading. At eleven she read Samuel Rogers's poem *Italy,* essays in *Chambers's Miscellany* about Italian politics, and, five years later, Silvio Pellico's *Le Mie Prigioni* and Farini's four-volume *History of the Roman State* (1820–1850), translated by W. E. Gladstone. Farini's record of Mazzini's deeds and words "formed an image of the ideal patriot, hero, and saint in my mind," and King writes that "From that moment I recognized Mazzini as the master-mind of the century, and the master and responsive note of my own mind." Farini's work also kindled her interest in the Italian patriots Guiseppe Garibaldi and Ugo Bassi, whom King was to write about in her first volume of poetry.

Her understanding of the political situation in Italy was greatly enhanced when, on her eighteenth birthday, her parents gave her permission to read *The Times* (London) daily. She writes that this permission "was unusual at that time, and at my age." Through the newspaper she followed the political upheavals in Italy. In her nineteenth year she began to write poems "without any likeness to others, and my style was formed at once." One of the first poems she wrote then was "The Execution of Felice Orsini," which took her a year and a half to finish.

Felice Orsini became the subject of her first mature poem through an unusual happenstance. Walking with her father down Regent Street one day, they saw a sign on a shop advertising "Portrait of Felice Orsini. Admission one shilling." Her father wanted to see the picture, which was by Madame Jirechau of Copenhagen, depicting Orsini in prison. King says that "the effect was instantaneous and indelible," that she "came away dazed," and for weeks afterwards "my whole brain was filled by him." She writes that "I found that my health suffered greatly from dwelling so intensely on such a painful topic;

and I had the sensation strongly that I was being dragged down to the grave by Orsini."

The fifty-page poem, not published until 1869, is divided into three parts. Part 1 is set in the streets of Paris, where the people await the execution of Orsini, and it reveals the thoughts of a speaker who shares his own despair and reports the comments of others in the crowd. The speaker is especially sad that no one is heroic enough to be by Orsini's side. Part 2 is set in the prison where Orsini awaits execution. It flashes back to three periods in Orsini's past and then gives an intimate view of Orsini as he is being prepared for the execution. Part 3, set at the scaffold, recounts the execution itself. The poem, like many of King's other works, is overlaid with allusions to Christianity. King was a devout Christian, and many of her poems are religious.

The verse itself shows skill: the poem has an irregular rhyme scheme and an irregular metrical pattern, both well suited to the subject. Particularly effective is the tension produced when the occasional iambic dimeter lines undercut the basic trimeter rhythm. King says that "the metre in which it is written is entirely singular and very difficult. I did not choose it; it came into my head, and I wrote the rest of the poem accordingly."

"The Execution of Felice Orsini" shows King's ability to seize an historical moment and reveal its drama. The poem conveys genuine emotion, but its effect would have been even more intense had it been less diffuse. The major critical complaint about "The Execution of Felice Orsini" and most of King's other long narrative poems is that she interrupts the focus with too much description of nature, too elaborate figures of speech, and too much historical detail. For example, in her overview of King's work in *The Poets and the Poetry of the Nineteenth Century* (1907) E. H. Hickey says that "'The Execution of Felice Orsini' has beauty; but it is, I think, injured by the fault one might expect to find in young work—want of condensation." However, King writes in *Letters and Recollections of Mazzini* about the poem that "I have always considered it the most remarkable I have ever written, and in many respects the finest."

Along with "The Execution of Felice Orsini" several other poems about Italy make up the first section of *Aspromonte, and Other Poems* (1869). In the preface King says that these were written when she was between eighteen and twenty-two years old and that she was publishing them ten years later "with the hope that they may find a few friends before they are quite out of date." The title poem recounts Garibaldi's capture by King Victor Emmanuel's Italian army at Aspromonte and his subsequent imprisonment at the fortress Varignano. The poem begins with an apostrophe to Garibaldi; of the first twelve lines nine begin with his name. "Aspromonte" describes the battle and Garibaldi's imprisonment and meditates on Garibaldi's role in Italy. King compares Garidaldi to John the Baptist, and the poem upbraids Italy for not being worthy of one "Who trusted that you were true!" Beginning with several stanzas of iambic pentameter and hexameter lines in an irregular rhyme scheme, the poem utilizes shorter tetrameter and trimeter lines as its tone becomes meditative rather than descriptive. The quickened pace suggests energy and fervor.

Other poems about Italy in *Aspromonte, and Other Poems* include "Battle Hymn," "Two Sonnets to Garibaldi," and "To the Memory of Orsini." Among these the most powerful is the second sonnet to Garibaldi, which describes him as he visits dying soldiers in a hospital, treating them like a father and leaving them with a sense of peace and love.

King's ardor for the Italian cause soon intensified. On Midsummer Day in 1859, with her father at an outdoor concert of George Friedrich Handel's music at the Crystal Palace, King was suddenly overcome by the desire to celebrate the Battle of Solferino, which, she learned later, had just occurred that day: "That Midsummer Day shines out as one of the most glorious of my life. The passion for Italy so completely absorbed me that my own life was of no importance to me in comparison; I only longed to be able to sacrifice it." Three years later she wrote her first letter to Mazzini, addressing him as "the mild father of my spiritual life" and offering to come to Italy to serve him in whatever way he commanded. Mazzini, who responded warmly, asked her not to come yet. He and King began corresponding regularly, and when her poem "The Execution of Felice Orsini" was privately printed, she sent a copy to Mazzini. He sent her a photograph of Garibaldi.

King's passionate friendship with Mazzini was suddenly thwarted by her parents, however, when in 1863 they forbade her writing to him at all, though she was allowed one final letter. In it King begs to be given "a place enrolled among your disciples." After a six-month hiatus she resumed her correspondence: she had become engaged to Henry King, a publisher with Smith, Elder and Company. He was also a supporter of the Italian cause and Mazzini. After her marriage she finally met Mazzini when he came to London on 30 January 1864, and in April she first met Garibaldi, also in London, shortly before the birth of her first child. In 1864 her husband published a six-volume edition of Mazzini's works.

LETTERS AND
RECOLLECTIONS OF
MAZZINI

BY

MRS. HAMILTON KING
AUTHOR OF "THE DISCIPLES"

WITH PORTRAIT

LONGMANS, GREEN AND CO.
39 PATERNOSTER ROW, LONDON
NEW YORK, BOMBAY, AND CALCUTTA
1912

All rights reserved

With grateful friendship
To Harriet King
Joseph Mazzini.   May. 29. 66.

Inscribed frontispiece and title page for Harriet Hamilton King's memoirs of the Italian nationalist, whom she considered "the master-mind of the century" (courtesy of Special Collections, Thomas Cooper Library, University of South Carolina)

Serious illness prohibited King from writing to Mazzini in 1865. From this point she became a semi-invalid for the rest of her life though the nature of her illness is not clear. In 1866, however, Mazzini came to the Kings' home, The Manor House, Chigwell, Essex, for the only overnight visit he paid them. King enjoyed long conversations with Mazzini as they walked in the gardens there, and she writes of her special pleasure in being able to have him see her two children. In April 1868 she was so ill that doctors gave her only one year to live. However, in October she felt well enough to translate two articles written by Mazzini on George Sand and Felicite Robert de Lamennais, included in volume 6 of the 1870 edition of Mazzini's works.

In 1869 King's career was marked by two events: her book *Aspromonte, and Other Poems* appeared, and she had a talk with Mazzini that was the impetus for her most famous, and longest, book, *The Disciples* (1873). The first half of *Aspromonte, and Other Poems* contains the Italian poems written ten years

before, and the rest of the volume is divided into "Dramatic Lyrics" and "Miscellaneous." These sections contain poems that suffer from heavy-handed moralizing and strained versification as well as poems that reveal imagination, discrimination, restraint, and emotional power.

Of the dramatic lyrics "Many Voices" is the strongest and most imaginative. It owes its interest to the ballad tradition. This first-person narrative has incremental repetition in a question-and-answer pattern that appears in all but two of the fourteen six-line stanzas. The speaker, presumably a man, has lost his love to death and feels abandoned. As he travels further and further from home, each rural scene he encounters gives rise to a question and an answer: "And what did the mill-stream murmur / Silver-sliding to its leap?" is answered by the speaker's "O weary, weary anguish! / Through the long days to weep!" Finally falling upon the grave of his beloved, the speaker learns that beneath the suffering of humankind remains the eternal love of God.

The effect of the question and answer in this poem is similar to that brought about by the repetition King uses in "The Children," in which the last line of each stanza is "But where are the children?" In this poem the speaker imagines his or her children before the throne of God.

Similar themes appear in "The Iris," which consists of sixty lines broken into two stanzas of iambic tetrameter, the first stanza describing despair and the second offering hope. On a July day the speaker goes into the garden at noon but "found there no delight, / For all the year was out of tune." The speaker worries about how she has been unable to ascertain God's will and has let the talents given by God go to waste. An iris tells the speaker that good may not come to her, but that a more significant purpose may be revealed: that it is sometimes more important to learn to suffer. This theme of learning to suffer appears in several poems in this volume, and here, as in several other poems, King alludes to the New Testament parable in Matthew and Luke of the servants and the talents. This parable suggests a kind of spiritual anguish when one fails to live up to God's expectations. King is perhaps writing about her own physical and spiritual suffering that seems to have been constant throughout her life. Her poems often concern the human struggle to discern the will of God.

Learning to suffer is also central in "De Profundis," a five-page, one-stanza poem of irregularly arranged rhyming tetrameter and trimeter lines. A speaker hears the voice of one lamenting the fact that she must die before fulfilling God's will. Another voice offers comfort by saying that "what thou hadst not strength to do / Is not required of thee." This same voice thanks God for the reality of suffering because suffering allows the "inner soul" to find its own consciousness, and therefore "Nothing is lost, for God is left."

In the "Miscellaneous" section the most effective poems are "The Indian Summer," "The Lady's Steps," and "North Winds." "The Indian Summer" illustrates King's talent for describing nature, particularly plants, with keen detail: "Half-stripped, the wooded banks lift high / A carven lacework of grey boughs, / Soft brown and gold against the sky." On an autumn Sunday the speaker observes summer's attempt to restrain the coming coldness and imagines the summer as the lover of the River Tweed, from which she must now have a final parting. The poem's lack of moralizing makes it superior to others in the volume. Also striking is "North Winds," seven stanzas of tetrameter triplets that convey a beautiful picture of the numbing effect of the coming cold: "The long marsh in the windy vale / With

sedges lightens and turns page, / Pointed one way before the gale." "The Lady's Steps," a narrative poem with an irregular stanza length and rhyme scheme, relates the flight of a woman from the house of her husband, who she learns is to be murdered for political reasons. She is hunted down by the murderers, but before she is killed, she tells them that they will see her again on the day of judgment. Then she calmly bares her neck so they can behead her. Since then the place of her death has been haunted. Less successful, but nevertheless interesting, are the two narrative poems "Fritz and Wilhelmina" and "Adelaide." "Fritz and Wilhelmina" is a brief poem about two royal siblings who grow up amid suffering and sorrow. Its haunting effect results from having "Fritz and Wilhelmina" as the last line in each stanza. "Adelaide," in three parts, is about thwarted love. It describes the effect on Adelaide of her elopement from a northern country to Italy, her husband's death, and her forced return home and imprisonment by her family. The poem ends with her realization that God has brought her peace and that God's love will recompense her for her suffering.

When *Aspromonte, and Other Poems* appeared, King talked with Mazzini about the poem she wanted to write to commemorate him and other leaders of the Italian republican movement. When she asked him what he would have her write, he replied that "it is not my words that you must speak, but the word that God gives to you." This comment later became King's defense when, after Mazzini's death, *The Disciples* was attacked as being Christian when Mazzini clearly was not, even though he was widely known as a highly moral leader. Once King had finished the poem, she sent it immediately to Mazzini in Italy, but he died on the day it arrived, before he was able to see it. Ironically, King's devotion to this non-Christian hero led her from Protestantism to the Catholic Church. In her *Letters and Recollections of Mazzini* she states that Henry Edward, Cardinal Manning, sent a priest to her home after he had read *The Disciples* because "he said it was an entirely Catholic book." Cardinal Manning "told me that I was a Catholic without knowing it, and that I had been one all my life." King adds that Cardinal Manning's appreciation of her book did not mean that he "approved of Mazzini."

The Disciples is a large volume made up of five poems. The longest poem by far is "Ugo Bassi," the story of the Italian monk who was priest to Garibaldi's troops and who became a martyr in the republican movement, which runs to more than 250 pages. This narrative in blank verse traces Bassi's miraculous effect on the poor and suffering as he

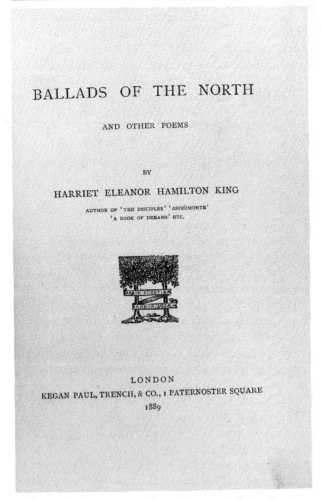

BALLADS OF THE NORTH

AND OTHER POEMS

BY

HARRIET ELEANOR HAMILTON KING

AUTHOR OF 'THE DISCIPLES' 'ASPROMONTE'
'A BOOK OF DREAMS' ETC.

LONDON
KEGAN PAUL, TRENCH, & CO., 1 PATERNOSTER SQUARE
1889

Title page for the 1889 edition of King's collection in which she combines fantasy, history, and social commentary (courtesy of Special Collections, Thomas Cooper Library, University of South Carolina)

ministers to them both physically and spiritually. The poem is related by Antonio Lotti, a boy whom Bassi has saved from pestilence in a country town and whom he takes with him to work as a lay servitor in the Barnabite hospital in Rome. It focuses on events from 1847 to 1849, when Bassi is tortured and executed because he will not lead authorities to Garabaldi. Bassi's place of execution was one of the sites King visited in 1873 on her only trip to Italy.

The poem is accessible even to readers who do not know Italian history, and having begun the poem most readers find it difficult to stop reading. Suspenseful narration alternates with careful description and powerful speeches by Bassi as well as some of the villains. King's skillful depiction of Bassi's life and death unifies the poem and propels it to its end. To appreciate the poem one must read the whole; excerpts cannot adequately illustrate its power, as many critics have noted.

Contemporary critics complained that the action is interrupted by too many tedious speeches and unnecessarily complex descriptions, but most found it a powerful and moving work. Hickey, for example, says that the poem is injured by the history inserted into it and that alongside the poetry is also "a good deal of metrical prose." William Morton Payne, writing in *The Dial* (May 1888), says that "Mrs. King's style is diffuse, and not always poetic; the intense emotion with which the work is charged alone saves it from wreck in many dangerous places." Payne also says that "the author's theme is so great that her work is borne over these reefs of prose; we forget to be technically critical when we read how such men as Bassi died." The reviewer for *The Spectator* (1874) agrees: "the story of how he lived and died for the cause is told with a power of pathos and description which makes us regret the more the interruption of tedious historical details." Eric Robertson writes in *English Poetesses* that "it is not easy to lay the volume down till it has been read through," and he adds that it is "a much more spontaneous and truthful exhibition of Italian feelings about the movement for freedom than any of Mrs. Browning's poems exhibit."

In 1885 a twenty-nine-page section of "Ugo Bassi" was lifted out and published separately as *Ugo Bassi's Sermon in the Hospital;* it was republished many times until 1924. This section appears about a third of the way into the larger poem and uses a vine as a parable for the relative amount of joy and pain meted out to humankind. Bassi argues that "love's strength standeth in love's sacrifice; / And whoso suffers most hath most to give." Bassi goes on to say that "no good / Or glory of this life but comes by pain." He tells his audience in the hospital that humans are linked to one another and often have power over one another's lives. He concludes by reminding his listeners that God will grant them the patience to endure and to suffer all for Christ's sake.

Aside from "Ugo Bassi" *The Disciples* contains "Overture," "Jacopo Ruffini," "Agesilao Milano," and "Baron Giovanni Nicotera." "Overture" explains that Mazzini "commanded" the author to write this book: "For he, the Seer, the Master, and the Saint, / Named me his poet, crowned me laureate / Of his Republic." Early in "Overture" King introduces her Christian theme by saying that Christ should be the model for human lives. "Jacopo Ruffini" is a twelve-page poem in heroic couplets that recounts Ruffini's decision to die rather than betray Mazzini, the one who has taught him the meaning of sainthood. This poem is tedious in its repetitiveness. "Agesilao Milano," in six-line stanzas of iambic hexameter, is a first-person statement of thanksgiving that Christ has not forsaken the speaker, who awaits his execution for killing the king of Naples. "Baron Giovanni Nicotera" is another poem about martyrdom. In six-line stanzas of iambic tetrameter it describes the horrors of the dank prison, where Nicotera and his men await their slow and painful deaths.

In 1883, ten years after the publication of *The Disciples,* King's next work, *A Book of Dreams,* appeared. This collection of thirteen poems juxtaposes the dream world and the real world from a variety of perspectives and in a variety of verse forms from ballad to dream vision. Most have an ethereal quality about them that seduces the reader into a dreamlike state. The lack of moralizing in this volume is striking in view of King's previous work. Only the last two of the poems are overtly Christian: "A Midsummer Day's Dream" and "Awake."

The most skillful of the poems are "A Dream Maiden," "Four Watches," "A Palace," "A Haunted House," and "A Midsummer Day's Dream." "A Dream Maiden," in ballad stanzas, describes a woman lying in bed, dreaming that she is roaming in "glittering dream-worlds." At the end the reader is unsure whether the woman is an elf-maiden masquerading as a wife and mother or a woman longing to be an elf-maiden. This blurring of reality is common to all of the poems in this volume.

"Four Watches" is arranged in four sections, one for each watch: "Noon," "Sunset," "Midnight," and "Sunrise." The poem is unified through references to a different flower in each watch and through a series of questions. The speaker stands in a shower of white and rose apple blossoms in a garden and asks "why am I standing all alone in this place?" The question in the "Sunset" section is "Why am I all alone among the roses here?" In "Midnight" the speaker stands amid orange blossoms. The last stanza is a series of questions about the speaker's emotional state and ends with the question "Dare I not look round me through the maze of orange-flower?" Finally, at sunrise, the speaker is surrounded by passion flowers as the presence of the long-awaited loved one is felt.

"A Palace" recounts a dream in which the speaker is all alone wandering through the rooms of a vast palace where no human being appears. In the final scene the speaker tries to flee through the rooms but finds that each room has four doors from which to choose. Ultimately the speaker arrives "at the inmost chamber of them all" in a state of great fear and awakens without knowing the cause of the fear. In "A Haunted House" a lovely angel-like being participates unseen in the life of a family that has both "health and wealth." The interest comes in the realization that the angel is in pain as she watches over the children and the life of the house, presuma-

bly because some small part of her longs to be human.

"A Midsummer Day's Dream," the longest poem in the collection (twenty-six pages), is a dream vision in blank verse. The speaker, worshiping in a cathedral, is struck by the way in which the crucifix is left alone at the end of the service: "The smoke from dying tapers curled around / The dying Christ, and He was left alone / Upon His Cross, without a worshipper." Part 1 ends with the speaker leaving the church. In part 2 the speaker is walking alone in the predawn darkness on Midsummer's Day and realizes that "I was walking all alone / Through the Garden of the Earth." The speaker sees the Mountain of the Sanctuary and sunrise over the Monte Rosa and then takes the Pilgrim's Way, passes the Station of Calvary, reaches the convent at the Mount of the Madonna, sees the Plains of Promise, walks a path around the Mountain of the Three Crosses, and comes back to the open country through beautiful hills where "Here it was joy to be alive and move; / For such a quickness and a springing strength / The glorious freshness lent to heart and limb." At the end of part 2 the speaker realizes that it is noon. Earlier the speaker has observed that Midsummer's Day is the longest day of the year and "if God should give / But one day in our lives for happiness, / Surely it would be kind to choose that day." The poem breaks off after the title "Part III." The poem's many beautiful descriptions of nature more than compensate for its labored allegory.

The reviewer for *The Spectator* (14 July 1883) praises *A Book of Dreams,* comparing it to "the sort of beauty which belongs to the best pictorial work of the 'impressionists;' such beauty as can be achieved when line and colour are suggested, rather than adequately rendered." This reviewer complains that the poems lack "that minimum of grip and definiteness which the most imaginative work demands, in order that it may leave a sufficiently sharp impression upon the mind. Mrs. King sings of things which cannot be carved, or painted, or spoken, but only sung." Hickey finds that this volume "was more sheerly poetry than 'The Disciples.'" She comments on the sensuousness of the poems, particularly her descriptions of flowers, "which Mrs. King can write of as very few can; the charm of colour, of sound, of sensuous exquisiteness." Eric S. Robertson writes that these poems are "phantasy-paintings, pourtraying feelings rather than thoughts."

King's next book, *Ballads of the North and Other Poems* (1887), also contains many poems that have a sense of fantasy about them. Many, too, concern the theme of suffering, which runs through all of King's work. This volume is divided into three sections:

Statue of the Italian monk and republican martyr Ugo Bassi in Barcelona; frontispiece for King's Ugo Bassi's Sermon in the Hospital *(1885)*

"Ballads of the North," "London Streets," and "Miscellaneous." Poems in the first section have an ethereal quality similar to that found in much Pre-Raphaelite verse. Particularly haunting are "The Ballad of the Midnight Sun," "The Haunted Czar," "The Irish Famine," and "The Glastonbury Thorn." Part 1 of "The Ballad of the Midnight Sun" is set in 1883 on the coast where a traveler has been cast up and languishes, near death, as the midnight sun appears "In one ethereal crimson glow; / As if the Rose of Heaven / Had blossomed for one perfect hour." Then an angelic being with golden hair and flowing white robes, "the Rose of all the World," comes to him, comforts him as the chill comes, and lies with him on the beach until the end. In part 2 summer has come; the Queen enters the music-filled summer palace, and "Where her looks fell was summer, / When she smiled was a dream." Suddenly the dance slows as all hear that "The pulse of the air is beating / Throbs of pain." At midnight the Queen

swoons, and within four hours she dies. As the mourners stand around her, a "faint flame" enters her body, and she sits up with "a smile as of thy secrets, / Paradise." At the end of the poem the traveler from part 1 is recalled; no one knows why he has not returned from his travels. The Queen hears this talk but simply sits and "In the golden shadow always / She is pale." The connection between the traveler's death and the Queen's sadness is made in such a slight way that the poem becomes all the more tantalizing. The beauty of the poem comes from its precise description and its verse form. The poem is in six-line stanzas in which the first, third, and fifth lines are in tetrameter, the fourth line is dimeter, and the last line is three syllables. This gradual diminution of line lengths gives the poem an eerie sound like that in John Keats's "La Belle Sans Merci," with its final dimeter line in each stanza.

"The Haunted Czar" is a powerful soliloquy by a noble who has murdered the czar Roman Romanovitch and seized power but who is now haunted by the specter of the czar and overcome with guilt for his crime. He imagines the final judgment when, ironically, Roman Romanovitch, who should be taken into the kingdom of God is not, while he, who should be consigned to hell, is redeemed through his own suffering and penitence. "The Irish Famine," set in Bantry in 1847, is spoken by Old Aileen, who is dying because of the famine and is brought back to life through the ministrations of a young man she imagines to be the Angel of Life. Old Aileen asserts that the poor "are naught in the world, we are little wanted here"; she tells the young man that the burdens of the poor are growing, and therefore his work is growing as well. She promises to pray to the Blessed Mother for him and thanks God that "He has spared me to behold thy face." This poem is in heptameter verse, an unusual form for King. "The Glastonbury Thorn" is spoken by a priest who has come to a remote place to convert souls to Christ and is discouraged that no one has responded to his teachings. After many months he prays to God about his poor harvest of souls. Called from his house by a spirit during the night, he is shocked to see that the staff he planted in the ground when he first arrived has become a living plant. From this miracle the priest learns that "Our Master needs no other help / When He would feed His own."

The other sections of this volume also contain interesting poems, especially "Working Girls in London," "Dives," and "The Siege of Strasburg." "Working Girls in London" is a series of questions and answers emphasizing that through poverty and suffering comes joy in Christ. "Dives" is spoken by the rich man in the biblical story of Lazarus the beggar. Dives regrets his shameful treatment of the humble beggar, admitting that it was only through Lazarus's humility that he could feel his own superiority. "The Siege of Strasburg" is a grim poem in blank verse that testifies to human suffering in war, especially the pain inflicted on women and children.

Writing in *The Academy* (16 November 1889), Roben Noel says that *Ballads of the North and Other Poems* combines the best qualities of King's previous work, her concern for human causes and courageous leaders, and "gossamer visions and fancies, showing an exquisite feeling for Nature." Noel compares "The Ballad of the Midnight Sun" to Samuel Taylor Coleridge's "Christabel," and he praises "The Haunted Czar" and "Dives" because they effectively teach the possibility of repentance through suffering. He also comments on the variety and skill of King's versification. Hickey writes, "I do not think Mrs. King has done anything which for sustained flight of imagination and subtle, delicate beauty of expression equals her 'Ballad of the Midnight Sun.'" She also praises "Working Girls in London," "The Haunted Czar," and "Dives."

King's final two books have many poems in common. In 1895 she published *The Prophecy of Westminster, and Other Poems. In Honour of Henry Edward, Cardinal Manning,* and in 1902 she included many of the same poems in *The Hours of the Passion and Other Poems.* Of particular interest in the first volume is "The Cardinal's Peace," which pays tribute to the cardinal's peaceful intervention in and settlement of the dockers' strike in August 1889. She met Cardinal Manning as a result of her own experiences at the docks trying to understand the issues and concerns of the workers. The title poem, "The Prophecy of Westminster," is about King Edward the Confessor and his pilgrimage to the Hermit of Thorney Isle. The Hermit tells Edward what is to befall the Church in England and what his role will be in building it.

King's final collection, *The Hours of the Passion and Other Poems,* contains mostly devotional poems, including some from earlier volumes. The most subtle and intricate poem is "The Sistine Madonna." In the poem's twelve six-line stanzas the Madonna speaks about her maternal feelings for the Christ child: "The splendours of the Saints in white, / Could not console me for that first / Hour when my Babe new-born I nursed." She says that in watching out for other mothers' children she is reminded constantly of her own child and the night of his birth, when she was able "to be alone / With Him, the Child that is my own." The volume has a great variety of genres and verse forms. For example, "The Hours of the Passion" is a series of speeches from a reluctant Christian alternating with reassuring and firm answers from Christ; "St. Peter" and "Simon the Cyrenian" are soliloquies; "Veronica" is an apostrophe to Veronica just before she wipes the brow of Jesus, thus making her veil a relic; "Mater Desolata" is an apostrophe; "Innocents' Day" is a narrative in triplets; "Make Haste" is a hymn; and "Katharine Douglas, R. I. P." is an elegy.

Clearly, once King entered the Catholic Church, her poetry became more devotional. The prose written near the end of her life, *Letters and Recollections of Mazzini* and *The Religion of Mazzini* (1913), both paid tribute to her hero and also proclaimed her deep religious conviction. *The Religion of Mazzini* was prompted, she writes, by rumors that many of Mazzini's followers were acting in opposition to Christianity and especially to Catholicism. She points out that Mazzini had been baptized a Catholic but became separated from the Church through the influence of anti-Christian groups. In this essay King argues that "nevertheless, the *inborn* Catholic survived, and uttered strange contradictions."

In writing about King's role in Victorian poetry of his day an anonymous reviewer in *The Spectator* (14 July 1883) said that surely critics of the future would not consider Victorian poetry "a homogeneous product" but see at least three kinds: "a healthy realism, a healthy play of the emancipated imagination, and an unhealthy compound of base realism and of insolent imagination." Of these three he saw King's work as an example of the second. Modern readers would probably agree. Although many will be put off by the religious poems that are overly emotional and predictable, readers today will like many of her lyrical poems. Not many modern readers have the time or interest to pursue a complex work such as *The Disciples,* but because of such work King deserves more critical attention than she has received.

References:
Waldo R. Browne, "New Memorials of Mazzini," *The Dial,* 52 (16 May 1912): 394–396;
E. H. Hickey, "Harriet Eleanor Hamilton-King," in *The Poets and The Poetry of the Nineteenth Century,* edited by Alfred H. Miles (London: Routledge, 1907), pp. 81–86;
Hickey, "Two Catholic Poetesses," *Dublin Review,* 168 (January/March 1921): 73–82;
Eric S. Robertson, "Harriet Hamilton King," in *English Poetesses: A Series of Critical Biographies, with Illustrative Extracts* (London: Cassell, 1883), pp. 367–374.

Lady Lindsay
(Caroline Blanche Elizabeth Fitzroy Lindsay)
(19 September 1844 – 4 August 1912)

Lucy Morrison
University of South Carolina

BOOKS: *Lisa's Love,* Moxon's Select Novelettes, no. 5 (London: Moxon, Saunders, 1880);

Caroline, a Novel (London: Bentley & Son, 1888);

About Robins. Songs, Facts, and Legends Collected and Illustrated by Lady Lindsay (London: G. Routledge & Sons, 1889);

Lyrics, and Other Poems (London: Kegan Paul, Trench, Trübner, 1890);

Bertha's Earl. A Novel, 3 volumes (London: Richard Bentley & Son, 1891);

A String of Beads. Verses for Children (London: Adam & Charles Black, 1892);

The Philosopher's Window and Other Stories (London: Adam & Charles Black, 1892);

A Tangled Web. A Novel, 2 volumes (London: Adam & Charles Black, 1892);

The King's Last Vigil, and Other Poems (London: Kegan Paul, Trench, Trübner, 1894);

The Flower Seller, and Other Poems (London: Longmans, Green, 1896);

The Christmas of the Sorrowful. A Poem (London: Kegan Paul, Trench, Trübner, 1898);

The Apostle of the Ardennes. A Poem (London: Kegan Paul, Trench, Trübner, 1899);

The Art of Poetry With Regard to Women Writers. A Paper Read at the Literature Meeting of the Women's International Congress on Wednesday June 28th 1899 (London: Hatchards, 1899);

For England. A Poem (London: Hatchard, 1900);

The Prayer of St. Scholastica, and Other Poems (London: Kegan Paul, Trench, Trübner, 1900; Boston: Small, Maynard, 1901);

Kitty's Garland (London: Kegan Paul, 1900);

A Christmas Posy of Carols, Songs, and Other Pieces (London: Kegan Paul, Trench, Trübner, 1902);

From a Venetian Balcony and Other Poems of Venice and the Near Lands (London: Kegan Paul, Trench, Trübner, 1903);

Godfrey's Quest: A Fantastic Poem (London: Kegan Paul, Trench, Trübner, 1905);

Lady Lindsay

Lays and Lyrics (Venice: S. Rosen, 1907);

Poems of Love and Death (London: Kegan Paul, Trench, Trübner, 1907);

From a Venetian Calle. Poems (London: Kegan Paul, Trench, Trübner, 1908);

Within Hospital Walls (London: Kegan Paul, Trench, Trübner, 1910).

OTHER: *Original Plays by Blanche Lindsay* (London: Privately printed for the author by Bradbury, Agnew, n.d.).

SELECTED PERIODICAL PUBLICATIONS–
UNCOLLECTED: "Some Recollections of Miss
Margaret Gillies," *Temple Bar,* 81 (September
1887): 265–273;

"Dora's Defiance," *Lippincott's Monthly Magazine,* 54
(1894): 577–649;

"The Salvage Man," *Pall Mall Magazine,* 3 (May–
August 1894): 397–409.

Lady Lindsay was a leading figure in London
society long before she began the literary career that
occupied the last twenty-five years of her life. She
walked in Venice with Robert Browning, received
Alfred Lord Tennyson's comments upon her watercolors, and mingled in the leading art circles of the
times, forming lifelong friendships with John Everett Millais, Edward Burne-Jones, and George F.
Watts. Although her sonnets are slowly being recognized and anthologized, most of her longer works
remain ignored. If Lindsay is noted at all, it is in her
role as the wife of Sir Coutts Lindsay, who founded
the successful Grosvenor Gallery.

She emerged as a literary figure only after
separating from her husband and enduring a debilitating illness in the 1880s. Having composed poetry
privately since childhood, Lindsay launched her
work into the public realm with considerable popular success. Her verses, disclosing social concern as
well as emotional depth, provide an original and
unequivocally female perspective upon the prominent themes of many of her male Victorian predecessors and contemporaries even while much of her
work is repetitive and somewhat facile. The true
value of her work lies beyond the conventional expressions to which she tends to adhere, and her fascination with legend, her concern for the poor, and
her special interest in the artist figure all lend insight
into the changing environment of the turn of the
century.

Lindsay was the second child of Hannah
Meyer Rothschild FitzRoy, the second daughter of
the famous Baron Nathan Meyer Rothschild, who
established the London branch of the finance house
that bears his name. The Jewish Rothschild family
disapproved of Hannah's marriage to the Christian
Henry FitzRoy, second son of George Ferdinand,
Baron Southampton, and the wedding on 29 April
1839 was attended by only one other member of the
Rothschild family, Hannah's younger brother Nathaniel. But Henry FitzRoy's political success and
charming personality gradually won the Rothschild
family's acceptance. He represented the borough of
Lewes in Parliament from 1837 until the end of his
life while rising to prominence in a variety of government positions.

Caroline Blanche Elizabeth FitzRoy was born
on 19 September 1844. Her older brother, Arthur
Frederick, had been born on 15 December 1842. Because of their father's career both children, who
were devoted to each other, quickly became accus-
tomed to visits from political leaders of the day in
their home on Upper Grosvenor Street in London.

Arthur's spine was severely injured when he
fell from a horse in 1848 and the family traveled
widely in their attempts to improve the invalid Arthur's strength. Blanche (as the family called her)
visited Pau in 1848 and subsequently stayed at Tun-
bridge Wells, Roehampton, and Brighton in England. The two children had a French nurse, and
her frequent journeys to France gave Blanche an
easy youthful facility with the French language. She
enjoyed visiting the theater and was especially close
to her father, who delighted in taking her driving as
well as taking her with him to his clubs. Arthur had
a classics tutor at their London home, from whom
Blanche took English grammar and literature lessons as well as Greek, and she began writing poems
for family members at the age of four. She was an
enthusiastic participant in children's activities
within the upper-class circles of London, attending a
court ball when she was ten and mixing with daughters of prominent families. Blanche visited France in
the summer of 1855 and continued to take French
lessons; concerns over her delicate health in 1858
led her mother to take Blanche and the sickly Arthur to Paris, visiting Schwalbach for its waters en
route. During these journeys Blanche sketched
whatever caught her attention, and she developed
the artistic skills that subsequently led to her marriage and acquaintance with prominent artists.

In November 1858 Arthur died peacefully in
Paris: this death deeply affected all the family who
returned sorrowfully to their home in London.
Blanche visited France again in August 1859 before
traveling to Scotland with her parents and on to
Brighton in the fall of that year. At this time her father's health was at its worst. He never really recovered from the shock of losing his son, and when the
press vilified him for alleged incompetence in his official duties, Henry FitzRoy resigned his government post shortly before his death on 22 December
1859. Within a year Blanche lost the two male figures to whom she was closest, and she was to explore her pain at both these losses, especially that of
her much loved elder sibling, in her subsequent
work.

Blanche traveled to Germany with her mother
in 1860 before returning home and the following
year resumed her art classes at Heatherley's, a private school on Newman Street. She passed the win-

Lindsay and her husband, Sir Coutts Lindsay, in front of their home, Balcarres Castle, in 1864; photograph by Thomas Buist (National Portrait Gallery, London)

ter of 1862 at Nice in France and traveled in Switzerland and Belgium before returning to London. She was presented at court on 16 May 1863 and became a dynamic and admired participant within artistic circles. In the summer of 1863 Blanche visited Sir Coutts Lindsay, a minor painter, in his London studio and, at the age of nineteen, fell in love as quickly as her mother had twenty-five years previously. Once again the Rothschild family had objections since Sir Coutts Lindsay was twenty years older than Blanche and had a mistress, the artist's model Kate Harriet Burfield, to whom he was devoted and about whom Blanche was ignorant. Nonetheless, the couple were married at her home in London on 30 June 1864 while Hannah lay ill in her bed. Traveling to Balcarres, seat of Sir Coutts's hereditary baronetcy near Fife, for their honeymoon, Lady Lindsay wrote to her mother that "I feel I have made a happy choice, and one which I do not think I shall ever have cause to regret."

Lindsay was indeed initially happy in her marriage and actively engaged with the duties befitting her station among the poor and suffering in neighboring Scottish villages. She devoted herself to developing the gardens, starting a school for girls to learn needlework, and forming a library for the village people at Balcarres. All these charitable social responsibilities gave her intimate contact with and knowledge of the sufferings of the lower classes—life experience she incorporated into socially conscious verse. The young couple returned to London in the fall of 1864 to live in a house with a studio in Grosvenor Square near Hannah, who died in December of that year. At the age of twenty-one Lindsay gave birth to a daughter, Euphemia, known as Effie, on 15 May 1865 and two years later to another daughter, Helen Anne, on 18 October 1867. Sir Coutts Lindsay began exhibiting at the Royal Academy in 1865 while Lindsay busied herself with her children and her watercolors as well as consistently practicing the violin playing for which she was renowned in their sociable circle of friends.

The Lindsays were prominent in London artistic circles and were close friends of many famous painters such as John Everett Millais and William Holman Hunt. Lindsay developed literary friendships with Robert Browning and Tennyson, and in the 1870s she became a prominent figure in London's social world, especially when the Grosvenor Gallery opened to national acclaim in 1877. Lindsay had contributed to the event not only a large part of her fortune and aesthetic talents but also her considerable social skills. She went into the dinner of the opening gala on the Prince of Wales's arm, and the event was attended by leading artists of the day, with admission by invitation only, as well as by many writers, including George Eliot, Henry James, and Oscar Wilde. The gallery presented the works of Edward Burne-Jones and James McNeill Whistler in a novel fashion, allowing each artist ample space for display, and a portrait by George F. Watts of Lindsay playing the violin welcomed visitors at the top of the stairs leading from the entrance. The Grosvenor Gallery was to remain a leading art gallery until its eventual closure in 1890.

After a successful first season the Lindsays traveled through Germany into Italy, where they spent several months and where Lindsay began the lifelong love affair with Venice that is prominent in much of her work. During the late 1870s the family divided their time between trips abroad, the Grosvenor Gallery, and their homes in London and Balcarres. Prince Leopold, Queen Victoria's youngest son, often invited himself to Balcarres for week-long stays, and friends such as Louise Jopling and Christine Nilsson were also frequent residents at the Scottish castle. Lindsay wrote two songs, "Fishermen of St. Monan's" and "Sometimes," which, with the assistance of her close friend, composer Arthur Sullivan, were published in the late 1870s. Lindsay's diary records her many social activities in London; for example, Tennyson visited her on 30 October 1879, Robert Browning paid a call on 14 November 1879, and Lindsay dined with Eliot on 23 March 1880.

But amidst this social whirl and shortly after her first publication, *Lisa's Love* (1880), a long short story for girls, the Lindsays' marriage of nearly twenty years fell apart. Sir Coutts Lindsay had never given up the mistress he had prior to marriage, and, after an emotional collapse at Balcarres in the summer of 1881 followed by a restorative trip to Germany, growing tension between the Lindsays resulted in Lindsay's permanent separation from her husband in November 1882. Lindsay and her two daughters made their new home at 41 Hans Place in London, where she was to live until her death, the top floor of the house serving as her studio. She retired from the spotlight of society and devoted herself to her daughters and to writing for the remainder of her life. She continued her trips abroad and some of her charitable social commitments while maintaining her friendships with prominent society figures. It was during this final period of her life that she emerged as a prolific and successful writer.

In July 1884 a fall down the stairs caused a contusion of the brain that increased her sensitivity to light and sound, so Lindsay was compelled to retire to St. John's Wood in the country to begin a slow recovery. During the illness that weakened her eyes Lindsay turned from painting to writing, and she dictated much of her work to her youngest daughter Helen in a darkened room lit by only one candle. Her first notable appearance in print was a short novel, *Caroline* (1888), in which the heiress to a large fortune is pursued by fortune hunters before finding true love. Memories of her long recovery clearly exerted a profound influence on much of Lindsay's subsequent work; thematic concerns with illness, death, and nature feature prominently. In her periodical pieces, published mainly in the late 1880s and 1890s, Lindsay provides further insight into her own character and opinions; for example, in "Some Recollections of Miss Margaret Gillies" (1887) she recalls her acquaintance with her former instructor in watercolors. Lindsay also contributed many stories to *Aunt Judy's Magazine* about characters named Lizzie and her father Mr. Roy, which are

veiled portraits of herself and her father and recount her own childhood recollections.

Gradually she recovered enough to enjoy sunlight once again, indulging her delight in natural scenes and an interest in ornithology that resulted in *About Robins. Songs, Facts, and Legends Collected and Illustrated by Lady Lindsay* (1889), a delightful book both for lovers of nature and for children. Lindsay records in her preface that "on emerging from a dark room after long illness and pain," her recovery was aided by spending time in the garden of her cottage and watching the robins that visited her there. She recounts many legends about the bird, emphasizing those connected with Christ, and provides relevant extracts from the works of many canonical authors, such as Geoffrey Chaucer and William Wordsworth, as well as a brief natural history. She illustrates each of the poems with sketches and beautiful color plates and provides many verses of her own, especially simple rhymes for children, as well as several songs.

Lindsay's first full volume of verse, *Lyrics, and Other Poems* (1890), secured her contemporary reputation. This volume demonstrates her ease with a wide variety of poetic forms while also establishing what were to remain many of her favorite themes. Dedicated to the memory of her mother, Lindsay's simple lyrics frequently explore the love of a mother for her child and deplore how the security of that relationship declines in adult years. Songs addressed to children consistently invoke memories of her invalid brother. There are also fairy-tale lyrics, Christmas ballads, and songs admiring agricultural workers and the simplicity of their lives. Religion is a dominant force in many poems as children are gathered to heaven while God guides readers through their lives. The "Songs of Nature" section celebrates robins and other beauties of the natural world while "Songs of Love" is divided into two subsections. In "Her Songs" the female protagonist longs for her beloved but doubts that he returns her affection and fears the complete dependency of her heart and happiness upon him. "His Songs" are similarly loving but admire the woman principally for her physical beauty while the male protagonist is far more confident of the return and security of his own love, is in control of his emotions, and expresses casual joy rather than heartfelt pain. Three longer religious poems conclude the volume, all of which demonstrate the challenges presented to those who try to adhere to God's teaching. The major themes established in this first volume—life as a struggle, with relief through religious faith; the beauties of the natural world; and the painful nature

George Frederic Watts's painting Portrait of Lady Lindsay Playing the Violin
*(1876–1877), which hung above the stairs of the Lindsays' Grosvenor Gallery
(private collection)*

of relationships—were to remain consistent subjects throughout her career.

In 1891 Lindsay published the three-volume novel *Bertha's Earl,* which relates the story of Bertha Millings's marriage to Earl Delachaine, who is more than twenty years older than the female protagonist. Clearly much of the novel is autobiographically rooted; for example, there are the age differences of the protagonists and the Delachaines' delight in their Venetian honeymoon. Lindsay explores in fiction what is also a dominant and recurrent theme of much of her verse: artistic aspirations in conflict with love. The year 1892 was also successful for her as she published *The Philosopher's Window and Other*

Stories, the novel *A Tangled Web,* and *A String of Beads. Verses for Children.* Dedicated to her daughters, the latter work demonstrates Lindsay's facility with rhyming in memorable songs, many of which recount familiar fairy tales and celebrate the simple pleasures of childhood. The volume, despite its celebration of the delights of gardens and of the Scottish shoreline especially, is occasionally tinged with autobiographical melancholy; "A Reminiscence" recalls toy-soldier battles between Arthur and Blanche while the speaker of "A Child's Dream" delights in her elder brother's company on a fairy voyage. For once, brother Tom doesn't laugh and say "'When I'm fourteen I'll go to sea!'" as Arthur did, but instead, he opts to remain in his sister's presence. Faith in God is again a dominant theme although the emphasis rests upon God's beneficence and guidance so that the speaker celebrates the joys of "A Winter's Morning" while, simultaneously, children are reminded to pray for less fortunate sufferers in the cold.

The title poem of *The King's Last Vigil, and Other Poems* (1894) stemmed from a dream Lindsay dictated to her daughter during the late 1880s. It details a king's fear of death until he is visited by God and taken to a meadow of flowers that represent the good deeds performed during life and thus ensure peaceful rest. Many of the poems in the volume are tinged with the sorrows of aging; "The Violinist's Farewell" tells of the sadness when a violinist's fingers give out. The collected "Sonnets" in the middle of the volume comprise some of Lindsay's finest poems since her work is at its best when she works within established forms. In "To My Own Face," currently anthologized in Angela Leighton and Margarez Reynolds's *Victorian Women Poets* (1995) and which her contemporary critics singled out for special praise, the speaker addresses a mirror and notes how her face has become marked with sorrow while she wishes she could recall her girlhood and youth. The speaker is ultimately reconciled to her altered image by recalling "God's own image thou—O human face!" Similarly intriguing is the sonnet "Love or Fame," which depicts a girl choosing fame over love at the Delphic temple and then returning many years later realizing that she has lived in vain despite popular acclaim. Life is nothing if she is not beloved, and she pleads to the oracle to reverse her former choice. Both of these sonnets are examples of Lindsay's work at its finest: they are emotionally vibrant without an excess of passion or overstatement, and they concisely present insight into the dilemma of a woman who chooses to follow a public career at the cost of personal happiness. Lindsay also includes lullabies, love lyrics, and translations in this volume, which was acclaimed by a reviewer for *The Times* (London) for its "generous sympathies, graceful fancy, skill and variety of versification, a wide reach of thought, and a broad range of theme."

In 1896 *The Flower Seller and Other Poems* appeared, with a dedicatory sonnet to her old friend, Edward Burne-Jones. The title poem records, in rhyme royal, the love of young Brunhild for the king she sees only at a distance as she slowly pines to her death. A poignant and emotionally charged poem, it reiterates several of Lindsay's consistent thematic concerns, including the divisions between rich and poor, the death of children, and the nega-

tive aspects of love. "In Sleep" poignantly recalls Lindsay's brother Arthur's death, and many of the poems collected in this volume explore death as a release from the pains of life, with an especial emphasis upon children's deaths leading them to heaven. This collection illustrates Lindsay's developing confidence after several successful publications, and the critics applauded her progression as a writer: "the thought has grown richer and deeper; the style is surer." This volume resounds with an easy command of poetic forms and a demonstrated ability of stylistic diversification, and even while many of her poems seem careless and overwrought, the *Daily Telegraph* noted that "in her sonnets Lady Lindsay is seen to best advantage."

Much of her work revolves around artists. In "Long Years After" Lindsay creates a reunion between youthful aspiring artists, one who has achieved fame, wealth, and success and one who has endured poverty and the loss of a wife and child as well as any dream of prominence. The negative effects of fame and poverty are dominant concerns; however, most of Lindsay's poems are more lighthearted, especially those in which she expresses her admiration and love for the natural world and its beauty and renewal. Lindsay records many memorable songs and ballads in a simple manner, some of which demonstrate her fondness for the Scottish environment in which she lived as a young wife, while she often writes loosely in the Italian sonnet form, which she varies in rhythm and rhyme. She ponders her own posthumous reputation in "Of Remembrance," fearing that only her physical attributes will be remembered. In the final section of this volume, "Lucinda's Letters," Lindsay presents a narrative sequence of fifteen poems in a variety of forms in which Lucinda expresses her desire for the presence of her absent lover. This sequence explores again the predominantly negative variety of emotions surrounding love, including doubt, pain, and absence.

More serious in tone and subject is Lindsay's next publication, *The Christmas of the Sorrowful* (1898), a short pamphlet that George W. E. Russell says "attained a wide popularity" with its "fresh" perspective on the subject of Christmas. The fourteen-stanza poem opens with conventional reflections upon the joys of the Christmas season and recounts familiar details of the first Christmas, but it quickly turns to consideration of those laboring under the multitudinous sorrows of life. Having depicted the struggles of the poor and the isolated, the narrator reminds readers how Christ, as a man, endured much misery upon earth. Frequently alone and hungry, Christ endured his own "Christmas of

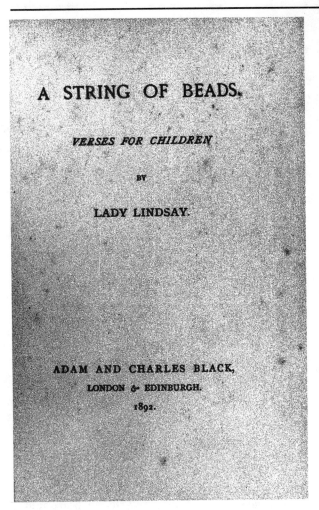

A STRING OF BEADS.

VERSES FOR CHILDREN

BY

LADY LINDSAY.

ADAM AND CHARLES BLACK,
LONDON & EDINBURGH.
1892.

Title page for a book of children's verse which Lindsay dedicated to her daughters Euphemia and Helen Anne (courtesy of Special Collections, Thomas Cooper Library, University of South Carolina)

the Sorrowful" so that those who suffer today should remember Christ in their hearts and experience Christmas as a promise of renewal.

The Apostle of the Ardennes (1899) is a seven-part narrative poem based on the life of Saint Hubert that maintains religious themes and demonstrates Lindsay's ability to construct a free-verse narrative, illuminated and diversified with interspersed lyrics. Hubert the Hunter defies God by hunting on Good Friday until he is struck by a holy vision. Having lost his wife and found God, Hubert renounces his pagan ways and spends ten years as a peaceful, devoted hermit in the same woods in which he once hunted. He is then appointed a bishop and earns the title of the Apostle of the Ardennes through his wise rule, faithful service both to God and to the poor, and his achievements in spreading God's teaching. Throughout, Lindsay's emphasis rests upon Christ as the savior of the world, and the work was highly praised; the critic for the *Westminster Review* suggested that "the stately verse of the poem makes it not unworthy of comparison with some of Tennyson's 'Idylls of the King.'"

Her contemporary prominence as an esteemed woman poet is indicated by *The Art of Poetry With Regard to Women Writers* (1899), which was published after Lindsay presented it at the Women's International Congress in June. In 1900 Lindsay published two volumes of poetry, *Kitty's Garland* and *The Prayer of St. Scholastica, and Other Poems*. While the former volume earned encouraging commentary for its simplicity and pleasing tone, the latter volume emphasizes religious themes. The title poem is Lindsay's version of the legend of St. Scholastica, and several other poems depict saints' lives, while much of the volume comprises local legends and songs in accordance with much of her previous work. She marks the dawn of a new century with poems in memoriam of two of her friends, John Everett Millais and Alfred, Lord Tennyson, noting that she will remember both men for their friendship while the future will applaud their work, and critics responded favorably to the range and music of the poems in this collection. Several poems in the volume also address the contemporary Boer War, honoring the dead while hoping that the peace of heaven might come to exist on earth. In 1900 Lindsay republished one of these poems, *For England. A Poem,* in pamphlet form, dedicated by permission to the Princess of Wales. According to Lindsay's cousin Constance Battersea, the patriotic poem was sold to benefit the Red Cross and earned £300 for that organization. The female speaker of the poem is proud of her husband's response to the appeal to go and fight for his country but notes that the women left behind suffer as well as the men engaged in battle. The speaker reflects upon marriage and misses her husband; she finds comfort in persistently waiting and praying, secure in the knowledge that God will guard her husband whether he lives or dies for England. It is easy to understand why this poem should have attained such popularity at the time of its publication: not only was it sold for a good cause, but the patriotic and religious message of the poem and its emphasis upon the women left behind during times of war also would carry an obvious appeal to the buying audience.

A Christmas Posy of Carols, Songs, and Other Pieces (1902) is aptly titled since this attractive volume consists of many simple lyrics and songs that all pay tribute to Christ's birth and to the ritual celebration of the occasion. Many prayers for the sad and poor are interspersed with familiar ballads and carols that praise Christ and celebrate his birth. "The Christmas of the Sorrowful" is reprinted in the middle of the volume, and Lindsay also incorporates foreign myths of Christmas; for example, "A Tradition of the Zuyder Zee" recounts how, on Christmas night, Dutch fishermen hear the bells of a town that sank beneath the waves when God no longer held the sea back from the town after its populace refused assistance to Christ. At the conclusion of the volume Lindsay provides the originals and her translations of a selection of verses from France, Burgundy, and Germany, which lend original perspectives upon familiar themes of Christmas.

From a Venetian Balcony and Other Poems of Venice and the Near Lands (1903), with pen sketches by Clara Montalba, was, according to Russell, "sold at Venice almost as a guidebook." Clara Montalba also provided sketches for a companion volume, From a Venetian Calle (1908), and both volumes consist of many light lyrical poems that demonstrate Lindsay's love of and familiarity with Venice and its legends although she had stopped visiting Italy by 1903. A religious vein runs through the first volume, in which Lindsay celebrates Venice and its scenery and relates many of the stories behind popular tourist sites. The second volume has a particularly successful brief lyric, "Casa della Angelo," relating the history of a miser's conversion to God and his subsequent glorification of the Lord. Having stated at the opening of the volume that the poems therein "are all absolutely original," Lindsay provides endnotes in which she outlines her sources and provides topographical descriptions and locations that document her poems. In "Maria Robusti" the protagonist chooses to serve her father and to honor her love for him over her own desires for artistic fame as the female protagonist decides that love is more worthy than fame—a further variation on one of Lindsay's favorite subjects. The volumes were favorably reviewed in The Times Literary Supplement (22 January 1904) as including "extremely pretty" verse that demonstrates "a keen appreciation of natural beauty, an ardent adoration of Venice, and a true lyrical gift," although the reviewer (referring to word choice and meter), went on to note that "there is no denying that Lady Lindsay is a little careless at times."

The second of her volume-length poems, Godfrey's Quest: A Fantastic Poem (1905), again bears a religious message as had The Apostle of the Ardennes, but here the message is more skillfully interwoven within a stronger narrative tale. The title protagonist pursues the glory of the sun's setting at the cost of all human relationships and interaction, eventually blinding himself in his pursuit and undergoing

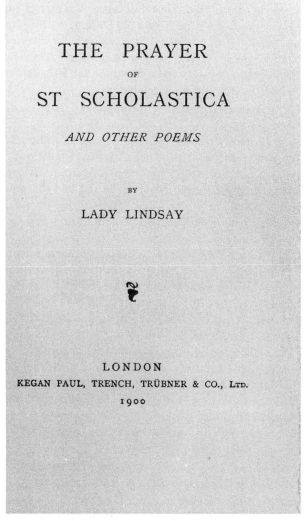

THE PRAYER
OF
ST SCHOLASTICA

AND OTHER POEMS

BY

LADY LINDSAY

LONDON
KEGAN PAUL, TRENCH, TRÜBNER & CO., LTD.
1900

Title page for Lindsay's collection that includes poems on both religious and patriotic themes (courtesy of Special Collections, Thomas Cooper Library, University of South Carolina)

isolation before reemerging into the world with only a faith in God as his companion. In the six books Lindsay skillfully explores a variety of human relationships, including the love of siblings, married couples, friends, and parents for their children, consistently providing minute localization that strengthens the verisimilitude of her wondrous tale. Godfrey is a fully fleshed character, overburdened with pride and desire, and clearly exhibiting humanity's selfishness and disregard of God within daily life. The youthful Godfrey who ran away in pursuit of his dreams returns as a broken old man, only to find that his sister Marjorie willingly welcomes and embraces him under the shadow of God's guidance and support. Notable too is Lindsay's endorsement of women's contentment with their designated societal role as caregivers as she extols Marjorie's willing acceptance of the hardships of life and emphasizes the contentedness to be found in faith. A reviewer for *The Times Literary Supplement* (29 December 1905) remarked that the "allegory is pleasing" and asserted that Lindsay "is master of a smooth, elegant, and facile verse, which carries her over her long course without weariness or excessive toil."

In 1907 Lindsay produced her last two collections of poetry, *Lays and Lyrics* and *Poems of Love and Death*. The latter is notable in that Lindsay includes a section titled "Talmudic Traditions," which acknowledges her Jewish heritage in contrast with the Christianity espoused and disseminated in much of her work. The volume includes poems thematically concerned with Christian forgiveness and suffering as well as a section titled "Nature's Voice" that delights in the world's beauties. "Unemployed" reveals Lindsay's continued social consciousness in its portrayal of the sufferings of a starving artist and his family, and "The Oracle," inspired by a dream, again suggests that life is worthless without love. "The Murderer's Wife" is a rare dramatic poem that deals thematically with both love and death, and although the review in *The Times Literary Supplement* (23 January 1908) noted that "nearly every poem in the book is kept from complete unity and beauty," the reviewer went on to remark that ultimately "the charm outweighs the negligence."

Lindsay privately printed and gave away quarterly pamphlets titled *Green Leaves* from April 1903 until the summer of 1912. These are in the form of chatty letters to friends filled with verses taken from her previous volumes and with anecdotes of and reflections upon her early life. Her final publication, *Within Hospital Walls* (1910), is dedicated to "all who suffer" and was written by Lindsay while she was struggling with a long illness that marred her final years. The volume has several of Lindsay's original poems intermingled with scripture verses and sayings, so that Sir Philip Sidney, Psalms, and Buddhists all share the same page. The book is clearly intended to encourage both hospital patients and their families, and the contents are marked by a devout religiosity, which emerges as Lindsay notes Christ's sufferings and encourages her readers to find faith and comfort in religion. She apparently found growing comfort in religion in her final years, dying peacefully at home on 4 August 1912.

In her own time Lindsay was a popular writer: her first volume of poetry went through two editions in its first year of publication while *The King's Last Vigil* attained similar success and *The Prayer of St. Scholastica* went through three editions in its first year in print and was also published in America. Critics responded favorably to her work but also consistently voiced complaints that modern readers probably share: that much of her work is repetitive and that she is often careless in word choice and meter, with her poetry giving the impression of hasty composition. While her continued publications during her lifetime demonstrate the popular success of her work, the critics' complaints seem to have consigned her to obscurity after her death. Despite these admitted faults, her poetry adds singular perspective into the end of the Victorian era and into the troubled transitional period of the early twentieth century. Lindsay's lyrics not only serve to determine contemporary popular tastes and concerns but also provide invaluable original insight into the ongoing struggles of women writers venturing into the public sphere.

Biographies:
Robert Henrey, *A Century Between* (New York: Longmans, Green, 1937);
Mrs. Robert Henrey, *Green Leaves* (London: J. M. Dent, 1976);
Virginia Surtees, *Coutts Lindsay, 1824–1913* (Norfolk: Michael Russell, 1993).

References:
Constance Battersea, *Reminiscences* (London: Macmillan, 1922), pp. 55–57;
Colleen Denney, "Introduction" and "The Grosvenor Gallery as Palace of Art: An Exhibition Model," in *The Grosvenor Gallery: A Palace of Art in Victorian England,* edited by Denney and Susan P. Casteras (New Haven: Yale University Press, 1996), pp. 1–36;
Paula Gillett, "An Exhibition Model," in *The Grosvenor Gallery: A Palace of Art in Victorian England,* edited by Denney and Casteras (New Haven: Yale University Press, 1996), pp. 39–58;
George W. E. Russell, "Lady Lindsay," in his *Half-Lengths* (Freeport, N.Y.: Books for Libraries Press, 1970), pp. 99–103;
A. M. W. Stirling, *Victorian Sidelights, from the Papers of the Late Mrs. Adams-Acton* (London: Ernest Benn, 1954), pp. 162–164.

Constance Naden
(24 January 1858 – 23 December 1889)

J. Jakub Pitha
University of South Carolina

BOOKS: *Songs and Sonnets of Springtime* (London: Kegan Paul, 1881);

What Is Religion? A Vindication of Freethought, as C. N. (London, 1883);

A Modern Apostle, The Elixir of Life, and Other Poems (London: Kegan Paul, 1887);

Induction and Deduction (London: Bickers & Son, 1890);

Selections from the Philosophical and Poetical Works of Constance C. W. Naden, compiled by Emily Hughes and Edith Hughes (London: Bickers & Son, 1893);

The Complete Poetical Works of Constance Naden (London: Bickers & Son, 1894).

The many friends and admirers who mourned the early death of Constance Naden would doubtless be surprised that it is her poetry, rather than her philosophical writings, that most interests scholars. However, despite the fact that Naden and her posthumous publicists, chief among them Dr. Robert Lewins, considered her poetry little more than a charming hobby to be set aside in favor of the promotion and elaboration of Lewins's doctrine of "Hylo-Idealism," she did attract considerable attention as a poet in her own time. The essayist and Liberal member of Parliament William Ewart Gladstone ranked her among the top eight women poets of the century (a list headed by Elizabeth Barrett Browning and excluding such luminaries as Felicia Hemans and L. E. L. [Letitia Elizabeth Landon]). Naden was one of the few writers of her time who drew praise from Oscar Wilde, and she was further distinguished when the first three stanzas of her poem "The Pantheist's Song of Immortality" were chosen in April 1890 as the passage set for the Latin Elegiacs section of the Examination at Oxford, Jesus College.

"But for the early death" is the phrase that recurs most often in writings about Naden; if not for her truncated career, most of her readers felt, she would have fully developed into a major thinker

comparable to George Eliot. What she did leave behind, though, provides an important intersection of science, gender, and poetry, as well as affording the reader an original poetic voice that sometimes contrasts sharply with the overweening sentimentality of much of Victorian verse. One of the foremost preservers of Naden's memory, George McCrie, wrote defensively against the insinuations of a "cult" forming around Naden, arguing that her works were still grossly undervalued by an ignorant public. The scientific and philosophical grounds of debate have shifted so dramatically since Naden's time that it is difficult to imagine how radical they were; evolution is no longer a rebellious creed but an orthodoxy, and Herbert Spencer, who cast a long shadow over Naden's life, is safely ensconced as the "father of sociology." In general, though, Naden's dedication to the realities and beauties of the material world make her a forward-looking thinker, and possibly given more time she would have become a well-known figure.

Constance Caroline Woodhill Naden was born on 24 January 1858 at No. 15 Francis Road, Edgbaston, a suburb of Birmingham. Her mother, Caroline Anne Naden, died less than two weeks later. Her father, Thomas Naden, an architect who later became the president of the Birmingham Architectural Association, surrendered the child to her maternal grandparents. She lived with Mr. and Mrs. J. C. Woodhill at Pakenham House, Charlotte Road, Edgbaston. Her grandfather was a jeweler with a good income. "Little Consie" grew up in a comfortable if somewhat insular home and perhaps as a consequence was a quiet and meditative child, notable only for her capacious memory and her intense dislike of any sort of falsehood. Her grandmother taught her to read using a book that presented words before letters (a synthetic approach to education later recommended by Herbert Spencer).

At the age of eight Naden was sent to a small Unitarian day school kept by the Misses Martin. The school eschewed competition as an organizing principle so even her teachers had little idea of the true extent of her talents, and Naden avoided advertising them if possible. She did gain a reputation, however, as a delightfully inventive storyteller, especially when among younger girls. After graduating from the school in 1875 Naden continued her education by reading a wide range of books, mastering her grandfather's large and miscellaneous library. She found Reverend R. A. Vaughan's *Hours with the Mystics* (1856) particularly fascinating; Vaughan, a Congregational minister and neighbor, was renowned for his intellectually intricate sermons. Little is known about Naden's religious upbringing except that, at various times, she went to the Mount Zion, Wycliff, and Church of the Redeemer Baptist churches. One of her chief interests at this time besides reading was flower painting; one painting was accepted by the Birmingham Society of Artists, but the next year two were rejected, and these rejections may have discouraged her pursuit of an artistic career.

In 1876, in the resort town of Southport, a chance meeting occurred that strongly influenced the course of Naden's life. Robert Lewins, a Scottish surgeon who had served in many of the British

army's most difficult campaigns, perceived her still underutilized intelligence and urged her to continue her schooling. Lewins had, perhaps, an ulterior motive for fostering Naden's continued intellectual development: after retiring from the army he had devoted his time to spreading the doctrine of "Hylo-Idealism," also known variously as "auto-centric Solipsism," "automorphic egoism," "Hylozoic Materialism," "Hylo-Phenomenology," "monism of autocosm," "solipsismal egoism," "Autoplasticism," "Autopsicism," and "Autocentrism." The *Oxford English Dictionary* defines "Hylo-Idealism" as "the doctrine of R. Lewins that reality belongs to the immediate object of belief as such; material or somatic idealism, sensuous subjectivism." It was intended to unite the disparate claims of materialism (*hylo* = matter) and idealism. Although nothing exists outside of the physical, idealism is still crucial in the creation of the universe within the brain of the perceiver. Naden's most effective metaphor in explaining the idea is the rainbow, since two people looking at the same rainbow will see different colors due to minute differences in the wavelength of light. The most striking aspect of this idea was its denial of any god outside of the self; indeed, Thomas Carlyle singled out Lewins as the most annoying of a new breed of scientifically based atheists. Following their meeting in Southport, Naden and Lewins exchanged letters about Hylo-Idealism, with Lewins eventually converting her to its importance. He later published parts of their correspondence under the title *Humanism versus Theism; or, Solipsism (Egoism) = Atheism* (1887).

Naden returned to school in 1879, first studying botany at the Midlands Institute, where she took first-class certificates in the science and art department examinations. She also studied French and German there, making a lasting impression on her German professor by her ability to translate, at sight, a passage of ancient Greek into modern German. In 1881 Naden entered the Mason College of Science, where she studied biology, chemistry, geology, physics, and zoology. At Mason College she became deeply interested in the "synthetic philosophy" of Herbert Spencer, which inspired her pursuit of all varieties of scientific knowledge. All signs pointed to greatness. During a trip to Coventry, Lewins convinced Naden to undergo a phrenological examination; the examiner was struck by the resemblance of her head to that of George Eliot.

Constance Naden's career in poetry began in 1881 as well, with the publication of *Songs and Sonnets of Springtime*. It is not a unified work, since most of the poems had been composed at odd moments during the years between day school and college, but it often displays a sensibility that is at once artful and direct. The subjects range from her own childhood (in "Six Years Old") to a philosophical poem, "Das Ideal," written in German and dedicated to Lewins; Naden also included translations of various German poets, among them a lilting version of Johann Goethe's "Wandrers Nachtlied II." Hylo-Idealism, if it had any real impact on *Songs and Sonnets,* reinforced Naden's tendency toward close observation of the physical. Perhaps the most characteristic and best-known poem of the volume is "The Pantheist's Song of Immortality," which draws on John Keats's "Ode to Melancholy" in presenting the stoic optimism of a young woman on her deathbed—an unfortunate foreshadowing of Naden's own fate. "The Two Artists" anticipates her future poetic style with its efficient mockery of a painter frustrated by his inability to capture in paint the bloom of his beloved's cheek; his younger sister gleefully increases his frustration by informing him that the source of those rosy cheeks is in a bottle upstairs.

Songs and Sonnets of Springtime was generally well received by critics, and Naden was given credit for having a fluent style. Although the emotional range of her poetry was often mentioned, the lighter poems were most often preferred. Later reviews of her work, particularly those written after her death, would often praise her poetry as only one aspect of her broad intelligence, but at this stage she was primarily a promising young poet. William Gladstone's high opinion of Naden's poetic skills was based, it seems, entirely on this first volume. Naden also began publishing scientific and philosophical pieces in many different periodicals, ranging from the *Journal of Science* to the *Agnostic Annual.* She published these articles under her full name, "C. N.," "Constance Arden," and "C. A." Naden spent the summer of 1881 touring Europe with her friend Ellen Brown, visiting Belgium, Switzerland, and Paris. Her grandfather died in December, bringing an otherwise triumphant year to a gloomy close.

Naden had found her intellectual and social milieu at Mason College, and the once withdrawn child became a forceful presence. Deciding not to pursue a degree in favor of greater academic freedom, she continued to produce writings and speeches on Hylo-Idealism and the ramifications of evolutionary theory for individual and social ethical development. She was a member of the Birmingham Ladies' Debating Society and eventually became its president. Because of Naden's quick intelligence and devotion to what she saw as truth, she was a feared debate opponent; however, because of her consistently good humor and fine manners her popularity continued to grow. In the spring of 1883

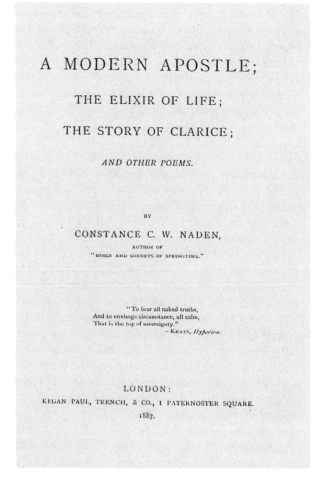

A MODERN APOSTLE;

THE ELIXIR OF LIFE;

THE STORY OF CLARICE;

AND OTHER POEMS.

BY

CONSTANCE C. W. NADEN,

AUTHOR OF
"SONGS AND SONNETS OF SPRINGTIME."

"To bear all naked truths,
And to envisage circumstance, all calm,
That is the top of sovereignty."
—KEATS, *Hyperion.*

LONDON:
KEGAN PAUL, TRENCH, & CO., 1 PATERNOSTER SQUARE.
1887.

Title page for Naden's collection that includes her poem cycle "Evolutionary Erotics"

Naden traveled abroad again, this time to Italy (Rome, Venice, Naples) with her friend Miss Rock. In that year she also published her pamphlet *What Is Religion? A Vindication of Freethought* under the initials "C. N.," positing that science would eventually replace religion and that Hylo-Idealism would reconcile poetry, philosophy, and science. When the Birmingham Natural History and Microscopical Society formed a new sociological section dedicated to the exegesis of Spencer's fledgling science, Naden joined and quickly became its leading member. She also taught, for a time, at a home for friendless girls. Continuing her increasingly public career, Naden won the Panton Prize at Mason College for an essay on the geology of the district and in 1887 won the Heslop Gold Medal, the highest academic honor bestowed at Mason, for her essay "Induction and Deduction," which would be published posthumously.

Naden had trouble finding a publisher for her second book of poetry, *A Modern Apostle, The Elixir of Life, and Other Poems* (1887); it was rejected by an unnamed "eminent firm," despite the fact that Naden offered to defray the entire cost of publication; apparently the publisher was concerned about the theologically unusual subject matter. The volume as a whole represents a considerable advance over the earlier one, particularly in terms of consistency. "The Modern Apostle" is a long narrative poem in somber ottava rima (in itself a special accomplishment) that tells the story of Alan, a preacher of "pantheistic socialism," and Ellen, a devotee of the abstract, particularly mathematics. He dies in her arms after attempting to quell a riot he is indirectly responsible for. It is atypical in its tragic ending and tendency toward melodrama, but it does explore the theme that preoccupies Naden in this collection: the tension between reason and love, mind and heart. The pinnacle of Naden's poetic efforts are four poems that are collectively titled "Evolutional Erotics": "Scientific Wooing," "The New Orthodoxy," "Natural Selection," and "Solomon Redivivus." Each tells a tale of love spiced with scientific terminology, and Naden manages the difficult task of satirizing both romance and logic; in "Natural Selection," for example, the scholarly and drab narrator loses his sweetheart to an inane but flamboyant rival and concludes that "Ah no! for since Chloe is false, / I'm certain that Darwin is true!"

The reviewers' praise was almost unanimously directed at the lighter verse. The key words, used in a variety of forms, were "charming" and "humourous"; a Birmingham newspaper found the combination of playfulness and nobility especially appealing. Naden's underlying philosophies, when noted, were usually disregarded as unnecessary to the enjoyment of the work. Oscar Wilde, however, in his review in *The Woman's World,* praised both Naden's skill in versification and her courage in subject matter. Although Naden may not have anticipated it or much desired it, her poetic timbre was most appreciated in its comic form, a result that itself illustrates a kind of aesthetic Darwinism.

In June 1887 Naden's grandmother died, an event that initiated the last stage of Naden's life; for, although Naden was a devoted granddaughter, she now possessed a considerable fortune and freedom of mobility. In September she embarked on a nine-month trip across Europe to Constantinople and on to Cyprus, Palestine, and Cairo. Naden and her companion, a Mrs. Daniell, next sailed to India, where they were introduced to many members of the highest society; Naden also met with various reformers, and she was particularly interested in the campaign against infant marriages. While in India, Naden caught a fever that kept her at Mount Aboo for seven weeks. When healthy enough to travel, Naden returned not to Birmingham but to London,

having decided after her grandmother's death to live there permanently. Naden lived in a series of apartments before purchasing a recently built house at No. 114 Park Street, Grosvenor Square. She had also decided to stop writing poetry, which possibly led her to enter even more fully into public life. Establishing herself again as a skilled defender of Spencer, Naden became a member of the Aristotelian Society and also joined the Royal Institution.

Naden, in line with Spencerian thought on the subject, was a great supporter of charitable organizations as an alternative to state-sponsored aid, and in 1889, the last year of her life, her charitable efforts intensified. In April she hosted a meeting to raise funds for the new Hospital for Women; at that meeting the medical training of women for service in India was discussed, a topic that had been of special interest for Naden since her visit there, and the result was several hundred pounds in donations. Naden also became more active politically, canvassing for the Liberal parliamentary candidate G. Leveson-Gower (who lost). Months later, shortly before her death, Naden was also negotiating the assumption of responsibility for the Campden Houses, which lodged women of limited means.

One of Naden's last public appearances was for the feminist cause, which had also been an abiding interest for her. As early as December 1883, writing in the *Mason College Magazine,* Naden had been plainspoken on the position of women in society, observing that a young woman in a corset "may be called rather a criminal lunatic than a slave, since her tortures are voluntary." Although her poetry is rarely overtly feminist, many of the "love" poems, humorous or not, explore the delicate negotiations of power in female/male relationships. On 19 November 1889, Naden gave a lecture in Deptford for the Women's Liberal Association, arguing forcefully for the extension of suffrage to women.

Naden's industriousness masked a steadily deepening illness. Even her friends had little idea of the seriousness of her condition until, after consultation among various doctors, the leading gynecological surgeon in Great Britain, Dr. Robert Lawson Tait, was summoned. Naden was afflicted with ovarian cysts and, although Tait had an extremely impressive success rate with ovariectomies, it was simply too late. It appeared for some time after the surgery that she might recover, but Naden weakened and died on 23 December 1889—a month short of her thirty-second birthday. She was buried on 28 December at the Old Cemetery on Warstone Lane in Birmingham, at her mother's side.

Lewins quickly began efforts to preserve her work, gathering her philosophical writings and having them published as *Induction and Deduction* (1890). Naden inspired considerable reverence in her friends and colleagues, and the national press mourned the passing of a promising mind who, it was mournfully ventured, might well have accomplished something completely revolutionary. Gladstone's high opinion of her was sealed only after her death. There were few dissenting voices, among them *Sylvia's Journal,* which was embarrassed that so much had been made of so little, although it laid most of the blame on Naden's overenthusiastic followers. The most ignoble "tribute," though, came from Herbert Spencer himself, who, after comparing Naden to George Eliot, felt compelled to add that "I cannot let pass the occasion for remarking that in her case, as in other cases, the mental powers so highly developed in a woman are in some measure abnormal, and involve a physiological cost which the feminine organization will not bear without injury more or less profound." His remark was apparently met with some outrage, and he tried to explain himself and soften his generalization in a later letter to Lewins.

As a poet, Constance Naden enlarges our perspective on Victorian culture. Although some poets attempted to incorporate the ferment of Darwinism and its corollaries into art, Naden alone conveys the impression of a mind at ease with those potentially destructive ideas, making, to use C. P. Snow's famous formulation, one culture out of two. The fact that Naden was a woman further increases her value to posterity, as her singular utterances add to the range of voices only now being rediscovered. As a

philosopher she was perhaps unlucky: although essentially correct in her vision of a secular Western culture, Naden attached herself to a short-lived philosophical terminology. Hylo-Idealism appears in no history of philosophy, but its basic tenet that the mind is a physical phenomenon served as a corrective to the Victorian fascination with spirituality and was in a sense a forerunner of modern cognitive science. Her contemporaries' view of Naden as a half-finished colossus seems, now, to have been shortsighted; given what Constance Naden did accomplish, modern readers will not spend much time wondering what might have been and instead will appreciate the art that remains.

Biography:

William R. Hughes, *Constance Naden: A Memoir* (London: Bickers & Son, 1890).

References:

James R. Moore, "The Erotics of Evolution: Constance Naden and Hylo-Idealism," in *One Culture: Essays in Science and Literature,* edited by George Levine and Alan Rauch (Madison: University of Wisconsin Press, 1987), pp. 225–257;

Phillip E. Smith II, "Robert Lewins, Constance Naden, and Hylo-Idealism," *Notes and Queries,* 25 (1978): 303–309;

Smith and Susan Harris Smith, "Constance Naden: Late Victorian Feminist Poet and Philosopher," *Victorian Poetry,* 15 (1977): 367–370.

Caroline Norton
(22 March 1808 – 15 June 1877)

Dan Albergotti
Auburn University

See also the Norton entries in *DLB 21: Victorian Novelists Before 1885* and *DLB 159: British Short-Fiction Writers, 1800–1880.*

BOOKS: *The Sorrows of Rosalie: A Tale with Other Poems,* anonymous (London: Ebers, 1829; Boston: C. S. Francis, 1854);

The Undying One and Other Poems (London: Colburn & Bentley, 1830; Boston: Crosby, Nichols, 1854);

Mrs. Norton's Story Book (London: J. Harris, 1830);

Poems (Boston: Allen & Ticknor, 1833);

The Coquette, and Other Tales and Sketches, in Prose and Verse, 2 volumes (London: E. Churton, 1834); republished as *Kate Bouverie and Other Tales and Sketches in Prose and Verse* (Philadelphia: Carey & Hart, 1835);

The Wife and Woman's Reward, anonymous (3 volumes, London: Saunders & Otley, 1835; 1 volume, New York: Harper, 1835);

A Voice from the Factories (London: John Murray, 1836; Boston: Putnam, 1847);

The Natural Claim of a Mother to the Custody of Her Child (London: Privately printed, 1837);

The Separation of Mother and Child by the Laws of "Custody of Infants" Considered, anonymous (London: Roake & Varty, 1838);

A Plain Letter to the Lord Chancellor on the Infant Custody Bill, as Pearce Stevenson, Esq. (London: Ridgway, 1839; New York: Rogers, 1922);

Lines (On the Young Queen Victoria) (London: Saunders & Otley, 1840; Philadelphia: Carey & Hart, 1840);

The Dream, and Other Poems (London: Colburn, 1840; Philadelphia: Carey & Hart, 1841);

The Child of the Islands: A Poem (London: Chapman & Hall, 1845; New York: Francis, 1846);

Aunt Carry's Ballads for Children: Adventures of a Wood Sprite; The Story of Blanche and Brutikin (London: Cundall, 1847);

Letters to the Mob, as Libertas (London: Bosworth, 1848);

Caroline Norton; engraving based on a portrait by John Hayter

Tales and Sketches, in Prose and Verse (London: E. Churton, 1850);

Stuart of Dunleath: A Story of Modern Times, 3 volumes (London: Colburn, 1851; New York: Harper, 1851);

English Laws for Women in the Nineteenth Century (London: Privately printed, 1854);

A Letter to the Queen on Lord Chancellor Cranworth's Marriage and Divorce Bill (London: Longman, Brown, Green & Longmans, 1855);

The Lady of La Garaye (Cambridge & London: Macmillan, 1862; New York: Bradburn, 1864);

Lost and Saved, 3 volumes (London: Hurst & Blackett, 1863; Philadelphia: Lippincott, 1863);

Old Sir Douglas, 3 volumes (London: Hurst & Blackett, 1867; Philadelphia: Lippincott, 1867);

Bingen on the Rhine (Philadelphia: Porter & Coates, 1883; London: Walker, 1888).

PLAY PRODUCTION: *The Gypsy Father,* London, Covent Garden, May 1831.

OTHER: *La Belle Assemblee; or Bell's Court and Fashionable Magazine,* edited by Norton (1832–1834);
The English Annual, edited by Norton, 1834–1835;
The Keepsake, edited by Norton, 1836;
Elizabeth Melville, *A Residence at Sierra Leone: Described from a Journal Kept on the Spot, and from Letters Written to Friends at Home,* edited by Norton (London: John Murray, 1849).

Caroline Norton is primarily remembered for the notorious scandal surrounding the breakup of her marriage, for her influence on British divorce and custody legislation, and for her novels. Virtually all modern critical work on her writing focuses on her fiction and nonfiction prose. Her first and deepest literary interest, however, was poetry, and it was through her verse that she attained her greatest contemporary esteem.

In an essay in the June–September 1840 issue of *Quarterly Review* Henry N. Coleridge ranks Norton at the top of a list of female poets including Elizabeth Barrett and calls her "the Byron of [our] modern poetesses." Coleridge had in mind the Byron of *Childe Harold's Pilgrimage* (1812–1818) and the tales rather than the Byron of *Don Juan* (1819–1824), but some of his contemporaries took exception to the comparison regardless. In many ways, though, it is a good one. Like Byron's poetry, Norton's contains much energetic and passionate expression, and her early poems often concern a central character's disappointment in love. Norton also shared Byron's tendency of working autobiographical issues into the fabric of verse. In addition she stands beside Byron as one of the most prominent nineteenth-century practitioners of the Spenserian stanza. Coleridge's high ranking of Norton in his list of women poets and the comparison to Byron indicate the degree to which Norton had achieved fame and respect through her poetry during her lifetime. Her impressive poetic achievement, which ranges from romantic laments on the futility of love to extensive and eloquent calls for charity and social reform for the less fortunate, has not yet been fully evaluated by modern scholars.

Caroline Elizabeth Sarah Sheridan was born on 22 March 1808, the third of seven children. She was the granddaughter of the famous playwright Richard Brinsley Sheridan. Her father, Thomas Sheridan, died while serving as colonial secretary at the Cape of Good Hope in 1817, leaving his wife, Caroline Henrietta Sheridan, with small children (three of them girls) and little money. The widow

was able to support her family through novel writing and by the assistance of the duke of York, who gave her apartments in Hampton Court Palace.

As a child Caroline showed an early interest in literature, composing and illustrating a small volume titled "The Dandies' Rout" at the age of thirteen. At sixteen she was sent away to boarding school at Shalford in Surrey. During occasional visits to Lord Grantley's nearby Wonersh Park she attracted the attention of a young man named George Norton. Caroline was beginning to display the remarkable beauty that would win her so much attention during her adult life in London, and he fell immediately in love with her. When she was still only sixteen, he made clear his intentions of asking for her hand in marriage, but he was willing to wait until she had grown a bit older and could make her own decision. The decision that she made three years later was strongly influenced by her family's encouragement and her lack of dowry. Caroline had been introduced into London society in 1826 and was in her second season of this life when George Norton renewed his proposal in 1827. She accepted, despite hardly knowing him, and the couple were married on 30 June 1827. It was the most fateful day of Caroline's life.

The match of Caroline Sheridan and George Norton was a poor one from the start. She was beautiful, strong willed, and quick witted; he was dull and weak, though capable of demonstrating a violent temper. He was deeply impassioned by her striking beauty, but she apparently felt no strong attraction to him. Their married life was filled with disputes, quarrels, and resentments, interrupted only occasionally by brief periods of calm. It would ultimately dissolve in open hostility and public scandal.

In 1829 Caroline Norton published her first serious volume of poetry, *The Sorrows of Rosalie: A Tale with Other Poems.* It was published anonymously by John Ebers, but Norton's authorship was soon well known. It is the least polished of her works, but this is quite understandable since she composed the title poem four years earlier, when she was only seventeen. *The Sorrows of Rosalie* is a three-part poem detailing the deception and seduction of the humble Rosalie by the upper-class Lord Arthur in a first-person narrative. Arthur ultimately abandons Rosalie and takes their child away from her, a plot development that resonates with poignancy for those readers familiar with Norton's later struggle for access to her own children. While the poem is the least consequential of her mature works, it demonstrates the poet's early interest in championing the less for-

*Letter from Norton to William Lamb, Lord Melbourne, written in 1837 after she
was separated from her husband (Clarke Olney Papers, Special Collections
Department of the University of Georgia Libraries)*

tunate and in displaying the oppressed state of women. The poem also shows her first use of the Spenserian stanza, a form to which she would return in more mature works.

The Sorrows of Rosalie sold well and was praised by James Hogg, "the Ettrick Shepherd," in the *Noctes Ambrosianae* of the April 1830 *Blackwood's Edinburgh Magazine*. It was a convenient time for literary success as Norton gave birth to her first son, Fletcher, on 10 July 1829. She would later claim, "The first expenses of my son's life were defrayed from that first creation of my brain." Norton had strong maternal feelings, and the arrival of her first child did much to alleviate the initial disappointment of her marriage. The earliest years of the 1830s thus became the happiest period of her domestic life.

The title poem of Norton's second volume, *The Undying One and Other Poems* (1830), is a four-canto poem that presents a variation on the legend of the Wandering Jew. Rather than adopt the traditional figure of Ahasuerus, Norton renames her cursed protagonist "Isbal" and makes the futility of love the chief torment of his ceaseless existence. The poem begins with Isbal revealing the awful secret of his curse to his current love, Linda. Through the four cantos, he tells of his successive loves for Edith, Xarifa, and Miriam and of the agony he suffers in having outlived them all. Beyond his romantic exploits, he also reveals that he has lived a life of various adventures. At the end of the poem Linda also dies, leaving Isbal once more completely alone. The poem's theme is the impossibility of true love;

Canto IV opens with an extended discussion of the desirability and the futility of such a state. With the knowledge that the author herself did not marry for love, a reader can imagine Norton's inclusion of personal sentiment here.

The Undying One was well received overall though contemporary critics uniformly complained that Norton was wasting her powers on a hackneyed subject. Her Wandering Jew, however, is not the common sort of poem on this theme, but rather, in the words of the reviewer for the September 1830 issue of *Fraser's Magazine,* "a Byronian of the purest pattern." Indeed, this poem displays the kind of solitary, brooding hero and excessive passionate expression that led to Coleridge's comparison of Norton to Byron ten years later. The volume established Norton as a significant figure on the British literary scene.

In 1831 Norton was presented at court and late in the year gave birth to her second son, Brinsley. At this time she began to turn her literary efforts to editing and contributing to gift books and annuals. She boasted that she earned £1,400 in a year for her gift book contributions of poetry and short fiction. She published in *Friendship's Offering, The Amulet, The Keepsake,* and others. She edited the influential "women's periodical," *La Belle Assemblee; or Bell's Court and Fashionable Magazine* from 1832 to 1834. She also edited *The English Annual* (1834–1835) and *The Keepsake* (1836).

The early 1830s also marked the development of Norton's intimate friendship with William Lamb, Lord Melbourne (widower of Lady Caroline Lamb). She met him in 1830 after she had made a series of petitions to her family's Whig connections on behalf of her husband, who had lost his seat in Parliament in the general election earlier that year. Melbourne soon became a regular visitor to the household, calling on Caroline Norton nearly every day. George Norton did nothing to discourage these visits, and in fact he encouraged the close friendship in hopes of pecuniary advantage. In such hopes he was rewarded as Melbourne in his authority as home secretary bestowed on George Norton a metropolitan police magistracy in April 1831.

In the fall of 1833 Norton gave birth to her third son, William, but this event occurred amid dire times in the marriage. The period 1832–1835 was marked by several violent quarrels between the couple, one of which involved George Norton's physical abuse of his wife just weeks before she gave birth to William. Many of these quarrels and disputes were the indirect result of George Norton's deteriorating finances, which weighed on him constantly and fed his smoldering temper. In the latter part of this period newspapers started reporting rumors about the nature of the intimacy between Caroline Norton and Lord Melbourne. While these speculations were untrue and Caroline had given her husband no reason to suspect her, the publicity must have embarrassed and hurt him, especially since he was keenly aware that his wife did not return his passionate love.

Despite this domestic turmoil Norton continued her literary endeavors. In 1835 she published *The Wife and Woman's Reward,* which was regarded as her first novel though it actually contains two separate works of fiction. Her name was withheld from the title page, and the work sold poorly. In 1836 she published *A Voice from the Factories,* her first poem to show explicit social concern. The "voice from the factories" is the voice of the poor children of England who are being abused by unregulated industry. Calling on a patriarchal government to modify its system and expecting to influence public opinion, Norton with this poem prefigures Barrett's concerns and goals in her 1843 poem "The Cry of the Children." The incidental similarities between the two poems are striking enough to suggest that Barrett took her cue from Norton.

A Voice from the Factories also marks Norton's return to the Spenserian stanza with which she had begun her poetic career, but these stanzas are much more assured and graceful than those of *The Sorrows of Rosalie.* The unusual choice of the stanza for this work is also worth noting. Rather than using it for a work of romance or fancy, Norton employs the revered form of *The Faerie Queene* (1590–1596) for a frank poem on contemporary social issues and thus makes a bold break with the traditional use of the stanza.

While Norton's poetry was becoming stronger, her marriage continued to deteriorate. In spring 1836 the couple had a bitter quarrel about the meddling of one of his cousins, a Miss Vaughn, and the general dislike that each family held for the other. The couple remained angry throughout the day, and the next morning, while Caroline was away from the house, her husband packed up the children and spirited them away, first to his cousin's home and then to a third location. When Caroline learned that her children had been taken, she frantically searched for them and, failing, sought refuge with her family. Her husband made an inadequate offer of terms for separation, threatening to sue for divorce if she did not agree to them. She did not, and in May her husband made good on his threat, naming Lord Melbourne, then prime minister, in a criminal conversation suit for £10,000.

THE

LADY OF LA GARAYE

BY THE

HON. MRS. NORTON.

MACMILLAN AND CO.
London and Cambridge.
1862.

[*The Right of Translation is reserved.*]

*Title page for Norton's poem in which an aristocratic couple
finds satisfaction in charitable works*

The naming of Melbourne was due far less to legitimate suspicion (the evidence suggests not only that Caroline Norton was innocent but also that her husband believed she was) than to political motivation. George Norton's sympathies and his friends were Tory while Melbourne was at the center of the Whig government in power. Whatever the reason for the suit, it is clear that it had no merit. The trial took place on 23 June 1836, and the jury acquitted the accused without leaving the box. The evidence had been so weak that Caroline Norton and Melbourne were not even called upon for their defense. Although she was legally vindicated, the damage of publicity surrounding the trial and of the insinuations of the gossip papers had been done. Ever since Caroline Norton's name has been quickly associated with scandal.

Though George Norton had been defeated in court, he still had the right under English law to sole custody of the children. He had the power to keep them away from his wife, and he did. Outraged at her husband's spitefulness and her powerlessness in the matter, Norton resolved to take on the unfair system itself. She spent a great deal of her time during the late 1830s lobbying for a change in the law through private letters to and conversations with her political friends and through the publication of such pamphlets as *The Separation of Mother and Child by the Laws of "Custody of Infants," Considered* (1837) and *A Plain Letter to the Lord Chancellor on the Infant Custody Bill* (1839). Her tireless efforts paid off in summer 1839, when Parliament passed the Infant Custody Bill, legislation granting women the right to apply to the courts for the custody of their children. Fighting to reverse the wrong of her own personal situation, Norton had struck a blow for the rights of all women in England. Her own problem, however, was not resolved as her husband had sent their sons to stay with relatives in Scotland, where the English law did not have jurisdiction. He thus managed to separate Norton from her children for two more years.

Norton's poetic career was revived in 1840 with the publication of *The Dream, and Other Poems.* This volume again reflects autobiographical issues and Norton's interest in promoting sympathy for the less fortunate. The title poem begins with an extended section praising parental love over erotic love. The scene depicts a mother watching her sleeping daughter. The daughter awakens and is instantly disappointed to learn that the dream she was having is not real. She relates to her mother the contents of her dream, a veritable catalogue of natural and man-made beauty viewed by her and an unknown male companion (whom the daughter is apparently too naive to recognize as a lover). At the end of her story she laments the transitory nature of this paradise vision. The mother upbraids her daughter for selfishness, pointing out that all people suffer and that nothing is perfect, especially not conjugal love. Upon hearing this the daughter wishes for an early death to avoid such disappointment, but the mother again scolds her child for wishing to escape the common lot of all, sorrow. She adds that her daughter's behavior is especially offensive when so many of the suffering poor bear their sorrow with quiet dignity, and she ends by instructing her child to think less of her earthly lot and more of her moral responsibilities and her spiritual life. The daughter feels chastened at the end of the poem, resolving to live her life in the example of her mother.

It is easy to read the autobiographical relevance of this poem. The daughter's disappointment at the imperfection of reality reflects Norton's own well-known disappointments and sorrows. The mother's scolding and instruction suggests the poet's resolve not to wallow in self-pity but to dedicate her life to helping fellow sufferers, as she had done by publishing *A Voice from the Factories* and lobbying for the Infant Custody Bill. The volume was warmly received by Coleridge in the *Quarterly Review,* where he compared her to Byron, and by the critic in the December 1840 issue of *Dublin University Magazine,* who asserts that "highly as her earlier productions have been esteemed, her last work will elicit still warmer approbation."

In the early 1840s Norton gained increased access to her children but at a terrible cost. During the Christmas season of 1841 her husband finally relented to a small degree and allowed the boys to spend part of the holidays with their mother. In September 1842 a tragic accident further softened her husband's attitude. George Norton and his three sons were visiting Miss Vaughan's estate in Yorkshire. One day the youngest child, eight-year-old William, was thrown from his horse. He sustained no broken bones and only a bad scratch on his arm. The minor wound was poorly treated, though, and William developed massive blood poisoning. His mother was called for, but the child quickly worsened and died before she could arrive. This was a terrible loss for the woman who deeply loved and longed for her children. After William's death her husband became more conciliatory, and so Caroline Norton finally attained partial custody of her two remaining sons.

In 1845 Norton published her most ambitious poem, *The Child of the Islands,* the longest of her poems, carefully structured in Spenserian stanzas. The work is divided into six parts, the relatively short "Opening" and "Conclusion" sections surround four longer cantos: "Spring," "Summer," "Autumn," and "Winter." It is a remarkable work, not only for its structure and scope but also for the strength and audacity with which Norton argues for the poor. The "Child of the Islands" is the infant Prince of Wales, but the poem is no vapid birthday ode in praise of the aristocracy. Instead it illustrates the gulf between the rich and poor in England in order to instruct the prince on his moral responsibilities upon becoming king.

In the first section Norton considers the universality of parental love and contrasts the state of most people to the prospects of the young prince. "Spring" broadens the contrast to encompass what Benjamin Disraeli called England's "Two Nations,"

the rich and the poor. Here Norton chastises the fortunate ones who show no pity for those beneath them. "Summer" continues the contrast and calls on the "Child of the Islands" to honor those deserving people whose stations are beneath his, specifically mentioning the need for universal education. "Autumn" contains some of the most moving arguments on behalf of the poor, particularly stanzas 45 and 46, in which Norton calls for England to take moral responsibility for the condition of its lower classes. "Winter" compares sickness and death as they are experienced by the rich and the poor. In the concluding section Norton boldly reminds the prince that death is the great leveler and that sympathy for the poor is divinely commanded.

The Child of the Islands was enthusiastically reviewed, and Norton remarked in an unpublished letter, "I care more for it than anything else I have written." The critic in the May 1845 issue of *Tait's Edinburgh Magazine* called it "the finest production its authoress has yet given to the world," and J. G. Lockhart, though not caring for the poem's political sentiments, called it a "brilliant volume" in the *Quarterly Review* of June–September 1845. Modern readers are likely to appreciate its structure and its enlightened positions on the welfare of the poor but may find its length a drawback, as did the critic for the March–June 1845 *Westminster Review,* who nevertheless praised its poetical merits highly. Whatever the final judgment on its artistic success, *The Child of the Islands* stakes a strong claim as the most significant work of Norton's poetic career.

In 1845 Norton again found herself at the center of controversy. Since 1841 she had developed a close friendship with Sidney Herbert, then secretary to the Admiralty in Sir Robert Peel's government. The nature of their relationship is unclear, but at the time London gossips assumed they were lovers. In December 1845 Norton was rumored to be responsible for the leak of the Corn Laws repeal story to *The Times* (London), having supposedly gleaned inside information from Herbert, who was then war secretary and very close to Peel. The question of repeal was the most highly changed political issue of the time, and the controversy surrounding the newspaper story led to Peel's resignation. The rumor of Norton's involvement in the leak was completely false but so sensational that George Meredith would adopt it forty years later as the central episode in *Diana of the Crossways* (1885). The heroine of the novel, Diana Merion, is carefully patterned after Norton's notorious public image. Her family objected to Meredith's portrayal, especially to his resurrection of the Corn Law rumor that had since been disproved. In subsequent printings Meredith included

"TELL my sister not to weep for me, and
        sob with drooping head,
When the troops are marching home again
        with glad and gallant tread,

Page, with illustration by Alfred Fredricks, from Norton's Bingen on the
Rhine *(1883), a poem about a soldier serving in foreign lands*

a note reminding his audience that the novel "is to be read as fiction." The remainder of the 1840s passed in relative calm for Norton. In 1847 she published a volume of children's verse, *Aunt Carry's Ballads for Children.*

Although Norton had signed a separation agreement with her husband in 1848, she found early in the next decade that it provided her no legal protection. In 1851, having discovered that his wife's mother had left her a small legacy, George Norton cut off her allowance. In the subsequent dispute Norton learned that the agreement she had signed in 1848 was not valid and that her husband still had legal right to her income and no responsibility for her expenses. During the legal wrangling that followed, George Norton was apprised that Lord

Melbourne upon his death in 1848 had also left his wife a legacy. He vehemently attacked his wife in court during a petty suit for the bill of repairs made to her carriage and revived rumors of the supposed Melbourne affair in a letter to *The Times*. In her defense Norton wrote a long response to *The Times*, again challenging the fairness of English law.

Norton devoted much of her time in the mid 1850s to lobbying for reform in laws affecting women's rights within domestic unions. She again petitioned her influential friends and published pamphlets, including *English Laws for Women in the Nineteenth Century* (1854). Her efforts were once again rewarded when Parliament passed the new Marriage and Divorce Act in 1857. This landmark legislation allowed women to be considered as distinct individuals within a marriage contract and granted wives the right to own property and to protect their income from their husbands. As she had in 1839, Norton struck a major blow for English women. Though she did not align herself with some of her more radical feminist contemporaries, Norton accomplished more for women's legal rights in England than any of them during her time. The legislation she influenced paved the way for further reforms, such as the Married Women's Property Act of 1870 which extended the right of wives to own property.

From the early 1850s Norton turned primarily to fiction, publishing *Stuart of Dunleath* (1851), *Lost and Saved* (1863), and *Old Sir Douglas* (1867). Her final major poem, *The Lady of La Garaye* (1862), is based on the legendary lives of the count and countess de la Garaye. The young couple is shown to live a life of plenty and indulgence until the countess suffers a fall from her horse and sustains injuries that prevent her from bearing children. The couple experiences a deep melancholy at this news, but ultimately they discover that the best balm for their own emotional pain lies in working to alleviate the suffering of others. Thus, they convert their château into a charity hospital. Norton's last poem again reflects autobiographical interests as the lives of her characters—their suffering and then their turning outward to others—seem to represent the pattern of her own life, her sorrows (to which had recently been added the death of her oldest son, Fletcher, in 1859) and later devotion to charity. The poem was highly praised in the January 1862 issue of *Edinburgh Review*.

In February 1875 her husband died, and Norton was finally freed from the marriage that had caused her so much pain. Two years later she married the historian Sir William Stirling-Maxwell, a longtime friend, on 1 March 1877. However, just three months after entering into a marriage that she actually desired, Norton died on 15 June 1877 at the age of 69.

Caroline Norton's life was marked by a remarkable energy and indomitability. Constantly threatened by the circumstances of a disastrous marriage, she refused to be beaten down and fought tirelessly for her own rights as well as for those of others. She became a successful poet and novelist while maintaining a prominent social life in the face of scandal. Few of her contemporaries matched her will and resilience, and fewer still could claim to have exerted such influence in as many different arenas.

Letters:

The Letters of Caroline Norton to Lord Melbourne, edited by James O. Hoge and Clarke Olney (Columbus: Ohio State University Press, 1974).

Bibliography:

Dale E. Casper, "Caroline Norton: Her Writings," *Bulletin of Bibliography,* 40 (June 1983): 113–116.

Biographies:

Jane Gray Perkins, *The Life of the Honourable Mrs. Norton* (New York: Henry Holt, 1909);

Alice Acland, *Caroline Norton* (London: Constable, 1948);

Alan Chedzoy, *A Scandalous Woman: The Story of Caroline Norton* (London: Allison & Busby, 1992).

Papers:

Collections of Caroline Norton's letters, papers, and manuscripts are held by Harvard University; Yale University, the Altschul Collection; the Pierpoint Morgan Library, New York; the Huntington Library, San Marino, California; and the British Library.

Eliza Ogilvy

(6 January 1822 – 3 January 1912)

A. A. Markley

Pennsylvania State University, Delaware County

BOOKS: *Rose Leaves* (n.p. Privately printed, 1845);
A Book of Highland Minstrelsy, illustrated by Robert Ronald McIan (London: G. W. Nickisson, 1846);
Traditions of Tuscany, in Verse (London: Thomas Bosworth, 1851);
Poems of Ten Years, 1846–1855 (London: Thomas Bosworth / Edinburgh: John Menzies, 1856);
Sunday Acrostics, Selected from Names or Words in the Bible (London: Frederick Warne, 1867).

OTHER: Elizabeth Barrett Browning, *Poems,* with a memoir by Eliza Ogilvy (London: Frederick Warne, 1893);
Peter N. Heydon and Philip Kelley, eds., *Elizabeth Barrett Browning's Letters to Mrs. David Ogilvy, 1849–1861, with Recollections by Mrs. Ogilvy,* with a memoir by Ogilvy (New York: Quadrangle/New York Times Book Co./The Browning Institute, 1973; London: John Murray, 1974).

In 1846 a collection of poetry, *A Book of Highland Minstrelsy,* quickly attracted the favorable attention of readers and reviewers in both England and Scotland. The richness and depth of feeling in these new interpretations of ancient Scottish folklore made a name for the twenty-four-year-old poet Eliza Ogilvy, a young woman who had just begun to attempt to balance her creative impulse with her duties as a new wife and mother. Ogilvy would continue to write poetry throughout her long life, but her work was largely forgotten in the century following her death. In 1971, however, a private collection of letters to Ogilvy written by her intimate friend, Elizabeth Barrett Browning, was offered for sale. The subsequent publication of these letters managed to recall Ogilvy from complete obscurity although her poetry remains largely unanthologized and unread. Nevertheless, the quality and the wide range of her work are remarkable, and many of her poems have a vitality and a richness that reward the modern reader. Perhaps the greatest value of her

work is the profound insight that it offers into the attitudes, passions, and life experience of a woman in nineteenth-century Britain, particularly in its startling reification of the joys and agonies of motherhood during the Victorian era.

Eliza Anne Harris Dick was born on 6 January 1822 in Perth, Scotland, the daughter of Louisa Wintle and Abercromby Dick. Little is known of her childhood except that she spent several years in India with her sister Charlotte in the late 1830s. The girls probably traveled there to spend time with their grandfather, Dr. William Dick, who served as chief surgeon to the East India Company in Calcutta. After returning to England, Eliza Dick married David Ogilvy (1813–1879), also a member of an old Scottish family, on 6 July 1843.

Eliza Ogilvy gave birth to her first child, Rose Theresa Charlotte, on 19 March 1844. Motherhood seems to have brought to her an enormous degree of artistic inspiration. A letter from David Ogilvy to an aunt written soon after Rose's birth reports on his wife's recovery and his new daughter's health. In his letter he enclosed a poem that is among the earliest of Eliza Ogilvy's known works, titled "A Natal Address to My Child. March 19th 1844." David Ogilvy tells his aunt that the poem was actually composed on the day of the child's birth, and he explains that his wife had begun the poem in a serious mood but that "the Muse ran away with her." This address to her new daughter is remarkable for the realistic manner in which Ogilvy describes the infant's appearance, her "puggy nose," swollen, twisted mouth, and red, dry skin, as she lies screaming in her nurse's arms. In the final line the address breaks off as the speaker exclaims humorously, "Oh! how she squalls!—she can't bear rhyme!"

Unfortunately Rose did not survive long past her first birthday. After her death on 7 July 1845 Ogilvy struggled to express through her poetry her intense suffering at losing her child . The result was a thin, privately printed volume of poems with the poignant title *Rose Leaves* (1845). Ogilvy bore six

Eliza Ogilvy in 1864

more children over the next twelve years: Louisa Mary (1846–1870), Alexander William (1848–1887), Marcia Napier (1850–1940), Walter Tulliedeph (1852–1927), Angus (1855–1928), and Violet Isabel (1857–1954). Nevertheless, Rose's short life and her death continued to haunt Ogilvy's poetry, and the theme of a mother's anxiety over the health and safety of her infant often resurfaces in her work.

Ogilvy's first commercial success, *A Book of Highland Minstrelsy* appeared in 1846, only a year after the publication of *Rose Leaves*. Ogilvy described herself in this project as clinging to the traditions of her Celtic ancestry, a sort of nostalgia that she ascribed to her Scottish temperament. Each of her lyrical treatments of anecdotes from Scottish folklore and legend is preceded by a prose headnote explain-

ing the tradition or story underlying the poem's theme. The poems in the collection can be categorized under two general headings: those concerning the speaker's memories of past misfortunes and those concerned with dark superstitions, stemming from ancient Celtic history and often involving the supernatural.

An excellent example of the poetry in *A Book of Highland Minstrelsy* is "The Vigil of the Dead." The prose headnote to the poem explains that, according to old Scottish legend, after a burial took place, the spirit of the deceased was obliged to keep watch over the graveyard at night until replaced by the spirit of the next townsperson to be buried there. At such a time the spirit would be allowed to move on to the heavens on a "Dreeng," or meteor, which the

THE BOOK

OF

HIGHLAND MINSTRELSY.

BY

MRS. D. OGILVY.

WITH ILLUSTRATIONS

BY

R. R. M'IAN.

New Edition.

LONDON AND GLASGOW:
RICHARD GRIFFIN AND COMPANY,
Publishers to the University of Glasgow.
1860.

Title page for Ogilvy's first commercial success, a collection of poems based on stories from Scottish folklore (courtesy of Special Collections, Thomas Cooper Library, University of South Carolina)

author suggests may refer to the aurora borealis. Ogilvy considers the dreadful state of a poor ghost in this situation, eagerly counting over his neighbors, and considering and reconsidering the likelihood that each will die in the near future—constantly hoping for a speedy release from his tenure in the graveyard. The writer then speculates on the sheer terror that this waiting period must impose on the souls of those who have no hope of salvation, and must anticipate during this interim period the dreadful retribution that awaits them.

The poem that follows this introduction is a powerful dramatic monologue written in swift anapestic tetrameter couplets in which a recently deceased young herdsman describes the accident that took his life and speculates on the most likely candidate from among his former neighbors for the next death in the community. At the poem's midpoint the reader learns that the soul who will replace the speaker will be his own newborn infant. The speaker describes the agony that his widowed wife will suffer at losing her baby and ends his speculation on the death of his child with a prayer to Death that his child not long be left alone as the guardian of the graveyard. Here Ogilvy deftly turns the father's concern for speeding along his own term as warder of the graveyard to his concern that the spirit of his infant child be spared such an undeserved penance. As in her volume *Rose Leaves,* the poet's fixation on infant mortality works its way into her poetry, reminding modern readers of the level of anxiety concerning infant mortality that accompanied parenthood in the Victorian era.

Another poem, "The Spinning of the Shroud," again demonstrates Ogilvy's focus in this volume on the difficulties of motherhood, particularly the potential for losing children. Here the poet describes the old Highland tradition requiring a new bride to begin immediately spinning the yarn to make her own burial shroud. Ogilvy uses the rich imagery of the sights and sounds of summer to emphasize the youth of the young bride who is spinning her thread. As she imagines the life that lies before her and the home and the children she will have, the young woman finally asks why she must be subjected to such a dark custom. To this question the winds reply that when the time comes for her to die, she will be all too happy to embrace the comfort of the grave after suffering the losses that life has in store for her.

The poem titled "Imprecation by the Cradle" demonstrates the range of Ogilvy's poetic voice in *A Book of Highland Minstrelsy* by revealing her strong views concerning the lot of women in contemporary Britain, a concern shared by many of her fellow poets. In a format recalling that of the old English ballad a young mother addresses her infant son, telling him of the sorrow she has suffered at having been abandoned by his father before their marriage. She describes the fair "Lady Ellen," who stole her lover's heart, and calls down a curse upon Ellen's marriage to him, including a few poignant stanzas in which she cautions her child not to look like his father, not to smile like him, and not to speak like him. In the second part of the poem the child in turn addresses his mother, now apparently dead, and describes to her how her curses on his father and Lady Ellen have all come to pass. The child promises that he will win back the wealth, the rank, and the pride that his father denied his mother and himself by pursuing a glorious career as a soldier. Far more than merely an echo of an ancient Scottish anecdote fashioned into poetic form, this poem's candid exposure of the wrongs that women suffered if abandoned and left with a child is a scathing critique of the mores of contemporary society concerning the treatment of the "fallen" woman.

A reviewer in *The Athenaeum* (9 May 1846) wrote that *A Book of Highland Minstrelsy* was a credit to the accomplished mind of the young poet and praised Ogilvy for the depth of feeling with which she treats the characteristics and superstitions of the Scottish Highlanders. Another contemporary review in *The Literary Gazette and Journal of the Belles Lettres, Arts, Sciences, &c.* praised Ogilvy as well worthy of the "temple of fame" and claimed that the collection evidenced the fact that the poet, like George Gordon, Lord Byron, must have been nurtured among the beautiful scenes of the Scottish highlands. The reviewer then speculates on the extreme wealth of inspiration such natural scenery can have on the artistic temperament. The popularity of *A Book of Highland Minstrelsy,* which included illustrations by Robert Ronald McIan, is attested to by the republication of the book in both 1848 and 1860.

In 1848 the Ogilvys moved to Italy, and Eliza became close friends with Elizabeth Barrett Browning, whom she met in June 1848 while visiting Florence. From 1848 through 1852 their two families spent much time together and often traveled to such places as the Bagni di Lucca, Venice, and Paris. At one point the two families were neighbors, when the Ogilvys rented the upper floor of Casa Guidi while the Brownings were living on the floor below. Eliza Ogilvy wrote two memoirs of Elizabeth Barrett Browning in later years, one a short version written in a commonplace book and another that she wrote for Frederick Warne and Company for inclusion in their 1893 edition of Browning's *Poems.* These memoirs provide an invaluable source of information regarding the Brownings' and Ogilvys' lives in Italy from 1848 to the early 1850s, and they paint a particularly vivid portrait of Elizabeth Barrett Browning. Ogilvy describes Browning's appearance and her gentle personality in great detail, and she includes fascinating accounts of discussions and arguments between the Ogilvys and the Brownings on such topics as religion, politics, art, and especially poetry. It appears that Ogilvy and her husband disagreed with the Brownings on the issue of poetic composition, "depreciating their [the Brownings'] favourite assonance, and insisting on the more complete consonance of accurately responsive rhymes." Ogilvy also reports that the two couples disagreed on the issue of whether poetry should be composed to be understood by the masses, the Brownings feeling that it was to be intended for the "Higher Intellect" while the Ogilvys professed a more democratic view of the audience that a poet should address.

Illustration for opening lines of "Parting on the Brig," in A Book of Highland Minstrelsy *(courtesy of Special Collections, Thomas Cooper Library, University of South Carolina)*

Nearly forty of Elizabeth Barrett Browning's letters to Eliza Ogilvy survived and have been published. Written from 1849 up to Browning's death in 1861, the letters provide a wealth of information about the two families during these years. The letters offer rare insight into Browning's personal life and her attitudes and feelings about her own poetic compositions as well as those of her husband and the works of other contemporary poets; unfortunately Ogilvy's letters to Browning have not survived, and thus much less is known about Ogilvy's personality, her thoughts, and her work as a poet.

One of the most important aspects of the friendship between Ogilvy and Browning seems to have been the common experiences they shared as mothers. Ogilvy gave birth to her third child and her first son, Alexander, in September 1848, just after becoming acquainted with the Brownings. After several miscarriages Browning gave birth to her only child, Wiedeman, known as "Penini" or "Pen," in March 1849. In her memoir Ogilvy describes both Browning's anxiety for her baby's survival before delivering him, and the occasion of Pen's birth, upon which Ogilvy became the first

Manuscript for Ogilvy's memoir of Elizabeth Barrett Browning that was included in the 1893 edition of Browning's Poems; *the manuscript shows marking by the publisher's in-house editor (Browning Institute)*

person after his nurse to hold the newborn infant. Although Browning never mentioned it to her directly, Ogilvy describes her friend's grave concerns for Ogilvy's infant Alexander, who seemed pale, weak, and ill suited to survive, as Pen Browning was growing more robust every day. The letters and memoirs reveal such details as the two mothers' shared worries over the sicknesses through which their children suffered, their debates over the proper ways to raise their children, mundane details concerning the children's care and clothing, and such insights into each woman's personality as when Ogilvy had to administer a dose of medicine to the infant Pen because, as Ogilvy explained, Elizabeth Barrett Browning could not bear to cause any living thing pain or discomfort.

Two surviving letters written by Browning to her sister Arabel and another to Mary Russell Mitford contain some of the only impressions that have survived concerning Eliza Ogilvy's personality. Browning wrote to Mitford in April 1850, describing the Ogilvys as "cultivated and refined people" and calling Ogilvy "a pretty woman with three pretty children, of quick perceptions and active intelligence and sensibility." Browning's letter to her sister Arabel, however, dated March 1850, is far more revealing. Here she writes of the Ogilvys that, "quick sympathies, fine tastes, & a great deal of kindness, make them agreeable friends & neighbours. I am not drawn into love with Mrs. David Ogilvy . . . with all her prettiness, liveliness, intelligence, & feeling . . . there is wanting somehow the last touch of softness & exterior sensibility—I like her much . . . like her society, respect her good qualities, feel an interest in her actions & sentiments . . . there is just a want of softness in the character . . . a want of tenderness, somehow." In a second letter to Arabel dated May 1851 Browning again referred to the Ogilvys as "Most agreeable fellow-travellers . . . full of intelligence & good humour . . . Really clever in their knowledge & apprehension of pictures & churches," but she again intimated that despite their delightful friendship, Ogilvy was not her ideal soul mate.

Undoubtedly Ogilvy's close relationship to the Brownings from 1848 to 1852, a time of intense poetic composition for her and for both of the Brownings, had a strong influence on her own sense of herself as a poet and on the work that she produced during these years.

In 1851 she published her third book of poetry, *Traditions of Tuscany, in Verse,* with the London publishing house of Thomas Bosworth. This volume is very much an Italian version of *A Book of Highland Minstrelsy,* in which Ogilvy composed poems based on her experiences in Italy and on the Italian traditions and anecdotes to which she had been exposed. An example of one of the more successful poems in the *Traditions of Tuscany* collection is "Alla Giornata." As in *A Book of Highland Minstrelsy,* Ogilvy provides a prose headnote to explain the inspiration for the poem. While traveling in Pisa, she writes, she came upon a beautiful yellow-marble palace, on which a fragment of chain hung down from the lintels of the door beside an inscription, "Alla Giornata." The author reports on the products of her research into the legendary explanations of this inscription. The story involves a certain Count Lanfreducci, who, having been released from a period of enslavement by the Algerians, was able to restore himself to his former wealth in his native city and thus hung the chain on his palace as a dedication "Alla Giornata," or "Unto the day," of his freedom. In the poem she effectively recounts the tradition of the chain and its inscription before moving into a consideration of the symbolic nature of a particular day—a day characterized either by great joy or great grief—in every human life; her example of grief containing another haunting echo of her own pain at losing a child. The poem is an impressive philosophical speculation, and Ogilvy's ingenious use of the repeated phrase "Unto the Day" is both striking and highly effective.

"A December Day in the Campagna, Rome" is another outstanding example of Ogilvy's achievement in this collection of poems on Italy. The poem offers a rich description of the beauty of the Italian countryside in December, heavily contrasted with the thick, driving snows of a December day in Scotland. The speaker's speculations on the vast changes wrought on the Italian landscape in the time since the days of the Roman Empire add a profound philosophical texture to the poem's visual power. Although one reviewer dismissed this volume by alleging that Ogilvy had listened "too long and too submissively" to Alfred, Lord Tennyson and the Brownings, many of the poems in this volume are impressive achievements. A contemporary critic, D. M. Moir, in his *Sketches of the Poetical Literature of the Past Half-Century* (1856) compared the collection to *A Book of Highland Minstrelsy,* citing both as evidence of the imaginative, energetic, and accomplished mind of the poet.

In 1856 Ogilvy published a collected edition of her poetry, *Poems of Ten Years, 1846–1855.* The subject matter of this collection covers an impressive range that spans from aspects of motherhood, to Scottish remembrances and experiences in Italy, to the poet's reactions to contemporary political events. Several of the poems respond directly to

Ogilvy's husband, David Ogilvy, circa 1865

events in Ogilvy's life, and particularly her travels, during these years. In the poem "Despondency" written in 1850, for example, the speaker describes her exhaustion from the difficulty of constant travel, and in "Farewell to Florence" written in 1852, the poet looks back over what her years in Florence have meant to her. Narrated on a rainy final day before returning to England, in "Farewell to Florence" the speaker chastises the city for denying her one last opportunity to see it in the splendor of beautiful Italian weather, and she regrets that such bad weather will be all too familiar to her once she has returned to her native country.

A noteworthy poem in this collection is "Newly Dead and Newly Born," in 1850, written at Casa Guidi—a powerful piece in which Ogilvy

again returns to the familiar theme of a mother's anxiety over the life and health of her child. In this poem Ogilvy describes a young mother who hears the chanting of a Florentine dirge and smells the burning censers of a funeral procession while watching over her newborn infant. Ogilvy deftly captures the shudder that the young mother feels during this experience, herself only just narrowly having escaped the risk of death during childbirth. Likewise she subtly depicts the mother's natural fear for her baby, constantly looking at it and listening out for it to assure herself of its safety. The specific importance of her daughter Rose in Ogilvy's poetry is illustrated in the haunting and lyrical "A Family Picture" of 1852. Here the speaker sets the stage of her noisy cottage, active with romping children, and in a stanza devoted to each of Ogilvy's four children as of 1852 she describes each child's appearance and personality. The melancholy speaker then admits that she always includes her lost firstborn daughter when counting her children. In a poignant conclusion she describes how her image of this daughter's spirit takes on new proportions even as her other children grow, and she favorably contrasts the "angel-smile" of her first daughter's spirit to her living children's "passion-storms."

Several of the works in *Poems of Ten Years* also demonstrate the great emotional passion with which Ogilvy devoted herself to the turmoil of contemporary Italian politics. It was a particularly turbulent time in Italian history; Grand Duke Leopold II of Tuscany, who many had hoped would be a strong leader in the fight for Italian liberation, had fled Florence only to return soon afterwards under the protection of the Austrians who were occupying the area. In "The Austrian Night Patrol, Florence" from 1851, Ogilvy chooses strong language to depict the Austrians in occupation in Florence as cruel conquerors and the natives of Florence as oppressed slaves, their freedom compromised by Leopold's shameful actions and apparent cowardice. Ogilvy described her political poems as having been written "in the passion of the living struggle." Two years later she would also find poetry to be an outlet for her reactions to British involvement in the Crimean War (1853–1856). Elizabeth Barrett Browning praised her friend, who apparently had relatives among the soldiers, for being able to produce poetry during the anxious days of the war.

A final politically minded poem in *Poems of Ten Years* is "Charon's Ferry" a sharp bit of social commentary from 1853 in which Ogilvy depicts a relentless Charon who refuses to take the spirits of the dead across to the Elysian Fields without payment despite the fact that the pathetic souls explain they had nothing on earth but want and despair. Browning praised this poem for its "stroke on the head of the modern bigots from the end of his [Charon's] black oar."

When the Ogilvys returned to Great Britain after their four years in Italy, they lived at various times in Perth, Edinburgh, Peckham Rye, Lower Sydenham, and Forfarshire. Throughout these years, as she raised her six children, Eliza Ogilvy continued her career as a writer. She contributed poems to the literary annual *The Keepsake*. In addition she contributed stories for publication in *Chambers's Edinburgh Journal*, an inexpensive weekly periodical with an extremely wide circulation throughout the nineteenth century. In

Camilla Crosland's *Landmarks of Literary Life, 1820–1892*, Crosland includes a letter from Browning dated September 1852 asking her to send the issues of *Chambers's Edinburgh Journal* in which one of Ogilvy's stories had appeared. Crosland explains in a headnote to the letter that Ogilvy is "a lady better known by her initials E. A. H. O. than by her full name, and recognized as a writer of clever stories and able criticisms, as well as of spirited poems." In 1867 Ogilvy published *Sunday Acrostics, Selected from Names or Words in the Bible,* a collection of religious puzzles drawing on both her linguistic ability and her strong religious background.

After her husband's death in 1879, Ogilvy spent the next twenty-one years at Bridge of Allan, near her father's home. She then lived at Ealing, with her daughter Marcia Ogilvy Bell until her death on 3 January 1912, three days before her ninetieth birthday. Despite the fact that she gradually lost her eyesight, collections of her unpublished manuscripts attest to the fact that Ogilvy continued to write poetry up until the end of her life. Her work continued to be characterized by its diversity; poems that remained unpublished in her lifetime include such titles as "Victoria and Her People," "Work for Work's Sake," "The Ant and the Bee," and "A Ditty in Praise of Good Wine." In many of her later poems she continues to draw on situations from her own life, such as "The Lord Hungerford," a poem about the ship that had taken her to India in 1838, or the light "Grannie's Birthday," written in January 1885 on the occasion of her sixty-third birthday.

In a particularly poignant poem from these manuscripts, "Allan Water August 27th, 1887, (on the death of Alexander Ogilvy)" Ogilvy returned once again to the lament for a dead child after the drowning of her adult son Alexander. Addressing the Allan River that took her son's life, the speaker in this poem asks for the return of her child. When the remorseless river laughs at her request and points out that she has returned the woman's son, the speaker clarifies that it is the living man that she wishes back. In a conclusion typical of the fatalism that runs throughout Ogilvy's poetry, the river points out that blame is useless; Fate had "foredoomed" her son. Forty-two years after the death of her infant daughter Rose, Ogilvy again found in her poetry an outlet for expressing the agony of losing a child, here the thirty-nine-year-old Alexander. The persistence of this particular theme in Ogilvy's work continuously and passionately reifies this aspect of the experience of Victorian motherhood. Ogilvy celebrated life in her poetry, from the joy and the suffering of parenthood, to passionate reactions to political events, to the love of place and local culture in the highlands of Scotland and the scenic countryside of Tuscany, offering through her poetry a glimpse of her experiences as a nineteenth-century woman.

Bibliography:

Andrew Boyle, *An Index to the Annuals (1820–1850),* vol. 1 (Worcester: Andrew Boyle, 1967), pp. 213–214;

Gwenn Davis and Beverly A. Joyce, *Poetry By Women to 1900: A Bibliography of American and British Writers* (Toronto & Buffalo: University of Toronto Press, 1991), p. 211.

References:

Virginia Blain, Patricia Clements, and Isobel Grundy, *Feminist Companion to Literature in English: Women Writers from the Middle Ages to the Present* (New Haven: Yale University Press, 1990), p. 809;

Camilla Dufour (Toulmin) Crosland, *Landmarks of Literary Life, 1820–1892* (London: Sampson Low, Marston, 1893), pp. 234–235;

Frederick C. Kenyon, ed., *The Letters of Elizabeth Barrett Browning,* volume 1 (London: Smith, Elder, 1898), pp. 445–446;

Angela Leighton and Margaret Reynolds, eds., *Victorian Women Poets: An Anthology* (Oxford & Cambridge, Mass.: Blackwell, 1995), pp. 299–303;

D. M. Moir, *Sketches of the Poetical Literature of the Past Half-Century,* third edition (Edinburgh & London: William Blackwood, 1856), p. 306;

John Mackay Shaw, *Childhood in Poetry. A Catalogue, with Biographical and Critical Annotations, of the Books of English and American Poets Comprising the Shaw Childhood in Poetry Collection in the Library of Florida State University* (Detroit: Gale Research, 1967), p. 1922.

Papers:
Some manuscripts and letters are held by the Browning Institute.

Emily Pfeiffer

(26 November 1827 – 23 January 1890)

Kathleen Hickok
Iowa State University

BOOKS: *The Holly Branch: An Album for 1843,* as Emily Davis (N. p.: Privately printed, 1843);

Valisneria; or, A Midsummer's Day's Dream, a Tale in Prose (London: Longmans, Brown, Green, Longmans & Roberts, 1857);

Margaret; or, The Motherless (London: Hurst & Blackett, 1861);

Gerard's Monument; and Other Poems (London: Trübner, 1873; enlarged edition, London: Kegan Paul, 1878);

Poems (London: Strahan, 1876);

Glân-Alarch: His Silence and Song (London: Henry S. King, 1877);

Quarterman's Grace and Other Poems (London: Kegan Paul, 1879);

Sonnets and Songs (London: Kegan Paul, 1880; Delmar, N. Y : Scholars' Facsimiles & Reprints, 1998); revised and enlarged as *Sonnets* (London: Field & Tuer/Leadenhall Press / New York: Scribner & Welford, 1886; revised and enlarged, London: Field & Tuer/Simpkin, Marshall/Hamilton, Adams / New York: Scribner & Welford, 1888);

Under the Aspens: Lyrical and Dramatic (London: Kegan Paul, Trench, 1882);

The Rhyme of the Lady of the Rock and How It Grew (London: Kegan Paul, Trench, 1884);

Flying Leaves from East and West (London: Field & Tuer/Leadenhall Press / New York: Scribner & Welford, 1885);

Women and Work: An Essay Treating on The Relation to Health and Physical Development of the Higher Education of Girls and the Intellectual or More Systematised Effort of Women (Boston: Ticknor, 1887; London: Trübner / Edinburgh & London: Ballantyne, Hanson, 1888);

Flowers of the Night (London: Trübner, 1889).

SELECTED PERIODICAL PUBLICATIONS–UNCOLLECTED: "The Tyranny of Fashion," *Cornhill Magazine,* 38 (July 1878): 83–94;

"Woman's Claim," *Contemporary Review,* 39 (February 1881): 265–277;

"The Suffrage for Women," *Contemporary Review,* 47 (March 1885): 418–435;

"The Posthumous Critics of a Dead Poet, and Deathless Poetry," *Journal of Pre-Raphaelite Studies,* 1 (Fall 1988): 87–101.

In her writing Emily Pfeiffer addressed many Victorian controversies, including the debate over women's rights and status, the cultural struggle between science and religion, the tension between art and politics, and the economic and class structure of England. She believed in freedom, justice, and the ultimate triumph of human conscience. First and foremost a poet of sonnets, lyrics, dramatic monologues, ballads, and blank-verse drama, Pfeiffer also published political essays, travelogues, and a few mixed-genre works. Despite ill health and insomnia, Pfeiffer wrote tirelessly about the struggles of women, including single women, working-class women, foreign women, and "ruined" women. Her literary career connects her with such authors as Alfred, Lord Tennyson; Elizabeth Barrett Browning; George Eliot; and the Pre-Raphaelite poets Dante Gabriel Rossetti and Christina Rossetti.

Emily Jane Davis was born on 26 November 1827 to the former Miss Tilsley of Milford Hall, Montgomeryshire, Wales, and Thomas Richard Davis, an army officer. Her father, an Oxfordshire landowner, was devoted to art, particularly painting. At age fifteen Emily prevailed upon him to publish (privately) *The Holly Branch: An Album for 1843,* containing tales, legends, and melodies she had written accompanied by her own illustrations. Subsequent financial problems precipitated by the failure of his father-in-law's bank prevented Captain Davis from providing his daughter with a thorough and systematic education. However, in 1850, when Emily married Jurgen Edward Pfeiffer, a wealthy German merchant living in London, she acquired both the means and the leisure for independent study. The couple had no children, and Emily's husband encouraged her literary, artistic, and political activities.

Title page for Emily Pfeiffer's first adult work, which combines a realistic tale of Victorian daily life and a fairy story with erotic undertones

mothers are alienated from their young daughters, and their attempts to guide the daughters' choices are ineffectual as youthful vigor asserts its own needs. The realistic scenes of the framing tale are initially handled with wry humor. The account of the narrator's invalid mother screening her reading by avidly pre-reading and then rejecting books such as Henry Fielding's *Amelia* (1751) and Johann Wolfgang von Goethe's *The Sorrows of Werther* (1774) is highly comedic. The fairy narrative, on the other hand, ends in tragedy. The imagery shows the influence of early Pre-Raphaelite poetry, prose fantasies, and paintings, with lush natural descriptions and an emphasis on women's beauty embellished by long flowing hair and classical drapery. *Valisneria* anticipates the allegorical fantasy and suggestive imagery of later works such as *Goblin Market* (1862) by Christina Rossetti and *Sylvie and Bruno* (1889) by Lewis Carroll.

In 1861 Pfeiffer continued the theme of motherhood, publishing *Margaret; or, The Motherless,* a long narrative poem dedicated to the memory of her own mother. Young Margaret can be compared with the orphaned Aurora of Browning's 1857 verse novel *Aurora Leigh;* Margaret's natural high spirits and inquisitiveness have been dampened by her inept woman guardian. Inexperienced and poorly advised, Margaret marries an older man, a German prince whom she does not love, basing her decision on his reputation for maturity and intellect. This marriage soon comes to grief; the husband divorces Margaret and sends her home to England, where she falls in love with a fatherless physician. Her second, happy marriage is almost prevented by Margaret's scruples about attaching the social stigma of divorce to her fiancé. The poem can be read in part as a plea for more-humane divorce laws in England.

The initial portrayal of Julia, Margaret's guardian, is almost Byronic in its humorous rhymes and its characterization of her as a "light" woman:

In 1857, at the age of thirty, Pfeiffer published her first mature work, *Valisneria; or, A Midsummer's Day's Dream,* a prose fantasy comparable to Sara Coleridge's *Phantasmion* (1837). The tale is full of oblique eroticism, fairy episodes, and Romantic imagery, with a realistic frame tale of female innocence, modern marriage, and disillusionment with eros, pleasure, and idleness. Mixed in tone, *Valisneria* asserts Victorian values of duty, moderation, and restraint along with engagement in daily life and social relations. Besides the critique of idleness, the poem contains an indictment of the Victorian marriage market, a warning against overindulgence in erotic or romantic love, and a comic denunciation of women's limited role in nineteenth-century society. Relations between women—especially mother-daughter and peer relations—form an important subtheme. Both the realistic narrator and the fairy heroine have female associates whom they love profusely but also fear and envy as rivals. The

Julia was light as any tendril curl
    Which cast its trembling shade upon her brow,
And with that shade a doubt, if Time—the churl!—
    Had wrought there on his own account ere now.
Julia had beauty still, enough to make
    Her protest against Time the more pathetic;
Was gay and graceful, kind for kindness' sake,
    Given to change, loquacious and aesthetic.

She had a mind which, like her curls, was rock'd,
    But never rudely shaken by life's breezes;
She lov'd Italian cities, where she stock'd
    That mind with ghosts of pedestals and friezes;
Classic remains unclassified, which haunted
    Her brain thereafter like the curious ware

In a Jew's shop, which no one ever wanted,
   Which came from, and which went to—heav'n knows
   where!

Like *Valisneria,* this poem vacillates between satire and melodrama. By its conclusion Julia has become a sympathetic character, and the two women are reconciled. A happy ending asserts Pfeiffer's characteristic values of love, hope, faith, and a serious purpose in life for women.

In 1873 Pfeiffer published *Gerard's Monument; and Other Poems,* all of which are more internally consistent in tone. Noteworthy short poems in *Gerard's Monument* include "Martha Mary Melville," a Patient Griselda tale in verse; some affecting lyrics ("Love Unrequited," for example, which is, surprisingly, about aging); various meditative sonnets about love; and "The Chant of the Children of the Mist," an allegory about Victorian estrangement from God that expresses the need Pfeiffer saw for a united reassertion of religious faith.

The title poem, "a metrical romance," treats the conflict between a woman's love for her brother and for her husband, who is a goldsmith. Valery cannot appease either man as they both require all of her time, love, and attention. After her husband speaks harshly to her dying brother, Valery turns her back on him and pines away to death. The final image is of Valery draped over her brother Gerard's monument, dead.

In a notice of the first edition of *Gerard's Monument* (quoted in *Under the Aspens: Lyrical and Dramatic,* 1882) a reviewer for *The Spectator* noted the overall pictorial quality of the poem: "Here is a picture which Mr. Millais might transmute into canvas and colour":

> Valery, proud and patient maid,
> Half in sun and half in shade,
> Sitting still in the morning hours,
> Sorting, binding meadow flowers,
> Laying them three, and two, and one,
> On a grey stone slab in the eye of the sun.
> The orchard grass was high and green,
> The sea a breadth of quivering sheen;
> The morning sky was deep and blue,
> Where boughs and blossoms let it through;
> The apple blooms hung white and red
> Over the maiden's burnished head.

The wedding scene is reminiscent of "The Eve of St. Agnes" (1820) by John Keats and "The Haystack in the Floods" (1858) by William Morris, which are both (as is "Gerard's Monument") attacks upon medieval heroism. The heroic aims of Valery's bridegroom are overcome by rain and gloom, betrayal and decay, and ultimately death; the following stanzas illustrate this development:

> The sun shed gold upon the sands,
>   Dropped jewels in the sea,
> The morn that saw them join their hands,
>   It rose so royallie.
> The goldsmith trained his eagle sight
>   To look upon the sun:
> "Mine eyes, ye'll have to race the light
>   Before the day is done!"
>
> He brought his palfrey to the gate:
>   "Ho, curve thy neck with pride,
> Mine own good steed, for 'tis your fate
>   This day to bear the bride.
> Ho, songs of thrush and nightingale,
>   Give notice to the skies,
> And greet our Valery of the Vale
>   When she shall bless our eyes."
>
> The throstle and the nightingale
>   They raised a merry shout,
> And greeted Valery of the Vale
>   When blushing she came out.
> The throstle and the nightingale
>   They piped so loud and clear,
> That no one heard the peewit's wail
>   That echoed from the mere.
>
> Upon her head the fleur-de-lis
>   Was plaited for a crown,
> And all about her, till her knee,
>   Her golden hair fell down.
> A silken train was vain to seek
>   In presses old and bare,
> So Margery combed, and combed so sleek,
>   Her lady's silken hair.
>
> Then by the diamond-dancing sea
>   They go, and if there stir
> A breath, deep-laden it will be
>   With incense from the fir.
> And so to Saviour's Church they come,
>   And enter at the door,
> Where the groom had waited sad and dumb
>   A little month before.
>
> The sun might beat upon the shore,
>   But Saviour's Church was cold;
> The spices float from copse and moor,—
>   It only smelt of mold.
> The sun might break upon the glass,
>   But Saviour's Church was dim;
> And brokenly the sunbeams pass
>   The carven cherubim.

The imagery of the poem's final scene also resembles a Pre-Raphaelite poem-painting, such as Dante Gabriel Rossetti's "Beata Beatrix" (1863). It also recalls Christina Rossetti's "In an Artist's Studio" (1861, published in 1896), in which a beloved model is repeatedly and unsatisfyingly painted by an obsessed artist. There are even echoes of Chris-

tina Rossetti's "The Convent Threshold" (1862) in
Valery's agonized struggle for self-control:

> Oh, Christ! it was a moving sight,
> That face so beautiful, and white
> Of its own pallor, and the beam
> That smote it with a silvery gleam!
> The lids half closed upon the eyes,
> The orbs uplifted to the skies
> As in an ecstasy of prayer,–
> But on the lips a dumb despair.
> The linen flutings of her gown
> From breast to frozen feet swept down;
> The slender hands that joined in prayer
> Rose upward from the bosom bare.
> Her perfect limbs the coffer prest,
> As in an agony of rest.
> There Valery lay all cold and meek,
> With icy tear-drops on her cheek;
> So having learnt to pray and weep,
> She may attain to holy sleep.
> Fair as she left the goldsmith's bed,
> She lay on Gerard's tomb–stone dead.

For the rest of his life her remorseful husband strives
in vain to reproduce Valery's image accurately on
Gerard's monument. Eventually the wind and sea
claim the tomb. Local legend has it that the goldsmith's bellows and tools can be heard beneath the
waves as his ghost toils on, ceaselessly trying "to perfect some grace / Of memory on the imaged face."

Poems, published in 1876, was the making of
Pfeiffer's reputation; it is the richest and most versatile
book of her career. With *Poems* Pfeiffer established a
firm and lasting reputation for her fine lyrics, particularly for her sonnets. Among the comments included
in the "Extracts from Private and Press Notices" appended to the 1888 edition of Pfeiffer's *Sonnets* was Oliver Wendell Holmes's remark that Pfeiffer's sonnets
reminded him of John Milton's poems; Algernon
Swinburne's comment that he was "struck by their singular power and freshness of thought . . . and expression"; and, in *The Spectator,* a reviewer's statement that
"In not a few of the sonnets . . . there are flights of
imagination, to our minds, of which almost the greatest of English sonnet-writers might, and possibly
would, have been proud; they are, to our mind,
among the finest in the language."

In 1929 Vita Sackville-West included Emily
Pfeiffer in an essay on women poets for Harley
Granville-Barker's *The Eighteen Seventies.* Sackville-
West quoted from Pfeiffer's 1876 sonnet "Peace to the
Odalisque" as an example of feminist poetry at "the
very beginning of all this stirring about women's
rights, and women's equality" that characterized the
1870's. Here is the opening octave of the first of Pfeiffer's two sonnets on this theme:

> Peace to the odalisque, the facile slave,
> Whose unrespective love rewards the brave,
> Or cherishes the coward; she who yields
> Her lord the fief of waste, uncultured fields
> To fester in non-using; she whose hour
> Is measured by her beauty's transient flower;
> Who lives in man, as he in God, and dies
> His parasite, who shuts her from the skies.

One other overtly feminist poem in the 1876 volume
was "Ode to the Teuton Women," a critique of patriarchy, which anticipates Pfeiffer's later, even more
radical feminist poem "Outlawed."

Repeated themes in *Poems* are the devastating effects of woman's repression; the confusion into which
science has thrown religious faith; the triumph of love
and poetry over death and despair; and the frustrating
imprisonment of the spirit in the flesh. These themes
are carried by images of flight, illumination, infinity,
fertility, and frustrated desire. All of these themes and
images are integrated in the sonnet titled "The
Winged Soul":

> My soul is like some cage-born bird, that hath
>   A restless prescience–howsoever won–
>   Of a broad pathway leading to the sun,
> With promptings of an oft-reproved faith
> In sun-ward yearnings. Stricken through her breast
>   And faint her wing, with beating at the bars
>   Of sense, she looks beyond outlying stars,
> And only in the Infinite sees rest.
> Sad soul! If ever thy desire be bent
>   Or broken to thy doom, and made to share
> The ruminant's beatitude,–content,–
>   Chewing the cud of knowledge, with no care
> For germs of life within; *then* will I say,
> Thou are not caged, but fitly *stall'd* in clay!

"Hymn to the Dark Christmas of 1874," also from this
1876 volume, affirms hope, love, innocence, music,
and Christmas over sorrow, despair, skepticism, sin,
and death in a foggy and cold December when several
railway accidents occurred in England:

> Time and to spare when the children are gone to their rest,
>   To open your minds,
> And to build up the fragments of science as each one thinks best,
>   As he fancies or finds;
>
> To tell of a Universe having nor centre nor soul,
>   Drifting no whither,
> Making and moving itself without purpose or goal–
>   Hither and thither;
>
> To essay, sons and daughters of men, to grow cold to the voice
>   Which your progress has led,
> To silence the cry of the heart, and affect to rejoice
>   In the Fatherless Dread.

In a June 1876 *Contemporary Review* essay titled "Evolution and the Religion of the Future" Anna Swan-

wick commented that "Hymn to the Dark Christmas" was "an eloquent protest against the desolating doctrines propounded by modern science."

"Childe Rupert, the White Ermingarde, and the Red Ladye," a Pre-Raphaelite medieval ballad of innocence triumphant over temptations of pride and sexuality, is another of Pfeiffer's best works that appeared in 1876. Childe Rupert is a knight, and the White Ermingarde is his lady. As in the prose fantasies of William Morris, such as *The Wood Beyond the World* (1895), and the medieval ballads of Dante Gabriel Rossetti, such as "Sister Helen" (1853, 1870), the story follows the convention of good and bad ladies. Ermingarde is associated with the color white, the angelus, the sheep, and a white rose. The Red Ladye is likened to a snake, a wolf, rubies, and hemlock. The young hero must resist the temptations of idleness, luxury, sexuality, and power if he is to achieve his knighthood and win his true love. When Rupert leaves on his quest, Ermingarde challenges him to kneel in prayer and breathe her name whenever he hears the angelus. Fidelity to this promise saves him from the enchantments of the sorceress.

Each stanza consists of one quatrain that advances the plot followed by another that carries the emotional content of the action. The sensuous and symbolic accompanying quatrains, their imagery drawn mostly from the natural (or sometimes the preternatural) world, act as a refrain or chorus, adding both lushness of tone and implied moral judgment to the tale. Here is the scene in which Ermingarde and Rupert first see the Red Ladye:

> A shadow cross'd the brooklet's face,
>   It trembled at a sound;
> The lady started back a pace,
>   The knight looked boldly round.
>   O the sliding of the snake
>   Through the sun-browned grass,
>   And the silence of the birds
>   As they feel it pass!
>
> He turn'd and met a fiery glance,
>   Which struck him as a glaive;
> She saw a bloodless face advance,
>   And blood-red tresses wave.
>   When the rose retires, the hemlock
>   Stands forward in the dusk;
>   How the air grows hot and heavy
>   'Neath the leaden fumes of musk!
>
> The ashen face rose proud and fair
>   From a robe of cramoisie;
> Said Ermingarde: "Sweet-heart, beware!
>   It is the Red Ladye."
>   When you see the she-wolf's track
>   At even on the snow,

>   Keep a watchful eye and steady,
>   And be wary as you go!

The Red Ladye is a memorable femme fatale; as in Samuel Taylor Coleridge's "Christabel" (1816) and Mary Elizabeth Coleridge's "The Witch" (1892), the innocent hero can resist her beauty and her courage but not her vulnerability. After Rupert has trampled her with his horse and she lies bleeding behind him, he cannot leave her in that condition:

> He put aside her silken vest,
>   With trembling hand I wis;
> He stanch'd the wound upon her breast;
>   She thanked him with a kiss.
>   O balmy life of Paradise
>   Begotten with a breath
>   O spirits of the tainted air,
>   Whose freight is death!
>
> . . . .
>
> And then like an angel's wing, as fleet—
>   Reding as blest a rede—
> There swept a breath all fresh and sweet,
>   Of mushrooms from the mead.
>   We never may know how spirits pass
>   Through forms of earth, but are ware
>   Of the warning voice and the saving touch
>   Of their heaven-timed care.
>
> Childe Rupert stood on his feet and cried,
>   "I see thee a goblin sprite,
> With never a wound in thy haggard side,
>   While I am a recreant knight!"
>   Sweet the smile of dreaming babe,
>   Or of saint who stifleth moan;
>   But the laugh of the lost is curst, and rings
>   More hollow than a groan.

Saved by the angelus, Rupert returns to Ermingarde with new respect: "He said, 'I knew you for the White,— / I know you for the Wise.'"

Pfeiffer's next publication, *Glân-Alarch: His Silence and Song* (1877), was another chivalric verse tale, reminiscent of Sir Walter Scott's *The Lay of the Last Minstrel* (1805) or Tennyson's *Idylls of the King* (1872). Pfeiffer's intent, stated in the preface, was "to revivify a typical moment of that past which lies at the root of the present through which we are living, and the future to which we aspire." She wanted to impart a more human character to the Middle Ages; however, reviewers did not think she achieved this ambitious goal. Critical response was mixed as the following press notices, appended to the 1878 edition of *Gerald's Monument,* attest: *The Nonconformist* reviewer wrote, "We fully perceive the high ideal of love and its mission which Mrs. Pfeif-

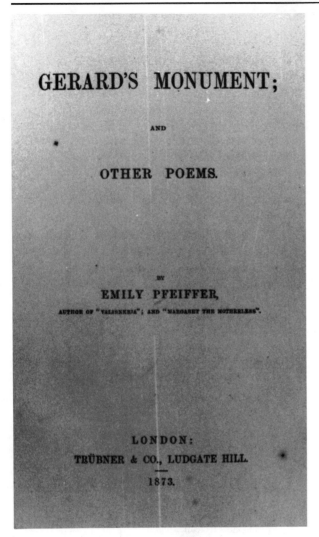

GERARD'S MONUMENT;

AND

OTHER POEMS.

BY

EMILY PFEIFFER,

AUTHOR OF "VALISNERIA"; AND "MARGARET THE MOTHERLESS".

LONDON:

TRÜBNER & CO., LUDGATE HILL.

1873.

Title page for Pfeiffer's first collection of poems. The title piece chronicles the tragedy of a woman torn between love for her husband and loyalty to her dying brother.

fer teaches us in this poem"; the *Whitehall* reviewer, calling Pfeiffer "a true woman-poet," recommended the book for "the description of British scenes and fashions"; and, also judging her as a poetess, the reviewer for *The Spectator* observed how "her lines flow on with sweetness and grace." Only the reviewer for *The Academy* seemed to take her point, noting that the story "is less concerned with external movement than with spiritual motives and their relation to two human hearts." Pfeiffer did not attempt another poem of this kind until *The Rhyme of the Lady of the Rock and How It Grew* in 1884, in which she mixed contemporary responses with the details of heroic myth.

Quarterman's Grace and Other Poems, Pfeiffer's next volume, appeared in 1879. Grace is an English peasant's beautiful, restless, and dreamy daughter, whose hymn singing reaches the ears of all the par-

ish, high and low, like Pippa's in Robert Browning's *Pippa Passes* (1841). Grace is a natural, untutored singer. Not only is she beautiful to look at—a work of art herself—but she is also an artist. During the week she sews at home with lace and bobbins and thread: "O' week-a-days it was a sight / To gladden eyes made sore by weeping / To see those hands of touch so light, / Those feat and fluent fingers, leaping / Amongst the dancing bobbins, till– / The slender threads each turned and twisted, / She set them down at her sweet will, / And fresh ones for the dance enlisted." Her work seems picturesque: it is likened to a dance—but Grace expresses her inner spirit through this employment. On the Sabbath, with her hands idled by religious custom, she finds other modes of expression.

"Grace" also refers to the state of grace that the heroine achieves while singing in church. Afterward, musing upon the contrast between her narrow rural life and the sensual glory of the universe, she is transfixed by a vision of St. Cecelia (patron saint of music) and follows her in "unappeased desire" up a steep, dangerous mountain to the brink of destruction. Falling asleep in her reverie, Grace feels herself falling; she is rescued (awakened) suddenly by the church organist, an "angel" who "she knows will save her soul from death."

The poem seems to be in part an allegory of female innocence and the temptations of sensual desire, from which a woman may be rescued by the love of one good man: "And the hand that is holding her hand will guide / Her unused feet on the mountain side." The poem concludes with a moral: "From this true song of Grace it well may seem / That there is hope for maids that fall in dream." Grace's temptation foreshadows the sensuality and the sexual fall of other Pfeiffer heroines.

For example, another long poem in this volume, "Madonna Dunya," received special notice on publication, Geraldine Jewsbury remarking that it "lives within one like an influence." Taken from a Russian legend epitomizing, Pfeiffer thought, "love of children and reverence for the maternal relation," this story chronicles a fallen Madonna who returns one cold night with babe in arms to her former household to beg for admission. For the sake of the child they take her in, but only provisionally; after a year they will decide whether she may stay. During that year Dunya is stricken with the Black Death. She turns the baby over to the household and fights the illness alone so as not to infect him and the others, but she prays to the Virgin Mary to feed him, "If his poisoned fountain [herself] should soon be dry!" All day the unweaned baby cries, but at night he gurgles happily and then peacefully sleeps. Members of the household creep in to find out why this is so, and they discover the Virgin Mary, in jewels and a golden stole, nursing the laughing baby.

In this volume Pfeiffer also continues her attempts to reconcile mythological and scientific, religious and cynical, views of the earth and our place upon it. The dramatic monologue "A Vision of Dawn" is typically Victorian, reminiscent of Tennyson's *In Memoriam* (1850), his prophetic lines in "Locksley Hall" (1842), and his speech in "Morte D'Arthur" (1842)–"The old order changeth, yielding place to the new. . . ." Like George Meredith's 1883 poem "Lucifer in Starlight," it is cosmic in its perspective, staged in outer space, with grand mythological figures such as Titans and gods:

> Through the tremulous air, straight on through the ether
>   pure
>   To that midmost heaven whence nothing can rise or fall,
> I flew with my thought; there it hung as an eagle secure,
>   And the cup of the earth grew to sight as a burnished
>   ball.
>
> . . . .
>
> The Titan hurled as I guarded mine ears and eyes
>   From the crash of the falling spheres that hailed fiery
>   death
> Each against each,–from the flames as of hell, and the cries
>   Of a universe lost in the storm of my passionate
>   breath.
>
> But lo, the music and measure were alway the same,
>   The symphony weaving for ever its circles of sound,
> As the stars on the floor of the universe guarded their flame,
>   Or yielded it, fairer for use, when they left the
>   round.
>
> And the earth sped on, though the Titan had failed from
>   sight,
>   It was gold on the sun-side, silver anent the moon,
> And it spun to the tapering point of its garment of light
>   As a weaving worm that is closing its own cocoon.

Here Pfeiffer expresses a sense of being poised between the medieval world of love and faith and the modern world of alienation from those values. Yet her vision is of the dawn after all, and she prophesies a rebirth of love to succor the human race in an unimaginably different future day and time. Pfeiffer was a great believer in human evolution, which she defined in an article ("The Suffrage for Women") for the *Contemporary Review* in March 1885 as "the slow triumph of the spiritual nature over the brute." Two sonnets addressed to "Dr. Wilhelm Jordan, the Great German Poet and Apostle of the New Faith," two more titled "Love's Eclipse," and a final sonnet "To S. J." reassert this hope for the triumph of love and reaffirm its importance to human life on this planet.

The Wynnes of Wynhavod: A Drama of Modern Life writtren in 1880, was a play that Pfeiffer originally hoped to produce; however, unsuccessful negotiations with managers of plays induced her to give up the idea. The play is a melodrama of inheritance and dispossession, with a villain, a poet-aristocrat hero, a courageous and literate heroine, and a happy ending. Written in blank verse and advertised as "a drama of modern life," this play also is possibly indebted to *Aurora Leigh*. Pfeiffer was sometimes compared to Elizabeth Barrett Browning; the entry on her in the *Dictionary of National Biography* pronounces: "As a poetess, Mrs. Pfeiffer resembled Mrs. Browning. . . . she was uplifted by the same moral ardour and guided by the same delicate sensitiveness. Her sentiment is always charming. Her defects are those of her predecessor–diffuseness and insufficient finish." *The Wynnes of Wynhavod* appeared in *Under the Aspens: Lyrical and Dramatic* in 1882.

Throughout the 1880s, working chiefly in the sonnet form, Pfeiffer published *Sonnets and Songs* (1880), *Under the Aspens: Lyrical and Dramatic,* and *Flowers of the Night* (1889). Not only the artistic achievement of Pfeiffer's sonnets but also their political intent continued to meet with critical approbation. In a comment included in "Extracts from Notices," appended to the 1888 edition, Theodore Watts is quoted as remarking of *Sonnets and Songs:*

> Assuredly, no lover of poetry can read Mrs. Pfeiffer's . . . without pleasure and admiration. Apart altogether from its purely poetical qualities, writing so sweet of temper and so noble of tone could only, I think, have come from one of those benevolent Englishwomen of our time, who are in the van of good thought and good work . . . bringing about that emancipation of humanity which we hope for–that final emancipation, I mean, from the tyranny of ignorance and wrong.

A representative example of Pfeiffer's work toward that "final emancipation" is the sonnet "To the Herald Honeysuckle," in which she expresses lyrically her belief that sexual love is not unwholesome or unchaste, and certainly not unnatural, for women as well as men.

Two interrelated themes are prominent in the lyrical poems of *Under the Aspens:* nostalgia for childhood and the portrayal of devastated innocence. The autobiographical, nostalgic poems include "Invocation to Memory" (about Pfeiffer's mother), "A Wind from off the Sea" (about her father), "A Remi-

Binding for Pfeiffer's 1876 collection, which established her reputation as a poet

niscence" (from her childhood nursery), and "The Bower among the Beans" (a memory of childhood games and puppy love). The two themes blend in "A Lost Eden," a retrospective account of a five-year-old's sudden awareness of mortality, particularly the mortality of her mother. This piece is beautifully written, with vivid imagery of flowers, gardens, apples, indeed of a domestic paradise lost.

Another initiation poem in *Under the Aspens,* one that exemplifies Pfeiffer's sympathetic treatment of sexuality and the fallen woman, is "From Out of the Night," a six-hundred-line dramatic monologue spoken by a ruined woman poised on the brink of a river. She is a motherless working girl seduced and betrayed by an upper-class lover. At the end of the poem the speaker flings herself into the river and drowns. The beauty of the poem lies in its portrayal of the naturalness of the woman's sexual and romantic feelings:

> It was May-time, within and without us, above and beneath,
>   It was May with the lark in the sky and its mate on the ground,
> It was May in our hearts, and the wonder had broken its sheath
>   With all blossoming things, and flowed forth as the waters unbound.

The narrator of "From Out of the Night" may be related to Marian Erle, the ruined woman in Browning's *Aurora Leigh*. As with Marian Erle, the poet's romantic idealization of the fallen girl is intended to result in the reader's contempt for her seducer.

Similarly, the three-sonnet sequence "A Protest" (dated 1885 and included in the 1888 edition of *Sonnets and Songs*) offers a feminist analysis of the cultural dynamics of prostitution. Here Pfeiffer indicts not only the men who patronize the "martyrs" and "frail victims" of man's lust but also the pure wives and mothers, the "queens who claim to reign in right of this foul wrong." It was Pfeiffer's consistent philosophy, as it was Browning's, that women writers should not turn away from sordid realities but should expose and confront them so they might be changed. The first of the three sonnets begins, "Let no man charge thee, woman if thou art, / And therefore pitiful, to veil thine eyes / From any naked truth whereof the cries / Reveal the anguish."

Flowers of the Night continues with sonnets on death and change and lyrics of grief and self-consolation written after the death of Pfeiffer's husband. It also contains strong poems reflecting Pfeiffer's political views. Arguing for woman suffrage in the *Contemporary Review* in March 1885, Pfeiffer had declared that "in the matter of legal justice, the woman is still to a great extent an outlaw." She continued, "A foreigner well read in our literature, well informed on our social life" would find it "unaccountable . . . that the being from whom the offspring of Englishmen were to be so jealously guarded should be the one to whom Nature had confided them in their hour of utmost need." Similarly, the feminist poem "Outlawed" in *Flowers of the Night* protests that custody of young children was assigned by law to fathers instead of mothers. Pfeiffer's tone is sarcastic and angry throughout: the "outlaw" of the title, "this terror, this name of fear . . . / this vampire that fastens and thrives / on the tender young lives of the children,– / this fiend from whom the children must be protected," she reveals, "IS–their MOTHER!"

In 1882 a warehouse fire at the London establishment of Kegan Paul, Pfeiffer's publisher, destroyed the plates of six volumes of Pfeiffer's works stored there. A planned volume of her *Collected Works* was announced, but it was never published because Pfeiffer, who was fifty-five years old in 1882, was too ill to carry out the necessary editing. Thus Pfeiffer's poetry published before *Flowers of the Night* became inaccessible to the next generation of readers, and the longevity of her reputation as a poet suffered as a result.

The Rhyme of the Lady of the Rock, and How It Grew is mostly prose: part travelogue, part heroic poem, and part contemporary dialogue about women's rights and abilities. In structure it resembles Tennyson's *The Princess* (1847). It purports to be the story of the conception, composition, and reception of the title poem, told by the poem's author, a woman. Lengthy interposed commentaries (in prose) offer a lively debate about the merits and meaning of the poetic narrative. The embedded poem is based on an old Scottish legend, retold so as to condone female sexual self-determination and condemn male brutality and arranged marriages. Executed with humor and grace, the book's self-effacing frame elevates the poem to prominence, gives it a sympathetic reading, and provides a spirited defense for its author and for the project of reconstructing old legends from a feminist perspective.

Between 1878 and 1888 Pfeiffer published several prose essays on the pressing feminist issues of the decade: women and education, work, suffrage, trade unionism, dress reform, wife beating, and so on. Most appeared in the *Contemporary Review* or the *Cornhill Magazine*. Pfeiffer thought the accelerating progress of women's rights would inevitably lead to social revolution. In her *Contemporary Review* article "The Suffrage for Women" she dismissed the opposition to woman suffrage thusly:

> Those who have noted the humanizing nature of woman's influence through all the ages of the past, those who have seen it diffusing itself in new spheres of activity in our own day, and who have felt the comfort and added strength of its help in many a social difficulty, must surely be very blind if they can still be startled by, very timorous if they can still fear, the last revolution of a wheel which has been so long in motion.

Flying Leaves from East and West (1885) is a collection of political and artistic commentaries in travelogue form based on Pfeiffer's 1884 trip through Eastern Europe, Asia, and North America. Among the political topics addressed were class and race relations in the United States and the degraded status of women in harems in Turkey. Pfeiffer's analysis of ancient Greek culture is reminiscent of Amy Levy's poem "Xantippe" (1884), in which the wife of Socrates criticizes her husband's contempt for women. In *Women and Work* (1887) Pfeiffer produced evidence documenting women's ability to endure hard work and meet mental challenges. Specifically Pfeiffer argued for allowing women access to higher education and to well-paid employment.

In addition to being a poet and essayist, Pfeiffer was also a painter. In *Flying Leaves* she wrote, "The lion has so long been the painter, that he is apt too wholly to ignore the aspect which his favorite subject may take from the point of view of the lioness. If the latter will sometimes tell the truth, and tell, not what she thinks she ought to see, but of what she really sees, many an intellectual picture which has hitherto satisfied the sense of mankind, may be found to be somewhat out of focus." Pfeiffer admired her controversial contemporaries, the Pre-Raphaelite painters and poets. *Flowers of the Night* contains several poems to accompany paintings by Edward Burne Jones: "To E. Burne Jones, on His Picture of the Annunciation" and "Suggested by the Picture of the Annunciation by E. Burne Jones," both written in 1880, and "King Copehetua and the Beggar Maid, Suggested by the Picture of E. Burne Jones," written in 1888. In 1882 Pfeiffer wrote a lengthy defense of the morality of Dante Gabriel Rossetti's poetry, which Robert Buchanan had attacked as "fleshly" in the *Contemporary Review* a decade earlier. John Campbell Sharp, professor of poetry at Oxford, extended this attack in the July 1882 number of the *Contemporary Review* to include *The House Of Life,* which appeared in its final form in Rossetti's *Ballads and Sonnets* (1881). Pfeiffer's rebuttal to Sharp, titled "The Posthumous Critics of a Dead Poet, and Deathless Poetry," was scheduled to run as the lead article in the July 1883 number of the *Contemporary Review,* but for unknown reasons it did not appear. She argued that the union of body and spirit portrayed in *The House of Life* constituted "not an abasing of the spirit to the flesh, but a taking up of the flesh into the spirit."

In this essay Pfeiffer also defended contemporary poets (such as herself), whose duty is to state the case for their times, to bear faithful witness to the confusion and discord of the era:

> if there come times in the world's history which poetry is in its own way constrained to record–times when the jarring elements are too loudly heard, and when the resolutions hardly find place within the scope of the performance–art, which is form, must suffer from the conditions, but I cannot in faithfulness withhold its testimony. That the days through which we are living and trying in patience to possess our souls, are days which answer to this description, can hardly be denied. . . . The whole thinking world seems traveling in pain together, and we know not how long it may be be-

fore,–we know not indeed if ever again,–a paramount organizing power will appear to give substance and coherence to the antagonizing elements.

Clearly Pfeiffer's own poetry pursues this mission. More optimistic than Dante Gabriel Rossetti, Pfeiffer succeeded both in bearing witness to the pain and anxiety of the late Victorian period and in imagining its elusive resolution.

Emily and Jurgen Pfeiffer left no heirs except one niece, who inherited their collection of paintings. The rest of the Pfeiffer estate was expended on projects connected with Pfeiffer's political goals, including opening an orphanage for poor children, funding the School of Dramatic Art for women, and erecting Aberdare Hall, the first residence hall for women students at University College, Cardiff, in South Wales. Pfeiffer envisioned an egalitarian future free of class oppression, sex discrimination, sexual violence, and hopeless poverty. She consistently asserted the importance of personal courage, love, and faith in attempting to create such a world. In her poetry and prose, as in her political life, Pfeiffer was as progressive, humane, and artistic as her times and her talents would allow. If her work seems somewhat dated, the tribute she wrote in "The Lost Light," on the death of Eliot, may apply equally well to Pfeiffer's own poetic legacy:

> So hast thou sought a larger good, so won
> Thy way to higher law, that by thy grave
> We, thanking thee for lavish gifts, for none
> May owe thee more than that in quest so brave–
> True to a light our onward feet must shun–
> Thou gavest nobler strength our strength to save.

References:
Kathleen Hickok, "'Intimate Egoism': Reading and Evaluating Noncanonical Poetry by Women," *Victorian Poetry,* 33 (Spring 1995): 13–30;
Hickok, *Representations of Women: Nineteenth-Century British Women's Poetry* (Westport, Conn.: Greenwood Press, 1984), pp. 30, 31–32, 90, 104, 167, 230;
Angela Leighton and Margaret Reynolds, eds., *Victorian Women Poets: An Anthology* (Oxford: Blackwell, 1995), pp. 338–343.

May Probyn
(1856 or 1857 – 29 March 1909)

Marion Thain
University of Birmingham

BOOKS: *Once! Twice! Thrice! and Away!* (London: Remington, 1878);

Who Killed Cock Robin? (London: Literary Production Committee, 1880);

Poems (London: Satchell, 1881);

A Ballad of the Road, and Other Poems (London: Satchell, 1883);

Christmas Verses, by Probyn and Katharine Tynan (London: Catholic Truth Society, 1895);

Pansies (London: Elkin Mathews, 1895).

SELECTED PERIODICAL PUBLICATION—
UNCOLLECTED: "Robert Tresilian," *The Sea-Side Annual* (1880).

May Probyn is one of a group of little-known nineteenth-century women poets in whose work there has begun to be a revival of interest. Critics are now recognizing that the witty social criticism that was a major theme for these poets is important to understanding the period. Probyn as an individual has so far received little critical attention, but her humor and satire, which break the sentimental stereotype of Victorian women's poetry, and her astute commentary on the position of women deserve to be rediscovered. Because Probyn was never a popular or successful poet, information is scarce. In fact, a review of *Poems* (1881) in *The Westminster Review* (October 1881) begins, "Who May Probyn may be we know not."

Juliana Mary Louisa Probyn was born in France to British parents, Julian John Webb Probyn and Mary Christiana Spicer Probyn. Probyn's three younger siblings were born after their return to England, in Esher, Surrey. The dedication in Probyn's collection *Pansies* (1895) is addressed to the sister and brother who survived to adulthood and relates how close they were as children, as well as suggesting that they all were educated at home.

Probyn's first book was published when she was twenty-one years old. *Once! Twice! Thrice! and*

Away! (1878) is a romantic adventure novel about the Kilcorans of Feversham Priory: Diamond, the plucky young heiress, escapes a marriage of financial convenience planned by her father and ends up with the man she loves. The novel has the feel of an historical romance, but it is difficult to judge the time of its setting since it incorporates elements of both the medieval and the Victorian. The novel *Who Killed Cock Robin?* was Probyn's second book. It was published in 1880 by the Literary Production Committee after Probyn won second prize in their competition for amateur authors. The novel follows the fortunes of a man and a woman in the small community of Chilvester. Flirtatious Phyllis, sister and houseguest of the village curate, is irresistible to Robert Tresilian (Cock Robin), the local schoolmaster and poet. The novel records their love and, ultimately, Tresilian's tragic death. The British Library has records of another story published by Probyn, also in 1880, called "Robert Tresilian." Since the story appeared in *The Sea-Side Annual,* a journal produced by the same Literary Production Committee, it seems reasonable to assume that the two works are connected, if not actually the same.

A note in the front of *Who Killed Cock Robin?* identifies the author as "May Probyn of Weybridge," suggesting she spent some time there after her childhood in Esher. By 1881, however, when her *Poems* was published, Probyn had moved away from Surrey and was sharing a house with her sister, Dora. This house was the Fernleigh, from which she addresses the preface to *A Ballad of the Road, and Other Poems* (1883). The full address, which reveals the house to be in Hillworth, Devizes, is given in two letters that she wrote from there to Vernon Lee (Violet Paget). Probyn was at this address with her sister at the time of the 1881 census, and she was still there at the time of writing the second letter to Vernon Lee, in 1883 or 1884. The fact that the Fernleigh household employed three servants and that neither of the sisters had an occupation suggests that

243

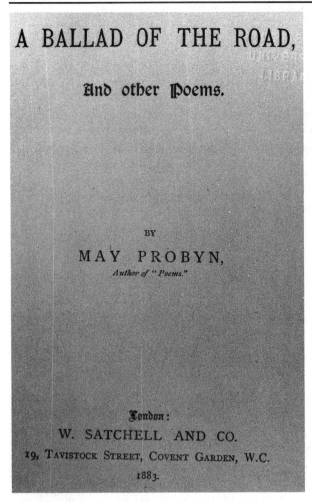

Title page for May Probyn's second collection of poems, which combines conventional romantic ballads with acute social satire

their family was reasonably well off, certainly from at least a middle-class background.

The move from prose to poetry was a good one for Probyn, and her first two volumes of verse are much more mature than her efforts at fiction. Perhaps the least successful verses in *Poems* are Probyn's dutiful attempts at social criticism—the turgid "At the Workhouse Door" and the long and conventional "City Chimes." However, this volume contains mainly fanciful, enigmatic poems, at which Probyn excels. Another prevalent type in Probyn's work is the short, songlike poem, characterized by repetition, a strong rhythmic drive, and suggestive content. Some are more akin to the ditty or nursery rhyme, such as "Jacobite Snatch," "At the Fancy Fair," and "Dandelion Clocks," while others are less whimsical exercises in the use of strict verse structures. Probyn's fondness for French forms is one of the striking features of her work: *Poems* contains triolets, villanelles, and ballads. *The Westminster Review* critic points out that Probyn has just missed the

fashion for these verses and speculates that her collection would have been better received six or seven years before; yet, the review continues, she brings a fresh voice to these forms. There is no doubt that one of Probyn's strongest features in this book is her careful crafting within these fixed structures—the strong drive of the form carrying evocative content.

The subject matter of much of her poetry is love and the games played between men and women in the name of love. *The Westminster Review* critic praises Probyn for writing "love-poems, which are neither tediously sentimental nor cheaply sensual." "Soapsuds," one of Probyn's longer poems, follows the wooing of the washerwoman Sally, who refuses to be seduced by the traditional games of romance. "Swinging" follows the psychological contortions of a young woman who wants to remain aloof from her lover but is too eager to manage it. These emotions are nicely observed and wittily represented. Probyn is at her most interesting, though, when she plays with the conventions of the Petrarchan love poem, in which the beloved woman is nearly always a distant, silent figure seen only through the lover's eyes. Given Probyn's interest in the woman's part in the game of love, it is not surprising that she develops a subtle strategy for giving a voice to the silenced woman of the traditional love poem. While Probyn does not allow the woman to speak directly, she clearly implies that the male narrator is misguided in his interpretation of her expression; one can assume, then, that the woman's real meaning is the opposite of the narrator's interpretation. Probyn thus satirizes the traditional love poem by exposing the male lover's suit as based on a misunderstanding of the frustrated female beloved. "In February" is a good example of this type of satire. The epigraph for the poem is from a work by Sir Walter Raleigh and is used by Probyn to highlight her theme: "The lass saith 'no' and would full fain— / And this is love, as I hear sain!" In the language of love "no" spoken by a woman is taken to mean "yes" by a man: "And all the while you wish it so—! / My love—what makes you answer 'No'?" This satiric deconstruction of the Petrarchan love poem is continued in *A Ballad of the Road, and Other Poems,* in poems such as "Villanelle."

At her best, Probyn challenges, satirizes, and questions the conventions of her literary heritage in *Poems.* In "Dante's Wife," for example, Probyn presents one of the Western world's great love stories in a new light. If Beatrice was Dante's mistress, what then of his wife, Gemma? Probyn's sonnet, narrated by the eponymous character, gives voice to a woman who has been silenced twice over—once by being the object of Dante's poetry and not its speaking subject, and again by being always second to Beatrice, who constantly eclipses her in the Western literary tradition. Gemma's testimony confirms that his treatment of her does not compare well with his adoration of Beatrice:

I think you count me as a faithful thing
For rocking children, and for comforting–
A little set aside as soon as wed.

Even though Beatrice's name is not mentioned, a comparison between the poet's treatment of wife and of mistress is implicitly made by the wife's description of her relationship with Dante. Their relationship appears the opposite of everything we expect of the mythical affair between him and Beatrice. This focus on the woman who was passed over in the romantic myth draws a contrast between wife and mistress, real and ideal woman.

The book received a positive response in the long critique in *The Westminster Review,* as well as in many shorter laudatory press notices (some of which were quoted in the front of her next volume). Probyn was reviewed as a minor poet who shows much promise. This attitude is most clearly expressed by the critic in *The Westminster Review:* "It is positively fascinating to read these bright, pure verses after the silly schoolboy imitations of Swinburne with which young writers have wearied the world over-much of late."

The section of ballads that begins Probyn's second volume of poetry, *A Ballad of the Road, and Other Poems,* is comprised of conventional, largely sentimental romantic tales. The title poem concerns a highwayman who spares a girl her gold and her life in return for her daffodil posy. He is later about to be hanged for his crimes when the girl, struck by his gallantry, recognizes him as the lover she lost years ago when he went to war and saves him from this fate. "Jane Shore," the other long ballad, is another quasi-mythological tale of a woman in love. Jane Shore is thrown out of her home by her mean husband but finds love with the king of her land. She lives happily with the king until his early death but then is accused of sorcery and hounded to her own demise. These romances are at times somewhat implausible, even within their own frame of reference, but Probyn's talent for musical verse is apparent, particularly in "A Ballad of the Road."

The lyrics in this volume often still have the enigmatic, Romantic quality that was evident in *Poems,* and a section titled "A Nosegay from a French Garden" again reflects Probyn's interest in strict French poetic forms. What is new to *A Ballad of the Roads* is a concern with the real world, particularly

Vernon Lee (Violet Paget), the author and critic who introduced Probyn to a large circle of women writers; painting by John Singer Sargent (by permission of the Trustees of the Tate Gallery)

the lot of women, rather than simply the fantasy world of romance. This engagement with life shows itself in two ways–in Probyn's choice of the stories of real women as her subject matter and in the astute social criticism that emerges in this book. In a letter to Vernon Lee from 1883 or 1884 Probyn writes, "'Mary Trent' is a true story, I am sorry to say. It happened, word for word, to an acquaintance of our's half-a-dozen years ago." Like the ballads, this poem concerns the fate of a woman in love, but "Mary Trent" differs strikingly in Probyn's decision to set the tale in a non-Romantic milieu. Probyn's attempt to use what were usually considered the trivialities of women's experiences as valid poetic subject matter likewise signaled a new direction in her work. "Changes," for example, is about the value of the feminine domestic role, suggesting that its importance is not recognized until it is gone.

Probyn's satiric perspective on relationships between women and men is particularly evident in the seven witty triolets of "A Nosegay from a French Garden." These poems are markedly different from the turgid social-conscience poems in her last book. For example, two consecutive triolets,

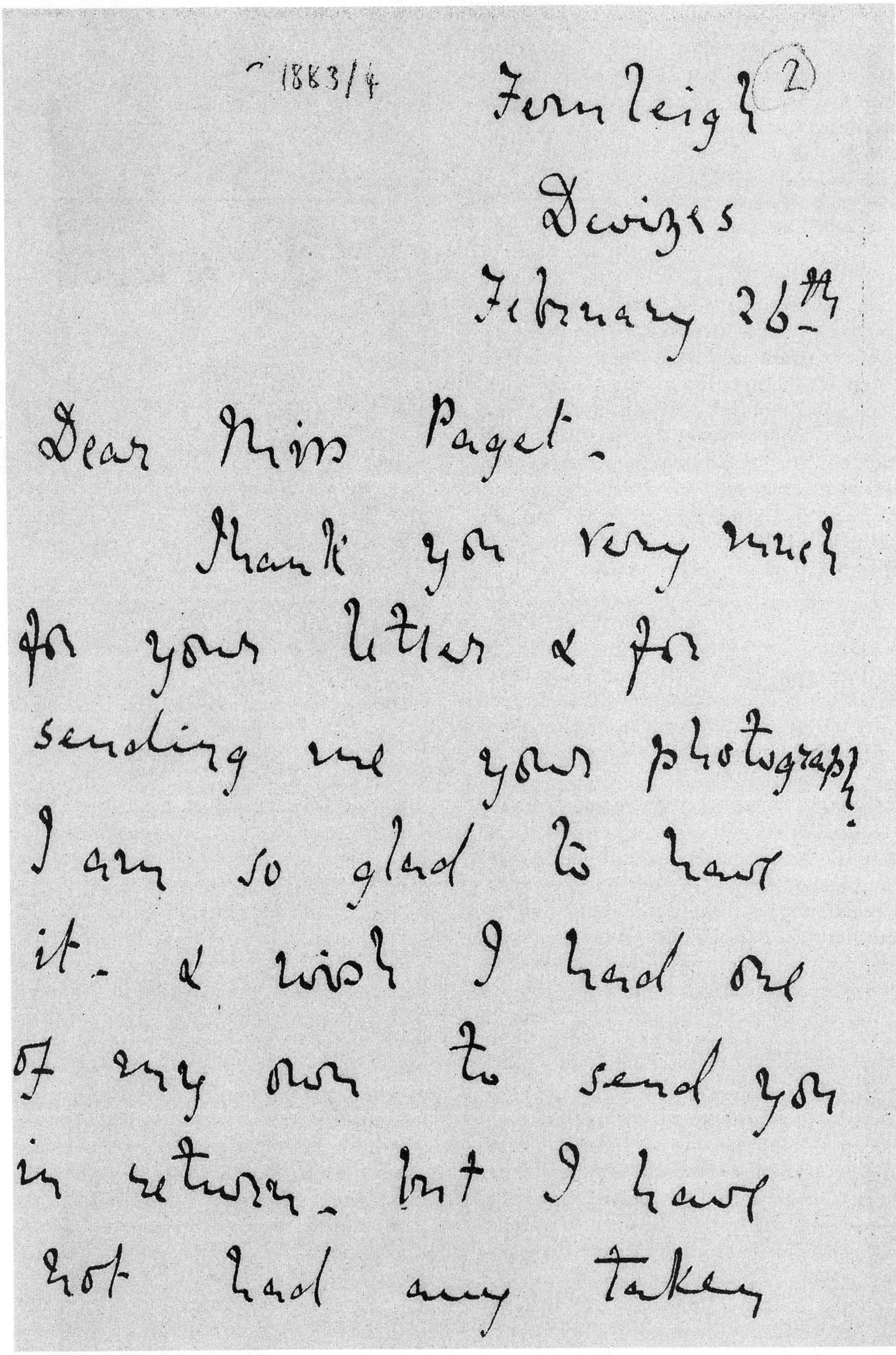

1883/4

Fernleigh ②
Devizes
February 26th

Dear Miss Paget,

Thank you very much for your letter & for sending me your photograph. I am so glad to have it. & wish I had one of my own to send you in return. But I have not had any taken

Pages from a letter to Paget in which Probyn acknowledges the factual basis for her poem "Mary Trent"
(Vernon Lee Archive, Somerville College, Oxford)

in the master's work[4] would be intolerable in a disciple's. but perhaps I have not studied his work enough to be a good judge. "Mary Brent" is a true story, I am sorry to say. it happened, word for word, to an acquaintance of our's half a dozen years ago. I think you are right about the "faculty.

"Before" and "After," present a cynical but humorous analysis of marriage wherein the idealized relationship is shown to be a dream and the difficult reality becomes apparent. In "Frustrated" Probyn satirizes the assumed right of men to possess women through their gaze by depicting a woman who actively avoids the male gaze, to the intense frustration of the narrator:

> Not a thing could I see
>   But her coalscuttle bonnet!
> Fair enough she may be–
> Not a thing could I see!
> 'Twould give shelter to three–
>   What induced her to don it?

At other times, however, Probyn is not so playful and paints a grim picture of sexual relationships between men and women. In "The End of the Journey," for example, a destitute Indian woman tracks down the father of her child, who is white, happily married, and not expecting the past to catch up with him. In a grotesque parody of their previous sexual union, he plunges his knife into her heart. Probyn offers a more subtle analysis of sexual relations in "Going to Market," an allegory regarding the place of female sexuality in the economic market, whose title suggests a reference to Christina Rossetti's "Goblin Market."

One of the main subjects of Probyn's social criticism is the objectification of women in society. In "As the Flower of the Grass" she perfectly illustrates this conception of woman as a perishable commodity. The poem shows a man dancing with the belle of the ball. The woman, like a beautiful flower, is discarded when the season ends, however, and a newer, fresher plaything is found for the next year. The imagery used to convey the theme is striking, as is the musicality of the form. This theme is successfully continued in "Ballade of Lovers." Probyn's exploration of the objectification of women is, however, best exemplified by "The Model"–one of a series of nineteenth-century poems that deal with artists' models, also including Michael Field's "A Portrait" and Rossetti's "In an Artist's Studio." "The Model" vividly evokes the difficulties faced by the Victorian woman who sought her identity as the subject, rather than the object.

The reviews for this volume were mixed. In *The Athenaeum* (3 March 1883) it was reviewed along with collections by Alfred Austin and Henry Rose. The two men are assessed damningly while Probyn is praised with a pointed comment: "the poems contained in Miss Probyn's new volume are decidedly above that class of verse which is generally printed solely for the author's gratification. . . ." Probyn was reviewed as a minor writer alongside other minor

figures, but she is nonetheless seen as successful in those terms. The reviewer in *The Academy* (10 March 1883) congratulated Probyn on her mastery of French verse forms as did the critic in *The Athenaeum*. *The Westminster Review* (April 1883), on the other hand, opined that her work in this volume was not original and simply reflected the influence of many other writers.

Although most of the reviews for Probyn's first two poetry collections were positive, she did not achieve much recognition for them. Alfred Miles mentions her only briefly at the end of volume 8 of his anthology *The Poets and the Poetry of the Century* (1898) and includes none of her work. There is little record of her having much contact with the literary scene of the time. *Poems* was dedicated to Thomas Westward, whom Margaret Reynolds in *Victorian Women Poets: An Anthology* (1995) identifies as "an aspiring poet in the 1840s who had once sought out Barrett Browning because he admired her poetry and corresponded with her in the 1840s and 50s." It seems quite likely, then, that this was a literary friendship. There is no evidence, however, to suggest that the dedication to Alfred, Lord Tennyson in *A Ballad of the Road* implies a personal acquaintance.

Probyn may not have known Tennyson or the other famous poets of her time, but she did have close contact with the aesthetician Vernon Lee. It appears that initially their mutual publisher, W. Satchell and Company, functioned as the point of contact between them. The first extant letter to Lee thanks her for a copy of one of her books, which she sent through Satchell, as well as for "having written so kindly to Satchell about my poems in the autumn. He let me see your letter and I need not tell you that it gave me a great deal of pleasure." Lee acted as the nucleus for a circle of women poets who knew her and in many cases knew each other through her. Thus Probyn was drawn into contact with A. Mary F. Robinson, a contemporary poet and close companion of Lee. In the same letter to Lee, Probyn writes that she has been reading Robinson's *Handful of Honeysuckle,* and she praises it highly. Her admiration of Robinson's poetry is evident in her use of a quotation from it as the epigraph to "A Nosegay from a French Garden" in *A Ballad of the Road.* A second letter from Probyn among Lee's papers (written in 1883 or 1884) is much more familiar and suggests that Probyn and Lee came to know each other on a friendly as well as professional basis.

While Probyn was part of Lee's circle of women writers, exchanging work and criticism with both Lee and Robinson, she sought the fellowship of other writers as well. In the late 1880s she made an unsuccessful attempt to associate herself with Wil-

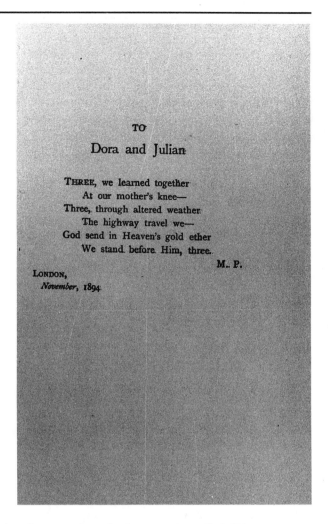

TO

Dora and Julian

THREE, we learned together
At our mother's knee—
Three, through altered weather
The highway travel we—
God send in Heaven's gold ether
We stand before Him, three.

M. P.

LONDON,
November, 1894.

Title page and dedication page for Probyn's final collection of poems, written after her conversion to Catholicism

liam Butler Yeats and a small group of other writers inspired by Irish fairy tales and folklore, as R. F. Foster reports in *W. B. Yeats: A Life* (1997). Probyn's desire to join Yeats's group is difficult to explain since nowhere does her work evince a Celtic style or subject matter. Probyn's friendship with Katharine Tynan, who had met and admired Yeats, may partially explain it.

For many years after *A Ballad of the Road, and Other Poems,* Probyn published only occasional poems in journals such as *The Marygold,* and by the time her final volume of poetry, *Pansies,* was published in 1895, her other work was long out of print and she had moved to London. *Pansies* appeared with a note from her publisher, Elkin Mathews, acknowledging her long silence and saying that: "Miss Probyn is a convert to Catholicism and her new book will contain some fervent religious poetry often tinged with mediaeval mannerism." The Bodleian Library in Oxford holds a proof copy of *Pansies,* which Probyn inscribed to Mrs.

Katharine Hinkson (Katharine Tynan's married name). The friendship with Tynan, a passionately Catholic woman, was likely bound up with Probyn's conversion. Indeed, in the same year that Probyn gave her the copy of *Pansies* they wrote a tiny, seven-by-ten centimeter book of verses together. *Christmas Verses* was published by the Catholic Truth Society and priced at one halfpenny. It collects four poems by Probyn and two by Tynan, all of which seem aimed at a church congregation and which deal nearly exclusively with the story of Mary and Jesus.

Given this new focus in Probyn's life, the emphasis on religion that is the most notable feature of *Pansies* should come as no surprise. The book was originally intended to end with a poem describing a miracle, set in medieval times. The proof copy held by the Bodleian is one of only three that contain the poem; it was withdrawn before the book was printed for reasons that remain unclear. Many of the poems in the volume have as their focus a Christian topic or more general moral lesson. Accompanying this new focus is a much more serious and somber tone. Even the poems about love have a chilling quality. "Lord John" describes a brother murdering his sister rather than letting her go off with a suitor; "Love in the Lane" shows lovers parted never to be united; and "Cophetua" describes a daughter's feelings as she is forced to marry by her father. In this collection Probyn's poetry often has a portentous quality rather than its previous whimsical tone. But there are still a few musical, upbeat poems in her previous style, and there is a collection of poems in the usual variety of French verse forms near the end of the volume. The two triolets, "A Mésalliance" and "The End of the Season," are in the same vein of teasing social criticism featured in *A Ballad of the Road*. Yet Robinson also uses these strict forms more reverently, as in the set of rondeaux taking Jesus, Adam and Eve, and religious teaching as their subjects.

Probyn's religious poems are not all simply celebratory. "A Legend," for example, attempts to work out the tensions between Probyn's new religion and her writing. The poem is about living a life of unfailing Christian charity, but it also comments on how this life for a woman can be incompatible with intellectual occupations. The woman speaker in the poem has little time to herself to read or write. Similarly, "Soeur Louise de la Miséricorde" deals with the pull between two different kinds of life and, on a deeper level, with the irreconcilable tensions and desires in the social roles of the Victorian woman.

Despite Probyn's conversion, she does appear to be satirizing religion in some poems. "Ite ad Joseph" is typical of the kind of slightly humorous, suggestive poetry by Victorian women that gently undermines the establishment. In the poem a soul begs St. Joseph for mercy after being shut out of Heaven by St. Peter, who insists the soul should not be let in. Joseph, sympathetic to his case, organizes a strike in Heaven in order to force God to overrule Peter, bringing everyone in Heaven down to the gates. Finally, "God Almighty looked from His Throne, / And saw He was left in Heaven alone." Joseph's strike action works. God sends the message:

"Go say that St. Peter must change his mind.

Without court, without singers, am I to stay

Till what time St. Joseph has got his way?

If St. Joseph's prayers are to empty Heaven,
Go say that his client must be forgiven."

This odd poem seems to be a parody of divine justice and the workings of redemption. Heaven, like earth, is shown as subject to economic pressures, and God can be forced to change his mind by strike action.

Probyn's title for the collection, *Pansies,* is significant in that it points to the importance of garden imagery throughout her poetry. A common metaphor of the Victorian era was the feminine sphere as a garden, with the beautiful lady as the flower within it. Outside the walls of the garden lay the dangerous world of intellect, public affairs, and men. Probyn's "Virelai" can be read as a critique of this image of the feminine sphere. In this poem a dweller "In the garden of the king," a sumptuous space of birds, flowers, and soft breezes, finds this beautiful space no consolation for her lack of freedom and the lack of access to the real world. Probyn's rebellion against this traditional image of the feminine sphere can also be seen in her epigraph to *Pansies:*

De mon jardin, Voyageur,
Vous me demandez une fleur?
Cueillez toujours—mais je n'ai,
Voyageur, que des pensées.

(You are asking me, traveler,
for a flower from my garden?
Gather all you wish—but,
traveler, I have only thoughts.)

"Pansies" was a common name for volumes of poetry, as it punned on *pensées,* a wordplay made more explicit here by the epigraph. This pun has a special resonance for Victorian women as it linked the feminine with the intellectual, in direct contrast to the conventional association between woman and flower.

Pansies was reviewed in *The Athenaeum* (29 June 1895) in comparison with one of Lady Lindsay's collections: Lindsay's work is clear, to the point, and moral, but uninteresting; Probyn's poems are "not easy to read or to follow, but they are distinctly interesting and impressive." Their fault, if anything, is to be too indistinct and intense. The reviewer praised the religious poems and noted that the collection was well crafted overall—"something that has been made, not something that has grown." *The Academy* (20 April 1895) was more effusive in its praise, judging *Pansies* to be for the most part "delightful" and "packed full of a quite peculiar refreshment which, so far as we know, has no counterpart in modern verse."

Despite the generally good reception of this book, no more was heard from Probyn before she died of heart failure on 29 March 1909 at the age of fifty-three. Her estate was worth a little more than seven thousand pounds; she left all her personal belongings, among which she lists her books, to her sister Dora, along with her house and an income. Some of her other property she left to her brother. Given the cynical view of wedlock expressed in her poetry, it is no surprise that she never married.

Probyn's style developed through her three books of poems from the fantastic to the realistic to the portentously religious. Some themes, however, were constant. Her use of strict French forms is a particular hallmark of her poetry, as is her lively analysis of relationships between the sexes and of the social roles of women. The latter interest, occurring most often as a subtext, is the main reason for renewed interest in her work. Probyn was never a successful or well-known poet, and she was not remembered after her death. The

faults of her verse are obvious: she can at times be trite, melodramatic, and sentimental; but her good work is interesting, and the critical reception of her work reflected this. By and large the reviewers saw her as a minor poet but a good one who crafts her poems particularly well. Notably, in 1881 a review of *Poems* in *The Pall Mall Gazette* praises her for her rare gift of humor, and it is this quality, particularly the wry humor seen in her satire, that distinguishes her from lesser writers. It remains to be seen what her late-twentieth-century audience will make of her.

Reference:

Angela Leighton and Margaret Reynolds, eds., *Victorian Women Poets: An Anthology* (Cambridge: Blackwell, 1995).

Papers:

The Bodleian Library holds a proof copy of *Pansies* containing a poem that was withdrawn before the book went into print. Two letters from Probyn to Vernon Lee (Violet Paget) are held in the Vernon Lee Archive at Somerville College Library, Oxford.

Adelaide Anne Procter
(30 October 1825 – 2 February 1864)

Cheri Lin Larsen Hoeckley
Westmont College

See also the Procter entry in *DLB 32: Victorian Poets Before 1850.*

BOOKS: *Legends and Lyrics: A Book of Verses* (London: Bell & Daldy, 1858);
Legends and Lyrics: A Book of Verses, Second Volume (London: Bell & Daldy, 1861);
A Chaplet of Verses (London: Longmans, Green, Longmans & Roberts, 1862).

OTHER: *Victoria Regia: A Volume of Original Contributions in Poetry and Prose,* edited by Procter (London: Victoria Press, 1861).

In 1866 Charles Dickens wrote an introduction to a posthumous edition of Adelaide Anne Procter's collected works, which has been, by far, the most influential biographical work on Procter. Dickens knew his subject well, not only because he had a long-standing friendship with her father, Bryan Waller Procter, but also because she was one of the most popular poets to appear in Dickens's periodicals *Household Words* and *All the Year Round.* According to Dickens, in December 1854 he was invited to lunch at the Procter house. That day he brought with him an issue of *Household Words* that included a poem by a poet whom he had been publishing and admiring for nearly two years but whom he knew only as Miss Berwick. The following afternoon he learned that he had spoken favorably of the poet and her poetry to his contributor's mother, in the contributor's presence, and that Miss Berwick was the pseudonym chosen by Adelaide, whom he had known since her childhood. Dickens's biographical introduction captures Procter's lively and well-connected literary family and the sober piety of her poetry. However, the imaginative novelist omits or minimizes many facets of Procter's life—her devotion to Roman Catholicism, her vigorous involvement in women's rights and her vivacious humor—that contribute to an appreciation of the richness and the often complexly ironic texture of her poetry.

Adelaide Anne Procter (Collection of William B. Thesing)

Procter was born on 30 October 1825 in London. Her father, Bryan Waller Procter, was a successful lawyer who also published poems under the pseudonym Barry Cornwall. Her mother, Anne Skepper Procter, was the stepdaughter of the prominent judicial figure Basil Montagu, who counted William Wordsworth and Samuel Taylor Coleridge among his extensive circle of friends. In addition to his legal texts on limiting capital offenses and on bankruptcy law, Montagu was a biographer and editor of Francis Bacon. When Adelaide was born, her parents were living in a bustling house at 25 Bedford Square with her mother's mother and stepfather. Adelaide was the oldest of six children, three boys (two of whom died early) and three girls. The children were part of the daily activity at 25 Bedford Square with regular visits from such Victorian luminaries of literature as Dickens, William Makepeace Thackeray, Leigh Hunt, Thomas Carlyle, and

Christina Georgina and Dante Gabriel Rossetti; stage stars that included Fanny Kemble; and social reformers such as the MP Benjamin Leigh Smith and his family. In the midst of this household activity Adelaide acquired an early love for poetry. Before she could write, she had her mother record her favorite passages in a tiny album so that she could carry them with her. Her intellectual appetites extended beyond verse to an interest in Euclidean geometry and fluency in French, German, and Italian.

In 1851 the three Procter daughters, Adelaide, Edith, and Agnes, broke away from their household religious practices and followed the lead of an Italian aunt, converting to Roman Catholicism. In her chapter "The Montagus and The Procters" from *In a Walled Garden* (1895) Bessie Rayner Parkes writes that the "one thing" Adelaide "never mentioned was her own conversion." In spite of Adelaide's silence on the topic, Catholicism indelibly marked the lives of the three women. Agnes eventually joined the Order of Irish Sisters of Mercy, and Adelaide engaged regularly in the philanthropic endeavors of the Catholic Church in England and relied heavily on Catholic images in her poetry.

Before her poems ever appeared in print they had gained praise by circulating in manuscript form among her many friends, a practice that quite likely provided her with an auspicious set of early critics, given the literary backgrounds of her family connections. In 1843 her first work, "Ministering Angels," was printed in *Heath's Book of Beauty,* one of a plenitude of richly illustrated books of verse that came out annually as gift books in the early nineteenth century; the annuals were often filled with poetry by women beginning literary careers. In 1853 Procter submitted her first poem to *Household Words* under the pseudonym Miss Berwick, and her work continued to appear regularly in Dickens's periodicals until he ceased publishing *Household Words;* it then appeared in *All the Year Round* for the duration of her life. Dickens's periodicals, of course, questioned some middle-class institutions but adhered to fairly standard sentimental representations of gender. Many of Procter's ballads, legends, and lyrics could be read as straightforward praise for domestic virtue and suited the family audiences of *Household Words* as well as its editor. In his biographical introduction Dickens limits his critical assessment of Procter's poetry and concentrates on other aspects of her life. His single mention of her authorship praises her initial submission to his journal as "possessing much more merit" than "the shoal of verses perpetually setting through the office of such a Periodical."

In addition to the contributions Procter made to Dickens's periodicals, two of her poems appeared in *Cornhill Magazine,* and two appeared in *Good Words* during the 1850s. In 1857 Procter also became the most frequent contributor of poetry, as well as an occasional contributor of prose on women's issues, to *The English Woman's Journal,* which began publishing that year under the editorship of Procter's childhood friend Bessie Rayner Parkes. *The English Woman's Journal,* in contrast to the general-interest stories and domestic tales provided by Dickens's periodicals, catered to an audience who sought and expected engagement in such topics as women's education, female employment, and wives' property rights.

Parkes and Procter were two of the women in a group that became known as the Langham Place Circle for their participation in a variety of women's rights activities out of offices in London's Langham Place. Some of the central figures of the group included the painter and essayist Barbara Leigh Smith, the art historian and social critic Anna Murphy Jameson, the translator and ballad writer Mary Howitt (as well as her daughter Anna Mary Howitt), the painter Eliza Fox, and the poet Matilda Hays. Before they occupied offices in Langham Place, these women had come together in each other's homes and agitated for the reform of marriage and property laws, calling themselves the Married Women's Property Committee. The ad hoc committee sought to abolish Victorian coverture laws that made all of a woman's property automatically her husband's when she married. Like Procter, several of the women on the committee were known as poets or writers and hoped to use their reputations for public influence. In fact the women on the committee enjoyed sufficient recognition as authors to prompt *The Saturday Review* to write a column on 24 May 1857 that dismissed their efforts as "the petticoat rebellion . . . of a few literary ladies whose peculiar talents had helped to place them in a rather anomalous position." The women gathered signatures for petitions and lobbied Parliament throughout 1855 and 1856. Their goals were marginally acknowledged with minor changes in marriage laws that were part of the Matrimonial Causes Act of 1857. The women involved were disappointed in the particular outcome but began devoting their attention and their resources in Langham Place to other efforts to improve women's general opportunities for employment and education.

In addition to sharing sensibilities about women's roles and literary activity, Procter shared affectionate attachments with many of the women in the Langham Place Circle. She and Parkes had strong

Letter from Procter to an unidentified gentleman (Collection of William B. Thesing)

family connections and had known each other since childhood. Anna Jameson was a friend of Adelaide's mother, Anne Procter, and frequently referred to her friend's daughters (and the other younger women in the circle) as her "nieces." Procter's attachment to Matilda Hays is reflected in the dedication to *Legends and Lyrics: A Book of Verses* (1858), where she honors Hays and amplifies that testimonial with a quotation from Ralph Waldo Emerson's *Essays* (1844): "Our tokens of love are for the most part barbarous. Cold and lifeless because they do not represent our life. The only gift is a portion of thyself. Therefore let the farmer give his corn; the miner, a gem; the sailor, coral and shells; the painter his picture; and the poet, his poems." Hays returned the poetic gift after Procter's death by publishing the poem "In Memoriam, Adelaide Anne Procter" in the April 1864 issue of *The English Woman's Journal*.

In 1859 Jessie Boucherett came to the Langham Place offices and organized the Society to Promote the Employment of Women (SPEW). According to Boucherett's 1 March 1864 essay about Procter in *The English Woman's Journal*, Procter took time away from an already active poetic career to work as the society's "leading person" and "animating spirit." She diligently attended to SPEW duties that ranged from writing circulars to mailing out subscription receipts. While working in that capacity Procter also edited and contributed to an anthology titled *Victoria Regia: A Volume of Original Contributions in Poetry and Prose* (1861), which was published by the Victoria Press, a printing company staffed entirely by women and housed in the busy Langham Place offices. Some of the contributors under Procter's editorship of the *Victoria Regia* included her father, Bryan Procter, and many of her associates from the Langham Place circle, as well as Hunt; Thackeray; Alfred, Lord Tennyson; Geraldine Endsor Jewsbury; Harriet Martineau; Coventry Patmore; Matthew Arnold; Anthony Trollope; John Forster; and Caroline Norton.

Procter contributed her poem "Links with Heaven" to the collection. The poem's celebration of "Mothers of Dead children" who "give Angels to their God and Heaven" exemplifies the kind of piety and sentimentality that critics have historically used to dismiss Procter's poetry. In this case Procter's specific celebration of maternal sacrifice and sentimental piety should also be considered in the context of the larger project she was editing and promoting. Under her editorship and the managerial guidance of Emily Faithfull at the Victoria Press, *Victoria Regia* was produced to create more jobs for women in the printing industry and to display women's capabilities when they were given the training and the opportunity to engage in occupations traditionally considered male domains. Undoubtedly Procter saw value in this role of maternity; her mother, to whom Procter was deeply attached and who had lost two sons as children, might be said to embody this sanctified maternal postion. The traditional role, however, was not the one Adelaide chose to pursue as she worked in the Langham Place offices for women's independence. The sentimental view of femininity suggested in "Links with Heaven," then, becomes not the definitive representation of womanhood but one of a range of possible femininities that includes economically independent women and women working in professional collectives. Procter's belief in that nuanced range of female roles becomes evident in the two published collections of her poems, *Legends and Lyrics* and *Legends and Lyrics: A Book of Verses, Second Volume* (1861).

In addition to her many efforts with her associates in Langham Place, Procter acted independently to improve the condition of women in mid-Victorian England. In 1862 Longmans published a book of her poetry, *A Chaplet of Verses,* which she wrote for the benefit of the Providence Row Night Refuge for Homeless Women and Children, a shelter run by Catholic nuns. "Ministering Angels" reappeared here, but it was one of only three poems in the thirty-one-poem collection that had been published previously. Her introduction for *A Chaplet of Verses* emphasizes the particular economic vulnerability of women and the risks of degradation and predation they face on the street. Her concern for supporting the shelter is clearly more motivated by a desire to provide shelter for "women and children utterly forlorn and helpless" than to purge the London streets of sexual sin. In other words, the introduction suggests that Procter locates the moral strength of the Night Refuge in its physical protection for a vulnerable population, not in its role in policing female sexuality. The collection has a decidedly Catholic emphasis, as evidenced by the prayer with which Procter concludes her introduction: "May the Mother who wandered homeless through inhospitable Bethlehem, and the Saint who was a beggar and an outcast upon the face of the earth, watch over this Refuge for the poor and desolate, and obtain from the charity of the faithful the aid which it so sorely needs." Several of the lyrics–not only "The Names of Our Lady" and "The Shrines of Mary" but also "Birthday Gifts"–continue this adoration of Mary. Mary symbolizes female purity and spiritual devotion. In Procter's verse, however, she also contributes an element of female intelligence and independence, which is never in conflict with proper femininity. Moreover, Procter's repeated emphasis on Mary as "Queen of Heaven" ("The Annunciation") must have resonated particularly with the Victorians, whose sovereign demonstrated a kind of earthly female leadership, albeit a domesticated one. In case her readers should miss the connection, Procter reminds them of it in "The Jubilee of 1850" by referring to "our Queen" with an ambiguity that could mean either Mary or Victoria, the usual recipient of English praise during a Jubilee:

> Pray to her Saints, who worship
> Before God's mercy Throne;
> Look where our Queen is dwelling,
> Ask her to claim her own[.]

At some point in her philanthropic work, which included visiting the sick and promoting education for the poor, Procter seems to have been exposed to tuberculosis. After several months of continuing to write, to maintain her charitable activities, and to attend to her administrative duties in Langham Place, in 1862 Procter went to Malvern near the Welsh border, hoping for relief from an illness the Victorians diagnosed as consumption. Despite these efforts to seek "the cure" in Malvern, she took to her bed the following year and was bedridden for fifteen months. Procter's biographers have frequently recounted the narrative of her lingering illness and peaceful death in the presence of her mother and sister shortly after midnight on 2 February 1864. Especially when coupled, as it often is, with selections from her poems such as "The Angel of Death," the deathbed tale reinforces the image of the poet as self-deprecating, somber, and pious. The narrative effect conveys a fairly apt but only partial sense of Procter's life. To understand fully Procter's personality and to appreciate her poetry, readers need to remember other anecdotes from her life that convey a sense of her liveliness, her ready wit, her female camaraderie, and her boldness of purpose. Those traits are all reflected throughout her letters and in the biographies written by her friends Boucherett and Parkes. Though he lets the witty moments pass without comment, Dickens gives some hints of

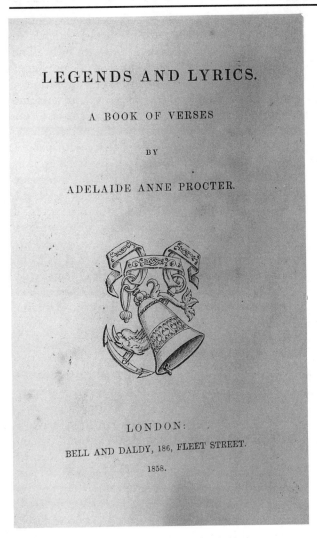

LEGENDS AND LYRICS.

A BOOK OF VERSES

BY

ADELAIDE ANNE PROCTER.

LONDON:

BELL AND DALDY, 186, FLEET STREET.

1858.

Title page for Procter's first book

this humor when he quotes extracts of the letters she sent home from her 1853 visit to her Catholic aunt, Emily de Viry, in Turin, Italy.

For instance, Procter delights in a lengthy description of an evening she spent dancing at a peasant engagement party—not only with male guests and the groom-to-be but also with the bride-to-be. Procter clearly enjoys the festive gaiety, particularly after her Italian hosts recover from their shyness and assure her that she will not be without a partner for the evening. In the end, she tells her family, she had to drag herself home "so dead beat with the heat that" she "could hardly crawl about the house." As the instance indicates, neither Procter's devotion to Catholicism, nor her unwavering political commitments, nor even her hardworking nature ever squelched the joyous exuberance that permeated her life and frequently appears in the cleverness of her poetry.

Taken alone, like certain aspects of her character, titles of Procter's poetry can mislead and rouse in contemporary readers an antipathy toward the kind of religious moralizing that Victorians frequently employed to justify surveillance of women and female submission to male rule: "Cleansing Fires," "A Crown of Sorrow," "Milly's Expiation," "Strive, Wait, and Pray," "The Angel of Death," "The Story of the Faithful Soul," "Life in Death and Death in Life," and "The Warrior to His Dead Bride." Her titles rarely convey the multifarious texture of Procter's poetry. One is tempted to underread her references to holiness, Christian duty, and God's strength as calls to feminine domestic virtue. Her individual poems repeatedly juxtapose images and language from the various facets of her life as devout converted Catholic, women's rights advocate, political agitator, and professional poet. Procter's choice of tropes embed her poetry with a complex understanding of mid-Victorian women's spiritual, sexual, political, and economic positions. Her combination of sources and referents creates poetry that displays a devotedly spiritual and domestic surface and also stringently critiques the political and economic injustices that she worked to eliminate for Victorian women.

No careful reader of Procter can deny that many of her poems are not only sentimental but also formally simplistic. Works such as "Treasures" and "One by One" display her occasional proclivity for unimaginative quatrains and repetitive rhymes. In her own century Procter's use of regular meter and her inclination toward spiritual themes attracted the attention of religious composers. Sir Arthur Seymour Sullivan (of the nineteenth-century operatic team Gilbert and Sullivan) set her poem "The Lost Chord" to music. Other lyrics, including "Per Pacem Ad Lucem," "I Do Not Ask," and "Evening Hymn," survive in many standard twentieth-century hymnals. Critical fixation on formulaic features of her poetry, however, can mask a finely tuned ironic voice and artistic ingenuity that allows Procter to combine critique of traditional women's positions with Catholic theology and domestic scenarios. In her 1996 essay in *Victorian Women Poets: A Critical Reader,* Isobel Armstrong argues for this complexity behind a simplistic surface as a trend in Victorian women's poetry. Armstrong includes Procter in a set of female poets who "share a capacity to produce a poem with a simple moral or emotional surface that actually probes more complex questions than its simplicity suggests." Tempted by the apparent "simple moral or emotional surface" of her poetry, one might say that Procter divided her energies between help for the poor, Catholic worship, women's rights activities, and writing poetry. More precisely, she ordered her life and created her poetry so that she could combine these divergent interests in her everyday work and writing and make them a part of her humorous delight in the world. Procter's poetic voice and her daily activities allowed her to engage in various interests simultaneously.

Her narrative ballads, or "legends" as she labeled them, as well as many of her lyrics, display this double-edged use of the languages of domestic ideology and conventional piety, often augmented with traces of her wit or boldness of character. "A Legend of Provence" is the tale of a runaway nun who returns to her convent repentant to find her transgressions—and the broader, adventurous life that prompted them—miraculously erased from history and her monastic place restored. While the erasure suggests an absence of female sexuality rather than a deep engagement in female sexual pleasure, it also indicates a fantasy of a woman's control of her destiny without suffering either societal criticism or bodily consequences for her choices. Not all of Procter's heroines are protected in their public activities by religious habits. In "A Legend of Bregenz," for instance, a Tyrol dairy maid during the Austrian Wars learns that troops are about to invade her homeland, so she steals a white charger to ride home and warn her country people of the invasion. She succeeds, survives, and is remembered every night in Bregenz when the warder calls her name at midnight. In this case the secular heroine acts boldly and with martial intentions. She succeeds in her nontraditional feminine acts of bravery and goes on to have her memory preserved not with some private honor but rather with the nightly ritual publication of her name on the street.

Procter brought issues of women's proper roles to the world of her own readers in "Three Evenings in a Life." This poem about a woman living in London with her brother was first published as "Three Evenings in the House" in the 1858 Christmas issue of *Household Words*. Inexplicably, the heroine is called Alice in *Legends and Lyrics* but named Bertha in the periodical version. With the revised title "Three Evenings in a Life" the heroine, Alice, rather than the dwelling, becomes the focal point of the poem. The other characters become satellites revolving around and reflecting back on Alice. The three other characters—her brother Herbert, her lover Leonard, and her sister-in-law Dora—repeatedly and almost willfully misread Alice to justify their selfish ends. Furthermore, with "life" rather than "house" in the title of the book version, portions that describe place figure more definitely as

metonymic of Alice's psychological and economic conditions. Procter clearly sees Alice as impeded by practices that foster gendered social inequalities. While not entirely eradicating sympathy for her loyal heroine, the poet comments critically on that heroine's choices to remain limited by immediate social restraints when she is presented with alternatives that range from rural independence to emigration to a professional artist's career. Overall the poem suggests that the "duty" to which Alice ought to answer is not a myopically private one but rather a more public, even global, calling that would protect her from the rejection and displacement she suffers from the shallow trio of her brother, her intended lover, and the woman both men eventually choose over Alice. That protective public life, in marked contrast to much of domestic ideology, does not come at the expense of Alice's independent material security but is rooted in an understanding of a single woman's precarious economic condition and of the physical peril that excessive self-forgetfulness might cause in a Victorian woman's life. The poem, then, displays Procter's interest in suitable marriage, work for women, women's social conditioning, relations between women, and female vocations. "Three Evenings in a Life" is a tour de force in the style of narrative irony at which Procter excelled and that allowed her to appeal to differing readerships simultaneously. In one work she combines the rhetoric of domestic ideology with a markedly less conservative rhetoric of women's rights activism to suggest that the most honorable female duty lies not in unexamined self-sacrifice but in economic self-sustenance and in stewardship of talents that might allow a woman to leave her home.

Likewise, her most frequently anthologized work in the twentieth century—the trilogy "A Woman's Question," "A Woman's Answer," and "A Woman's Final Word"—relies on the same powerful irony to capitalize on the language of domestic ideology while critiquing male political and economic oppression of women in courtship and marriage rituals. Lyrics that more overtly portray long-suffering women, such as "Too Late," can also be read as bitterly chastising family members and suitors who keep women from taking control of their futures and let the women be destroyed in the process. Similarly, her dramatic monologue "My Journal" suggests a deep passion in the speaker's former years and implies that a woman's calm domestic devotion might mask a turbulent personal history.

Procter turned both her earnestness and her irony to contemporary issues other than women's rights. For instance, she wrote highly critical poetry about both the Crimean War and the Irish question.

In "The Lesson of the War" the speaker delivers a pacifist response to the deaths of British soldiers in Crimea. She details the cost the war has exacted in the lives and homes of British families who never saw "the bleak Crimean shore" but who lost loved ones and began to doubt their leaders. "An Appeal" is her scathing lament against "The Irish Church Mission for Converting the Catholics," in which she argues for the freedom to practice Catholicism in Ireland. As she writes:

> Deny them, if it please thee,
> A grave beneath the sod:–
> But we do cry, O England,
> Leave them their faith in God.

In these poems Procter departs from the docility of much of her verse. Furthermore, her refusal here to veil her criticism in the irony on which she often relies suggests that her own "faith in God" emboldened her to step out of traditional domestic roles and into the public arena, not only to speak to other women but also to denounce government policies.

There is no denying the moral tone in Procter's poetry. However, the spiritual language and imagery of the poet can lead readers, especially twentieth-century feminist readers, to misjudge the object of the moral. Only on a cursory level do the poems exhort a self-sacrificial domestic female duty. Female duty and political agitation for economic independence are two sides of the same coin for Procter, the coin of religious duty. Through the skillful irony of her poetry Procter is able to invoke spiritual language to condemn a range of economic and political injustices against women and rhetorically to subject the perpetrators of that injustice to God's chastening.

Biographies:

Jessie Boucherett, "Adelaide Anne Procter," in *English Woman's Journal,* 13 (March 1864): 17–21;

Charles Bruce, ed., *The Book of Noble Englishwomen: Lives Made Illustrious by Heroism, Goodness, and Great Attainments* (Edinburgh: Nimmo, Hay & Mitchell, 1891), pp. 445–452;

Charles Dickens, introduction, in Procter's *Legends and Lyrics: A Book of Verses* (London: George Bell, 1892), pp. xiii–xxiv;

Bessie Rayner Parkes, *In a Walled Garden* (London: Ward & Downey, 1895).

References:

Isobel Armstrong, "A Music of Thine Own: Women's Poetry–An Expressive Tradition?" in *Victorian Women Poets: A Critical Reader,* edited by Angela Leighton (Oxford: Blackwell, 1996), pp. 245–276;

Gill Gregory, "Adelaide Procter's 'A Legend of Provence': The Struggle for a Place," in *Victorian Women Poets: A Critical Reader,* edited by Leighton (Oxford: Blackwell, 1996), pp. 88–96.

Papers:

The most significant collection of Procter's letters is found among the papers of Bessie Rayner Parkes Belloc and those of Barbara Leigh Smith Bodichon at Girton College, Cambridge University.

Arabella Shore
(1820? – 9 January 1901)

and

Louisa Shore
(20 February 1824 – 24 May 1895)

Natalie M. Houston
Duke University

BOOKS: *War Lyrics: Dedicated to the Friends of the Dead. By A. and L.,* by Arabella and Louisa Shore (London: Saunders & Otely, 1855; enlarged, 1855);

Gemma of the Isles, a Lyrical Drama, and Other Poems: By A. and L., by Arabella and Louisa Shore (London: Saunders & Otley, 1859);

Hannibal: A Drama, anonymous, by Louisa Shore (London: Smith & Elder, 1861); republished, as Shore, introduction by Arabella Shore (London: Richards, 1898);

Fra Dolcino, and Other Poems: By A. and L., Authors of "War Lyrics," by Arabella and Louisa Shore (London: Smith, Elder, 1870);

The Citizenship of Women Socially Considered, by Louisa Shore (London: Savill, 1874);

An Answer to John Bright's Speech on the Women's Suffrage, by Arabella Shore (London, 1877);

Elegies, by Louisa Shore (London: Privately printed, 1883);

Dante for Beginners: A Sketch of the "Divina Commedia." With Translations, Biographical and Critical Notices, and Illustrations, by Arabella Shore (London: Chapman & Hall, 1886);

Elegies and Memorials. By A. and L., by Arabella and Louisa Shore (London: Kegan Paul, Trench, Trübner, 1890);

Poems: With a Memoir by Her Sister, Arabella Shore, and an Appreciation by Frederic Harrison, by Louisa Shore (London & New York: John Lane, 1897);

Poems by A. and L., by Arabella and Louisa Shore (London: Richards, 1897);

First and Last Poems, by Arabella Shore (London: Richards, 1900).

OTHER: Henriette Etiennette Fanny Reybaud, *A Daughter of the Malepeires: A Tale of the "Ancien Regime,"* translated by Arabella Shore (London: Remington, 1885);

Journal of Emily Shore, edited by Arabella and Louisa Shore (London: Kegan Paul, Trench, Trübner, 1891; revised edition, 1898); edited by Barbara Timm Gates (Charlottesville: University Press of Virginia, 1991);

"The Present Aspect of Women's Suffrage Considered" and "What Women Have a Right To," by Arabella Shore, in *Before the Vote Was Won: Arguments for and against Women's Suffrage,* edited by Jane Lewis (New York & London: Routledge & Kegan Paul, 1987), pp. 282–315, 354–365.

SELECTED PERIODICAL PUBLICATIONS-UNCOLLECTED: "The Novels of George Meredith," by Arabella Shore, *British Quarterly Review,* 69 (1879): 411–425;

"The Character and Poetry of Madame de Sevigné," by Arabella Shore, *British Quarterly Review,* 180 (1884): 424–430;

"Shelley's Julian & Maddalo," by Arabella Shore, *Gentleman's Magazine,* 263 (1887): 329–342;

"Modern English Novels," by Arabella Shore, *Westminster Review,* 134 (1890): 143–158.

In November 1854 Louisa Shore, like many others in England, was shocked to learn of the disastrous cavalry charge near Balaclava in the Crimea. Descriptions of the terrible losses suffered by the Light Cavalry regiments first reached England on 11 November, and the newspapers were filled for weeks with discussions of the mistakes in leadership that resulted in the aristocratic, dandified cavalry regiments attacking the Russian gunners with sabers. Shore included a poem about the tragedy in a letter to her older sister Arabella, who gave it the title "War Music" and sent it, without Louisa's knowledge, to *The Spectator,* where it was published on 25 November. Louisa Shore's poem thus preceded by a fortnight the publication on 9 December in *The Examiner* of Alfred, Lord Tennyson's more celebrated response to the battle, "The Charge of the Light Brigade." Louisa and Arabella each contributed a few more poems about the war to *The Spectator,* and in January 1855 they published these verses as *War Lyrics: Dedicated to the Friends of the Dead. By A. and L.* The volume sold out within two weeks. Shortly thereafter the sisters published a second edition with additional poems. The poems in *War Lyrics,* although topical, display themes that are evident throughout both sisters' work, including a focus on women's roles and on the social and national significance of personal grief.

Although Louisa was the more skilled poet and received more critical attention, without Arabella's encouragement she would probably never have published any of her poems, which she wrote for her own enjoyment and self-expression. The sisters published several volumes of poetry together and jointly edited their older sister's journals for publication. Arabella's textual contributions to poems published under Louisa's name are explicit in some works, while in others they are implied in Arabella's prefatory notes. In addition to their joint works, Arabella published translations and critical essays. Both sisters were early supporters of woman suffrage, but Louisa's shy and retiring personality contrasted with Arabella's involvement in political causes and intellectual debates.

Arabella and Louisa Catherine Shore were the second and third daughters of the Reverend Thomas Shore and Margaret Anne Twopeny Shore. Arabella was born between 1820 and 1823, Louisa on 20 February 1824. Their father, whose independent religious views prevented his accepting preferment in the Church of England, supported the family by tutoring young men, including Charles John, Earl Canning; George Francis Robert, third Lord Harris; and Granville George Leveson-Gower, second Earl Granville. He also wrote several theological works and classical studies. The world of Louisa and Arabella's early childhood in Bedfordshire and then at Woodbury Hall in the New Forest is described in the journals of their older sister, Margaret Emily, who was born in 1819. With their elder brother, Richard, and their youngest brother, Mackworth Charles, the three Shore daughters were educated at home by their father in a "healthy atmosphere of wise freedom and mild restraint, of mental culture, of open-air joys and observations of Nature," as Arabella described in her memoir of Louisa in the latter's *Poems* (1897). They were taught several languages, read widely in literature and science, and joined their father's male pupils in conversations about philosophy and politics. Emily's journal entry for 3 January 1833 suggests that their literary endeavors began early: "In the afternoon there was a fall of snow, and we began to speculate what we should do if every flake was a piece of gold money . . . we would have a noble library, and printing-presses for us children, to print all the productions of our pens." Emily was a poet and a naturalist at a young age and published accounts of her observations of birds in the *Penny Magazine.* Louisa also wrote poems as a child but hid them; she was haunted by nightmares in which members of her family read her poetry aloud despite her protests.

In late 1838 the family moved to the milder climate of Madeira in the hope of helping Emily recover from tuberculosis, but she died there six months later. According to Arabella's memoir, Louisa was also considered to be in "delicate health" and was quiet and "lacking in vigor" as compared to the other Shore children. Her shyness would remain throughout her life her most distinctive feature: Arabella claims that "self-assertion was impossible to her."

A year after Emily's death Richard Shore went to India; the rest of the family returned to England, settling at Sunbury, Middlesex. There Arabella and Louisa grew closer to their younger brother, Mackworth. When he immigrated to Australia, probably in early 1841, the loss of his companionship added to their grief over Emily's death. Louisa's poem "Man Flutters in the Cage of Destiny," dated December 1841, describes the human individual as "a being made to mourn and to be mourned," one who struggles against constraint and grasps at delusional joys. The second stanza offers one response to grief:

> Ah no! though sorrow be their mortal lot,
> There are who can endure and murmur not;
> There are who hallow uncomplaining years
> With a perpetual flow of quiet tears,
> Gaze on the captive fluttering in his cage,
> The wind-swept billows tossing in their rage,
> The fretful infant, with a smile and sigh,
> And whisper "Till grief tamed me, such was I."

The death of her eldest sister and the absence of her younger brother would remain significant sources of Louisa's poetry throughout her career.

The family moved to London in 1845 so that Margaret Anne Shore, who was in poor health, could receive medical care. Three years later Louisa and her parents moved to Kent; Arabella remained in London but corresponded and visited frequently with her sister. During an eighteen-month sojourn in Paris from 1851 to 1853 Louisa and her parents met Robert and Elizabeth Barrett Browning.

Arabella and Louisa Shore's father, the Reverend Thomas Shore; their older sister, Emily; and their younger brother, Mackworth (drawings by Emily Shore, from Journal of Emily Shore, *revised edition [1898], edited by Arabella and Louisa Shore)*

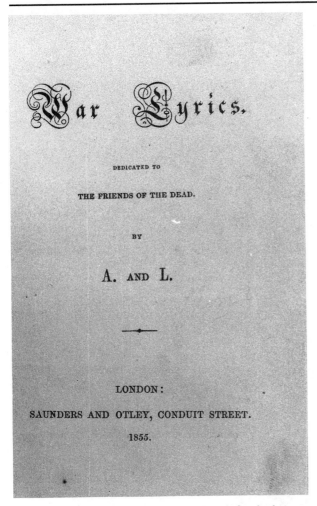

Title page for Arabella and Louisa Shore's first book, a collection of poems about the Crimean War

War Lyrics comprises fifteen poems, each signed with *A.* or *L.*: six are by Arabella and nine by Louisa. In contrast to much Crimean War poetry, only one poem, Arabella's "Inkermann," purports to represent a particular battle. Instead, Arabella and Louisa consistently represent the effects of the war on family members at home, especially women. The dedicatory poem, Louisa's "To the Friends of the Dead," addresses the volume's large intended audience:

> Oh! wives and mothers! sons and brothers,
>   And sisters of the dead!
> And daughters, too, and fathers—who
>   Will not be comforted!

The Crimean War was the first English war to receive extensive media coverage. William Howard Russell's reports in *The Times* (London) stirred up public opinion regarding the management of the troops, and Roger Fenton's photographs captured for the first time the actual faces and places of the war. As idealized representations were replaced with documentary realism, Britain's conception of war was radically altered. Louisa's poem about the charge at Balaclava, like Tennyson's, was written in response to newspaper reports, and its final stanzas describe the readers in England as participating in the event:

> Doubt not, I say, the hearts of all
>   A grander music made,
> When dancing to that funeral,
>   Than ever clarion played.

> And Music in our hearts at home
>   Re-echoes, as we read,
> The rapturous harmonies that come
>   From an immortal deed.

Many of the poems in the volume deal with the responses of women to the Crimean conflict. In Arabella's "The Maiden at Home" a young woman whose lover is fighting in the Crimea worries:

> He who last summer pressed my hand
>   With such a long farewell,
> Now fights in yonder murderous land—
>   Last night perhaps he fell.

She imagines him in various battle scenes and notes that

> In stories of heroic deeds
>   His name is never missed;
> I kiss the word my dim eye reads
>   In the immortal list.

Frustrated by the distance between them, she cries:

> Oh! these dull limits to enlarge,
>   This blank with life to fill!
> Oh! to have been in that grand charge
>   Up Alma's deadly hill!

The grief of the soldier's betrothed is a familiar sentimental trope of war poetry, and this poem fulfills such generic expectations. Yet the "blank" of the speaker's existence, cut off from the excitement of war, realistically designates the peripheral role allotted to most women; and the speaker's irritation at her "dull limits" points to the feminist principles that later became visible in Arabella's work for the woman suffrage movement. Louisa's "When She Went Forth" describes Florence Nightingale, and Arabella's "The British Soldier" takes up questions of gender and patriotic sentiment. The Shore sisters' first volume constitutes the only sustained poetic response by women to the Crimean War and provides a useful contrast with the patriotic bombast of much war poetry written by men. Arabella and Louisa's poems are no less patriotic; but by focusing on the emotional responses of those left at home in England, particularly women, they illuminate the complexity of the public response to the conflict.

In 1859 the sisters published another joint collection, *Gemma of the Isles, a Lyrical Drama, and Other Poems: By A. and L.*; Louisa wrote the title poem. Their mother died that same year, and Mackworth, who had never returned to England, died in 1860. In 1861 Louisa, encouraged by the interest of her classical-scholar father, published a lengthy verse drama about Hannibal that she had drafted when she was twenty-one and had frequently revised and expanded since. The notice of *Hannibal* in *The Athenaeum* (18 May 1861) said that the subject could have been better treated in an epic and was "fettered by the form" of the drama. But the reviewer singled out noteworthy passages and declared that "the writer is unmistakably a poet." The story, and particularly the heroism of the ultimately defeated Hannibal, held particular interest for British readers in the years immediately following the Crimean conflict. Arabella republished the drama in 1898, after Louisa's death, believing that it was her sister's most cherished work; the reviewer for *The Englishwoman's Review* (15 July 1899) considered its "massiveness of thought and expression" out of place in "these days of small things."

After their father's death in 1863 Arabella and Louisa lived together for eight years in the family home in Kent before moving to Berkshire. After the publication of their *Fra Dolcino, and Other Poems* (1870), the title poem of which was by Arabella, Louisa became convinced that there was little audience for their work. For the next twenty years she resisted her sister's urging that they continue to publish.

Throughout the 1870s and 1880s both sisters were involved in liberal causes, most particularly the suffrage movement. In her essay *The Citizenship of Women Socially Considered*, which was published in the *Westminster Review* in July 1874 and reprinted as a pamphlet the same year, Louisa contends that traditional modes of education for women and the social coercion of drawing-room chivalry combine to keep women in an inferior position. She contends that Victorian notions of a woman's appropriate role and essential nature are culturally specific: "Let us remind the upholders *par excellence* of 'feminine delicacy and refinement' how very different are and have been the ideas attached to these words in other ages and other countries, and maintained with obstinate persistence, and confidence that they rest on the immutable sanction of nature and religion." She attacks the social codes governing courtship and marriage and insists that if

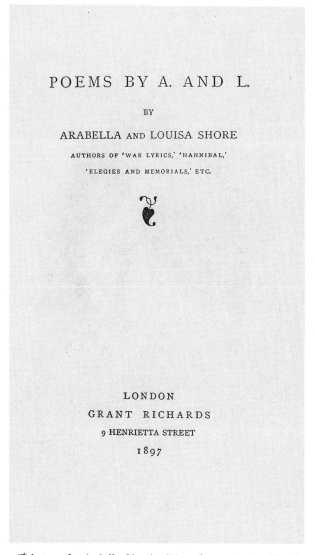

POEMS BY A. AND L.

BY

ARABELLA AND LOUISA SHORE

AUTHORS OF 'WAR LYRICS,' 'HANNIBAL,'
'ELEGIES AND MEMORIALS,' ETC.

LONDON
GRANT RICHARDS
9 HENRIETTA STREET
1897

Title page for Arabella Shore's edition of poems by herself and her deceased sister

women are to exercise their purported ameliorating influence they must be highly educated and free to pursue serious interests. Neither Louisa nor Arabella married, and they lived together until Louisa's death in what Arabella called a "dual life." This arrangement allowed them the intellectual and personal freedom that they advocated for all women. Arabella wrote critical essays on literary topics, and some of her lectures to suffrage organizations were published in journals such as *The Englishwoman's Review*. Her *Dante for Beginners: A Sketch of the "Divina Commedia." With Translations, Biographical and Critical Notices, and Illustrations* (1886) provides her own translations of key passages, as well as historical commentary and simplified literary criticism to guide readers through Dante's work. The sisters became friends with George Meredith in 1873 after John Morley encouraged Louisa to write to the nearly unknown writer, whose work

POEMS

By LOUISA SHORE

With a Memoir by her Sister
ARABELLA SHORE
And an Appreciation by
FREDERIC HARRISON

JOHN LANE: *The Bodley Head*
LONDON & NEW YORK
MDCCCXCVII

Frontispiece and title page for Arabella Shore's posthumous edition of her sister's poems, published in the same year as Poems by
A. and L.

she admired. They corresponded with other literary figures, including Robert Browning.

Louisa's most important lyric poem, *Elegies* (1883), dates from this period. It was highly praised by Browning and Meredith, both of whom saw it in manuscript. After it was rejected by a leading journal, Arabella had it printed privately in 1883. Her prefatory note explains that

> The following verses are an attempt to revive, as far as loving portraiture can do it, two brief lives extinguished many years ago. Little known in the world, and now remembered by few, this sister and brother, Emily and Mackworth Shore, had yet traits of nature which, had time been allowed to the one and happier conditions for due development to the other, might have set their names amongst such as are not forgotten.

The poem consists of three numbered sections; the first describes Emily as "a flame extinguished soon," before she could fulfill her "appointed beauteous task":

> But now her little lifetime seems a dream,
> So long ago, and so unknown she died.
> ....
> Now all that girlhood, now that flushed, intense,
> Young fever, are a whisper of the night,
> A faint sweet resurrection, a strange sense
> Of absence unexplained till morning light.

The longer second section deals with Mackworth, whom Louisa knew better than she had her oldest sister. The essential difficulty of memorial poetry is made explicit in a passage that was frequently quoted in contemporary notices of the poem:

> In what strange lines of beauty should I draw thee?
> In what sad purple dreamshine paint thee true?
> How should I make them see who never saw thee?
> How should I make them know who never knew?

The third section of the poem moves from these highly personal considerations to the general questions of faith that grief raises, and it examines the substantiality of memory:

> The form Love meets advancing through the gloom,
> Is but the reflex of her own desire,
> Flashed on the glass, as in a darkening room
> We meet ourselves.—Love once within the tomb,
> Shall not that reflex of herself expire?
> Can any form our thought may fashion here
> Have life beyond this bounding atmosphere?

The poem promises that "Earth yet shall know, / By a new light, the secret of her past" and envisions a "perfect Race to be." Louisa exhorts these perfected future generations to remember the past:

> Forget not, Earth, when thou shalt stretch thy hands
> In blessing o'er thy happy sons and daughters,
> And lift in triumph thy maternal head,
> Circling the sun with music from all lands,
> In anthems like the noise of many waters—
> Forget not, Earth, thy disappointed Dead!
> Forget not, Earth, thy disinherited!
> Forget not the forgotten! Keep a strain
> Of divine sorrow in sweet undertone
> For all the dead who lived and died in vain!
> Imperial Future, when in countless train
> The generations lead thee to thy throne,
> Forget not the Forgotten and Unknown!

This attention to the lost and forgotten recalls the insistence in *War Lyrics* on the social and national functions of memory, which are here extended to a larger vision of humanity. In his critical appreciation of the work, published in the sisters' collection *Elegies and Memorials* (1890), Frederic Harrison writes that "The dominant and absorbing idea of Louisa Shore in poetry was to treat it as a school for the great problems of life—to hold on to the heroic, to the religious, in poetry—religious, be it said, in a human, not in a theological sense." This reflective and philosophical quality is apparent in much of Louisa's poetry, even when the ostensible subject is highly personal. With George Eliot's "Oh! May I Join the Choir Invisible," and Margaret Woods's "Praise to the Unknown Dead!," Louisa Shore's "Elegies" was included in the Positivist hymnbook *The Service of Man*.

Elegies and Memorials also includes Louisa's "A Requiem," subtitled "On Reading Some Verses about a Poor Woman Seen Carrying the Coffin of her Infant in her Arms to the Burial." Like *Elegies*, it is concerned with the forgotten, the "dead darlings of the past" borne "by disappointed souls" and laid to rest "to no triumphant requiem." Arabella's poems in *Elegies and Memorials* include "'In Memoriam,'" which describes her experience as a reader of Tennyson's 1850 poem:

> My secret finds its twin in yours,
> And in that twinness its relief.
> . . . .
> I thank you—love and loss I've felt,
> As you, and never word would come;
> Till your sweet wand its magic dealt,
> I thought this child of tears was dumb.

After reading Tennyson's poem she says, "An 'In Memoriam' in our hearts, / A marble table, ever dwells."

Arabella's "Young Boatman" describes Mackworth's adventures in Australia, and her "Dejection and Hope" allegorizes her progress and that of her "gold-locked, star-eyed brother" in climbing the mountain of life. Strikingly, Arabella describes herself as "A grey-haired toiler . . . content, for pain / And weariness, with little gain." His striving to satisfy desires that she has stilled in herself ends in disaster, and Hope becomes food for the scavenging wolf of Despair. One purpose of the Shores' memorializing poetry seems to have been the reaffirmation of their lack of interest in material or worldly desires, although the volume also includes explicitly political poems.

The preface to *Elegies and Memorials*, unlike the introductory sections of most of their other books, is unsigned, and it combines references to Louisa's and Arabella's poems as if they were written by one person:

> The two poems called "Lamentations" and the "Story of Woman" were written, perhaps in too much bitterness of spirit, about seventeen years ago; and it may be thankfully said that the "Woman Question" has assumed a very different aspect since then. Not only have many wrongs—and some especially flagrant ones—been redressed, but the whole spirit in which the question is handled is so enlarged and elevated, and woman is herself pressing forwards on so hopeful a path, that in England at least many of these utterances must sound like exaggerations. But the world in general, though it begins to move, has not yet reached such a hill-top of justice and humanity that such appeals can be regarded as uncalled for.

FIRST AND LAST POEMS

BY

ARABELLA SHORE

·

AUTHOR OF

'FRA DOLCINO' AND OTHER POEMS

AND EDITOR OF THE

'JOURNAL OF EMILY SHORE'

LONDON

GRANT RICHARDS

1900

*Title page for Arabella Shore's final book, the first collection
devoted solely to her own poetry*

In the second part of Louisa's "Lamentations"
Mother Earth speaks, blaming man for mistreating
and confining woman:

> Thou madst this queen thy slave,
> In falsehood, fear, and shame;
> . . . .
> Rebellious and reviled,
> Or crouching and caressed,
> A goddess or a child,
> But still a slave confessed,
> Caged in the jealous East, toy-sceptred in the West. . . .

The speaking Earth links the fate of all women
across the globe with that of the fallen woman,
"HER that fell / To shameless shame for thee," and
exhorts Man to "Rise up, a nobler Brother, loose
thy Sister's chain!" Louisa's poem presents some of
the same ideas as her essay *The Citzenship of Women
Socially Considered,* in which she emphasized the
many ways in which men keep women confined.

Arabella's "The Story of Woman" is even
more explicit in its feminism. After listing various
forms of slavery disguised as admiration, such as
the jeweled woman in an Eastern harem and the idealized object of troubadour love poetry, Arabella directly addresses male oppressors on behalf of
women:

> Wide is the world, and scant
> Her plot marked out by you;
> She asks no royal grant,
> For she is free-born too:
> Give her her *human* rights, and see what she can do!

Arabella and Louisa's poems have many thematic and emotive similarities, although Louisa's
tend to be somewhat abstract while Arabella introduces more concrete and topical details. Louisa is
the more skillful poet: her lyrics are technically less
flawed, her rhythms smoother, her word choice
never jarring. Little is known about the dynamics of
the sisters' collaboration, as few manuscript materials survive, but Arabella's memoir of Louisa suggests they frequently discussed their work with each
other. The Shores were writing poetry at a time
when the novel was seen as the dominant genre for
social commentary. Arabella's 1879 essay "The
Novels of George Meredith" in the *British Quarterly
Review* says that the novel is "the successor of the
poem" in "the sense in which that is at once the ef-
flux of the spirit of the age and the interpreter of human nature," and she admits that few readers are
willing to put forth the effort required to understand
poetry. Yet, convinced of their literary merit and intellectual substance, she continued to write poetry
of her own and to publish and republish her sister's
works.

In 1891 the Shores published selections from
the notebooks of their older sister as *Journal of Emily
Shore;* it was well received, and another edition, illustrated with drawings by Emily, appeared in 1898.
As Barbara Timm Gates points out in her 1991 edition, the published journal is not simply Emily's
text: Arabella and Louisa's annotations reshape the
work to fit her sisters' views fifty years after her
death. The extent to which any of Arabella's or
Louisa's poems are the work of a single poet is also
unclear. Because Arabella frequently signed the introductory notes to their volumes and arranged for
their publication, she sometimes appears to be a
controlling editorial presence. Yet Louisa's influ-

ence on her sister's poetry is also apparent over the forty years of their joint publishing career. Their close relationship involved more than purely literary matters: Arabella's warm memoir of her sister recalls "years of the closest, most unbroken union; all the closer, no doubt, that two markedly distinct personalities viewed and handled the stuff of which that life in common was made up." Unfortunately, no written record exists of Louisa's perspective.

Louisa Shore died on 24 May 1895. Her obituary in *The Englishwoman's Review* (15 October 1895) comments that her life "was one of those whose existence adds stability to the woman movement as we know it in England. It was out of homes filled with a rich atmosphere of culture and family affections that the nineteenth century renaissance for women began." In 1897 Arabella published a collection of Louisa's work as *Poems: With a Memoir by Her Sister, Arabella Shore, and an Appreciation by Frederic Harrison.* The volume includes some early unpublished poems, among them two sonnets about the Crimean War. It also includes "Fragments from an Unwritten Novel," written in the 1840s, which, Arabella explains in a note, is not autobiographical but "purely fictitious . . . thrown off in passing moods or youthful imaginative feeling." She says that Louisa's "taste for emotional poetry and for melancholy themes, as well as a want of belief in happiness in general, led her to an involuntary preference for depicting unrequited and despairing attachment." By juxtaposing sentimental and rather derivative poems such as "Like to a Statue," "Life's Jewels," and "My Heart Prostrate" with four poems from *Elegies and Memorials,* the volume highlights the striking absence of conventional love poetry from Louisa's later work. Among the early poems, however, "A Last Avowal," the confession of an aged speaker to the object of her early unrequited love, has great affective power.

Poems also includes several unfinished verse dramas that Louisa apparently kept secret. Arabella's note recounts how she found the fragments tucked away in odd places after Louisa's death:

> The verses were scrawled with pen or pencil in most irregular fashion, often on blank leaves of tradesmen's account-books, on scraps of old letters and memoranda, the pencil notes sometimes almost effaced, and the handwriting not rarely all but illegible. They were covered, moreover, with hundreds of female fancy heads, sometimes very beautiful, which she had through life an irresistible propensity to draw whenever she had pen or pencil in her hand.

"Irene's Dream" opens with Irene, who is obviously a portrait of Emily Shore, narrating a dream in

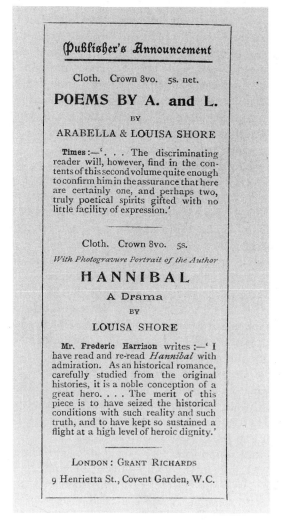

Publisher's announcement in Arabella Shore's First and Last Poems

which she encounters a band of fairies. In another fragment the hero Florestan comes to the fairy valley and falls in love with Irene, who is thought to be mad because she shuns the human world and lives alone. Eventually, according to Arabella's piecing together of the fragments, Irene returns to the human world. There she is deserted by her lover and eventually resolves to improve the human sphere that she has somewhat unwillingly rejoined. Arabella notes that in the later written fragments, in which the heroine's detachment from the human sphere and involvement in the fairy world are detailed, the figure of Irene is to some degree a self-portrait of Louisa. Louisa's retirement from the world and satisfaction in quiet dreaming intensified in her later years, and the energy of the planned drama is clearly in the dream sequences rather than in the projected reform section that is outlined in Arabella's notes and is apparently based on conversations with Louisa.

A second volume edited by Arabella in 1897, *Poems by A. and L.,* includes Louisa's verse drama "Gemma of the Isles," another fairy story, and an expanded version of "Olga," a second dramatic fragment that was published in *Poems*. In "Olga" Arabella adds sections to connect the existing fragments, performing an explicit act of textual collaboration that was surely based on years of conversation and mutual criticism with her sister. In this instance Arabella admits that she has added to her sister's text; there is no way to know what changes she may have introduced elsewhere in her sister's work. Other poems by Louisa include some of the early war lyrics and some translations from French and Portuguese. *Poems by A. and L.* also includes a republication of Arabella's "Fra Dolcino," a series of poems about a Franciscan monk mentioned by Dante who set out to reform the corrupt church.

After republishing all of her sister's poems and fragments, Arabella republished her own in *First and Last Poems* (1900). The volume includes poems originally published in *Gemma of the Isles, a Lyrical Drama, and Other Poems,* in *Fra Dolcino, and Other Poems,* and in *Elegies and Memorials,* as well as some previously unpublished early and late works. Her final poem, "Death and Immortality," written and revised from 1881 to 1899, demonstrates Arabella's strong intellectual commitments. The poem locates the origin of religion in the human need for comfort when faced with the mystery of death. She rejects conventional Christianity and claims that love endures in human memory: "Oh our loved Lost! why lost, when safe ye rest / Shrined in the hearts that cannot cease to see." The personal losses and memories documented in Arabella and Louisa's poems, as in many other Victorian elegiac texts, serve a larger spiritual purpose, according to Arabella:

> O Human Love! when step by step we trace
> Our path, and find at every stage thy place,
> We learn the Deity we cannot see
> Is a more beautiful Humanity.

Belief in a humanistic "one great Law" that governs the natural as well as the social world spurs her rejection of the church in "Fragment From Unwritten Poem (Between Two Creeds)." In addition to these philosophical poems, the volume includes four sonnets written in 1855 about Empress Eugenie, Queen Victoria, Nightingale, and Charlotte Brontë; and a long narrative poem, "Annette Meyers," which details Meyers's seduction and subsequent ill treatment by her lover and her murder of him. Most striking in Arabella's treatment of the murderess is the mingling of love, explicit sexual desire, and hatred that characterizes Meyer's unequal and abusive relationship: "The fiend she hates, the idol she adores, / Joined in one form that still her fancy lures." Although Arabella may not have been as skilled a poet as Louisa, her works contribute to the study of Victorian women's history as well as to late Victorian poetry.

Read autobiographically, Arabella's early poem "The Ungifted," first published in *Gemma of the Isles, a Lyrical Drama, and Other Poems* and republished in *First and Last Poems,* suggests that she was aware of her lesser poetic gifts:

> Nature, gifting, loading others
> From her treasury,
> Siren-sisters, poet-brothers,
> Only left out me.

She says that the burning of her passion goes largely unexpressed, because "From my utterance doth in steam / Half the soul escape," and she longs that she might "For one hour, to one alone, / What I am, appear." The early promise shown by her siblings—Louisa and Arabella frequently describe Mackworth as a poet, although no work by him was ever published—may have contributed to Arabella's taking on the role of editor and promoter of Louisa's poetry.

Arabella Shore died on 9 January 1901. Without her encouragement, assistance, and forcefulness, Louisa Shore's works might never have been published; without the companionship and literary critiques offered by Louisa, Arabella might not have continued to write poetry throughout her life. The complexity of their collaborative relationship can best be appreciated by reading their poems together: shared subjects and images abound in these works. Their explicit attention to women's roles and status and their independent spiritual beliefs make their poetry distinctive, and their elegiac or memorial poetry has political and religious dimensions that transcend the purely personal or topical. The writings of Arabella and Louisa Shore have much to offer students of literature, of Victorian culture, and of women's history.

Reference:

"Miss Louisa Shore," *Englishwoman's Review,* new series (15 October 1895): 269–271.

Elizabeth Eleanor Siddal
(25 July 1829 – 11 February 1862)

Whitney A. Womack
Purdue University

BOOK: *Poems and Drawings of Elizabeth Siddal,* edited by Roger C. Lewis and Mark Samuel Lasner (Wolfville, Canada: Wombat Press, 1978).

In the 1850s and 1860s Elizabeth Siddal was synonymous with Pre-Raphaelitism. Images of Siddal's pale complexion, flowing copper-red hair, long neck, and large-lidded eyes haunt the canvases of the Pre-Raphaelite Brotherhood. She served as a model for paintings by Walter Howell Deverell, William Holman Hunt, John Everett Millais, and Dante Gabriel Rossetti, who eventually married Siddal, his favorite model and muse. Her life has become the stuff of myth and legend, making it difficult for biographers to separate fact from fiction. A continuing morbid fascination with Siddal persists, largely stemming from the many artistic representations of her as a "pale lady of death," from her lingering illnesses and mysterious death, and from the infamous exhumation of her coffin in order to retrieve her husband's buried poetry.

While Siddal has not been forgotten in the years since her death, her artistic and literary achievements have received almost no critical attention. Siddal was a prodigious artist, completing more than one hundred drawings and paintings in just one decade of activity. Her art was admired by some of the most important figures in Victorian culture, including John Ruskin, who became her patron; Robert Browning; Alfred, Lord Tennyson; Ford Madox Brown; Coventry Patmore; and Algernon Swinburne. While art was considered a fine amateur pursuit for ladies in the nineteenth century, for a woman to aspire to a professional career in art was unusual. Despite cultural constraints, Siddal studied art, both with Rossetti and at art school, and exhibited her works alongside other Pre-Raphaelite artists. Siddal's poetic corpus consists of fifteen complete poems plus a few fragments, none of which was published during her lifetime. Although her brother-in-law William Michael Rossetti published all fifteen of Siddal's completed poems in a variety of books and articles between 1895 and 1906, they

Elizabeth Siddal in 1855; drawing by Dante Gabriel Rossetti (Ashmolean Museum, Oxford)

have been excluded from the canon of Pre-Raphaelite poetry and were not collected until 1978. Critics have tended to dismiss Siddal's verses as derivative or as mere confessions of her relationship with Rossetti. While Siddal shared many techniques and themes with male Pre-Raphaelite poets, her poetry also challenges many of their assumptions about gender and provides a new vision of the Pre-Raphaelite woman.

Elizabeth Siddal—known to family and friends as "Lizzie"—was born on 25 July 1829 in Holborn, London, to Charles Crooke Siddall of Sheffield and Elizabeth Elenor (Evans) Siddall of Hornsey. Named after her mother, Lizzie was the third of

Clerk Saunders *(1854), an etching by Siddal inspired by Sir Walter Scott's ballad*

in the morning until eight in the evening, in cramped conditions.

In 1850, while working at Mrs. Tozer's, Siddal was "discovered" by Walter Howell Deverell, a young painter connected to the Pre-Raphaelite Brotherhood, or PRB. Created in 1848 by Rossetti, Hunt, and Millais, who met as students at the Royal Academy, the PRB was a semisecret society of artists, poets, and critics who set out to challenge the conventions of academic art and looked back to Italian and Flemish artists before the High Renaissance for inspiration. They were particularly interested in medieval and literary themes. In 1850 the PRB created a short-lived monthly magazine, *The Germ,* to showcase their art and poetry. They faced criticism and ridicule from the art world, but their revolutionary aesthetic was championed by Ruskin, who wrote two articles for *The Times* (London) in 1851 on their behalf. While the PRB is famous for its representations of women, it is not generally remembered for its female artists and poets. Yet there were important women Pre-Raphaelites, especially Siddal and Christina Rossetti, sister of Dante and Michael, who published many of her poems in *The Germ* under the pseudonym Ellen Alleyne. Although the PRB dissolved in the 1850s, its influence can be seen in art, design, and literature through the end of the nineteenth century.

Hunt later recounted the tale of Deverell's discovery of Siddal, a discovery that would have a profound impact on the PRB:

> He [Deverell] bounded up, marching or rather dancing to and fro about the room and, stopping emphatically, he whispered, "You fellows can't tell what a stupendously beautiful creature I have found. By Jove! she's like a queen, magnificently tall, with a lovely figure, a stately neck, and a face of the most delicate and finished modelling . . . she has grey eyes and her hair is like dazzling copper and shimmers with lustre as she waves it down. And now, where do you think I lighted on this paragon of beauty? Why, in a milliner's back workroom when I went out with my mother shopping . . . I peered over the blind of a glass door at the back of the shop, and there was this unexpected jewel.

Thus began Siddal's career as an artist's model, a profession viewed by Victorian society as questionable if not outright immoral. Like prostitution, modeling involved the conspicuous public display and sale of a woman's body. The sensual and suggestive nature of Pre-Raphaelite art, as well as the predilection of the Pre-Raphaelites to suffer from a sort of Pygmalion syndrome and fall in love with their models, made working as a model for the PRB a par-

eight children. While "Siddall" was the family spelling of the name, Lizzie eventually adopted the spelling "Siddal," apparently at Rossetti's suggestion. The Siddall family possessed a coat of arms (consisting of three birds and the word "Honour"), and their ancestors once lived at Hope Hall, near Sheffield. Siddal's own family was in reduced circumstances, however, and Charles Siddall ran a retail business on the Old Kent Road. In his biographical sketch of Siddal, William Michael Rossetti tried to minimize her shopkeeping roots and her family's ambiguous class position. Her contemporaries tried to downplay the class disparity between the Siddalls and the Rossettis; Hunt stated simply that Lizzie was "gentle, with the manners of a lady." Little is known of Siddal's childhood beyond the fact that she had an ordinary education and, like her brothers and sisters, was apprenticed to learn a trade. Siddal became a milliner's apprentice at Mrs. Tozer's fashionable bonnet shop in Cranbourne Alley, where she earned £24 per year exclusive of board and lodging and worked long hours, often from six

ticularly dubious position by contemporary standards.

Persuaded by Deverell's mother, Siddal sat as Viola for Deverell's *Twelfth Night* (1850). She then modeled for Hunt, first as a British girl in his painting *A Converted British Family Sheltering a Missionary from the Persecution of the Druids* (1850) and then as Sylvia in *Valentine Rescuing Sylvia from Proteus* (1850–1851). Siddal's most legendary modeling job was sitting for Millais's *Ophelia* (1852), one of the best known Pre-Raphaelite paintings. Following the Pre-Raphaelite precept of fidelity to nature, Millais painted the landscape portion of the canvas outdoors, on the banks of a river in Surrey. Later, during the winter months, Millais had Siddal come to his studio to pose as the mad, drowning Ophelia. She wore an antique silver brocade gown and, to create the effect of a drowning woman, floated in a tin bathtub filled with water, which was heated by only a few small candles. On at least one occasion Millais became so engrossed in his painting that he did not notice the candles had gone out; by the time Siddal was pulled from the tub, she was numb and fell ill with a severe cold.

Siddal began modeling for Rossetti sometime late in 1850, first for sketches of his highly erotic painting *The Return of Tibullus to Delia* (1851). Siddal and Rossetti's relationship was soon more than just that of an artist and his model, and there is speculation that the two were secretly engaged as early as 1851. No formal engagement announcement was ever made, and there were apparently no plans made for a wedding. Siddal, who Rossetti nicknamed "The Sid" and "Guggums," spent much of her time at Rossetti's studio at 14 Chatham Place, Blackfriars. William Michael Rossetti and other contemporaries tried to rewrite Dante Gabriel Rossetti and Siddal's unconventional, even scandalous, relationship by suppressing evidence of their long premarital relationship and by comparing them to Robert Browning and Elizabeth Barrett Browning, the great literary romance of the nineteenth century.

After 1852 Siddal modeled exclusively for Rossetti and was known as his "stunner." Christina Rossetti immortalized Siddal as a model in her poem "In an Artist's Studio" (1856): "One face looks out from all his canvases, / One selfsame figure sits or walks or leans . . . / He feeds upon her face by day and night, / And she with true kind eyes looks back on him." In the poem Christina Rossetti critiques the artist's consumption of the model, using almost vampiric imagery to describe this relationship. Siddal posed repeatedly as Beatrice, a literary figure with special significance for Rossetti, who had rearranged his given name (Gabriel Charles Dante) to reflect his passion for and identification with the medieval Italian poet Dante Alighieri. Siddal modeled as Beatrice, Dante Alighieri's unattainable ideal woman, for *Beatrice at a Marriage Feast, Denying her Salutation to Dante* (1851), *The Meeting of Dante and Beatrice* (1852), *Dante Drawing an Angel on the Anniversary of Beatrice's Death* (1853), *Dante's Dream at the Time of the Death of Beatrice* (1856), and, most famously, *Beata Beatrix* (1864). Rossetti's *How They Met Themselves* (1851–1860) provides an eerie premonition of Siddal's early death as a pair of earthly lovers confront their own apparitions.

Siddal was not content to be only a model and by 1852 began to create her own designs, working in oil, watercolor, gouache, pen, and pencil and sharing Rossetti's studio on Chatham Place. Her first completed work, *We are Seven* (1853), based on the poem by William Wordsworth, shows the influence of the angular Pre-Raphaelite style. In 1853 she was at work on her *Self-Portrait* (not completed until 1854) on a painting titled *St. Agnes' Eve,* and on a painting based on Tennyson's "The Lady of Shalott" (1832), depicting the fateful moment when the Lady of Shalott turns to look at Lancelot. Reportedly Siddal had discovered Tennyson, her favorite poet, as a child when she read several of his verses printed on a piece of paper that had been used to wrap butter. Siddal's *The Lady of Shalot* was among the earliest Pre-Raphaelite representations of this poem and is the only one to depict a correct weaving technique. Siddal drew several other pieces inspired by Tennyson's poetry and attracted the attention of Emily Tennyson, the poet's wife, who reportedly wanted her to do illustrations for the 1855 Moxon edition of Tennyson's *Poems,* although the publisher did not include any illustrations by Siddal. Siddal continued to look to literature for inspiration, completing a drawing of *Pippa Passes the Loose Women* (1854), based on a scene from Robert Browning's poem *Pippa Passes* (1841), and a woodblock etching and later a watercolor of *Clerk Saunders* (1854–1857), based on one of Sir Walter Scott's ballads. *Clerk Saunders* is taken from the story of a young man who is killed by the brothers of his beloved and later appears to her as a ghost. *Clerk Saunders* was part of Siddal's ambitious (but unfinished) project to illustrate Scott's collection of border ballads, *Minstrelsy of the Scottish Border* (1802), and was later purchased by the president of Harvard University, Charles Edward Norton.

By all accounts Rossetti was extremely supportive of Siddal's artistic endeavors and admired her work. In a letter to Ford Madox Brown in 1854 Rossetti wrote that "Her power of designing even increases greatly, and her fecundity of invention and

Dante Gabriel Rossetti, the Pre-Raphaelite poet and painter whom Siddal married in 1860

facility are quite wonderful, much greater than mine." They often tackled the same subjects, and in 1856 they each produced a painting depicting a medieval woman seeing a knight off to battle: Siddal's *Lady Affixing a Pennant to a Knight's Spear* and Rossetti's *Before the Battle.* The two artists even collaborated on a painting, *Sir Galahad at the Shrine of the Holy Grail* (1855–1857). The inscription of the painting reads "EES inv. EES & DGR del.," meaning that the composition was created by Siddal and the painting was executed by both of them. Rossetti completed a number of interesting sketches of Siddal in the act of painting, including *Rossetti Sitting to Elizabeth Siddal* (1853) and *A Lady Seated at an Easel* (c. 1854).

Although some later critics, most notably Oswald Doughty, dismissed Rossetti's praise for Siddal as lovesick rantings, Ruskin recognized her talents and corroborated Rossetti's high opinion of her art. Ruskin and Siddal first met on 11 April 1855, after he had purchased nearly all of her drawings from Rossetti. Ruskin proposed a patronage agreement, whereby he would settle £150 per annum on her and take her art works up to that value. Ruskin, who nicknamed Siddal "Ida" after the heroine of Tennyson's poem *The Princess: A Medley* (1847), gave her instruction in oil techniques and encouraged

Rossetti and Siddal to marry in order to conform to propriety.

Siddal soon suspended her art work because of illness. Always in poor health, Siddal had become alarmingly ill in 1854 while visiting Barbara Leigh Smith's country estate at Scalands. Smith unsuccessfully urged Siddal to either enter a hospital in Sussex or return to London and enter Florence Nightingale's Harley Street Sanitorium. She was seen by several doctors, who variously diagnosed her with consumption, curvature of the spine, neuralgia, and phthisis and alternately prescribed both stimulants and opiates. When Siddal's symptoms returned in 1855, Ruskin took charge of her health care and sent her to be examined by the eminent physician Sir Henry Acland, who could find no organic disease and claimed that her illness was simply the result of "mental power long pent up and now overtaxed" and prescribed the "rest cure," a remedy often suggested for ambitious or artistic women. Ruskin financed a trip to the south of France during the winter of 1855–1856 to help restore Siddal's health, with the admonition to her that "you must try to make yourself as simple as a milkmaid as you can, and only draw when you can't help it." Siddal later traveled to British health resorts at Bath, Hastings, Clevedon, and Matlock, where she tried a hydropathic cure. Her continuing ill health led her friend Georgiana Burne-Jones, wife of the painter Edward Burne-Jones, to ask in bewilderment "How was it possible for her to suffer so much without developing a specific disease?" Some biographers of the Pre-Raphaelites, specifically Helen Rossetti Angeli and Doughty, have accused Siddal of being a hypochondriac who used her illnesses to lure and manipulate Rossetti, though there is no proof to substantiate these claims. By the middle of 1857, Siddal had to give up Ruskin's pension because her health prevented her from fulfilling her part of the contract.

The high point of Siddal's artistic career was the Pre-Raphaelite Exhibition at Russell Place, Fitzroy Square, in 1857. A number of her paintings and drawings were on display, including *We are Seven, Pippa Passes the Loose Women, Clerk Saunders, The Haunted Tree,* and *Study of a Head.* Later in 1857 several of Siddal's pieces were chosen for a traveling exhibition of British art that visited America. Also in 1857 Siddal spent several months studying at the School of Art in Sheffield.

While Siddal's artistic career is fairly well documented, the evidence about her poetic career is much more sketchy and it is very difficult to date her poems with any certainty. Scholars generally assume that she began writing sometime in 1854, sev-

Dante Gabriel Rossetti's painting Beata Beatrix *(circa 1864–1870), a posthumous*
tribute to Siddal, who is depicted as Dante Alighieri's Beatrice (Tate Gallery, London)

eral years after she began her association with Rossetti and the PRB. Roger Lewis and Mark Samuel
Lasner, the editors of the only complete edition of
Siddal's poetry, believe, however, that Siddal had
probably been writing poetry since her childhood.
While Siddal continued to write up until her death
in 1862 and completed fifteen poems, there seems to
have been no attempt by Siddal or Rossetti to seek
their publication during her lifetime, and they apparently were unknown outside of the family. In
fact there is no recorded mention of her poetry until
three years after her death, when Rossetti approached his sister Christina about the possibility of
including six of Siddal's poems in her forthcoming
volume, *The Prince's Progress* (1866). Christina rejected the proposition, however, claiming, in a letter
to Dante, that the poems were "almost too hope-
lessly sad for publication." Rossetti then put the poems aside for the rest of his life. After Rossetti's
death his brother, William Michael Rossetti, titled
the poems and published them in series of books

and articles on the Pre-Raphaelites: *Family Letters and
a Memoir of Dante Gabriel Rossetti* (1895); *Ruskin: Rossetti: Pre-Raphaelitism* (1899); "Dante Rossetti and
Elizabeth Siddal," in *Burlington Magazine* (1903); and
Some Reminiscences (1906). There is no way of knowing if Siddal considered these poems finished and
ready for publication.

Many critics have read Siddal's poetry as simple autobiographical confessions of her troubled relationship with Rossetti; Doughty, for example, describes her poems as "plaintive little love-sick
verses, all pathos and self-pity." Like Christina Rossetti, Siddal employed a deceptively simple and
primitive style, which has undoubtedly contributed
to such reductive interpretations. Siddal shared the
Pre-Raphaelite interest in the ballad tradition, and
several of her poems, particularly "True Love," reflect the influence of Scott's border ballads. The two
major themes of Siddal's poetry are the "passing of
love" (the title given to one of her poems) and death,
and these themes are often interwoven. Many of her

poems represent melancholic women trapped in death-in-life situations who yearn for an escape from this world.

Siddal allows her women personae to exhibit anger, defiance, and self-reliance, characteristics not often associated with Victorian womanhood. In "Love and Hate" the speaker is a betrayed woman who does not sit by quietly and passively but instead venomously rails against the lover who "stole my life away." She tells her lover that "The blasts of heaven shall strike thee down / Ere I will give thee grace" and that though she once had a "great love" for him, "now great hate / Sits grimly in its place." The poem "Dead Love" is one woman's warning to another about the fleeting nature of beauty and love. A "bonny face," the speaker argues, may attract a man, but it will not guarantee constancy or lasting love, for "love was born to an early death / And is so seldom true." The speaker asserts that only in heaven can one find true love:

> Sweet, never weep for what cannot be,
> For this God has not given.
> If the merest dream of love were true
> Then, sweet, we should be in heaven,
> And this is only earth, my dear,
> Where true love is not given.

Christina Rossetti claimed that this was her favorite of Siddal's poems, "piquant as it is with cool bitter sarcasm." Siddal's "At Last," one of her longest poems, has a strong-willed female speaker who is dying of a "great love." Despite her condition, the speaker has the presence of mind to give her mother detailed instructions for her burial and to make provisions for her young son.

Two of Siddal's most intriguing and satirical poems, "Gone" and "The Lust of the Eyes," are written from a male perspective. In "Gone" the speaker is a male lover who has lost (perhaps by death) his beloved, his "tender dove," but remembers her only by the material objects he associates with her; he longs "To touch the glove upon her tender hand, / To watch the jewel sparkle in her ring." In the speaker's memories his beloved has no voice, agency, or body.

Siddal's "The Lust of the Eyes" provides interesting commentary on the voyeurism of the Pre-Raphaelite poets. The superficial and sadistic speaker of the poem makes it clear that he cares only for his beloved's outward appearance and that for him love is not transcendent but merely physical and earthly: "I care not for my Lady's soul / Though I worship before her smile; / I care not where be my Lady's goal / When her beauty shall lose its while." While he is content to gaze at her

"wild eyes" now, he matter-of-factly states that he will abandon her when "their starlike beauty dies." In the final stanza the speaker wonders "who shall close my Lady's eyes / And who shall fold her hands," implying that she will die from his betrayal. The poem can be read as a biting indictment of the male Pre-Raphaelite artists' adoration of the youth and beauty of their models.

Critics have rightfully identified "A Year and a Day" (c. 1857), Siddal's longest poem, as her masterpiece. The poem is Siddal's retelling of the story of Ophelia, who, in the second half of the nineteenth century, had become an important cultural icon. There were competing Pre-Raphaelite representations of Ophelia, including the Millais painting that Siddal had modeled for and one by Arthur Hughes, both of which were shown at the 1852 Royal Academy Exhibit. In "A Year and a Day" Siddal gives her Ophelia-like speaker (who is never named) a context, subjectivity, and voice to express her frustrated desire, all of which are denied to her in artistic and photographic representations. The poem begins with the irony that although it is springtime, the season of rebirth and renewal, the speaker yearns for death as an escape from this world. The landscape described in the poem—with its river and tall grasses—is reminiscent of Millais's painting. In the second stanza the speaker lies in the grass and imagines it folding over to cover her body, as if she were already in the grave:

> I lie among the tall green grass
> That bends above my head
> And covers up my wasted face
> And folds me in its bed
> Tenderly and lovingly
> Like grass above the dead

In the third stanza she tries to articulate her troubled mental state, explaining that "Dim phantoms of an unknown ill / Float through my tired brain; / The unformed visions of my life / Pass by in ghostly train." The speaker has difficulty distinguishing between reality and memory; when a shadow falls on the grass, she is reminded of "The shadow of my dear love's face— / so far and strange it seems." In the final stanza a silence and calmness overcomes the speaker, and she imagines herself lying in the grass "Like beaten corn of grain," describing the violent harvesting process whereby the best part of the wheat is beaten out and the rest is left to fertilize the fields. The implication is that the best part of the speaker, her love, has been beaten out of her, leaving her as a mere shell of her former self.

Little is known about Siddal's life during 1858 and 1859, what might be called her "lost years."

POEMS
AND DRAWINGS
OF
ELIZABETH
SIDDAL

Edited by Roger C. Lewis
and
Mark Samuels Lasner

THE
WOMBAT PRESS
1978

Frontispiece—a self-portrait (1853–1854) by Siddal—and title page for the first complete collection of Siddal's poetry

Sometime during 1858, for reasons not fully known, Siddal and Rossetti's engagement of more than seven years was abruptly called off. There has been speculation that the break was prompted by Rossetti's infidelities with his other models, particularly with Fanny Cornforth and Annie Miller. For the twenty-two months that Siddal and Rossetti were estranged, there is almost no information about her life, and it is presumed that she spent this period with her family in Southwark. Siddal's father died in 1859, the same year she turned thirty. His death left his widow to tend to the family shop and to support her other unmarried children (including three daughters and Harry, her mentally handicapped son). Without a patron or the support of Rossetti, Siddal faced an uncertain future.

In early 1860 Siddal was desperately ill again and called for Rossetti, reportedly to say good-bye. Rossetti, believing she was on the verge of death, rushed to her side in Hastings and renewed his marriage proposal. Fulfilling a promise made years earlier, Rossetti married Siddal on 23 May 1860 at St. Clement's Church, Hastings, in a ceremony performed by a Reverend T. Nightingale. The wedding came as a surprise to the Rossetti family, who were informed by a hasty note written by Rossetti the day before the ceremony. Christina reported to Bessie Parkes, a close family friend, that "Gabriel has married poor Lizzie at last." With Siddal's health somewhat restored, the newlyweds traveled to Paris and Boulogne for their honeymoon. After they returned to their newly expanded quarters at 14 Chatham Place, Siddal became pregnant with their first child. On 2 May 1861 she delivered a stillborn daughter. Although there are stories that Siddal underwent a period of temporary insanity, in which she acted as if the child were alive, later in 1861 she was well enough to spend time with Jane Morris, wife of poet and artist

275

William Morris, at Red House and was at work on a mural project in Brighton. Siddal did, however, become increasingly dependent on laudanum, an addictive opium-based medication, during this period, taking up to one hundred drops at a time to help her sleep and keep down food. William Michael Rossetti speculates that it was around this time and under the influence of laudanum that Siddal wrote the poem "Lord May I Come" (c. 1861). The speaker of the poem is a dying woman who paradoxically equates life to night and death to day and beseeches God to remember her and take her in "Holy death."

On the evening of 10 February 1862 Siddal dined out at Sablonniere Hotel, Leicester Square with Rossetti and Swinburne, who had become a dear friend of Siddal's. Siddal, who may have been pregnant again, and Rossetti returned home together at eight o'clock, but Rossetti went out again. When he returned after eleven o'clock, he found Siddal unconscious, with an empty laudanum vial on her bed table. The renowned surgeon John Marshall and three other physicians were called to her side and attempted to pump her stomach. Despite their efforts, Siddal died at twenty minutes after seven on the morning of 11 February. Although a coroner's inquest on 12 February returned a verdict of accidental death, all of the evidence points to the fact that Siddal committed suicide. She apparently had pinned a note to her nightdress that asked Rossetti to "take care of Harry," her simple-minded youngest brother, but it was reportedly removed by Rossetti's friend, Ford Madox Brown so that the family could avoid the stigma that came with suicide. The circumstances of her death were not completely secret, though, and an obituary in the *Sheffield Telegraph* (28 February 1862) contains a veiled reference to her laudanum addiction, claiming that Siddal had "a secret habit which has proved fatal to many."

Siddal was buried in the Rossetti family plot, next to Dante's father, in West Highgate Cemetery on 17 February. A distraught Rossetti placed the sole manuscript of his poems in her coffin before the burial, tucking them between her cheek and the folds of her hair. Rossetti claimed that since the poems were chiefly inspired by and addressed to Siddal, she should have them with her always. There were rumors that Rossetti saw Siddal's ghost every night for two years after her death and he quit their apartment at Chatham Place because it reminded him of Siddal. He moved to Tudor House, 16 Cheyne Walk, Chelsea, which he shared with Swinburne and the writer George Meredith. During the spiritualist craze of the 1860s Rossetti even attempted to contact Siddal through a spirit medium. Rossetti painted *Beata Beatrix* in part as a tribute to his dead

wife, his Beatrice. The painting depicts Beatrice, eyes closed and head lifted toward the sky, at the very moment of her death as she is conveyed from earth to heaven. A dove, Rossetti's symbol for Siddal, drops a red poppy in Beatrice's hand; the poppy traditionally symbolizes both sleep and death, but it is also obviously connected to opium. When Rossetti died in 1882, Theodore Watts-Dunton's obituary in the *Athaneum* (15 April 1882) claimed that Rossetti "felt her [Siddal's] death very acutely and for a time ceased to write or take any interest in poetry. Like Prospero, indeed, he buried his wand. . . ."

In 1869 Rossetti decided to return to his poetry and to retrieve the poems that had been buried with Siddal seven years earlier. Rossetti, who had never visited Siddal's grave, dispatched a friend, Charles Augustus Howell, to exhume the body and recover the poems. On 10 October, Howell had the grave disinterred. Part of the Siddal legend is that when the coffin was opened, the witnesses found her body perfectly preserved, looking as if she were still alive. Her famous red hair, according to the legend, was as brilliant as ever and had continued to grow after death, filling the coffin. Three pages from the exhumed manuscript survive, one of which is in the British Library. Rossetti published these recovered works in his *Poems* (1870), the volume that prompted Robert Buchanan's famous essay in *Contemporary Review* (October 1871), "The Fleshly School of Poetry," condemning Rossetti's "fleshliness" and eroticism. This essay contributed to Rossetti's nervous breakdown in 1872, which led him to attempt suicide by a laudanum overdose, just as his beloved Lizzie had done ten years earlier. He never remarried and died of Bright's disease on Easter Sunday, 9 April 1882.

Since her death Siddal has maintained an ambiguous place in popular imagination, and her story has been taken up and rewritten by each succeeding generation. She has been understood alternately as a victim, a feminist, an incubus, and a heroine. Her popularity soared in the 1890s when cheap platinotype reproductions of Rossetti's paintings were made widely available, making her a cultural icon. Critic Jan Marsh compares the impact of these reproductions to posters of celebrities such as Marilyn Monroe in the later twentieth century. Wilde and other members of the Decadent movement were strongly attracted to the ghostly image of Siddal, the famous "pale lady of death." In 1898 William Michael Rossetti, who was gradually publishing Siddal's own poems, capitalized on her popularity and name recognition by titling a new edition of Dante Gabriel Rossetti's poetry "The Siddal Edition." In the twentieth century Siddal became the subject of biographies and a character in countless novels and films. Violet Hunt's biography *The Wife of Rossetti* (1932) was based largely on hearsay and personal reminiscences of the remaining Pre-Raphaelites and their descendants. Hunt claimed her goal was to depict the real Elizabeth Siddal, and in the biography she paints Siddal as a tragic victim, asserting in her preface that "Like another Iphigenia, she was sacrificed and slain that the PRB might conquer and live." Inspired by Hunt's biography and a revival of interest in the Pre-Raphaelites, the modernist poet H. D. wrote a fictional autobiography of Siddal, "White Rose and the Red" (1947–1948), which was never published. Siddal is also a chief character in Paula Betchelor's novel *Angel with Bright Wings* (1957), Paddy Kitchen's novel *The Golden Veil: A Novel Based on the Life of Elizabeth Siddal* (1981), Gillian Allnutt's seven-part poem *Lizzie Siddal: Her Journal* (1981), and William J. Palmer's mystery novel *The Hoydens and Mr. Dickens* (1997). Film depictions of Siddal and the Pre-Raphaelites include Ken Russell's film biography *The Private Life of Dante Gabriel Rossetti* (1969) and a six-part BBC miniseries, *The Love School* (1979).

While Siddal will likely remain a figure veiled in mystery and legend, she should also be studied as a woman who challenged Victorian gender constraints and pursued professional careers in modeling, art, and literature. While her poems are few, they are fascinating revisions of traditional Pre-Raphaelite themes and ideals. Siddal's poems strive to give a voice to and context for the idealized and silent heroines in male Pre-Raphaelite art and poetry. Her depictions of angry and defiant women who voice their discontent are unusual in Victorian women's poetry. Serious critical reassessment of Siddal's poems has been hampered by their inaccessibility though in recent years they have started to be anthologized. The one edition of Siddal's complete poems, Lewis and Lasner's *Poems and Drawings of Elizabeth Siddal* (1987), was published by a small press and had a limited run of only five hundred copies. William Michael Rossetti claimed that "one must fairly pronounce her to have been a woman of unusual capacities, and worthy of being espoused to a painter and poet," but she is worthy of being remembered not just as the wife of Rossetti but as a talented painter and poet in her own right.

Bibliography:
William Fredeman, *Pre-Raphaelitism: A Biblio-Critical Guide* (Cambridge, Mass.: Harvard University Press, 1965);

Biographies:
Violet Hunt, *The Wife of Rossetti: Her Life and Death* (London: Bodley Head, 1932);
Jan Marsh, *The Legend of Elizabeth Siddal* (London & New York: Quartet, 1989).

References:
Helen Rossetti Angeli, *Dante Gabriel Rossetti: His Friends and Enemies* (London: Hamish Hamilton, 1949);
Maggie Berg, "A Neglected Voice: Elizabeth Siddal," *Dalhousie Review,* 60 (1980): 151–56;
Susan P. Casteras and Alicia Craig Faxon, *Pre-Raphaelite Art in Its European Context* (London: Associated University Presses, 1995);
Deborah Cherry and Griselda Pollock, "Woman as Sign in Pre-Raphaelite Literature: The Representation of Elizabeth Siddall [*sic*]," in *Vision and Difference: Femininity, Feminism, and Histories of Art,* edited by Pollock (London: Routledge, 1988), pp. 91–114;
Sandra M. Donaldson, "'Ophelia' in Elizabeth Siddal Rossetti's Poem 'A Year and a Day'," *The Pre-Raphaelite Review,* 2 (1981): 127–133;
Oswald Doughty, *A Victorian Romantic: Dante Gabriel Rossetti* (London: Frederick Muller, 1949);
Alicia Craig Faxon, *Dante Gabriel Rossetti* (New York: Abbeville Press, 1989);
Lila Hanft, "Woman 'in an artist's studio': Pre-Raphaelitism, Female Authorship, and the Construction of Gender," dissertation, Cornell University, 1991, pp. 143–246;
William Holman Hunt, *Pre-Raphaelitism and the Pre-Raphaelite Brotherhood,* volumes 1 and 2 (London: Chapman & Hall, 1913), pp. 61, 70,–73, 349;
Jan Marsh, *Pre-Raphaelite Sisterhood* (New York: St. Martin's Press, 1985);
Marsh, *Pre-Raphaelite Women: Images of Femininity* (New York: Harmony Press, 1987), pp. 21–24, 90–99, 109–110, 138–142;
Lynn Pearce, *Woman/Image/Text: Readings in Pre-Raphaelite Art and Literature* (Toronto: University of Toronto Press, 1991);
Roger Peattie, "William Michael Rossetti and the Siddalls," *Journal of Pre-Raphaelite and Aesthetic Studies,* 2 (1989): 19–26;
William Michael Rossetti, "Dante Rossetti and Elizabeth Siddal," *Burlington Magazine,* 3 (1903): 273–295;
Frances Winwar, *Poor Splendid Wings: The Rossettis and their Circle* (New York: Blue Ribbon Books, 1933).

Menella Bute Smedley
(1820? - 1877)

Deborah A. Logan
Western Kentucky University

BOOKS: *The Maiden Aunt* (Boston: Littell, 1848; London, 1849);

The Story of a Family (London: Hoby, 1851; Boston: Littell, 185?);

The Use of Sunshine, a Christmas Tale (London, 1852; New York: Appleton, 1852);

Nina. A Tale for the Twilight (London, 1853);

Lays and Ballads from English History (London: Lumley, 1856);

The Story of Queen Isabel, and Other Verses (London: Bell & Daldy, 1863);

Twice Lost (London: Virtue Brothers, 1863; Boston: Loring, 1864);

Linnet's Trial (Boston: Loring, 1864; London: Virtue Brothers, 1871);

A Mere Story (London, 1865);

The Colville Family (London, 1867);

Poems (London: Strahan, 1868);

Poems Written for a Child (London: Strahan, 1868);

Child-Nature (London: Strahan, 1869);

Child-World (London: Strahan, 1869);

Other Folks' Lives (London: Strahan, 1869);

Two Dramatic Poems (London: Macmillan, 1874);

Silver Wings and Golden Scales (London & New York: Cassell, Petter, Galpin, 1877).

OTHER: "A Very Woman," in *Seven Tales by Seven Authors,* edited by Frank E. Smedley (London, 1849), pp. 268–332;

Boarding-Out and Pauper Schools Especially for Girls, edited, with an introduction, by Smedley (London: King, 1875).

Born in Great Marlow, Buckinghamshire, Menella Bute Smedley was the daughter of Edward Smedley, a clergyman, writer, and tutor, and Mary Hume Smedley. Sources differ about Menella's exact year of birth, which is placed between 1815 and 1820; during childhood her fragile health necessitated her living in Tenby for several years, presumably with relatives. The oldest of five children, Menella was later educated at home, receiving a thorough grounding in the classics—a rare privilege for a Victorian girl—that served her well in her writing career. The family lived in London until her father's failing health forced his early retirement to Dulwich. Like many Victorian daughters Smedley assumed her father's professional responsibilities—acting as his "amenuensis," according to one source—as his health continued to deteriorate.

Literary interests were endemic to the Smedley family, providing influences that helped shape Menella's writing career. An encyclopedia editor, Edward Smedley's only volume of poems was published posthumously, while Menella's brother Frank is best known for his novel, *Frank Farleigh.* More directly, Smedley's Aunt Hart, who wrote children's literature, encouraged her first efforts at writing, which were published under the pseudonym "S. M." Smedley, who never married, lived a productive life as a writer of poetry, novels, stories, and plays and as a philanthropist devoted to the education and training of pauper children. Several of Smedley's books are geared toward children, such as *Poems Written for a Child* (1868), *Child-World* (1869), and *Silver Wings and Golden Scales* (1877).

Smedley's interest in children assumed a more practical form in the 1870s when she became a district visitor to pauper schools. Seeking to improve education opportunities for pauper girls, Smedley's work with Mrs. Nassau Senior, an inspector of the local government board, resulted in a Blue Book on the topic (1873–1874) and, in 1875, *Boarding-Out and Pauper Schools Especially for Girls,* for which Smedley edited and wrote an introduction. Earlier, a letter to the reformist periodical *The Magdalen's Friend* (1862) signed by M. S. B. (one of various pseudonyms used by Smedley) pleads eloquently that poorhouse girls be permitted to possess a small amount of cash as a preventive against their being forced into prostitution in times of economic duress: the correspondent "ventured to intrude these remarks," hoping to "prevent the inmates being exposed to the temptations which beset the friendless and destitute." Smedley's use of various pseudonyms throughout her life makes identifying her as the author of this letter both speculative and plausible. Its content is

with "The Conquest of England," the first part of this collection features poems recounting the exploits of Geoffrey of Anjou, Earl Strongbow, Eleanor of Bretagne, Henry III, and King John of France, some comprised of two or three lays. The Norman Conquest and reign of William the Conqueror marks the bloody beginning of English history:

> Duke William Stood on the Norman shore,
> With all his merry men round;
> And he will sail the blue seas o'er,
> To land on English ground.
>
> Saint Edward made him, ere he died,
> Heir to the English throne;
> But Saxon Harold, in his pride,
> Hath seized it for his own.

After detailing the Battle of Hastings, the narrative concludes by describing a monument, ancient yet still erect, "eloquent / Of Harold's fame and fall."

Recording another pivotal moment in English history, "The English Merchant and the Saracen Lady" traces the adventures of Gilbert à Becket. Taken captive on a voyage to the Holy Land, he falls in love with Zarina, a Saracen maid "Of virtue and beauty rare," and is so enamored that he learns her language in order to teach her Christianity. She converts because of her love for him and plots their escape to England; but their plans are thwarted, and Zarina is imprisoned while Gilbert escapes to "the noblest . . . of all earthly lands." Several years pass before Zarina escapes, running to the harbor weeping and repeating the only English word she knows: "London." In the chivalric style typical of the period, the sailors vow,

> . . . let it never be said that men
> Look'd on a woman in sore distress,
> And gave no aid to her feebleness!—
> The maiden shall sail with us!

After many months of begging her way across Europe Zarina arrives in London, relying now on Gilbert's name as her only means of communication. The strange story of the beautiful foreigner who wanders London's streets early and late calling his name finally reaches Gilbert, who

> . . . took that happy wanderer home,
> He placed her at his side;
> O'er desert plain, and o'er ocean's foam,
> She hath come, with her changeless love and faith;
> And now there is nothing can part, save death,
> The bridegroom and the bride!

After Zarina's heathen name is changed to Mathilda, the couple is married in a Christian ceremony.

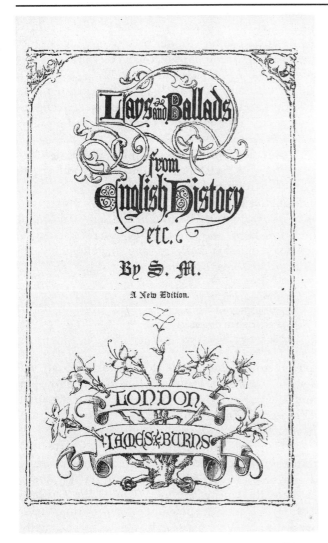

Title page for Menella Bute Smedley's 1856 collection of poems that recount the stories of English and Scottish royalty

consistent with her interest in the well-being of young girls made sexually vulnerable by poverty and orphanage, an interest more fully articulated in her 1875 introduction to *Boarding-Out and Pauper Schools*.

Little else is known about the personal details of Menella Bute Smedley's life, prompting one source to conclude that the writer is best known through her literature. Smedley's literary themes demonstrate her interest in English history, myths and fairy tales, Irish culture (which forms the social backdrop for the 1852 novel *The Use of Sunshine, a Christmas Tale*), Italian independence (as exemplified in the 1863 novel *Twice Lost* and selected poems), gender issues, religious faith, and death. *Lays and Ballads from English History* (1856), beautifully illustrated by engravings depicting knights in armor and ladies veiled in draperies, methodically traces English monarchical history reign by reign. Opening

Their union is later blessed by one who becomes a significant figure in British history, as the author explains in the notes accompanying the poem, the "famous Thomas à Becket, archbishop of Canterbury in the reign of Henry II." One of Smedley's earlier novels, *Nina. A Tale for the Twilight* (1853), employs similar themes of abducted girls, valiant Christian soldiers, seraglios and orientalism, pirates and ruffians, and political intrigues involving monarchical succession.

The second part of *Lays and Ballads* features poems treating Robert the Bruce and Douglas of Scottish history. Bruce's tragic death results in Sir James's transporting his heart to its final resting place in Palestine, again emphasizing the strong element of Christianity undergirding the history depicted in this volume. The themes of love that transcends all boundaries, of interactions between Christian and "heathen" values, of the exoticism of Middle Eastern cultures, and of the imperialist pride that casts England as the world's greatest nation are addressed elsewhere in Smedley's work, although with less of the unquestioning celebration of British values than is evident in this collection.

The title poem of *The Story of Queen Isabel, and Other Verses* (1863) features a long narrative stylistically similar to the lays and ballads of the 1856 volume. Notable in this collection is Smedley's increasingly vocal criticism of restrictive gender roles and inequities, a social standard romanticized through the medieval courtly love tradition and legitimated by Christian precepts. Although "scarce fifteen," Princess Isabel lives in the castle of her betrothed in order that

> . . . she might learn his ways,
> Make her smooth brow a mirror for his smile,
> And practise, ere she vow'd, a wife's submission.
> Wives should have grown all perfect by such practice.
> Perhaps they wearied in the exercise. . . .

Like the Pre-Raphaelites and Alfred, Lord Tennyson in his *Idylls of the King,* Smedley participated in the neomedievalism popular during the mid- and late-Victorian period. But the promotion of Christian values so central to her writing frequently borders on didacticism, and Smedley was unwilling to address the connections between religion and gender roles that are more apparent to modern readers. A typical Victorian daughter in her devotion to her curate father and his mission, Smedley, as her work with pauper girls attests, channeled her Christian beliefs into more practical, rather than literary, modes of reform. Her literary themes, on the other hand, while promoting Christian values, also depict strong heroines who are loyal and courageous and do not hesitate to confront life-threatening events in defense of their convictions. The novels *Twice Lost* (1863) and *Linnet's Trial* (1864) and the tale "A Very Woman," (1849) for example, feature heroines who are drawn in terms of strength, loyalty, and intellectual vigor rather than feminine fragility.

Smedley is not without spiritual doubt, however. "Out of the Depths" appeals to God but "In vain our strong cries touch the Throne": "We faint beneath this burning sky, / Upon this barren steep, . . . We fail beside this darken'd bed, / Where dies our life's last light." As is typical of Smedley, even in spiritual doubt her concerns range beyond herself to incorporate souls throughout the world:

> Souls we would give our souls to save,
> Are Wandering far and long:
> Ah, shut them in the sinless grave,
> Life does them such deep wrong!

The poem concludes with the comfort of God's response but also a reminder that doubt and pain and the lack of peace on earth are inevitable: "Yea, strive, and shrink, and die; / I spare thee not a single tear, / Yet fear not,—*It is I.*"

Other poems in the 1863 volume attest to Smedley's fascination with Italian independence, an interest shared by her contemporary, Elizabeth Barrett Browning, in her *Casa Guidi Windows* (1851). "Cavour" depicts the widow of the patriot who died at Villafranca. In her grief she melodramatically rejects onlookers' pity, proclaiming wildly, "Here lies Cavour; a man / Who built the throne of Italy, and died." Smedley laments another Italian patriot in "Garibaldi at Varignano," a general berated by his country even as he fought for her independence: "She struck him who struck not again, / But fell while shouting her name." There may be rest for the dead, but not for those left behind:

> Can you give him back to his Past,
> Crush'd by your hand, for your sake?
> . . . .
> Chain'd on the soil he saved
> And conquer'd at last, by his own!

With a final appeal to "Italy, royal and free, / Forget not the means in the end!," the poet acknowledges the political controversies surrounding Garibaldi. Yet her admiration for him continues undiminished in three subsequent poems: "An Anniversary, September 7, 1860" ("Shout for royal Victor! let your *vivas* ring! / Shout for Garibaldi, greater than a king!"); "September 7, 1862"; and

"Garibaldi Impeached. September, 1862." Smedley's haunting romance, *Twice Lost,* presents a more fully developed account of Italy's fight for independence. Ranging from South America to England, from Wales and Ireland to Italy, and recounting the lives of several generations of families involved in the struggle that so compellingly captured the writer's imagination, *Twice Lost* attests to Smedley's skill as a storyteller, a skill only hinted at in her shorter poems.

Poems (1868) offers the most comprehensive collection of Smedley's poetry. The poet's fascination with characters of mythic proportions receives clearer definition in "A Character" whose qualities, interestingly, do not include knightly heroics or aristocratic connections. "So noble that he cannot see / He stands in aught above the rest," he rejects fame and praise; he is uninterested in contests of physical prowess, though "never passing by a woe, / Nor sitting still to watch a wrong." He is a person of sharp insight and faith, of

> Out-looking eyes that seek and scan,
> Ready to love what they behold;
> Quick reverence for his brother-man;
> Quick sense where gilding is not gold.

He also possesses "voluntary grace, . . . careless grandeur of a soul, . . . True sympathy," qualities lacking in Smedley's earlier heroes, whose quasi-mythical status and divinely appointed aristocratic connections distance them from ordinary experience and limitations. This character, with his humility and lack of a name, represents the sort of Everyman hero other writers of the period, such as Thomas Carlyle and Matthew Arnold, sought to define through their writing:

> For such a leader lifts his times
> Out of the limits of the night,
> And, falling grandly, while he climbs,
> Falls with his face toward the height.

But Smedley is careful to follow this celebration of modern masculine values with the strategically placed "A Contrast," a poem presenting women's character strengths thwarted by the social compulsion to marry and serve a husband. The poem is also significant for its depiction of the double standard with respect to premarital sexual relations. The heroine's girlhood joys and innocent pleasures are haunted by the specter of inevitable marriage looming in her future:

> Yet, under all, the feeling lurks,
> As ever since the world began,

> To make a helpmeet for a man
> Is Woman's perfectest of works.

The girl is represented as a beautiful flower waiting passively to be plucked, since all "Must finish in the name of wife." However, she retains enough spirit and imagination to resist (for a time, at least), resulting in her mother's distress and in the reluctance of potential suitors to be burdened by a difficult bride. Although others gloomily predict "Her day shall come," she remains for the present "A dream with no interpreter."

Then follows a sequence difficult to interpret in its euphemistic allusiveness. The girl matures and, "reluctant and ashamed," falls in love. What happens next is less clear: after asking God's protection for this "tender bloom," the narrator then exclaims:

> God bless the deed! for it is done,
> The moment is proclaimed at last;
> A word divides her from her past;
> Her song is sung, her life begun.

Whether the deed in question is her emergence into womanhood, falling in love, a declaration of love ("a word"), or sexual consummation (suggested by the eroticized garden imagery in this passage) remains indeterminate, nor is it clarified by her "confession" at the poem's conclusion.

The young woman eventually meets and marries a man whom the narrator paints in a somewhat unflattering light. Arrogant and cynical from a life of privilege and bored with his colorful sexual exploits, his one qualification is that he loves her. Unprotected from his "unholy past . . . Of which she must not ask nor speak," the social pressure to marry is demonstrated by those "who might rescue" her but choose to "stand afar," relieved only that she is married at last. But this love match, like most, eventually suffers from disillusionment and from his harsh treatment—harsh because it stems from his own guilty past—of his loving bride. Hoping to clear the air between them, the bride confesses that he was "not the first." After an intense inner struggle the husband realizes that, compared with his own past, his wife's indiscretion is minimal; the humility and love for him demonstrated by her confession serves to transform him into a husband who, rather than taking his wife for granted, now "looks at her with reverent eyes."

Other subjects in *Poems* include the loss of a child in "Windy and Grey the Morning" and "The Fisherman," missed opportunities for romance in "A Meeting," loss through separation or death in "A Remembrance," desire for the more palatable world portrayed in paintings in "Waiting for the Tide," and death in "Once Upon a Time." Another death poem, "'Wind me a Summer Crown,' she said," anticipates in death a better existence, in which pleasant memories are sweeter—"Your mother's tones shall reach you still"—and painful memories—"the false love that broke your heart"—are forgotten. But the greatest reward is the promise of a divine "Face which you shall see; / And wish for nothing more."

The separation of lovers is also the topic of "The Letter," written in the form of a letter by a woman waiting for a soldier to return from war. The letter writer recounts nightmarish dreams in which "I see you lying wounded, with your face upturned to the light / And I cannot stoop to kiss it." Later, sitting alone by the fire, she senses his presence in the room, a spectral visitation implying death, "but when I turned, you were fled." She struggles with hope and fear—"it never lets me rest . . . it is wearing me out"—and worries that her despair has diminished her beauty and thus her appeal to him. She observes that even in battle men become "brown and fierce, . . . erect and swift; you have always something to do," unlike women: "Ah, you men are happy! you live with a burst and a dash; / Weeping wastes us away, but work ennobles you." The poem ends abruptly with the soldier's return, which causes his lover to look ten years younger.

The social criticism implicit in this poem is somewhat undercut by the idea that the man's absence causes his lover to wilt, while his return instantly recovers her youthful bloom. However, the poem highlights another sort of gender-based issue, one Smedley herself was no doubt forced to confront throughout her life. Victorian social history was shaped in large part by "The Woman Question," the running debate over the social role of women, whose lack of anything useful or productive to occupy their time was regarded as a visible sign of men's suitability to control the culture economically and politically. During this time women increasingly demanded more fulfilling lives than those provided by the conventions that relegated them to a separate domestic sphere. They wanted productive labor, economic stability, and the training that could secure them with a livelihood. As an unmarried woman Smedley probably confronted her culture's prejudice against spinsters who pursued careers for remuneration or worked in the public realm. Nothing is known of the reasons Smedley did not marry; like many women who nursed ill and aging parents and helped raise younger siblings, she may have found herself well beyond the conventional age for marriage before she was sufficiently free from family responsibilities. Whether she was

single by choice or circumstance is impossible to determine and, more importantly, immaterial; Smedley's legacy as a writer and social activist speaks eloquently for women's capacity for action once freed from compulsory social constraints.

Another poem that addresses women's issues is "Slain," which depicts a fallen young woman being comforted by her mother as she dies. Although the standards of the time dictated "once fallen, always fallen," she is cast as a martyr—"she's young to be crowned with the saints"—and an innocent babe. The narrator voices the grieving mother's silent thoughts:

Did some one break her heart with a word,
Having grasped it at first as a prize?
Did it flutter from his hand, like a bird
Which goes a little way, and then dies?

He remembers the joy of her face,
The love in her smile, and the light,
When, shrinking, she met his embrace—
Bring him here, let him look at her to-night!

The poem calls for men to accept responsibility for their illicit relationships, the results of which are almost always ruin and even death for the women involved. Some moralists argued that even a single misstep results in eternal damnation; Smedley's appeal to compassion presents the fallen woman as an innocent victim who deserves a place among the saints for her suffering.

Reflecting other contemporary issues and events, *Poems* features more verses on the Italian campaign—"Ampola" and "Our Welcome to Garibaldi"—a compelling eulogy "On the Death of Prince Albert," and a criticism of the reluctance of European nations to come to the aid of Poland's famine victims ("In the Meantime"):

Land in the midst of rich Europe that starvest,
Stretching thy hands, in thy weakness sublime!
This is thy seedtime, be sure of the harvest,
Martyrs are earning it in the meantime!

Also timely is "A Plea for Beauty," the poet's response to the issues raised by a passage from Charles Darwin's *The Origin of Species* (1859): "Nature cares nothing for appearances except in so far as they may be useful. . . . Some naturalists . . . believe that very many structures have been created for beauty in the eyes of man. *This doctrine, if true, would be absolutely fatal to my theory.*" Smedley, like many Victorians, found her spiritual faith challenged and tested not only by Darwin's controversial theories but by a range of scientific discoveries that marked the era. "A Plea for Beauty" is more than simply a lament for what seemed like the death of beauty and even of God:

> I heard there was no place among the powers
> For Beauty; that she stands not in the plan;
> That even the tints which glorify the flowers
> Came but for use, and not for joy to man. . . .
> Tell us, what makes the beauty beautiful?

Nature, the poem asserts, "endears" and "touches us to tears"; "the Voice proclaiming all things good" provides beauty as a banquet "for our grateful eyes and hearts." Recalling William Blake's celebration of the senses as media through which to know God, Smedley in a sense abandons her Christian didacticism and Victorian utilitarianism to cast beauty as a divine gift designed solely to guide us through life's difficulties.

Other poems address spiritual doubt from the perspective of a seemingly unshakable faith that still asks questions. "What We May See," for example, wonders

> Why must new Hope be ever born in troubles and in fears?
> Why must the grey cloud rise and break before the Day appears?
> Why breaks it into bliss for some, and why for some in tears?

Such variety in human fate is dramatized in "Two Journeys," which depicts the tragedy of a young mother who shields her infant while witnessing her husband's murder. Maternal love aligns with divine love as the poet asks:

> Oh, must not mother-love be strong
> To cover its darling thus?
> Is there never an angel clasp and song
> To do as much for us?

As such poems illustrate, Smedley's perspective is refreshing in its unflinching perception of life's random inequities; hers is not a faith which avoids reality by focusing exclusively on a rewarding afterlife. In the poem "What Hearest Thou?" the narrator is nearly overwhelmed by cries of human anguish and nature's chaos. Beyond all else, however, she hears the voice of God, although distant and dimly perceived:

> I hear God speak,
> It is the only sound,
> Through clamour, sob, and shriek. . . .

A final example of Smedley's perennially optimistic spiritual searching is "The Future," which begins with a mysteriously veiled figure who "wanders through my dreams," resisting the poet's attempts to learn its identity or see its face, although she has intimations of the figure's divinity: "The rapture of that smile can teach / More than a century of tears." The narrator feels contact with the figure not as "phantom-grasp that melts away" but as the touch of Life itself. The poem's concluding stanza emphasizes a spirituality not blinded by moralistic platitudes but shaped by an honest acknowledgment of the often debilitating effects of life tempered by a carefully cultivated faith:

> We know the lesson; but a cry,
> Bitter and vast, is in our ears;
> One life of fruitless misery
> Shakes all our wisdom into tears.
> Thronged by the clamorous griefs that say,
> "Behold what *is*, forget what seems,"
> I can but answer, "Welladay;
> There *is* that figure in my dreams."

Smedley's poetic interests are also evident in her plays. Written as poetry rather than prose, the plays seem intended more as closet dramas than plays for performance, although she does provide stage and character directions. *Lady Grace* (included in *Poems*) dramatizes the title character's attempts to heal familial breaches created by the distribution of her late husband's wealth. Lady Grace's honest efforts to rectify the situation are cruelly misinterpreted by the younger generation, whose tests of her character prompt her to persist in her efforts despite their resistance.

The volume titled *Two Dramatic Poems* (1874) features the plays *Blind Love: A Dramatic Poem in Five Acts* and *Cyril: Four Scenes from a Life,* the subtitles of both emphasizing their poetic, rather than dramatic, qualities. *Blind Love* describes the relationship between Hope and her fiancé Raymond, whose resentment over his blindness and resulting dependence on his family breeds ambivalence toward the adoring Hope. Committed to serving as Raymond's handmaiden for life, Hope is thrilled to learn of a new medical procedure that could restore his eyesight. Raymond regains his vision, but through the trickery of Hope's beautiful, jealous cousin Avice he confuses her for Hope. Even when the error is corrected Raymond leaves Hope to marry Avice and is banished from the family out of respect for Hope. Motivated solely by selfless love, Hope releases Raymond from his commitment to her, although the loss of her "hope" leaves her crushed and broken:

> You have killed me now;
> You have taken all from me, even my thoughts. . . .
> All is lost: . . . All lovely days and faiths innumerable,
> Which made up all my life, lie in this tomb,
> This tomb whereon I dare not write a word,

Because there is no word to write upon it
But false, false, false!

Years later the marriage between Raymond and Avice is revealed to be strained. Hope, realizing she is dying, again proves her goodness by promoting reconciliation first between Raymond and his father and second between husband and wife. At Hope's deathbed Raymond sees his "life is going down into this grave" and admits that his is "the greater sin." With its didactic tone, its emphasis on "true" over false love, and its melodramatic deathbed confessions and reconciliations, *Blind Love* is typical of the instructional "fiction with a purpose" that appealed to Victorian audiences. Also typical is the character of Hope, who, like most Victorian angels, is so pure and good that she dies of a broken heart; her devotion, compassion for those who wrong her, and commitment to others' reconciliation mark her as one martyred by life's cruelties.

Divided into parts rather than acts, *Cyril* begins with a choice destined to affect the course of the protagonist's entire life. Cyril decides to forgo the life of ease and wealth to which he was born, including a lucrative marriage to a beautiful, well-dowered lady, to pursue a vocation as an impoverished cleric. Part 2 details the trials he undergoes in his efforts to aid the poor and destitute; his life is difficult, but he never regrets his choice. In part 3 Cyril finds love at last, though with a girl of the lower classes; although she has no dowry, hers is an inner, spiritual beauty. In an unexplained plot twist, however, she swoons suddenly and dies, leaving Cyril devastated to have found love so late and lost it so soon. Part 4 takes place "Thirty Years Afterwards," when Cyril's old college friends reunite, finding that Cyril has never married and never regretted the vocational choice he made so early in life. Still working for the poor, Cyril's eloquence before parliamentary reform committees is legendary. Yet oddly, the narrative concludes abruptly with Cyril's unexplained death and his vision of the afterlife beckoning to him. Smedley's primary dramatic heroes—Lady Grace, Hope, and Cyril—manifest those qualities of integrity, compassion, and honor she outlined earlier in "The Character."

As is the case with many women of her day, the details of Smedley's life are elusive. Literary scholarship has been further hampered by the literary conventions of the time, whereby the authors of works were identified simply by pseudonymous initials or as "The authoress of. . . ." According to many traditional biographical sources Smedley's greatest claim to fame is as the sister of Frank Smedley, although her literary output, in terms of quantity and range of genres, far surpasses his. In the absence of biographical details, Menella Bute Smedley's body of work must stand alone as her legacy. Her promotion of spiritual searching, compassion, gender equity, and social change marks her as, in her own terms, "A Very Woman" of the Victorian age, although one with remarkably modern sensibilities.

References:

Stanley Kunitz, ed., *British Authors of the Nineteenth Century* (New York: H. W. Wilson, 1936);

Angela Leighton and Margaret Reynolds, eds., *Victorian Women Poets: An Anthology* (Cambridge: Blackwell, 1995).

Henrietta Tindal
(1818? – 6 May 1879)

Lee Anna Maynard
University of South Carolina

BOOKS: *Lines and Leaves* (London: Chapman & Hall, 1850);
The Heirs of Blackridge Manor, a Tale of the Past and Present, as Diana Butler, 3 volumes (London: Chapman & Hall, 1856);
Rhymes and Legends (London: Richard Bentley, 1879).

SELECTED PERIODICAL PUBLICATIONS–
UNCOLLECTED: "The Spirit of the Vanished Island: A Poem," *Once a Week* (8 November 1862): 545–546;
"Notes Taken at Hampden Concerning the Greatest Squire of That Ilk," *Once a Week* (10 January 1863): 64–69;
"The Strange Story of Kitty Canham," *Temple Bar* (May 1880): 341–350.

Inspired by some of Henrietta Tindal's fugitive pieces, the acclaimed novelist, dramatist, conversationalist, and letter writer Mary Russell Mitford wrote on 30 November 1841 to the then Henrietta Harrison: "next to Miss Barrett, the most remarkable woman probably that ever lived, I know no one of whom I entertain such sanguine expectations." Mitford went on later to include Tindal in the "Female Poets" chapter of her *Recollections of a Literary Life; or, Books, Places and People* (1852). Although largely forgotten in this century, Tindal's poetry struck a chord in her own time, particularly with women readers. In fact, Queen Victoria read Tindal's poems. Perhaps what won the admiration of her contemporary readers is what modern readers also find exciting in her poetical works: Tindal juxtaposes the oft-occurring events of nineteenth-century womanhood with well-known (and frequently royal) historical events, thereby investing the domestic sphere with a majesty and dignity seldom found before in poetry.

As with her literary output, little is now known of the details of Henrietta Tindal's life. She was born Henrietta Euphemia Harrison, probably in 1818, to a well-to-do country family. Her father was

the Reverend John Harrison of Ramsey, Essex, Vicar of Dinton, Bucks; her mother, Henrietta Elizabeth Wollaston Harrison, was the elder daughter of Thomas Wollaston, Esq., of Moor Court, Hereford, and Bishop's Castle, Salop. Her mother and her father, a Whig clergyman, doted on Henrietta and her sister, Margaret. Although Margaret was physically weaker, both sisters apparently had poor constitutions and were prone to illness. Through a combination of these factors Henrietta Harrison had the time to take advantage of the plethora of available resources in the fine library of their country estate, concentrating her reading most heavily on the early English poets. She began to have somewhat of a literary reputation in her early twenties on the basis of fugitive pieces and poems circulated within her own social circle. Mitford writes to Miss Anderdon in the spring of 1841, describing the young poet as writing "well even now–will write *very* well–is tall, fair, and stately, decidedly handsome, from grace and expression, cares for nothing but literature and art and her happy home."

In 1846 Henrietta Harrison married Acton Tindal, a solicitor, and moved to the Manor House at Aylesbury. The next year she became pregnant with her first son, Nicolas, and on 28 November 1849 Mitford wrote to congratulate her on the birth of another boy, Acton Gifford, as well as on the birth of her first book of poetry. Henry Chorley's footnotes refer to the book as "a little, forgotten volume chiefly of early verses." In naming the 1850 volume *Lines and Leaves,* Tindal ignored the advice of her literary friend Mitford, who cautioned against "one of those leafy or flowery titles. . . . They are of bad taste, and bad omen. . . . No! No leaves!"

Lines and Leaves consists of some romantic, immature poems as well as works based on history and legend. "The Infant Bridal" was one of the most popular pieces in the volume, and it was a favorite of Mitford's, for she includes it in her *Recollections of a Literary Life,* praising Tindal for her painterly de-

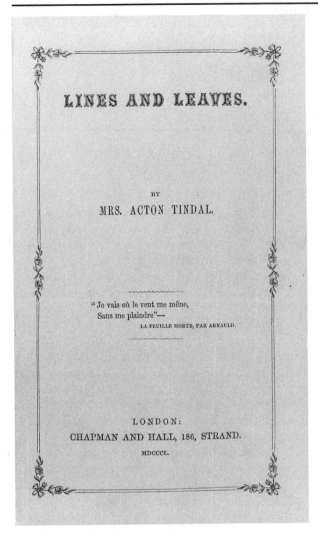

LINES AND LEAVES.

BY
MRS. ACTON TINDAL.

" Je vais où le vent me mène,
Sans me plaindre"—
LA FEUILLE MORTE, PAR ARNAULD.

LONDON:
CHAPMAN AND HALL, 186, STRAND.
MDCCCL.

Title page for Henrietta Tindal's first volume of poems

scriptions. The poem is based on the marriage in 1477 of the four-year-old Richard, duke of York and the three-year-old Anne Mowbray, duchess of Norfolk. Like the ill-fated bride and groom, who die virtually on the heels of their marriage, the subject of "The Burial in London," a young American girl, expires. In both poems, however, Tindal impresses upon the reader that the innocent children have gone to a better, more serene place. The innocence of children is a theme that runs constantly through much of this first volume of verse; although the young subjects often die, they can, as in "The Baptism of the Gypsy Babe," survive to retain, the poet hopes, the goodness and purity of childhood through the intervention of God. Not all readers were impressed with Tindal's style of poetry: Sir James Stephen criticized her work as too melancholy and plaintive.

The next few years saw times of great change in Tindal's personal life. Not only did her sister,

Margaret, die after a long, painful illness, but her friend and correspondent Mitford died after a carriage accident in January 1855. Tindal later repaid her debt to Mitford by assisting Henry Chorley in writing the introduction to the collected *Letters of Mary Russell Mitford* (1872). Her sister's death left Tindal sole heiress to her family's fortune. The poet had a third son, Charles Harrison, and wrote a three-volume novel, a well-written and witty romance titled *The Heirs of Blackridge Manor, a Tale of the Past and Present* (1856), which she published under the pen name Diana Butler. On 18 May 1858 Tindal bore twin daughters, Margaret Sabina and Henrietta Diana.

Tindal made at least three contributions to periodicals around this time—a poem, a report, and a story. "The Spirit of the Vanished Island" first appeared in the 8 November 1862 issue of *Once a Week*. The historical event/legend on which Tindal based this poem is also the basis of Felicia Hemans's "Indian Woman's Death-Song." Hemans's poem, published in *Records of Woman* (1828), relates, like Tindal's, the last thoughts and actions of a Native American woman who, upset by her husband's infidelity, has determined to kill herself and her child by rowing down the Mississippi River in a canoe toward a waterfall and certain death. In the earlier poem the child is female, while in Tindal's poem the child is male; whereas the heroine of the Hemans poem hopes to save her daughter from being hurt by men, the mother of Tindal's poem wishes to prevent her son from toughening into manhood. While "The Spirit of the Vanished Island" lacks the raw passion of "Indian Woman's Death-Song," it does offer an almost photographic depiction of the spirit and her surroundings, and Tindal's high verse raises the tall tale to mythic proportions.

Less sensational in nature are the contributions that arose from Tindal's genealogical research. In the process of discovering that she was the sole representative of the families of Wrotham, De Plessetis, Durant, Wroth of Loughton Hall, Gough, Carrington of Ramsey, and Harrison, which had their beginnings in the thirteenth century, she found the basis for her article "Notes Taken at Hampden Concerning the Greatest Squire of That Ilk." This article on John Hampden appeared in *Once a Week* on 10 January 1863. In "The Strange Story of Kitty Canham," which was published posthumously in the May 1880 issue of *Temple Bar,* Tindal relates the story of her great-great-aunt (through the Gough branch).

Although ancestry was important to Tindal, it was members of her immediate family who were to shape her poetic career most profoundly. On 18 December 1867 Henrietta Diana Tindal, one of the poet's twin daughters, died. The emotional effects of the loss can be seen throughout Tindal's second volume of poetry, *Rhymes and Legends,* her most mature and accomplished work, published posthumously in 1879. Tindal dedicates the volume to her children, including her deceased daughter, who "can never be forgotten by her mother." A real preoccupation with death pervades the volume, with the vast majority of the poems dealing directly with ghosts, dying, or graves.

Rhymes and Legends begins with "The Eve of All Souls," an irregular fragment comprised of ten individual poems. The premise of the fragment is that the narrator, spending the night in a cathedral on All Souls' Eve, falls asleep and encounters ghosts who tell their tales in the ten poems. The ghosts represent groups who are often forgotten, marginalized, or simply overlooked—such as scholars, factory workers, slaves, women who die in childbirth, good wives and mothers, and children. Tindal's verse is at its best and most powerful in "The Oppressed," "The Cry of the Oppressed," "The Death in Childbirth," and "The Rising of the Children." In "The Oppressed," an introduction to "The Cry of the Oppressed," the narrator hears hoarse voices rushing toward her from every corner of the cathedral. The tired, frustrated cries cause her to question whether those who live in comfort have obeyed God's will in relation to the poor. The souls argue that the more fortunate have not been true to divine will in "The Cry of the Oppressed." The phrase the "many who served the few" describes their lives and deaths. They have been taken from their homelands and sold; virtually imprisoned in hot, airless factories; drowned in rotted, overcrowded freighters; and always hit hardest by any plague. All of these troubles have occurred before the unseeing or uncaring eyes of the wealthy. The final quatrain urges the narrator and her ilk to walk into any neighboring street and discover whether or not they are so hard-hearted as to be undisturbed by what they see.

Although "The Death in Childbirth" was written in memory of Emma Matilda Purey-Cust, Tindal's grief over the loss of her own daughter is evident in her almost wistful descriptions of the dead mother and baby reunited under a peaceful green mound and of the mother's soul following her child's. Most affecting, however, are Tindal's imaginings of the pains of the mother, both physical and emotional. In a surprisingly realistic yet tasteful manner, Tindal relates the effects of the difficult delivery on the mother's body and her mental torment at never seeing the child she has loved unseen for months. Tindal's tribute to women who die in child-

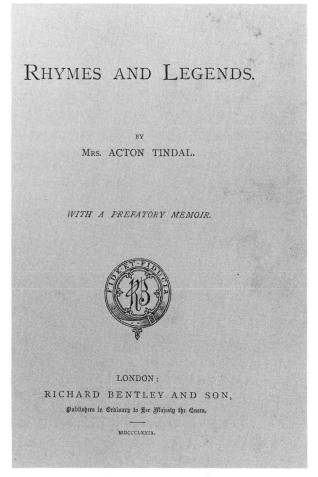

Title page for Tindal's second volume of poems, many of which reflect a preoccupation with death

birth is emotional but not bathetic, and it sheds light on the nobility of spirit of these short-lived mothers.

The grieving mother finds some outlet in "The Rising of the Children." Tindal's narrator dreams that the children awake, as if from a peaceful slumber, all rosy and glowing with health, unaffected by the decay of the grave. All have forgotten why or how they died and feel only a sense of security and belonging. They have dreamed beautiful dreams in their moldering tombs, serenaded by the lullabies of their mothers. While the poet takes comfort in these images, the reader is left wondering why Tindal's own child, who would seem to be the cause of the narrator's waiting up in the church on All Souls' Eve, makes no appearance. The children are treated as a group, not as individuals.

Perhaps the memory of her child is too sacred to be included within a fragment based on a superstitious notion, but later in the volume Tindal does include a poem titled "H. D. T." Tindal's emotions run the gamut from joy at the thought of being united in heaven with her dead child, to fear at the thought that her daughter will not remember her or will have changed, to aching sadness at having to leave her beloved child outside under the snow, to pain at seeing her now twinless daughter unwrapping gifts at Christmas. "H. D. T." ends with questioning and fear, not with the relative assurance of "The Rising of the Children," because "H. D. T." deals with the fate and complex emotions of those adults left behind on earth to grieve.

Queen Victoria, who was grief stricken over the death of her husband, requested copies of two of Tindal's poems that are included in *Rhymes and Legends*–"To the Most Illustrious Mourner in the New Year, 1862" and "On the Hartley Colliery Accident." Tindal wrote the first poem on the event of the prince consort's death on 14 December 1861, and in it she attempts to console the queen, who must bear the weight of a nation's troubles and sorrow as well as her own personal grief. Again, Tindal stresses the majestic spirit of a mourning wife and mother, who in this case has the added responsibility of the monarchy. The woman's point of view is prevalent in "On the Hartley Colliery Accident" as well. More than two hundred workers were trapped in a mine pit and few survived. Tindal focuses on the waiting of the mothers and wives gathered for days around the edge of the pit, capturing their fear and helplessness as they pray, sob, and strain to hear or see anything that offers hope of life. Queen Victoria, who sent anxious telegrams to the mine, is commended for her "womanly" compassion and empathy. This noble behavior above all, Tindal predicts, will guarantee the monarch's place in heaven.

Rhymes and Legends centers on the ideas of grief and women's dignity and strength. While some poems, such as "The Most Illustrious Mourner" and "On the Hartley Colliery Accident," directly hit upon these themes, others add import and power to Tindal's concept of womanhood through association. "The Imprisoned Princes," which tells of the imprisonment and impending death of Edward V and the duke of York; "The Lament of Joanna of Spain," which relates the misery and madness of the daughter of Ferdinand and Isabella; "Isabella of Valios"; "St. Mary Magdalene"; and "St. John Baptist" are all based upon events of great historical or religious importance. By writing of friends who died in childbirth and grieving widows and mothers in the same style and by including these works together in the same volume, Tindal validates the nineteenth-century female experience as poetic, dramatic, and powerful. Tindal died on 6 May 1879 after a lifetime of poor physical health, and although she has been critically neglected since, her strong literary legacy is breathing new life today.

References:

Angela Leighton, "Henrietta Tindal," *Victorian Women Poets: An Anthology,* edited by Leighton and Margaret Reynolds (Oxford: Blackwell, 1995);

Mary Russell Mitford, *Letters of Mary Russell Mitford,* edited by Henry Chorley, 2 volumes (London: Richard Bentley, 1872);

"Tindal, Henrietta Euphemia," *The Feminist Companion to Literature in English: Women Writers from the Middle Ages to the Present,* edited by Virginia Blain, Patricia Clements, and Isobel Grundy (New Haven: Yale University Press, 1990).

Margaret Veley

(12 May 1843 – 7 December 1887)

Staci L. Stone
University of South Carolina

BOOKS: *"For Percival," A Novel,* 3 volumes (London: Smith, Elder, 1878; Philadelphia: Lippincott, 1879); republished, 1 volume (London: Smith, Elder, 1884);

Mrs. Austin, Harper's Half-Hour Series, no. 139 (New York: Harper, 1880); republished as *Mrs. Austin by Margaret Veley and Othello the Second by F. W. Robinson,* Seaside Library, volume 337, no. 139 (New York: G. Munro, 1880);

Damocles, 3 volumes (London: Smith, Elder, 1882); republished as *Rachel's Inheritance; or, Damocles* (New York: Harper, 1882); republished as *Rachel Conway,* Seaside Library, volume 71, no. 1436 (New York: G. Munro, 1882);

Mitchelhurst Place, A Novel, 2 volumes (London: Macmillan, 1884); 2 volumes, Harper's Franklin Square Library, no. 411 (New York: Harper, 1884); republished, 1 volume (New York: G. Munro, 1884);

A Garden of Memories; Mrs. Austin; Lizzie's Bargain, 2 volumes, Macmillan's Colonial Library, no. 47 (London & New York: Macmillan, 1887);

A Marriage of Shadows and Other Poems, with biographical preface by Leslie Stephen (London: Smith, Elder, 1888; Philadelphia: Lippincott, 1889).

OTHER: "Milly's First Love," in *Tales from Blackwood,* new series, 21 (Edinburgh: Blackwood, 1880), pp. 18–96.

SELECTED PERIODICAL PUBLICATION– UNCOLLECTED: "Twice by the Sea," *Hourglass* (July 1887).

Margaret Veley was a writer whose prose and poetry appeared repeatedly in the *Cornhill Magazine* and other popular magazines alongside the works of Henry James and Thomas Hardy. Although she enriched the periodicals of her day and garnered much praise, her works have largely been forgotten. Most of Veley's poetry originally appeared in periodicals; her single poetry collection was compiled posthu-

mously by Sir Leslie Stephen, editor of the *Cornhill Magazine* from 1871 to 1882. Titled *A Marriage of Shadows and Other Poems,* it was published in an edition of 750 copies in 1888 by Smith, Elder, and Company.

A Marriage of Shadows comprises thirty poems, ranging from Veley's first published poem, "Michaelmas Daisies," to poems presented in her prose work to unpublished pieces, such as verses she scribbled in Christmas cards. *A Marriage of Shadows* was received favorably, as a review in the 28 July 1888 issue of *The Spectator* reveals: "while we admire greatly many of the grave poems, we think that the humorous poems have the advantage over them that they are so pointed and edged that no one can miss the unity of drift." The review also states that "An intensity of feeling . . . runs through almost all the poems, and raises them to a level far above that of even excellent amateur verse."

The second of four daughters, Margaret Veley was born on 12 May 1843 to Sophia Ludbey Veley, whose father was rector of Cranham from 1818 to 1859, and Augustus Charles Veley, a solicitor in Braintree, Sussex. After her early education by masters and governesses, she completed a term at Queen's College, Tufnell Park in London. Throughout her studies, Veley showed an aptitude for the French language and a great affinity for French literature. She also appreciated several British authors, such as George Eliot and William Makepeace Thackeray, and particularly admired Jane Austen, preferring her works to those of Sir Walter Scott.

Veley's literary aspirations arose while she was a child; she began writing religious poems at the age of thirteen. A little later, she attempted a mock heroic piece, "The Blue Princess," in which a fairy godmother who despises "blue" (intellectual) ladies grants a princess's wish for the gift of learning, which brings disaster.

Before Veley turned to writing as a career, she occupied herself with her studies and by teaching Sunday school. Although her students were devoted to her, Veley's religious beliefs clashed with those of a newly employed clergyman and she surrendered her post, though not her opinions, which Stephen describes as "liberal." According to Stephen, Veley's "divergence from the conservative and high-church principles of her closest connections showed the real independence of thought which was generally concealed by her extreme gentleness of manner." Although Stephen believes Veley veiled her liberal political and religious beliefs from her conservative family, these opinions are discernible in Veley's works, such as the poem "Out of the Darkness" (1875) and the prose piece *Mrs. Austin* (1880).

An auspicious year for Veley was 1870, for in that year she placed two literary pieces in two different periodicals. Her first published piece, a poem in *The Spectator* (April 1870), "Michaelmas Daisies," is a celebration of the flowers also called aster or Arctic daisies. The opening six-line description–beginning "Daisies on the emerald lawn"–is repeated at the conclusion of the piece, enveloping the elegy to other seasonal flowers and plants. Floral imagery, as seen in this piece, was a favorite motif of Veley, as the titles of other works indicate: "Almond Blossom" (1881), "A Town Garden" (1883), and "A Garden of Memories" (1886). She also took an avid interest in researching the meanings of flowers; Michaelmas daisies stand for afterthought, or farewell.

Five months after *The Spectator* published "Michaelmas Daisies," Veley's story "Milly's First Love" (1870) appeared in the September edition of *Blackwood's Magazine*. In this story Veley's repeated interruptions to instruct the reader and her witty presentation of manners and courting are reminiscent of Jane Austen's style. Seventeen-year-old Milly Hope's first love is Matthew Warburton, for whom Bella Mannering has "been laying snares" for eight years. The entrance of John Eversley to Drayford society almost upsets the Milly Hope–Matthew Warburton engagement, as "Our little Milly was dangerously near her waking" from her false admiration of her fiancé. However, the romantic tale concludes with the marriage of Milly Hope and her first love and with a statement of the author's regret for the fate of her heroine: "I cannot be angry with Milly for her first mistake. 'But the pity of it! oh the pity of it!'" Veley's humorous depiction of situations and characters and her use of parenthetical comments to undercut the text, which appear in this first prose piece, become characteristic of Veley's style as displayed in her later works. Sentimental and troubled romances also recur throughout her poetry and prose.

For example, Veley's next published prose piece, "Lizzie's Bargain," presents the sad outcome of the romance between Lizzie Grey and Ernest Fletcher. Initially published anonymously in the *Cornhill Magazine* in May and June 1877 and published under her name in book form ten years later, the story describes Lizzie's sacrifice: at Thorpe Fletcher's suggestion she gives up Ernest, and in return Thorpe Fletcher is supposed to assist his nephew financially. However, Ernest's sudden inheritance renders such assistance needless, so part of the bargain remains unfulfilled. Two and one-half years later, Lizzie, depressed and miserable, is still refusing Thorpe Fletcher's economic support despite her distressing situation until she suddenly decides to marry him: "Lizzie Grey did not seem to think that bargain had turned out badly for her."

The second poem in *A Marriage of Shadows*, "A Shadow on the Dial," consists of 428 lines in varied meter. This poem had not been published prior to its appearance in Veley's posthumous collection, but was written in 1873. As they are in much of her poetry, death and love are the primary topics in this poem. Veley states that mortality makes love more valuable because "Is not June sweeter that December comes? / And blossoms that they fade?" She then further elevates Death, calling it "a king" and "great" and attempts to welcome old age, but fails due to fear. The poem concludes with a prayer: "Then send Thy final message–a white flash / To snap the thread, and light me to Thy feet." The poem thus presents a cyclical attitude toward death, just as it relates death and aging to the seasonal cycle. *The Spectator* 1888 review describes this poem as "full of vigour."

Another early poem is Veley's "Out of Darkness," which was written in February 1875. The iambic pentameter verse is separated into two sections, "Night" and "Morning" and opens with a crippled girl praying "To one God only–black Forgetfulness!" because she resents God and Jesus for her "distortion." The girl passionately hates those who pity her and those who "preach your Christ," just as she detests God, who is loved while she is repulsed. However, the morning brings a change of heart as she is "new born since yesternight" due to a renewal of religious faith. A dream of walking with her love in a paradise has restored her belief in God, and since it is because she is afflicted that she can truly appreciate the promise of the dream, she asks "'Have mercy, God / Nor heal me of the pain that is my soul!'"

The late 1870s was a difficult time for Veley, despite her literary success. In 1876, Veley's sister, Alice Holmes, moved to Penzance due to her failing health, and Veley was nursing her when she died in July 1877. Veley's father died two years later on 19 January 1879, and Veley, accompanied by her mother, moved from Braintree, where she had lived for thirty-five years, to London. The sadness of these successive deaths was relieved briefly by the marriage of Veley's youngest sister, Constance, to Alfred E. Warner in 1878. However, Constance suffered from ill health as well, and traveled to various resorts to convalesce; Veley accompanied her sister on trips to Switzerland and to the Riviera prior to 1884, when Constance's health worsened, forcing her to remain in London.

Another death that affected Veley was that of Frederick Walker in 1875. The thirty-five-year-old Walker was a landscape painter who had been an illustrator for the *Cornhill Magazine* since 1863. Veley remembers him in the elegaic "The Unknown Land," composed on 12 February 1876. The poem exhibits Veley's habit of varying her metrical form and stanzaic arrangement as she offers a contemplation of death and poetic vision of another land where the afterlife occurs. Inspired by Walker's paintings, Veley imaginatively describes an otherworldly place, which is a favorite topic for her, as evidenced by "A Marriage of Shadows" and "The Level Land."

The title poem of *A Marriage of Shadow,* written in 1878, was not published until ten years later, with the publication of the collection. In the "Prologue" Veley describes a man observing various shadows: "the shadows of bygone days, the shadows of hopes and fears," and, "saddest of all," the shadows "from the Land of Might Have Been." The poem then moves from a realistic world at "Sunset" to "The Land of Shadows" and again returns to the more real setting of "On the Bridge." Sunset begins the poem because, at this time of day, shadows are their largest, before they disappear completely (the men on the bridge face the setting sun):

> With shadows grey and long.
> With slim fantastic shapes that slip and glide,
> Follow and run,
> That lurk, and waver in uncertain flight
> And fear the sun.

Then Veley focuses on a solitary figure, probably the same man from the "Prologue," whose introspection makes him oblivious to a passing woman whose shadow merges with his shadow for one moment. And though "this one man sees nought," his shadow stirs as her shadow passes. During the night, the shadows "fly afar to Shadowland" while their master and mistress sleep; Veley paints this phantom destination as a barren, desolate place:

> Strange is the pathway—strange the final shore—
> A hollow earthen-coloured waste
> (That might be a forgotten world
> From life and splendour hurled),

> Girt by a mountain range, lies low for evermore,
> Shrunken and dead.

Against this bleak landscape, the shadows "Dance through the silence of the windless nights," while the man's shadow pursues the woman's shadow until, near dawn, "The flying shadow shapes were fused in one." Upon daybreak, the shadows must return to their owners; thus the female shadow makes her way "Unto her lady's feet" as the "bridegroom shadow" rejoins his master. When these shadows cross again on the bridge, the man notices the other shadow, and gazes at the woman who casts it as "He felt within his soul a strange remembrance rise." The woman reminds him of his deceased love, and she observes his startled stare as the "wedlock of their shadows" causes her to glance at the man.

In the "Epilogue" Veley writes about her actual creative act; the shadows are her somber personification of the imagination: "A shadow hand lay side by side with mine, / And ever as I wrote it penned a line." She asks readers to excuse the failure of her writing to capture fully her vision, which has come from "Out of the shadows of an unknown night." Mixed with this romantic mingling of shadows on the bridge and in Shadowland is the threat of death, "the Unknown shadow." Veley concludes "A Marriage of Shadows" by connecting these two themes: "If like a shadow, or a passing sigh, / Love, thus made perfect from the world must die, / Scorn it who will, I will not scorn it—I!"

Highly praised, though entirely unlike "A Marriage of Shadows," is Veley's "A Japanese Fan." Veley's literary relationship with Leslie Stephen and the *Cornhill Magazine* began in September 1876, when her "A Japanese Fan" first appeared. As Stephen recounts: "I was then editor, and she sent me the poem with a letter of introduction from her friend, Mr. Meredith Townshend, for whose services in the way of literary advice and encouragement she often expressed her gratitude." The poem, arranged into lines alternating between trochaic tetrameter and an anapestic foot, opens with rhetorical questions that set the scene: two people trapped in a parlor by a thunderstorm investigate "all the treasures / Gathered here." The speaker's companion studies the glasses, chess pieces, china plates and cups, and a tapestry while the speaker contemplates a fan "Lying here—bamboo and paper / From Japan." The speaker understands this relic and explains it to the companion by translating the Japanese scroll depicted on the fan. The speaker describes a past romance between an "ardent" lover and "a lady, small of feature, / Narrow-eyed, / With her hair of ebon straightness / Queerly tied" who waves "the fan of

Sir Leslie Stephen, editor of Margaret Veley's A Marriage of Shadows and Other Poems (1888)

pictured paper," which "Might have been / Fairy wand, or fitting sceptre / For a queen." As do most of Veley's literary romances, this love story ends sadly as the Japanese woman betrays the man, who is forever changed by the experience. The speaker then presents what may be the thoughts of the betrayed lover or an introspective self-examination:

> I can almost see her, touch her,
>   Hear her voice,
> Till, afraid of my own madness,
>   I rejoice
> That beyond my help or harming
>   Is her fate—
> Past the reach of passion—is it
>   Love—or hate?

This ambiguous stanza lends credence to the speaker's concluding statement to the companion: "my story might as well be / Japanese!" "A Japanese Fan" is one of Veley's most praised poems. George Saintsbury calls the poem Veley's "chief work," describing it as "really something of a positive masterpiece of quiet ironic passion, suitably phrased in

verse," and a 28 July 1888 review in *The Spectator* calls the piece "a poem of very delicate irony."

Closely following the publication of "A Japanese Fan," Veley's "A Closed Book" appeared in *The Spectator* on 13 January 1877. Rather than again using a varied poetic form, Veley expresses her vision in thirteen quatrains in which three lines of pentameter are followed by a line in dimeter. The speaker of the poem reminisces about a book read as a child and contemplates perusing it again but decides against such an act because the emotions and reactions evoked then might not be repeated: "How if the fear, whereat my pulses quickened, / Should not be there?" The speaker appreciates the author's work, but fears that "Perhaps I read the book he meant to write, / Not that he wrote," and so the book remains closed. Veley also admonishes against attempting a return to an idealized past at the conclusions of both *Mrs. Austin* and *Damocles* (1882).

Since March 1872 Veley had been working on yet another romantic tale with a pessimistic conclusion, *"For Percival,"* which was first serialized in the *Cornhill Magazine* from September to December 1878 and immediately thereafter published in three volumes in 1878. This work is Veley's best known; it was published in England and the United States, where it went through six editions with three publishers. The story focuses on Percival Thorne's loss of love, inheritance, self-respect, and political fame. Stephen truly admired *"For Percival"*—in the preface to *A Marriage of Shadows* he says that the novel "appeared (and still appears) to me to be marked by very rare qualities which are not always to be found in more popular novels. It had true literary distinction: a graceful, clear, and pointed style, a strong sense of humour, and a keen perception of character approached by few of her contemporaries." Though *"For Percival"* may have been "warmly welcomed by many readers," such as Luke Ionides and his wife, who befriended Veley, Stephen believed that the sad ending of the novel diminished its popularity because most readers expect and demand happy conclusions. Despite the ending, a review in *The Spectator* (27 December 1884), following the republication of *"For Percival"* in one volume, remarked that the novel "gave the world assurance of a novelist of no ordinary promise," and a review in the 16 February 1887 *Illustrated London News* praised the novel, echoing the speculations of many readers by attributing the unsigned piece to Thomas Hardy.

Veley's next publication was a three-quatrain poem titled "October" that was initially published in the November 1880 issue of *Harper's Magazine*. The poem describes the changing seasons as a woman anxiously awaits the summer. But "something heavier than the autumn leaves / Has hidden eyes that looked for summer-time." The trees will awake "from their forgetful sleep" during winter, but the woman will not; nor will anyone "keep / A little leaf or flower that she has seen!" This issue of *Harper's Magazine* also included Veley's "The Level Land," in which Veley returns to a favorite theme: in this poem the other-wordly landscape is an Edenic scene. The speaker desires "a level land I love" and proceeds to describe this place, which is "A land of sunny turf and laughing rills, / A land of endless summer, sweet with dew." Despite the gaiety inspired by this environment, the speaker is unable to escape her concerns about sin, pain, doubt, and the "Burden of Duty." Veley decorates her idyllic land with amaranth and asphodel, which she borrowed from the poems of John Milton, Alexander Pope, and Alfred, Lord Tennyson. She later regretted using these flowers, as Stephen reports: "She was uncomfortable at having used the poetically commonplace flowers, amaranth and asphodel, and looked them out in a French dictionary . . .[she remarked] 'I came to the conclusion that I know no more of amaranths and asphodel than I did before, since the poets' flowers—Mr. Tennyson's for instance—are evidently not related to their earthly namesakes.'" Veley's statement was prompted by her discovery that amaranth is a wild garlic and that asphodel is a medicinal, turnip-shaped root.

While publishing in the *Cornhill Magazine,* Veley had become acquainted with Stephen, and had befriended his second wife, Julia Prinsep Stephen. She was Veley's model for *Mrs. Austin,* though Leslie Stephen did not think it a realistic sketch of his wife. This prose piece, initially published in the *Cornhill Magazine* in April and May of 1880, details several romances: a failed relationship of the past, between Mrs. Austin and Gilbert South, Frank Leicester's current crush on Mrs. Austin, South's romantic intention to reignite the passion he still holds for Mrs. Austin, and the final, unexpected union of Tiny Vivian and South. The tale's moral is for lovers to avoid seeing old flames because such an encounter will shatter the idealized dream of the past.

Stephen included in *A Marriage of Shadows* a verse Veley had enclosed in a Christmas card to his wife: "A Christmas Card. To J. P. S." The four tercets (three-line stanzas) of iambic pentameter—beginning "Ere yet, Old Year"—detail Veley's wishes for her friend: "Tell her my Christmas thoughts are hers again, / Tell her, O year, I long that she may live / Glad in all gifts that all good years can give." However, this cheerful greeting becomes melancholy as Veley mentions sadness and loss, which she hopes, if they occur, "even *that* may flower /

With loving thought." Stephen also selected a birthday poem Veley dedicated to her friend Luke Ionides for publication in *A Marriage of Shadows:* "A Birthday Wish. (L. A. I., March 10, 1881)." The speaker of this verse, which follows the poetic form of "A Closed Book," wishes that Time, rather than halting, would "Take nought away of happiness bygone, / Bring nought but good."

Veley used a floral motif in "Almond Blossom," first published in *Harper's Magazine,* where it was accompanied by an illustration that appeared as the frontispiece for the August 1881 issue. In ten rhymed triplets, the speaker addresses his "Love," who stands "With almond clusters in your clasping hand." The illustration depicts a woman holding a bouquet of these flowers (which symbolize hope) and accompanied by a man (presumably the speaker). The poem contrasts the mortality of planted gardens, architectural wonders, and human life to eternal blooms that "are not dead—the flowers can never die." Veley's allusion to John Milton's elegy *Lycidas* (1638) in the fifth stanza emphasizes human mortality, a mortality that flowers escape as they return each spring. Although these flowers will outlive the speaker's love, the poem ends sentimentally since the blossoms would not be identical without the woman's presence:

Because to these

Pink sprays of almond, for a little space
Your musing smile, your blossom-perfect face,
Give a supreme and solitary grace.

In 1882 Veley's prose piece *Damocles* was published serially in the *Cornhill Magazine* from February to December. It was republished in book form, first under the title of *Rachel's Inheritance; or, Damocles* (1882) and later as *Rachel Conway* (1882). The novel details Rachel Conway's interactions with two men, Charles Eastwood and Adam Lauriston, neither of whom she marries and concludes with a melancholy heroine who only realizes her true feelings when she is unable to act. Similar to Veley's *Mrs. Austin, Damocles* warns against revisiting an idealized past, for fear of brushing "the bloom off . . . remembrance." The final chapter, "The Picture Speaks," begins with thirteen lines of iambic pentameter that describe Adam Laurison, who "Never glad / Was he with sweetness of his lady's eyes, / Nor joy he had content to die because someone dead." The portrait is of Lauriston's deceased wife, and the painting—similar to the painting in Mary Braddon's novel *Lady Audley's Secret* (1862)—is mysterious and beautiful, becoming important as the key to Rachel Conway's curiosity. Like "Lizzie's

Barmouth N. Wales.
Sept. 3rd 1870.

Dear Sir

Mr. Townsend's note enclosing your letter and cheque has been forwarded to me here, where I am staying for a few days, and I cannot acknowledge the latter — which is more than I at all expected — without thanking you for your kindness in giving me a chance when I was utterly untried and unknown to you.

A disappointment or two, and a good deal of suspense, such as I

had always expected and feared, would, I should think effectually take the bloom off a first success, but, thanks to you and to Mr. Townsend, I shall have as long as I live only the happiest recollections of my first attempt.

I shall indeed be glad if one of these days a second should meet with the same good fortune but however that may be I shall always remain

Sincerely & gratefully yours
Margaret Veley

Letter from Veley to her publisher, William Blackwood, about the first publication of her short story "Milly's First Love" in the September 1870 issue of Blackwood's Edinburgh Magazine (National Library of Scotland)

Bargain," this melancholy story concludes with a moral: "People talk of life as a vale of tears till the expression is repulsively hackneyed. Rachel was astonished when she suddenly discovered the meaning of it."

In "A Town Garden," published in the August 1883 issue of *Harper's Magazine,* Veley again returns to her fascination with flowers. The five eight-line stanzas offer a depressing poetic description of a city garden, where flowers "With scanty, smoke-incrusted leaves" are watered by "foul droppings from the eaves" and struggle "through the stagnant haze." The grime of the city, "Where men make money, buy and sell," has infected the garden, and the speaker contemplates transplanting the blooms to the country. However, the speaker decides the town garden is preferable since the "dole / Of lingering leaves shall not be vain— / Worthy to wreathe the hemlock bowl, / Or twine about the cross of pain."

Veley also initially published "Mother and Child" in 1883, in the April issue of *Century.* This

sentimental verse relates the death of a child, but it ends on an optimistic note since the memory of the child will remain intact, undisturbed by a separation from the mother that is a result of choice, of maturation, rather than a fateful death: "For a house that once has known / Tiny feet on stair and stone— / . . . Keeps remembrance of the dead." Death is also the topic of Veley's poem, "Of the Past," initially published in the February 1884 issue of *Harper's Magazine.* The ten-quatrain poem is an elegy for the woman who wears a circlet "on her head; / She is a queen, and she is dead."

Also in 1884 *Macmillan's Magazine* published *Mitchelhurst Place* as "by the Author of 'For Percival.'" This novel was highly praised by a reviewer for *The Spectator* (27 December 1884), who states: "Miss Veley's pages are bright with flashes of insight, and abound in touches of sympathetic tenderness." The reviewer also states that "*Mitchelhurst Place* is a story which rivets the attention from the first page to the last, and the writer's management of her plot is perfect." The story details the romances of Barbara Strange as she chooses between her two suitors: the tutor Reynold Harding and the poet Adrian Scarlett.

Stephen included three poems from *Mitchelhurst Place* in the collection *A Marriage of Shadows.* "At Her Piano" is taken from the chapter entitled, "Barbara's Tune," in which Barbara Strange plays the piano while Reynold Harding admires her. The verse is purportedly composed by Adrian Scarlett, who had observed Barbara playing a beautiful melody on an untuned, aged piano the previous summer. He knows that "Love had made the music right." The sonnet entitled "Autumn Berries" in the collection appears untitled in the chapter describing a girl dropping a cluster of red berries, which is scooped up and treasured by her admirer. The poem is also supposedly by Scarlett, who transforms the prose description of this scene into a Petrarchan sonnet. In chapter seventeen, Adrian Scarlett reads to Amy Wilton another sonnet that voices his romantic emotions: "if you alone– / Should hear the passionate pulses of my heart!"

Another poem published in the same year is Veley's "Private Theatricals," which appeared in the September 1884 *Century.* The poetic persona is an actor playing the hero of a comedy, as he describes in the first section, "Before the Curtain Rises": "I am the happy hero of the play, / With Love, and Luck, and Valour on my side." Despite the auspicious fate for this character, who wins the lady's love and defeats the villain, in the second section, "After the Curtain Falls," the actor playing the part does not succeed with the actress because in reality, "it was the Villain she preferred– / The Villain all the while!"

Stephen included in *A Marriage of Shadows* several short verses gathered from holiday cards. One such piece, "A Christmas Card. To E. I.," dated December 1884, also appears in *A Marriage of Shadows.* The addressee is probably Veley's friend Mrs. Luke Ionides. Apparently, the card that she inscribed bore two printed quotes, one from William Shakespeare's *The Merchant of Venice* (1600)–"Fair thoughts and happy hours attend you"–and an anonymous line: "May Christmas come laden with every blessing!" Between these two lines Veley inserts two quatrains of iambic tetrameter that conclude with "To tell you I defy them both / To *say* ought sweeter than I *mean!*" *A Marriage of Shadows* also comprises two additional Christmas poems, which are undated. One is addressed to "Sweet Sister mine," whom the speaker encourages to reflect on Christmas memories, though she will never find "One Christmas earlier than my love for you." The other Christmas card seems to be addressed to Mrs. Ioni-

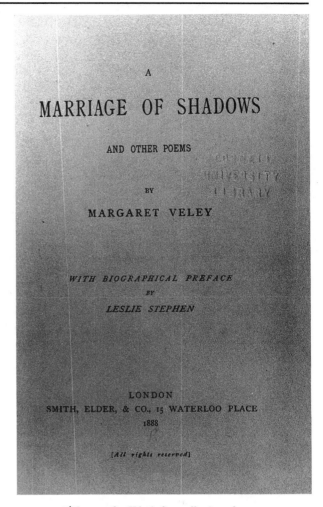

*Title page for Veley's first collection of poetry,
published posthumously*

des, whom Veley probably met in the summer 1879, and was probably written in 1885, since the dedication displays the dates "1879–1885" and describes their initial meeting.

Her sister Constance Warner died in May 1885, and Veley dedicated *A Garden of Memories* to her: "Thus far in my work I have had my sister's sympathy, and I shall have it no more. Even in her weakness she cared for the beginning of this story, chose it to be a remembrance of her." First published in the *English Illustrated Magazine* in July, August, and September 1886, and collected in book form the following year, this prose piece describes a walled garden situated in a poor section of Brenthill, next to the factory and tenements owned by Thomas Brydon, who wishes to purchase the property in order to build improved housing for his workers. Miss Wynn, who owns the garden, refuses to sell because she hopes her lover, Philip Wargrave, will one day return to his beloved garden where she will be waiting for him. When the affianced Philip War-

295

grave does arrive, Miss Wynn has agreed to sell the garden, and Thomas Brydon hurries to build the cottages so he can again see Miss Wynn, whom he loves. When *A Garden of Memories* was published with *Mrs. Austin* and "Lizzie's Bargain," the July 1887 *London Quarterly Review* published a laudatory review of the two-volume set: "They are but sketches, but at every point they show the instinct and the master-touch of genius. The writer does not need a sensational story or a cunning and wonderful plot to excite and to enchain the interest of her readers. Every paragraph is fresh and engaging, and her writing is as sweet and pure as it is charming."

Although "A Game of Piquet" is undated, the poem seems to allude to Veley's personal experience with the death of one of her sisters, perhaps that of Constance. It is a provocative poem that connects the ancient and medieval conception of death as a skeletal figure, as presented in Hans Holbein's series of woodcuts titled *The Dance of Death* (1523–1526, published 1538), to Veley's own association of death with piquet, a card game:

> Silent I saw her stand,
> Pallid, in trouble sore,
> While from her hanging hand
> Slipped downward to the floor
> Black cards, whose ominous
>   Array
> Fate had not suffered us
>   To play.

This poem, too, concludes on a mournful note as the speaker calls out to God for comfort, but "No love the unknown land / Invades, / And Death played out the hand / Of Spades."

Veley returns to the topic of romance in the undated poem "A Lutanist," comprised of trimetric verse arranged in stanzas of two quatrains that she doubles occasionally. The title applies both to an actual musician who plays the lute for a female employer and to the employer, since the musician "should linger mute" without her: "For I am but the lute, / And she the lutanist." She is a queen who keeps her lutanist in a turret of her "stately house." The musician's compositions have attained a godly, legendary status; princes make payments of gold to hear the music. However, the musician now cares solely for the woman, not fame or fortune.

"A Student" is another undated poem and was probably influenced by Veley's experience as a teacher. The twenty-four-line poem warns scholars to acknowledge life itself rather than to focus solely upon their studies. In it, Veley depicts a student impervious to actual experience: "He shrinks alike from laughter and from tears" and does not heed liv-ing men. Instead, "His pathway lies 'mid visionary throngs,'" as he recognizes only "ancient songs," chronicled fears and hopes, and "ages vast and dim." However, as "He dreams of bygone days, with thoughtful brow / . . . Life stands still, and, startled, whispers 'Now!'"

The undated "A Wish" is a short poem (three six-line stanzas) that brings New Year's tidings. The speaker imagines "the Little Year, / Like a pedlar with his pack," who will stop and cheer people by allowing them to choose from among the wares in his pack as he travels throughout the world. Also undated is "First or Last? A Wife to Her Husband." The poem—a combination of Veley's favorite themes of love, death, and afterlife—presents the belief in the possible reunion of this couple in another world, so that their final kiss before her death may either be the first or the last. Veley continues her obsession with death in "A Dream of Life and Death," also undated. Here, Veley paints dying as a competition ruled by Death: "While high above the ardour of the race / Sat Death, enthroned o'er all with quiet face." The speaker initially struggles against Death, but then states:

> Is my life short? I measure not its flight,
> Let me maintain it on a level height,
> That I may look thee boldly in the eyes,
> Not gazing upward as a suppliant dies.
> Let me live nobly, nobly yield thee all—
> Thou shalt preserve me, Death, from future fall!

Veley's final publication prior to her death is the six-quatrain poem "His Calendar," first published in the 1887 *Bairn's Annual*, and later included in *A Marriage of Shadows*. In this short poem, the speaker wishes someone identified only as "Steenie" a cheerful life:

> May his days be rose and green,
>   With the blossom and the leaf—
> Golden-bright with sunny sheen,
>   Never, never grey with grief.

Veley died unexpectedly on 7 December 1887, due to a throat infection. Her obituary in *The Times* (London) consists of three lines stating only the basic facts: age (forty-four), date, address, and father's name. No mention of her literary accomplishments is made. She was survived by her mother and one sister, Mrs. Webb. Veley's grave is beside those of her father and sister Alice Holmes in Braintree Cemetery, where she was buried on 10 December. At the time of Veley's death, she was writing another novel, set in the country. She had completed the first of three volumes and outlined the entire story, indicating familial relations and dates, but Leslie Stephen thought the fragment "too incomplete and too much in the nature of an introduction to justify publication."

As do many of the poems in *A Marriage of Shadows,* the undated poem, "One of the Multitude," which concludes the volume, focuses on death; it begins "When I am dead!" In the poem the poetic persona envisions her grave, and what the world will be like without her. Through this persona, Veley voices her own desire that her writing will remain after her death:

> And if, when I am gone,
>   Some words of mine live on,
> They shall be only, in the world's great day,
> Like a brief echo that from far away
>   Comes with familiar sound.
> It wavers to and fro between the hills
>   Above, around,
>   The silent air it fills
> With lonely speech that knows no change,
>   But wanders, clear and strange,
> And has no help of living lips or eyes.
> A little while the sound may go and come
>   Though he who uttered it be dumb,
> A little while it lingers ere it dies.

Sadly, Veley's words have not lived on. Forgotten for many years, Veley's literary contributions merit examination; her imaginative descriptions, witty sketches, and poetical arrangement should be reassessed. Although appreciative of her talent as a prose writer, in his biographical preface to her one collection of poetry, her editor Stephen remarks of Veley's poetry that it "showed real talent but—well, not quite of the first order." However, as *The Spectator* review of 1888 states: "Miss Veley, if she had lived, might have surpassed greatly as a poet the considerable reputation she had made as a novelist."

References:

John W. Birknell, ed., *Selected Letters of Leslie Stephen, 1882–1904,* 2 volumes (Columbus: Ohio State University Press, 1996);

Gillian Fenwick, *Leslie Stephen's Life in Letters: A Bibliographical Study* (Brookfield, Vt.: Ashgate, 1993).

Papers:

The unpublished pieces mentioned by Leslie Stephen, such as the "Blue Princess" manuscript, and the novel fragment, have not been located. Veley's letters to William Blackwood are at the National Library of Scotland, and another letter is in the Stoker Correspondence at the Brotherton Library, Leeds.

Lady Jane Francesca Elgee Wilde

(27 December 1821? – 3 February 1896)

Karl Beckson
Brooklyn College of the City University of New York

BOOKS: *Ugo Bassi: A Tale of the Italian Revolution,* as
Speranza (London: Saunders & Otley, 1857);
Poems, as Speranza (Dublin & London: J. Duffy,
1864);
Driftwood from Scandinavia (London: Bentley, 1884);
The Believer, as Speranza (Dublin: J. Charles, 1885);
*Ancient Legends, Mystic Charms, and Superstitions of
Ireland,* 2 volumes (London: Ward & Downey,
1887; Boston: Ticknor, 1887);
Ancient Cures, Charms, and Usages of Ireland (London:
Ward & Downey, 1890);
Notes on Men, Women, and Books (London: Ward &
Downey, 1891);
Social Studies (London: Ward & Downey, 1893).

TRANSLATIONS: J. W. Meinhold, *Sidonia the Sor-
ceress* (London: Parlour Library, 1849);
Alphonse de Lamartine, *Pictures of the First French
Revolution* (London: Simms & McIntyre, 1850);
Lamartine, *The Wanderer and His Home* (London:
Simms & McIntyre, 1851);
Alexandre Dumas *père, The Glacier Land* (London:
Simms & McIntyre, 1852);
Emanuel Swedenborg, *The Future Life,* (London: J.
McGlashan, 1853);
Wilhelmine Canz, *The First Temptation; or "Eritis Sicut
Deus,"* 3 volumes (London: T. C. Newby,
1863).

OTHER: "Jacta Alea Est," anonymous, *Nation*
(Dublin), 29 July 1848;
The American Irish (Dublin: W. McGee, 1878);
"Concluding Portion," in *Sir William Wilde's Memoir
of Gabriel Beranger* (Dublin: M. H. Gill, 1880),
pp. 131–176;
Essays and Stories, by Lady Wilde (Speranza), in *The
Writings of Oscar Wilde,* volume 14, by Oscar
Wilde (London & New York: Keller-Farmer,
1907).

A noted patriotic poet who established a reputation with her fiery, inspiring verse during the Irish

Lady Jane Francesca Elgee Wilde

potato famine of the mid 1840s by signing her poems with the pseudonym Speranza (a name meaning
"Hope"), a diligent researcher of Irish folklore and
folkways, a feminist who sought to end social inequalities, and a noted translator, Jane Francesca Elgee (as Lady Wilde) maintained her fame despite being overshadowed by her son Oscar, who on his
American lecture tour in 1882 was referred to by the
American Irish as "Speranza's son." Also noted for
her eccentricity and wit, she was the subject of an article in the *Boston Pilot* (28 September 1889) by William Butler Yeats, who remarked that "London has
few better talkers." When Wilde achieved renown

for his brilliant plays, she wrote facetiously: "I must now pose as the Mother of Oscar."

Descended from Anglo-Irish Protestant forebears (the Irish ruling class known as the Protestant ascendency, for no Catholic was permitted to hold government posts until 1829, when the Catholic Emancipation Act was passed), she was nevertheless convinced (without any evidence to substantiate her claim) that her family "originated in the sixteenth century from Italy and Elgee is an Irish corruption of the name [Algiati]." Even her date of birth is questionable, for there is no record of it, nor is there any record of baptism. When in 1888 she applied to the Royal Literary Fund for a grant, she gave her date of birth as 27 December 1821 (her contemporaries regarded 1826 as the year of her birth: Brian De Breffney suggests 1825). Born in Dublin, Jane was the fourth child (the third died at the age of three) of Sara Kingsbury Elgee and Charles Elgee, a solicitor and the eldest son of the Archdeacon Elgee of Wexford. Since formal education for girls in her day was uncommon, Jane was educated by tutors, who stressed contemporary European literature and the classics. In *Hearth and Home* (30 June 1892) she remarked: "I was always fond of study, and of books. My favourite study was languages. I succeeded in mastering ten of the European languages. Till my eighteenth year I never wrote anything. All my time was given to study."

In 1845, at the beginning of the potato famine—more than eight hundred thousand people would die during the following six years—she was drawn into the Irish crisis when Thomas Davis died of scarlet fever at the age of thirty. In his *Tribute to Thomas Davis* (1947) Yeats records the symbolic moment when Elgee, encountering Davis's funeral in a crowded Dublin street, asked a shopkeeper: "Who was Thomas Davis? I have never heard of him." He answered that Davis was a poet. Yeats continues, "She was so struck to find so many people honouring a poet and one she had never heard of, that she turned Nationalist and wrote those energetic rhymes my generation read in its youth." In *Home and Hearth* (30 June 1892) she recalled: "Since I had caught the National spirit, all the literature of Irish wrongs and sufferings had an enthralling interest for me; then it was that I discovered I could write poetry."

Her first submission as Speranza to the radical organ of the Young Ireland party, *Nation* (21 February 1846), was a translation from German of a poem titled "The Holy War," which characterizes the people as "rising in pride" and calls for a hero to lead them, a theme that recurs in her poems. In an ac-

companying letter to the editor, she signed her name with another pseudonym, John Fanshawe Ellis, which she also used in publishing prose and verse. Her disguise, however, was soon penetrated, as she later recalled in the *Freeman's Journal* (4 February 1896): "One day my uncle came into my room and found the *Nation* on my table. Then he accused me of contributing to it, declaring the while that such a seditious paper was fit only for the fire."

Jane's early reputation as a poet rests on poems written between 1846 and 1848, works that depict the suffering during the famine. In the *Dublin Review* (April 1865) a critic notes that her "gloomy series of images recalls to us the awful state of the country—the corpses that were buried without coffins, and the men and women that walked the roads more like corpses than living creatures, spectres and skeletons at once . . . and, far as the eye could search the land, blackened potato-fields, filling all the air with the fetid odours of decay." However, a member of the Royal Society of Literature later contended in volume seventeen of *Transactions of the Royal Society of Literature* (1895) that her poems were "especially marred by the intense strain she subjected herself to, which prevents her ever approaching naturalness."

Nevertheless, her defenders, such as the anonymous critic in the *Irish Fireside* (2 September 1885), wrote that the language of her prose and poems "in its passionate ardour, in the advocacy of liberty, in denunciation of tyranny, rose to the majesty of Demosthenic eloquence," as in "The Voice of the Poor," which had appeared in the *Nation*:

> Before us die our brothers of starvation:
>   Around are cries of famine and despair.
> Where is hope for us, or comfort, or salvation—
>   Where—oh! where?
> If the angels ever hearken, downward bending,
>   They are weeping, we are sure . . . [.]

In the issue of 21 January 1847 her poem "The Stricken Land," later reprinted in *Poems* (1864) as "The Famine Year," indicts the cruel injustice of Irish corn (that is, wheat) shipped to England while the Irish starved:

> Weary men, what reap ye?—Golden corn for the stranger.
> What sow ye?—Human corses that wait for the avenger.
> Fainting forms, hunger-stricken, what see you in the offing?
> Stately ships to bear our food away, amid the stranger's scoffing.

The final lines depict the ultimate appeal of those who have died as a result of English indifference: "A ghastly, spectral army, before the great God we'll

Lady Wilde as a young woman (courtesy of the William Andrews Clark Library)

stand, / and arraign ye as our murderers, the spoilers of our land."

Elgee was also preoccupied with the hundreds of thousands who had fled from Ireland during those years and those who had either died en route to the New World or had died on their arrival or shortly thereafter in hospitals (in 1847 sixty thousand Irish arrived in New York, and in one year one hundred thousand arrived in Canada). The result was her poem "The Exodus":

"A million in a decade!"—of human wrecks,
    Corpses lying in fever sheds—
Corpses huddled on foundering decks,
    And shroudless dead on their rocky beds;
        Nerve and muscle, and heart and brain,
        Lost to Ireland—lost in vain.

In 1848, when revolutions erupted throughout Europe, Elgee envisioned the possibility in Ireland in her poem "Courage" (later retitled "The Year of Revolutions" in *Poems*) for the 22 April issue of the *Nation:*

Lift up your pale faces, ye children of sorrow,
The night passes on to a glorious to-morrow!
Hark! hear you not sounding glad Liberty's paean,
From the Alps to the Isles of the tideless Aegean?

The familiar attempt to arouse the Irish sounds again in this poem: "On, on in your masses dense, resolute, strong / To war against treason, oppression, and wrong. . . ." Yet she did not believe that

democracy was the alternative to oppression; as she wrote to a Scots friend, "Why should a rude, uncultured mob dare to utter its voice? Let the best reign, Intellect and Ability. . . ."

During this time Elgee was so swept up by revolutionary fervor that in a review of a book on the nationalist Daniel O'Connell (responsible for the passage of the Catholic Emancipation Act) she wrote in the *Nation* (8 July 1848): "If a government stands in the path of that people, and refuses those demands which it was only placed in office to execute (for a government is not organized to control, but to execute a people's will), that government must be overthrown." Three days later, in response to such views in the *Nation,* the editor Charles Duffy was arrested on a charge of treason and the files of the paper confiscated. For the new editor Elgee wrote "The Challenge of Ireland" for the 22 July issue with a new call to the Irish: "And are there no men in your Fatherland / To confront the tyrant's stormy glare / With scorn as deep as the wrongs ye bear. . . ."

In the 29 July issue a prose piece appeared titled "Jacta Alea Est" (the die is cast), unsigned but written by Elgee, who with the eloquence of an impassioned orator challenges England, whose "recent acts" of suppression have "justified us before the world. . . . Oh! For a hundred thousand muskets glittering brightly in the light of heaven, and the monumental barricades stretching across each of our noble streets, made desolate by England. . . ." But a starving, decimated, demoralized nation was clearly unwilling or unable to take up arms.

Significantly, in August 1849 Queen Victoria was cheered rather than hissed on her visit to Ireland. Nevertheless, Alexander Martin Sullivan, a later editor of the *Nation,* wrote in his *New Ireland* (1877) that Elgee's "revolutionary appeal" was "exquisitely beautiful . . . in fact a prose-poem, a wild war song. . . ." Since Elgee's call for revolution was written after Duffy's arrest, she was concerned that he might be cited as the author of "Jacta Alea Est." To her Scots friend she wrote: ". . . I shall never write sedition again. The responsibility is more awful than I imagined or thought of." As later recalled in *Irish Society* (31 December 1892), when the attorney general read aloud Elgee's article with its inflammatory rhetoric at Duffy's trial, Elgee reportedly stood up in the gallery and announced: "I am the culprit, if culprit there be." Although this dramatic moment contributed to the legend of Lady Wilde in later years, no such report appeared in any publication at the time of the trial. She later wrote to her Scots friend: "I was amused at that imputed heroic act of mine becoming historical," but she resented that "our grand Revolution" had ended in "shielding itself with a lady's name. . . ."

Elgee's ardent patriotism waned as many revolutionary Young Irelanders were either deported or forced to flee to America. Her fame, however, had been meteoric, for within three years she had emerged from obscurity and was known throughout Ireland. With the excitement of politics now gone, she turned to translating J. W. Meinhold's Gothic romance *Sidonia the Sorceress*, which appeared in 1849 without her name on the title page in order to demonstrate that she had not undertaken the translation "for celebrity." Her son Oscar would later claim that when he was a child, the novel was his favorite reading.

In 1849 Elgee met Dr. William Wilde, who at thirty-four was well known in Dublin society, for he had reopened the old St. Mark's Hospital as the Ophthalmic Hospital and Dispensary for Diseases of the Eye and Ear for the Poor, the only British hospital that taught aural surgery. Dr. Wilde was to publish many books on subjects such as Irish archeology and folklore, travel, Jonathan Swift, and aural surgery (a volume that on its appearance in 1853 established his international reputation). He was also the editor of the *Dublin Quarterly Journal of Medical Science;* in addition he was the commissioner overseeing the Irish medical census, for which he was knighted by Queen Victoria in 1864. After completing her translation of Alphonse de Lamartine's *Pictures of the First French Revolution* (1850), Elgee and Dr. Wilde were married on 12 November 1851 in St. Peter's, Dublin.

An ardent feminist, Wilde found it difficult to accept a passive role as a wife. In an essay titled "The Bondage of Woman" in *Social Studies* (1893) she wrote that "women still weep and toil, as they have ever done, that man, the lord of the world, may find existence made easier and pleasanter by the ceaseless devotion and patient self-sacrifice of the inferior, at least, the weaker sex." Curiously, however, in a letter to a correspondent, she was also capable of expressing an opposing view: "I would be a much better wife, mother and head of a household if I never touched a pen." In her essay "Genius and Marriage," also published in *Social Studies,* she contended that women often have "many and grievous faults in married life, very irritating to a literary husband and a man of genius." In the same essay she suggested the means of maintaining domestic tranquility: ". . . when all the family are Bohemians, and all clever, and all enjoy thoroughly the erratic, impulsive, reckless life of work and glory. . . ."

Her first child, christened William Charles Kingsbury (always called "Willie"), was born on 26

Wilde's husband, Sir William Wilde, drawing by Thomas Herbert Maguire, 1847 (courtesy of the William Andrews Clark Library)

September 1852. Wilde continued her translating despite the birth of her son, publishing in that year *The Glacier Land* by Alexandre Dumas *père,* an account of Dumas's tour of Switzerland in 1832. On 16 October 1854 she gave birth to Oscar Fingal O'Flahertie (the first two names drawn from Irish legend): "Is not that grand, misty and Ossianic?" she wrote to her Scots friend. In the same letter she is convinced that "God has lavished blessings on me." Yet she concludes ruefully: "Life has such infinite possibilities of woe."

By 1857 the Wilde family was living at 1 Merrion Square, an elegant house in the most prestigious section of Dublin, and on 2 April, Wilde gave birth to Isola Francesca Emily. During these years Wilde contributed reviews to the *Dublin University Review,* devoted much time to socializing with friends and associates, and attended to her growing children (although she also had six servants to assist her in running the house). In 1858 she began the translation of a German novel by Wilhelmine Canz that was finally published in three volumes in 1863 as *The First Temptation; or, "Eritis Sicut Deus"* (the Latin subtitle means "Ye shall be as God," echoing the serpent's remark to Eve in Gen. 3:5).

In 1864, the year that began with Dr. Wilde's knighthood, Jane Wilde became Lady Wilde, a title

Lady Wilde as Speranza, painted by George Morosini (from Richard Ellmann's Oscar Wilde, *1988)*

In addition the volume includes "Thekla: A Swedish Saga," her major achievement of 690 lines in a rather bewildering variation of stanzaic lengths from four to twelve lines. This ballad, an adaptation of a work that Lady Wilde discovered in Sweden, evokes the Narcissus myth: gazing into a mirror, Thekla "beholds, with inward praising, / Her own beauty in amaze." Moreover, the poem echoes Samuel Taylor Coleridge's "The Rime of the Ancient Mariner" and "Christabel," involving Thekla's "witchlike beauty [that] bodes no good. . . ." Yet by the end Thekla is pardoned by God for the Faustian pact that she had entered into for the destruction of her seven children before they were born in order to retain her beauty.

The volume was generally well received by Irish reviewers, the *Freeman's Journal* (8 December 1864) regarding her poems as "preeminently characterized by the beauty of their imagery, their truthfulness to nature and the purity and simplicity of the phraseology in which our gifted countrywoman conveys her musings, her thoughts and her very emotions to the reader." The *Dublin Review* (April 1865) praised her "extraordinary influence on all the intellectual and political activities of Young Ireland" but noted the "peculiar and powerful but monotonous rhythm" of her poems. The English reviewer in the *Athenaeum* (London) on 18 March 1865, however, was critical of her "grandiloquent generalities, tricked out with imposing but not striking metaphors."

A sudden upheaval in Lady Wilde's life occurred in December 1864, when an unstable young woman, Mary Travers, charged her with libel because of a letter that she had written to Travers's father, a professor at Trinity College, Dublin, suggesting that Mary's bizarre behavior might be construed as an "intrigue" between her and Sir William. Ten years before, when the nineteen-year-old Mary had been his patient, he had befriended her, perhaps because he sensed her instability. She said, on the other hand, that an "intimacy" had arisen between them over the years. Testifying at the trial, Mary claimed that she had been raped by Sir William in 1862; however, she had continued to see him and accept his gifts. He had even introduced her to Lady Wilde and invited her to their Merrion Square home. At the trial Lady Wilde insisted that nothing improper had occurred between Mary and Sir William. After hearing the testimony the jury awarded Mary a mere farthing (a quarter of a penny), apparently the value of the damage allegedly done to her, but Sir William's court costs amounted to £2,000.

On 23 February 1867 the Wilde family was devastated by the sudden death of Isola, just two

that delighted her and that perhaps stimulated her to resume writing verse. In *Duffy's Hibernian Magazine* (March 1864) she published "Work While It Is Called To-day" which depicts God's questioning of the Irish:

> I gave you a land as a Garden of Eden,
> Where you and your sons should till and toil. . . .
> What have ye done with my land of beauty–
> Has the spoiler bereft her of robe and crown?

The Irish respond with one of Lady Wilde's favorite themes: "Our prophets and wise men are heard no more; / Our young men give a last kiss to their mothers, / then sail away for a foreign shore." In the following month the periodical published another of her poems, "Who Will Show Us Any Good?," which again calls for a leader to resuscitate "Suffering Ireland! Martyr-Nation!"

Late in 1864, as "Speranza," Lady Wilde published *Poems,* its contents dating back to the 1840s with many translations or adaptations of works by European authors, such as Alphonse-Marie-Louis de Prat de Lamartine, Friedrich von Schiller, Girolamo Savonarola, and other authors not identified.

months before her tenth birthday. "My heart seems broken," Lady Wilde wrote to a friend. "Still I feel I have to live for my sons and thank God they are as fine a pair of boys as one could desire." For several years Lady Wilde responded to social invitations with a brief note: "I do not go out into evening society at present." However, when her friends protested that they never saw her, she began to invite them to her "At Homes" on Saturdays between 4:00 and 7:00 in the evening. Writers, artists, doctors, musicians, and university professors were her guests; as a result she became the most prominent hostess in Dublin.

By the mid 1870s, however, Sir William's health began a long, slow decline, during which time Lady Wilde wrote "The Soul's Questioning" for the *Dublin University Magazine* (April 1876). The poem, completed in the previous year, raises the question of whether or not there is an afterlife:

Can this be the end of all?–the power of beauty and birth,
The splendours of youth and brain, the laughter and songs
     of mirth–
A nameless thing of horror, to be hidden away in the
     earth?

Sir William died on 19 April 1876 at age sixty-one. The lord mayor of Dublin, the president of the Royal College of Surgeons, and other mourners of distinction made up the funeral procession, which the *Express* (24 April 1876) noted was "one of the most imposing that has been witnessed in the city for a long time." The *Freeman's Journal* (20 April 1876) wrote on the day after Sir William's death that he had been "ever helped and sustained by the grace and social brilliance of Lady Wilde."

Not only was Sir William's death a shock to Lady Wilde, but the discovery that he had left the family only debts and liabilities was perhaps an even greater blow. As though to maintain her stability, she wrote during the summer of 1876 the final chapter to the memoir of the eighteenth-century illustrator and antiquarian Gabriel Beranger, which Sir William had written before his death. Later that year she wrote a poem for the *Dublin University Magazine* (January 1877) titled "In the Midnight," which recalls the manner in which her husband read to her: "Read till the warm tears fall my Love, / With thy voice so soft and low. . . ," a soothing lyric that departs radically from much of her former verse.

Continuing financial difficulties, intolerable loneliness, and separation from her sons (Willie in London establishing himself as a journalist and Oscar at Oxford University) convinced her that she must move to London. Before departing from Dub-

lin, she learned, to her utter delight, that Oscar had won the prestigious Newdigate Prize at Oxford for his poem *Ravenna:* "Oh Gloria, Gloria! Thank you a million times for the telegram–it is the first pleasant throb of joy I have had this year." Later in 1878 she wrote a pamphlet of forty-seven pages titled *The American Irish,* which, while admiring those who had immigrated to America and had flourished there, devotes much space to the history of English oppression. Indeed, she even suggests that America should purchase Ireland from England. Commenting on the piece, the *Sentinel* (1 January 1879) remarked: "She remembers the days of old with a vengeance. . . ."

On 7 May 1879 she left Ireland to live with Willie in London in Ovington Square, Chelsea. She soon entered the world of journalism herself, writing social news, reviews, and leaders for such newspapers and magazines as the *Pall Mall Gazette,* the *Queen* (a weekly magazine designed for "ladies' reading"), the *Burlington Magazine,* the *St. James's Magazine,* and other publications. Meanwhile, Oscar, establishing a reputation as the "Aesthete of Aesthetes" (as *Punch* labeled him), was moving in celebrated circles. At first Willie was pleased at his brother's success, but in time antagonism developed between them.

After living for three years in Chelsea, Lady Wilde and Willie moved to Park Street, a more fashionable area near Grosvenor Square, where she continued her salon for distinguished visitors, who included Yeats and George Bernard Shaw (both at the beginning of their careers), Oliver Wendell Holmes, Bret Harte, George Moore, John Ruskin, and Robert Browning. Later memoirs of visitors noted her odd dress, though over time they may have added picturesque details.

With Oscar's engagement to Constance Lloyd in November 1883, his mother wrote to him: "live the literary life and teach Constance to correct proofs and eventually go into parliament." Of Willie, she wrote, "take warning by Willie," an indication that his drinking and unreliability were beginning to disturb her. Meanwhile, she wrote *Driftwood from Scandinavia* (1884), based on not only notes of her travel in Sweden but also her linking of Swedish and Irish legend, history, and antiquities. Early in 1887 Lady Wilde published *Ancient Legends, Mystic Charms, and Superstitions of Ireland,* which utilizes the material collected by Sir William for his *Irish Popular Superstitions* (1852).

In November of that year Oscar became editor of *Woman's World,* to which in January 1888 his mother contributed a poem of 227 lines in blank verse titled "Historic Women," which celebrates

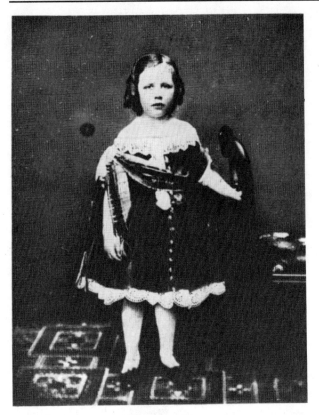

Wilde's son, Oscar

"Strong, splendid souls that chafed at human wrong" from the Bible through history and literature, including allusions to such figures as Cleopatra, Joan of Arc, and Queen Victoria. Clearly the intent of the work is to inspire readers with the ideal of womanhood, a common subject in Victorian poetry. In 1890 Lady Wilde published *Ancient Cures, Charms, and Usages of Ireland,* which Yeats cited in the *Scots Observer* (1 March 1890) along with her *Ancient Legends* as "the fullest and most beautiful gathering of Irish folklore in existence."

With the publication of *The Picture of Dorian Gray* (1891), Lady Wilde, ignoring many of the denigrating reviews, wrote to Oscar: "It is the most wonderful piece of writing in all the fiction of the day." Meanwhile, she collected her own reviews and articles in *Notes on Men, Women, and Books* (1891), which discusses such figures as Alfred, Lord Tennyson; George Eliot; Edward Bulwer-Lytton; Harriet Martineau; William Wordsworth; and Benjamin Disraeli. At this time, when Oscar was in Paris at work on *Salomé* (1894), Lady Wilde wrote to him: "Your fame in Paris is becoming stupendous. . . . You are indeed taking a high place in the literature of the day and I am very proud of you." In 1893 another of her books appeared: *Social Studies,* a collection of previously published articles with such titles as "The Destiny of Humanity," "Genius and Marriage," "Irish Leaders and Martyrs," "The Vision of the Vatican," and "The Poet as Teacher."

By 1894 the antagonism between Oscar and Willie (caused by Willie's dependence for money on their mother following his divorce from an American newspaper owner and his increasing reliance on alcohol) disturbed Lady Wilde, who wrote to Oscar: "*He has never injured you.* Why should you hate him? . . . Come then & offer him yr. Hand in good faith. . . . I shall hope to see you soon—if not I'll die of grief." Reconciliation did not occur between the brothers, but Oscar—as though to placate his mother—dramatizes the moment in *The Importance of Being Earnest* when Cecily urges her guardian: "However badly [Algernon] may have behaved to you in the past he is still your brother . . . you will shake hands with him, won't you, Uncle Jack?" Indeed, they do shake hands. Unfortunately, Lady Wilde's declining health prevented her from attending any of Oscar's plays, but she read the reviews avidly.

When in April and May of 1895 Oscar was arrested and tried for "gross indecency," his mother reportedly said to him: "If you stay, even if you go to prison, you will always be my son, it will make no difference to my affection, but if you go, I will never speak to you again." On 3 February 1896 she died of subacute bronchitis in her Oakley Street, Chelsea, home; two days later she was buried in Kensal Green Cemetery. She wished "to be buried *quite privately* and for no one to come to her funeral." Her only mourners were Willie and his second wife, Lily. Despite her own ill health, Constance left Italy to visit Oscar at Reading Prison to inform him of his mother's death, which deeply distressed him.

The obituaries generally adopted a kindly estimate of Lady Wilde's personality and literary achievements. In England the *Athenaeum* (8 February 1896), though critical during her lifetime, now wrote that "under the mask of brilliant display and bohemian recklessness, lay a deep and loyal soul and a kindly and sympathetic nature." *The Times* (London) of 7 February 1896, calling her "a distinguished member" of the Young Ireland Party, praised her verse "of virile and passionate rhetoric." In Ireland obituaries generally ran to several columns, the *Freeman's Journal* (6 February 1896) calling her "a woman of the most versatile attainments, genuine intellectual power and commanding character," and in a veiled allusion to Oscar's disgrace, the *Dublin Evening Mail* (6 February 1896) commented that Lady Wilde had "a great deal of the shadows of this life to encounter."

Biographies:

Horace Wyndham, *Speranza: A Biography of Lady Wilde* (London: Boardman, 1951; New York: Philosophical Library, 1951);

Patrick Byrne, *The Wildes of Merrion Square: The Family of Oscar Wilde* (London & New York: Staples Press, 1953);

Eric Lambert, *Mad with Much Heart: A Life of the Parents of Oscar Wilde* (London: F. Muller, 1967);

Terence de Vere White, *The Parents of Oscar Wilde: Sir William and Lady Wilde* (London: Hodder & Stoughton, 1967);

Joy Melville, *Mother of Oscar: The Life of Jane Francesca Wilde* (London: John Murray, 1994).

References:

Karl Beckson, "The Importance of Being Angry: The Mutual Antagonism of Oscar and Willie Wilde," in *Blood Brothers: Siblings as Writers,* edited by Norman Kiell (New York: International Universities Press, 1983), pp. 115–136;

Brian de Breffny, "The Ancestry of Oscar Wilde: Speranza's Ancestry: Elgee–the Maternal Lineage of Oscar Wilde," *Irish Ancestor,* 4 (1972): 94–103;

J. S. Crone, "Bibliography of Lady Wilde," *Irish Book Lover,* 20 (1932): 74;

Richard Ellmann, *Oscar Wilde* (London: Hamilton, 1987; New York: Knopf, 1988);

James Edward Holroyd, "Brother to Oscar," *Blackwood's Magazine,* 325 (March 1979): 230–240;

William Butler Yeats, "Lady Wilde," *Boston Pilot,* 28 September 1889; reprinted in *Letters to the New Island,* edited by Horace Reynolds (Cambridge, Mass.: Harvard University Press, 1934), pp. 76–82;

Yeats, *Thomas Davis Centenary Address* (London: Blackwell, 1947);

Yeats, "The Tragic Generation," *The Autobiography of W. B. Yeats* (New York: Collier, 1965), pp. 188–193.

Papers:

A major collection of Lady Wilde's letters to Oscar and other correspondents is in the William Andrews Clark Memorial Library, Los Angeles. Smaller collections of her letters are in the University of Reading Library; the Royal Library of Sweden; the National Library of Ireland; the New York Public Library; and the Houghton Library, Harvard University.

Books for Further Reading

Armstrong, Isobel. *Victorian Poetry: Poetry, Poetics, and Politics*. London: Routledge, 1993.

Armstrong. *Victorian Scrutinies: Reviews of Poetry, 1830–1870*. London: Athlone, 1972.

Armstrong, Joseph Bristow, and Cath Shorrock, eds. *Nineteenth-Century Women Poets: An Oxford Anthology*. Cambridge: Clarendon, 1996.

Bethune, George W., ed. *The British Female Poets with Biographical and Critical Notices*. Philadelphia: Lindsay & Blakiston, 1848.

Bivona, Daniel. *Desire and Contradiction: Imperial Visions and Domestic Debates in Victorian Literature*. Manchester: Manchester University Press, 1990.

Breen, Jennifer, ed. *Victorian Women Poets 1830–1901: An Anthology*. London: Everyman, 1994.

Claridge, Laura, and Elizabeth Langland, eds. *Out of Bounds: Male Writers and Gender(ed) Criticism*. Amherst: University of Massachusetts Press, 1990.

Clarke, Norma. *Ambitious Heights: Writing, Friendship, Love—The Jewsbury Sisters, Felicia Hemans, and Jane Welsh Carlyle*. London: Routledge, 1990.

Cross, Nigel. *The Common Writer: Life in Nineteenth-Century Grub Street*. Cambridge: Cambridge University Press, 1985.

David, Deirdre. *Intellectual Women and Victorian Patriarchy*. London: Macmillan, 1987.

De Shazer, Mary K. *Inspiring Women: Re-Imagining the Muse*. Oxford: Pergamon, 1989.

Ezell, Margaret, J. M. *Writing Women's Literary History*. Baltimore: Johns Hopkins University Press, 1993.

Faderman, Lillian. *Surpassing the Love of Men: Romantic Friendship and Love between Women from the Renaissance to the Present*. New York: Morrow, 1981.

Gilbert, Sandra M., and Susan Gubar. *The Madwoman in the Attic: The Woman Writer and the Nineteenth-Century Literary Imagination*. New Haven: Yale University Press, 1979.

Gilmour, Robin. *The Victorian Period: The Intellectual and Cultural Context of English Literature, 1830–1890*. London: Longman, 1993.

Hale, Sarah Josepha. *Woman's Record; or, Sketches of All Distinguished Women from the Creation to A.D. 1854*. New York: Harper, 1855.

Hickock, Kathleen. *Representations of Women: Nineteenth-Century British Women's Poetry*. Westport, Conn.: Greenwood Press, 1984.

Homans, Margaret. *Bearing the Word: Language and Female Experience in Nineteenth-Century Women's Writing*. Chicago: University of Chicago Press, 1986.

Johnson, Wendell Stacey. *Sex and Marriage in Victorian Poetry*. Ithaca, N.Y.: Cornell University Press, 1975.

Kaplan, Cora. *Salt and Bitter and Good: Three Centuries of English and American Women Poets*. New York: Paddington, 1973.

Landow, George. *Victorian Types, Victorian Shadows: Biblical Typology in Victorian Literature, Art, and Thought.* Boston: Routledge & Kegan Paul, 1980.

Leighton, Angela. *Victorian Women Poets: Writing against the Heart.* Charlottesville: University of Virginia Press, 1992.

Leighton and Margaret Reynolds, eds. *Victorian Women Poets: An Anthology.* Oxford: Blackwell, 1995.

Levine, Philippa. *Feminist Lives in Victorian England: Private Roles and Public Commitment.* Oxford: Blackwell, 1990.

Lootens, Tricia. *Lost Saints: Silence, Gender, and Victorian Literary Canonization.* Charlottesville: University of Virginia Press, 1996.

McGhee, Richard D. *Marriage, Duty and Desire in Victorian Poetry and Drama.* Lawrence: Regents Press of Kansas, 1980.

Mermin, Dorothy. *Godiva's Ride: Women of Letters in England, 1830–1880.* Bloomington: Indiana University Press, 1993.

Moers, Ellen. *Literary Women.* New York: Doubleday, 1976.

Montefiore, Jan. *Feminism and Poetry: Language, Experience, Identity in Women's Writing.* London: Pandora, 1987.

Parrinder, Patrick. *Authors and Authority: A Study of English Literary Criticism and its Relation to Culture, 1750–1900.* London: Routledge, 1977.

Robertson, Eric S. *English Poetesses: A Series of Critical Biographies, with Illustrative Extracts.* London: Cassell, 1883.

Ross, Marlon B. *The Contours of Masculine Desire: Romanticism and the Rise of Women's Poetry.* New York: Oxford University Press, 1989.

Rowton, Frederic. *The Female Poets of Great Britain: Chronologically Arranged with Copious Selections and Critical Remarks.* London, 1848.

Rowton, ed. *The Cyclopedian of Female Poets.* Philadelphia: Lippincott, 1852.

Showalter, Elaine. *Woman in Sexist Society: Studies in Power and Powerlessness.* Eds. Vivian Gornick and Barbara K. Moran. New York: Basic Books, 1971.

Stephenson, Glennis, and Shirley Neuman, eds. *ReImagining Women: Representations of Women in Culture.* Toronto: University of Toronto Press, 1993.

Stodart, Mary Ann. *Female Writers: Thoughts on Their Proper Sphere and on Their Powers of Usefulness.* London, 1842.

Swindells, Julia. *Victorian Writing and Working Women: The Other Side of Silence.* Cambridge: Polity Press, 1985.

Vicinus, Martha. *The Industrial Muse: A Study of Nineteenth-Century British Working Class Literature.* New York: Barnes & Noble, 1974.

Vicinus, ed. *Suffer and Be Still: Women in the Victorian Age.* Bloomington: Indiana University Press, 1972.

Wharton, Grace, and Philip Wharton. *The Queens of Society.* New York: Harper, 1860.

Williams, Jane. *The Literary Women of England.* London: Saunders, Otley, 1861.

Contributors

Dan Albergotti ....*Auburn University*
Crys Armbrust ....*University of South Carolina*
Karl Beckson ....*Brooklyn College of the City University of New York*
Carol A. Bock ....*University of Minnesota, Duluth*
Florence S. Boos ....*University of Iowa*
Denise K. Comer ....*University of South Carolina*
Siobhan Craft Brownson..*Winthrop University*
Marya DeVoto ....*University of North Carolina at Chapel Hill*
James Diedrick ....*Albion College*
John Ferns ....*McMaster University*
Janet Gray ....*Princeton University*
Kathleen Hickok ....*Iowa State University*
Cheri Lyn Larsen Hoeckley ....*Westmont College*
Natalie M. Houston ....*Duke University*
Gloria G. Jones ....*Winthrop University*
Linda A. Julian ....*Furman University*
Harriet Devine Jump ....*Edge Hill University College*
Becky W. Lewis ....*University of South Carolina*
Deborah A. Logan ....*Western Kentucky University*
A. A. Markley ....*Pennsylvania State University, Delaware County*
Lee Anna Maynard ....*University of South Carolina*
Kathleen McCormack ....*Florida International University*
Lucy Morrison ....*University of South Carolina*
Suzanne Ozment..*The Citadel*
Tony Perrello ....*University of South Carolina*
J. Jakub Pitha ....*University of South Carolina*
Daniel Robinson ....*Widener University*
Eijun Senaha ....*Hokkaido University*
James R. Simmons Jr. ....*Louisiana Tech University*
James I. St. John ....*Forest Lake Presbyterian Church, Columbia, S.C.*
Staci L. Stone ....*University of South Carolina*
Beverly Taylor ....*University of North Carolina at Chapel Hill*
Marion Thain ....*University of Birmingham*
Richard Tobias ....*University of Pittsburgh*
Whitney A. Womack ....*Purdue University*

Cumulative Index

Dictionary of Literary Biography, Volumes 1-199
Dictionary of Literary Biography Yearbook, 1980-1997
Dictionary of Literary Biography Documentary Series, Volumes 1-17

Cumulative Index

DLB before number: *Dictionary of Literary Biography*, Volumes 1-199
Y before number: *Dictionary of Literary Biography Yearbook*, 1980-1997
DS before number: *Dictionary of Literary Biography Documentary Series*, Volumes 1-17

Cumulative Index

H

K

Cumulative Index

X

Y

Z